The Earth Caretaker Way

Walking Backwards into the Future

and Remembering What We Already Know

Tim Corcoran

and Julie Boettler

Book Cover by Janie Stapleton

Illustrations by Janie Stapleton, Julie Boettler, TJ Putnam

First published by Kindle Publishing

ISBN: 979-8-218-96888-5

Books by Tim Corcoran

Growing up with a Soul Full of Nature – One Man's Story of a Childhood Filled with Nature as a Teacher and Friend

Mt. Shasta the Beautiful – The Shasta Photo Project Volume 1, 2, 3, 4, 5, 6

Santa Cruz and the Central Coast- A Photography Celebration of a Love of Place

The High Sierras Volume 1

The Oregon Coast Volume 1

CONTENTS

CONTENTS

DEDICATION

I dedicate this book to the Earth. She gives us life. She gives us purpose. She gives us beauty defined. The Earth has inspired my life.

Stop for a moment and consider this incredible being, our Earth. Nowhere in any universe, as far as we know yet, I'm talking millions and billions of planets, and stars, and as far as we know, this miracle called Earth, is the only living planet that can be home to humans. That fact is beyond comprehension, and I am so grateful and honored to call Earth my home. Earth, this book is literally for you.

I also dedicate this book to my spiritual mentor, teacher, guide, and friend, the Earth Keeper. He is one of the inspirations behind me writing this book, and I am honored to give voice to his teachings and visions.

Coming Home To Nature

For thousands of years our ancestors laid the foundation for us to have a close, personal relationship with nature. These people of the Earth lived as one with the land. They were Earth Mind, no separation, Earth Heart, nothing but love and respect for our Mother Earth.

To be mothered is to be loved, protected, and inherently connected. This is what good mothers do for their children. We humans are children of the Earth.

Since our ancestor's time of living directly with nature, when Earth caretaking was intrinsic for survival, we have left the land, and lost our sense of purpose of caretaking. How did we get to this place? As humans began to explore the world, we shifted our way of life from hunters to agriculture. We switched to a mindset of ownership of the Earth and began trying to control and divide up land.

We segmented parcels without considering that we need all of its parts working together to have a balanced ecosystem. As predators, humans try to conquer, but what we do to manipulate one section of land affects the other.

To make a radical change we need to tell the truth. Through time and innovation, in the quest to make our lives easier, we inadvertently pushed nature away. We moved into a world that made our Earth our adversary to conquer.

As we disconnected ourselves for convenience, we lost our love and respect for the land and animals. We lost our wonder. Our lives have become about using our planet for power and wealth. We got lost and we made war on our Earth.

The knowledge our ancestors acquired was disregarded with no thought of future generations. Many humans have lost the ability to feel Earth's pain and loss. We have poisoned our life-giving waterways and oceans, and are desecrating our land. All with no heart, no love, no thought of right or wrong. The worst parts of humans have been unleashed.

Thousands upon thousands of animal species have become extinct. Each extinction unnecessary, and a forever wound to the collective human soul.

Our quest for an easier life through advancing technology has caused us to forget about our Earth connection. We need to be reminded that we can have balance in both.

Our Earth is very patient with us, but patience does run out. There comes a tipping point when what we do to our planet can't be reversed. Whether it is a natural disaster or human caused disaster, a new way will be birthed.

So, here we are at the edge of the cliff ready to fall off. Many of us still wanting to be in denial of this because it isn't convenient.

The truth is all the pain that is being created is completely unnecessary. With this understanding, this book was written to bring hope to a new way. The Earth Caretaker Way.

If we embrace this birthright and become Earth Caretakers as our everyday way of life, the Earth can begin to heal herself.

We could emerge into a time of The Earth Keeper Age. The age of respect, and love, and sustainable abundance for all. The only thing preventing this, is us. This is a defining moment in human history on the Earth. This is our time. What will we do? Can we and will we rise to this opportunity?

The good news is we know what to do. We have the knowledge. We have science. We have creativity, and genius. We have the answers, and I have great hope.

I hope with all my heart, a fire will ignite, and this book will spawn action into the Earth Caretaker Way Movement. My goal is billions of people committing to this way of life.

Now is a time for heroes. It is no accident that we have been born during this time of change. This generation and the next, are here in the most important time of human history. You have a sacred purpose as an Earth Caretaker.

This generation has been preordained to take on this Calling. It is up to the individual if they choose to initiate themselves, by acting on the challenges before us.

We can say this is a burden or it can be an exciting time of innovation, creativity, and of a global community coming together.

We need to take responsibility for our actions. We need to walk backwards into the future and remember what we already know. We need these skills to navigate our way.

We are born with a connection with nature, but as we grow, we may lose conscious touch with that relationship. Regaining that awareness and connecting with nature so intimately, that you know you belong as a part of it, can be life turning. You are no longer an outsider feeling as if you are in a museum looking through glass. You feel a complete sense of belonging. You are home.

I have been fortunate to have never lost my connection with nature. Being in it and of it, and teaching others how to appreciate it, rather than fear it, has been my life's work. I created Headwaters Outdoor School in Mount Shasta, California in 1992 to help people come back to the one source that heals and nurtures us all.

The Earth Caretaker Way builds our personal relationship with our Earth. It emphasizes what it is to be a human of integrity and honor. It includes inspirational teachings to get out into nature without fearing it. The intention is to create leaders to guide us into a new future of Earth Caretakers.

There are three core teachings in this book, Nature Awareness, Wilderness Skills, and Earth Philosophy. Our awareness in our environment is the bridge between the physical and the spiritual.

Studying science, our Earth's history, animals, and their behaviors, and practicing essential physical, life skills are all ways that draw us closer to the natural world we live in.

The spiritual work teaches that everything, including trees, rocks, and animals are alive and have their own consciousness. We can become them, and they can become us. When people are empathically interconnected with nature, they are willing to do the right thing.

One of the reasons this world is in the state it's in, is that our leaders are detached from nature. When we spend time in nature, we learn empathy for other beings. We inherently know, everything affects us, and it becomes harder to make bad decisions.

In my previous book, *Growing up with a Soul Full of Nature*, which I co-wrote with my wife, Jean Sage, I shared some of my childhood experiences in nature until the age of 17. *The Earth Caretaker Way* revisits those memories. It picks up after many years of working at wildlife attractions, breeding programs, and in wildlife rescue.

After an initial backstory of how my outdoor school and the teachings in this book came to be, each chapter's intention is to share inspiration and suggested activities. It encourages you to live your best and most effective life, by rekindling your personal relationship with nature. We all need this connection, from the human heart to the Earth heart, to ignite our passion of being of service.

The majority of this book was created through a collection of my personal stories, writings, poems, and reflections of my life experience. Some of the writings have been transcribed from my talks in my classes that I teach at Headwaters. Others are from my teachings and stories in my Tim Talk series, on our Headwaters Outdoor School Podcast, and YouTube Channel.

As a side note, I started recording Tim Talks on our land during the COVID-19 pandemic lockdown. I wanted to continue to offer these teachings, and help keep our students connected with the Headwaters land, as an anchor during times of chaos. More than ever these insights are needed during tumultuous times.

The way we will all excel is to learn to get creative and pivot during changes and disruptions. This is how we continue to not just survive, but continue to grow, and thrive.

I have also included writings, and quotes from some of my heroes and friends, that are inspirational and make us consider who we are at our core.

***

Julie Boettler has many integral roles as the caretaker of Headwaters. She runs our outdoor nature school alongside me, and takes care of the land, our dogs, and the people here.

Julie has her own, rich life experience to share, and has co-written this book with me. We have included many of her own stories and insights to add to these teachings. Julie's writings are printed in italics to recognize her contributions.

***

I am honored to share some of my personal stories. I hope you will be inspired to get out and build your own relationship with nature, and join us in being a caretaker of our Earth. - Julie

***

I give you my word, I live these teachings. This book is who I am, an Earth Keeper. The Earth Caretaker Way is from my heart, and my life's experience. I've shared what I have learned, and honesty is the most authentic way to teach.

Open any page of this book, in any order, and it will speak to you. Read it through, over and over. Each time may stir up a new thought or an ability to relate to an experience of your own, or it may reunite you with a connection you may have forgotten about or had dismissed.

Sitting around a campfire in the Marble Mountain Wilderness, I asked my students in our class to help create a list of actions they could take home to apply in their daily life, to maintain their connection with nature.

Many of the chapters in this book are based on those actions. I have expanded on them as a guide, with suggestions to help you live as an Earth Caretaker in your everyday life.

The journey of this book will lead you from, *Answering the Call of the Earth Keeper*, to what it is to *Be an Earth Caretaker*, to enhancing your *Nature Awareness* and expanding on your interaction with nature, to becoming more self-reliant through mastering *Wilderness Living Skills*, to communicating with the spirit of nature through *Earth Philosophy*, to manifesting your dream life and *Living a Life of Service*, and ultimately to joining our global community in *The Earth Caretaker Way Movement*.

My dream for all people is to have a personal relationship with nature by reconnecting with our Mother Earth. She is our human life force, we are one and the same.

I believe that a new rise in human evolution and consciousness is ready to become our new baseline for living. If enough people become aware, and it doesn't take all that many, this shift will take place. I believe this in the very core of my being.

I am a dreamer. It is part of my medicine. We dreamers dream big and find solutions to make them happen.

Get out in nature and build these skills, and stand up and speak for our Earth without holding back.

Nature is for everyone. I plead with all adults to share this with their children. The children need to consciously claim their birthright to stay connected to nature. They have been born into a time where their life choices can make a pivotal change in our future and the health of our planet. Our Earth's health and all living beings depend on the next generations.

The Earth is calling you. She's calling you Home. I'm honored that you are curious enough to read this book. Take in these words, and hopefully they will inspire you to live fully, and protect this land we live on and with.

The world needs you. We have a clear choice. What will we do?

Thank you for participating in the Earth Caretaker Way Movement and enjoy. - Tim Corcoran

Chapter 1
Answering The Call Of The Earth Keeper

At thirty-five years old, I was well on my life path, and felt a calling to buy land. Early in my childhood I had dreamed of having a piece of land to call my home. The feeling was so strong I felt it in my blood, my bones, and most powerfully in my heart and soul. I knew this was an important part of my life's purpose. I didn't know why, but I knew I had to begin searching.

At the time, I was living in Santa Cruz, California. A place I love, with dense Redwood and Doug Fir covered mountains, and wild beaches hugging the edge of the Pacific Ocean.

I regularly visited a place called Franklin Point, within Gazos Creek State Park. This rocky overlook became a power spot for me. I first visited this beach with my father when I was twelve. The moment I stepped onto the beach I knew I was returning home. It was my place.

The twinkling lights of Earth spirits hovered over the sand and water's surface. I was not alarmed; I had seen Earth spirits observing many times before in sacred places. I feel a sense of peace and acceptance when they are around.

This beach was home to majestic birds of prey, including Golden Eagles. There were countless varieties of seabirds, Plover, gulls, and cormorants. Coyotes, rabbits, and deer lived within the plant life of the rolling dunes.

Elephant seals and pelicans were always there to greet me. While whales, dolphins, seals, and otters frequently swam by.

Playing with crabs and watching otters fish was paradise for me, decades later, it still is. I will always visit this shoreline as one of my sacred pilgrimage destinations.

Historically, this beach was home for California Grizzly Bears and the Ohlone people. I still walk in reverence with them whenever I visit, knowing they are both waiting for their return time.

A few decades ago, this beach was not visited by many people. I was able to do a four-day vision quest there without encountering another person.

I sat on the cliff with occasional wave breaks spraying a salty mist about me. I prayed for clarity on my next step in finding my land and what it was I was looking for. The call was strong, but I needed signs to help show me the way.

As I dropped into deep, day long meditations, visitors came to me. One coyote came every night and often stayed for hours. Sometimes sitting near me, and sometimes circling around.

I was visited by a native ancestor that spoke with me all night about trusting the calling and not giving up. He told me that once I found the land, I was to make it my home. I was to protect it and share it with others, which seemed contradictory at the time.

He told me to love the land. To allow it to heal my past wounds and make me whole, so I could move forward into a place of Earth Caretaking.

At that point I wasn't sure what an Earth Caretaker was. I had strong visions about it, but it wasn't yet clear what it meant for me.

I was also visited by the plant and animal spirits of the land there. Through a felt understanding, they let me know that this native ancestor was the keeper of that land.

1

He was aware of me at that beach, since my first day there as a child with my father. Memories surfaced of countless times I felt watched and protected by this guardian.

I completed my quest with his support and guidance, and walked back to the trailhead to share my amazing experience with a friend. Leaving no room for doubt, I told him, "I'm going to Mt. Shasta. That's where I'm meant to be. When I get there, I'll find my land, it's calling, and I have to go."

When I was twelve years old, I had completed my Rite of Passage by solo climbing Mt. Shasta, and that's when my connection with the great mountain began. Since that time, I hadn't spent any serious time around the mountain. Here it was 23 years later, and I was being pulled to Mt. Shasta, about to make one of the biggest decisions of my life.

In the book, *The Call of the Wild*, by Jack London, the dog, Buck, heeded his call to go back to the wild, and followed a wolf into the wilderness. My primal call had also come, and there was no turning back. Within a week I was on the road north.

***

Finding My Land

My previous wife at the time, and I, met up with a wonderful realtor. After looking at a few properties, he came across a 32-acre listing that had come up for sale that day. We headed down an undeveloped, dirt road, barely making it there in four-wheel-drive. Affirming chills prickled down me. We approached the area and my life changed in the most dramatic way, forever.

I immediately felt my ancestors speaking to me. I became excited and deeply in tune, as if I had been there before. My inner bear was stirring, and I was feeling primal.

Walking the forested land, a sense of home, belonging, purpose, and friendship came over me. I hadn't walked far when I came across a ten-foot wide, flowing creek. It wandered through the length of the property. It was late summer and the fifth year of a drought, and the abundant Dale Creek invited me in. I stepped onto a rock with the water swirling around me.

It was hard to find property with year-round water, but I also knew this land was special because I could *feel* it.

I was a falconer, and I worked with injured birds of prey. For 17 years I had a Red-Tail Hawk with one eye, named Porsche, who was one of my power animals.

An affirmation that this was my land came floating down the stream towards me. It was a bright red, center tail feather of a mature, Red-Tail Hawk, not even wet yet. I picked up the feather and knew that the hawk's spirit, and my ancestors, were speaking to me. That was my sign coming to me down the creek, *my* creek.

The land rushed into me. A oneness happened. In that moment nothing else existed. Sometimes the Earth speaks to me through the land, through the trees, through the water, through the mountains. Mystery is good in life. Sometimes you know something, and that is enough.

I looked up at an elder pine tree and noticed I was being watched by an Earth spirit. There are many Earth spirits and Earth Caretakers, and they don't have to be human. I understood this Earth Caretaker in particular, resides within this land. He is a Caretaker of the Caretakers. He is a guide that watches over this land, and now me. I know him now as the Earth Keeper, my friend, my teacher, and life companion.

I signed the papers that day and the land was mine to caretake, and live and teach on. This was a defining moment in my life. I was home.

Land ownership is a strange thing. I don't own the land, but in this culture, I do on paper. I feel it is my land to take care of until I move on into another life, and then the next person will take it on. I am protecting it for now.

***

I spent the next year getting to know the land. My friend, a wolf-dog my previous wife and I had rescued, named Joseph, was always with me.

We were asked to trap a wolf that had been reported by concerned parents. It was hanging out with school children at their bus stop in the Santa Cruz area, along a riparian forest.

The kids called him Casper. He would stay with them, and then disappear like a ghost when adults would arrive.

It took some time, but we were able to catch the wolf and we brought him to our home. After a couple of escapes, and over time, we were able to get close to him and hand feed him. We were fighting for his life as the S.P.C.A.'s intention was to destroy him. They feared he was a threat and not capable of living out a humane life.

Working on the wolf's behalf, we were able to connect with a county supervisor and plead our case to him. We won custody of Joseph, and our relationship and bond grew.

Being a wolf, Joseph could not be controlled. We had a trust between each other that went far beyond our understanding in our brains. Our relationship was spirit itself, beyond understanding.

Joseph had a way of awakening spirit in all things. When Joseph was around, the medicine of the land was fully alive. I came into Joseph's life to give him the freedom on the land he needed to work his medicine. Allowing his spirit to roam free.

I now think of Joseph as a living, spirit guide, brought into my life to lead me to this land. Today my secret name for this land is Joseph's Place.

Joseph could disappear, seemingly at will, and reappear when needed. Like the great Chief Joseph of the Nez Perce tribe, who he was named in honor of, both were noble souls.

***

What is the purpose of humans on this Earth? When I found my land near Mt. Shasta, little did I know, my answer to that would come from the land itself.

My land, "Joseph's Place," spoke to me that first year. My new life's purpose was revealed. I was to be the caretaker of the land for the rest of my life, and find someone to continue caring for it when I return to my ancestors.

I was to keep the land healthy for all living beings, plants, animals, and people too. This is how Headwaters Outdoor School began. I was to bring people to the land. I was told to teach them how to care for it, and love the Earth by reconnecting with it through experiencing a personal connection with nature.

Decades later, my journey into Earth Caretaking has been a privilege, and a tremendous joy. I have learned that one true purpose of humans is to be Earth Caretakers. It's a gift we have, and we can do it well.

After many years of Earth Caretaking, our land is healthy. Plants, animals, and people thrive living here amongst each other. Thank you, Joseph.

We are very good at destroying the Earth, but we are even better at caring for it, protecting it, engaging with it, creating with it, loving it, and living with it.

If we put our energy toward caretaking, this purpose for humanity could bring us all together for this higher cause. We could truly live in paradise on Earth.

One day we'll wake up. The Earth will certainly remind us. Earth Caretaking is a higher purpose well worth exploring.

In hindsight, I was called by the mountain, by the creek, by the hawk, and most of all by the Earth Keeper. We knew each other from the past. In my logical mind it wouldn't make sense, but my inner vision told me all I needed to know.

My ancestral guides conferred with the mountain on my behalf. Through a series of seemingly unrelated events, they moved me to Mt. Shasta. I had no choice but to listen. Everything else was drowned out. The Earth Keeper, the elders, had called me home to this land.

***

I Am An Earth Keeper

I have found my place. I am the physical manifestation of Earth Keeper to our Earth. This is what I will be forever. This will not change. No matter the time or space, this is what I am. I know this to my core being. I am Earth Keeper, an eternal protector and caretaker and lover of Earth.

This message came to me in February 2015 on the Kohala Coast of the Big Island of Hawaii. The Earth Keeper from our Headwater's land, visited me as I was in a deep trance meditation. He came across the ocean in a very dramatic way, and delivered this message as a validation. It humbly moved me to my core as my truth. - Tim

***

The Earth Keeper's Words

Some of my writings are a collaboration between the Earth Keeper and myself. I've been hesitant about sharing my connection with the Earth Keeper because this relationship is personal to me.

3

It is also difficult to explain matters of spirit in our modern culture. It is hard for people to believe that there is more to our world than the physical. What we think we see with our eyes through our logical brain is a wonderful thing. Yet, in these matters of spirit, it often closes the doors to deeper ways of our natural world that the mind just cannot comprehend.

I would be grateful if you honored me and the Earth Keeper by keeping an open mind. I have included the Earth Keeper's words throughout this book, and noted them in bold print with his initials. E.K.

***

The Earth Keeper – My Friend

I continue to speak with the Earth Keeper. I sit outside, sometimes late into the night when it's quiet, and he shows me visions of the potential fate of our world. Some of these visions I understand, and many things and places he shows me I don't know yet, but I'm guessing someday I will.

I see the Earth Keeper on the land and within the trees, observing as a protector. Sometimes I receive guidance, sometimes not, but it's good to know he's here.

Chapter 2
Be An Earth Caretaker

Humans have a purpose for our lives that has been with us from birth. Caring for our planet and our fellow Earth travelers is the gift of who we are. All life, plants, and animals care for the Earth by how they live. This happens perfectly.

Reclaiming this purpose brings meaning to life. We become who we are meant to be, Earth Caretakers. This is the base of all my teachings, to wake you up, to re-mind you of who you are, and what you are here to do. Everyone needs to do some-thing to recreate balance in one's immediate environment.

Caretaking the Earth is not something you do on the side. It's in *how* you live every day, and in every decision you make. It doesn't interfere with other aspects of your life, but it is the core focus within each aspect. Caretaking is vital to sustaining our lives.

Your calling is not the thing or occupation you do, it's *how* you live your life. Does this path have a heart? ... and are you kind? If you answered yes, then you're already on purpose.

What does it look like to be an Earth Caretaker in the industrial world? The technology world? The service world? The teaching world? The political world? The military world? The entertainment world? How does that Being inside you show up every day in every decision you make, no matter what your occupation is?

How will what you do currently and in the future affect other humans, animals, the planet, the universe?

Our planet needs us to be heroes. This is a time to be extraordinary. It is a time to prepare mentally, emotionally, physically, and spiritually. My hope is that you become a person of action and get to work. Your Earth needs you to speak up and share your truth.

Defending our Earth is not a choice. Our heart knows what is right. Not taking action in these trying times is a type of soul death, it's a wound to your very soul.

To save our planet from ourselves, live your life and protect your Earth as if it is sacred, because it is. This shift in conscious empathy must happen. The path of an Earth Caretaker is the human way of love.

We must change our current underlying way of thinking from a Taker Society to a Leaver Society. Each person holds the key to this. I do it, you do it, and on and on, until that elusive number of awake people create the moment where the new way of living becomes our baseline.

If sixty percent of Americans find a personal connection with nature, we would have a huge change in global warming almost instantaneously. It's like the crumbling of the Berlin Wall. When an entire culture has a paradigm shift in their perception, a divisive wall can come down quickly.

***

I was born an Earth Caretaker. As a kid I created a stunning, urban wildland on a quarter acre in my backyard. I have always felt plant's feelings and their energy call to me. My deep empathy for all life kept the door open to receiving their communication. I've always felt watched by the plants and animals, and I watch them as well. I feel a mutual love and bond with them.

As far back as I can remember I have always taken care of animals, birds, reptiles, fish, and insects. I've always helped the Earth, even when most people didn't notice that something needed help. I have felt my life has been a gift. Helping is a way for me to give back in gratitude.

Caretaking was always my medicine; it was what I knew and learned growing up as a child of nature.

In the defining moment of finding my land, I knew I was being ordained to grow into this role more consciously and more personally.

My wish for you is to find your personal Earth project and bring out the Earth Caretaker in you.

"To truly love our planet, you must care about it and ALL that live upon it more than anything else." – The Earth Keeper

Seeing Wounds

To heal our planet and ourselves, we need to first see the truth, speak the truth, and feel the truth no matter how uncomfortable it is. We need to practice empathy and face our whole truth to move forward and make an honest change.

Humans are in an extinction crisis. The challenge on a larger scale is that most humans aren't truly aware of what is happening to the Earth on a personal level. For many people there is a lack of empathy, feeling the Earth's pain, sadness, fear, and confusion.

We hear about global warming, forests being burned and cut down, oceans being poisoned and depleted, and animals being killed to the point of extinction, but for many people it all seems so far away. The effects haven't hit them directly hard enough yet.

Sometimes it's not always a conscious choice to look the other way, most people have busy lives and are simply trying to survive in the human world. The thought of losing our Earth is too big to wrap their heads around, so many people do very little to nothing, and stay in denial.

We don't want to look at the destruction of our planet and let it truly sink in because we don't want to feel our own death. We are afraid and so we act as if it will all be fine – but it's not.

***

Headwaters Outdoor School has been going strong and thousands have been touched by our teachings over the years, but the escalation of climate change has been weighing heavy on me.

The chaos of 2020 and the few years prior, was brutal for our Earth, and all that lives upon her. It hit everyone hard and forced us all to take a time out.

We are coming out of one of the darkest times in our modern history of the abuse of our planet by corporations and the U.S. government. Shocking environmental atrocities are still being executed daily. However, there are those who are revealing these hidden abuses and making a hard stand to stop them.

Many of these people exposing the shadows are our youth. This gives me a spark of hope to continue to ignite a passion in others, to move into action and change this destructive trend.

I do know that this can no longer be done passively. We cannot wait for collapse to change what is broken. Shifting the trajectory of the decline of our planet into healing will take much more effort on a grander scale.

We need to globally come together economically, politically, and socially to find solutions to our problems and implement them.

We have been warned that we are using up the Earth's life-giving resources faster than she can replenish herself. Scientists can mathematically see when we will no longer be living life as we know it.

Humanity is not sustainable at the rate of our consumption. We are continuing to add to our global population at an average of 385,000 births a day. That's 140 million people a year!

This is no longer sci-fi storytelling. We are here. The present day *is* the future that we were warned about, only it has come much sooner than was originally projected.

We cannot afford to wait for those in denial to do something to help. We are the ones who need to inspire others to follow our lead through our actions.

This is an overwhelming task, and the question is, do we have the focus and desire and commitment to save our Earth? I don't know, but I do have hope.

***

What stops us from doing the right thing? Laziness, comfort, pressure from others, convenience, cost, denial, disconnection.

I was lucky to grow up with wonderful mentors who taught about the ways of life through nature. As a result, in my early years I not only saw the beauty of nature, but all around me the wounds.

I grew up near the Santa Cruz mountains in a bountiful oasis near a reservoir, along the tree-lined Stevens Creek. It was a lush valley with fruit orchards, meandering creeks, and woods. It was a Garden of Eden but is now unrecognizable as such. Congested with houses, mini-malls, apartments, tech companies, concrete, and pollution, it has become known as the Silicon Valley.

It broke my heart every time a new road, subdivision, or business was built. I had established such a deep connection with its vast natural reserves.

My sacred spaces were being destroyed and I had no one to share my confusion and sadness with. To the best of my knowledge, no one around me saw or felt what I did. My friends thought I was crazy, so I held my feelings in.

I was very angry and scared, but I had to learn to keep seeing the wounds or risk losing my awareness of our natural world by shutting down.

I learned to carry the wounds within myself, and I used them to motivate me to work for our Mother Earth.

Witnessing what was happening to my little corner of the world, I could only imagine what was happening in other parts of the country, and around the world.

The more I studied, the more fanatical I became. I became an Earth warrior ready to do battle with anyone that destroyed the beauty of old growth forests or threatened to fill in marshland for condominium projects.

The angrier I became, the more depressed I was. I was spiraling out of center, and willing to do the same kind of harm to those who were harming *my* Earth.

It was nature who taught me to let go. The victim of all the devastation taught me that she and her beings would survive long past man's demise. A few earthquakes, disease, hurricanes, extreme storms, and climate changes, that bore the extinction of animals and plants so vital to man's survival, would cleanse her surface, and heal her wounds so she could start all over again. Like a dog shaking water from its fur, we would all disappear, and she would continue to heal.

I don't believe that the spirit of Earth wants that - she needs mankind as much as mankind needs her. Like a good mentor, she is telling us a bit more forcefully to change our ways or lose them.

She couldn't be more desperate at this point, but she is still hopeful and still trying to salvage her resources.

Instead of becoming more fanatical, I released my anger into the Earth, and I connected with her spirit on an internal level.

***

As you begin to embrace your place in nature your world unfolds a thousand times bigger, and it can be exhilarating. Being present with these amazing new insights can also be a painful journey as you bear witness to the losses.

The more aware we are we also see the overwhelming damage. Where in the past we might have walked much of our life with blinders on. We either ignore it for the sake of our own sanity, or we see the damage regularly and it puts us in such a negative state of mind, that we're not able to see the positive things in life.

There are times when best intentions, commitment, desire and being present aren't enough to ward off feelings of hopelessness. There are days when every time you read the news there is nothing but bad on all fronts.

Those are the times when we lose our innocence and focus, and we are willing to give up and callously say, "What does it matter anyway? I'm only one person." Yet, those are the times when we need to be the most vigilant to our deepest desires.

We don't like to look at wounds or damage. We don't want to carry the burden of feeling the sadness, but this expanded awareness also gives us the opportunity to make the changes needed.

Take on feeling big feelings as your personal medicine, own your empathy. Your extra sensitivity is a superpower when channeled in a healthy way.

We do need to feel anger and sadness, but we can't let it take us over. Those feelings have a place in our being to motivate us, but they can't become us if we are going to be effective in helping our Earth heal.

We need to set boundaries with our emotions, so they don't become crippling. We are here to also enjoy this world and thrive in this gifted lifetime, and learn bountiful lessons.

One way to fully interact with nature is by having fun. Climb mountains, run the rivers, hike, fish, play, and take in those joy-filled moments.

***

After I read, *A Sand County Almanac*, Aldo Leopold became a hero for me. I finally felt understood and found someone who dared to speak up and act. Reading his words, I knew I was not alone.

"One of the penalties of an ecological education is that one lives alone in a world of wounds. Much of the damage inflicted on land is quite invisible to laymen. An Ecologist must either harden his shell and make believe that the consequences of science are none of his business, or he must be the doctor who sees the marks of death in a community that believes itself well and does not want to be told otherwise."
- Aldo Leopold

***

We are creating genocide with the Earth and its Beings. We have the power to kill our Earth. We also have what we need and the power to save it.

If you truly want to change the world, educate yourself and become aware of what our Earth needs. Read, ask questions and be curious. Part of education is intellectual, but it's also through direct observation.

Years ago, a pilot who had taken classes with me, had dedicated his life to flying over clear cuts around the world. He would publish incredible photographs of them to show others the truth. I'm very educated on the planet and what it needs, but when I saw those photographs, it blew my mind at the damage we've done.

I used to naively drive through Oregon admiring the gorgeous forests and striking wildlands. When I saw the photographs from the air, I learned about the practices of the unethical logging companies. I saw how they would clear cut the forests down to a graveyard of stumps, and leave a short swath of trees along the roads, so the rape of the land was not visible.

I soaked up those images that were so painful, but I didn't allow them to ruin my life. I let what I saw motivate me and I got even more involved. I began educating as many people as I could about what is happening behind the frontline news.

I don't blame the individual loggers; they are making a living by providing what we all need. The problem is the greed of the companies in taking our Earth's resources in an unethical, and unsustainable way.

We need to become aware of wrongdoings by shifting our perspective, identifying, and acknowledging the truth. We need to feel what the destructive effects are, and then heal the damage.

***

The previous leader of Brazil has made a horrible impact on the environment. He has been responsible for destroying 10,000 square miles of rainforests. Can you imagine how many Earth people lost their homes in that process? Can you imagine how many animals lost their lives? How many waterways were destroyed? How long, if ever, until the Earth will be able to heal that wound?

The destruction continues today, every day, and as a global collective we are not doing enough about it. We are not consciously feeling the damaging effects of that loss. We don't allow ourselves to feel the truth of those atrocities. We blame natural disasters for the warming of our planet, and don't take responsibility that it is us that is creating those disasters. We are destroying our life-giving resources and it's madness.

***

One of the worst murders imagined was incited by the 2016 U.S. administration. Four days before they left office, they took wolves off the endangered species list. They allowed a mass murder to take place, for no other reason but cruelty.

Within a matter of three days, the state of Wisconsin wiped out 218 wolves in a public wolf hunt. Many of the wolves were pregnant females and pups in their dens. It was not an ethical way to control predator populations. It was an act of pure evil. They murdered those magnificent animals out of fear and greed.

When the government delisted the wolves from the Endangered Species list and opened it up to a public hunt, it signaled that predators are not of value. Poaching incidents rose, and it is estimated that another 100 wolves were killed that same year. Within one year Wisconsin's wolf population declined by over 30%.

These stories of the wanton killing of animals, or any other inhumane acts do not stay in the headlines for long. They get buried and forgotten, while the destruction continues.

People need to protest and march. If you're doing it for the wolves, you're doing it for the planet. When one species is wiped out, the concentric circles of negative effects continue to cause damage, long after the initial loss. I'll continue to repeat this over and over, all lives affect each other.

***

It is hard to hear these negative stories. We don't want to feel bad about ourselves. However, we should not live in guilt. Guilt should only be a fleeting emotion to spark you into change. It is a reminder to clean up mistakes.

It's ok to feel sadness, but then come back to center. We are always gifted with moments to choose the right thing. Turn your anger and wounds into action to do something for the good.

If you see damage to your waterways and parks, educate people and do what it takes to protect your community's resources.

Healing the Earth is part of your personal healing. Your involvement makes you part of the solution. If you're not helping, you're not much better than those who are doing the physical damage.

The planet is tired. The circle is broken. We take more than we give back. We are exhausting our resources. The Earth is not indispensable.

Imagine our Earth healthy and full of healthy humans, hold that good vision and make it so. Nature happily accepts our help.

It's time for people to get off their butts. It's your Earth, it's your children's Earth. There is no excuse for not being involved in making the planet better. It's your home. Protect it.

Today I heard a billion birds hit buildings and die. I cried. What can be done?

Reconnect And Begin To Heal

I was driving into Santa Cruz in heavy traffic when I saw movement out of the corner of my eye. In an instant a Red-Tailed Hawk hit a truck and the explosion of feathers rained down.

I pulled off at the next exit and headed back to the site in hope of moving the bird off the road, but sadly, the bird had become the road. I often think about it, as it reminds me of how at odds we are with nature.

We can't stop progress, nor would we want to, yet humans are constantly assaulting the natural world. Maybe the death of one hawk seems insignificant, but think about all the animals you see every day that have been struck by cars and lay mangled by the side of a road.

Do you remember the Passenger Pigeon, the Great Auk, the Ivory-Billed Woodpecker, the Heath Hen, or the Labrador Duck?

Did you know that the California Grizzly Bear, so prominently and proudly displayed on the state flag, used to roam the shores along the Pacific Coast 100 years ago? Now they no longer exist in our world except on a flag.

Our greed and over harvest have declared war on the environment. No forest or shoreline, mountaintop or sea bottom is safe from the demands of our consumption. The madness in this short-term thinking is that humans could be the cause of our own extinction.

***

The early Native Americans loved the land. They were the land, and the land was them. Living upon the land and depending on its plants and animals for survival, for shelter, for water, for their spiritual and emotional needs, gave them a personal relationship with all creatures.

When the Europeans declared these people of the Earth heathens and barbaric and took away their traditions, they sought to destroy the spirit and the pride of a nation.

The wounds linger within tribes today. In this act of genocide, the modern world has also lost much of the traditional knowledge that has sustained our Earth's balance.

The more distance between human and nature, the greater the unhappiness becomes. I can't tell you how many adults come to me in tears, after having spent a couple of days on our land and in our classes. They tell me how isolated and lonely they had felt prior to coming to our land. They feel happy and full now, but don't understand why they are crying. These men and women have been touched, some for the first time, by the Earth and her slow meaningful rhythms.

When I tell them they are simply connecting with nature and their true selves, it's almost more than they can comprehend. The city and the frantic pace of their lives have held them captive until that moment.

I marvel at the disconnection created by hours of mindless social media, and marathon video games. Dumbing-down a generation already muted by lack of truth-filled education, lack of exercise, lack of real food, and alienation from all that should give them sustenance – the Earth. We accept this lack of moderation of distractions, and we call it entertainment.

***

There are many ways to honor your relationship with the Earth. When caring people, who imagined a world without wild animals and plants, created Earth Day, they brought that potential outcome into the awareness of many people in the world.

There are activists who sit in trees to save old-growth forests, there are many organizations that fight unethical corporations in court, and there are everyday people who plant gardens and trees. We can all do something.

The Earth Will Remain

It took 65 million years for the universe to create our planet and a place for humans to be created. What a miracle. What took 65 million years to create, humans have come close to destroying in 50 years.

I know that human's interaction with the Earth and the outcome is still truly a mystery. I will not know the outcome in my lifetime, but I do hope I live long enough to be a force for change and witness a positive shift.

I also now know I don't have to save the Earth. I don't have to carry that burden anymore. I've carried it for most of my years. In fact, it's somewhat arrogant to even think that way. While that perception motivated me to teach about nature and fight to save land, it also took its toll on me physically and emotionally.

Our planet is capable of taking care of herself, she's done it perfectly for billions of years. Whether humans remain as a part of our Earth is an unknown. I do know humans would be missed, just as all the extinct species of plants and animals are missed. I also know the Earth will remain and heal her wounds in Earth time.

***

So, where do *I* go from here? I must still be a teacher. It can't be any other way. To inspire my students, I must not live in a place of sadness and despair as I see the wounds to our Earth. I will continue to teach from my heart and heal my sadness through right action.

From this point on I will become a new kind of warrior for the Earth, one that lives in a way that is respectful. One that shares my knowledge and love for the Earth in a positive way, one that fights the good fight, but not from anger.

I will make a difference whenever I can. I will not burn myself out. I know from a place of intellect, personal connection, and love, that our Earth will care for herself as she always has.

My legacy will be in my students, friends, family, my art, and my land. Knowing the influence of my wild, fun, engaging time with the land and water, and its animals fills me up.

As a being of the Earth, it is truly my birthright to live what I love on planet Earth. I carried a weight in me for so many years and now it has been lifted.

I will live the same wonderful life and do the same wonderful work. I will engage with the Earth in the same enjoyable way, and all the while much, much lighter in knowing that our planet will handle the big picture. I will fully commit to doing my part with the gifts I have been given, and that will be enough.

***

One last thing to say on this, I'm writing this sitting on a hill on the Kohola Coast on the Big Island of Hawaii. On land created from volcanic fire and grown into a garden of immense beauty.

I look across the vast Pacific Ocean, and I see Humpback Whales rising and spouting. Their population is growing back to health.

In the 1860's there were nearly 700 whaling ships here, brutally killing whales for oil for light and fuel.

Ironically, what saved the whales from complete extinction was the discovery of oil in Pennsylvania. Oil from whales was not economical any longer. Whale hunting slowed and eventually it was banned.

Now whales are considered sacred animals, honored, and loved. It will be a joy to discover what will replace crude oil as we acknowledge our Earth itself as sacred.

Whales came to winter in paradise. People came and killed the whales. Whales came back with human help. I sit and watch and wonder. What will be next? All the while knowing today, I will swim in gratitude in the Pacific Ocean with these whales close by. I will immerse myself in that life-giving water listening to their song.

I will be a warrior for the Earth for good, kindness, love, and hope. I know that if I only had one life to live, it would be on this good Earth.

A Call To Action

Right now, at this very moment our Earth and all her beings are on the run. It's not too late to reverse this.

The world's problems are so big and overwhelming, but focus on a small task each day. It may seem insignificant, but you do make a difference in that small world, that ecosystem, and that is significant.

Every action and thought creates a change, and every action is meaningful. Start today.

Finding Hope

Right the wrongs and carry great hope. Even if we are weighted down by negative circumstances, without hope we have nothing.

I do have hope that we can figure out what we're going to do, to continue living on this Earth in beauty for all beings.

I have tremendous hope the Earth will be OK in the long run. She has been through major extinctions before, and she has come back to this beautiful being that she is now. Even if we fail to ignore the ever-present signs of her dis-ease, she knows how to take care of herself.

She hasn't however had to come back after a loss of humans. If we continue to damage the Earth, will she be able to come back from us? I think the answer is yes.

So, then the question becomes, will *we* be able to come back? I think that answer is also yes, but on a much smaller scale. To avoid mass extinction on a human level, we must change our behavior.

There is hope everywhere. Every day I see the sunrise and the sunset, the moonrise, and the moonset. That's hope. That is something we need, and I count on it every single day.

I see water flowing, trees growing, and butterflies passing through. I observe varieties of birds fledging babies in my garden, and it gives me hope. They know how to live.

I'm finding hope for our Earth, and for this crazy species called human beings. I read about some of the young people from Generation Z being the newest Earth warriors. They are coming together to make nature and humanity healthier.

They are marching, they're writing letters, they're educating themselves and educating others. More of our youth are participating in their communities and traveling the world, volunteering where help is needed.

I have true hope that this generation is the right one for the time. I know they're going to grow into themselves and make a huge difference. That gives me hope.

We often only see the bad news, and there is a lot of it, but we need to research the good too. It doesn't always make the headlines, but good things are happening in every moment.

The positive stories give us motivation and a reason to get up every day and fight for what we love. We can feel the sadness and the pain, and then we need to get off our couch and work for the planet and for each other. It's possible. It's doable. I have great hope and I mean that.

I see the bad and it is scary. There are a couple of extreme potential futures and many in between. One possible future is a great reduction in the human and animal populations, and the diversity on the Earth. If that happens, our planet will come back, and maybe we will too, but none of it has to happen. We have a big say in how it turns out.

Let's work for hope and help the planet heal, and know we're not alone.

Nature Sanctuary

After I purchased my original 32 acres, I partnered with friends to acquire additional land. We purchased connecting parcels to caretake as a wildlife sanctuary.

I have also encouraged other friends to purchase land in the area as well for this same reason. Some of the people live in houses on their land. Some people camp on their land. They are separately owned parcels, but they are maintained with the land and animal's best interest in mind. I have loosely called these adjoining properties, the Headwaters Land Trust.

These connected parcels are vital for animal habitat. Animals need large sections of fenceless space to roam and feed.

Imagine if hundreds or thousands of people worked together to do this same thing. This is a way to be caretakers as individuals, while working with a community.

Instead of a homeowner's association, we could have an Earth Caretaker's association. We would maintain our own land or yard in a way that is also of benefit to wildlife and to the surrounding land. Instead of dogmatic rules on appearance, there would be suggestions of what would be congruently helpful to the wildlife across all connected parcels.

One Dream

I have one simple dream, that humans wake up and care for our planet. Our current technology is so advanced it can help in massive ways. We know how to live sustainably, and we have the ability to invent new technologies as needed.

I've seen the world come together for the greater good. During World War II, the world came together to stop the Nazis and the imperial Japanese, in basically five years. It can be done. It must be done.

Many problems must be handled at once; racism, poverty, global warming, overpopulation, food production, getting off our dependence on oil and coal, over logging, over mining, abuse of the ocean, air, land, and animals.

More land and all wildlife need to be protected. Not a single extinction should be allowed to happen. If humans came together, we could take on the problems of famine, war, slavery, gross wealth, corruption, and discrimination.

We have the intelligence, but we are the only animal that has come close to destroying our own home. Yet, we also have a tremendous ability to create beauty.

We created these problems, and we can fix them. With an honest assessment, facts only, it looks really bad. Although, I believe it only takes 5% of the population, if completely united, to change the world. So, what am I going to do to wake people up?

I may be a Dreamer, but this Dream must come true, and it can. Any other alternative is surely madness. Now is our time, we must get to work. Dream big and live well with our precious planet.

- The Dreamer

We humans are supreme predators. So good that we made it this far in every environment on our planet. - So good that we kill each other. - So good that we kill our Earth and the beings that live upon it. If we took our predatory nature and redirected that power for good, for love, for peace, for right living, wow, we'd become Earth Caretakers. It's within our reach.

Heroes

Where are the heroes? Who are they? Our Earth asks, our animals ask, our trees and oceans ask. Truth can be very painful. The time has arrived for truth to action. The time of heroes has arrived.

Be a voice for animals who need your help. If you see a wrong being done, speak up. It is better to act, than to not say or do something to right a wrong and fail that animal. If you know better, then be the one that will do better.

Wake up and find that place inside and change course! There is no time to wait. The time is now and past. The moment of greatness and purpose and wonder has arrived.

In these times you will find out who you are and find your place in the battle for our Earth. It's time to be a free thinker, and for words to become action. This is Earth-human time.

There is no higher honor than defending our Earth. So, hear the cry for help. It's your time to be a hero.

Guardian For Birds

Birds are in severe trouble. Global Warming, human overpopulation, use of pesticides, massive building of roads, and huge buildings are affecting birds and their migratory patterns.

To give you an idea of what millions of birds are facing every day, think about these questions: How many countless birds fly into buildings in their migratory pass at night, fall to the sidewalk and get swept up like garbage in the morning? How many countless birds get hit by cars? How many birds are poisoned from pesticides on plants, or affected by them by softening their eggs and making them crack? How many birds are shot for fun, not with honorable and skilled hunting, but just killed randomly? How many birds are lost to house cats? How many birds are affected by the loss of forests from fires and storms?

Imagine what it's like for a bird to go through a hurricane or tornado or a forest fire. Add to those dangers, the bird's challenge of survival from their natural predators. Our birds are in trouble folks.

You have probably heard the story of how coal miners took canaries down into the mines. Birds are very sensitive to the environment around them. If the air was unsafe, the canaries would die, and the coal miners would quickly leave the mines.

This scenario is what's happening in our world. Birds are telling us there's a problem! We need to pay attention and act quickly to remedy this.

If birds can't live here safely on our planet, the birds are telling us neither will we. They're telling us by giving their lives up, and it's sad.

Can you imagine a world without the beautiful colors of songbirds or hummingbirds? Can you imagine a world without gulls and pelicans on the ocean? Can you imagine a world without eagles or wild turkeys? It wouldn't be a world I'd want to live in.

Birds are the greatest teachers for us if we allow them to be. To help these wonderful beings you must be committed to observing them. A willingness to take time to be with them and follow them with your eyes. Not to just check a species of bird off a treasure hunt list, but to get to know them individually. What color are they? What do they eat? How do they live? Where do they build their nests? What needs do they have?

Study what birds are endangered in your area? What can you do to help them? Can you improve their habitats?

One way you can help birds is to turn your yard into a bird sanctuary. Landscape with plants that feed birds and shelter them from predators. Supply water and quality bird seed.

We all need to care for our birds. Not only are they an umbrella species that affect our entire ecosystem, they are also beautiful gifts of the heart.

Be of service to the Earth. How are you a part of the problem? How are you a part of the solution? Now show up!

13

Justice For The Earth

Human Evolution As Earth Caretakers – Healing The Earth

If you go back in human history long before gardening, when we were hunter gatherers, that was as pure as you get with the Earth, those could be tough times, but harmonious times.

There came a time in our history when we started to grow food, and a lot of things changed for the good, and a lot of things changed for the bad.

Once we started agriculture our population grew. We put up fences, marked our territory, and made our human and animal neighbors enemies to keep them from taking our food. We killed animals that ate our food, and then we domesticated animals for food and became disconnected.

We stopped looking at animals as friends and brothers and sisters. We took our sacred relationship with animals and turned them into working slaves. We went from loving them, and caring for them, and respecting them, to treating them like property.

As we started to raise animals in enclosed, crowded spaces, their quality of life went down quickly. We lost our way and our connection with the Earth.

Move forward a thousand years and we now have one of the darkest things humans do, factory farming. This evil is truly something that needs to stop immediately.

As we started to grow plants, as beautiful as it was, we created another problem. We grew them so intensely there was competition for nutrients and light, and of course animals tried to eat them, and ironically, we started poisoning plants and animals to protect our food.

I am challenged daily with deterring animals and insects in my own garden. In our ongoing challenge, we humans took it to an extreme. We created chemical fertilizers, and poisons, and started factory farming.

These chemicals not only kill animals, but they absorb into our food, and the runoff gets into our water, and we are killing ourselves. There are over 800 deadly chemicals embedded in our soil. We know this, and yet even today we continue to add it into our food source. This is the definition of insanity. Ultimately, we all suffer for this.

***

Our culture has implanted in us that we are better than. Even if we don't consciously believe that, it's there. We need to know that there is nothing more important than something else. Judgment clouds truth.

Nature does not create inferior or superior beings, only beings. All of Earth's beating hearts are interrelated: one heart.

If humans believe that we are superior to other living beings, our future on this Earth will be in peril. Our soul injustices will grow in countless forms: Patriarchy, racism, sexism, homophobia, classicism, ageism, environmental destruction, cruelty to animals, and violent acts will continue, and eventually equal our end.

All beings have an inherent right to justice. Humans have become the masters of injustice, and so we can change injustice to justice. It begins with you, right now.

To make real change in our world we must seek justice for all living beings. Earth justice is linked to social justice. Human oppression is tied to the oppression of animals and nature. We will not change the cruelty that humans inflict on each other, without also changing the cruel acts towards animals and nature. What humans do to nature we do to ourselves.

Before we can change anything, we must own what we did, we must tell the truth. Admit what we have done and then stop it and do it differently.

We need to take responsibility for the pain and suffering animals go through in our factory farms, mis-run zoos, circuses, sport hunting, and fish farming. To pretend it is not happening is soul death to us.

To be a feeling, loving, caring person and not do something to change this abuse is wrong. It destroys our sensitivity, and our self-respect.

Knowing our behavior, I'm still not going to call us bad, we are learning how to live on Earth. Maybe we need to go through this dark mess, to come out the other side to find the beauty of how to garden in a good way.

Organic gardening is catching on again. Animals are being raised in a beautiful way and are being cared for. People are educating themselves more, and learning where and how the animals were raised for their meat. Many farmers are making sure no pesticides are used to grow their crops.

Think of the resources 8 billion humans use. By choosing to live simply, being mindful of what you buy and not over-consuming, makes a huge difference, and allows others to live. Your choice in organic, humane, and fair-trade food, especially makes an impact on the lives of others.

How you spend your money is a powerful statement to the producers. Where there is a demand for products or services that's what will be made available. Buy food that supports our planet's health and supports the people who grow or raise it.

Be mindful of food that is wasted. Half of all food from our own homes, restaurants, and grocery stores is thrown away. That is an amazing amount of resources used, and food and lives wasted.

I've tried to shop in ways that are better for the planet. By no means am I perfect, but I'm making a genuine effort in being mindful of my consumption.

At Headwaters this is a constant challenge. We feed our students and staff members three meals a day for seven months. We have an organic garden, and have raised our laying hens, and keep our own honeybees, but we also need to supplement what we don't have.

Our neighbors raise livestock, and while we do purchase their meat on a small scale, we cannot afford to supply our entire school all year.

Every expense makes a difference in the stability of our small business, so it is very hard to not cut corners, and many times we do. We have a lot we can improve on, and we are always striving to do better without losing the quality of what we serve.

Each one of us Earth lovers must make it part of our life to give our best in being mindful of our impact in this world. When we do this, we build our self-respect and find our place in this life. From this place, many paths become clear, and our lives become more meaningful.

Love animals with all your heart. Help animals with all that you have available to you. Fight the good fight in a good way, and I believe one day the horrible things humans do to our Earth, to our animals, and to ourselves, will stop.

We must unite as protectors of our Earth. When this happens, humans will advance in our evolution. We will get to our next level of living life. It may happen soon or much later. Earth Time is patient. The hope for our future depends on how we treat our Earth.

We have also done amazing things. We have created the National Park system and have saved wild lands and waters. We are making wrongs right again.

We are supposed to be here. We are not an accident. We are not a mistake. We are a gift to the planet, but we are at a defining point where we need to make drastic changes immediately.

You start repairing the broken circle by repairing the circle you are in control of now. You have control of your personal circle. Repair the bigger circle by making yours whole.

Nature never forgets. Leave it alone and it will return. Give it a helping hand, and it will return more beautiful than ever. Through our partnership with our Earth, we can right our wrongs.

Volunteer-Be Of Service

Live for the Earth. She lives for you. If you see a job that needs to be done it's yours to do. If you need help, ask.

Everything you do for nature will send out concentric rings that make our world a better place. Find a cause and fight for it through right, loving action. Know that you are caring for *your* caretaker, Mother Earth. This is full circle living.

It's not enough to love our Earth. In these most troubling times, we must fight for our Earth. It's an honorable fight. Choose your battles, then go to work.

"I have hope for our Earth, she knows how to survive, but the human being?..." - E.K.

Mono Lake- Bird Time

In 1988 I was very lucky to spend two weeks living on the isolated and rugged islet, Krakatoa in Mono Lake. I was helping a group of bird-lovers band and study the nesting California Gulls, in the hope of using the finding to support the fight to save Mono Lake. The lake was dropping to a dangerous level, due to feeder streams being diverted to water lawns in the Los Angeles area.

As the water drained, the Gulls were vulnerable. Coyotes and other predators were able to get into their nesting grounds and eat the young birds and eggs. We saw much evidence of this, and it was tragic.

A grass-roots environmental group called; "Save Mono Lake Committee" had started up in the lakeside town of Lee Vining. This battle was immensely important.

The vast Owens Lake, and many creeks and rivers in the valley had already been drained to a dust bowl. Mono Lake seemed to be doomed. This was the classic tale of David and Goliath, and became one of the great environmental stories of our time, as a judge eventually stopped the theft of water from the feeder streams.

There is still work to be done, but this was an amazing achievement for our Earth, which started as a grassroots movement.

One thing I learned from this experience was the great truth from anthropologist Margaret Mead, *"Never doubt that a small group of thoughtful, committed citizens can change the world; indeed, it's the only thing that ever has."*

***

Mono Lake was drained severely and is still slowly coming back. It will now take vigilance, patience, nature, and healing work.

My time on the lake was a treasured experience. There is no doubt that this lake is sacred. To live on that island with the gulls was a true, peak moment in time. It was an opportunity that I have unforgettable, boundless gratitude for.

Nature will heal itself. If we get out of the way she'll do her own thing to restore balance, but if we can help, then why not?

There are countless moments each day that give you an opportunity to be a hero for nature.

Wild Lands And Oceans

The idea of State Parks, National Parks, Wilderness Areas, Wildlife Refuges, and Ocean Refuges were initiated by U.S. citizens and visionary presidents. This movement to save land spread throughout the world. Proof that world-wide cooperation in saving our planet is more than possible.

I have great gratitude for these forward thinkers. In 1864 Abraham Lincoln saved the magnificent, open land of Yosemite Valley and Mariposa Big Tree Grove by designating them as state protected land. Years later, Theodore Roosevelt, along with naturalist, John Muir, further protected Yosemite by saving it as a National Park.

Imagine all the trees, plants, bodies of water, mountains, meadows, animals, fish, insects, birds, and reptiles that have been protected. What also needs to be known is that countless people helped to make that happen. Landscape painters, explorers, hunters, fishermen, and naturalists, helped to save the wildlands and ocean by expressing their love of nature in their own way.

I invite you to study those that laid this foundation. One of my mentors once said, "Remember those that dug the well." Honoring good people is a way to keep great things happening through inspiration.

I will always honor and respect President Jimmy Carter for saving more land in Alaska, with a swipe of his pen, than all saved lands in the other 49 states. If he hadn't made that bold move, much of that precious land today would be under oil and gas, and mining destruction.

President Barack Obama went on to make history by being the person to save the most land and waterways than any other president prior. He has protected millions of acres of land and waterways, but for reasons unknown, this achievement mostly went unrecognized by the people. This truly is a heroic accomplishment that will have nothing but positive, lifesaving results for generations to come.

Let's set our sights now on saving at least 50% of all land on Earth. This will save most of Earth's remaining species, including ourselves, and turn the corner on planetary destruction.

Genius is the ability to live in an environment in a way that is good for all Beings. We must save wild land for nature to thrive.

Being of service is love manifesting into right action.

Forward Thinking Caretakers

Aldo Leopold, along with a few other people, started the movement to create the Wilderness Act of 1964. This created wilderness areas throughout America. Wilderness areas are truly wild, as land has always been throughout nature's time.

The Wilderness Act was established with the foresight that we are saving pure, wild land for the sake of the land itself, and for the protection of all the Beings who dwell within it.

People are encouraged to spend time in the wild lands, but this land is for the land and Beings to thrive. It is not protected solely for human use, but for humans to fully live.

Wilderness areas are waiting for you. Wilderness is where the Earth gods go to fully be in pure nature.

We find humility in the wilderness. It's in that humility that we find ourselves as a part of a universal spirit within everything. With this knowing we become good, reverent beings and cannot help but to protect what we are a part of, and love.

"Consciousness is awareness of ourselves, and our place in the Universe. Consciousness is knowing our place in the natural world. Knowing that we belong on this Earth! Knowing how we affect all life. Caring about all life. Caring for all life as best we can. Becoming an Earth Caretaker, evolving into an Earth Keeper. Living our calling. Calling Home to the Earth. We have arrived. Home. Now be thankful and enjoy. It's ok." - E.K.

Volunteer Your Time For Nature

When fighting for the Earth, the greatest gift you have to offer is yourself. With your brain, your hands, your legs, and your heart, find ways to volunteer your time for the Earth.

You're not doing it for money or to feed your ego, you're getting involved because it's the right thing to do.

Check out your community, who's cleaning up the rivers? Who's helping wild animals in wildlife rescues? Who's sending out letters to politicians to make improvements happen on a larger scale?

Find a way to volunteer. Come up with your own ideas and be a leader and make it happen. The great gift of volunteering your time for nature is that you get to be out in it. You get to interact with her in a healing way. Often, that means if you're restoring a damaged creek bed, you get to be physically, emotionally, and intellectually fully involved. You are restoring the natural flow of nature while doing the same for yourself.

Build your relationship up with nature while you're making the world a better place to live. By doing this you are becoming a steward of the planet. You're having fun. You're getting exercise. You're hanging out with good people, and maybe making new friends and creating a new community.

You can return to these locations year after year, and observe and feel the healing of place. That is the reward, a sense of greater purpose and making a difference on our planet.

In the sixties and seventies our country went nuts damming up wild rivers. Many of these dams are no longer needed and they harm wildlife and the ecosystems. Going into the future, help is needed in taking down dams that are doing more harm than good, and restoring the land around them.

Hundreds of people tore down a dam on a big river in the state of Washington and helped with the process of restoring the river. They planted native trees and vegetation, and created wildlife habitat. They worked with the river to create pools for fish and native, aquatic life.

Returning to the river after the work was completed, you would never know there was ever a dam there. Nature remembers and knows how to heal herself. She'll do it on her own, but when we help, it speeds the whole process up. We lead the way, and nature takes over and goes to work.

What a beautiful partnership, and why wouldn't there be? We're all the same, we are of this Earth.

Wake up every day and ask yourself, what can I do today to make the world a better place? Please realize that you are a gift, and you can offer the greatest gift to our planet, to all life, by being of service.

We Belong Here

Find the gift that we are. We are supposed to be here. Being born into difficult times means we have a Call to greatness to use our talents and skills. We are born to be Earth Caretakers. Many people have lost sight of this and need to be reminded.

Humanity is very immature right now. We are young and still learning. We are a complicated species, but we are also special, and we belong here. Feel gratitude for the blessing of being born into this life.

We are all connected, and we are not more important than a toad. We all have a place on this Earth, and a purpose here for each other. The toad is perfect for what it's here for, and so are we.

I sit with the land and ask – What is the human being's purpose on planet Earth? The answer – Enjoy participation. What more could you possibly want?

Imagine Every Day An Earth Day

Imagine every day is a day to celebrate the Earth. Each day begins with conscious awareness of your home. As you celebrate your possessions, imagine that you take the same celebratory joy in your Earthly home.

Imagine a day when you are stressed, and you drive to a place outside the city where you can hike a short distance, and sit beneath a beautiful old tree, and listen to the caws of ravens or the hawks screeching.

Imagine such a place where you can find comfort, solace and quiet from a hard day. A place where you can connect with yourself again. A place where you find the replenishment you need, to return to the space of your beautiful things, with gratitude for all that life has given you. Imagine what your world would be like if that place didn't exist.

Upon your return home, while admiring the sky on a full-moon night, fully taking in the clarity of beauty of that moment, even as traffic noise fills the air, you can still connect to the mystery felt by your ancestors.

Whether you love the Earth quietly or loudly, love it whole-heartedly.

Where To Start?

We need to build a relationship with the Earth first. We need to play on Her, and with Her, and protect Her. Once you know love of our Earth, and are touched when you go into nature and know it is Home, Earth-heart, one heart, Earth-mind, one mind, Earth-body, one body, then it's a must happen situation.

The best Earth Caretakers are the people who can feel the pain of the Earth and let it motivate them to take action. Building your nature awareness will strengthen your lifelong personal connection with nature.

Go into the wild, listen and follow what you feel. That's it, you're on your way.

Part 1

Nature Awareness

Awaken your senses and welcome the wild in. Build your personal relationship with nature by rewilding your heart.

Chapter 3

Awaken Your Senses

Our senses are the doorways to a deep personal connection with our Earth, and all that lives upon her. The more we develop them the more amazing they become. They are limitless in their potential. Building a relationship with your senses allows you to trust them as reliable friends.

Unnatural scents assault our senses, so we shut down our smell. We take in constant noise daily and our hearing is muted. We've dumbed down our senses in this modern world and we need to bring them back to life.

We gain knowledge through thinking. We also process information gathered from our physical senses. Through our heightened senses, comes our wisdom through our experiences.

When you are attuned to your senses your body communicates with you through this physical language. You can use your senses as tools to connect and tune into nature.

When our senses are heightened our world becomes more profound and more alive. Our heightened five physical senses open us to our sixth sense, which leads us into the spiritual, or mystical world of nature.

Our sixth sense or intuition is emotional intelligence. Our gut is where this primal wisdom dwells.

Nature is the ultimate teacher for developing our gut feeling. By getting out into the wilds we have endless opportunities to perfect this skill and live fully. In those moments of awareness are the sacred experiences.

The land becomes brighter as we observe more keenly. We stop only being observers passing through. We become an active part of the living process of life, truly in love with all of what the Earth has to offer and all the Earth is.

***

Coming home to nature is about being aware of the rhythms of the Earth. It's about paying attention to full moons, witnessing the trees bud in the spring, and drop their leaves in the fall.

Part of the reason global warming has exceeded scientist's estimations, is because modern man's desire for an easier life than his ancestor's, has almost eliminated his connection with nature. We have lost our direct awareness of our environment's needs.

Living in nature's flow isn't always convenient, but we need to find balance in our pace. Our desire to conquer nature has distanced us from magic and wonder. Many people engage passively, and their relationship with nature is cognitive through television documentaries.

Throughout most of our lives we attempt to separate ourselves from nature out of comfort and convenience, causing a feeling of emptiness in our hearts and souls. We become so sheltered we lose that sense of fully being alive.

We wear heavy layers of clothes, so we don't feel the weather. We wear thick shoes, so we don't feel the ground. We build houses and buildings that keep us from feeling, seeing, smelling, and hearing nature.

Coming home to the natural world is where many people long to be. Finding one's personal connection with nature, is finding one's power. Finding one's power is what creates miracles and change.

It's not always easy to connect with raw nature. Many of the great wild areas that were accessible have been developed. The few, natural recreation areas that we have set aside near the outskirts of suburbs and cities, have lists of rules about staying on the designated paths, and what you can't do and where you can't go.

There is minimal adventure in exploring these controlled spaces. We need those open spaces, but there is also a craving demand for the freedom of wild space. We have lost the respect and care for our Earth because we no longer live in it, but upon it.

***

Think of a time when you were moved by a sunset or felt peaceful sitting under a tree. Perhaps a bird migration caught your eye as you drove, sealed within your car, and you felt an inexplicable yearning. Remember the last time you were caught in a storm, and it made you feel alive, even humbled?

The more distant people get from knowing the Earth, the greater their unhappiness becomes. There are usually tears of sadness for all that they've missed in their rapid paced lives. As they awaken their senses, those tears turn to gratitude for finally having the experience they've been unknowingly craving. Our heightened awareness makes everything brighter and more beautiful.

They have been touched, some for the first time, by the Earth, and her slow-moving rhythms. They are connecting with nature and their true selves. They finally have a feeling of belonging, and not feeling isolated. The frantic pace of their lives had held them captive until that moment.

Our culture doesn't always allow for quiet time. Earth-connections aren't supported in most schools, and home life is so busy there is barely time for family dinners once a week.

One of the greatest gifts a parent can give their family is quiet time in nature, whether it's at the beach, or in the mountains or desert or in their backyard.

Many of the kids I work with have no ability or desire to spend time by themselves. They want to be entertained from the outside in, rather than entertaining themselves.

Eyes glued to a screen, constant blaring music to numb the mind, and shopping malls, acting as playgrounds, are defining the character of our lost youth.

It worries me of what our planet will be like in twenty years. Our children are growing up in a world so removed from the very force that gives us life and sustains us.

We all enjoy the convenience and comfort of our warm houses and all our toys. We are social creatures by nature, but it's all about balance. Get quiet sometimes and tune back in.

What Nature Brings To Our Lives

We must be *committed* to developing a personal connection with nature as a foundational part of our life. This cannot be something on the side we fit in.

At some point the spirit of the Earth that lives within us, becomes who we are. It becomes a driving reason to live fully.

A true, nature connection contributes to our physical body's health, enriches our mind and beliefs, and fills our soul and spirit. This restores balance in all aspects of our life, in love, work, play, family, and community.

Our physical, mental, emotional, and spiritual aspects of ourselves must be in balance, and not dominate the other, to be at our best. When all is in harmony, we are content, we feel we are on the right path and life works.

Wake Up Aware

Greet the day in a conscious way. Each one of your senses needs to wake up. Look for the beauty that speaks to you and let your eyes soak it up.

Look wide and feel the land through your eyes. Look closely, find the detail in patterns. Find the colors that call to you. Feel gratitude for the gift of sight.

Wake up your smell. Breathe in the air, the ground, trees, flowers, water. Be thankful for the gift of smell.

Wake up your ears. Listen near and far. Listen to the individual sounds and the symphony, the birds and insects, the wind and water. All are the songs of the Earth. Be thankful.

Feel the land with your bare feet and hands. Know that you are a part of it. Taste the air, leaves, and water. Blend it all together inside yourself. Wake up in a blessed way with gratitude, and your day immediately becomes amazing.

A willingness to be aware allows you to recognize when help is needed. All of this takes minutes, it's well worth the time. Make it a great day for all living beings by living well.

End The Day

End the day with completion, reflections and learning from your day. Observe the light move to dark.

Watch the night sky and dream upon a star. Find your star, the one that calls to you and speaks to your dream, reach up, and touch it.

Offer gratitude for the day. Contemplate those highlights. Remember your peak moments, the ones that became medicine, that stay with you for life.

Take a night walk or sit. Breathe that sweet air and know what a gift it is to be human on our sacred Earth.

A Good Morning Lesson

Picture this, I'm on the Big Island of Hawaii. I awaken and walk down to the shoreline, and sit with a massive Kiawe tree, relaxing and enjoying the view. Whales are jumping, boats are cruising, turtles are swimming.

A shorebird joins me, walking around me and sitting next to me. I could reach out and touch this bird. What a sacred moment we share.

After a while, this bird starts to peck the ground next to me, and lo and behold, a massive ant trail. Here I was, right next to this trail, and I was so focused on the ocean and the bird that I missed this ant universe. This bird showed me the trail, and my awareness expanded. I enjoyed my bird time and all that it showed me. What else was I missing?

Beauty Is A Vibration

Beauty is felt within, it is heard, smelled, tasted, and then seen. Your senses trigger memories. Smells of home and sounds of special moments.

Thank your senses, your body, for being able to take in and experience everything. Never take it for granted.

Gathering Memories

Of course, I am in awe of the gorgeous, expansive views, but my eyes are also drawn to the details. The tiniest of highlights; shapes, colors, textures, and lights that make up the whole view. I'm drawn to the small parts that make the grand vistas what they are.

There is not a moment that slips by without my eyes catching the light sparkle on a leaf, pierce through a raindrop dangling above, or outline the silhouette of a back-lit, twisted branch.

I am often drawn to step off my intended path to squish a mossy rock, pressing my hand deep into the loamy, wet, brilliant green.

Seeking contrast, my fingers run along the crackled, flaky bark of an elder, cedar tree.

I welcome in the sweet smell so deeply of a sugar pine, that I fill my lungs completely with its cotton candy essence.

With a child-like slurping of a popsicle, I taste the citrus icicles dripping from a fir tree's needles, taking in the bright, freshness of the forest.

I stop and tune into the distinct, far away call of the Sandhill Crane's early, spring arrival, while breathing in the warm, medicine winds that come and go so quickly, that I'm not certain it wasn't a dream.

Deep inside me I feel a premature mourning of the time in which I won't be on this physical Earth. I find myself soaking up and collecting memories of my abundant life, to take with me on the unknown journey that is to come someday.

I am gathering sacred moments for a time when I do leave this body. I want to re-member all parts of my physical experiences, and all the senses I have been gifted.

Do we have our physical sensations when we pass on to a different way of life? I don't know, but I will take these treasured memories with me just in case, to reconnect me with my Earthly Home. - Julie

Let your senses feel love individually, and then in harmony.

Enhance Your Vision

One of the gifts of being human are our amazing eyes. Being top of the food chain predators, our eyes through time have become a most serious tool when in nature. What's more incredible is that our eyesight can be enhanced with some simple exercises.

Free your eyes from your brain. Your brain controls what you see through your thoughts. It communicates to your eyes where and how to look. Sometimes your eyes will miss what's so apparent because of preconceived thoughts.

Quiet your mind and let your eyes wander. When they see something that interests them, they will get back in touch with the brain. This will improve your eyesight significantly. The only thing that limits your visual awareness are your thoughts getting in your way.

Your eyes have their own consciousness. Give them freedom to wander. This is how our Earth loving ancestors saw their environment. Set your eyes free and see where they lead you.

***

The Apache scouts were sometimes called the shadow people. They learned to look into the shadows where animals knew to hide. When they fought the U.S. Calvary, they used this knowledge of the deer to evade the soldiers.

Look beyond the edge of a forest and into it. Let your eyes filter through the trees, like water meandering through grass, over the branches and under. Notice the layers of underbrush and the grand canopy towering above.

Travel deep into the shadows. See more than you allowed yourself to see before. Learn to see into darkness. See designs in the shadows. There's a whole other layered, shadow world there. Then follow the gap between those dark spots until you see light. You will see far beyond your imagination.

***

When searching for animals in the environment, don't only look for the whole animal. Look for their body parts like a tail, nose, and legs. Some animals may be covered by branches or grass. Once you see a leg, then the whole animal will come into focus.

Take your time. If movement catches your eye, pay attention, and then focus on the animal emerging.

Animals use all their senses, but visually they rely on seeing movement to alert themselves to possible danger.

When you do spot an animal, stay with them as long as you can. Follow a bird through the sky or trees. Watch it until it is completely out of sight. You will gain tremendous knowledge.

Through careful observation, your relationship with an animal will grow on an intimate level, watching it go about the business of living life. Sharing in another being's life shows respect, and it's also fun being so engaged.

***

If your intuition says, look around that tree, do it and see what's there. As a photographer, I know by simply moving my body to the side or getting higher or lower, laying down, or walking a few feet in any direction, can completely change my view and my photograph. Get curious, get up close and shift your perspective to see the same thing differently.

Climb a tree and take in the views. Crawl through brush and observe through primal eyes. Use the existing landscape features to help you see more, and look up, always look up.

Owl Eyes

Owls don't see in the complete dark, but they do have amazing eyes that allow them to see well at night by collecting light from the moon and stars.

Our ancestors learned to open their eyes wide, which helped greatly for night vision. As they discovered, it became a great tool for seeing landscape in the daytime as well.

Stretch your eyes like you stretch your muscles. With wide-open eyes, we don't see perfectly clear, however, we do take in much more of the larger landscape. When we notice a movement or shadow or color or something that's interesting to us, then we can switch to a sharper, focused vision.

Use owl eyes with slow barefoot walking as a meditation. Connect on a heart level and feel yourself as a part of the landscape. Learn from our owl friend and open your eyes.

I See The Earth

Sometimes I see the Earth in highlights. Sometimes I see the Earth in shapes and patterns. Sometimes I see the Earth in colors. Sometimes I see the Earth in music.

It's in these moments, some of them a flash, some of them so much more, that I touch all that is good and real. I know I belong as a living part of this immense place I call Home.

The Earth speaks through my eyes to my soul. They wake up inner journeys within me and set fire to my better self.

Acknowledge the beauty you see, and it will live within you.

Go And Look

When you look at plants in a forest, a hedge, a meadow, anywhere, if it's brighter in some way it could be calling you. It might be showing you its beauty in a more detailed way, teaching you another way of seeing.

This is often how plants speak to the world around them, and engage with others. Sadly, we often ignore the call, and we never know what we've missed. Go and look.

The Silver Leaf Palm

After arriving at my rental cottage on the Big Island of Hawaii, I looked out the window and a silver leaf palm tree called to me. It was brighter than bright, among a forest of colorful, tropical plants.

A couple of days later it called me again. I walked over to it and found a whole world unto itself living on the palm.

Inside every other large leaf was a wasp nest. In front of every nest was a Golden Orb Spider. On every leaf was a green gecko.

I noticed all three animals were helping each other to live. The wasps were in the back of the leaf, building an intricate, chambered nest. They were artists in progress.

They cared for the eggs as well as any human mother cares for her baby waiting to be born. It was inspiring.

The Golden Orb Spider built a masterful web across the front of the leaves. The golden spider itself was two inches wide and was exquisite.

The spider babies inside a carefully and lovingly woven sack, were awaiting that sacred moment when they would birth into our world.

On the edge of the leaf was a gecko. It was art and color at its best, wearing brilliant greens and reds. The lizard ate the insects that were coming onto the leaf, with the intention of eating the spider and wasp babies.

The wasp protected the lizard from birds by warning them. The spider was always on the lookout, and ate the insects that came into the leaf to eat the plant.

The top edges of the leaves had stringy fibers hanging down to frame this living masterpiece.

I gave a thankful blessing to that amazing palm tree for the gift of that experience, and for expanding my awareness of our incredible planet.

A spider, a lizard and many wasps, all serious predators, were getting along for the greater good. Who is the wiser? Humans or the spiders, lizards, and wasps? Just wondering.

The Bee And The Orchid

Today I watched a bee fly into an orchid flower for pollen. The flower closed upon the bee. I saw that the bee was vibrating inside the flower. To my amazement the flower opened, out came the bee, dazed, and confused and covered with pollen. Off the bee flew to the next orchid. Pollination complete.

To witness this moment was a lifetime gift. Careful observation without judgment is required to allow nature to teach us her ways. Sit, be still, and observe. That's it.

Woods Walk

I walk into the woods with the eyes of an artist. My God! I can't believe the beauty I see! Sculptures, paintings, carvings, patterns, shapes, and colors. It's an art museum. All of it. The living Earth and all its beings, art and nature as one.

I walk into the woods with the eyes of a scientist. My God! I can't believe what I see! All green things, leaves, grasses, bringing in the sunlight to grow the forest and meadows. I see the web of life, it speaks to me of how life works, it's amazing.

The science of how our Earth works is a living miracle and it's comforting to know that I am a part of all of it. I just love knowing this. Science, nature, and humans as one.

I walk into the woods with the eyes of a caretaker. My God! I can't believe the work I'm being called to do! Trimming trees, moving rocks, making animal habitats. I am the Earth. I work for the Earth. Life's purpose, oneness, fun. I see all that needs to be done in my woods. Home at last.

I walk into the woods with the eyes of a tracker. My God! I can't believe what I see! The ground is nothing but tracks. Tracks up trees, down holes, across creeks, nests, bites, fur, scat, broken branches, bones, and holes.

The forest is alive with tracks, each is a story, each is life, each is nature's art, animal art. To be a tracker is a guarantee of a good life. My God, I love the woods!

Nature's Art

Shapes and patterns bring us into the intricate beauty of nature, often leading our eyes into surprises such as faces, signs, and symbols. Sometimes these signs can be very meaningful to us, and sometimes they're just fun to find and thought provoking.

Look at rocks and trees and see what is looking back at you. I've found the face of a Native American man looking north on the eastern slope of Mt. Shasta, half the size of the mountain.

Sometimes shapes speak to us by inviting us further into what we're looking at. Shapes within objects don't have to mean anything other than being nature's art.

Some images have been seen by all people for hundreds of years, and some symbols are personal just for you. Whether nature is speaking to you symbolically, or you're just enjoying nature's artwork, it can only be good to look more inquisitively into this fascinating Earth.

Color

Color is one way our Earth and all its living beings speak to us. Each color has its own language. It's an ancient language that we can remember. In fact, we already know it.

When color calls to you, for example, a red flower, or a green leaf, go to this color and feel it, smell it, look at it, listen to it.

Paint with your eyes. Look into nature and mix colors. Sense what each color *feels* like to you. What colors call to you? Color speaks to our higher selves. Color heals, color inspires, color connects us to our Earth through emotion.

Spend time with colors and find your color's language. Each human has a primary color. What is yours?

How many colors of green are there in a forest?

"Earth Keepers see new colors never known to humans. Earth Keepers see brighter." E.K.

Chasing Rainbows Is A Worthy Journey

When you think you've got the rainbow and find out you don't, well, that's the moment to believe in faith, magic, and other possibilities.

Look beyond the rainbow. There's more for you to see. The colors of the rainbow live within each living being. Find them there.

Look Again

When I see an animal, when I see a forest, when I see ocean waves, when I see mountains, I know when I first look, I see the surface of what's physically visible to my eyes.
On second look I wander into the soul of those sacred beings. I connect with my kindred spirits.

My eyes journey up and down the trees, and I'm led into their roots. I travel through timber and spot the squirrels, and fox, and insects. I wander through the grasses, and flowers, and creeks, following the heart of the forest.

The ocean waves take me on a journey to the depths beyond sight. The mountains take me inside. Losing myself in the labyrinth of the Earth's tunnels, is where I find my Earth-Self.

When I look inward, I always find that I am home right here where I belong.

"There is no beauty unless you perceive it. Where does this perception come from? There must be a place inside our being where beauty lives. Find that place and live in beauty." -E.K.

Look Up And Expand Your World

We tend to be single minded in what we do, we're purpose driven. So often, when we walk in nature, we tend to look forward or down at our feet. We forget we have an entire Universe just above us.

Learn to look up. Expand your awareness by looking up at trees. Look at the shapes of the bark, and then follow the trunk up and notice how the branches stretch towards the sky.

Imagine the tree reaching towards the sun, grabbing the sunlight, and bringing it down to you. Bring that energy of the sun into the whole universe of the forest.

As you look up and see those sun rays coming down into the tree, imagine yourself as a ray of sunlight going into the tree and filling it up. Feel its life force all the way to the roots. That can be a soul filling moment.

Maybe you're at the bottom of a cliff looking up, notice the shapes, the colors, the cracks, the little caves, and indentations.

When you look at a mountain, follow it from the bottom up to the top. See the details of it and the magic of the mountain. See how it reaches for the sky and brings the sky into it.

If you look with your heart open, and your mind open, and a willingness to connect, a fusion takes place, you become the sky and the mountain. That place where they connect is a true power spot.

Looking up has tremendous advantages in expanding your awareness. It's an entire world we sometimes forget.

***

I found my land over 30 years ago and when I look up, I realize how much the trees have grown every year. I literally feel like I can see them grow.

Mt. Shasta is a power spot. I've spoken with many loggers and other people who live in this area, and they all say that your average evergreen tree grows about two feet a year, depending on how much water and sunlight they get.

Here in the Mt. Shasta area the growth rate can be double that estimation. It's amazing, and I feel like I've been a part of their lives for all those years. I've watched them grow, I've appreciated them, I've nurtured them, and all that interaction with the trees has made my life more fulfilling.

When we choose to let in more of this world we live in, our lives become richer, and we are more inspired to do good for the Earth. We have more motivation in difficult times to be kinder people, and help where help is needed. We give smiles and encouragement to others much more freely because we are full and have that energy to share.

It always comes back to taking time to let the goodness of our world in. Over time, those moments we invest in ourselves to expand our awareness, are worth the wonderful payoff.

Tune Into Your Surroundings

Earth Sounds

Put your head to sleep, open your heart, your whole being, and let the Earth speak to you. Sounds – wind blowing, water running, birds singing, insects buzzing, and rustling leaves.

Put your ear to the ground and listen. Stop and listen often. Listen in layers. Take in one sound, then another, one by one until they blend into one universal song.

Don't try to understand it, just feel. Voice the sounds through song and chanting. The sounds will speak for the Earth, for the Beings that live on the land, and in the water.

In that most primal part of you, where no human busyness exists, you will know oneness.

Thank You Owl

Charlie Storm Owl had suggested I sleep in a bear lay to challenge myself while I was in the Marble Mountain Wilderness. I was still new to backpacking, and definitely fearful, but we were a big group, and the bear lay wasn't too far from our camp circle.

In the daytime that seemed like a good idea. Most of the bears in these wilds avoid people and we had already disturbed their space setting up camp there. So, I found a dished out, dirt patch in a thick stand of trees and left my sleeping bag to retreat to later that evening.

We went about our day and evening activities with our nature awareness class, blindfold walking, tracking lessons, and nighttime stalking games.

After the activities ended, the other students headed off to bed. It wasn't until then, that I remembered I thought I was brave earlier and left my bag downhill in the woods.

I grabbed my flashlight and headed off to find my sleeping spot. I made it through the meadow and entered the old growth woods.

Pushing undergrowth twigs and branches away from my face, I was getting frustrated. I couldn't see past a few feet from my flashlight's beam, and right on cue as in any scary story, the last of my battery's life died.

Sweating and tangled up in the overgrowth, I started to panic. It was pitch black in the dense brush and I didn't know where I was, or which way was up. I called out a few times to anyone who I thought may be nearby in their tents, but no one answered.

I was embarrassed at first to ask for help, but after a while when no one replied, I was just scared. The Marble Mountains are abundant with bears and mountain lions, and I was alone with no vision, no sense of where I was, and no sleeping bag.

I felt a stump next to me and sat down. I remembered what Tim had taught us earlier. If you are lost, stop, take deep breaths, and listen. I wiped away an escaped, fearful tear, took a few deep breaths, and cupped my ears like a deer, and waited.

In the distance, I heard a faint Great Horned Owl hoot. I waited, and then another call. My heart leapt. I knew which direction the owl was in. Earlier in the evening, Charlie had called in this Great Horned Owl to our camp circle. It stayed there with us for hours.

I took a few, soft steps so I could still hear it between the snapping of twigs under my feet. A few pokes in the face later I made it out of the dark canopy into a meadow.

I let my eyes adjust and was startled, as the low moon lit up a few gleaming eyes. At that point I just went for it, and crossed through the tall skunk cabbage praying, "Please be deer, please be deer, please be deer."

I stopped again with my own deer ears cupped, and heard the trickling of the spring water flowing just below our main camp circle.

I picked up my relieved pace seeing one of the class helpers, Rich, still sitting up next to the fading campfire. I told him my predicament, and he joined me with his flashlight, on the hunt to retrieve my sleeping bag.

Clearly, I wasn't ready to push myself into staying out in the bear lay, but I was grateful for the lessons on using all my senses to be more attune with the environment.

"Whey O Whey O" are some of the first sounds the ancients put together and sang." - E.K.

There is something to hear in silence. Nature speaks volumes through silence.

Pick out the individual ripples that make up the rushing river. Start with the trickle and follow it until you hear the collective roar.

Listen to rocks, don't ignore them. There's a lot to hear.

Munching

I was frustrated not knowing what was eating the kale and lettuce in our greenhouse. I wasn't seeing who was munching on my plants, and the thought came to me to go in there at night.

I went into the greenhouse after dark and waited in silence. It took only two minutes to find my gardening nemesis. I heard chewing, and stalked in that direction, flipped on my flashlight, and there was a grasshopper chomping away on the leaves. For the size of the little grazer, it was remarkably loud.

I learned that night, if one of my senses isn't getting the result I was hoping for, then try another one.

No song is more beautiful than a trickling creek. Our very souls sing this creek song.

Smell The Environment - Smell Yourself Into Awareness

Follow The Scent

Smell, then see what journey that scent takes you on. Track it, get curious. Don't underestimate the power of a smell. It can lead you on a life changing adventure.

Be Aware Of Changes Through Smell

Smell the daytime and smell the night. Smell nocturnal flowers. Smell the seasons. Smell the weather. Smell the metallic scent of snow coming. Smell the ground after a rain. Know your world through smell.

Senses Of A Bear

I was teaching a class in the Yolla Bolly Wilderness with a dozen students. We had stalked to the edge of a meadow to observe, which I knew was a feeding place for bears in the magic hour, just before dark.

A mother bear and two cubs came out to feed. As mom and the cubs grazed by, out came a 600-pound male. Our hearts pounded; we remained quiet. We watched for 20 minutes, and the male suddenly stopped, his nose twitching. He could smell humans but could not see us. In this wilderness bears get hunted so they have a healthy respect for humans.

***

It's said bears can smell 2100 times better than humans. Depending on the species and weather circumstances, a bear can smell 20-40 miles away from a scent. So, if a bear is a mile away and you're outside cooking a steak, they will no doubt know the location. A bear can smell roots deep in the dirt. Their world revolves around their nose.

***

A slight shift in the wind and the bear was on high alert. The curious male stood on his hind legs but couldn't see us. He sniffed again and got visibly angry. He growled and scratched the ground and charged, full speed and headfirst, into an old growth Ponderosa Pine. I thought it would knock him out.

He repeated this two more times, standing upright, and looking in our direction. We didn't move, not one inch. He spun around and darted back into the woods, thankfully away from us. Now that's what a good sense of smell can do.

***

Dogs, wolves, coyotes, and foxes, have great eyesight and hearing, and incredible smell as well. Anyone who has ever walked with a dog knows this. I'm often very envious of dogs. They inspire me to improve my smell. When the snow blankets our land, I can finally see the tracks the dogs smell.

I'm quite sure our ancestor's sense of smell was much better than ours, if that's true then we can get ours back. Through modern times we've downplayed our use of smell, as modern life just doesn't require it for daily survival. We favor our eyes and our intellect more.

To bring our smell back, all we need to do is be aware of it and use it every chance we get. Think of our senses like muscle memory, they will come back stronger. It will make our lives much more alive with all our senses working as they were meant to be.

Smell a pleasing scent fully. Breathe it in. It will become you. You will know this smell intimately as a great joy. Our sense of smell is linked to our memory. When I smell fresh bread, I'm taken right back to being a kid when my mom baked bread.

On your next outing, take in every scent you can, and smell what happens.

Emotional Aromatherapy

Scents keep me grounded in stressful or frustrating situations. When I am in traffic for long periods of time, I get agitated to the point of almost panicking. I feel trapped.

I have found that by keeping a piece of angelica root on my dash I can lightly scratch it and the scent brings me back to the sweat lodge, which is a calming place for me.
Find the scent that calms you and brings you back to center, and keep it close by.

Smell colors. Smell the color green. Describe it with all your senses. This is how to know color as a being. When you know color, you can animate color and bring it to life.

Taste Everything

Be present with your food. Food is a vital part of our lives. We spend huge amounts of money and time around food. Yet, many of us give very little thought to our food, we just suck it down and we're done.

Engage your senses when eating. Food will become more enjoyable. Engage your sixth sense and food will become spiritual.

Pay attention when you pick a carrot and eat it. Smell it first, in your mind's eye do you know where it grew? Do you smell the other scents in that environment? Feel its texture, then taste it and then notice if its flavor is more prominent. There is so much to learn from this. Happiness is often so simple.

Eating wild foods connects us to our ancestors and our Earth. We remember the good life—living with the Earth—This makes us happy and brings us home.

Taste a flower after a bee has visited it. You will begin to know the secret knowledge that only bees know.

Drink From A Spring

Notice how alive and alert you feel when you drink from a spring. Think of what the gift of water from the Earth brings, the energy, the beauty, the sounds, and the peacefulness.

Why does drinking from a spring make you happy? Spring water is pure life force coming out of the heart of the Earth. Taste the Earth.

Taste the wind. When you do, all things the wind blows through will be with you.

Touch And Feel

Touch is vital for nurturing our soul. Pay attention to the texture of what something feels like, as well as the sensation of what you feel inside.

Cuddling a baby, petting an animal, holding a hand, squishing clay, splashing water, all adds to our soul growth.

Feel

Touch something with your eyes open and then with your eyes closed. What details do your hands feel that your eyes didn't notice?

Would you recognize the same tree trunk with your eyes closed as you would with them open?

Get to know your environment on a personal level by engaging your sense of touch. Don't only admire flowers with your vision and smell, also feel them with a light touch. Some are soft or smooth or fuzzy or prickly. Some are thick and some are so thin you have to almost imagine feeling them.

Feel textures and temperatures with your hands, and when appropriate, with your face. Take it all in as a felt memory that has now become a part of you. Recall the sensations and how they trigger different reactions. Experience life fully by being a part of all of it.

When it's safe, go naked in nature. The warmth of the sun is heaven sent. Remove barriers. Let that primal self inside you out and be free.

Barefoot

Growing up I rarely wore shoes. Most of our ancestors barefooted or wore moccasins, allowing them to feel the Earth through the thin hide.

I'm sure if I look back on my life, that early connection of barefooting and not having a mother who constantly told me to put my shoes on, is one of the things that built my intimate connection with the Earth.

Your feet are amazing beings unto themselves. Every part of your body is unique and should be treated as a gift. Your feet hold your body up!

There are countless pressure points and power spots on the bottom of your feet. When you touch the ground and walk, you are feeling all the living beings that live in the dirt. You are feeling the living Earth itself. Sacred ground. Sacred walk.

Use your feet as you would your hands. Your feet are receptors of information and have their own sense of intelligence. The connection comes up through the Earth and into you, and back down into the Earth.

Let your feet feel, gather information, interact, and speak directly with the Earth. Let your bare feet be your teachers. They have a language of their own. Give your brain a rest and let your feet guide the way.

Barefoot connection is the best way to be close to nature and communicate with the Earth. You will receive the Earth medicine and reawaken memory in your feet. That day will be a homecoming.

***

When I was young, I read about a Native American man named Ishi. He was the last California Native from the Yahi tribe. It's a sad story, but I would recommend studying Ishi. He was an incredible, empathic man.

There were many lessons learned about his life. One that stood out to me were how strong his feet were and how they built up callouses. My feet were strong like that. It was how I lived life when not in school or in public buildings.

Ishi had the skills and ability to make protection for his feet, but he chose not to because it was his way of life. It would have cut off an invaluable source of information he needed to live efficiently.

***

I know a lot of you are thinking if you walk barefoot, it's going to hurt. Well yeah, it's going to hurt initially. You will need to build up the toughness of your feet, but as a benefit it will force you to slow down and observe and build your awareness.

Until your feet can tolerate longer periods of time, wear shoes with thin soles. Boots are tools that can be used if you're carrying a heavy backpack or when you need protection. Everything has its uses, but the more you can barefoot, the more you will read the Earth.

Let your feet massage the Earth and let the Earth massage you. Shoes can be helpful, but barefooting is one of the best things we can ever let kids do. Feet speak to the rest of the body.

Our students at Headwaters Outdoor School feel a huge sense of freedom and joy when they spend weeks and even months barefoot. Their primal, authentic self emerges. They slow down and feel as a part of nature, no longer removed from it.

Our apprentices that have grown up at Headwaters through many summers, often on their return home, go through a withdrawal from the freedom and personal connection they have built with the land.

It's not unusual for me to receive phone calls from concerned parents a couple of months after my apprentices leave from a summer on our land. They tell me their kids came home from Headwaters fired up with an enthusiasm for life, but it seems to have worn off.

33

When I ask to speak with the kids, I find that they are more depressed and have fallen back into old patterns of playing too many video games, and not getting enough nature time. I encourage parents to make the time to get them out to rewild and reconnect.

A couple of my apprentices confessed that the only way they could deal with being confined in a classroom all day wearing shoes, was to secretly cut out the soles so they could feel the ground. They did this in a scout way so they wouldn't get in trouble.

I must admit, that once I heard their way of adapting to an unnatural environment of an urban setting, I beamed with pride. I didn't let on to their secret because it wasn't hurting anyone.

Sometimes we get way too overprotective out of fear of someone getting hurt, and in doing so, we end up hurting them in other ways. They found a simple fix to be able to feel that sense of freedom.

I've always said, rules and signs are made to be interpreted. Going barefoot is not a high crime. It is sometimes a saving grace.

Tree Climb

I'm a little nervous about heights but I challenge that fear when climbing trees. One day I was going to do a tree sit meditation, and I climbed one of our huge fir trees with a blindfold on.

Surprisingly, I was able to see more of the tree with my eyes covered. I felt my way up and eventually back down with much more confidence than with my eyes opened. I "saw" every crack in the bark with my hands and felt, with a true knowing, how strong a branch was, rather than guessing if it could hold my weight.

I wasn't only feeling the tree's shape, but I saw it in my mind's eye and knew where to reach for the next branch. I learned that sometimes I can see more through touch, without the judgment of my eyes.

Walk Softly

Pay attention where your feet go. It matters. Be aware. When walking in a meadow lift your feet up instead of dragging them. Your feet make a difference, be gentle with the life below.

Walk with love. Our feet take delight in caressing our living Earth.

I walk with the ancients when I walk barefoot, and they walk with me.

Your Sixth Sense And Your Primal Self

The unspoken language of all living beings shows up in countless ways, some universal, some personal. Your sixth sense, or intuition, is about feeling, it's an all knowing.

To bring your intuitive sense alive, you must be willing to be wrong. It takes a journey of trial and error to get to the place where you know you can trust your feelings.

Often, a truth felt, is a chill across your shoulders or down your spine. It could be a knot in your stomach, a gut feeling.

Another phrase for intuition is your inner-vision or inner-knowing. We are born with this gift from the unseen world. It is a part of who we are. If your inner vision has gone to sleep, wake it up. Practice, have faith, take risks. Nature is the best teacher for this silent language. This is one of the main ways animals communicate.

Your brain is your tool, but it doesn't have to run the show. Use your intuition as a guide and trust your heart as well. Intuition is true knowledge that, if followed, leads to wisdom.

Primal Self

Every person needs to get to know a being that lives inside all of us, the primal self. This being was born into our ancestors, who needed this primal self to survive in a wild world.

We are the Earth. We come from it, and we go back to it. Our ancestors were wildlings, wild men, and wild women.

We survived from our earliest days because we became great predators. We learned to work together, to kill and to protect. We are not unlike other pack animals. It makes perfect sense why we domesticated wolves to live and work with us.

At our core we are the supreme predators of this Earth. We can adapt to almost all environments and are able to eat an enormous variety of food sources.

Our primal self is alerted when we get a gut feeling. Primal moments can be when you're confronted with a life-threatening situation and there's no time to think in your complex brain. The primal self instinctively knows what to do and responds. We intuitively get out of the way, and it saves our life.

When we build a relationship with that part of ourselves, it's truly a committed, loyal friend. It's never failed me, and I've had many near-death encounters.

Our primal self in nature is that wildness of all animals living within us. The wildness is all the places that have touched you in your life, and all the places that touched your ancestor's lives, that now dwell in you.

We hold back way too much in our modern lives, keeping our inner wilderness in a cage. These beings within us must get out to be fully alive. This feeds our primal self, keeps it ready to protect us and care for us.

It's in the primal moments, that fine line between life and death, that we find peak experience. This is where we find life. This is one place where great learning can take place, leaps in consciousness, and closeness to spirit. For me, this is where my ancestors and I unite.

***

Our ancestor's senses were alive with Earth. Wonder lived inside us. Curiosity was our way. Service was survival. Hard, meaningful work was a given.

We evolved through loving nature. Nature has been our spirituality, our Mother, our friend. Our definition of beauty came from trees, sunsets, sunrises, animals, birds, color, and shapes.

Love kept us in love with ourselves, each other and all that roamed the Earth. Love was alive, a living, motivating energy.

The Earth loved us by giving us life, food, water, shelter, and fire. Love was real and tangible. You could touch it and feel it. Every day was precious, as it really could be your last. Our primal selves instinctively protect what we love.

Our wildness came out through fighting, protection, and hunting. It came out through ceremony, dance, music, and song. It came out through play, tree climbing, and running with our dogs and horses.

Our modern world has tamed our wildness. There is no one to blame, it just happened.

We make war on each other and our planet Earth, and we don't even know why. We've stopped feeling empathically. Our predator has gone bad, no control, no wisdom, living through false fear, and pointless anger.

We've become lost and we don't even know it. We are living like strangers on our Earth, our Home. We must find ourselves again through nature in service, love, hard work, kindness, gratitude, and mindful living for our Earth, and for all future generations.

One way to start righting the wrong is to build your relationship with your wildness, your wild man and wild woman. Let them play by having adventures, by exploring, climbing trees, climbing the mountains, running the rivers, following creeks, chasing dreams, and being with wild animals. Get off your butt and get out on the land and in the water.

Be the trees, be the eagles, be the wolves, be the oceans, be the rivers, be the meadows. Be all of it! Live abundantly.

Express your love and passion wildly for our Earth, our land. Give your predator something to do, be creative. Use the predator inside for good, for harmony. Do this and humanity's troubles will dissipate.

Build a friendship with your primal self and let it out. Don't be over-controlled by a modern society that has thrown out thousands of years of Earth living. Keep your brain working, your heart open, and your wildness right there at your edges, ready to go.

Wildness must be honored, it's who we Earthlings are. When that wild man or wild woman is channeled for good, the magic in your life, humanity's life, and in our Earth's life will be set free.

Come Back To Your Senses
Use your intuition to enhance your physical senses.
Walk with your eyes covered to enhance your inner vision.
When you listen do you hear what someone's heart is saying?
Smell and taste a memory back to life.
Touch someone's soul with a hug.

Stop And Look Deeply

If a place in nature looks inviting, it's calling you. Go to that spot and lay down and absorb it like a sponge. Soak up what's there for you. So much good will come your way.

In nature let your feelings be your guide. Expand your awareness. It will be an adventure. If you see it, trust it, believe it. It could be the beginning of something remarkable.

Use Your Senses For Protection

You may wonder when you would ever need your primal senses heightened in your everyday life.

I went to San Francisco to visit my friend, Ben, and was so overwhelmed by all the chaotic energy of the people, and the lights, and cars and buses, and construction noise. I started to tune it all out and shut my senses down. I was feeling agitated, and almost panicky.

I hadn't realized I was tuning out until I found myself in a dangerous situation. I had walked underground to the B.A.R.T. train station and was the only one there waiting for the next train. It wasn't until I felt the hairs on the back of my neck tingle, that I knew something wasn't right. I spun around and there was a man hovering two feet behind me. I pivoted quickly and ran back up the steps and walked to a different station where there were other people.

I don't know what he was up to, but I know it wasn't good, and I wasn't going to wait to find out. I didn't second guess myself, I trusted my feeling and got away.

Sometimes you need to tune out a bit because feeling everything can be overwhelming. Just remember to pay attention enough to know what is happening in your surroundings.

Vision Walking

Go out in nature on a barefoot walk with your eyes wide open. This wide vision practice becomes a meditation that can take you into a higher state of consciousness.

As you walk, let your eyes open wider. Let the landscape in. You will notice the beauty highlights, the shape of a leaf, the color of a deer, the glitter of the water, the color of the sky through the trees.

You begin to feel beings in the woods. Whether it's birds or spirits or bears, it all starts to come alive. Taking in everything through your senses, those beings start to live in your body. You are hearing more, and you're smelling more.

Touch trees as you walk by with your hands, or your face, or your legs. Notice your feet touching everything as though they were your hands. Imagine your feet massaging the Earth, feeling the stone, feeling the dry leaves, feeling the water and sand and mud.

Bring all your senses into the barefoot walk, including your inner vision. Your heightened senses are doorways into new awakenings.

Imagine yourself walking through veils of fog as you go further, and further, and then sit and observe in a place that calls to you. Look for a special place that when you look at it, you know that's where you have to be. You feel it grabbing you and pulling you in, let yourself go there. Let go of control.

Let your senses guide you to those sacred spots and when you get there, fully engage. If it's a creek, get in the water, and feel the water or at least put your feet in it.

Roll around in a meadow. Get your whole body involved. Climb a tree. Let yourself sink in and become a part of that environment.

A sense of place develops and even though you may have never been there, it's your spot now, it belongs to you. You are the Earth Caretaker of that spot. You have an investment in it. It called to you.

Get so connected with that space that you will always want to protect it. When you are in that place you become an Earth Caretaker. You don't even have to think about it. It just comes so naturally to care for what you love.

Vision Walking could go on for 20 minutes or for an entire day. You can go out into the wilderness and walk for days that way.

You don't need to take anything that makes noise or creates distraction, shut your phone off. Unless you have a very concerning medical condition, if something comes up, you'll figure it out. Before phones we figured it out, take a little risk.

If it's cold, of course be warm, but don't overdress and let clothes push you away from the Earth. Be as natural and wild as you can. Let the wild human out. Be free.

Feel your ancestors. Ask your ancestors to walk with you. Ask the birds to fly with you. Let go of attachment to outcomes and leave judgment behind. Judgment creates walls of separation. Enjoy those moments as they come and go. By letting go there will be another moment to appreciate.

Take in those moments where there's nothingness, maybe no sound, no control of any kind, you are there with a sense of belonging, and a sense of just being. Those are amazing moments that often provide you with the greatest insights of your life.

It's an essential part of life to get out and Vision Walk. Make the time to do it. You'll find excuses not to, but make it a priority.

This time spent opening your senses fills you up by connecting you to the planet. The Earth's energy literally becomes your energy. The closer you feel to our Earth, the more you will feel that she needs us to live in a good way. Awaken your senses and Vision Walk home.

Nature awareness is a continuing state of being. There is no end to this wild journey. Jump in, pay attention, and live fully!

Reminders To Strengthen Your Senses:
* Slow down, get quiet, pay attention, and tune in to your environment.
* Free your eyes from your brain and change your perspective often.
* Listen for the minutia sounds and widen your awareness to the collective noise.
* Smell the daytime and smell the night.
* Taste a variety of flavors through varied temperatures and textures.
* Feel textures with all parts of your body.
* Practice using your intuition daily. Make a game of it so there's no pressure.

Chapter 4
Communicate With Nature

Communicating with an open heart, through our intuitive side, is the doorway into an animal or plant being. It is a direct spiritual connection through a universal language.

It takes a willingness to listen to learn the language of other living beings. You may remember these languages from past times when you were living with our Earth ever so closely. When you come to a place that feels familiar you can track this back to cellular memory.

Trees and plants and animals know this language of connection. We know it too. We only need to pay attention to relearn this skill.

Often, we get a feeling of All Knowing that can't logically be explained. As we trust in this knowing it leads us to deeper conversations.

A soft pretense is needed. This says we're open and peaceful and noninvasive. We need to almost disappear as a part of our surroundings and become the landscape.

Communication happens with plants and animals through feeling, sight, sound, touch, and taste. It helps to look with owl eyes, wide and soft, and a nonaggressive body posture. Perhaps most important, have a willingness to put your ego aside, and listen with a loving, heartfelt interest.

Learning the language of nature through your heart is like learning a foreign language. Once you have the basics you sink into it, and it flows. The Earth wants us to interact with her.

Communication can be many things and for many reasons. It can be as simple as being in gratitude while connecting with another level of life.

Communication can be used to seek knowledge, to ask a plant what medicinal uses it has or to ask a tree if it's ok to climb it. Many of our indigenous ancestors asked animals for their permission to hunt them.

For any communication to take place, we must get out of the mindset that we are better than others. The truth is we're no better or worse than any species on Earth. Each plant and animal are perfect for how they live.

To converse in a humble and open way is to show love and respect. Take time to consider how nature communicates with you. Trees, rocks, water, and animals are a good place to start.

Observe their qualities, learn from them, and use those qualities so you don't lose them.

No Limits

You must first put your time in nature. No shortcuts, just get out there and be in nature. There's no answer to how long. One day you will be in nature, and it will be different, something has noticeably changed. Your whole being will gently blend into the land. You won't feel solid. You will feel fluid as if you could walk right through trees. You could even enter a tree and become it.

A feeling takes over, you become forest, land, water, there is no separation. Feeling becomes your form of connection, you just know things. There will be no need to ask why. Why, will become unimportant.

This will become a moment in your life that will propel you to the next level in your relationship with the Earth. It is a stepping off point. The forest awaits you. Live limitless.

Nature Speaks

All our senses allow nature to speak to us. Feeling, smell, and sound are languages to be learned. They speak so clearly, that we awaken to our world just by being present with these senses open.

Nature speaks through color, shapes, patterns, texture, light, and shadow. Tracks on the Earth are stepping stones left for us to follow into our Earth's living soul. Memories hidden within, are all waiting for their door to open to us.

Nature endlessly speaks through our eyes. To learn nature's language, we must become more passive and accepting with our eyes. Our eyes will take us deeper into our Earth if we control less, and trust more in nature's teaching.

As the Earth speaks through our senses, practice gratitude, feel wonder, be content without the need to understand intellectually. This will be your vehicle to greater oneness with our Earth, and yourself. This will lead you to a fulfilling life, and a life well lived is good for all.

Animals Speak In Symbolism

Observe patterns of when animals start showing up in your daily life or over long periods of time. They become symbolic messages. Eventually you'll be able to trust what they are saying and understand the conversation they are having with you.

The first step is the awareness that something is even there. They've been there all along waiting for you to pay attention and engage.

Show Interest In Your World

When I come out of my house in the morning, I greet Mt. Shasta with voice. I thank the birds for singing me awake. I talk with plants that call to me. Sometimes I speak audibly and sometimes I speak silently inside. Either way, nature responds through feeling and a knowing.

Humans can also receive communication from other beings in a way we may not fully understand but we must trust. Be good with the mystery. Let it unfold.

Much of the response from nature that comes to us, we never know in our brain. It absorbs into our being. If we try to figure it out, we can lose it. There is a fine line between understanding in the brain and intuitive knowing. That place in the middle is the world of no limits, where all is possible.

Imagine that other forms of communication can happen than what we are familiar with. Our intuition is the bridge for much of this interaction.

When you're hot and tired from a long hike and you hear a creek in the near distance, it calls to you – communication. It calls to you through sight and sound. When you jump in, it communicates cold, comfort and aliveness, a good feeling, pleasure, and fun.

Talk to the creek. What lives in you? Where are you flowing? What is your source? Can I drink you? Can I fish in you? Include the rocks, fish, and plants in your conversation as well.

This is all about respect and a personal relationship with nature. Talk to the Earth herself. Why wouldn't we speak to the being that gives life to us or the beings that live upon her?

With practice, speaking with nature becomes natural. When this becomes our normal way of living, all lives benefit.

Stones

The stones have tales to tell. Listen and learn the language, you will find it familiar. Once this language comes alive in you it will never be forgotten. You will remember and know things even though you don't know how. Slow down and you will get an ear full.

Take Time

I'm looking at an old growth, apple tree flowering right now, and it's gorgeous. Part of the reason it's gorgeous is because those flowers mean so much more than simply the beauty that they're showing me.

They are filling up and nourishing the honeybees, and the mason bees, and the bumblebees, and the hummingbirds.

Those blooming flowers are potential. They are the future. They are going to be apples. Every year that tree will give life-giving flowers and apples to so many beings.

I don't just walk by that apple tree every day without acknowledging it. I stop and I take a moment to connect with the tree through gratitude, and appreciation of what it gives, and what it does.

I don't always have to stop. Walking by, I can look with gratitude and appreciation, and let my logical mind go, and connect with my heart for just a few moments.

Taking time to connect, might be with a lizard on the trail looking at you, after just coming up from sleeping all winter. It may have just emerged from under rocks when it was cold, and is taking its first breath, and feeling the sun for the first time. Maybe you could even feel the warmth along with that lizard, and share the experience.

Taking time to connect is not hard. It can be a quick walk by, or you can stop and sit with something. Have a willingness and an awareness to make a connection.

We get so busy and forget to take those moments, and we miss so many opportunities to develop a closer relationship to the natural world.

Each day we can engage in a profound and rich way with the Earth, and all her beings, by simply taking the time.

The key to all relationships is giving our time to what we love, whether it is with a person or a tree or an animal. Express your love through that undivided attention. It's simple. Just do it.

Sharing Space

Share space with another being in nature. We do this well with humans, such as when we fall in love or in close friendships. In these spaces, two people can just be in each other's presence – no words or thoughts. We do this with our pets and it's comforting.

As I'm writing many parts of this book on the Big Island of Hawaii, a gecko visits me, and eats the bugs off my notebook and my arm.

Like other predators, I could kill this gecko if I wanted, but a trusting communication has developed between us. The gecko is my friend. He inspires me to write from the heart. He's beautiful, he's fun to be with, and he's also so, so colorful. Green body, red spots, and blue sides – my favorite colors. Gratitude to the gecko. Keep eating those biting bugs. Keep sharing my space.

Often when an animal or a reptile or insect comes into our space, we don't invite them in. We move them away or we try to kill them. When this happens, we lose a chance to share space. We lose so much, and we'll never know just what we've lost.

I realize some animals aren't the type we like to share space with, such as mosquitos, rattlesnakes, and yellowjackets. Although, even these animals can be wonderful teachers for us. If we stay calm and welcoming, they will stay with us in a peaceful way, as they feel what we feel. They teach us to move through fear and judgment.

***

I was teaching a class of sixteen people in the Mojave Desert in Arizona. As we were hiking, we surprised a large Mojave Rattlesnake. It came to alert and began to rattle. In this instance most people would run or kill the snake or at the very least consider it a nasty being.

If we practice our human gift of empathy, and become the snake, we can see this encounter in a different light. If you were living in your home, going about your business, and a group of large humans surprised and surrounded you, that would put you on alert. We don't extend the same grace to the snake as we want for ourselves.

This behavior creates separation, distance, and fear. The rattlesnake doesn't spend its waking moments devising ways to hunt and kill people. It is simply trying to live. Remember we are in this life together. We are all fellow travelers on this Earth, and we can be kind.

As my students came upon the snake, at full rattle alert, ready to strike, I asked the class to sit in a circle around the snake. This was testy because usually when in the presence of a wild animal, you must give them an out or you become the out, if they choose to flee the situation.

We had about eight feet of distance from the outer circle to the snake. I asked the students to think calm, loving thoughts toward the snake. Right away, it stopped rattling and laid down.

I then asked the students to think aggressive thoughts, and immediately the snake sprang upright, coiled and rattling. Then we returned to calm bodies and minds and the snake relaxed.

This will work with all animals, including insects and believe it or not, humans. Now you're asking, what if it doesn't work? This can happen, so be aware. Trust your intuition and your primal self to act accordingly. Chief Dan George once said, *"Sometimes the magic works, and sometimes it don't."* This is simply part of the mystery of life. It keeps us from getting complacent and keeps us humble.

My wife, who I love dearly, doesn't have a good relationship with yellowjackets. Very few people do, especially if you've been attacked by one or even worse, a whole nest. That's not something you forget. The memory gets stored in your body.

In the summer, we like to eat out on our deck. Yellowjacket scouts find our food and soon others follow. They drive my wife crazy flying around her, getting in her food. They leave me alone, but I'm sitting right next to her. Why? The answer is simple. They feel her fear and they're attracted to her uneasy energy because their energy is similar to hers at that time.

I put out a calm energy, and they usually don't bother me. If you approach a yellowjacket nest though, all bets are off. They will attack you. Wouldn't you defend your home?

Sometimes a mosquito lands on you with the intention to bite and you squash it. That's between you and the mosquito. In the natural world, all beings kill and eat to live, that's the truth.

As we become closer to nature, we realize we are a part of nature, and sometimes come from a place of love, and sometimes we participate in the killing and eating just like all other animals. We humans are different though because we can make choices. We have options. We have our big brain, our compassionate heart and soul. We have free will.

Talk To Nature

We have the gift of voice. No other animal or Earth being can speak as we do. We talk to our dogs, horses, cats, and parrots, and we talk to ourselves.

Our voice, when used in a good way, is a true gift. Use your gift of voice and talk to trees, deer, squirrels, insects, flowers, forests, and meadows. Ask questions. All your curious thoughts need to simply be voiced.

If you want to climb a tree, ask it for permission, and then feel the answer. Responses come if you remain open, usually as a feeling, and sometimes as a voice inside.

Keep conversing. Have full conversations. I do it all the time. Your internal mind might think you are crazy. Put that thought to rest, as it's simply crazy *not* to talk to nature. I'm confident that our ancestors did it daily, never even considering that it could be strange.

Nature's Language

The universal language of nature is energy. Nature in all forms already reads our energy. We are the ones that need to get quiet and listen and feel nature speaking.

We need to adjust our speed of what we are connecting with, so we can relate and consciously interact.

Animals are the easiest for us to see the results with, but the same interaction or communication happens with plants, trees, rocks, and water, we simply need to adjust our energy to theirs.

Nature may not need us to listen, but it will thrive with being heard. Build relationships. Acknowledge nature and engage with it to animate it. It can then interact with you in return. We need to slow down enough to learn nature's language. It has become a foreign language to us, but it's a uni-versal language. Like music, you feel it as One verse.

You don't need a translator; we are wired for this understanding at birth. Slow down to resonate at the same frequency, just like radio signals tune in, we can do the same.

Learn As You Go

When you are open to connecting with nature, you draw more experiences to you. A signal seems to go out to the universe that you are available.

Along with the amazing experiences you will have, come the calls out where help is needed. You may not feel qualified, but no one is initially. You become qualified by your willingness to help when help is needed. Once you put that intention out, you begin to learn as you go.

Golden Eagle In The Road

When animals know you are aware they will communicate with you more. Julie had left for town, but then returned in a hurry. She was troubled when she jumped out of the truck.

She had driven around the corner and said there was a Golden Eagle in the middle of our dirt road calling out. She got out of the truck and ten feet away the eagle continued to call out.

She said she told the eagle to wait there, and she would be right back with someone who could help. The eagle hopped off to the side of the road, and she drove back home to find me.

I've worked with Golden Eagles many times in rehab work and falconry. They are magnificent birds. To have a Golden Eagle in the middle of our road, in the forest, didn't seem possible. I had my doubts and questioned Julie's claim. She insisted she knew what a Golden Eagle was, and there was absolutely no doubt as to what she saw.

I grabbed my leather glove and a wool blanket, and we drove right back to the place she had last seen the bird. We started our search in a thick patch of prickly, manzanita shrubs. Soon enough I saw the bird's tracks and verified that, yep, it was a big Golden Eagle.

We continued our search for 30 minutes. Maybe the eagle had been able to fly off just far enough to be out of sight? It was a hot day and birds get stressed, and overheat easily, which would put the bird in mortal danger.

After a few moments of doubt, there she was, perfectly camouflaged in the brush, panting and ready to surrender in hopes of help or acceptance of her fate.

Julie asked me what she needed to do to help, and I replied quite sincerely, "Be willing to get hurt." She took a deep breath with a committed sigh and said, "And then what?" I told her to hold up the blanket stretched out as a distraction, and I would come up behind her.

Golden Eagle talons and beaks are very powerful, and it can be a dangerous capture. When rescuing animals, you need to have a plan, and then just act.

I spoke with the eagle through my intentions and telepathically. I told her I was there to help her. In one smooth move I grabbed her with my glove and held her legs just above her talons. My God, what an amazing spirit this eagle was.

Julie draped the blanket over the eagle's eyes to keep her calm. It was so hot outside we had to hurry back to our land to uncover her. Fortunately, we were just around the corner.

Her wings were not damaged, but she was very thin. She was full-grown, but still young. Although eagles can soar at 10,000 feet, and see prey from such a great distance, she hadn't been able to hunt well on her own.

My guess is that in her quest to learn to hunt in her first year out of the nest, she didn't do so well for a few days. She began to starve and was too weak to fly.

So, there she was, waiting for Julie to show up and find her. To me this is the amazing part of this story. This wasn't a random situation. This eagle landed in the woods and stood in the middle of our road calling out to Julie. Through her own instincts she felt a communication connection with Julie. She knew there was help close by, and made it known that she needed us.

She landed in a place where a falconer, and animal and bird rehabilitator lived. If she had landed anywhere else, she may have not made it due to her condition. She found us.

***

This is an example of the Great Mystery at work. On some magical level there is a communication that happens. We call this knowing, this Mystery, the Spirit that moves in all things. Nature is the greatest teacher of this unseen realm. Our sixth sense, our intuition, is the entrance to this world.

There's so much more to the world than what we know physically, but when we open to different forms of communication, we discover anything is possible.

We experience so many more levels of existence, and amazing things happening we can't really identify or give words to. These magical connections occur more often as we recognize them, and they eventually become a part of our daily lives.

***

This eagle story has a happy ending. I did not have the time required to rehabilitate the eagle myself, so I found a local bird of prey rehabilitator.

Two weeks later, the eagle had been fattened back up and was released back into the wild. She has a tag on her now for observation, and she is flying and thriving over the Scotts Valley in Northern California. What a gift, and what an honor to be a part of this being's life.

Animals come to us and give us experiences like this, and when recognized and honored, they become sacred interactions. By participating in life, and not staying on the sidelines, we were aware of that eagle's needs, and she was given the opportunity to live a new life.

These experiences give me great hope in our world. They tell me we can save our planet if each one of us stays open to what the Earth and all her beings are saying to us, and act on it.

Next time you see an eagle, stop, and soak it in. Let it inspire you to change the world.

When an animal comes into your space, take time to ask about its life. Once you do, you'll be led on a sacred journey and get a glimpse of another being's life.

All animals have curiosity. They want to connect with us as well. Birds look down and wonder what we're up to. Stop and watch them checking you out.

Notice the small animals as well. They have secrets to share. Pay attention and listen.

A Special Bond With Our Pets

I had a chimney sweep and masonry business in Santa Cruz, California for over thirty years. I have met many interesting people through this work, and I cherished their life stories they shared with me as I worked.

On one job I was on, I was building a stone fireplace hearth and I connected with the couple's dog, Blue. They noticed my interaction with Blue and knew I would appreciate their incredible story.

Two years earlier they had moved to Santa Cruz from Boulder, Colorado. They had to leave their dog with their friends in Boulder until they were able to get settled in their home. They would then go back and bring Blue to their new home in Santa Cruz.

Unfortunately, one day their friends called with the bad news that their dog was missing. This couple was grief stricken as the weeks and months went on, and there was no sign of Blue. Time passed and they had to move on with life.

Six months later they opened their front door, and there was Blue. Their dog, who had never been to Santa Cruz, traveled from Colorado to California to find his people.

He had crossed through neighborhoods, cities, roads, wilderness, and through various weather conditions to find them. He found food and water, and I'm guessing some help on his incredible journey. Love was his guide back to his human family.

This is a mystery, and at the same time it's not. When trust, love, commitment, kindness, and courage become our guide, and when we get out of our logical minds and jump into the Mystery, anything can happen. Nature teaches this. Animals teach this.

Follow

Let your eyes look up a tree, then follow the tree down to the ground. Imagine the roots and follow them into the Earth. Ask no questions, just feel. Come back slowly. Then sit next to the tree and stay open.

Soul Language

Why are we drawn to pick up certain rocks? Why do they call out to us and catch our attention?

What is beauty to us? Some things seem universal, and some things are only beautiful to certain people.

The living Earth speaks through her beauty. We see beauty and we are touched, and often inspired by dramatic views. They fill us with wonder and dreams.

Sunsets and sunrises speak to our own inner beauty, we feel good watching them. We hear the Earth speaking.

The Earth speaks in flowers, and bees, and colors, and shapes, and clouds, and mountains. The Earth speaks in sounds, and smells, and taste, and views, and senses that are so simply profound it speaks to my soul.

We rarely think the Earth can show us something so important that we feel it in the core of our being, so we rarely listen. When we do get that feeling we don't always track it back to the Earth.

What speaks to you?

Soul View

Today I witnessed a view across the open sea, a sunset in volcanic fog. A word came into my mind, Soulview. This view ignited a fire in my own soul. Soulview is now my word I'm giving away to share.

The Shade Tree

Next time you are hiking and you're hot and tired and sweaty, when you see a tree go to it. The shade rejuvenates and fills you up with new energy. Just know this tree called you, this tree cared for you, this tree is your brethren on this Earth.

"All living beings from rocks, to plants, to insects, to reptiles, to amphibians, to birds, to mammals, to people, have song within them. To know these beings is to know their song." - E.K.

Earth Songs

Put your head to sleep, open your heart, your whole being, and listen to the Earth speak to you. Let sounds follow you – wind blowing, water running, birds singing, insects buzzing, leaves rustling. Feel the individual sounds, the songs, the symphony. Don't try to understand it, trust.

Gather a song from the Earth. Close your mind and voice the sounds through melodic chants. Start quietly and build up to a full belly song. Be the music that sings goodness into each day.

Join the choir that sings the song of the Earth. Be the conductor of the trees and let the sound unite the instruments of a forest, a meadow, mountains, creeks, and the ocean.

Sing to the Earth, it will sing back. Listen as your song echoes. The landscape absorbs your sound and energy, and sends it out into the world and back to you.

Receive this song with an open heart. Know that when you do, you're receiving the heart vibration of the entire landscape that was touched by your song. Your song touched every single living being, and it came back to you, in your song.

When certain sounds call again and again, they become your sounds. Lose yourself in Earth sounds to connect with our universal song.

The sounds will speak for the Earth, for the beings that live on the land and in the water. In that most primal part of you, where no human busyness exists, you will know oneness.

Sing the Song of the Earth. The song will do the rest. No time or space, just song.

Sing joy into your life. Sing songs when you're in the woods. I promise you the trees love it.
They told me so.

My Song

Today I heard the Earth sing my song. It came from the wind, the birds, the insects. It was my song for my soul.

When songbirds sing, I remember to sing with them.

Listen to the one cricket, then the choir. Then the one again. Offer gratitude for the Cricket Song.

The Moon's Song

In 1968 when our astronauts were on the far side of the moon, they heard a song coming from the moon. This was buried in the NASA archives for many years and recently released.

I heard this recording from the astronauts. It is beautiful and amazing. This sound touched the astronauts deeply. It was a mystery.

All things have song and sound. To know our moon has a song is a reminder of the wonder of all life beyond our Earth. Scientists now believe that it helped to create the universe.

I want to hear the songs of Mars, Saturn, Jupiter, and of all the planets. What a joy to be alive in our world where there is so much to explore.

The space between, is the silence between thoughts, which forms, and articulates the thoughts. Allowing that space between is how you hear nature.

The Creek Called My Name

It sang to me. I felt its song in my bones. Suddenly so much that's been troubling me made sense. I listened more intently and then jumped in.

Immersed in nature's gift of water, I was fully alive and refreshed. For a long time, I became the creek, one in the same. It's where I needed to be. The song called me in.

I'm so thankful I heard the song. All that is good in our world is in the creek.

Listen to a babbling brook, it will make you laugh, they never run out of things to say.

Write A Story

Go into nature with pen and paper and see what comes into you. Tell the story of a tree or the land. Explain what you see and how it feels. Deal with proper grammar later. Write freely. I know you will be amazed.

Keep your writings in a sacred journal on an Earth altar. These writings may only be for you, or they are to be shared. You'll know in time when to tell your story.

Tell A Story

I live to tell a story. I want to share my story with those I care for, those I love, and for those I respect. It's in the telling that I bring my story to life.

My story teaches those I tell it to, and I learn so much more by reflecting on my story. In telling my story I bring those I tell it to into my life, my space. It's an intimacy that is lost today.

Our quest for modern life has ended the art of storytelling on a personal level within our communities. Now we listen to the radio, podcasts, watch T.V., delve into the news, and isolate ourselves in our books. These things in themselves aren't bad, but when personal storytelling is lost it becomes a collective soul loss.

Storytelling is how we passed on knowledge. Long before writing we told our story, about our lives, about what we witnessed, about what we felt, about our fears, our anger, our joy. We shared our hopes and dreams through story.

Story was entertainment, belly-laughing fun. Telling a story is uniquely human. Telling a story is inspirational medicine.

Listen To A Story

For a story to come alive, to truly come alive, as a *living* story, one that survives the march of time, it must have listeners. These listeners must give life to the story by being fully present, with all senses alive, as the story is told.

To intently listen to a story is a full circle gift. The storyteller tells the story and gets the gift of reliving it and learning more from it, or just being entertained again and again by the story.

The listener gets to be entertained and learn. If it's a grouping of people, it becomes a true bonding for the community. Many times, it becomes sacred space and the bond that holds the community together.

To listen fully to a story is to give a wonderful gift to the storyteller, and to the story itself, and all the places and beings within the story. It gives meaning and purpose to their lives.

Even when the story is about people, and animals and places in the past, long gone, the story gives them life. This can only happen when we fully listen with all our being, and senses open to receiving.

Sit with a tree and ask it to tell you its story.

Talk to the Earth and it will talk with you. You will know it and feel it. When you do you will not be able to damage and destroy it without feeling it yourself.

The Council For All Beings

Our students participate in a ceremony called the Counsel for All Beings. They sit in the woods for a few minutes connecting with something on or within the Earth or Universe. They become that Being, and then ask it what humans can do to help them. They decorate themselves as that Being and they represent them as their voice in the Council.

Once they have transformed themselves, they gather in our roundhouse. One by one they approach me, and another person who is representing the human world. That antagonist person represents someone who is unaware of their effect on the planet.

One of my high school apprentices, Stewart, who participated in this ceremony touched my heart during this activity.

Stewart is normally a very quiet person, who spends a lot of time observing and reflecting. He is not someone who has a lot of words, but the words he speaks can be powerful.

Stewart chose to represent the small worlds. He represented the tiniest of Earth's Beings that many times get overlooked. The words that Stew gifted us with were these. *"I am the small worlds. I give beauty to the bigger things that live among us. Like the moss that grows on the trees. I am being ignored. Pay attention."*

Listening can be more powerful than a lot of words. Stewart has reminded us of this truth.

Learn the Language of Nature
Allow quiet moments. Welcome them. Be willing to listen. Get up in the morning and listen. Sit out at night and listen. What's whispering to me? Just listen. My ears ring with a silent knowing... There are no more questions.

Chapter 5
Connect With Plants And Their Elementals

Plants are great communicators within themselves and with other parts of the Earth. Plants speak through an inner feeling. Talk to the plant world, slow down and listen to their language.

When we come from a place of where we think we know more than the plants then the communication shuts down and we lose that connection and knowledge.

Learn how to be kind to plants. Be of service by tending a garden. So many lessons and values can be learned from nature and put into practice by taking care of plants.

Plant Language

Growing up I loved plants. I knew each plant in my garden as a friend. I grew them from seed and protected them and nurtured them with water, sunlight, and most importantly with love.

I noticed that the plants were living individuals, and often seemed to glow from the inside out. They spoke to my heart with color, shape, and patterns. I felt what they felt on a heart level.

I would sit with my plants and enjoy the shared space. I learned that they have their own way of living, different from mine, but both are wonderful.

One day sitting in my garden I gained an awareness that plants have their own languages. They speak to each other in one language and speak to other species, such as humans, in another.

I learned to listen to each plant, and this has always been the baseline of how I garden. I tend the whole garden, but also interact with the individuals to take care of their needs.

I involve all my senses, and gratitude runs through me knowing we share this Earth together. I never take that for granted. Their life means life for me.

With my heart guiding my eyes I often see and feel more. More colors, shapes, and movement. I am reminded that I am not alone and never have been. There's so much life to discover. The journey into plants is a journey of layers of life with no end, only endless beginnings.

Be Still

Sometimes it's ok to just enjoy things being wonderful. You don't always have to do something that targets an end. Enjoy the moment of being. Who better to teach that than plants? That's what they do.

If something comes to bother them, they can't run away. They must stay there and deal with it. Plants are the ultimate observers of life.

Be Kind Enough To Know

How does a plant feel when you come into its space? How am I affecting it? Good, bad or nothing different?

47

Be the kind of person who is aware enough and kind enough to ask the question. If it's not ok, how can I shift that? Right there in that moment, being willing to ask that question will change your approach to life forever. Stop and think how you are affecting the world around you. Are you enhancing those around you or taking away?

Acknowledge other beings. Speak to nature, to plants and animals. They are listening in their own way. Energy intention is universally received. Talking with plants and trees is directly talking to our Earth's living spirit.

Make It Personal

Each year I pull up cedar and pine tree saplings that pop up in our vegetable and flower gardens. I allow them to grow at least six inches and then I pot them. I give each baby tree a name, and when our outdoor school students show up in the spring, I set them out for adoption.

As soon as people see a being has a name, it becomes personal to them. They acknowledge and honor the tree as a living being. They instantly want to care for it and nurture it. They begin to build a connection to the tree, and they are invested in protecting that little being. As the tree grows, their relationship grows through their interaction.

When our students take one of our trees home, they are taking a part of the energy of the land, and it links them to their experience here.

When they care for their tree, they are carrying the medicine of their experience out into the world. The energy is shared, and it grows. When you make relationships with nature personal, people care.

Harvesting Wild Plants For Food And Medicine

One of the greatest ways to connect with our planet is to eat our planet. When you eat directly from the Earth, it becomes a profound personal experience. That's what all our ancestors did for thousands upon thousands of years. Our direct ancestors lived completely off the land until modern times.

Eat plants in nature like an animal. Get down on the ground and smell them, chew some leaves, and eat without using your hands. Enjoy the plant in its purest state of being.

Feel the plant travel through your body, freshly harvested, still alive. Feel its energy merging with yours, giving you a charge of life force. Share your gratitude for it giving its life to give you life. What a noble life purpose that is.

If you want to connect to the Earth, drink its water, harvest its plants, and harvest its medicines. Many of the common weeds that we pull out of our gardens are the best edible and medicinal plants.

When you harvest a plant appreciate what the plant is offering. Before you pick a plant, offer gratitude and appreciation. Have a willingness to observe whether it's a home for another animal, and if it is, then move on to another plant. If it feels right, harvest it in a good way that allows the plant to continue to grow.

You've heard the saying, "You are what you eat". If you harvest a plant in a violent way, that energy goes into you. So, take the time to honor it in a beautiful way. Cook it or eat it raw with heart and love, and the plant will nourish you and give you life. Especially with medicinal plants, you need to have positive energy and good intentions.

When you are foraging, there is the thrill of a hunt, but you don't have to kill it, harvest only parts of it. Plants thrive with that approach. I've seen many plants eaten by deer, and they grow back faster.

Plants have their own language, their own way of being, and they compensate for situations that nature brings their way, including being harvested by humans.

I strongly encourage you to make wild plants a part of your life. In searching for plants, you'll broaden your awareness. Your senses will awaken, as sight, smell, touch taste, and hearing all come alive in the quest for edible plants. This is a wonderful way to teach children and spend family or community time.

When you cook with wild edibles and make teas and salves, you're literally working with nature to make a better life. Mother Earth wants all her children to become happy, to become good, to live well, so that she is well. So, harvest wild plants with reverence, and take in the living energy when they are freshly picked. Food is medicine, treat it as sacred as it is.

Introduce Yourself

A weed is only a nuisance because we don't know what its uses are yet. Spend time with the plant and learn what its qualities are.

Some plants will take a lot longer to develop a relationship with. Some poisonous or prickly plants are challenging to get to know. With time you will learn their beneficial aspects and befriend them, maybe after relocating them, but you will have more respect for their life purpose and how they contribute to the whole.

Learn Their Story

Consider the plant being that you are eating. After all, it gave its life for you to have your life. Think of the animals that depend on the plant for life, for food, and shelter. Consider the overall environment the plant lives in and how everything depends on each other.

If you didn't harvest the food yourself, see in your mind's eye the being living and where it grew. What was growing around it? Who picked it? What was their journey from where it grew to your table?

If you're eating an animal, see the animal in its environment living wild and free or on a farm. How was it raised? Did it live alone or was it with others? What did the animal eat? Give blessings to the food it ate.

Honor the being by creating a sacred meal. See the plants and their energy entering your body, filling you up and giving you their life force. Give it thanks and blessings.

If you do this visualization, you'll find your food will nurture your whole being. You will consider more what you are eating, and naturally you will make better choices that benefit all.

Appreciate Your Plants

Don't forget to smell flowers by putting your nose right into them. It's an honoring, it's a blending, it's wonderful.

Observe the plant reaching towards the sun. Think about how we feel when we're outside and stretch out and soak up the sun's warmth with gratitude. That is also what they're doing.

Look at how the leaves are shaped. They manage the sun. They bring it into their being so they can grow. This is the basic process of photosynthesis. They stretch out and adapt their shape and direction to reach for life.

Plants give humans and animals life. They make our air breathable and create our dirt. They are our selfless growing companions. Plants only ask for respect and life in return. Give a plant a blessing of gratitude and watch it flourish.

Play Music

During some of our classes at Headwaters, we take the students to our greenhouses to show them where we grow our food. One day, our friend, Gabe, was working in the greenhouse while listening to the radio. One of the young girls got excited and blurted out, "That's so nice that you play music for the plants!"

I smiled and refrained from saying anything, other than to agree with her. I then let what she said sink in. She was right. The plants take in and respond to the energy around them. It is important to be aware of what they are exposed to.

Shortly after that, I hung wind chimes close by as a way of thanking the plants for what they give us.

Working With Children Is Similar To Gardening

We are planting seeds with our teachings and our actions. Those bits of life wisdom will take root. When the timing is right, if nurtured, they will grab onto those defining moments and run with them, and then just watch them grow!

49

Plant Communicator

George Washington Carver was a renowned plant chemist, and one of the great geniuses of American history. He invented crop rotation and developed innovative uses for many agricultural crops. He was famous for creating peanut butter and over 200 uses from plants such as oils, dyes, food, and medicine.

George Washington Carver was a black man who grew up around great prejudice and hatred towards black people in the South. He was self-educated and knew from childhood he had a gift. He could talk to plants, and they could speak with him.

He was once asked how he came up with his ideas. He said that he would get up at 4:30 in the morning and walk alone in nature. The spirits of the plants would talk to him and give him information on what to create, and he would listen. He would then go back to his laboratory and do the chemistry.

He humbly said he found that whether you talk with a flower or silently commune with people, they all give up their secrets if you love them enough.

"People came right after flowers arrived on this planet. We owe our lives to flowers." - E.K.

Flowers, Flowers, Flowers

I think almost every human being can agree that flowers are jaw-dropping beautiful, and inspiring. When I walk out into a meadow and I look at each flower, one after another, each one is an individual gem that is astoundingly perfect. Their delicate beauty overwhelms me.

They put a call out on the wind through their scent, through their beauty, through their color, and their shape, to the bees and hummingbirds, and other pollinators, that they're ready, willing, and able to do their part to make the world full of life.

Flowers teach us about bringing beauty into our world, and they are true Earth Caretakers. Flowers are food for many living beings. The pollinators travel from one flower to the next and produce more flowers. The flowers feed the animals, and they create habitat.

One being is not better than another, we all have a role to fill in our natural system to support life. Just like our own human bodies, everything within our body makes the whole, and every living thing on the Earth makes the Earth. It's so simple, and yet so powerful, and so true.

Start spending time with flowers. They have a subliminal way of teaching. You often don't even know exactly what you're learning, but you are receiving a blessing.

Sit by flowers, lay in a meadow, and roll with them, enjoy them, admire their details. Look at the stamen in the middle, and then expand out to all parts of the flower. Look down the stem to see what insects are living on the flower. Look at the tracks on the ground by the flower.

Spend time looking at the individual, and let your eyes expand out to all the flowers in the area. Immerse yourself in them. Become the flowers and let them become you.

This is not new age mumbo jumbo; this is just the magic of life. Take the time and allow yourself to explore these possibilities.

An average person walks by flowers and doesn't even bother to look. Somebody else might go by and notice a little flower and acknowledge it, but they just keep on going. Be the one who takes it to the level where you build a relationship with that flower.

By sitting with a flower, and getting to know it as an individual, they will come into your being. They will become medicine in your life. They will inspire you to do great things, and be a better, more aware person. You might not even be able to track it back to those moments you had with the flower, but that's how the essence of the flower works, it gives.

I absolutely love growing flowers. One of my favorite things is to create flower arrangements. I consider it working with the Earth to create Earth art.

I pick a variety of flowers. For a while I used to have trouble even cutting flowers because I love them so much. After spending time with them, I realized they are going to die back, and I don't have to be greedy, and take every flower. I take one here, and one there. I'm sensitive to the plant. I let it speak to me. If the plant says no, then I don't take it.

When I pick a bunch of flowers, I'll pick some interesting wild plants, and branches, and leaves, and odds and ends from nature. Then I'll make arrangements and bring nature into my home. The flowers complement my house, and I get to look at the beauty all the time.

While in the process of making the artful arrangement, I'm continuing to learn to be in direct connection with nature. I'm opening my senses by smelling the flowers, by feeling the flowers, by truly seeing them up close.

Give flowers to people. Sometimes you can give one little flower, or you can make a monumental arrangement. It's a great tradition to give flowers to someone on holidays and birthdays, but do it anytime. You make the world better by brightening someone's day.

In my school camp we put flower arrangements on the tables because it makes us feel good. There are so many beautiful blessings that come out of building a relationship with flowers, and appreciating them, and sharing them. So, grow flowers, spend time with flowers, make flower arrangements, photograph flowers, draw flowers, cook with flowers, get creative.

Have gratitude for flowers and the medicine will live within you. A heart full of flowers is a lifelong blessing.

We've Met

I see light shine on a flower and as that light reflects into me, I know this flower. We've met each other in that place, our place, a place for us. A timeless moment of friendship to be cherished and honored.

"Live as if you are a flower blooming in spring after a long winter snow. Call to the bees, and the hummingbirds. Call to the sun. Bring the sunshine into your very soul. To do this is to be fully alive and one with life." - E.K.

Plants Are A Bridge Between Worlds

Get to know plants on their level, on their time, and you will know our Earth-heart. Plants are life for all living things. The diversity of plants is the beautiful Earth loving soul connection to all life.

Sing to the plants, they will be listening. You may get a song from them as well; plants sing songs from our Earth through all our senses.

Let plants awaken your senses and join their world. They will let you in. Plants will introduce us to Earth spirits. Plants play with those elements, that's how they thrive.

When I think of good values such as kindness, love, respect, peacefulness, fun and wonder, I believe plants are teachers of these things.

Plants fill me up with love and wonder, beauty, and hope. Just when I think I can't be anymore full of plant wonder, a plant gifts me with a flower and a new journey begins into that flower.

<u>Helpers Of The Plant World</u>

Elemental Beings, Earth Nature Spirits, and All That is Real

There is a whole other level of how plants live called Elementals or Earth Spiritual Beings. They live in gardens and around the Earth. I know it's a huge subject, and I know a lot of people who are even dedicated to the Earth, that struggle with believing this.

In general, if we don't physically see something, we don't usually think it is real. Sometimes visually we're not even convinced of what we're seeing.

The non-physical realm is always left up to interpretation so it can be a bit perplexing and mystifying, but I will tell you now, I give you my word, I'm not lying about this. What I'm sharing with you is the absolute truth as I know it, and I am one of the most grounded people you will ever meet.

51

People have known about Elemental Beings for years. One teacher of this was Rudolf Steiner, the founder of the Waldorf education system. The gardeners of Findhorn, the beautiful, famous garden in Scotland, work with the Elementals, as we do on our land in Mount Shasta.

Plants need soil that is alive, and the roots need to be able to go down through it, and pick up all the nutrients from the water coming through. Plants need space and they need the sun. These things are needed for all plant growth.

The other vital factor for them to thrive are Elementals. Humans have trouble understanding Elementals, and that's partially a good thing. These Earth Spirits nurture the plants on a spiritual level.

We need to consider the fact that plants are living beings. They have their own feelings and expressions of energy. Do we believe that we are the only ones who enjoy life? Do we really think that plants can't express love in their own, unique way? Can we honestly believe that plants don't enjoy beauty or the gift of life and living? If you struggle with this understanding, then this lesson is still waiting for you.

Elementals or Earth Spirits are the caretakers and protectors of the plants. They are the ones that help them grow and give them spiritual energy.

"There are specific Earth Spirits that caretake flowers. The Being of the flower itself is food for Earth Spirits." - E.K.

***

These beings are not generally physical. They live on what I would call another plane of existence. I'm telling you this while I'm sitting in the woods on a log, breathing physical air, next to a running creek. I am in the physical plane, but if I just took a step a little further, I would still be in the same place, but I wouldn't be visible. I would be sharing space in another layer of life, and I believe there are many layers of life.

Just as there are many layers of life in the forest, and many layers of life in the creek, and in the ocean, and many layers of life in a garden, there are layers of life in our bodies.

To get to this perspective, you need to take a leap. It doesn't need to be that hard. We can't see cell phone, radio, or television energy waves, but we know they are there allowing us to communicate and send and receive information. We accept that as something we don't see physically, but we know that connection is real.

We all agree love exists. It's an incredibly powerful thing. We all want it. We all need it. You can see it in somebody's smile, but you can't actually see the energy of love or physically grasp it or contain it, but we feel it and know it is real.

So, why couldn't there be something more than just us? Isn't that just a little bit preposterous to think that the physical world is all there is?

The exciting part about this is that if we want to access more of the Elemental world, then we can. It's there for us to explore, to figure it out, to find the keys. If we don't want to, we can just enjoy our life in the physical world, knowing there's so much more, and have great peace knowing that.

"Elemental Beings or Earth Spirits are the tenders of the plant world. They are to flowers like water and sunlight. They feed and nurture the plants. They will show themselves to us when they feel we need to see them to understand more about caretaking plants." - E.K.

***

Over the years there have been stories and movies made up of fairies, and making light of them in a funny way, and yes, there are Beings kind of like that. There are thousands of what I would call species of Beings. Some care for the water, some care for flowers, some care for trees, some care for certain types of landscapes, and individual plants.

One place you'll always learn about Elementals is in a garden. When you work personally with plants, they will sometimes show themselves. They will be more willing to show themselves as they feel safer around you.

"Earth Spirits don't like people in general. Humans are destroying what they love and thrive on." - E.K.

***

I've talked to Elementals many times. The message I get very simply put, is that humans are not overall liked by Elementals. They are very simple beings. They don't necessarily have complex brains with a diverse knowledge from a scholastic education. They have a job to do, and they do it well. They care for the plants and protect them.

Many humans have abused our plants. What do you think it does to Elementals when we take monstrous tractors and chainsaws, and cut down old growth forests? What is it like when machinery rips across the ground and destroys everything? How is the health of all beings when we put poisons on our plants? These actions are why humans don't have a great reputation in this part of the Elemental world.

The communication I have received is when we are peaceful and open, often they will show themselves. We'll see a flicker of light in a tree or a movement, or a sparkle under a waterfall. Many times, it won't be something we see; we will feel a presence there with us. You know you're not alone. You're aware there are many beings living around the ground, and above flowing water. As you develop this awareness you may see or experience more Elementals.

"Build homes for Elementals. They need a healthy habitat too." - E.K.

***

Sometimes people ask me what my experience is when I'm in the woods, and I know people don't believe this, but I'm never really alone. There are Elementals everywhere. I started my life relationship with them when I was a kid.

I was raised as a child of nature. I learned to live on and with the land. The land was my personal friend, teacher, and healer. The Earth was my place of safety, inspiration, and endless play and learning.

My mentors taught me the physical, practical skills in nature such as hunting, fishing, fire making, shelter building, tracking, and foraging for wild foods. The most important thing they taught me was Earth spirituality. They allowed me to be in relationship, as only a child's pure mind can be, with Earth spirits, and the living spirits of trees, plants, water, animals, and the Earth itself. They never told me that my relationship was wrong or not real.

As kids, we don't have all the dogma and the scientific labels that limits much of our awareness. Kids are completely open to the world they live in.

A lot of kids have friendships with Elementals. They see and feel them all the time. They may talk about it with their families, but they don't think of it as anything stranger than seeing a plant or a raccoon, or a deer in the woods. It's normal to them so they don't make it a big deal.

Somewhere around the age of nine years old we move from this pure perspective of seeing the world, to the logical brain. Often, the awareness of the world of spirit in nature fades away. This is a form of survival if a child wants to fit into a linear society.

The logical world and the science-based world do not allow space for Earth spirits or talking to trees. Sadly, we then lose our connection to nature's richer side, its essence, and wisdom, unless it is consciously nurtured.

I was gifted with mentors who taught me that anything is possible and there are no limits. The support from my mentors and my passion for being in nature allowed me to keep my Earth spiritual connection, while living in a science minded world. Both became wonderful to me and often fused together. It's fun when science catches up and explains what we already know.

One of the major keys to keeping kids connected to that world of Elementals is letting them be in nature as much as they can. Don't give them every store-bought toy to keep them occupied, particularly computers at a young age.

Let them play in the dirt and play with bugs. Let them play in the water. Let them climb trees and make toys out of things they find in nature. They will build their relationship, and hopefully carry it over into the linear world.

As they move into that busy life, help them to still go to nature and be free and in the moment, not always purpose driven. There comes a point where they can have both. To live in the logical world while aware of the spiritual part of our world, is the gift we dream of. We dream it for ourselves, but it's already there.

The only thing stopping us from engaging in the enchantment of our natural world is our logic putting limits on what we believe. Doubt creeps in when our mind won't free our thoughts.

When we manage our logical mind and put it to rest at times, these moments are remarkable. We allow ourselves the room to experience unlimited freedom. We pass through veils, to the endless depths

of our living Earth. We feel welcome, Home again, one with our planet. We reclaim our birthright to be a child of the Earth, Earthlings.

We understand that anything becomes possible, and yet so normal. That connection was always there, now we just know it on all levels. We may have felt it before or sensed it through our intuitive side, but now we know it as a clear, defining moment.

I also learned this from my Catholic upbringing. My childhood priest was my mentor and spiritual teacher. I was taught that nature was spiritual, sacred, holy. I learned that all life was beautiful, and most importantly, all living beings were much more than the physical, including humans. I learned to believe in miracles and that all life was a miracle.

If we look into a mirror, we see this amazing body looking back at us, eyes blinking and seeing, hands and feet feeling and moving. Even the mirror's reflection is a miracle.

As we look at this body in the mirror, without prior knowledge, we would not know that there is a beating heart or lungs breathing or blood flowing throughout, allowing our nerves to feel and sense.

Going deeper we wouldn't know of antibodies flowing in our blood to fight illnesses. This miracle lies within us. If we paid attention though, we would know through our inner vision. Even if we couldn't explain it, we would just know, as our ancestors did.

This is how our Earth is, and our forests, our mountains, and oceans. So much life lies beneath the ocean's surface, and the soil. We know there are microscopic organisms, we can't see them, but we know they are there. Before we even had microscopes, we felt them.

There is no end to the depth of what there is, and the miracles that lie within. Earth spirits are alive and well and tend the land as Earth Caretakers. The Sun and water grow all living things, as do Earth spirits. They tend to our Earth energy fields, the garden, the very souls of all living things.

"Currently there are eight billion people here on Earth and there are many trillions of Earth Spirits." - E.K.

***

If you are in your later years now and feel like you have lost your ability to sense energies, how do you get that back? Gardening is one way, the other is to spend time in nature.

Sit by a creek and observe. Imagine your heart opening and taking in all that there is. Look at the details of plants, and water, and rocks. Notice if you see something that looks a little different. Maybe a shape in the bark of a tree. Maybe a disturbance in the rippling water will speak to you. Maybe you'll see a face within a rock.

Often, I find heart rocks that remind me that I'm a loving being. I'm reminded that I'm not the only one that has a loving side, and when I come from love, I'm the best that I can be.

Trees, plants, water, rocks, insects, animals, all have a loving side. Why would that be exclusively for humans? That would be insane. Is love expressed differently for different beings? Of course! Part of the fun of being human is learning how to see and feel love in everything. It's the journey of discovering layers of life in nature. It's always about the journey.

What is beauty? Why do you see one thing as beautiful and another not? When you see beauty how does it speak to you? How does it feel in your body? What does it do to your brain?

Often in nature when you look at something, and beauty is reflected back at the same time, an Elemental, an Earth spirit, is there as a part of it, and they are looking back at you. When you're at your best they're happy and feel good. Quality time inquisitively observing, will help you open to the Earth spirits.

"Earth Spirits are in and around water. You feel their rush of energy under waterfalls." - E.K.

***

Another great way to connect is to sit by a plant and ask it to give you a story or a poem about its life and start to write. You'd be amazed at what comes to you.

Ask a tree or plant to show you the essence of itself, and then paint or draw it. You could draw it in detail or get expressive and draw what it feels like. It will come from the heart of the tree or plant, and it will be from your heart, and the connection will be made between the two.

Earth Elemental beings love wild spaces in gardens. They don't want it too neatly controlled. It's not natural for them. They need a wildness to their space for them to thrive.

Your heart intention of being a caretaker is picked up and felt by every living being in nature. Immediately, nature grabs your heart and wraps its heart energy around you. There's a fusion that takes place. What I'm trying to get across to you is that it's so simple.

We are all individuals, and we all have unique ways of expressing ourselves. Get in touch with those various ways of interacting and engage in your environment. It might be that you dance on a beach. It might be that you climb a tree, or you crawl through the woods. It might be that you sit in water and disappear and become the water. It might be that you camo up, and sit by a tree and become the tree. Those are all incredible things to do.

The point is to engage with your heart open, and if you want to see Elementals, be patient. It's going to take time to build their trust. Be open for them to show up and see what happens.

Write about your experiences, draw pictures, observe details, and have lots of fun. The Earth spirits are there with, you just like the animals in the forest. Pass through the veils into our Earth's beating heart and enjoy the world of Earth spirits.

"To meet an Earth Spirit for the first time, to know this meeting is sacred and real, to embrace this Being fully, this moment is a step to a higher personal evolution in one's life. This step must be taken to truly know our planet". - E.K.

Reminders:
*Sit with a plant, observe it, talk to it, and then listen, write about it, draw it, but first just sit.
*Learn about wild edibles, ask permission from the plant, and harvest a sacred meal.
*Sing to plants and listen to their songs.
*Recognize when a plant needs help and do something about it. Water parking lot plants.
*Be with the Elementals. Acknowledge them and respect them even if you don't see them.
*Create habitat for the Earth spirits by tending a healthy landscape.
*Be wise enough to know that we don't know everything, but if we stay open to all possibilities we just may.

When we steward the Earth, we leave behind the old ideas of ownership, of power and control over the Earth. Our relationship with our Earth becomes personal and wonder filled.

Chapter 6

Tend A Garden

One of the best ways we can learn to communicate with nature is to become gardeners, and interact with plants as they grow.

Get inspired, go out on the land, and practice the art of understanding plants. Learn what's edible and medicinal. Learn to talk to plants, and involve your senses.

Your home can be a wonderful place to start. Grow plants outside and inside. Through the simple act of growing plants, we awaken our inner caretaker and give it life.

Own who we truly are, as Earth Caretakers or Earth Gardeners. This is when we are at our best; when we co-create food gardens, wildlife gardens, flower gardens, and even water gardens.

Go into your garden without your phone and be fully in your surroundings, without interruptions. You'll find your bliss there.

Family Garden

From junior high through high school, I grew our family's food in our backyard garden, in Sunnyvale, California, which is now Silicon Valley. Back then Sunnyvale was all fruit orchards and wild land. Our yard was about a quarter of an acre, and I had a wonderful garden.

In the seventies a lot of great information was just becoming available to home gardeners. I was able to learn from reading, and I asked questions, and experimented, and learned as I grew. I also learned naturally from the garden itself, and the spirits of the garden.

The first thing I did was dig a hole for a pond that I then lined with cement. I collected wild grasses, tulles, cattails, mosses, and other water plants, which I planted around my pond.

I scavenged pine trees that had been thrown out in a lot by a grocery store. I brought in frogs, snakes, and fish that I'd caught, and soon the pond became my Garden of Eden.

I expanded beyond the pond, and created a fruit and vegetable garden. It was such a joy and feeling of self-reliance to be able to provide food for our meals.

The gardens became a great teacher for me, as I could experience first-hand the connection between nature, plants and man. I learned what it meant to be a steward of the land. As I did my caretaking of the gardens for my family, I also provided a haven for insects, raccoons, skunks, and countless varieties of birds.

I noticed when I quieted my mind and moved at nature's rhythm, I could hear the language of the plants. They spoke in their own unique way, and I could see spirits or beings that lived around the plants.

These mysterious beings of light created halos around the plants. The Earth spirits seemed to show up as flickers of light or shapes, and colors or quick movements.

I was amazed by these life forces around the plants. I knew by working with them and with the animals, I could create a partnership that would result in an abundant bounty.

I also loved sticking my hands in the dirt, getting a reminder that life exists below the surface. The more I learned about gardening, the more I learned that there were more living things in the dirt than above it. It almost became too painful to dig so much life up. The synergy between what's above and below was demonstrated every day in the growth of my garden.

The garden kept me nature-centered and inspired. I had incredible food, healthy pine trees and an amazing pond that I would get into on occasion. Feeling the lusciousness of the wet and mud helped to remind me of the good things in life.

All around me the woods were being chopped down. The mountains were being trucked away for sand, and the orchards were being wiped out for housing tracts. I can't imagine how I would have sustained my sanity, watching the destruction of my childhood paradises, if I didn't have that garden.

Being surrounded by the beauty of plants always makes me smile. One of my greatest joys is to lie in a sunny meadow and roll in the tall grass among the flowers. I once heard it said that flowers were how the Earth laughed. I'd have to agree.

Gardening speaks to the creative gift that humans have. We can adapt to different environments. This can cause destruction, but we also have the ability to co-create sacred spaces. We have the potential to enhance our environment by listening to its needs and desires.

Seeds Are Miracles

What better way to communicate with plants than to plant a seed. Give it a blessing, water it, watch it sprout, nurture it, and continue to give it blessings. Protect it from insects, protect it from too much sun, or too little sun.

Tend to it daily, sing to it, watch it grow into its different stages of life and admire the masterpiece this seed has turned into. Notice the patterns, colors, and shapes of the leaves. Touch it with your hands, face, and bare feet- plants love to be touched.

As a plant grows, and you're looking at it every day, you're creating a personal relationship with that plant. You don't even know it. This is something I want you to get, it always happens with any plant, wild or non-wild. The plant is communicating with you endlessly.

One way you are interacting is by showing love, tenderness, and care towards the plant, and offering it protection. That's incredible communication, but you can always go further.

As the plant grows it eventually fruits and you then have the joy of harvesting it, and taking its life in a good way. With good intentions you let its life become you by eating it.

When you eat the fruit right away the plant is still living, and its energy absorbs into your system and gives you nutrients to live. The plant becomes a part of you as you help raise it.

Think about that for a minute, what a remarkable thing that is. You start a plant from seed, you grow it, you nurture it, you protect it, then you eat it. That is a miracle, it gives you life, and you give it purpose, joy, pleasure, and the art of living as a plant. It's a mutually beneficial relationship with nature, on all levels from the physical, to the spiritual.

Eventually that plant wraps up its life. You harvest and eat the plant or put it in your compost and help co-create life by making living soil. Tending gardens all begins in the dirt.

In the next year smell the soil, feel it in your hands. Put that incredible dirt, that's full of worms and other living beings, in your garden and start the whole process over again. Imagine that multiplied, a garden full of plants, all yours to care for.

Take in that thought. The full circle art of gardening. Every part of life is a circle. The Earth, the sun, the moon, the seasons are all a part of that cycle.

The seeds you plant may live one year, or they may be trees, and live for a thousand years. The seeds will be food for humans, and food for animals. Think of the flowers, and the pollinators like bees, hummingbirds and bats that rely on them.

When we are in partnership with nature we learn to observe keenly. The plants talk to us, and we talk back. When a plant dies, we feel the loss. When a plant grows, we feel joy.

Through gardening we find our place, our gifts to nature. When we eat the plants, we live through nature. It's a direct daily experience.

Gardening is a unique offering that humans have. That level of attention and full circle living with nature can transfer to all areas of our lives.

What an honor to take part in growing another living being. Notice how you feel to be a part of creation. That's what an Earth Caretaker is. That's the true meaning of life, to be a part of creation. To be the Earth.

So, if you are having trouble seeing what a miracle is, then look at a seed and be an active part of that life cycle. There's nothing more miraculous than planting a seed of pure potential.

Nursery

I was watering our seed trays and a flicker caught my eye. I wasn't sure where it came from, so I turned toward the windowsill where the small potted containers were. Another movement. Dang it! It must be another plant eating insect burrowing in the soil.

Curious to see what I was dealing with, I held still. Slowly, the soil on the surface of the container cracked and broke open. A smooth, shiny object emerged. I watched in amazement, a sprout stretch awake and come to life, as a young, one inch plant. It unfolded itself so gracefully like a ballerina. It looked like a time lapse video happening in real time.

I felt my heart open, and tears welled up, as it reached for its first ray of sunshine. I was crying over a bean sprout! I have grown thousands of plants, but this was the first time I had witnessed the actual birth of one of these miracles.

I instantly felt maternal towards this being, and finally realized why greenhouses are called nurseries. Our little greenhouse is there to protect these young, plant babies, and of course I knew that, but that day I felt it with honor.

I stood a little taller, knowing I had helped to provide the nurturing environment, and the care it took to allow these daily miracles to happen.

In our nursery these plants burst into the sunlight for the first time and new life is born and tended to, and I get to be a witness to this as a humbled caretaker. As gardeners, we help plants thrive alongside other companions in a symbiotic relationship. They can grow alone, but the young ones thrive when they have elders of their own kind, as well as other species to interact with. There is a plant communication between them that is far wiser than any one of us. The elder plants always have knowledge to share. We all have something to offer each other to flourish.

Now, when I enter the greenhouse and I see a new start emerging from the soil, I sing Happy Birthday to it. I'm literally singing Happy Birthday to people's salad.

Each time someone eats the vegetables they are ingesting new life. The energy of a fresh, harvested plant is still alive and beating through it, and into them, merging with their own energy. I feel proud knowing when I grow plants, I am helping people to live.

Interact with your food source. There's nothing more personal than something that goes into your being and sustains your life, and becomes a part of you.

Create A Food Garden

One of the greatest endeavors you can do for yourself and for the Earth, is to work with nature and garden in a beautiful way.

Grow a little extra so you have enough if you lose some plants to animals or weather conditions. If you have an abundance, share with your neighbors, then preserve your harvest.

If you do kill rodents, do it in a humane way and put them out for other animals to eat. Think about it consciously. Offer a prayer.

Ultimately, if you are going to be a steward of the Earth, you must be able to tend a garden without being merciless to the animals that live on the Earth. This means use care, awareness, curiosity, commitment, and time.

Learning to grow food and sharing it is a way to bring community together. When grocery stores are closed due to emergencies, food gardens are valuable assets to have. Being independent and not in desperate need of someone else providing for you is a vital life skill.

Experiment with growing a variety of the same species of plants. As our climate changes, so will our ability to grow what would normally live and produce in that environment. Learn to adapt to our changing water availability and temperature changes, and diversify your crops. Some farmers and winemakers are already doing this.

Learn about aquaponic and hydroponic gardening when environmental conditions won't allow you to grow your food in different seasons.

There are so many books, videos and people to learn from. One of the great ways to learn is by experimentation. You will be so invested in those little beings as you watch those plants grow. Go tend a garden!

Community Gardening

During World War II people grew Victory Gardens in their yards instead of lawns to feed their families. Roughly 40 percent of all vegetables in the U.S. were grown in home gardens.

The origin of lawns or grassy areas near a home is believed to have started as a grazing area for livestock, which organically maintained itself. As ranching eventually became more of a specific trade, lawns became a wealthy status symbol. Only those with money could afford to have others tend their grass and upkeep their yard.

We have moved on from the need to have this manicured area be the majority of our property. There is still space for beauty and a place for gathering and play and for our pets, but there is also a need to create living resources and wildlife habitat.

Can you imagine going through a neighborhood in the U.S. and instead of green lawns, seeing gardens with food, and flowers, and berries, and fruit trees? Imagine the abundance of food in just one neighborhood.

People would work in their gardens and actually meet their neighbors. Ideas would be shared, and friendships would develop.

Create a garden in your yard. There are many apartments now that offer garden plots to their tenants as well as community garden spaces in cities. There's always a way to get creative and make space.

Learning to garden is a huge step in being self-reliant and making the world better.

Urban Garden

Wherever you live, create a wildlife sanctuary. It could be your deck in an apartment complex. It could be your backyard. The size and type of space doesn't matter. Creating a nature sanctuary is an act of kindness and nature will teach us to use our gifts.

I once lived in a second story apartment with a twelve by five-foot deck. I turned the deck into a wildlife sanctuary, and a sacred sit spot for myself. I filled it with plants that provided cover and food. I also supplied water and bird seed. I barely had room for my small chair, but I loved to sit and observe this wild world.

Every year Mourning Doves nested and fledged their young. Many birds came to visit. Hummingbirds buzzed by to feed; lizards, spiders, butterflies, and insects showed up.

An ecosystem developed, a sanctuary. Nature, with my helping hand, did what it does best, it created life. It brought me peace. It harmed no one, and only good came out of it.

Animals need cover for protection, food, and water. Add these things to any place and nature will do the rest. Even a crack in the walkway becomes a habitat. If you have a larger back yard, you can go crazy with it. Add a pond, a variety of trees, and ground cover.

Creating sacred space with nature makes that relationship personal. Watching this space grow into a harmonious environment, becoming home to so many beings, is fulfilling. This space will become your teacher of nature awareness, and you become its protector.

Imagine if thousands of people in cities created nature gardens, on their balconies, on their front lawns, and in their windowsills. Add these to existing wild lands around cities, then add city parks and vacant lots, and food gardens, and the results could be astonishing.

If you're a bird or another animal living around the city, such gardens and refuges could be lifesaving. Suddenly, cities become beautiful, bountiful places to live for all.

Grow a garden even if it's in pots on a deck. Nurture the plants and you will feel the benefits. Make this something you do your whole life. Being an Earth Caretaker is this simple and yet so important. Everyday actions can change the world, one nature balcony at a time.

The Darkside

Gardening can be a nurturing interaction and it can also become very ugly. In many commercial farming practices, as well as with personal gardens, poisons are put on the plants. This is the manipulative side of gardening. The poisons can kill countless birds, and animals that come in contact with the toxic plants and dirt.

Many times, this type of garden is a monoculture, just one plant species with nothing else allowed to live. It becomes a living-dead environment. When there is only one plant or type of plant and nothing else, it becomes sterile.

Even organic can be unideal, if there's not a consideration for the quality of the plant's life and the beings that live around it. Be mindful of that dark side of gardening. Learn how to communicate with your garden to provide it with what it needs to thrive in a healthy way.

Remembering Moxy

When my wife, Jean, and I first moved to our land, we were raising our young pack of dogs. We had a white, Shepherd puppy named Moxy. She was such a joy full of spirit and spunk.

We had a landscaper taking care of our new yard as it was growing in and unknown to us, he had used a chemical fertilizer. Even though he had used it with good intention, that ignorant mistake cost our puppy her life. She died a horrible death from chemical poisoning after chewing the grass. We were devastated.

I'm sharing this story because no matter how tempted you might be to use just a little chemical fertilizer *don't* do it. Those chemical companies are evil and there is *nothing* good that comes of their poison.

I know it wasn't just our puppy that died from the poison. Any bird eating the seed off the ground, chipmunk, squirrel, rabbit, or reptile would have died as well. Those poisons do not just evaporate and go away. They stay in the environment and continue to damage our Earth, and ultimately kill us.

Although it breaks my heart to share this story, I know I need to honor Moxy's life by preventing another life from being taken directly or indirectly in this way.

Edible plants taste better when you plant flowers in between them.

Consider Eating For The Earth

Eat good food from our good Earth. What you put into your sacred body is a direct reflection of how you treat the sacred Earth. Eat for a healthy Earth. Eat real food, drink fresh water. Eat with gratitude, and food will become medicine.

Love the animals and plants you eat. You honor them this way. Consider not eating factory farmed animals. Grow your own food. There's no better way to feel our living Earth.

Indoor Gardens

Grow house plants at home and at your work. Indoor plants bring a life force to your personal space. You get to know them as companions. They teach you Earth Caretaking in a very natural way. Bring your home and workspace alive with fresh air.

Phyllis

When I was in preschool, I took on the job of watering our house plants with pride. My sisters were away at school, so the house plants became my friends.

I would mist them with a spray bottle and talk with them. Sometimes I would take my friend, Phyliss, the Philodendron, into my room while I was playing.

Years later, our family moved across the country. When we unpacked the moving van, I realized I hadn't seen Phyllis. My dad told me they had to leave the plants behind, and I completely fell apart. My dad didn't know those plants were my friends. He didn't even know Phyliss had a name. He told me his friend was taking care of her, but it was too far away to go get her.

I know he felt terrible about the situation. He had no idea about my special friendship with that plant. He tried to get me a new plant, but it just wasn't the same. I watered the new plant, but I never connected with it in same way.

For children, having a living being to take care of is so important. It is easy for us to see that animals are alive, but to truly connect with a plant as a living being with its own form of consciousness, takes a child-like, open mind and heart. Give children the responsibility of tending a plant, and they will grow into life-long Earth Caretakers.

Plant A Medicinal Garden

Create a space to grow your own pharmacy. Learn about medicinal plants and grow your own. Some of these plants may be for salves, tinctures, or poultices. Learn what plants complement each other and thrive in a symbiotic relationship.

Treat all beings with respect and treat these plants as sacred friends. They are here for you if you listen.

"When using the plants as medicines or teas, visualize them giving you their healing essence, and again offer gratitude. The effectiveness is in the partnership and working together. This practice will ensure that these plants will be medicinal and truly healing." - E.K.

Wild And Domestic

Only harvest wild or domestic plants as medicine with an open heart. Talk or sing to the plants, don't violently yank off the leaves and fruit, be gentle and caring.

Take only a little from each plant, so they can grow back and stay healthy. If picking the whole plant, give back an offering of gratitude.

If an animal's home is damaged while harvesting a plant, you must repair their home. If any animal is harmed while harvesting, you must help it and offer good blessings if you kill it.

Always engage your five senses as fully as possible when harvesting, and engage your sixth sense by seeing the plant as a spiritual being.

Have fun. Don't rush. Often this type of harvesting can be a wonderful way to bring a community together.

After harvesting, continue to treat the plants as sacred by preparing and storing them with honor and integrity, and always offer gratitude and love.

Wild Gardens

I live in a wilderness garden. When I built my house, I made a commitment to the plants I had to kill, to restore what I had to dig up. I spent many hours talking with the plants and planning the layers to make the space better than I found it. I have now done that, and I feel good about it.

I didn't do it alone, my wife Jean, Julie our land caretaker, students, my friends, and my gardener, Gabe, all have been a part of it. The community has helped me to create this magical garden. It was my vision, but I had help to make it happen over the years.

Vision is needed to inspire, and leadership is important in following through with an idea.

Somebody must have an idea and be the one to step up and make it happen. Otherwise, that dream just stays in the thought process, and nothing ever happens. When you set a project in motion, and it's beautiful, with a little nudge and encouragement, people come forth.

People want to do the right thing. They want to be a part of a sense of place. They want to be of service, and they want to create. There is a bond in communal commitment to a task.

The forest food garden I created around my house is separate from my vegetable garden. It has raspberries, grapes and leafy plants that are edible. There are self-planted wild edibles like currants, elderberries, thimbleberries, blackberries, mushrooms, and sorrel.

There are medicinal plants in this garden including lavender, nettle, yarrow, plantain, and thistle. As well as herbs like; mint, sage, and thyme.

Of course, there are flowers and ferns and a large variety of trees, such as maples, cottonwoods, willow, dogwoods, and aspens all growing within the landscape of the native alder, cedar, fir, oak, and pine trees. I have planted a variety of grasses and bamboos, and I leave the meadow wild behind my house.

A tiered forest canopy can be an incredible food garden for humans and animals. They tend to be lower maintenance, and offer a variety of edibles throughout much of the year.

You know a garden has arrived when plants and trees start themselves. The garden becomes a living being, regenerating itself, and new plants and animals show up. Having uninterrupted time to settle in and thrive is an asset to any garden.

I found a photo of my wolf-dog, Riley, standing by a four-foot willow tree that I had planted in my front yard. That same tree, twenty years later, dominates the front of our house. It is magnificently huge. It is 40 feet high, and its branches spread out are almost as wide as it is tall. It is a home for birds, insects, and squirrels. Visually it is so freaking beautiful, I stop in awe of it every day.

***

We thin our surrounding woods for fire safety and for the health of the overall forest, but I also leave some underbrush and some dead, standing trees. Dead trees are still alive. They are just alive in a different way. When trees die, they take on another way of being. They become magnificent art sculptures and vital habitats.

There is a line where you cannot be too over controlling, or the space will be sterile physically and spiritually.

I do my best to use my intuition and compassion when gathering plants and caretaking the woods, just as I do when hunting or fishing. As a caretaker of the land, it is necessary to take some of the trees down, but as with any community, I am always aware of leaving the elders. A forest without elders is a struggling forest. It is like a child left without parents to fend for themselves without guidance.

If you are truly in tune with your environment, you can sense which plants are ready to be harvested, or which trees are willing to be cut for different reasons.

When you choose to pull one plant from the ground rather than another, pay attention as to why you did that. Was it your inner vision telling you that the plant you chose also chose you?

***

This forest garden has created ample beauty, shelter, and food for animals. After twenty years the garden is in its early stages of maturing. It is a fulfilling journey to witness a garden grow over time. The connection to all things growing and living in the garden creates a personal relationship with the individuals.

The habitats that are built over time take us into the very soul of the garden, the land, the Earth. We are a witness to so many stories, and sacred moments.

One of the benefits of a maturing garden is the community that gathers. This includes animals, reptiles, insects, butterflies galore, dragonflies, and spiders spinning their intricate webs.

We have a variety of birds that visit the feeders, and many have become lifelong residents. Some birds come through during their migration. Some birds of prey come to hunt the many mammals on the land, and even attempt to steal our chickens given the opportunity for a take-out dinner.

One of my passions is helping provide spaces in our forest gardens for birds to fledge their babies. Once the birds leave their nests, some of the birdhouses become squirrel, chipmunk or bumblebee homes. No vessel in the woods goes unused.

There are fifty birdhouses and nesting boxes around the house and gardens. There can be 200 birds fledging each year. I feed the birds high quality seed and suet and have water available for them. I give the migrating birds a stop over to rest and have abundant habitat available for those who stay.

We have countless squirrels, rabbits, chipmunks, voles, and deer that live here. They draw in predators like hawks, coyotes, foxes, fishers, martins, skunks, mountain lions, bobcats, bears, and periodically, a lone wolf passing through. One animal will attract another, always leaving their manuscript in the form of tracks, scat, scent, and fur.

Packrats, mice and gophers live here. I must admit, some of them make me mad when they attack my plants. Do I kill them all? No. On occasion though, I do, if they are in huge abundance or are becoming very destructive. Mice can be very invasive in my house, so I do have to trap them when they make a mess of my home.

***

With a variety of plants and animals, we now have a new animal to our land that has taken up regular residency. A family of Ringtail Cats has moved in. One of them initially moved *into* my house.

A chunk of my pie was missing from my kitchen counter. After initially wondering if Julie snuck in and ate it, I found the real thief looking down at me from my family room loft.

I thought about letting it stay. It was so cute peering down at me while I sat reading on the couch, but I knew its place was in the wild. My dogs also wouldn't be too happy about a new roommate.

After a few failed attempts, we trapped the ringtail. I released it out on the land farther away from the house and closed all the openings that I imagined it would fit through. Turns out a ringtail cat can fit through very small openings and knows a good opportunity when he sees it.

After a few more captures and releases I decided I needed to relocate it much farther away. I found an abandoned barn miles away and relocated it where it could hunt sufficiently.

A month later we discovered where there is one ringtail, there are others. We now have a handful of ringtails that have made our land their home. They show up in our trees and visit our staff on top of their tents, and peek through our skylights on our homes. They seek out interaction with us, and I feel blessed after so many years to have a new species of friends on our land. This is an affirmation that our land is healthy and still thriving.

***

I have four dozen fruit trees around my property. The abundant fruit brings in the birds, squirrels, and deer. Half the fruit from our trees goes to the animals, and half I eat, and share with our students. I consider the food the animals eat as my give back and an offering.

The joy of climbing the fruit trees every year, and harvesting the fruit, and making pies and jams, and juice with a community is one of the most memorable times for us. The gardens bring us together in joy and purpose.

We have honey bee hives in the gardens to help pollinate everything. We also have mason bees, bumble bees, wasps, and butterflies. I have intentionally planted many plants that attract these pollinators. I have gathered milkweed seeds from roadways and planted them all over our land to help the monarch butterflies who feed on the plant and lay their eggs on them.

Tending a garden, consciously planting it with native plants that provide food for birds and other animals, helps our wildlife greatly.

***

There are different stages of a garden that bring in layers of life. Fill stone walls with plants for frogs, toads, lizards and snakes and the garden becomes alive as a wildlife sanctuary.

Start with one small area and build the layers as you go. When you put love and care into a garden, growth speeds up. As it matures it creates and maintains itself. At some point you let go of trying to manipulate it into what you think it should be, and let it grow organically into what it wants to be.

Earth gardening is highlighting what is already there. The focus is bringing out the beauty, and making it more accessible for humans and animals to experience.

Remember to add art pieces and sit spots to stop and take it all in and observe, and feel, and wonder. Some of the art pieces I have in my garden are pretty, and some are just funny weird things that make people laugh. Art grabs your attention and draws you in.

A well cared for garden gives people a sense of place. The garden I have created is my garden, but it belongs to the Earth and all the animals that live in it.

Start with one plant and build a garden.

When you find edible plants, eat like an animal. Bite the leaves off. Lose yourself in the wilds, get primal, and be free.

Blueberry

When I was 12 years old my mentor, Bo, took me and his son, Claus, backpacking into a national forest in New Hampshire. After setting up camp, I went exploring on my own. I wandered into an open area along a creek. I saw a blueberry patch so full of ripe berries that all I could see was blue.

I love blueberries ripe off the plant. I smelled them and jumped into the bushes and started to feast. I filled my mouth over and over again. My face and tongue were soon purple.

I suddenly heard a noise and looked deeper into the blueberry patch. As my eyes filtered through the berries and leaves, I caught a movement. A mother black bear and two cubs! They were drunk on berries. Our eyes met and somewhere in that meeting, in that mystery place where all beings get along, we agreed to be ok with each other. That's abundance, that's blueberry medicine.

After peacefully finishing my afternoon snack, and taking a bag back to camp, I noticed a mother deer and fawn eating a short distance away. The blueberry thicket brought us all together. What a joy to feast together!

Make Your Garden Personal

Add your own beauty to your garden. Gardens attract people, and a garden with true loving Earth medicine can often change lives.

I like to build trails that wind and twist and are not always easy to follow. It forces people to be aware and focus on being in the moment. They wander and find sacred spaces to sit and think and wonder. This lets the garden take them on a journey where doorways will appear. When someone is ready to open their heart, they will truly venture into the garden's soul, and feel the life force within it.

Time in a garden with no agenda is vital, but quick visits can be good too. Remember nature doesn't work on the human clock. The passing of time in nature is elusive. What was it like for us before clocks and modern times? Go into nature and find out. I'm sure it will be quite revealing and freeing in spirit, body, and soul. Gardens are timeless.

It's good to have sleeping spaces in a garden so you can experience the life within it, in the dark third of the day. Nocturnal visitors arrive and plants take on a different energy than during the day. There are different sounds and smells. Only at night can you truly smell the Night Jasmine at its peak, letting off its perfumed fragrance. What a treat that is.

Add water features and your garden becomes extraordinary. Add bird baths, ponds, streams, puddles, hose drips, shallow water dishes for bees. Water attracts animals. Water is life. It's what makes our planet Earth the garden it is.

Water makes gardens vibrant living places. The sound of running water is calming as well as invigorating. Think of the power of reflections and how they can stop you immediately and cause you to gaze deeply into what you see.

***

The best gardens are semi-wild. Your garden needs its own medicine, its own strong life force created naturally and not overcontrolled. Your garden must have freedom to create itself. Gardens need this to be extraordinary and not sterile. These semi wild spaces are also great habitats where Earth Spirits thrive.

Create nature art in your garden. Make sculptures from wood and rock. These artistic places reflect your love and connection you have with your garden.

Get to know individual animals. In my garden I personally know many birds that come to feed, and they often greet me through song. I know individual toads and snakes and even spiders in various webs.

***

Gardens create stories, shared with community. These stories become living memories. I often reflect on our ancestors. I think of how important their stories were of the land they lived on for thousands of years. These stories held them together as a community.

Today we are often so busy doing, that unlike our ancestors, we need to reclaim the art of just being. Gardens can provide these moments for us.

Gardens can become the caretaker's legacy. They are our gift to nature, community, and the future. Long after we are gone, our gardens will grow on, inspiring people, and creating homes for animals. I think of gardens as magical kingdoms, power spots. I've traveled to many gardens, and I'm always inspired. Each one is a unique treasure.

Work and create with the Earth in partnership. Listen, feel, be curious, have fun, plant many living beings, water, nurture, rake, trim.

Photograph, draw and paint your garden. Receive a poem or a song from the garden. Let your inspiration go out through your actions and change the world.

Think like a garden. Be a co-creator of life, of love, of happiness, of inspiration. Gardens teach us the value of hard work, and commitment.

Our forests, our mountains, our oceans, our deserts, they are all gardens. Our Earth is a garden. Gardens are a community of individual beings that live for the whole, the greater good. They are life and death. They are stories, and dramas, and dreams, and hope. The individual becomes the whole. Humans can live this way, we must, if we want to continue in a good way.

Backyard Habitat

Turn your front and backyard into wildlife habitat by removing your lawn and planting native plants. Make your yard a sanctuary. Think like an animal. What do birds and animals need to live? Add water, a birdbath or two, a small pond, a bird feeder, and plants for food and cover.

Keep in mind that domestic and feral cats can wreak havoc on bird populations. It's estimated that billions of birds are killed by cats annually. I grew up with cats and I understand the difficulty in dealing with their instincts. Do the best you can but be mindful of where you place your feeders.

Trees are a must. Add rocks and decaying wood for places to hide. Let leaf compost buildup around the base of your plants until late spring before raking them up. There will be valuable insect eggs on the leaves that will hatch out as it warms up.

If you want a lawn, keep it small and let the grass grow at least four inches so it can be a habitat for smaller animals. Allow Dandelions to grow in your grass. They will amend your soil with nutrients it needs and attract honey bees. Most importantly, keep all chemical fertilizers and pesticides out of your yards.

Think for a moment if your neighbors also did this. How about throughout the world? This could be the new international people's park. This could be a huge amount of connecting land. Animals would come to these wild yards in large numbers.

Imagine what a city or suburb looks like to a bird flying over a city, without wild gardens. What would it look like with all wild gardens? It would look like home. It would be inviting to animals, and soon our cities would be full of life.

The plants and trees would clean our air, and draw in moisture to replenish the land. Change the world by working in partnership with our Earth and rewild your yard.

Run through a wildflower meadow. Let go and let wild!

Create A Forest Sanctuary

Our forests at Headwaters are sacred places with a variety of elder trees, younger understory trees, and plants. Creeks and springs meander through the forest floor. Wildflowers grow to the edges where evergreens meet the meadows.

We tend these forests in a way that is healthy for the animals and plants that live there. We also create spaces that invite people in to explore and stay awhile. We open spaces within the thick woods for the forest's health, but it's also not too manicured.

We want to encourage the wild, and at the same time create a space that relies on your curiosity to explore further. It may be enhancing a natural circle of trees or clearing a spring enough to watch a leaf travel by on its journey downstream.

We may set up a natural seat with a rock or stump, or in some spaces hang hammocks to encourage people to stay longer and sway in the trees.

Sometimes places invite a natural altar to be built, just out of appreciation, or we may add an Earth art piece. Some places are to be left alone, and in doing so is a form of caretaking by being a protector of what it is.

The main thing to keep in mind is your intention. When you are called to a place ask how you can honor it. What made it inviting to you? How can you highlight the natural beauty and enhance that feeling for others to enjoy as well?

Tending a forest sanctuary is not a one and done thing. It's an ongoing co-creative process that can be allowed to reveal itself organically.

The Whole Picture

When caretaking a large parcel of land, we tend to lose sight of the whole picture outside of our personal property's boundaries. A good way to focus on the overall health of the land is to work with a small piece of land. Start with a space on your property or yard that's ten feet in diameter. Get to know it. How does this little piece interact with a water source maybe only a few feet away?

Looking a few yards away, what should be cleared out? What should you leave alone? If you shift a stream's flow, how would that affect the plants and life along the bank? How does your action or non-action affect this microclimate ecologically, and spiritually?

How does this little parcel affect the immediate area around it? How does it affect the neighboring property? How does it affect your city, county, and state?

If you used pesticide or chemical fertilizer on your property, how would that affect that space and all its inhabitants? How would it affect your neighbor's property? How would it affect a honey bee's colony two miles away?

When you provide water and food for wildlife, how does that influence the surroundings? Track the effects of your piece of land on the whole picture. Everything is a track. The Earth is a track.

A drought in California affects a flood situation in another country. There are not separate skies for each country or different clouds, stars, Moon, or Sun. We are under the same umbrella, same sky, same universe, with the same oceans.

How we care for any space, no matter how small or big, influences everything. Make your land care personal, and you will be a master Earth gardener.

Flower Gardens

Garden for beauty, for your soul and for the pollinators. Grow an ornamental garden. Plants bring us peace, joy, and comfort. They show us love in many different forms.

We surround ourselves with plants, not often even knowing why we do it. It may not be in our conscious thoughts, but some part of us knows the importance of cultivating beauty.

Flower gardens create diversity in your landscape, but don't over trim it. You want it to be beautiful and neat, but not so much that it loses its medicine. You want a garden that is a little semi-wild and not sterile.

Even in a more manicured garden you want it to have a little wildness. Allow the garden to have a wild section within it, where plants just get to express themselves without being manipulated. That space is more for the Earth Spirits to thrive.

Remember to enjoy your garden. There is always work to do in a garden, but it's just as important to do nothing. Stop and notice the pollinators. Honor them for doing their job well. Get lost in a flower. Bees do.

When I'm planting flowers, I feel like I plant joy and help it grow.

Create A Healing Memorial Garden

My wife, Jean, came up with the idea of creating a memorial garden, to honor our loved ones. We have created a space to wander and sit and stay a while. We set the intention of making this space with reverence, and beauty, and appreciation of those we love.

Our community has helped add the features of the physical garden over the years. There is a winding stone path that meanders around manzanita and ceanothus bushes, and cedar, pine, and fir trees.

We have memorial spaces dotted along the paths, with flat stones as altars. Some spaces have pictures, some have trinkets that were special to our loved ones. There are some spaces that have special trees planted within them, and art pieces in others. Each space is unique for the individual. When we tend gardens and care for the Earth, we are caring for each other.

There is a small meditation structure on the edge of the memorial garden, which looks similar to a tea house. We have larger art pieces along the garden walk, and throughout the space there are natural wood and stone benches.

One of the main features of this area is a paved circle with a mosaic owl laid within it, that Jean made. The circle is surrounded by a two-foot wall made of slabbed rock, which creates bench seating for people during releasing ceremonies.

Our memorial garden is a place to remember our loved ones. It is a place to honor and celebrate them in a beautiful, wild, forest garden.

Our garden is about a quarter of an acre, but a memorial garden can be a three-foot strip of land, with stones representing your loved ones. The intention is what is important.

***

A memorial garden is a healing space. Enter with an open heart and clear head. Walk slowly and stop anytime something touches you. A feeling, stop. A light or color, stop. A space that speaks to you, stop. Whenever you stop, take a moment to let into your being what the gift at that moment is for you.

In our memorial garden taking the long-sleep, are eleven of our dogs, and a lifetime of memories of countless hikes in the woods, beach walks and shared sunsets with my best friends. My dogs will always live with me, in all ways.

My mom, dad and sister's remains are all in the garden. Every time I walk through the garden, my mom speaks to me through memories of being raised with love. My dad reminds me of our adventures in nature and building things together.

Some of our close friends, and Headwater's family members are memorialized in our garden. Sometimes people write letters or poetry for them. Our loved one's spirits don't live in the memorial garden, but when we talk with them, I believe they join us for a walk.

The memorial garden is a place for reflection upon one's life. While in the memorial garden, I often think of what my legacy is. Who or what have I touched? How will I be remembered? Will I be remembered at all, and does it even matter?

When I leave the garden, I've gained resolve to live my best life. My life is my masterpiece, I create it. My journey with myself, in the end, is what it's all about. I remind myself that it's my precious life to live the way I want, and in each moment, I have a choice. I leave the garden filled up, and ready to live fully and honor the gift that is my life.

Life, Death And Grieving In A Garden

Gardens are teachers of profound events that occur in our lives. Gardens often teach us quietly, but profoundly.

Tending a garden over several years, watching them grow, and knowing individual trees and plants, is one of the most rewarding things a garden can offer.

When we become close to a tree or plant, we watch them face extreme weather, and we can feel what they feel. We feel their thirst and their abundance, and we feel their fear and their joy. Your heart opens and their stories live in you.

Hope springs up in you for your trees and plants to have bright futures. We share life's journey with them. It's wonderful. Then something happens, a tree gets sick, you don't know why, you're not sure how to fix it. Over time or maybe quickly, it dies. What to do with the grief? Often the garden itself can be your healer. There is always new life to enjoy and celebrate.

Our Loved Ones Live On

A few years ago, an older, Curly Leaf Willow I planted near the entrance of my home fell over in a heavy snow. I loved that tree. It greeted me every day. It was a good friend.

Years later I still miss that tree. Sometimes I still see it as if it left its mark in the sky. Before my willow fell over, I had taken a cutting from the tree and rooted it in another location next to my dad's old home.

Today it's healthy and strong. It honors the memory of my dad who has passed, and the original tree it came from. Life goes on. What a gift to grow a garden full of friends and family.

The best place to find Spirit is in a garden.

Reminders:

*Get into a daily rhythm of caretaking your plants. Tend a plant from soil to seed to plant to fruit to harvest to prep to eat to compost. Put love into all you do.

*Participate in your garden. When you harvest fruit you've grown, acknowledge and appreciate it. Even though gardens take a lot of effort, don't just stay busy, *Be* in it while you are working.

*Garden for food, for beauty, for health, for service to others, for healing, for fun, for connection and companionship.

*Make a wildflower bouquet.

Chapter 7

Build Human-Animal Relationships

We humans are animals. How we treat animals is a direct reflection of a part of who we are, but not all of who we are. Sometimes there is much more.

Animals can be our greatest teachers. They can show us our best, and they can show us our very worst. Animals are our friends, our food, and our coworkers. They should have our total respect and love and care.

To be a true Earth Caretaker we must care for our animals first. Our greatest joy and greatest sadness will come from our animal relationships.

Think of all species on the Earth as one being. We need each other to be whole. Deep relationships matter, and many times you have no idea how much. It's important to honor them. Relationships require attention, maintenance, and nurturing.

Some relationships are for just seconds, in the way you connect when you look at another being. Some are truly soul connections that will never be broken. The most honest relationship you will ever have is with nature, and all its beings. There is no judgment. Your exchange is simple truth, with no games.

To build such an intimate trust, ask yourself what you are putting into a relationship from the inside out? When we are coming from love we are at our best, and our life journey becomes that much richer. Being of service to animals is the highest calling, and an honorable life purpose.

To be with wild animals, our egos must be put aside. We need to be genuinely curious about their lives. When this happens, they drop their protective armor and allow us to join them. We can return to the right relationship with all beings through honor, and respect.

Love a mosquito for maybe nothing other than it is perfect for what a mosquito does. There is good and purpose in every being. As soon as you perceive insects and other beings as less intelligent, you create separation, and you lose perspective. I cannot fly like an insect but that doesn't make me lesser than. We have different qualities for what our species needs to thrive.

When our fear is put aside, we meet animals at a new place and a new relationship is built. We truly think of animals as our brethren, our fellow caretakers in partnership. We understand our life's journey is one of togetherness and we are a gift to each other.

Talk with animals and they will talk back. Start by listening with your heart.

Catching And Holding Animals

When you see a beautiful snake or lizard or frog or insect it's okay to respectfully touch them and hold them. Of course, you need to be careful, and you need to know what you are doing, but there is no reason to be afraid of the common, non-poisonous critters.

I love snakes and they love me. They find me wherever I am in nature. I pick them up and share a moment of sacred space with them. Then they go off and live their lives.

There is the idea of leaving no trace and observing nature as a guest. I do believe there are sensitive areas like wetlands that are fragile and need extra care. You do want to treat nature sacredly, but when you have the chance to engage with an animal or insect safely, do it. Whether you are holding a grasshopper or a spider it's a way of connecting more on a personal level, and we humans need that.

What's humbling is that insects and reptiles go back 280 million years. Scientists believe once humans are gone, insects are going to live on for millions of years, which is very humbling.

Animals and insects and reptiles are such gifts. Be gentle with them. They may give you a bite, but so what? It's a momentary thing, and it probably means the critter was fearful. Animals are curious and want to be with you. Sit still and they will let you admire them.

Feed Birds

Put out a bird feeder and study them. Get to know them personally. Get to know their habits, their colors, their relations, what they enjoy and how they live. What are their skills to avoid predators? How do they play?

Taking interest is how you love nature in a pure way. When you feed birds, you are being of service. It is a life purpose. We need birds and now they need us to care and protect them. Share your bounty with animals.

Birds are a wonder made physical. As birds fly, they are constantly seeking, they are awareness masters. Today in Hawaii I fed bread and nuts to myna birds. Soon I had doves, two kinds of cardinals, and eight wild turkeys join me. All enjoyed my company and I enjoyed theirs.

Get out of your overactive brain and enjoy this world.

Animals Are Dreamers

Most people would say animals dream, but in truth we rarely consider it. Even animal lovers rarely consider on a heart level, the deeper natures of animals.

Animals need exactly what we need: love, safety, food, purpose, community, adventure, kindness, play, fun, Home, a purpose for life. Animals in our care depend on us to give this to them, or to allow enough space to have access to these most important needs. When we care for animals on a level of love and kindness that transcends the basic human-animal interaction, we all become the best we can be.

Be A Hero, Rescue Animals

Fight for animals. In our culture so many animals are tortured for medicine, food, and product testing. I mean horrible, beyond horrible torture is done to these innocent animals, cruelty beyond most people's comprehension.

Factory farming of chickens, cows, horses, pigs, rabbits and so many more animals is horrific. The torture of medical testing on rabbits, rats, mice, pigs, chimps, monkeys, dogs, and cats, and the endless killings is beyond comprehensible.

Many good books have been written on this subject, and many incredible groups are out there helping. Educate yourself to this darkness that lives in human culture throughout the world, and be a part of the fight to stop it all.

I will always be the voice for animals, and in doing so, I am unapologetically blunt about what I see and know. I may come off as offensive to some, but I am always truthful. There is no room to dance around this subject. Cruelty must be stopped.

My country, that I love, has some of the worst "legal" animal cruelty practices there are. Don't eat tortured animals. Not only is the cruelty so inhumane to another living being, you are also taking in that tortured energy into your body. It becomes a part of you.

Work to change this dark practice. Get involved. Tell the truth, don't hide it. Yes, it's uncomfortable and ugly, but we all need to do what's right. Be a hero.

Animals need our help. They tell us every day, just look into their eyes. If we continue to allow these dark practices and turn our head from the truth it will bring us to our end. Once you know something is wrong, and you still choose not to do something to change things, then this is the definition of evil. Remember that not only the act is evil, but so is your lack of action.

Ignorance, laziness, or lack of education does not exempt you from taking responsibility. You're either working for a better way or you're not. This may sound harsh, but we are at a turning point in human consciousness, and now it is our time to wake up and do the right thing. If we live through compassion, then anything is possible, anything.

Preventing a pig from being tortured, so it can be cheap food for humans, could be our greatest teacher of how to lovingly live on our planet. Compassion to animals equals compassion to humans, equals compassion to our planet, equals life for all. We can do it. We know how. The question is, will we before we can't?

Kindness Is Medicine

Next time you see an insect in your home, perhaps on a window trying desperately to get out, stop, don't kill it. Gently let it go back to its home outside. Show love. Show mercy. It matters to that one insect. It matters to you.

The Crabs

I love the beaches of Hawaii, especially the crabs that dig holes and tunnels in the sand. I love watching them and it's clear they love watching me as well. Yes, it's true, crabs can observe and love in their own way.

I'm also jealous that crabs can move all eight legs independently of each other, and their eyes too. That's amazing, I'd say a miracle.

One day I was laying back on the sand, and I felt a pressing. It dawned on me that a crab was trying to move me off its home, so I moved. I've observed countless people on the beaches that never take notice of these crabs, and crush their homes, and this saddens me. I just want people to care and walk around the holes. What happens when a hole is crushed? Can a crab get out? I'm not sure. There seems to be many crabs, so I believe they can.

Here's the good news if you're a crab, or a crab lover, when all the people leave the beach for the night, the crab's time arrives. The tide comes in and erases the footprints. The crabs do their work, eating, and digging their homes. I come back in the morning, and I see their industrious work. Life goes on, another crab day. The crabs and I don't really care what the crowds miss right at their feet, it's our secret.

Love Heals

We rescued a stray dog from the Big Island of Hawaii. He was an abused, pig hunting dog. He was beaten and starved and most of his teeth were broken off. He survived on the edge of a forest on the streets, in a neighborhood where people threw rocks at him.

A kind woman was able to give him a temporary, foster home. I saw his photo in a store window, and felt called to take him back home to California, to Headwaters, to Dog Paradise.

We named him Koa because he had a brindle brown pattern of fur, which resembled the Hawaiian Koa wood. He was shy and insecure, and we called him by a name that means *brave* and *unafraid,* in hopes he would eventually bring out those traits in himself.

Koa's face and body were a map of physical scars from his previous tough journeys in life. He was a bit nervous, but he didn't hold a grudge against the world. He eagerly tried to fit in our pack.

His heart was open to many, but shared with few. His love grew faster than his trust would allow. Those who were patient were rewarded with pure joy, and eternal, grateful love. Koa rescued abandoned hearts, including his own. He was a lover at his core, we just gave him a safe space to share his love. We were given a gift, and his name was Koa.

Our Domestic Friends

The collaboration between nature and humans, with animals, is a true miracle. With nature came dogs, our greatest companions. They work for us, they protect us, they love us unconditionally. My life has been wonderfully blessed because I've shared it with dogs.

Cats, while more edgy and wild, are also heart companions. When I was eight years old, I had a cat named Bootsy. He slept in my arms every night and ushered me through a very bad time in my life, with boundless love.

This kind of love is what humans need to give to the Earth, and to each other. Maybe then we would really know what peace is. It's amazing that a cat could teach this without a spoken or written word, only pure love, and loyalty.

Our Staff

My dogs have taught me all I need to know about love. They are my true friends and teachers. Our dogs at Headwaters are an integral part of our staff. They help break down people's walls of fear and pain quickly. They are the first ones I watch to see if my students and newcomers at our school are okay. Our pack will sense when someone is happy or hurt, either physically or emotionally, through their energy.

The dogs will help people open their hearts without reservations of judgment. They give comfort by being authentically themselves.

Bear, our Golden Retriever, was the best example of a healing, medicine dog. We worked in partnership. He would alert me when one of the students needed some extra attention. He sat directly in front of them, and put his forehead against theirs, and looked in their eyes. I knew then that person was hurting. Bear would be the first one to help them let their guard down and smile.

If someone was physically drained, Bear would lick their face obsessively until they came around. This connection was his gift he was born with. It was my job to pay attention and follow up by checking in with that person in need.

We don't usually plan to adopt dogs. The right ones show up when they need a home, and when we are in need of another member of the pack. Our pack size averages 6 dogs at any given time. Our older dogs eventually pass on, and new dogs and puppies hit the dog lottery and join us at Headwaters. Also known as, Dog Paradise.

The Headwaters Pack is the envy of most people. We have many people tell us that in their next life they want to come back as a Headwaters dog. They have all the fenceless land they need to roam and explore, and creeks and meadows and woods to play in, healthy food, warm homes, lots of pack members, and an abundance of people to play with.

We are their caretakers, and pack leaders, but we also have a beautiful mutual friendship. I would never run a school or live without a pack of dogs. They are that important!

Domestic And Wild

Our wolf dog, Riley, was a bridge between nature and humans. He awoke the innate wild within all of us by touching our soul.

Riley was a black, wolf-dog mix and had the best traits of both worlds. He was a protector, a scout, a teacher, a loyal companion, and a friend to all.

Riley was unique in that he loved to be loved, but on his own terms. He would cuddle as though he were a puppy, and then distance himself to oversee from just outside the fire circle. His eyes would flicker in the firelight, and his shadow would cast an ominous larger than life figure against the trees, but his gentle kindness always sneaked through with a lick across your cheek.

Riley wanted to be within the group, but always needed a sense of freedom. He needed to know he had a way out, and he could not be contained.

As Riley aged a bit his restless need to wander settled down more. He knew the couple hundred-acre boundary of the land, and was always on patrol day and night, making sure no predators were trespassing on his watch.

He was smarter than any animal I have ever known, and he could disappear and reappear as he needed.

In Riley's later years we took him on day trips into national forests so he could explore wilder terrain. His nose led him just far enough, but not so far that he didn't know where we were at any time. My only regret for him was that we never took him with us backpacking to the true wilderness. The risk of the wolf in him running off and causing trouble was too great.

When we would return from a wilderness trip he would jump in circles for joy at our return, and smell where we had been, through the scent on our clothing. That was the only way in this lifetime he could experience that true wild sense of place.

Now that Riley has passed, I know he is rolling in those wildflower meadows and running through the trees. He perches himself up on a high snowbank, and observes this beautiful Earth from a perspective much grander than here.

Riley gave us the blessing of feeling our own primal self through him. I am forever grateful for my friend for tapping into that part of my soul.

Kodi - My Animal Soul Companion

Kodiak was my 110-pound, Black Lab-Rottweiler dog. He was my gentle giant, my protector, my mirror, my boy, my friend for nine years.

Kodi's biggest gift to me was allowing me for the first time in my life, to love with one hundred percent of my heart, not holding back out of fear of judgment or abandonment. He was the first living soul who I could be completely myself with. He allowed me to experience ultimate love on this Earth.

He spoke through his eyes. Kodi and I were so tightly connected I knew his thoughts and he knew mine. He read my energy and responded to it, and we always looked after each other. I know he came to me to be one of my Earth spirit helpers.

***

I was recovering from a surgery and feeling weak. I forced myself to go for short walks and extend the distance a little bit each day. I pushed it too far walking into the woods, and I didn't feel like I could make it back home.

Kodi was staying close by my side. I stopped and asked him if he could share some of his energy with me so I could make it back to our house.

I put my hand on his back, and just in the asking I felt relief. Whether he sent his energy to me or not, I felt supported, and that gave me enough strength to make it back.

***

I'm so grateful that my nephew captured one of my favorite moments with Kodi in a photo. We were walking through a wildflower meadow in the Marble Mountain Wilderness. It was a warm, July day and the lush mountains were alive all around us. I remember feeling at home and free in the wilderness. I stopped and looked around, taking it all in, and I had a smile growing from the inside out.

Kodi was usually a very laid-back boy, but in this moment, we shared a moment of spontaneous joy. I turned around just in time to see him leap across a stream towards me, and literally jump for joy almost into my arms. He felt the same way I did. The wilderness filled him up, and Kodi filled my heart with a lifetime of wild love.

In his last year with me, I brought home my little girl, a Lab-Border Collie puppy, Cooper. Kodi and I had been so close I wasn't sure how he would act with a puppy joining us. My worries were put to rest the first night I brought Cooper home. Kodi was asleep, and eight-pound, seven-week-old Cooper inched her way up against his big, barrel chest. She cuddled in up against him for the night, and for the rest of his life. Kodi protected Cooper from harm just like he did me.

A year after Kodi passed away, Cooper was sleeping up against me in bed. I had dozed off with the T.V. and bedside light on, and awoke with Kodi standing on the bed over me. Cooper looked up at him and then me, questioning what was happening.

I smiled with no surprise at all and said, "Hi Bubba. It's ok Cooper. Kodi is just here to watch over us." I looked back over at Kodi, and he was gone, but Cooper was still looking up in his direction. I reassured her that everything was ok because Kodi is with us.

It's been eight years since Kodi passed, but I know, I don't believe, I know, he is one of my spirit helpers watching over me. I have felt him paw my back a few times. I see him on the land sometimes, and of course I always feel his comforting energy within me. I know we will be in the same place again someday.

Dog and wolf energy are what I connect with the most. I resonate with their traits, and I always feel their support and guidance. There is no judgment with animals. They are here to help us. They are guides and gifts. They want to be recognized and used for their help. It fulfills part of their purpose for being here with us.

Companions

Dogs have a desire to connect with humans. Our two Golden Retrievers, Bear and Jackson, both had a strong attachment to children, and especially babies. Whenever someone visited who had an infant, they would immediately cling on to the baby and stay by their side. Smelling them and licking them if allowed.

They would lay at the baby's feet and get anxious if someone carried them off. Bear and Jackson would follow the babies wherever they went.

On one occasion someone left their baby's toy giraffe behind. Jackson was so attached to that baby that he claimed the toy as his own to protect. I kept it on a shelf so he would feel ok about leaving it to go outside to play without it. When he wanted to check in on it, he would sit waiting by the toy looking up. I would bring it down for him to smell and lick and then put it back on the shelf. This attachment to the baby's toy lasted for the rest of Jackson's life, another nine years.

The day Jackson was passing away I put the toy giraffe down next to him for comfort. He stretched his nose out towards it and gave it a final smell and nuzzled into it. Within a half an hour he passed away, and I know he was more at peace saying his goodbyes.

Human babies always brightened Bear and Jackson up and seemed to give them a sense of purpose. They were born to be caretakers of human companions.

It is a special trait that we sometimes think only humans have, but other animals have the same empathic connection as we do. Many of them are drawn to other species as well. Gorillas, chimps, dogs, cats, and birds, are some of the animal species that not only have the capacity to love and care for another being, but the true desire to.

We need to remember that we don't own animals. We're not protecting our property. We are guardians of our soul companions, living alongside them.

The Cow That Gave Her Life For Me

I was raised partially on my grandfather's farm in Montana, so I've been around farm animals growing up. I've hunted in my younger years for food and fished my whole life.

I'm very aware of the horrors of factory farming, how animals are raised for food with no respect, and are tortured. I try to shop in a way where I buy food where animals are raised humanely, on a good farm, in open pastures.

There's always room for growth and learning, and it is one of those crazy dilemmas we face where we must eat things to live, and everything else in the world does as well. We're all eating each other in some way.

Plants have their own consciousness as well, and corporate farming is also unethical, so it doesn't just end with mammals.

When I first moved to Mount Shasta, my neighbor was raising cows and I thought that was the best way to get our meat. The cows were raised in open grasslands, in a loving way.

I felt it was important that I kill the first cow that I planned to eat. Every day I would visit with the cow, and she became my friend. I was young and idealistic, and I thought that would be a good way to connect with her, before I had to kill her. In the end it was a good way, but it was also very painful.

The day came that I was going to kill her. I was going to shoot her in the head with a .22 pistol so she would die instantly and not suffer. I tried to put myself in a space where I was going to be calming and loving, and do it in a beautiful way. I was so torn, but I also knew that I am a meat eater, and this was the most humane way that I could take her life, and then honor it.

When I arrived that day, she knew. She could feel my change of energy and my intention. She knew it was a different day, and for the first time she ran away from me. It was that unspoken, universal language, that inner vision we all have that alerted her of danger, despite our friendship. By far, this language is the most honest.

When I knew, she knew what my intentions were. It really threw me. I had to ground myself and get to the place where I was coming to her with love and not fear. I was finally able to go out in the pasture and bring her in and take her life. I cried and I cried, and it broke me a little, but also because of the relationship I had with her, I was able to truly honor her and have immense gratitude for her. The whole experience was painful and beautiful all at once.

The idea of killing our brethren animals is a never-ending dilemma in my life. That cow touched me and nourished me, and I am grateful for her.

Some people may say that it would be best to not eat meat, and that's a conversation worth having. For the purposes of this story though, on a personal level, the remarkable part of the story to me is how she knew. Animals are such pure beings. They don't have the baggage of the brain we have that carries so much knowledge, but also so much garbage that gets in the way of that pureness within us.

When we tap into nature, it's the most honest, direct kind of communication. It's always available for us. It is on a different level than the physical, and animals are masters of tapping into that knowing spirit that moves within all of us. That's simply how they live. We are all connected, and we can honor each other with respect. What one of us feels, we all feel.

Tillie

I fell in love with a chicken. She captured my heart through a song. One of our chickens got sick and the other chickens started picking on her and beating her up. I would find her isolated, and at one point she was bleeding pretty bad. I scooped her up and nursed her back to health. She stayed in my house with me for a while until she could go back out with the others.

I kept an eye on her and made sure the other chickens didn't pick on her, but she was alone when she was out with the other chickens. So, every day I sat down, and she would walk over to me and sit in my outreached hand.

For some reason I started singing Waltzing Matilda to her and she began to sing back with me. I would sing and she would babble and sing too, in her own way. I believe this was part of her healing. A sense of knowing someone cared. She had a sense of belonging. A connection with another Being that loved her.

I hadn't had any hands-on interactions with our chickens prior to this. Our chickens were pretty feral, so this was a special connection between her and I. A trust was formed very quickly.

Before Tillie, I bunched chickens together as a species, but once Tillie connected with me, I learned that they are individuals. They have primal instincts, but they have their own personalities. They are social and need the bond of another. Tillie talked to me verbally and through her heart, and I sang to her and loved her through mine. I became aware of the soul within her.

Tillie was sick but survived, and even thrived for a while on love. Over time her body became too small and weak for her soul. It trembled to get out and move on, but she stayed a while longer than she probably would have, I believe just to be with me, and share her love. Thank you, Tillie, for loving me back, and singing to my heart.

Bridges Between The Wild

Relationships between humans, horses, mules, and donkeys are profoundly amazing. Miners in America's Southwest desert rely on their donkeys to find water by smell and intuition. The miner's life is completely dependent on the donkey finding water. Without water, the donkeys and the miners would perish, and become the desert.

This absolute trust between the two, this partnership, is a miracle between man and nature. Everything we need to know about living with nature is in this relationship. To let go so deep that we might lose everything, our life, we must trust wholly and love completely.

If you take the time to get out of your human mind and meet horses where they live, you will find they can be amazing teachers, and more importantly true friends.

Take in the things we take for granted with horses, they carry us on their backs wherever we want to go, for pleasure, for work, for war, for thousands of miles, always willing. This relationship is another miracle.

Whole human cultures have been created and dictated by horses. The Comanche culture was a horse culture. Everything within their world was horse related. In fact, the final killing blow to the Comanche people was when the U.S. Army made a grotesque move by killing all their horses at one time. That was the end of the wild, free Comanche people. This was the power and interconnectedness that the horses had within their lives.

The American culture migration west could not have happened without horses. This true companionship between humans and nature is remarkable. We are nature, let's own it and start living from respect. Horses are our fellow brethren in our journey. What luck for us to be so close to such a special being.

My personal connection with mules has always been an immediate heart fusion. They are so intelligent and believe it or not, graceful when trail riding. I grew up helping a mule and horse packer in the Trinity Alps Wilderness in the summers. Each mule had my total respect and gratitude for what they were able to do when being of service to the human world.

They can be as tough as nails and protective when a predator is close by, and as sweet as can be, snuggling up to you for some affection. They have an independent mind of their own, but they are extremely smart and aware. There is a lot to learn from them.

Prey

Once or twice, I've had a grizzly look at me with a hunter's eye. My ancestors came forth immediately. My primal being was so very alive. My Ancestors showed the way. The bear lost me and moved on. I lived to see another day. It was intense and good.

Envision yourself hunted by one of nature's ultimate predators. What would you do?

Animals As Friends

There's a packrat that lives in my woodpile. One day I came out by my back door and there he was, sitting on a light fixture. He was looking at me and not running away. I knew this was unusual behavior, so I slowed down and took my time.

My curiosity and heart led me to put my hand out and touch his back. I pet him for a few minutes as he leaned into my touch. He went back into the woodpile, and from that day on, at certain times when I was around the woodpile, he would come out for some affection. It became a great friendship, which lasted a couple of years.

It's important to note that I could have tried to scare away the packrat or worse tried to kill it. It was making a mess in my woodpile and shredding up my kindling. This is a reminder to be patient, be understanding and show grace to other living beings.

All my life I have done this, and I've had countless wild animal friends. Some people would say leave wild animals alone, and I agree most of the time. There are those moments in time though, when two beings find an opening, a crack in the normal, and they come together.

These are sacred moments to be cherished. These moments build our trust and connection. These are moments to share. Allow them to happen.

Bees

If you have any doubts about the miracle of nature to create life and to heal, learn about bees. That's it. You'll get it. They are the perfect example of how to live in a sustainable community.

Then go eat a spoonful of honey and celebrate bees and give them gratitude for your life and all life on Earth. Honey bees are the sunshine in our lives. Let the Sun shine.

The Lone Wolf

One summer night a very special visitor showed up at Headwaters. A lone, male wolf wandered onto our land. For an hour he howled, searching for a female companion. The call pierced the silence, it was primal, and beautiful, and sacred, but it was not returned.

So many feelings came up for me. I thought how wonderful to hear this male looking for a mate, to bring wolves back to our area.

***

Wolves have just started to return to Northern California. Their travels from Northeastern Oregon and Idaho to find new homes is an inspiring journey. They travel alone for hundreds, and hundreds of miles, across roads, freeways, and ranches constantly in danger of being hit by vehicles, shot, or trapped, and yet they are still finding mates and starting new packs.

In Northern California within 60 miles of the Oregon border, we have had four packs of wolves take up residency. Three packs seem to be doing well, while the other pack of five black wolves have been murdered by poachers. Another pack of wolves in Southern Oregon were poisoned. These are unfortunate common stories of the fate of wolves.

***

That inner calling for this wolf to continue his species was stronger than all the roads and guns in his way.

My thoughts went to sadness as I thought of my European ancestors that murdered all the wolves from our lands.

I thought of future days when wolves might fill our wild lands again, with the medicine of predators. Restoring that unique wildness, that opens land, needs to be truly alive. I thought of the wolves I've known in my life, from the Canadian Wilderness, the zoos, the wildlife parks, and of course our own wolf dogs, Joseph and Riley.

Every time I look into a wolf's eyes I am mesmerized. I have changed. I am taken into the wolf's ways, and for a moment, I am wolf.

Everything from nature is a gift. I feel, personally, that the gift of dogs and all canines is beyond wonderful. We must protect our wolves – we owe them. I thought if wolves returned to our community how I would again have to lead the fight to save them from the ignorance and fear that would arise.

Then I stopped, shut down my mind, opened my senses and let this lone male wolf bless me and this land with his calling. What a healing it was for my soul. I sent him well wishes and visualized him with a female and pups in a safe place.

This animal, this wolf, reminded me of what matters the most in our world, which is to me being fully connected to our Earth. Thank you to that lone wolf. Good journey my friend.

My Friend Called Out To Me

The wolf has been on my mind. That feeling of true wildness wakes up a sleeping, primal spirit inside of me.

A wild, free brother desperately searching for a companion. Navigating through life's challenges. Trying to be unseen, and yet still noticed enough to not be fully alone.

A strange world he's wandered into. Finding pockets of Home as a refuge from the confusion. The space between the chaos is where his spirit resides. I'm going to meet him there.

A Toad's Lucky Day

I went for a walk with a friend and came upon my pond. A garter snake had a large toad by the leg. What to do? Leave the snake to eat the toad? I doubted the snake could actually swallow it. Or catch the snake and release the toad?

The second thought prevailed. I released the toad; its leg was ok. They both swam off. Was I right or wrong for interfering? I felt sad for the snake, but I knew it was a large snake and surely it had been a good hunter, it would hunt successfully again.

I knew this toad. I had seen it many times as I worked in the garden around the pond. It was the toad's lucky day. I'm happy with my decision. Today I was the toad's hero. Tomorrow it may be the snake's lucky day.

My Life With Animals

When I finished high school, in the 1970's, I went exploring in the Canadian Wilderness for a few months. It was a defining moment in time, but when I came out of the wilderness, I still didn't know specifically what I was going to do next.

I just had this monstrous vision quest in Canada, and I was clear I wanted to do meaningful work in my life, that made a difference in the world. I knew I wanted to work outside and with animals, and I knew it had to be something that I loved, that would challenge me to keep growing and be a better person. I wanted to work with good people who were kind and generous.

I couldn't afford to go to college, so I went right to work. I stopped in Oregon to visit a friend and got a job working on trails. It was a good job, but I was still wondering what was next when I got a call from a high school friend, John. He told me he was caretaking and cleaning the whale and dolphin aquariums at an animal park called Marine World Africa U.S.A. in Redwood City, California. He said they needed help caretaking the chimpanzees and elephants.

John knew speaking with animals and connecting with nature came naturally for me. I grew up working with farm animals and wildlife rescue animals, so this call seemed to be spirit driven. Working with animals and nature is why I came to this Earth. My wilderness journey brought this into my vision for my life.

So, I headed back down to the Bay Area, and took a job that was literally going to set the stage for the rest of my life. I didn't know at the time it would unfold into a highlight, but I could feel a momentum, a sacredness, I was about to step into the gift of my life at 20 years old.

***

There has been a lot of controversy over the years about animals in captivity. I have strong feelings about this subject. I'm a huge believer in the animal rights movement. I fight hard for farm animals, and animals in zoos and parks to be well cared for. I'm very skeptical of many zoos, which I think are more like prisons for animals.

We do need to allow our wild animals to remain wild and keep their spirit intact. Humans also need the wild to keep our own spirit alive. I generally agree that taking animals from the wild is not ok. I also think raising some animals in spacious, healthy habitats, in good breeding programs to be released in the wild helps their population.

When I was young, I didn't know all about the mistreatment of animals in some parks. Thankfully things have been changing for the better through awareness, education, and interaction.

Connecting animals with people through interaction can be a good thing. The hope is these animals in parks and zoos that are well taken care of and have quality lives, can become great ambassadors for nature. They entice and excite people to join animal organizations, donate money to save wild land, and volunteer their time to make the world a better place for animals.

***

My first day at Marine World, I was given the job of assisting the elephant and chimpanzee trainers in putting on shows. I also helped feed the elephants, chimps, the big cats, exotic birds, and many other animals at the park.

I had no idea what I was getting into, and I jumped right in. I was working under an elephant trainer's guidance, who was a nice guy, but also a wildly, crazy human. He showed me the elephant barn and told me there were seven elephants, but three of them were living there long term. There was Samson, the African bull male, Matidi, the African female, and Mardji, the female Asian Elephant.

The trainer told me the first thing I had to do was get accepted by the elephants. I asked him what that meant. He said I had to go in there and hope they wouldn't kill me. If they came after me, I had to fight back. He said elephants are a dominant animal and there is a hierarchy, and they would test me.

So, I went in and walked up to Samson, who was about 14 feet at the shoulders and I'm six feet, so you can imagine he's over twice my height. I approached him and he threw me with his tusk about 10 feet into the plywood wall.

I was hurting but I remembered the trainer told me I had to go after him. I didn't want to hurt animals, so I just ran toward him with a rake to scare him and I accidentally hit his eye. He screamed, and I felt so bad. I also thought I was going to die at that moment.

He could have simply crushed me, but he calmed down and his eye felt better. He looked at me and we just knew we were going to be okay. I gave him a big hug. It was a rough introduction, but it was all love from then on.

I worked at the park for five years, and many nights I slept next to Sam in the barn. He weighed 10,000 pounds or more and I never felt unsafe. It was the best sleep I've ever had.

Some of the greatest times of my life were working with these animals. I even had fun in the elephant barn in the mornings cleaning their poop. I would dance and joust with the elephants and play with them. I put fresh straw in there and they blissfully rolled in it.

I would feed them fresh fruits and vegetables and bread. I had set up deals with local produce people to give us all their premium leftover products.

I got to take them all for walks all over the park in the back belt, which was a wild area along San Francisco Bay. They were such good friends.

It was an incredible life, and at the same time I was also working with the chimpanzees. I had to also break into the family of chimps. Let me tell you something, I would take a crazy elephant, any day, to a crazy chimp.

When a full-grown, male chimp that's 160 pounds, and about 5 times the strength of a man and seven times the coordination, decides to come at you, it is terrifying. Often the only way you can stop them is to bluff. Chimps are very much a hierarchical society like human beings, and they're always testing each other. You must be taken in by them. You have to fit in with the group, and once you're in, you're in. I mean, you are like a blood brother.

The big male, Raffles, loved me from day one. He never tried to hurt me, and he became a beloved companion. In fact, I don't think I've ever loved another being as much as I loved him.

We had a soul connection from the start. It was such a joy to spend time with him, and he would help me with the other chimps. I had up to nine chimps at any given time, and we climbed the trees in the park and ran around.

Every day when I cleaned the chimp enclosure, I would blast rock music and give the chimps their own brooms to help me. We would dance and clean and have a blast. They would also come with me while I took care of all my other animal caretaking and feeding duties as well.

Many times, I would take one or two of them at a time to my home at night. I would bring them over to my parent's house for dinner on occasion. It was just an amazing, fun time.

I have a lifetime of stories from those few years of spending time with all the different animals. I created such strong bonds with all the elephants and chimps. Raffles, however, will always have a piece of my heart. He and I are connected through our souls. Brothers forever.

***

When barriers are dropped through trust, these profound human animal relationships are created. When these special moments happen in life identify them. Give them energy. Bring them alive in your life. Nurture them, like watering a plant, and watch them unfold.

Be aware as you are experiencing them. How are they affecting your life? How can you keep this going? How can you do it better? Be an active participant in your life and the creation of it, and these magical amazing things will come your way.

***

My position at the animal park allowed me to run educational programs for schools, and ethical breeding programs to help save species from endangerment.

Over the next decade I went on to work at the Alberta Game Farm in Canada, and the Crandon Park Zoo in Miami, Florida, where I oversaw relocating all their animals to a new location at a better facility.

With the knowledge I gained in those positions, I was able to help start a wildlife rescue and rehabilitation in Santa Cruz, California, and found a love for falconry.

When I worked with all these animals, it was an extraordinary opportunity and a powerful part of my life. It brings tears to my eyes knowing what an honor that was. Forty plus years later it is still a major highlight of my life.

There are moments when your life seems to move in an extraordinary direction. Opportunities arise for you to be involved in making the world a better place, and to bring joy to life. Meaningful work or moments show up. It's part of your challenge to identify those times and give them life by giving them your energy, your love or passion, your intelligence, your work ethic, and commitment to give your best.

Those magical times will tend to grow in your life and become extraordinary. Often, they will shape your life. They'll lead you down paths you could never have imagined you would have gone down. So many of those opportunities in our lives we pass by. We don't acknowledge them. We don't pay attention and we lose our moment.

Looking back now to when I was in my twenties into my thirties, when I worked so closely with those animals, I knew then it was something special and I didn't take it for granted.

I had many adventures with all the animals, and many extraordinary moments in the ordinary moments as well. You don't have to have grand encounters with exotic animals to feel that deep connection with another being. I get just as excited when I look into the eyes of a dragonfly and feel seen. Truly, it astonishes me every time.

Finding spirit in nature and companionship with animals is simple. Just get out there, open your heart and do it!

Chapter 8
Be Curious And Play

Ask questions, as many as you can of the Earth. Ask thousands of them. Be curious enough to ask the right questions for that moment and allow enough time for the answers to reveal themselves. It's the wonder that births questions, which leads you to discovery.

Curiosity is vital to develop our nature awareness skills. Curiosity in a way is somewhat like a living being inside us. It is a huge influence in developing and growing our lives. Build a relationship with that aspect of yourself by following that spark.

Address your questions directly to a tree, a mountain, animals, the Moon, an insect, clouds, birds, water, forests, oceans, landscapes, and continents. The quiet wonderment that posed the question will also give you the answer. In deep observation without judgment, you will experience the answers.

Some answers will come to our brain, some to our hearts, and some to our souls. Some won't come at all, or so we may think. That's when the mystery can take hold, then the answer becomes of little importance, almost a side thought.

That's when we realize, on an Earth-Heart level within us, that we know the answer, that we always have, and always will. The grand library of the universe is ours if we want it but when we go into the Mystery, we know the answer really doesn't matter. Be inquisitive, study life and let go of the need to know. Just live it.

Being curious is a way of saying I love you to the Earth. Your Earth-Heart expands, and an intimate connection is felt. Live a life of curiosity and you'll know all you need to know.

Curiosity In A Newborn

Any newborn animal from the moment of birth is curious. Curiosity is what leads all beings into life's journeys. It's the beginning of all teaching, and necessary for growth.

Encourage your curiosity and nurture it in children. Remember to forget your preconceived ideas. Open your vision back up to the empathic view of life through the eyes of a child. Feel the purity of that perspective. Follow a curious toddler in nature, and move through the world mimicking their actions as if it were your first time. When you expand your limiting filter, you will be astonished how much more there is to learn and experience.

Witnessing nature's miracles through pure innocence, satisfies a hunger for adventure, and yet leaves you thirsting for more.

Wander With Wonder in Nature

Nothing is more important to the development of any living being than allowing a sense of wonder to emerge at a young age. Wonder will guide a life. All beings know wonder.

Nature is the teacher of wonder. From those first days as a child to the last, we must wander in nature to know wonder. Support and nurture wonder and magic in children. It is the birthplace of ideas, which leads us to exploration, knowledge, and connection.

Without wonder we will be lost and not know it. Let wonder grow inside you and lead you to the greater parts of yourself. It is in this joyful discovery that makes life wonder-full. To be full of wonder is to be full of life.

You cannot have too much wonder in your life. You can have immense amounts of wonder, from the most amazing ah-ha moments, where you want to sing to the universe, to the simplest interactions.

Be open and curious and naive for a day in nature. Let go of labeling things. Get to know whatever you are curious about by reintroducing yourself as if it's your first encounter.

Glancing through the woods, take the path through the trees to that spot where the light is catching your attention. Those pathways in your life will lead you to amazing places. Appreciate the beauty and lose yourself in it. Even if it is just for a fleeting moment, go all in and soak it up. Let that beauty become a part of who you are and share your beautiful wonder with the world.

Where Would You Go?

I'm a great believer in exploration. I believe exploring comes from our born sense of curiosity to create, curiosity to survive, and curiosity to thrive in joy and wonder.

Gain awareness by studying and asking questions. Reading historical books about great explorers can light a fire in us. If you could go back in time, and not be in any danger, and participate in something amazing, where would you go and who would you be with?

Personally, I would travel with the Lewis and Clark Expedition to the American West, through the wildlands. I would be their naturalist. Or I would sail with Captain James Cook on all three of his voyages around the world. I would explore Australia and the Hawaiian Islands. I would sail up the coast of California to British Columbia and into Alaska.

I get sad sometimes thinking everything has already been discovered and we don't have that same opportunity, but there are other adventures awaiting us in this world, we just need to be curious.

We are only beginning to explore the vast spaces in between what we already know, as well as the expansive minutia of the unseen. We are just starting to actualize our potential of what we can do through our curiosity of exploration.

We recently sent a rover to Mars, and we discovered a vaccine to fight the global COVID-19 virus that threatened all mammalian life on Earth. It is vital for us to know that anything is possible. There's nothing we can't do. With this knowledge, there is hope, and with hope we are more likely to act.

There are reachable answers to solve so many of our problems. We have the ability. We need to stay curious and explore the unknown to find the solutions; explore space, explore the depths of our oceans, explore viruses, explore new ways of living, explore places we already know, but on another level to discover animals and species we have not identified yet.

We need to explore ourselves more intimately, and find out who we are and what we are all about. Why are we here, and what are we supposed to do with this amazing life?

Knowing what we have already achieved is positive motivation to continue to move forward and grow. It's our time to shine, and to step into action, of protecting and healing our home. We must find a way to all come together. It's going to affect us all. No one is going to get away from this global climate crisis untouched, and the only answer is that it starts with you. Give yourself an honest self-assessment of what you are doing to tackle this problem.

There is no accident that we have all been born at this time in this world. We are meant to be here, to make a difference. Everyone here now, no matter what age, needs to fully participate. Particularly younger people need to start a movement of making your life about caring for the planet. Let your actions inspire others. From there, it's up to something bigger than you and I. When we're giving our best, providence, that unseen collective power, moves in and lifts us to reach our intentions.

Look Up

You can change people's lives, just by teaching them to look up. It can reveal a new upper world for them. Most people look up briefly and don't take it all in and curiously study what's above them.

When I worked with chimpanzees and elephants as a trainer and caretaker at Marine World Africa U.S.A., sometimes I would take a few of the chimps on day trips. I always wanted to keep the chimps engaged with life outside the park whenever I could.

I would take them to a beach to run and splash along the shoreline. There were days when I would take one or more of my chimps on a walk at a California state park in a grove of redwood trees to play. The chimps needed to be free and let their wild out.

When I saw other people approaching on the trail, I would send the chimps up into the treetops. They would climb up a 250-foot-tall tree above the people along the trail.

Not one time did anyone ever look up and see the chimps. They were usually looking down at the ground or busy talking with another person. Part of me wonders if someone did look up into the redwoods would they see the chimps? Or would their logical mind discount what their eyes saw? I wonder.

I look under rocks because I'm curious. What do I miss when I don't look? Just wondering.

Science gives an answer to what we already know. Science is the language that satisfies the ego's curiosity, but don't let it quench it.

I have been led to believe that there are no new places to explore. "Hogwash", says the frog. "My pond is always changing."

A Plea To Parents

Please, get your kids out in all types of weather and different times of day and night. Encourage them to play in the mud, roll in the dirt, jump in the puddles, hold bugs, get cold, get hot, sweat, push comfort zones, and seek discomfort.

Let them be alone and have adventures. Give them guidance and then get out of their way. Let them experience life and learn their own lessons. Be there for support, and then kick them back outside to explore and entertain their own boredom. Allow them to grow through their insecurities, and their fears of the unknowns…to do otherwise is disabling.

In some ways overprotection is a form of abuse. Shockingly, the life skills are just not fully there. Get them out there, nature will do the rest. Nature will be their teacher and friend.

So Much Joy

Today I watched a little girl play in the surf. Back and forth, rolling in the waves, and carrying rocks up the beach to build a rock pile.

Sometimes you just have to roll in the surf and carry stones. It's good to be happy. It's good to play. The mind goes to rest, it's time will come soon enough. Just play.

Free Me!

Free your body from your mind on occasion. Your body has its own intelligence. It will lead you to places in nature that your mind never would.

When you arrive, wake up your wild self. Fully live with that wild woman or wild man as a part of you and take them on adventures. Free your spirit from your physical body. Have courage. Be an explorer. Let go of mind control, find freedom, and live wild.

Follow a stream of rainwater. Where does it lead and how did it travel there?

Non-Judgment

Play in the woods. Dance and sing in the woods. Get silly stupid in the woods. It doesn't matter that the trees and the animals are watching. They don't judge. Weirdos are ok. They're usually the ones that get things done and have the most fun.

Judgment creates separation, and false fear. A heart can't thrive when judgment rules the moment. Remove judgment and your open heart will pull the Earth into you. One Earth, one person, a good life full of wonder, full of love, full of kindness, full of Earth.

Follow Their Lead

Let curiosity show you the wonder of our planet. Watch another's curiosity and let it inspire you to explore from a different view. Watch young children and puppies playing in nature. They have boundless energy. They love getting dirty. Turning over rocks is taken to a fine art. Digging is never ending. Climbing is just a given. Insects are entertainment.

Crawl into the places that are uncomfortable and find comfort. Let children and puppies be your teachers. Wander, play and look up. Get out there and get dirty.

Seek Your Own Answers

There are times when it may be important to use a computer to search for answers, but for the most part, there is no medicine in the information.

It's in the journey of experiencing your own answers that you gain wisdom.

Chapter 9

Have A Sit Spot

A sense of place is waiting for all people. Let it call to you. Put aside your thoughts, and feel it.

A sit spot is a place to observe, in nature. Sometimes sit spots choose us and sometimes we choose them. Sometimes it's a partnership as the space draws us in. You may already know that place. Go to it and fill yourself up with what nature has to offer.

This spot is where you want to build your relationship with nature, a place to drop back in, not necessarily a time out. When you let go of mind clutter, there's room for profound moments to come to you.

When you repeatedly return to a personal space, it becomes a sacred place as it holds you, your energy, your thoughts, your dreams, your sorrows, your anger, your love, and your joy.

It is a place that teaches you and builds your awareness. Sleep there and experience it day and night.

Often, we love the larger view, but how often do we spend quality time with a flower or a rock or one tiny space in front of us? You can have a sit spot up in a tree and go out in incremental weather. Get your shoes off and feel this space.

Introduce yourself to all the beings in and around your space. Ask for help from the plants and beings that are there. They are your witnesses when you make life commitments. Talk to the spirits, sing songs, dance, laugh, and play.

Observe nature as it happens, and know you are a part of it. You are our Earth, and you belong there. This space will become a constant, trusted friend over the years. Let this place tell you its story. Who or what has been through there? Who has slept there? Who has died there? Who has celebrated there?

This is a place where sometimes you take nothing with you that will take you away from that very space. It's just you and that spot, taking in the natural sounds of the environment. There may be times though, you do bring an instrument or choose to sing or chant or meditate or write poems or stories or create art. You can build an altar in this space, and change it as time goes on.

It will be a place of inspiration, peace, and safety for you. This heart space will hold your medicine and remind you of what is real, of what matters most.

You will find that when you are not there physically, it will still call to you. When you feel that call you must go. Something will be waiting for you.

You can share sit spots with others, but have at least one spot that's just for you alone. As you get to know this place, you will feel what is happening to the Earth. You will feel when she is well, and when she needs help.

You may have this sit spot for a day or a week or years or for a lifetime. You can grow old with your sit spot until your last days, and when you pass on into the land of spirit you may find it again.

I wish you many wonderful sit spots in your life's journey. Go into nature, your sit spot is calling you home.

Concentric Rings

We humans are always moving and making noise. In the woods we're crunching branches, talking, crashing through brush. Our minds are busy with tasks, gossip, and false fears.

In this high-tech world, we're on our smartphones or thinking about them. We're always thinking ahead about potential issues that usually take care of themselves.

When we're with another person we never stop talking or thinking of what to say. Busy and noisy in our minds and bodies. The natural world passes us by every moment. We lose the experiences and treasures the Earth offers us.

Wherever we go in the world, we put out concentric rings, both with our physical bodies and our thoughts. The animals in the forest hear or feel us coming and disappear. Our concentric rings are like dropping a rock into a lake. The water is disturbed, and the rings travel outward, and our energy is felt.

We can learn to send out concentric rings that are peaceful, loving, and inclusive, and the animals will not flee from us. Better yet, we can quiet our minds and bodies and disappear. We become a part of the land. We belong, we find ourselves at home. This is a profound experience of recapturing our natural state of being one with the Earth. If we do this often, this oneness becomes our baseline state of being.

When you sit quietly, mind and body, the animals will come to you. Patience is a must. It's worth the effort to reclaim your personal connection with nature.

Removing our concentric rings and finding that oneness with the Earth is not only profound for your sense of place, but also a way to honor the Earth. Sitting with another being with heartfelt listening is an expression of love and respect.

I want to communicate with the spirit of each place I sit.

Sit Spots Have Guided My Life

Growing up in Sunnyvale, California, in the sixties, was a kid's dream. At the time it was mostly fruit orchards, and creeks with surrounding hills. Our backyard was a quarter of an acre, an amazing place for a woods-loving kid, and an emerging Earth Caretaker to grow up.

My favorite sit spot was a large apricot tree in a corner of the yard, standing alone, its branches spread out unencumbered. I grew up with this tree, from childhood throughout my teenage years. I would climb to the perfect limb and wedge myself in. I felt the tree pull me into it through love from within the tree, from peace within its branches, from safety, from its height. I found comfort and healing from being held in the tranquility of the tree.

When I sat quietly in the tree I would go into a meditation and feel my connection with my surroundings. I didn't know what was happening when I was younger, but I also didn't have the doubts of an adult.

I found myself leaving my physical body, traveling down into the tree, through the roots and into the Earth. I would become the tree and view life as the tree.

So much of what I could see and feel, I didn't understand in my logical brain, but I knew in my being that much of life on Earth isn't visible. That experience was profound for me. It gave me a life of wonder knowing there was more beyond the physical, and I carried that understanding with me my whole life.

My sit spot in the apricot tree became home to me, and a mutual friendship developed. I'd tell it my stories and ask it questions. I got to know that tree intimately because I took the time to be with it.

We think of great moments as big profound experiences, but often they are the simplest things that lead to big things. I watered the tree and pruned it. In the spring the tree would blossom with thousands of flowers. The floral smell was a gift to me, and to the bees and hummingbirds.

I would climb, and smell, and observe the beauty, while the bees and hummingbirds buzzed around me. Then the magic would really begin, the confetti blossoms would fall off onto the ground. I would lay on the solid blanket of petals and roll in them.

The green fruit would then appear and grow throughout the summer. I'd watch, I'd anticipate, I'd dream of ripe apricots. The day would come, and I would eat juicy apricots right off the tree like an animal without using my hands. Nothing tasted better in all of life. Each one I ate was a gracious present to my body, and to my taste buds. All my senses came alive. Eating those plump apricots became a sacred experience I could count on, year after year.

I harvested the fruit and gave it to my family. I put boxes of apricots at their peak ripeness in front of my house, and neighbors would pick them up and become transformed. When there is something in my life that is special to me, I find it so much better when others can enjoy it with me. I appreciate it that much more when I know it makes others happy as well.

This tree fed the birds and the raccoons, all the wildlife would stop by for an apricot. When we all had our fill, the extra fruit would fall to the ground and rot, feeding countless insects and rodents.

As fall came the leaves changed color and fell off the tree. The leaves would house helpful insect's eggs and then become compost, creating dirt to grow more trees and plants.

In spring, apricot saplings would sprout up, and I would plant them all around Sunnyvale. I watered them with my friends, and people wondered why so many wonderful apricots began to grow everywhere.

To this day I can't find an apricot that tastes as good as my tree friend's fruit. That moment in my life, the sharing of two lives, a boy and a tree, was profound for me. It nurtured my body and soul, and I loved it in return. That tree helped to raise me. It was a big part of making me into the man that I am today, a good human being.

All these years later I still feel my tree, and I smile inside and out as I retell my story. It lives through me as a part of who I am, my medicine I carry, and I am honored that the tree chose me to climb it.

Sacred Space

If you sit in a place
if chills come across your back
if your heart pounds
if your body feels excitement
if your body feels at home
if an animal visits you
if you have an epiphany
if you know you are in the right place
if this place feels like your place
then you know it's sacred space.
Then stay for a long while.

Notice transition spaces, places where forest meets meadow, or forest meets creek. These spaces have much to share.

Be quiet in nature. When you think you're quiet, that's the time to be quieter, until you disappear.

Focus on something in nature. After a short time, close your eyes, and then open them and look again. The results will be quite gratifying.

Tracking Life

One of the exercises I have my students participate in during our Nature Awareness Class is a three-day commitment. They choose a spot on the land that calls to them, and they mark off roughly a three-foot circumference boundary.

We introduce this when we are camping in the wilderness, but I also highly recommend that they carry this invaluable practice with them when they return home.

The students sit outside of the marked boundary and observe their space for a few hours in the morning. The idea is to observe this space from many different angles. Look in great detail at what is in the space, from laying down and looking up, and from standing above it.

I ask them to take notes and draw a map of every detail. There are no rules of what the map looks like. The map is to help them with their memory and reference points.

Many times, these maps become works of art. Some people draw plants, rocks, and sticks in realistic detail. Some people make marks that represent objects. Some people write out stories or poetry about the piece of land, and who lives within it. Other's use geographic coordinates for their reference. Their approach to this exercise really doesn't matter, as long as it helps them with their observation.

On the second day, I ask them to observe their sit spots for a couple of hours in the afternoon, to see if there had been any changes or any visitors that may have crossed through. I ask them to note the changes the temperature or weather may have made in their space.

Sometimes it feels as though the time passes quickly. Other times they may feel that it drags on, and they have trouble focusing or even staying awake during the observation time. The weather or bugs or other people or animals can also be distracting.

***

On one occasion, a student was standing up looking down on his sit spot to get a different perspective on his site. He was so into what he was looking at, he didn't notice a visitor walking up on him. Fortunately, another student who was sitting up on a rock overhang fifty yards away, shouted out to him that there was a bear behind him. The student spun around and there was the bear lumbering right by him, ten feet away with his head down, smelling the plants.

They were in a rolling meadow of Angelica plants, and tall wildflowers, and both were so focused on their terrain, they hadn't even noticed the other's presence until they were right upon each other. The student stayed still, and the bear walked by and headed back down the hill.

While this is not usually common for large mammals to show themselves in the middle of the afternoon, it shows us how when we blend into our environment, we are welcomed and accepted as a part of it.

***

By the third day, the students have become intimately familiar with their sit spot, and quite protective of it. They've made connections with plants or little beings that reside within it.

These are the small worlds that most people don't take time to get to know. They get bored and disconnected with what's going on under their feet, because they don't pay attention long enough to care.

On the morning of the third day, I have the students check their sit spots one more time. The staff breaks up into small groups and we visit each student's sit spots and have them tell us all about it. We ask them how they felt there. Why did they choose that space? Can they identify any of the plants or did they give any of them their own names? Did they notice any tracks? Did they notice any changes? Did they notice any visitors that passed through or nearby when they weren't there watching? Were they drawn to a certain part of their space, and if so, why?

We ask if they would be upset if we messed up that space at all. Just about every person who has ever participated in this activity got fiercely protective about their space and asked us not to mess it up. Many people have profound revelations while sitting in the same space looking over it for just a few days in a row.

Once they have shared their map, or story or poem or anything they wanted to share about their experience, we ask them to leave the space and do another activity while we make some changes.

We draw a rough sketch of their sit spot and then remove, add, or change things within the space and mark it down. We usually make ten to twenty alterations, depending on how much effort we think the student put into the exercise. We place the removed items, such as stones, sticks or plant parts in a bag, and tell them how many changes or additions we made.

After lunch, we give them their removed items and clues, and they have thirty minutes to an hour to figure out what we did to alter their space. We then come back around to each student to see if they were able to find the changes.

Most people do a really good job, and there are always some that impress us with how well they did, if we made it extra tough on them with nit-picky details. We help some students with clues and others just nail it all right away. It's such a fun challenge for everyone, and it introduces some of the most important life skills we should have. Awareness, expanded perspective, connection, mindfulness, self-observation, storytelling, and just being still.

Having a sit spot is an activity that will always prove to be invaluable.

An Unexpected Healing

The first class I took at Headwaters was the Nature Awareness Class in the Marble Mountain Wilderness, in Northern California. While we learned countless wilderness skills and life lessons, the tracking, sit spot activity was probably the most life changing for me. It became one of those defining moments in life that propelled me forward, by letting go.

I found my space on the hillside overlooking the vast valley, which was our classroom for the week. I marked off my three-foot space and immediately started talking to two small fir trees within it.

I felt a motherly protection well up in me. I was worried they wouldn't make it through the coming winter snow. I gave them a pep talk to lean on each other when the snow got heavy, and to help support each other's growth. They were only a foot tall, and I didn't think they had much of a chance.

I began to map out my site and got too much into my head about it. I was worried because I didn't know the names of the plants. I wasn't sure if I could remember where everything was. Was I doing this right? Am I going to be able to tell the staff anything about this spot in a couple of days? Is my cryptic map good enough?

As I started letting go of my fears of failing this exercise, I realized what I was really there for. My time sitting at this space had become a type of vision quest. While I was sitting there observing this space, and everything around it, through the hot afternoons and the rainy mornings, I began to open up to literally everything around me. I felt it all within me, as a part of me.

I cried for the potential loss of the little trees, and allowed myself to cry for the first time for the loss of my baby years before. I felt myself melting into the Earth and losing myself into my surroundings. I wasn't in any fear of not coming back, as I had feared before. I just felt held by a mother. By the Earth.

I had no intention of going into this place of grief, but as I did, I was able to shed the hurt, and felt the healing begin. I thought I was only at that sit-spot to learn physical tracking skills. What I learned was so much more.

I did learn the beginning skills of nature tracking, but I also learned how to track myself back, emotionally, and spiritually. I tracked back to the core of who I was before life's events built more walls than were needed.

I learned to observe by just being, through the comfortable, and the uncomfortable. I followed the tracks by allowing myself to be led. I learned how to clean the slate and do a do-over. I retraced what was, and what to let go of that was no longer relevant.

Having a sit spot, has many times over, triggered an unexpected defining moment in my life. If you are ready to change your world, just sit and be, and allow answers to your unknown questions to come.

Animals Have Sit Spots

All living beings have sit spots they spend time in that feels safe, and inspirational. They have places to observe our world quietly and peacefully. We have this in common.

Bears tend to choose prime sit spots, most often at an overlook. Whenever I find an empty bear lay, I lay down in it, feel the bear's energy, and enjoy the view.

Opening And Closing Sacred Space

A sacred space doesn't have to be a large area. It could be that you're walking in the woods, and you decide to go through a group of trees, and there's a beautiful oak tree. You sense it's a sacred space because of how it feels or looks.

You may walk through an opening in the trees to a meadow filled with wildflowers and it invites you in. You might walk up to a creek and there's a pool with your reflection in it, and you see fish swimming in there, and ferns growing on the edge, and it calls to you. You are drawn in by the shimmer and the sound of the water, and you know it's a sacred space.

 89

You can be taken to the next level of honoring sacred space and do a ceremony there, where you join the space with an open heart. You allow it to come into you and inspire you. Maybe you're with other people and you share the space together, allowing that energy to grow.

You can draw boundaries around a sacred space or allow the natural boundaries to define it, such as rock or tree circles. You can build a shelter within the space or an altar.

Some places are going to be sacred to everyone because of the spectacular beauty of a place. Other places are going to speak to you personally. Or maybe a sacred space will be shared by two people in love. It may become a bonding space for the couple.

Families can share a sacred space and build on their experiences and memories there. Communities can share a sacred space, which creates a common bond.

Open up this space or activate it by putting your intention into it. Create nature art there. A space becomes sacred because you have decided to make it so by putting your energy, your love, your respect, and your heart into it. We often forget to do this, and it can heighten the whole experience.

When you enter a sacred space, enter it in a way that's respectful and intentional, as you would to start a ceremony. Give it a blessing. Take a moment to breathe a space in, take it in visually. Get all your senses involved, including your sixth sense.

When you leave a sacred space, offer a blessing. Express your gratitude. Let it know you'll be back. Appreciation is so important. If you take that time in the beginning and in the end, it makes your experience so much more powerful. It becomes a highlight.

Have an opening when you join the space and have a closing. You don't have to spend two hours talking or do a dance, it can be very simple and quick. Feel your energy coming from your heart, from the part of your being that is honest and authentic. That is what is so powerful. If you don't do that you can still have a wonderful time. That space will still work on you subliminally, but if you open and close that space with an intention then look out, it will be a wild ride!

It's Ok To Be Bored

We tend to want to fill empty space with busyness. I am very guilty of this. There is always a task to do and not enough hours in the day to do them. Some days I find I am behind before I even wake up.

Sitting still to look at a sit spot or just to Be is tough for me. I spend half the time trying to let go of the to-do list in my head. I want to bring a journal with me because I don't want to waste my time being bored.

Once I finally get out of my busy head, I am so relieved. My energy shifts and my perspective clears. Everything that is there waiting for me to do will still be there when I leave my circle. In that moment, what I'm not doing is more important than what I feel I need to do.

As soon as my daily tasks drift out of my mind, I am open to clarity on what truly is important. Before those quiet moments, there was no room for anything else to come into me. There was no room for relationships with humans, my dogs or nature.

When I'm constantly busy I get randomly angry, and I forget why, until I realize I'm so disconnected with what is real. I have to be bored to get to the place where I'm not.

Having a sit spot helps me reunite with nature, with myself. When I'm physically on the ground I feel what is real. I become the ground. I see and feel life around me and within me again. I gain energy from my sit spot, and I am back to who I am. A human-Being.

Reminders:
*Walk and sit in nature every day. Breathe it in. Make it a requirement for your health. It's that vital.
*Make a space sacred through your intention.
*To know the Earth, you must sit with her. Observe everything.

Chapter 10
Soak In The Magic Hours

The magic hours are one hour before sunrise and one hour after sunrise, and one hour before sunset and one hour after sunset. This light is the purist light, as the light travels across the landscape it seems to illuminate the land from the inside out. It brings out the purist of colors. It is speak to the heart beautiful.

Seeing the glow in the light of this time of day, you don't have to be a photographer. Our eyes are our body's cameras. They take in the beauty and our body absorbs the light.

In the morning it's not just the light that makes the magic hours magic. The world that was sleeping is awakening in you. Birds and insects are waking up and bathing in the light. They share this time with you. Many mammals awaken to the light, and glow in it. Birds of prey begin flying overhead, always alert for a tasty animal that's not paying attention.

It's glorious to wake up and greet the beginning of the day. It sets the stage for the rest of the day to be only good.

At my outdoor school, my students and I often go for bear walks. These walks begin about one hour before sunrise. Looking for bears is our objective. It forces us to look deeply and quietly. We're out enjoying the magic morning hours when the Earth awakens, and it's a special time spent in silence.

When we return to camp for breakfast, which has been cooked over an open fire with love, well, all I can say is that it's the best food ever. We share our stories from our morning explorations with each other, while eating good food and enjoying a welcoming fire.

Back at camp is the first time we really speak with each other about our experiences. Sharing good stories with a good community, equals good living. Some of the moments we experienced together bond us, and some of the experiences are special just to us, in the way we soaked them in.

At breakfast time we have already been awake for four glorious hours, and we haven't even started the day.

When the late afternoon, magic hours come and the sun begins to set, again it travels low across the land, highlighting its beauty with the purist of color, shape, and shadow.

This is a time when many animals that have been resting in the heat of the day begin their night activities – feeding. Often when sitting still by a meadow, deer will come to feed, and that pure light will accentuate their beauty.

Magic hours create a oneness between the land and humans. We have an opportunity each day to look at beauty, bring it into our being, and appreciate it. We can keep the moments as personal medicine, remembering them often our entire lives.

The magic hour sunrises and sunsets create the changing light, which touches our being. It's perhaps most amazing of all if you're in the same location to see the sun rise and fall. I've watched countless sky, light shows, and each one blows my mind. Each one is the best.

Traditionally in the morning is when we sleep and eat breakfast, and in the evening, we eat dinner inside. Be committed to adjusting your routines to get out into the magic hours, and allow your life to become magic. That's Earth medicine, and nature's gift of heart – "Earth Heart."

Sunrise

That light at sunrise, right before the all so colorful light, before that orange, pink and red light. That light that has no named color. Look at *that* light, the timing must be perfect. This light will touch you in a way no other can. Go into that light and be swept into the Earth's soul.

Sunsets

I love finding changing light at day's end, and watching all colors paint nature's canvas. Watching sunsets with groups of people is a wonderful way to share Earth time together. Get up high and take in the views. Receive them. Gather sunsets inside of you. Every sunset I witness is a personal offering from our Earth to me. No matter who I'm with, no one sees sunsets the same way I do, it's unique to me, and the same holds true for you.

I run to catch the light on the mountain. When I arrive at my place with my camera ready, I look through the lens, and I realize the mountain caught me.

Light Painting The Landscape

The light is the paintbrush. All day every day, a new painting appears. Become a painter of light. Let your eyes observe the light. Reach out across the land, through the trees, through the mountains, through the clouds. Early morning light. End of daylight. Back light. Light filtered through fog.

As the light paints the land, notice all the colors and every variation. Endless greens, reds, yellows, colors that defy our reality. Notice how each color makes you feel. Feel it in your mind, feel it in your heart. Let it inspire you and connect you. Let it make you happy. Dream the light.

Observing light painting the landscape is witnessing the Earth as a master painter. The masterpiece changes moment to moment, always, a new painting, always bringing us deeper into the land, always bringing us deeper into the sea, always bringing us deeper into the sky.

Let yourself be amazed and lose yourself, get stupid and scream. Stand in the light, become the color. Moments like this feed our souls. Moments like this happen every single day.

A photographer sees the masterpiece, frames it, and snaps it. Each time, a new work of nature art is created as the light comes forth and highlights a dreamscape. Nature needs no touching up. Light painting the land and water reflects nature's inspiration. It's nature's magic. This is one way our precious Earth calls us home. Now go paint your landscape.

Stay Until The End

I was in Kauai, Hawaii with a dear friend at an incredible lookout. Below the viewpoint lay the lush Kalalau Valley, and beyond that the brilliant blue Na'Pali Coast. It may be one of the most magnificent views I've ever seen, and that's quite a statement because I've seen a lot.

As we watched the sun sink below the horizon, a man joined us for the view. Sunsets and sacred moments bring people together.

As we chatted with him, he mentioned he was on his honeymoon, although his new wife chose to stay in the car. She was bored.

At the most spectacular, drop-dead-beautiful point of the sunset, when the sun began to greet the ocean, we heard a car horn. It wouldn't stop. I thought it was an alarm.

Our new friend assured us that no, it was his new wife honking him back to the car. We tried to convince him to stay and finish the sunset. It was the best view on Earth, the best sunset, and a perfect view of a magical valley that was usually shrouded in fog.

He was torn, but sadly, he left and returned to the car, and I knew then the future of his marriage. Imagine a life with no time for sunsets. I felt sad for the guy, and maybe sad for her too. No one had introduced her to the magic of powerful, medicine moments in nature.

Every single day the Earth and Sun provide humans with the most amazing sunrises and sunsets. If you're lucky and live where you can see the sun rise and set, then go out and receive that blessing. Stay to the end, just when you think the show is over, that's when the whole sky lights up in a burst of color. It's worth the wait.

Santa Cruz Sunsets

I've watched thousands of Central Coast sunsets. In the watching I've observed my life. I would say that those sunsets have guided my life. I've learned who I am in those sunsets. I've found inspiration in those sunsets. I have found love in those sunsets.

As I've watched the sunsets become me and I them, they have carried me on my life's journey. In a sunset I'm anything I want to be. I travel to far off lands on the rays of the light, and when I land back in myself, I'm different and happy.

Sunsets have brought the dreamer out in me, and it's the dreamer that's been my good friend. Sunsets have been food for the dreamer and fill my soul.

I hope to drink up many more sunsets in my life. They remind me of what a wonderful world I live in.

Could Heaven be a big endless sunset? I'm in no rush to find out. I'll just keep watching all I can of *these* Heavenly sunsets.

Pack a picnic and greet the morning light. Stay out until the dark of night swallows the brilliant blanket of color filled clouds.

Chapter 11

Photograph Nature

Earth Caretaking through photography is one way I share my love of nature with people. Through photography, I'm able to show people how I see our Earth. Photography was a gift given to me at 12 years old, when my father gave me his Kodak 35mm camera.

I became an avid photographer in junior high school. I began in earnest, to document the beauty of the wonderful meeting of ocean and land, along the California Central Coast.

My love affair with the Santa Cruz Coastline started earlier when I was six years old. My father used to take me to the North Coast beaches to fish off the Davenport cliffs. He also shared his love of Big Basin State Park, and we hiked many trails through the Giant Redwoods.

My father was very quiet, so much of my time was spent in silence, just letting the land and sea come into me.

My mother loved sunbathing and she would take me to the boardwalk beach. We'd often rent a small place in the beach flats. We'd stay much of the summer, and I was able to play and explore the shore endlessly.

My father and mother are gone to the other world now, but those early years built a solid foundation of love and respect for the central coast. It was a dream place for a nature loving kid, and will always be in my blood. I found love and great friendships there.

***

When I received my first camera, the Sierra Club started to publish books of sacred places in nature with color photographs, and I was hooked. My camera became my friend.

Photography took me into nature a zillion times, and each time I fell more in love with our Earth. I had countless, and I mean countless adventures photographing nature.

The Earth Caretaker was born in me. My focus in life became clear to photograph nature as living art to teach about nature, and our Earth as a living being.

Through my photography I found I could share what I saw and felt. I could show the beauty, and the wounds. Photography became one of my ways of carrying the wounds without being overtaken by them.

Photographs in nature highlight themselves to catch my attention. I see the composition of the photo long before I hold the camera to my eye. This form of nature art has been a foundation for my life. It's become an expression of my life's purpose. It teaches through inspiration, through seeing first, then feeling.

I've used the art of photography to fight for our Earth, and it has brought me unmatched joy. It is my way of showing the art of nature, and it has taught me to look further into the landscape, sometimes so deep I lose myself in it.

Moments like this are precious in life, to be cherished and honored. Nature photography has taught me that nature looks back at me and comes into me.

I have gratitude for the coastlines, and the mountains, and forests for shaping my life, and for helping me to step into my purpose as a caretaker. I have worked to make a living, and to save our planet by connecting people with these amazing places.

***

When I became serious about photography, I fell in love with the Sierra Nevada mountains. To me the Sierras are humbling artistry. They are grand and ever so intimate.

I believe in going to the same areas over and over again, and that's when a place unfolds its intimate secrets. It's in that unfolding that wonderful photographs show up. Photographs that capture the love of place and awaken a sense of wonder in the viewer.

When I share my photographs, I hope people are reminded of what a treasure we have with our relationship with nature, and more people will go into it and find inspiration. I hope what I do brings out the dreamer's heart. I hope the dreamer dreams of ways to protect what we have and bring back what we've lost.

It's not enough to love a place, we must do more. In drinking in all that the land and sea give us, we must find time and a way to serve and protect these places, it is our obligation.

With nature art being a life purpose, I get to hunt beauty in the wilds and interact and play in a very personal way. As I reflect on my life, photography has been a true highlight of a life well lived and I feel blessed. It will always be my greatest expression of love.

***

At a young age nature photography gave me a way to be an influential warrior for the Earth. I saw its destruction happening before my eyes and I could document it.

I had heroes like David Brower, the 1970's leader of the Sierra Club that inspired me. Myself, and others like me, had a hopeful innocence that if we could educate others of what was happening to our planet, that it would awaken a good place inside people all over. We felt human beings would unite around a common cause to love and take care of our planet. Surely all would agree to this, how could it be any other way?

As I've traveled life's journey through the ups and downs of my maturing awareness of human interaction with nature, it's been very difficult to remain a positive warrior for the Earth. Thankfully, my personal connection with nature has saved me from falling into hopelessness. My true love of nature is my savior.

As a teacher and nature photographer, I have to ask myself, "I'm in my sixties now, there's only so much time left for me, what can I do?" Then I think of some valuable advice from another hero of mine. It reminds me to soak it all up and enjoy this world, *while* in the midst of saving it. Please read it slowly, and let it settle into you.

***

"One final paragraph of advice: Do not burn yourselves out. Be as I am- a reluctant enthusiast...a part time crusader, a half-hearted fanatic. Save the other half of yourselves and your lives for pleasure and adventure. It is not enough to fight for the land, it is even more important to enjoy it. While you can. While it's still here. So, get out there and hunt and fish and mess around with your friends, ramble out yonder and explore the forests, encounter the grizz, climb the mountains, bag the peaks, run the rivers, breathe deep of that yet sweet and lucid air, sit quietly for a while, and contemplate the precious stillness, that lovely, mysterious and awesome space. Enjoy yourselves, keep your brain in your head and your head firmly attached to the body, the body active and alive, and I promise you this much: I promise you this one sweet victory over our enemies, over those deskbound people with their hearts in a safe deposit box and their eyes hypnotized by desk calculators. I promise you this: you will outlive the bastards."
- Edward Abbey

A Global Defining Moment

The power of a photograph was never felt more than on Christmas Eve 1968. The moment of the Earth rising above the barren horizon of the moon was captured forever by astronaut Bill Anders on the Apollo 8 mission.

For the first time we saw our beautiful home. We saw not only life on Earth, but Earth as a living being. We saw white and greens and browns, and the blue water which equaled life.

95

It was unfortunately a time of great division, not unlike our worldly troubles now, but if for just a few moments those illusions of disconnection ceased, and all beings were one, united on a living, breathing planet, our Home, Earth.

Seeing our home gave us a sense of ownership, pride, and protection, and brought us together in awe as a global community. With a new perspective on our world, soon after the environmental movement was birthed, and I was fully in.

Every time I recall the moment those photos of our Earth were sent back to us; I choke up seeing our Mother Earth and all her beauty.

It took one change in perspective to shift people's awareness outside of their singular vision. Hearts were opened, many judgments were dropped, and a vital spark of enthusiasm to save our planet was ignited.

We can't unsee what we see. We know what we know, and we cannot shut our eyes to the truth of the state of our world. We can't pretend the problems will just go away without everyone's effort.

Yes, our world is big, and it can be overwhelming. At the same time, we are also able to see how very small it is in the overall view of just our universe alone. Sharing images is one of the best ways to share another perspective with the world. There is no judgment, only truth in what each person sees.

***

"We landed down and saw planet Earth and realized it was our beautiful and very small home. We realized things were not going so well down there and we felt we had to do something about it."
- Edgar Mitchell, NASA Astronaut Apollo 14

Protecting Nature Through The Power Of Photographs

In 1970, the year of the first Earth Day, we were studying the effects of pollution in school. A photo in *Life Magazine* showing a city shrouded in smog, practically made me choke. That photo is embedded in me and was a catalyst for me to become, a nature photographer.

Another powerful picture was of a pile of dead, Bald and Golden Eagles on a ranch in Wyoming, found by game wardens. Ranchers in helicopters had blown 500 birds out of the sky, proclaiming they were killing their sheep.

There is a photo book called, *The Place No One Knew* by Eliot Porter, of a sacred site, where petroglyphs etched by ancient hands are submerged under a man-made lake, known as Lake Powell. That place was a remarkable slot canyon with a river running through it in Utah called Glen Canyon. It was a place I had visited with my uncle before the deluge. When you walk into these canyons in the red rock country, it is impossible not to be awestruck. This astounding canyon was dammed and flooded to make the massive lake.

It took seventeen years for Glen Canyon to fill up with water, and now the dam, for which the beauty of the canyon was destroyed, is filling up with silt and becoming useless. It leaks so badly that Salt Lake City would have enough water for three years from the seepage.

There is talk of taking down the dam, which I hope happens, as the sadness of the flooding of that beautiful canyon still causes deep sorrow within me.

Studying that book, I saw how the power of photography influenced people's ideas about nature. My passion for photography was forever embedded in me and reinforced a sense of purpose. I am moved by photographs of both the beauty and the destruction of nature, as there is so much to learn from both.

Nature photography helps people to remember what we've lost. Perhaps future generations will recognize this and remember and help nature to bring itself back. Nature never forgets.

Photography is not only one of the most fulfilling parts of my life, it made me a keen observer of the natural world, and helped me find my place in it.

I believe my photographs have done justice to some of the great mountains, rivers, deserts, and oceans. I can take pride in knowing if that is all I have done in my life, I feel I have served my planet well.

Show Up

People ask me how I have been able to have so many peak experiences out in nature throughout my life. The only answer is that I'm out there. I'm out in those magic hours before the sun rises to watch the colors wake up the landscape, and hear the gathering of the birds.

I'm out at sunset while most people are eating dinner in front of the T.V. and I'm watching the animals emerge from the shadowed edges of the meadow.

I get off the trail, climb trees, and stop to see what is under the next log. In those moments when others think nothing is happening, I wait. I sit and wait, and the show begins. It never fails.

On a photography shoot, I stop and put the camera down to listen to a pack of wolves echo through the trees. I watch a herd of elk trample the dewy meadow, escaping the haunting calls. While caught up in the wonder of life, I find myself surrounded by a herd of bison, being absorbed up within their community as one of them.

There is no magic or special quality in me. I just show up, and stay open with curiosity, and it all comes to me. I become the land, and the land becomes me, as it could for anyone. There are no shortcuts. Get out in the woods! It's the best place to be.

Share What's Personal

Get out and notice nature. Capture it, in slices, in the way you see it. Cameras allow people to share with others what is interesting to them. It's a way of giving another person your perspective by seeing what you see, the way you see it. You can communicate what you see through images rather than verbally.

In our nature awareness class, I have students pair up with a partner. I give them an empty picture frame and ask them to walk around the land and hold up the frame to capture that space that calls to them.

You don't need a camera, and it doesn't have to be the perfect enhanced image. It's just perfect in the way you see it, and something personal you can share with another. It's an opportunity to see through another's eyes. The person framing the image only needs to show the composition, it is up to the viewer to feel their own personal interpretation.

The Nature Photographer

Wildlands become a nature photographer's pilgrimage places. Nature always calls us home. Our cameras come alive with the rawness of the place and when we capture that sacred wildness in our photographs, well then, we have climbed to the top of the mountain.

It's not about fame, money, or anything false. It's about the lure of a place, and sharing it, if we get lucky enough to do so. In the end, if the sharing doesn't happen, I think most photographers wouldn't change a thing. They would keep on going to the wild lands, making their pilgrimages to the places that call to their hearts.

I will never stop going to nature, and it will never stop giving me photographic treasures each time. I know I can capture amazing images, but I will also always leave humbled, that I still just couldn't quite capture that whole living grandeur on film, and that's ok.

Humans need humbling places like this. They remind us of just how small we are, but that we are also a remarkable piece of the whole. They remind us of how lucky we are to be born on this incredible Earth, and they continue to keep us going out in search of these sacred sites.

Slide Film

Once I complete a shoot, a journey into nature with my FM2 Nikon camera, I come home and mail my film in to be developed. This is when I really get excited. There's a profound joy of being on a shoot and engaging with the natural world in such an intimate way as only a film photographer can know.

Part two, of my journey is waiting for the slides to return, and looking at them on my light table. I get to relive the physical experience again. Every sacred moment that a photograph was taken, I relive in my slides. This process becomes sacred to me and it's something I cherish.

Part three, is when I choose my best images and enlarge them and create my books. Again, I get to relive all those sacred moments in nature. Sometimes I go into my photographs in this process, letting my eyes land on the details, and find completely new things within the photos I missed in the field.

Part four, brings more joy. I get to share my photographs with people. I get to tell my story. It's beautiful to see the joy the photographs bring to people and see how they get inspired to go to nature and

to protect nature. Again, this process takes me back to the precious time in the field when the photograph was taken.

Part five, is of course the best of all. I go back to nature and photograph again. My Nikon FM2 and my slide film, together we live a dream.

Capture images in a photo and carry the essence of them in your heart.

Light

A truly great photograph captures the image that shows the beauty and majesty of the moment it was taken in. How light plays with the physical surfaces of objects-be it light on a mountain in the distance after a storm or on a flower petal, is the lesson a nature photographer must learn and focus on to capture that moment.

If the picture is taken without consideration to the existing light, the photograph will be flat. A good photographer pays attention to the light, not just when taking a picture, but even when the camera is put away.

There have been moments when I have been so overwhelmed by the beauty of the light on a cloud or a mountain, or reflecting off the water, I can hardly contain the joy. It's always my hope that the photo I have taken will be as awe-inspiring to those who view it as it was for me.

As a photography diplomat for the Earth, I feel a great responsibility to instill in those people who don't get into nature, who she truly is through those images.

Go Into A Photo

Look at a perfect photograph of nature, and enter a world that before you really looked, you had no idea was there. Some people glare, some stare, some calculate its technical perfection, some notice the clouds, animals, mountains, reflections and then they move on. This is not a bad thing. In fact, it's safe to say that a photographer is always honored when someone enjoys their photograph.

My dream though, is that when someone looks, they look so deeply they're carried away into the photograph and travel through the scene. The hope is that they look far, and wide, and close, and that they travel beyond the borders. They find all the nuances of color and shape in the landscape and the photo jumps out into them. I hope it touches them, filling them with wonder.

My dream for them is that they forget themselves, for just a moment, they are in that place, and that place is in them. For just a moment, they lose all sense of time and space. That is this photographer's dream.

The Nature Of The Photographer

The photographer of nature sees what others don't. The photographer walks into the scene and finds the side acts. They find the heart and soul of nature and transform it to film.

The photograph goes into the eyes, and brain, and heart, and soul of the viewer. At that moment the photograph, and nature, and the viewer are one.

The Photographer And The Tree

A photographer takes a tree, perfect as it is, and adds more by capturing the varied yellows of a leaf, a beam of light through the fog or the frost glistening on the bark.

A photographer puts the image in a frame, or gives it borders. The artist pulls the tree out of the whole forest and shares it with the world. The highlighted tree brings joy, amazement, and connectedness, and reminds us we are a part of that forest.

When the environment invites you in, dance with the landscape. Share your excitement through your lens, through your art.

Chapter 12
Grok Nature

Grokking is a shamanic skill used throughout time to learn first-hand from nature. It's a skill to learn from animals, plants, water, the weather, the Earth.

It's a way to experience the world we live in from another being's perspective, empathically becoming the other being. It's a way of showing love, honor, and respect for another being's way of living and life's journey.

This must be done with no judgment. Judgment creates separation and closes the heart. Love and respect are vital, and must always be present. A sense of wonder is also needed. It's important to be deeply committed to be successful. Your whole being must dive into grokking. No back doors.

Grokking must be done only for good. It can't be done for control or manipulation. Much of what you will learn will be subliminal. It will just be in you. You'll become a more in tuned, compassionate person.

Children learn grokking naturally if gently encouraged and supported. Adults can learn also, but we have more doubt in our heads to get through.

One of the best beings to grok are trees. Trees live such long lives, by grokking them you can learn history, how they live, how they feel, what they need, and what they have witnessed. Trees can't move, they are master observers, a skill so vital to nature awareness.

Tracks can also be grokked. The master trackers, the bushmen of the Kalahari, hunt large antelope. Once they have been shot with poison darts, the antelope run ahead and die after days of wandering. The bushmen grok the tracks to follow the antelope. They see and feel the energy of the antelope. Many Earth peoples have this skill.

Grokking is a skill you are born with, and when practiced it becomes a tool for life. Put your hand over a track and feel the energy. Then coupled with the knowledge of the animal, follow what you feel. Only occasionally look at tracks, until you find the location of the animal or discover the answer as to what you believe happened to it.

When you grok an animal, you must bring in all your senses and think like an animal, move like an animal, smell like an animal, see like an animal, feel like an animal, eat like an animal, listen like an animal. Be the animal.

Animals, trees and plants have emotions as well. It may just show up differently. Be open to being empathic enough, to sense what they feel.

Humans can grok anything in nature, all possibilities are open. The only thing stopping you is your belief, and effort.

Earth Emotions

Our Earth has feelings and emotions. The closer you come to our Earth, the more you'll feel the Earth's beating heart, as your own. This will seem familiar to you in a distant way on a level outside of your mind. The mind will catch up in time.

Becoming The Wilderness

During our Nature Awareness Class in the Marble Mountain Wilderness, we have the students mud up, and camouflage their bodies with the surrounding vegetation. This activity is to enhance their awareness, and to also learn to blend into the environment to observe wildlife.

There is hesitancy at first from some of the students. It may be cold; they may think it's dirty or they may be self-conscious of what they look like. Once the group dives into the activity, it no longer becomes weird.

The students help each other get "dressed" for nature with ferns, and grass sticking out of their swimsuits and hair. They very much look like wild heathens, and they are beautiful, inside and out. There is laughter ,and big toothy grins, shining through their crackled, muddy cheeks.

We divide the group in half and have one group of people partially hide themselves, and blend into the environment. The intention is to still be physically visible, but to also disappear and become the place they are in.

Once the camouflaged students find their spot and sink in, we walk the other half of the group past them at a steady pace, to see if they can see those hiding, without pointing them out.

We will then walk back through the area slowly, and stop at each student's hiding spot, to admire their ability to blend in, and the raw beauty of each person in nature.

Some people are in trees, some are tucked under bushes, and some are sitting upright in the middle of a wildflower meadow. The students are transformed, and truly co-create themselves into nature's art. Human and nature become one living sculpture. Not only is nature beautiful, but we are astoundingly beautiful too. We need to remember that. We belong in nature.

Invitation

I was filling our bird feeders and heard the songbirds above me excitedly chattering, waiting for me to leave so they could swoop in and feast. I finished filling one feeder, and a Pine Siskin landed on a flimsy branch just above my head. The branch was bobbing up and down from the weight of the bird, but then it settled down and the bird tilted its head sideways to look at me.

I offered a soft hello, and slowly held my hand near the feeder with a little seed in it. I took a few, slow breaths and in my mind, I invited the bird to come sit on my hand. Internally I let it know that it was welcome to eat from my hand or the feeder, but of course it was their choice.

I sunk into the slower than slow energy of the moment, and the bird landed on my hand and ate the seed. It was wonderful feeling its feet adjusting its balance to my fingers.

Blending into the bird's comfortable level of energy, I felt honored that it chose to accept my invitation.

Know Your World

Grok the Directions; North, South, East, West. How do they feel?
Grok the elements; water, rock, wood, air, dirt, fire. How fast does their energy feel?
Grok insects as they crawl on you. What is their understanding of life?
Grok the night. Can you know it as a friend?
Grok the spirit of a forest. Do you know the trees as individuals?
Grok the universe. Can you feel humans as a humble part of the whole?

"Empathy. A gift given to humans. Use it wisely". - E.K.

Being Kindness

Last night in ceremony I was able to grok kindness as an energetic Being. I saw and felt myself as blue energy flowing through everything. I breezed through our meadow of flowers and took on the yellow

colors, and became green. It felt good, and then it was gone, I couldn't hold onto it. At least I know that is something I can work towards. Being Kindness.

Grok the forest fires. Grok the clouds and rain. Ask them for mercy and blessings.

Get Dirty!

There is a difference between dirt and grime. Get dirt on you. Become dirt. Dirt is a living being. There are millions of living beings that make up the dirt. Dirt used to be trees and plants and animals and humans. Grok it and become them. Get covered with the Earth. Maybe you'll find you're the cleanest you've ever been.

I Pissed Off A Chipmunk

I sat down on a log with the intention of being the log. My thoughts drifted to my everyday task list for a bit, and then I brought my attention back to being the log. I closed my eyes, took a breath, and then let it out slowly, melting into just being. I opened my eyes with soft vision, not focused on any one thing.

Moments later, a darting flash scurried in the distance of my peripheral. A chipmunk ran straight up to my feet and stopped, and looked up at me. I never moved my eyes and kept breathing into the log, into the Earth, sinking in.

The chipmunk hopped up on the log next to me, and then quicker than I was ready for, started to crawl up my back. I snapped back to what was happening in that moment, and I flinched. That split second of pulling back my energy from being the log, into questioning if I wanted the chipmunk to climb up on me, is all it took for the chipmunk to feel that there was something not right.

He immediately jumped down off the log in front of me, screamed, ran a few more feet away, turned back towards me, and chewed me out! I accidentally scared him, and he was pissed off about it. I couldn't stop laughing as I apologized to the chipmunk. He didn't take it very well and ran off into the woods, while I fell over on the ground cracking up.

I was amazed that grokking the log worked, and from that day on I never questioned the ability to shift my energy to match my intention.

To know anything in nature, you must become the thing. Sing it, chant it, dance it, celebrate it. Grok its joy and grok its fear, shift your perspective and you will have compassion.

Clouds

I moved through the clouds, to find spirits and I found trees.
I moved through the clouds, to find trees and I found stars.
I moved through the clouds, to find stars and I found a universe.
I moved through the clouds, and in the universe, I found a meadow of flowers and grass, and I was in it.

Stretching Awake

Have you ever stretched your dormant self-awake with a full body yawn?
Have you taken an endless breath felt throughout every cell?
Upon waking have you reached skyward for the nurturing sun, with a tingle of new life emerging from within?
After a time of rest have you felt stronger and more grounded, deeply rooted, encircled with a concentric ring of wisdom?
Have you found yourself standing taller after having offered others a place to rest within the embracing security of your limbs? If so... then you know what it is to be a tree in spring stretching awake.

Bird Song

Bird Song is an extraordinary language. Listen with a clear mind. Let the song become your song.

Watch the behavior of birds when they're singing. When you do that with an open mind and open heart, you will find that humans are not the only beings with advanced language. This awareness might lead you into the deeper realms of bird language, and bird life.

It might humble you in a good way, allowing for wonder to explode within you. A wonder for birds. As your heart expands, love will grow within you, respect will grow within you, happiness will be you. One day an opening will appear in a way we don't understand in our brain. We will move into the world of birds, the world of nature.

Go to the edge of where the sound stops. Move into that space where the bird stops singing. Enter at the edge of that space between and become the bird through that opening.

You will find yourself home again, in the place it all began, where you belong, as a part of nature. You will no longer be a person sitting in nature, you will be nature.

I look at birds as beings of living light, lighting up our Earth for all. Listen to a bird song.

Bird watch. That's it. Just watch.

Hike up creeks. Sit in them and grok them. Grok the fish and beings within them.
Grok a river all the way to the ocean. Who did you meet along the way?

Naturally Blending Into Our Environment

Humans instinctively tend to grok the environment and blend into the landscape where they live. Pay attention to the color of clothing humans wear in different environments. We tend to wear colors that imitate our surroundings. Of course, hunters do this intentionally and there are exceptions, but look around and see if you notice how we adapt to where we are.

In the desert climates people wear beige and light colors. Those lighter colors help to keep them cooler, but they also happen to be the natural colors of the desert surroundings.

In the mountains and forests people tend to dress in Earth tones, deep greens, and shades of brown.

People in the Caribbean wear a lot of pastels and sometimes bright colors, which mirror the ocean, reefs, and sky.

In larger cities, people tend to wear shades of gray and black, and more subdued colors. Of course, there are exceptions, but in general this is what I notice.

We also not only change the fabric for different temperatures for the changing seasons, but the colors themselves also tend to mimic the colors of the seasons as well. I notice people wearing pastel colors in the spring, bright colors in the summer, browns and warmer colors in the fall, and whites and darker colors in the winter.

No matter how much we remove ourselves from consciously being aware that we are literally a part of the environment, we instinctively gravitate towards being a part of it in one way or another. There is no separating us from who we really are. We are a part of nature.

Disappear into the wild lands and observe. If you can, sneak up on a croaking frog. If you can.

The Meadow

Today I smelled the scent of a wild iris in a meadow. This scent spoke to me of the butterfly that visited the iris.

The flowers spoke of Anna's Hummingbird, our garden honeybees, the wild bumblebees, and the very essence of the flowers, all scents mixing quietly in the breeze.

The gift of these smells coming into my body, once inside, became me. The flowers, the bees, the hummingbirds, the butterflies, the meadow, all of it, became me. I am the meadow.
I'm so grateful to be aware of this gift that I give and receive. I am certain the meadow, and all that the meadow is, gets all of me too. This is an amazing way of full-circle, Earth living.

Become A Thing

To know a thing in nature, you must be that thing. To be that thing, you must put aside yourself and open your heart. This is the doorway in, a way of asking, "Is it OK to be you?" This can be anything in nature, as all things are alive in their own way.

When that moment happens, when you observe the world through another being's eyes, when your heart is their heart, the world you thought you knew just changed forever. Your evolution as a human being just progressed. Your real journey has just begun. Don't stop, keep going. What joy the Earth has for you. Only goodness.

Be A Tree

Think of your life as the rings of a tree. The years pass, bringing drought, storms, insects, sun, friendship, community, togetherness, light, sky, spirit, song, love, peace, wisdom; a good, full, meaningful life. To be a tree is to live fully, to be alive—to be a part of the whole.

Make friends with cold and hot. Go into them and know them and you will no longer fear them.

"Look into a pool of water and see the Earth looking back at you. Your reflection is the Earth's reflection. Look in the eyes of any animal with love and respect. They will reflect back into you, their essence. Somewhere within this interaction a meeting will take place and you will know each other. To look at any being with an open heart is to open a door to a place where only goodness lives. We protect what we love. When you smell something in nature then at that moment you see something in your consciousness, or your mind's eye. You've been invited to go into what you see, however far or close or confusing. Explore, a wonderful surprise may be waiting for you. Remember the journey, the gift may be along the way. Happy Travels." - E.K.

Be Aware

Putting out peaceful energy will attract beings to you. Putting out angry, intense energy will send beings away from you. This is true for all beings whether they are human, animals or plants. Be aware and responsible for the energy you bring to a space.

Journey Into A Leaf

Look into a leaf and see the tree. Travel to known and unknown places. It will feel familiar and safe. A sense of belonging may overcome you, then you'll look again, and a new journey will begin.

"To fly like an eagle is sheer joy. Next time you see an eagle project your conscience to the eagle with an open heart. You will fly." - E.K.

If you could be any animal, tree or mountain what would you be? What is it about these Beings that call you? Follow that call.

The Spider And The Web

All my life, I've loved spiders. They are fascinating beings. As a kid I read a natural history book published in 1912 called, *The Life of a Spider* by Jean-Henri Fabre, and I was hooked. I began to enter their world with a different perspective.

To enter another being's world, we must put aside our egos and judgment. We must let go of any ingrained idea that might live in us that we are better than another being. Many humans think this way and most of the time, we don't even know it. To enter another being's world be open and enjoy sharing space with another fellow Earthling.

I've spent many hours observing spiders busy on the ground as well as in their webs. Spiders are master weavers. To me spider webs are nature's fine art. A backlit spider web with glistening dew drops is a stunning show of delicate, strong beauty. To a fly caught in a web however, it is terrifying and deadly. Another example of how wonderfully complex our Earth is.

I've always held spiders and saved them by carefully relocating them outdoors. I've also had spider friends living in my house. For months at a time, they have kept me company at my desk while I worked.

I have no fear of poisonous spiders, just respect and curiosity. I've been bitten by Black Widows twice when I unknowingly almost smashed them. I still love them. They were just protecting themselves. Animals feel our energy and react to it in different ways.

On average, one acre of land has thousands of spiders who keep the insect population in check. Without spiders our plant life would be desecrated, and all life would suffer. A healthy spider population means a healthy Earth.

***

One time I was camouflaged to blend in with a tree to observe wildlife. A herd of deer entered my space without seeing me, and a spider began to build its web across my eye. It was weaving back and forth from my eyebrow to my cheek.

It was one of those sacred moments for me that was too good to be true. A spider, bringing me into its world. A shared moment. I didn't move or change my energy. I enjoyed the deer as the tree. Eventually I gently moved the spider onto the tree and the deer moved on.

This was a good day on Earth's playground. Tree, deer, spider, and me.

Become Your Surroundings

You are a beautiful part of the whole. Develop a deep-rooted connection with the Earth knowing you are the Earth, not living outside of her. Become the wildness of the Earth and let her ignite you into action.

"Just as a blade of grass becomes a prairie, the human also will become the prairie, when he becomes a blade of grass." - E.K.

Reminders:
*Find compassion by grokking another being through curiosity.
*Become the wind and gather empathic wisdom from all you blow through.
*For five minutes a day have fun experiencing life through another being's perspective.

Part 2

Wilderness Living Skills

*Build your nature awareness and
reconnect with your Earth through engaging with its natural
resources.*

Chapter 13
Master Wilderness Living Skills

Mastering wilderness living skills is a necessity we've lost in our modern world. The art of living off the land and with nature in a partnership, has now become a hobby, at best, for some.

We now go to the grocery store and hardware store to buy whatever we want. We are entertained by movies, and constantly engaged with our cell phones.

Even though everything does in some way come from the Earth, and we depend on the Earth, we've lost that sense of that awareness, and that's a deep wound to us. Without that conscious awareness in the forefront, we make bad, impulsive decisions for the overall health of the Earth, and in turn our own health and wellbeing.

Our ancestors woke up every day with the Earth, knowing they had to decide if they were going to go hunting or fishing or foraging. They had to figure out how they were going to live that day. If they wanted to make a shelter, they had to figure out where to find the materials and cut the trees. If bad weather damaged their shelters, they had to repair them.

If they needed water, they had to make a vessel for the water to carry it to their camp. Everything they needed to live came directly from the Earth in its raw form.

Our ancestors didn't have capitalism, their job was the art of living. I think in our souls we long for that time. We didn't have to get a nine to five job and pay for an apartment, insurance, and cars. Our living was made by how we lived on the land and engaged with it. We worked hands on to feed ourselves, our families, and our communities. We all took responsibility to protect each other.

In general, that approach to life is gone for most humans. There might be a few primitive tribes left that are living that way, but in many cases, they are in grave danger of losing their sustainable way of life now.

Bringing wilderness living skills back is one of the traditions our school focuses on. We teach the art of wilderness skills, and how to live with nature without trying to control it.

These are all very important things to learn. Practicing the old ways that our ancestors lived before modern technology, just you and the land, is an incredible thing. Learning to do that is empowering and so freeing knowing you can directly work with the Earth and honor these skills and bring them alive again.

Being able to make fire so you can cook your food, stay warm, and make tools is a basic skill to learn. Imagine what life was like before fire.

Making shelters, for a place to call home, no matter how simple, provides protection from the environment and weather.

Our bodies are over eighty percent water. We need clean water to live, it is vital. Without water we'd pretty much evaporate and disappear. Our ancestors didn't have to worry much about clean water, most of it was naturally clean.

Isn't it fascinating that we now destroy everything we need to live? We know what not to do, and yet we continue to pollute ourselves. So, now we need to learn to purify our water.

If you're going to live in the wilderness you need to get food by hunting, trapping, fishing, and gathering plants.

Clothing is made with tanned hides and wool. Wild foods are preserved by drying, smoking, salting, and pickling. Medicine is made from the plants you harvest.

I strongly encourage you to bring back the art of these skills, and master them, and pass along the knowledge. It all benefits you. Learning these ways of our past allows you to move forward with confidence.

The Earth shows love by providing a home, food, water, shelter, air, gravity, companionship with other species, and boundless beauty to thrive in.

Being self-reliant is a form of Earth Caretaking. Bringing the old skills alive is a way to connect personally with the Earth. Even if you don't need them to live your life, do it for fun. Everything you do adds to who you are and creates a stronger relationship with our living home.

Life Skills

Wilderness living skills are physical life skills that will help you to survive in nature. More than that, wilderness skills are truly there to allow you to live in nature in any environment and thrive, not just survive.

You don't have to be in an epic survival situation to be in the wilderness. Go out with the intention of living with the wilderness, blending in with our environment as a part of it, instead of battling it and trying to conquer it. Go with the flow of nature. Adapt and admire our human ability to do so. Not all beings are capable of living in different elements and environments, but we are. Honor those skills we have been born into.

Just as we learn to drive and use computers, and take care of our own finances, learning wilderness skills are extended life skills outside of the home. We have adapted to what we need to know in the urban and semi-rural environments, where most of us live, but we are missing the basic life skills outside of our modern homes.

In times of natural disasters in cities, many amenities are not available, and we are in positions where we cannot feed or shelter ourselves if our banks are closed or technology shuts down. We don't know what we can eat or find safe water to drink. We become helpless and must rely on outside help to save us. We haven't learned some basic life skills to be self-reliant, and in turn be in a position where we can help others.

We should learn this while in nature, but we all should know these skills within our households. Many of these living skills are not taught at home or in schools any longer.

The pandemic was a wakeup call, especially for Americans. We tend to pay other people to do tasks and actively live our lives for us. When the trades people weren't available to help us, we either froze in our tracks or we rose to the need and figured it out.

I think many times that if one of our ancestors were to show up in our lives in present day, they would need help in showing them how to operate many devices, but they would have the basic knowledge of how to find food, how to find water, how to build shelter, how to make fire, and how to navigate by the landscape and sky.

A young child would know how to do these things as they were growing up. Now, in general, we are lacking those abilities. We really don't know how to take care of ourselves if our electricity goes out for even a day.

In the United States, survival reality television shows have become popular because those outdoor living skills have become foreign to us. They are a novelty to us, we see them as primitive, and not useful in our daily lives. Yet, if we knew some of those basic, outdoor living skills, they would no longer be labeled survival, they would just be living skills. We wouldn't be fearful of being outside without our cell phones.

I admit as an adult, before I had started taking wilderness skills classes, I really hadn't made a campfire. I didn't have a fireplace in my home, and hadn't done much camping outside of a group situation, where the leader made the fire for us.

When it came time for me to make a basic campfire with a match, and even a lighter, I didn't do very well getting it lit and then keeping it going. I didn't think it was going to be that difficult. After watching others who knew what they were doing, and then actually being taught what it takes to build and maintain a good fire, I have a great skill now, and a good relationship with fire.

 109

I have learned what type of fire is needed for different situations and tasks. Whether it be for a group campfire outside or in a shelter, a fire for cooking, roasting, baking or a personal campfire for warmth, I know what to do, and what type of wood is best for each situation.

I learned how to also make a fire by friction with a bow drill and a hand drill. Being able to take care of myself and others is self-empowering and allows me to have a sense of purpose. I can teach others, even when they are too embarrassed to admit that they too don't have much, if any, experience with fire making. I can relate to them and help them learn to help themselves.

Being self-reliant creates personal empowerment, which equals freedom, and will aid you in future life situations. Even if you never use any of these skills, you will have gained the confidence in knowing that you can take care of yourself and others, by knowing edible and medicinal plants, knowing how to build shelters in varied terrains, how to make tools out of items around you, how to build a fire or how to get clean drinking water.

Even if it's just for fun, go out and practice your skills, and reconnect with your Earth through engaging with its natural resources. Become a kid again and learn as you play.

The Gift Of Earth Living

Your day could be like this. At first light, you blow your coals from your previous night's campfire into flame, by adding a few pine needles and small sticks. The fire warms you and heats your coffee, and cooks your breakfast.

Your day might include walking your landscape, looking for tracks, possibly hunting for your next meal or fishing the creek or lake.

In the midday you might build a shelter and make it home. Each day becomes a celebration of the Earth by living with the Earth in partnership.

How can we bring this into our modern lives?

Harvesting

Plants taught me to see the world in a more intricate way. I learned to pay attention to the subtle differences in the shapes of leaves, and became aware of the infinite variety of colors. Plants provide access into the layer of mysteries of nature and life. They can grow in the most difficult places, like the cracks of sidewalks. A plant's tenacity toward life is remarkable. Think of burned-out landscapes where everything seems to be destroyed, and within a month new green growth will sprout.

When I knew I wanted to live off the land, I learned to identify as many plants as I could. I had to learn to use different eyes to see the plants for their various uses. I had to use hardware eyes to know which plants or trees would make good shelters, fire, cordage, and tools. I needed to use my grocery store eyes to find food and medicines.

I knew there would be times when plants would be all there was to sustain me. Although it was important to stay alert to the plant's uses, it was also important to also see the plants with an artist's eye, and appreciate their beauty and smells.

One of my favorite things to do on my adventures was to walk along the tree-shaded creeks observing the plants. I would create a menu with what was available as I walked. I knew that watercress loved the moistness of creeks, and could provide a comforting soup when steeped in water with a little chicken bouillon added.

There were so many plants dancing merrily on the banks that provided nutrition in addition to beauty, that I never felt scarcity in my wandering.

Never Too Old

The students at our outdoor school range from seven years old through adult, with the majority being in their teens and twenties.

One memory that stays with me, was a wilderness skills class where we had two seventy-nine-year-old women participating. They were planning a trip across the United States to explore the national parks. They wanted to feel prepared, and confident that they could take care of themselves if they needed to.

One of our staff members is in his seventies and one is in his mid-eighties, and they have been in the woods for many years of their lives, so the student's ages weren't that out of the norm. What struck me differently about these wonderful women is that they were just then starting in their lives to get out on their own, hiking and camping, and they were so enthusiastic about it.

It was such a joy to watch their youthfulness when they were making their shelters, and giving fire by friction a try. They had no shyness about asking our teenage apprentices for help in teaching them. In our camp, one of the unique, and special things is that there really isn't much of an age gap when it comes to teaching and learning new skills. The students all learn and play and teach each other.

When learning new skills, please don't ever be shy about jumping right in no matter what your age or ability level is. We should never leave this Earth with the regret that we wish we would have tried all that we could while we were here.

Those wonderful, wise women gave the younger students an opportunity to be teachers, and the kids were given the blessing of witnessing what it is to live life fully, with grace and adventure their entire lives.

"Notice how you affect the woods. Just notice." - E.K.

Shelters

Camping without tents and building a beautiful shelter out of bark, plants, and trees is literally a way to fully immerse yourself in nature. Earth shelters create security, protection from the elements, and a cozy home. They give us comfort. Crawling into that shelter and sleeping in it, you'll know what a bear feels like in a den. Your shelter will create a space for the Earth to hold you safe. Building a shelter is letting the Earth take care of you.

Learning to build a primitive shelter from what is around you is empowering and fun. If you have the luxury of time, you can get very creative and make it a work of art. Make it blend into the landscape in such a way that it feels like home. Whenever you build a structure, make it with the intention of not taking away from the specialness of the land, but to build and co-create beauty *with* nature. Enhance the landscape without disrupting it. Take pride in your efforts and make your shelter absolutely gorgeous.

An Earth shelter is a sight to behold. It's as if the shelter reaches into our primal soul, invites us in and calls us home. When we enter a primitive shelter, we lay down on the soft leaves, look up at the arranged sticks and branches and bark, and sink into admiration. We relax and let go, safe and dry and warm. It's a peaceful feeling to be in an artful shelter.

Our bark shelters in our school's camp are an example of a functional structure that are works of art. Each structure incites wonder, and blends into the esthetics of the environment.

***

It's vital to learn the skill of shelter building, as it might save your life one day. In rainy, windy, snowy conditions your shelter will make the difference between life and death. It can be important for your safety, and it can also just mean you will have a more comfortable night.

Your shelter may become your home for one night or for many. When you feel safe your heart opens, your curiosity grows, and you explore the land more freely. The art of shelter building can be most helpful in this quest to build a personal relationship with nature.

Most importantly, shelters must be functional. They must be built strong and weather-proof. Your commitment to detail will always make the difference. When you think you're done building, put in more time on the details. Water dripping in, and wind blowing in the smallest of cracks can make for a rough time. Detail, detail, detail.

Utilize what's in the surrounding terrain to build up thick floor insulation. Never put your shelter under a dead tree that may fall or in a low area that could flood.

Get out in nature and have adventures, and build shelters in lots of different landscapes. Start with one night out and extend it from there. Each time you go out you will learn what worked and what didn't work. Continue to improve your structures, until you get very efficient at it. You can become a master builder in no time. Your shelter will be a reflection of the person you are. It will make a statement to the land itself.

Earth Shelters

Shelters of all kinds are amazing testaments to man-kind's creativity. Shelters that are as small as a twig lean-to, to the Taj Mahal, are structural statements as to who we are.

Earth shelters are constructed from what is available in our wilderness environment, and in their simplicity can be some of the most beautiful structures in the world.

My first shelter-building teachers were the woodland animals who built masterful debris-huts. I would observe the squirrels, pack rats, and beavers, busily gathering sticks and piling them on top of each other, to create mounds three feet thick. The thickness and height would act as a protective wall from predators.

I would make small debris huts by putting up ridge poles and stacking branches on top. To ensure a weatherproof structure, I would cover the branches with debris like pine needles, dried ferns, moss, or bark.

A fancier structure called a wickiup, consisted of small trees and saplings covered with outer layers of bark. Some of my shelters had more than one room.

My favorite shelters when I was a kid were dug into the Earth. They could only be reached by crawling under the roots and into an underground space, which was cool in the summer and relatively warm in the winter.

I had shelters along creeks, and shelters on hillsides overlooking valleys. Over time I had a network of shelters scattered over a wide-ranging territory that were rarely seen by other people, but were havens for me when I explored.

The important thing about a shelter is it allows a person to feel at home in the wilderness. My shelters gave me places where I could center myself and find peace.

I always kept my shelters clean and made them beautiful. A good shelter can blend with the environment and become an Earth sculpture.

I built one of my favorite shelters in my backyard. When developers started to cut down the forests and fruit orchards in the Silicon Valley, I decided to befriend them to scrounge their leftover scraps. I would collect plywood, two-by-fours, nails, old windows, and roofing material. A couple of friends and I would haul the "booty" to my backyard, where we built a three-story structure next to a pond I had made.

This make-shift hotel had sleeping quarters, a living room, and a room at the very top that had a sensational view and a deck. It had a locked door, and you had to crawl up the middle on a pole to get to any of the levels. I decorated the outside with bird feeders, and put a telescope on the top deck so we could watch the stars on clear nights.

I papered the walls with nature pictures and old maps that I'd torn, from well-read National Geographic magazines.

One room had art objects I had found in nature. I collected unique pieces of wood, flowers, and leaves that became dried arrangements, and animal bones that looked like sculptures.

I often made my primitive Earth shelters so a fire could be built within them. I would also build them near creeks as often as possible so I could have fresh water.

Playing around like that really taught me about the basic necessities of life, and it taught me how to be creative with what was available. It inspired me to think bigger. It broadened my awareness and interaction with my surroundings.

***

I believe shelter building is a great way to engage city people in being comfortable in nature. Most people are incredibly creative if you leave them alone to create their own shelter.

Many adults become kids again when they build their shelters. It reminds them of their fort building days as an adolescent, and while they are creating their space, it seems they have an endless internal and external smile, and a sense of adventure.

I encourage them to always treat their shelter as a sacred space. I also encourage them to build natural Earth shelters when they backpack. I remind them to not damage their surroundings, and to dismantle their shelter and leave no trace.

I tell them to bring a tent as back up, but to also challenge themselves in different environments with a variety of natural materials. If they get cold or wet, then they will have learned a lesson for the next time.

Shelter building is one of my favorite creative times to play, and yes, I have spent many nights in the cold and soaking rain as I was growing up. I learned what not to do, but what great stories of my adventures I had to tell.

***

My Uncle Bill took me up to the deep snow in the mountains of Colorado, to teach me how to build shelters in an inhospitable environment. We dug snow caves that had two or three rooms connecting them by a network of tunnels. I took inspiration from the movie, *Nanook of the North*, and built an igloo with windows that we made, by cutting chunks of clear ice from the frozen lake.

During our winter class at Headwaters, we spend a couple of nights 7,000 feet up on Mt. Shasta. The students build a personal snow cave, as well as a group igloo. They carve out nooks inside the caves and igloo to hold candles, which glow on the inside and out.

Those nights sleeping up there are the most magical nights. We feel the sense of sleeping inside the mountain and being held by the Earth. Even during blizzards, it's one of the quietest, most peaceful night's sleep one can have. The temperature is warmer inside a snow cave than in a tent, and those are special moments that are never forgotten.

***

There is no reason for people who are stranded for a time in the wilderness to ever die from exposure. Use the materials available to build a simple home that keeps you dry and relatively safe. Observe the animals around you. Where are they building their shelters, and what are they building them with?

Take advantage of fallen logs and hollowed out trees. Watch for low ditches that may fill with rainwater. Become a part of the environment you're in and blend in.

I highly recommend going into your local woods or park and start building. Camouflage your shelter and see how many people even know you're there. You'll get an insight as to how aware, or not, we humans are. I will also give you a little hint, most humans never look up. You may have to get a little creative and build a temporary structure due to local laws, but don't let that stop you from having fun.

Sleep Under The Stars

Sleeping under the stars is a primal thing. When you don't need shelter, get outside under the open sky.

When I grew up and began backpacking, I always slept under the stars. Only when it rained or snowed did I make a shelter or sleep under a tarp or a reclaimed army tent. I would just sleep on a pile of leaves or pine needles with a blanket or an old, army surplus, sleeping bag under the canopy of stars. I loved it.

I truly believe the openness allowed me to sink deeper into the soul of the Earth. The Earth, the trees, the rocks, all held me, and I felt protected. My senses expanded and my awareness grew. Watching shooting stars was my favorite way to fall asleep.

Sometimes animals would check me out during the night. Often, I was asleep and would find their tracks in the morning, and see who had come into my camp. I was visited by deer, bear, raccoons, skunks, mice, owls, coyotes and even a pack of wolves when I was in Canada.

When you sleep out it's you and the wide-open land and sky. It's wonderful, humbling, and amazing. Stretch your routines and sleep out with no roof above. Sleep in different places. Sleep next to water, near rocks, under trees. Sleep in the open. Enjoy a campfire with friends. Tell your stories, and enjoy being in nature with no walls.

Fire Making

Rubbing sticks together to make a coal, putting the coal in a tinder bundle, blowing it into flame, and igniting a fire that keeps you warm, cooks your food, and gives you light, is a miracle!

Fire by friction is an amazing art to create fire. Think about it, how did that skill come to us? I've read there could be up to sixty ways of making fire by friction. Imagine, each culture around the world had their unique take on how to do it. How did that ever happen? From what I know, it happened pretty much around the same time in human history.

I think there is a communication line throughout human life and nature life. We call it the Spirit that moves through all things. Language is difficult sometimes to come up with a word that properly states what you know is true, but when you tap into that energy field of information, all you need to know is there.

Maybe the people in Africa, Australia, Europe, and the Americas tapped into it around the same time. The same synchronicity happened with drumming as a spiritual practice to go into a higher state of consciousness, and that's true for a lot of other things.

Often, when I've been making a bow drill fire, I'll have a moment where I'll have a flush come over me. I'll close my eyes and see myself in another life, as a person living in the wilderness. I see myself making a fire or I'll see my ancestors doing it.

I see how I was dressed and how I lived. Maybe it's a flashback, I don't know exactly. It's a magical moment of connection with my grandfathers and grandmothers who made fires, for thousands upon thousands of years. I can relate and their knowledge lives in me.

Before Fire

Imagine what life before fire was like for our ancestors. What do we take for granted that they didn't have? No light, no warmth, fear of the dark and the unseen, no gathering place for the community, no cooking food, no way to fire-harden tools, and no sense of safety.

When we figured out how to make fire, it advanced us as a human species. It was a giant leap into who we are today and what we are capable of. Prior to fire making we had to rely on forest fires from lightning strikes. Our skills were birthed out of a deep need for survival. Nature taught us how to live.

Within a community there was a fire tender who had the critical job of making sure the fire stayed lit. Some North American tribes made star fires to help insure there was constant fuel. They used long logs that were laid out in a star pattern, meeting in the center of the fire. As they burned, they were pushed farther into the fire's center.

It's astonishing looking back at how far we've come, and at the same time how we still use some of the same skills we used so long ago. Efficient skills, most times, are simple techniques. We can still learn new, old skills if we go back in time, learn from our elders, and pay attention.

Fire Tender

Fires, like other beings in nature, can have a shadow side. Practice safety, be respectful of the powerful energy of fire. Be humble and aware so you don't become complacent and accidentally start a wildfire. Remember you are in the home of many beings such as trees, animals, and birds. Being safe and respectful is the honorable thing to do.

It's one thing to build a fire, and it's another to maintain a fire so that it gives off light and heat without smoke. It's an art to work a fire, it becomes a meditation, and a peaceful joy. The fire is a living being that you birth and tend to until it burns out.

When a group, ceremonial fire is shared, the best fire tenders are those that go unnoticed. They quietly tend to the fire and keep it at just the right size, appropriate for the gathering. Fire keepers step in to tend the fire and slip back out, without distracting the group by poking at it constantly. They allow the fire to draw people's attention into it without disturbance. A masterful fire tender has a connection with the fire and communicates with its energy.

I've sat by hundreds of fires. Some of my greatest dreams and visions have come from my fire time. Working a fire is magic, it's sacred time.

Personal Empowerment

I've noticed that kids gain their self-empowerment when they begin being able to take care of themselves. When people gain their independence in nature they are plugged back into their Source. They generate their own power and are then much less likely to give it away.

Learning to make fire by friction is a vehicle to self-empowerment. We don't have to rely on a lighter or light switch to have light or heat. We can use those modern conveniences, but we don't have to. We can turn to nature and be self-reliant. We gain confidence by generating the energy of fire. By igniting its energy, we are animating the life of the fire, and we feel it inside of us as well.

Connecting with the potentiality of the energy of fire that is within the wood, is not about the physical skill so much, as the connection with the spirit of the energy within it.

Ultimately, when we are teaching our outdoor students fire making, the importance isn't so much about the student learning the physical skill, the intention is about how did they grow from the experience? As mentors we ask ourselves, did they gain self-confidence, self-esteem, and a personal connection with nature by interacting with it one on one?

Yes, we want to teach people to be self-reliant, but the main focus is, did we help them to grow as a better human?

Fire Cooking

Cooking over a fire will often take you back to your ancestor's time. You might even have an ancestor join you by the fire, or you might have memories of your past, living wild upon the Earth, cooking over a fire.

It is truly an art to cook over a fire. At some point with practice and patience, you'll achieve a oneness with the fire, and cooking becomes easy and creative.

Cook Over A Campfire

During our wilderness skills class at Headwaters, we teach many primitive cooking techniques. We cook vegetables and a whole pig in an underground steam pit, sun dry meat, smoke fish and beef for jerky, spit roast meat over a fire, sun dry fruit for fruit leather and pemmican, heat rocks in a fire for hot rock boiled soup, and we cook meat and veggies on a flat rock in a fire pit. We have students make stick bread and ash cakes, and we bake cobblers and stews in a Dutch oven over hot coals.

Cooking over a campfire brings community together. It invites conversation and welcomes knowledge, and becomes a shared joy.

When we backpack, we bring along food, but we also gather wild edibles, and sometimes go fishing so we can have fresh food. We do all our cooking over a fire the whole trip.

During our winter class, the students build their own shelters, make and tend their own fire for a night, and cook their own dinner. This is always a magical night for everyone. Sometimes the weather is very challenging, and other times it is so quiet and calm, it can be the most peaceful and magical nights the students have ever experienced.

We give everyone some basic ingredients, and it's up to their own creativity of how they choose to put it all together and cook it. When people engage with preparing their food and interact with the fire, they reclaim some of their primal, Earth-living instincts. There is always an opportunity for problem solving for sure, but that is part of the experience.

Fires are living beings. When you cook over a fire you have a relationship with it, especially if you are tending it to cook your food. There is a constant interaction with it.

There is a feeling of pride when you make your own fire and cook food over it. What may seem like small tasks are actually very big accomplishments for people who don't usually do this. Each small success builds people's self-confidence and self-esteem, which in turn allows for more self-reliance. This one night out is life changing. It brings people back to the basics of living with nature.

In the morning when we all gather back as a group for breakfast, everyone has stories to tell. They share ideas of what worked and what didn't work for them. So much learning comes from even one night out, that you could never gain from a book. Once you experience putting your skills to use, you gain wisdom and not just book knowledge.

***

115

A memory that will always be a part of me was a snowy, winter night out. I was cooking over a small fire in the woods, and was heating a flat rock to cook my sausage, onions, and bread dough on.

I was so happy to be out in the woods with a blanket of snow on the ground, and stars twinkling through the opening of the tree canopy. My mind was completely preoccupied as I was putting the sausage on the hot rock, and I got a sense someone was behind me.

Snow insulates nighttime sounds in winter, and creates a stillness like none of the other seasons. People's crunching snow steps can be heard, but not a wolf's.

Standing in the moonlit tree's shadow, was Riley, our wolf-dog, with his head curiously drooped just enough to enhance his primal, predator silhouette. After a brief startle, I welcomed him into my fire circle to share in my primitive, gourmet meal. He humbly stalked in to receive his sausage, and then retreated outside the firelight circle to sit and watch over me.

Making my own fire by friction in the woods, cooking my meal on the rocks, and enjoying the stillness of a winter night with my wolf friend watching over me, was a magical moment that will forever be a part of me.

Eat Wild

When you engage with plants and create with them, you get to know them personally. If someone just tells you the name of a plant, you are likely to forget. If you interact with them and have a conversation and build a relationship with a plant, like you would when you meet a person, you will remember them.

There are an abundance of plants that are edible, but need to be prepared first, by either a leaching process or by cooking them. Acorns from the giant oak trees in California fed many of the Native people. They were their main food staple and were a good source of protein and fat. They had to be boiled down and the water changed multiple times.

So, how did we learn how to do that? We figured that out through curiosity, experimentation, and maybe intuition.

Educate yourself on edible plants and experiment with your own recipes. When you are backpacking, this knowledge will help provide you with an abundance of fresh food.

***

When you harvest plants for food, when you hunt or fish for your food, when you raise animals for food and kill them, what you learn is those living beings you eat become you. That oneness connects you to everything physically and energetically. You feel completely nourished.

You truly understand that some other living being, be it a plant or animal, must give its life up for you to live. You don't take it for granted, it's a gracious exchange of energy.

This truth can be tough to take if you love what you eat. It's humbling, and it forces you to be respectful and kind and loving to all things. All beings want to live.

If you love something it will then become you, and live in a way, through you. Raise plants with honor. Hunt with honor. Raise animals with honor.

Respect the individual. When foraging for food or plant medicine, be mindful of how much you take from a single plant. Allow them to continue to flourish and spread. This should be the approach to any resource we use to live.

Always give back to the Earth to keep the circle of life full and healthy. If you take, you must give back. Be a human that leaves all that you touch better.

Fishing

"Think like a fish, think like a fish, think like fish" – that was my mantra, as a friend and I tramped through brush toward Gray's Falls on the Trinity River in Northern California. It's a beautiful place near the Hoopa Valley Reservation, where the river creates a cascading waterfall, and tumbles and rumbles into deep pools below. This is the place where the salmon congregate as they make their final push upriver to spawn.

As we got closer to the sound of the river, we came upon an old-timer on his way to the fishing holes, and who incredibly, told us of all the hot spots. Most fishermen wouldn't tell a single person where their prime spots are, so we figured our encounter was heaven sent, and destined to provide us nature's bounty.

He told us of one special hole that was a perilous place in the middle of the rapids, which meant we had to cross the river. He told us the earlier we got there the better, because only two or three people could fit out there at one time.

He said the best way to catch them was to use a #1 hook without a barb on it. The elder suggested a bit of red cloth tied to it. The salmon don't eat on this journey because they are in such a state of frenzy making their way to the spawning grounds. They will strike out, however, at any red object that comes near them.

With the sound of the river near us, and the welcomed advice from the generous guy, I was pumped and anticipating some of the best fishing of my short life.

Fishing is a great tool for learning about inner awareness, and like learning about edible plants; it's a great opening into the hidden realms of nature.

Thinking like a fish should be easy, since their brains are minuscule, but they are very difficult to catch, as they are instinctual thinkers. Because the fish react instinctively, they are aware of the slightest changes in light and noise.

My experience of watching a bear fish with Uncle Bill, reminded me what I had to do for a successful catch. I had to be quiet, stalk and crawl to the fishing pools so the fish wouldn't see my shadow or feel the vibration of a heavy footfall on the ground.

I had to use my senses; smell, sight, hearing, touch, and inner vision. I had to become one with the environment and think like the predator who feeds upon it. I had to think like a bear, otter, or heron.

I would imagine myself as an osprey or an eagle soaring high above, so as not to cast a shadow. With eyes so alert that a flash of the fish's tail would trigger my predator instincts, I would dive silently down to catch the fish hiding in the shadows of the rocks.

As we approached the falls, the sunlight against the wet skin of the jumping fish, looked like sparks of electricity dancing off the water. That quick glance sparked within me a vision of the complete lifecycle of the salmon, from the time they lay their eggs, the hatching, and the desperate swim of the newly born, from the river to the ocean.

I envisioned the ocean where they spend years facing the hazards of killer whales, sharks, seals, and fishing boats, and yet, miraculously find their way back upriver to the spawning grounds, to ensure the survival of their species. I felt the power of the salmon journey, and I felt deeply connected to the spirit of the fish.

As we made the steep climb down into the canyon, we saw a couple of fishermen claiming their rights with the flick of the rods. We also noticed some kids about our age casing the place.

As the salmon frenzy began to calm, the fisherman started to leave, knowing that they could dangle the red cloth all day and not one would bite. The other kids however, had brought treble hooks that they weighted, casting over the pools as soon as the last of the fishermen had left. It was an illegal way of catching fish, as the hooks, when jerked, could hook the side of the fish's belly.

Large numbers of salmon can be caught this way. There is no sport or craft involved in this type of fishing - it's for the greed of the take only.

We were just about to intervene when a Fish & Game warden appeared and arrested the kids, confiscating their knives and fishing equipment, and saving us from the potential bloody brawl. I hate the ruthlessness of humanity, particularly in relation to the creatures of the world who can't fight back.

I was confident from having studied the river, and how the other fishermen fished, that we could start our day early and be successful. We got up at 3:00 a.m. in the moonless night, as we wanted to be the first ones there. Though we had flashlights, they were not very helpful in the unfamiliar terrain. I slipped in the darkness, and tumbled down a cliff about fifty feet, almost killing myself in the fall, but at sixteen the feeling of indestructibility was enough to heal any wounds. I dusted myself off and kept moving.

It was important to be there at the "magic hour", that time right before dawn, as the sky is just beginning to lighten. It's the time that our ancestors and the poets say we can slip between the two worlds – the physical and the spiritual.

It sure felt sacred out there as great blue herons, river otters, eagles and all kinds of critters stirred and prepared for their daily survival. My friend and I slogged through the leg-numbing, snow-melted waters to reach the rock where we sat shivering, until the first rays of the sun blessed the Earth.

As the pools began to light up, we dropped our lines. Within an hour we each had caught three salmon, which was the limit. We couldn't believe how easy it had been. It was time to give the rock to others who had gotten up early, but not as early as us.

As we slogged back through the icy waters, there seemed to be an energy shift. We all sensed something. It was as if electrical impulses were charging the air and everything around us. Everyone felt it, and we all started to yell excitedly to each other. "What do you see?" was the question circulating up and down our piece of river. Finally, one of the fishermen yelled, "Steelhead!"

I had never seen one, and in the time it took for me to say steelhead, the river was streaked with lightning bolts of silver energy. The water was pulsing and shooting up all around the salmon and us.

Like salmon, the steelhead travel from the Pacific Ocean up the rivers to spawn further in. I was paralyzed with excitement, hypnotized by the motion and the energy, as one of the old fishermen brought me back into my body by yelling to put some salmon eggs on a hook. It seemed instantaneous as my roe-baited hook hit the water, and my line went screaming upriver, and just as quickly came screaming back.

It was mayhem from one side of the river to the other, up and down, and I held onto my rod for dear life. The old guy yelled that I had a big one. I was putting all my energy into trying to reel it in. I was jerking the rod trying to get it in one motion, as the old guy appeared from nowhere whispering in my ear, "Softer, softer now. Not so hard, you'll lose her. You gotta work her. Let her come to you." The fish kept zigzagging and before I knew it, there was a crowd around me on the banks of the river shouting encouragement and advice.

It was one of the most connected moments in nature that I had ever felt. I loved that fish for that moment. I fought it for 45 minutes, my energy waning as I pulled it closer and closer, and finally the decisive moment, as someone came to my side with a net in hand ready to scoop the giant into our world. He put the net to the tail first, and the fish feeling the net gave one more struggle for freedom, wiggling and lurching and jumping, loosening the hook, and flying into the river and downstream.

I couldn't believe it! How could the guy be so dumb – you always put the head in the net first. I was ready to explode, grief-stricken and exhausted from all the work with nothing to show for my efforts. Then it struck me, that fish had given me the most incredible 45 minutes of my life, and it was now free. It fought with everything it had to get up that river to make sure its species survived. It was one of thousands, but that didn't matter. It was the one that would ensure the steelhead lineage.

My anger quickly became happiness. I realized that the fish's survival was more important than a good hearty meal. I never fished the same after that. I became a catch-and-release fisherman.

I felt that the spirit of nature rewarded me with a sacred moment. It said, "You're doing a good job. You're one of the good ones. Keep it up. Here's a gift." Its gift was the awareness of the connection we have with all things.

***

A year later, on the same river, in the same spot fishing for salmon, I hooked a big one. It made a 14-lb steelhead look puny. I fought her for about an hour and a half, finally landing her on the riverbank. She must have weighed over 40 pounds, and as I hauled her in and my eye caught hers, she started laying her eggs right there on the grass. I quickly let her go, hoping there were enough eggs left in her for the next generation.

I will never forget the look, however. It touched me to my soul. It spoke of a lost generation, and the struggle she had had for the last seven years surviving the ocean, and the sharks, and making it this far. Struggling to return to the place of her birth, only to be caught by a boy. I prayed that her journey would end successfully.

***

My favorite place to fish were creeks, they are a playground for the imagination. I was always on the move, exploring, looking for snakes and crayfish, and harvesting wild edibles.

You can give yourself a solid meal from fish and wild edibles, which graciously bonds you with the environment.

After a day of fishing the creeks, my Uncle Bill and I would spend the night in an old, log cabin he kept up in the Rocky Mountain Wilderness. It was wonderfully rustic with a big fireplace, a couple of bunks and kerosene lanterns.

Once the fish were caught, eating them was just as much an art form. We would cook our catch over the open fire with a pad of butter and some wild herbs. Even now my mouth waters thinking about those long-ago fish feasts.

I miss the companionship of my uncle, and the days of pure joy alone with him in that wilderness. He showed me that eating just the filet is like eating only the cake and not the frosting. I remember him insisting that I eat the entire fish.

The first time I popped an eyeball and a fish cheek into my mouth, it was blind faith that he would be right, and that I would enjoy the taste. Having that eyeball stare back at me was creepy. I wondered if the spirit of the fish remained in that eye, and I wondered what it was thinking.

***

One of the creeks I used to love to explore and fish, was Stevens Creek, in what is now Silicon Valley. It used to be a lush place where ferns and beautiful Columbine flowers would hang off edges of rock, and clean water would riffle down through a little waterfall, making eternal ripples in the pool below.

Maybe I would find a snake or a newt prowling along the clear bottom. I would hear frogs croaking, and chickadees chirping happily, in the sun-dappled leaves in the trees. I could drink the water and feel the cool liquid spiraling to my stomach.

Some of my greatest memories are fishing with my dad in Stevens Creek. Being an aeronautical engineer for Lockheed, kept him busy when I was growing up, but he would always find the time to be with me and teach me outdoor skills.

We took the two-canvas covered, wooden kayaks we built together, to the Stevens Creek Reservoir where we would fish. We'd gig frogs that we'd cook and eat, along with our fish catch.

Even though my dad wasn't much of a talker, I would love spending time with him. I liked just being with him, and no words were needed. He was an honorable, truthful, and caring person, and I am thankful for that time.

The enchanting memories of Stevens Creek are all that's left of the spirit of the place. The destruction started slowly. One day I would find garbage somebody had tossed. Another day I would find a 50-gallon drum of disgusting liquid, oozing into my pure, creek water.

Dead fish began to appear everywhere. Eventually all the household junk, including refrigerators and furniture that people were too lazy to dispose of properly, were dumped. With each new pile of garbage, I would cry for the slow loss of life and beauty, and finally Stevens Creek became lifeless. Today it's a cemented water channel filled with pollution.

***

Luckily, Coffee Creek in the Trinity Alps in Northern California, has not suffered the same fate. It's an iconic wilderness area accessible to Bay Area adventurers. I've often fished the creek that runs into valleys, surrounded by steep cliffs and huge boulders strewn along the banks.

I loved hiking and climbing the cliffs, and I always kept a stringer of fish hanging from my belt. The downside was that the stringer would invariably attract yellowjackets. I was never bothered by them, and a few buzzing around seemed quite harmless. They are, however, quite the carnivores, and they can eat a fish rather quickly, so I had to pay attention to protect my haul.

I always try to find a connection with a creature, and this time was no different. I stumbled along the banks trying to protect my fish, and trying to befriend a few yellowjackets that would have nothing of it. They were not there to commune with me on a spiritual level. They were mean and they were hungry.

In my stumbling and bumbling I stepped on a rotten log, broke it in half, and was suddenly swarmed by an entire hive of the aggressive creatures. Their biting and stinging was unmerciful. My string of fish went flying as I flailed to protect my face, and other exposed body parts. I jumped into the creek hoping the water would save me from the painful bites, but those creatures are ruthless when angered, and they got me even under the water.

It took about 20 minutes for them to retreat. They were determined to make a feast of me. Every time I went underwater, holding my breath for what seemed like an eternity, some of them would still be waiting when I surfaced. I had to swim underwater and downstream to escape.

It was a humbling experience to be overthrown by such tiny creatures. They taught me that not all of nature's creatures are wonderful, particularly yellowjackets. They can be quite dangerous if a nest is

119

around a camp or a group of them go after food. They follow their target relentlessly. Our dogs have been victims of their swarms, and run at the first buzz they hear.

There had been a time in my life when I thought I would love everything in nature, and find peace with even the most treacherous of creatures, but my peace with yellowjackets has not always been so peaceful. Like all predators and gnarly plants, they are nature's wake-up call.

***

The call to hunt and fish is instinctual. As a boy, I loved the feeling of self-sufficiency every time I put a pole in the water. I pretended to be a pioneer whose family depended on the spoils of the hunt. I often fantasized about being one of the last, great mountain men.

There is one place in the High Sierra's that takes me back to a time where I imagine the solitary, mountain man would go in the summers, just for the sheer pleasure and beauty of the terrain. I often went there with my dad and friends.

It was a perilous and difficult hike, as the trail was not well traveled. It was made even more difficult by my asthma, which was exacerbated by the high altitude at 10,000 feet and the uphill climb. It was hard to watch my dad and friends chug up the mountain past me, while I had to stop and rest and catch my breath. I learned to push through some of those limitations, but I also learned that I had limitations. Reaching the lake was worth every breathless stop, however. It was and is a breathtaking place that gives truthful meaning to "God's country".

Twenty years ago, the fish were so plentiful you could almost talk them into your net. One day I literally caught 60 fish – catch and release of course. I would like to say it was pure genius and intuition, but it was really the ants that showed me the trick.

As I was trying to figure out the best spot, I let my awareness be my guide. I observed a spot where fish were coming into the shallows, and wiggling up to the edge of the shore to suck in ants that cruised by.

I had never seen such a sight, and since I couldn't put ants on my hook, I figured that the fish probably would eat any of the local critters. I went on the hunt for the best hook critter I could find. Fortunately for me, and unfortunately for them, it was grasshoppers. That observation of the ants gave me one of the best fishing experiences of my life.

***

A fishing story isn't complete unless you have a story about the "huge" fish that got away. With my new driver's license in hand, my fishing buddies and I were headed into the Central Valley, in a Corvair convertible with our poles, shotguns, and bows and arrows. We were a sight, I'm sure. The plan was to hunt for doves and rabbits with the guns, take carp with our bows and arrows, and fish for catfish at night.

The Central Valley was filled with grazing cows and bulls in our dove hunting grounds. I had one bull chase me for what seemed like a mile before I could jump a fence to safety.

Doves are hard to hunt because they fly very fast and they swerve, so we had to focus on them, while trying to also focus on not being charged. It was pure adrenaline fun.

The second day, we fished for carp with our bows and arrows. They liked to swim in the shallows among the tule reeds, so bows and arrows were the best. It always reminded me of pictures I had seen of how the indigenous people had hunted a hundred years ago.

Most people think carp doesn't taste very good, but roasted slowly over a fire, they're as gourmet as a meal can get.

The most fun I had on that trip was sitting on the bridge at night, fishing for catfish and talking to my buddies. We'd lean our poles on the side of the bridge railing with our lines dropped into the water. The lines had little bells on them that would ring if a fish nibbled, so all we had to do was wait for the bell to ring while we partied away.

We'd been catching fish off and on for most of the night when my bell started to ring, but it didn't seem like an ordinary jingle. I had the feeling that this was one big fish. I was far enough away that I had to scramble and run to reach the pole. I was running as fast as I could when the rod yanked flush with the railing, and then flipped up through the air and into the river.

I shined my flashlight into the river, hoping some miracle would give it back to me, only to watch my reel being hauled away at what seemed like 90 miles an hour. I knew that was a big fish, I knew that was the kind of fish that books are written about – but it got away.

Not only did this monstrous fish that would have made me famous, get away, but it also got my rod and reel. It was some of the finest equipment money could buy, and I had worked long hours to buy them. My one hope was that the fish was able to shed the hook and get free.

***

Hunting and fishing with friends is a bonding experience that also speaks to the primal parts of our being. Like any venture, we need to be vigilant, so we don't take it to extremes. I can certainly understand how easy it is to kill more than one needs. There is a killing frenzy mentality that can overtake you once you're focused on the hunt. You can never close your heart if you're a hunter or fisherman.

To fully connect with nature, we need to understand that killing is also a part of nature's rhythm. It is how humans have survived for centuries before supermarkets. It's the way people lived in nature, how they participated in the cycles of life and death.

Taking life is a great responsibility. Responsible hunters and fishermen respect the process. They take only what they can eat, which honors the life of the animal they have killed.

We need to be humble again. We need to come back to center within ourselves, and the center within our community. Our extremes have created chaos and alienation.

People make personal changes in their lives because they want to, or because something hurts bad enough. I think the same options apply regarding people's attitude toward nature. Small groups of concerned people will always act locally and globally, but it will take the felt loss of a healthy planet before many people will act.

Tools

The knowledge of crafting the bow and arrow traveled throughout the planet, through that unspoken language of universal energy. We went from throwing spears and rocks, to the efficient hunting tool of the bow and arrow.

The only continent that did not use the bow and arrow was Australia. They have what's called the atlatl, but the Aboriginal people were so masterful using it that they didn't need a bow.

When my ancestors, the Celts in Northern Europe, got the bow and arrow it changed life forever. Can you imagine having to hunt a herd of bison or a bear with your hands or a spear? The bow and arrow changed everything, unfortunately, it made humans better at killing each other as well, but that's another story of the darker side of human nature.

Bow and arrows can be used for something beautiful or something very ugly. The same holds true with fire. Many things have a shadow side, including us. Many things can be a tool and gift, or a weapon and a hindrance.

When you learn to make your own bow and arrows, you gain an appreciation of the craftsmanship that goes into creating these primitive tools, as well as an appreciation for the commitment it takes to hunt successfully with them.

Bow hunting brings the human-animal interaction closer on a personal level. It can be considered a more honorable approach to hunting. Tracking animals also becomes much more of a necessary skill to learn, as well as the awareness of an animal's lifestyle and habits.

Learning to track and read the manuscript left by animals, plants, trees, and weather is learning to read the Earth. It's like being taken into a storybook. When you learn the skills, this open book becomes sacred to you.

I would highly recommend crafting your own bow and arrow before you go out and buy a commercially made bow. Start with the craftsman's skills and then venture farther if you choose. It will remind you to stay humble, by connecting with the animal close up, and you will choose your shot more carefully and respectfully. It becomes personal, because it is.

Hunting

Dawn was a few hours off. The marsh smelled of waterfowl. The occasional squawk or quack filled the blackness as I tried to quietly crawl through the tulles. My 12-gauge shotgun seemed a bit heavy for my 10-year-old arms, but I was determined to find a place to sit quietly and wait for the first light.

I wanted to get to my spot a couple of hours before dawn. I knew that slogging through the wet marsh and tulles would create a disturbance. The concentric rings of that disturbance would need to settle before I could become invisible to the birds.

This was my first duck hunting experience with my dad in the Merced National Wildlife Refuge. It was full of countless ducks and geese, and other migratory birds that come to these marshlands for rest before their journeys' north or south.

I was ready. I was excited and went over all the rules that I had been taught about hunting birds. I had to aim a bit ahead of the bird as it flew, so I wouldn't miss when I made the shot. We didn't have a hunting dog, so I had to shoot over open water so I could see where they landed when they fell. If they fell into the tulles, they would be lost.

As the sky lightened, the sound of waking birds was deafening. One by one they would start to fly. I had my eye and my aim on a mallard as it flew over. It was a beautiful bird, flying low and fast in the dawn light, its wings whistling in the cool, morning air.

I led the bird and fired. Boom! It was like the bird had hit a brick wall. It tumbled and spiraled and hit the water. It was flapping and spinning and squawking – wounded, but not dead.

My father matter-of-factly told me that I had to go out there and break its neck. The thought was gruesome, and each step into the marsh was painful, as I knew that I would have to have the courage to break its neck when I reached it.

As I approached, it stopped flailing and I prayed that it had died, but such moments are rarely that easy, and I found it to be exhausted and wounded. The bird's eyes met mine in a forever moment. As I picked up the poor creature from the water, I apologized. "Sorry my friend, I have to kill you. I didn't do the job right to begin with. Please forgive me." I held the bird to my chest and wrung its neck, then stood there in tears holding it in my hand.

My father shouted, "Get back in here! There's more hunting to do." He knew however and understood the sacred responsibility that comes with hunting. He knew how difficult it was to experience killing an animal for the first time, but he also knew hunting is taking life, and life feeds upon life. Yet, even knowing that each animal has its own unique place on this Earth just like us, it's still hard to kill a being that has a right and a desire to live.

A good hunter respects the bond between hunter and prey. Some indigenous Earth people would pray before and after a kill to announce their good intentions, and to give thanks to the animal spirit. The hunters considered that the spirit of the killed animal entered their being when they ate it, and that they had a responsibility to honor the soul of that animal. They believed that the animal spirit would be present the next time they went on a hunt. It would assist them, so that others of its kind would give up their lives when needed.

I remembered these stories, and I gave thanks to that duck for giving its life to me. I knew that duck and the others that I killed that day, would provide food for my family for quite some time. When I killed, I would often sit quietly with the animal, admiring its form, thankful and reverent for what it was about to give me. The animal would often come to mind for days after I had taken its life, its spirit reminding me of the gift it gave.

I didn't always hunt with a shotgun. I've found hunting with a self-made tool much more rewarding. I searched for two weeks looking for the perfect Y-shaped stick to make a slingshot. I fastened an old piece of rubber from a tire's inner tube to the prongs, and I had one wonderful slingshot. I practiced shooting small stones at river rocks along a creek, and I became a pretty good shot, at least at stationary targets.

One of my first kills with the slingshot was a typical young boy, thoughtless act. I saw a robin from my bedroom window perched on the telephone wire in the front yard. I aimed, not thinking I would actually hit it. Not only did I hit it, I demolished it with the velocity of the careening rock.

I loved robins. They were always the first bird to sing praise to a new day in the morning, and give thanks for the day at dusk. I loved their color. I loved watching them peck worms out of our lawn. I helped them after rainstorms by picking worms out of our gutter and putting them on our grass for them.

So, when I found the bird dead from a big hole in its chest due to my rock, I felt horrible. I vowed not only would I never kill another robin, but I would also protect all songbirds for the rest of my life. It took some regretful experiences to gain the understanding from my own thoughtless, impulsive actions. I learned how one can make bad choices that result in consequences you can't take back.

Even today, as a result of that negative experience, I have continued to turn it around into a positive, and I have created a sanctuary on my land where hundreds of migrating songbirds come to eat, drink and rest. I have dozens of nesting boxes and a sacred space for them, where even my dogs are not allowed to go so they won't be disturbed.

After having killed that robin, I knew that I had to eat what I killed out of respect for the creature. To randomly kill animals for no other purpose than to kill is a wanton cruelty and disrespect for all life. The next day I made a small campfire in the woods, and I roasted that tiny creature, along with some squirrels that I had shot, and consciously ate them with reverence.

Many Native American tribes would construct buffalo shields in honor of the buffalo that they killed. The best tribal artists would decorate the shields, which they would sometimes burn in ceremony, honoring the creature that gave them life.

The robin gave me my first "medicine" feathers, and her wings were dried and used as power objects. Meaning, I was then aware of using the qualities of the robin in times of need. I called on the tenacity, endurance, and joy of that bird many times.

In addition to slingshot hunting, I learned how to set dead-fall traps and snares for rabbits. One of my traps had snared a rabbit, and I found it hanging upside down and still alive. I approached quietly, but the rabbit was terrified and started screaming. The sound was so human-like and penetrating, that I literally began to spin from confusion and fright. I had to sit by a tree and calm myself before I could go back and cut the rabbit down.

Luckily for the rabbit, and for me, he had not been injured. The snare had caught him around a leg and the chest, so he was just scared. I held him for a minute while I apologized and petted him, and then let him go. I suppose I could have killed him, but his fear was so palpable that I could only feel compassion, and felt that it wasn't his time to go. It was meant to be a teaching experience for me.

I think a good hunter knows when to keep an animal and when to let one go. It's a visceral, heart connection that you can have with an animal, rather than kill for pleasure and power. Being aware of that potential connection is important when you are in the woods.

Listening to your intuition leads to a greater connection with the natural world. Part of that asking is that you must be willing to hear, "No" and respect that voice in the moment, without maybe a clear understanding as to why. We tend to take what we want when we want it, rather than allowing room for another option to present itself.

I had many hunting experiences as a kid, but truth be told, they have always been difficult. I suppose it's because I wasn't really hunting for survival, but for experience.

One of my first hunting experiences was in the Trinity Alps with a family friend, Bob. He was a handsome man, muscular, six-foot-four and square-faced, with thick eyebrows, and sharp green eyes.

The thing I remember most was that he wore the same outfit every time I saw him – blue jeans, a blue jean shirt, chunky, black work boots, and a very big watch that had all kinds of gadgets on it.

Bob took me to an area in the Trinities where very few people went. We backpacked in the wilderness about five miles, and scouted the area for three days without our rifles. The time spent scouting was to connect to the land, read the animal tracks, and keep our eyes peeled for any good size bucks.

Bob said that we weren't there to take the largest animal. The biggest bucks were the strongest, and were needed to help keep the deer population strong during the breeding time.

When hunters only go after the trophy animal, the deer populations breed smaller deer. With a significant loss of large bucks, they aren't able to pass on their genes.

The best hunters don't try to alter the balance in nature by bagging the trophy animal. It is better to follow the example of the deer's natural predators, such as the mountain lion. The lion is more likely to take something smaller, because the big bucks are harder to kill, and it poses too great a risk of injury to the mountain lion.

The abundance of wildlife in that spot in the Trinities was almost overwhelming. I saw bears, wolverines, marten, and fishers.

The deer tracks were a road map to where the best hunting spots could be found. We started early in the morning and walked quietly along a deer trail. We decided to part ways so that Bob was on one side of the valley, and I was on the other. The idea was to flush the deer down to the end of the valley, into a box canyon that we had discovered the day before.

I soon heard a deer footfall snapping the dry twigs in the distance. I stopped and sat motionless, hoping he was coming my way. A young buck came into view perhaps fifty yards away, stepping warily,

ears alert, sniffing the air. It was not stopping to feed, even though there was a bounty of lush plants at its feet. It sensed my presence, but it couldn't smell or see me.

I took aim. I had the deer in my sights, and I felt from deep inside that it was right to pull the trigger. I made a good shot.

The deer was dying, blood was coming from his mouth, and his eyes were wide open when I approached. I held him around the neck and cried. Even though my intuition said that it was my deer to take, my heart was heavy from the killing.

Bob came running and he was very supportive, as he knew the thrill and the pain of one's first deer kill. We dressed out the deer, cleaned him up, and took him back to our camp, ecstatic that we would be eating deer steaks over a campfire that night. It was some of the best eating I had ever had.

I used all parts of the deer. I took the hide home and made it into rawhide, for lashing my shelters. I also used a large piece to stretch over a wood rim to make a drum. The deer legs also made wonderful handles for rattles. Being able to use the whole deer made me feel like the hunter of old, who didn't waste one bit of his kill, and honored its life completely.

As good as our meal was, it was my game, and Bob was feeling a bit out of sorts because he hadn't gotten a deer. For two days we scoured the mountains, and though Bob was an excellent hunter, the deer eluded us. They managed to stay just far enough away so there was no clean shot.

I remember on the third day, we were up on a promontory taking in the incredible view and looking for deer. Without warning, a crack sounded loudly behind us, and a bullet flew through the bushes right by our heads. Bob looked at me and said, "That's it, I give up deer hunting." To my knowledge he never hunted deer again.

Some of the other hunters wanted our spot on the promontory, and they were sending a deadly message. We had no idea where the shot had come from, but we knew it wasn't far off because the loud pop and the bullet reached us at about the same time.

I tell you to this day, I believe that it was a message from spirit and nature saying it's time to go home gentlemen. We had spent two days without being able to get close to any more deer. Nature was inviting us to leave, and when we didn't get that message, it sent another message in the guise of a wacko hunter with a 30.06 and a bullet flying by our heads.

***

My good friend, Charlie, gave me a Cherokee teaching. He told me that a person is like a tree with two big forks growing from the trunk. The forks represent our dark side and our light side. If you lean too far to one side, the branch splits off the tree and you're no longer whole. Life's great challenge is finding the right balance between our dark and light natures.

Working With Your Hands

If you go out into nature you can't simply just live by wonder, and miracles, and love of Earth. You must have physical skills that allow you to live in the wildlands. In our outdoor school we teach wilderness survival skills, but I think of survival as something you are thrust into by accident, and you must fight to live.

We also like to teach these same skills as Earth living skills, where you are learning to live with, and in nature, instead of battling it.

We would have a tough time doing many of these skills without our incredible hands. Our hands are tools that help us to build tools. They allow us to create and interact physically with our world. They are almost their own living beings, but we take them for granted because they work independently, as well as *with* our whole body and mind, all day without too much conscious thought.

Appreciate your hands. Take care of them and develop their abilities. Feel true gratitude if you are lucky enough to have a good, working pair of hands. You can literally build the world around you.

When you are working with knives or other tools, think of them as an extension of your own hands. Get as comfortable with the tools as you are your own body. Tools are an extension of your energy. You give them life force.

Your knife will become your closest friend. Treat it with care, and it will become a living being full of your life force. Respect the power of your knife, keep it sharp. When using it, be aware, and it will always work with you in a good way.

One thing I notice when working with my students, is that some of them are just not fully in their body. They struggle with what in my mind, are very basic movements. Either they haven't been taught to use their hands with certain tools, and don't have much experience with hands-on activities, or they are just unsure of themselves and need practice and encouragement.

You can literally build a relationship with different parts of your body, and it is as simple as just appreciating them. Becoming more aware of your body and how amazing it is, allows you to master physical skills to the point where they become second nature to you.

When you are crafting and focused, it becomes an intuitive, spiritual time. The practical side of working with your hands unites with the artistic side and creates a flow.

It's no small thing to think about the enormity of what your hands are to you on a personal and practical level, and how the things you can do with them expands out to affect the entire world.

I think one of the great challenges for all human beings is to learn to let all the wonderful tools we have, like our hands, guide us into using them for the greater good. Use them for acts of kindness and love that support all living beings.

What Are You Going To Master?

You can always learn the physical wilderness skills, but until you use your nature awareness skills, and call up your personal medicine, and the spirit within the craft, you will only be a good craftsman, but not a master of those skills.

Crafting the perfect bow or any Earth tool can be a lifelong journey. To be masterful in wilderness skills, you need to bring in the spirit and awareness into your craft, to take it to an artist level. A fire maker without heart medicine is just a mechanic.

One way to describe and compare the difference between a craftsman and being masterful, is that anyone can learn how to play an instrument and play a tune, but a true master musician is able to tap into another level of greatness, where you become the open vessel, and the music plays through you.

So, hone your nature awareness and wilderness skills, and allow your connection with the Earth, and the unseen spirit to flow through you. In time, you will be masterful in your art.

Woods Tips:

*Communicate with rocks, trees, water, elements, and animals. Observe their qualities, and learn from them to work with them. Use those qualities so you don't lose them.
*Take a hands-on class to learn skills. Practice your skills and then go play in nature. Have fun!
*Create wild edible plant recipes and add them to your meals.

Chapter 14
Follow Tracks

I believe the art of tracking is an important skill for anyone that's serious about living a life with nature. Our ancestors were true masters in learning these Earth's ways from birth. Tracking was the way of life for our ancestors, it literally meant life.

Tracking becomes a doorway into the depths of nature. The mastered art of tracking is transparently seeing the manuscript left by animals, plants, elements, and humans. Seeing intimately into the landscape leads us into the spirit of the land.

Tracking is a spiritual practice as well as a practical one. It's also quite simply a tremendous joy. When tracking, we become more alive. We touch our ancestors. They awaken us. Our bodies become an awareness being, a fusion takes place, and at some moment within the tracking, we are the land- the good Earth. It's a true natural high.

I've always believed the beautiful tracks animals leave on the ground are their art, their signature. They are also the art of storytelling. When you learn to read this manuscript, the animals tell you their story. They take you into their world. When we take the time to read this story, we honor them. It's respect, it's love of nature, and it's always fascinating.

Tracking is also needed as a skill if a person chooses to live on the land in an Earth living way. If hunting is needed to live, then knowing where animals go and when they go, is necessary for survival.

When a hunter tracks an animal and makes a kill, it becomes personal. The journey of tracking takes us into the animal's life, which builds our respect for them. The kill becomes a spiritual and practical experience. When we eat the animal, it becomes food for our whole being. We take in the cells and energy of that animal, and it becomes us.

Anyone can be a tracker. Anyone can look at a track with wonder and let it take you into its story. To be a great tracker you must dedicate your time studying the tracks and the being that made them.

Whether you become a serious tracker or just do it for fun, remember that tracking is so much more than just a footprint. Tracks are trails, rubs, scratches, bite marks, scat, lays, hair, or fur, digs, dirt mounds, broken branches, scents, tastes, and sounds, anything that leaves a disturbance or alteration of a space.

When tracking, you find one sign, which then leads you on a journey into nature's stories, and ultimately into your own. Make tracking a part of your life, and you'll never be lost.

Create Tracking Boxes

Mark off a small space on the ground in any terrain, a meadow, a forest, a beach, or your own yard. Sit outside of it and take notes of what you see and feel in this space. Visit this space daily and record your findings.

Look from all sides of the space. Look close up, and step back and see what is happening from farther away. Lay down and look from ground level, and then stand above it. Make sure you look up as well. What is in the vertical space above the ground?

Look at every rock and every single track that's been made in this spot. Look at every flower, every plant, every shape, every color. Look at spiders and ants. Discover the stories the sit spot tells. What did that ant do? What did that spider do? Where did that track come from?

Visit this space at different times of day and night. What has changed over the course of hours or days or weeks? Did plants die or blossom? Has an animal passed through? Did insects eat the foliage? Has the morning dew highlighted a glistening, new spider web across an imprint in the ground? Has the wind wiped your space clean?

Keep in mind a tracking sit spot can be both a physical exercise, but also have a spiritual intent. It doesn't have to be either or.

It may seem initially that this is a sedentary activity, and you may fear that boredom will set in quickly. There are times you will need to slow yourself down to take it all in, but you will also find that this is a very active, ever-changing view into the small worlds.

So often we forget to look at the smaller world beneath our feet. When we pay attention, we feel we are on another planet we didn't know existed. In reality, we have arrived at the ground beneath our feet, home.

There are so many unknowns in every moment waiting for you to figure out. Get to know the small worlds, and they will tell you the stories of the bigger ones.

When you stay with this activity daily, one day you'll realize you are a tracker. When you leave your sit spot you will subliminally start to read the Earth through curious observation. There is power in knowledge and self-reliance.

Everything Is A Track

From the smallest ant trail to the Grand Canyon, we can follow tracks. Lay down for an intimate look at an ant trail, and while you are there, smell it. Most often we can smell ants, even before we see them. The scout ants mark their trail to guide the worker ants to food sources. The acidic smell is made of pheromones and natural chemicals.

Stand at the overlook rim of the Grand Canyon and let your eyes follow the bends of the river, and the gradating lines along the rock cliffs, to see how the water and wind carved their way through the terrain. After you track with your eyes, get down in there and hike the giant track.

We can see, and smell, and feel, and taste, and even sense the tracks on this living Earth. Where there is life, there will be tracks. Get to know your Earth by reading her story of creation.

Intuitive Tracking

Take tracking to a spiritual level. Soak up the medicine of the animal by *being* with it. Follow the animal until you no longer see their tracks, then become the animal. Think like the animal and follow your intuition. Track the animal's energy. Honor the Being by getting to know it on all levels.

Hold your hand over a track. Close your eyes, feel. Close your eyes tighter and see the animal in your mind's eye. Open your eyes quickly and look down the trail. Walk with the animal in its footsteps.

Sit in an animal lay. Soak up their energy. Be empathic and feel their stories, and you'll gain more wisdom than you could ever read in a book. Time shared this way is special and yet normal.

Woods Walk

I walk softly into the woods with the eyes of an artist. My God! I can't believe the beauty I see! Sculptures, paintings, carvings, patterns, shapes, and colors. It's an art museum. All of it. The living Earth and all Its beings, art and nature as one.

I walk into the woods with the eyes of a scientist. My God! I can't believe what I see! All green things, leaves, grasses bringing in sunlight to grow the forest and meadows. I see the web of life. It speaks to me of how life works. It's amazing. The science of how our Earth works is a living miracle, and it's comforting to know that I am a part of all of it. I just love knowing this. Science, nature, and humans as one.

I walk into the woods with the eyes of a caretaker. My God! I can't believe the work I'm being called to do! Trimming trees, moving rocks, making animal habitats. I am the Earth. I work for the Earth. Life's purpose, oneness, fun. I see all that needs to be done in my woods. Home at last.

I walk into the woods with the eyes of a tracker. My God! I can't believe what I see! The ground is nothing but tracks. Tracks up trees, down holes, across creeks, nests, bites, fur, scat, broken branches, bones, and holes. The forest is alive with tracks. Each is a story, each is a life, each is nature's art, animal's art. Being a tracker is a guarantee of a good life. My God! I love the woods!

Track Life

Track patterns. Notice the shapes of objects in nature and how the shapes can call to you. Track sound and smell and taste.

Be an observer. Study humans. They become predictable. Track yourself. Put the time in and track your way around the world. You'll never be bored.

Put that smartphone down, then go out in nature. That's how you become a good tracker.

My eyes follow the trails before me and lead me on a journey before I even walk them.

Smell A Snake

We were scrambling along a ledge of granite, just above a mountain swimming hole. We were looking for a flat spot to jump off, traversing hand over hand, just under the ledge.

Tim told me to stop and not to move. My fingers were gripping the bottom lip of the shelf and I couldn't see above me. He told me he smelled a snake. I thought he was kidding at first, and then I smelled it myself. I back stepped down the rock ledge onto the flat ground, and of course, being a snake lover, Tim had to find it.

He followed the scented trail and searched into the cracks of the rock shelf. He didn't end up finding the snake, clearly, we had scared it off. The scent was strong, and it doesn't come off your hands easily. That is one track that stays with you.

Remember to use your nose. Many times, your sense of smell will tell you all you need to know before you see something too late.

Search And Rescue

I used to volunteer with the sheriff's department searching for lost people. A young boy had gone missing, and had been out in the woods overnight in the Santa Cruz Mountains. I spoke with his mother to get an idea of the boy's personality, and to see what his experience was in nature. She gave me a pair of his shoes and I held them for a few moments to make a connection with the boy.

I found his tracks behind their house and off I went. I followed his prints, broken branches and kicked over rocks. Intuitively, I headed in the direction where I felt the boy would go. I let the landscape and terrain help guide me.

About a half mile from the house, I felt the boy. I turned and right next to me was an old, downed log, and under the log, covered in leaves was the boy, scared and sleepy, but warm.

He knew instinctively to shelter himself, and cover up with leaves and stay put. He followed his intuition and paid attention to what the Earth showed him. The boy lived, and what an adventure story he had to tell.

On another search in the foothills of the Sierras I found a middle-aged hunter who had been lost. The signs and tracks led me to him.

When I got close, I was excited to see him sitting in the open clearing on a log, but then sadly, I realized he was dead. He had passed from hypothermia, and had probably given into the fear of being lost and panicked, and just gave up.

Unfortunately, the log he was sitting on could have saved his life by crawling under it, and covering himself with debris like the boy had done. The Earth always provides answers. The endless question is, will we listen?

Something to keep in mind, whether you are tracking people, animals or just going for a hike, make sure you periodically stop and look behind you and identify a landmark. The terrain looks much different coming back the other direction.

When tracking, the focus tends to be on the ground or the immediate surroundings, and looking ahead. Be sure to look behind you as well, so someone doesn't have to track you!

Tracking Is An Art Form

Tracking is a lifestyle, it's the way you see and interact with the world. Tracking expands into more answers, and more questions, and it keeps growing. Tracking is curiosity in motion.

Ask animals what they're doing, where they're going, what they want. To be curious about another being is to love them.

Some of the most amazing ways to expand your world are simple. Follow tracks and embark on journeys of endless wonder, and exploration. It's a lifetime of work, of joy, and connection to the richer parts of our Earth.

Study The Craft

Today we are blessed to have many incredible trackers that have shared their knowledge in books. I recommend reading and using them. They will help take your tracking to a higher level much quicker than starting from scratch.

Learning from others can help accelerate the timing of your knowledge, but only putting in the time to study tracks will develop your wisdom and skill.

Daily Actions:

*Ask the world to show you something new.
*Pay attention to the small worlds.
*Look up, always look up.
*Mark off a small section of your yard and check it daily for any changes or visitors.
*Stop often and use all your senses. Nature will tell you a story every day.

Chapter 15
Conquer False Fear

F.E.A.R. - *False Evidence Appearing Real,* is what may keep us from going into nature. Fear of insects, fear of wild animals, fear of birds, fear of getting lost, fear of being cold, fear of being hot, fear of poisonous plants, fear of drowning, fear of injuries, fear of getting dirty, fear of clouds -Yes, it's a thing! Fear of the night, fear of sleeping outside, fear of crazy people!

Fear is what keeps us from climbing a tree or going in the water. Fear keeps us from going down that trail, not knowing what's around the corner. Fear is what keeps us from drinking the water.

The fear of being uncomfortable is what keeps us from flourishing with the natural world. The list of fears seems endless and yes, I've witnessed all this and more.

If our Earth ancestors, our ancient grandfathers, and grandmothers could see this list, they wouldn't believe it. It's sad and unnecessary for any of us to fall victim to these fears.

We must overcome these false fears to fully engage in our lives. Our alternative is to stay in our homes and cities, having no relationship with our Earth.

Whatever your fears are, face them head on, challenge them, demystify them. Take their power away by going to nature anyway. Educate yourself and ask for help. Do what it takes. We're talking about your life, your relationship with the good Earth.

Maybe ten percent of our fear is valid and something we need to pay attention to. Use your body and your intellect to ask when something is your real fear, or someone else's that you've taken on. Track back your fear, identify it, understand it, and build a relationship with it so you can manage your fear.

It helps to go back in our history and see what or who put this fear in us. We must ask ourselves, does this serve me? Does it keep me from being my true self? Does this fear keep me from living fully?

Unconsciously, fear can make our decisions for us, it puts limits on us, and shrinks our life experience. Politicians base their campaigns on our fears.

False fear is a type of bully that takes up a lot of energy. You need to challenge it and not let it control you, and take over. Ask the Earth and all her living beings to help you conquer this false fear. Risk is one of nature's teachings. Embrace risk and you will find freedom.

There may be a voice in the back of your head that torments you saying you can't do it. Put it to sleep. Be smart, there are some things you can't do safely. There are mishaps that can happen, but use your intelligence and your intuitive side. Use your sixth sense to let you know when something is not okay, then pay attention.

Put the false fear aside and experience nature more personally, and create that intimate bond with the Earth. When you are one with the Earth you will take on becoming an Earth Caretaker. You will protect her, and care for her, and live your life in a way that honors her. You'll also have a hell of a lot more fun, joy, and adventure as well.

***

False fear keeps us from having adventure. I see so many kids who are truly overcontrolled. When I was growing up, my parents kicked me out the door into the woods, and that was how I became my own man. Kids need guidance, but experiencing life through adventure is how you learn to grow through challenges.

I'm not faulting parents; I know they get scared. I know the fear is real, but when you don't allow your kid to get in the mud, to walk off trails or to climb trees, you are putting limiting boundaries on their life experience. Excessive boundaries set primarily through fear, narrows their vision of what's out there in the world.

When we keep kids from exploring, interacting, and connecting with the Earth, they may never do it in their life, and will have a huge piece of themselves missing.

Where the connection becomes foundational, rooted within a person, is in childhood. As an adult we sometimes feel lost, and that we are missing something, and you have to reclaim that because you didn't get it in childhood. As an adult it is not impossible, but so much more difficult.

Allow a child to be rooted in a love of the Earth at a young age. It is a benefit that will stay with them forever. Even if they forget it, as they get caught up in their everyday lives, they'll come back to it. Adventure is a key to this, and false fear is what keeps us from adventure.

***

You deserve a personal relationship with nature. It's your birthright. Reclaim it. Think for a moment about this, we drive cars every day. In my opinion, nothing is more dangerous and crazier than driving at high speeds, within a few feet of other vehicles doing the same thing, but with no control over what the other person is paying attention to. Going into nature and facing our fears is nothing compared to driving. So, get out into the woods. Oh! Also, please drive safely.

Taking Smart Risks

I know my life is so rich today because I love trees. I know trees personally because I spent countless hours climbing them, building treehouses, and living in them as a kid.

I always have kids, and adults, climb trees. I take a risk and encourage them to do it because I believe strongly, people need to climb trees. I believe it is a bigger risk not allowing them to climb trees, and depriving them of that necessary connection with an elder of the Earth. There is so much wisdom that would be lost if people did not connect with trees.

A few years back we had a private school class come to Headwaters. After a week, they went back home and talked about the great time they had, and shared how they climbed trees. To my shock and disappointment, one mother, who wasn't even on the class trip, came from fear of not knowing how safe it had been for the kids, and convinced their school board to not allow the kids to return to our school if they were allowed to climb trees again.

Questions arose about our school's insurance policies. That to me is insanity. A world filled with selfish lawyers and crooked insurance scammers have dictated our lives.

The kids returned the following year and one of the first questions they asked was if they were going to get to climb trees again. The parents who denied them the opportunity, never even told the kids they were forbidden to climb trees. They put us in a terrible position to make it seem like it was our decision.

I believe in telling the truth. I don't believe in secrets in our camp. So, I told the kids exactly what had happened. It was a teaching they needed to learn because it affected them directly. We spoke of false fear based on no knowledge of a situation, only assumptions, and over control out of fear.

The kids were truly crushed, but I had to follow the wishes of the school board, or they would never let the kids come back.

***

I know there is so much here at Headwaters for people to learn because they are encouraged to experience nature hands-on.

I could not run a business based on fear of being sued, that's not a life I am willing to live. I take a risk, because I feel the risk is minimal, compared to the risk of not providing opportunities for kids to fully be in nature.

If you overprotect a child or if you over protect yourself as an adult, you miss the glory of being alive on this Earth. You miss interacting with our Earth in a way that allows you to be an Earthling. You become separated from your truth.

131

I'm going to repeat, I'm not saying do crazy, reckless things, but don't allow false fear to rule your life. Allow yourself to have adventures, go create them. Look at maps. Aldo Leopold once said, *"I don't think I want to live for the day, when there's not a blank spot on the map."*

I can remember in high school sitting with my friends and looking at topographical maps, and saying, "That's the wildest place in the Sierra Nevada mountains, let's go!" When summer came, we threw our backpacks on and we went, and that was foundational for me.

Every person's physical capabilities and tolerances are different. Get to know yourself. Honor yourself, but also push the limits to stretch the scope of your life. Push the edges. Be an explorer.

The most dangerous animal in the woods are humans with false fears.

The Woods Are Calling Me
Who is in there calling out? What do you want from me?
It's dark and scary and an unknown place, but still I'm pulled in. One step at a time I enter. Who is calling me?
Who is beyond that first row of brush? Who is calling me?
Each step I take I'm further in, but I still cannot see. Who is calling me?
My heart is beating, I cannot hear. Who is calling me?
I smell the loamy, inviting Earth. But who is calling me?
I feel an encouraging breeze pushing me along, I wait for an answer against a mossy, elder fir for who is calling me.
I feel a knowing welling up, my vision widens and the darkness fades. I know who's calling me...It's the spirit of the forest...the trees are calling me.

Fear Of Silence In Nature

So many people don't go out into nature because they have a fear of silence. A fear of quiet stillness. I don't believe this is a real fear. It may originate because we are raised in a very noise ridden world.

A recent scientific report stated there are only three places left in the entire world that are truly quiet, with only nature's sounds. That is shocking.

As we grow up in this modern world, we simply don't even know true quietness, what a missing that is for us. Maybe this fear of silence came from how foreign it is to us now.

***

One of our new apprentices came running back into camp in a panic, after just a few minutes of a half hour sit to observe the land around her.

We asked what had happened, and she said she couldn't handle the silence. It freaked her out to not hear cars honking and sirens going. She was from a city and those were the sounds that were in her comfort zone.

As the summer progressed, she sunk into nature's rhythm and realized there were so many sounds in the "silence" of nature, that it could be just as busy sounding as a city. There were birds squawking, insects buzzing, squirrels chattering, trees blowing in the wind, and water rushing and percolating over rocks. She realized she wasn't alone in nature, and she took comfort in that.

***

True silence of self, connects you on a heart level with the sound of nature-silence. Break through this fear of silence and find blissful peace on the other side.

Fear Of Boredom

One of the biggest fears some of our young students have when they first arrive at Headwaters, is that they are going to be bored. They don't want to have a sit spot, not because they are afraid of being in the woods alone, they can see other students close by. They are afraid they will be bored, and can't sit still for an hour without their phones, filling space between their thoughts.

We instruct the students to pretend they are naturalists exploring this new space they will be sitting at. Their task is to return to the group circle to describe to us what they discovered. We tell them to imagine that we are aliens from another world, and we don't know anything about this planet of theirs.

We have the students sit in spaces close to our camp, so they feel comfortable with the distance. When we call them back an hour later, you would think they have been on a month's expedition when they return full of excitement.

We ask them to share their stories of their time in their sit spot. What did they notice? How did they feel? What did they hear or smell?

It is hard to break the habit of technology addictions, but once people are away from their babysitting devices, they realize that the world around them is still going, and there is so much to experience. Eventually boredom is a positive word because it means there is some free time to explore.

At the end of our week-long classes, we ask the students to share something about their time spent on the land, and every time we have this closing circle, one of the most common favorite things is, that they loved having so much free time to be on their own to explore.

The school age kids especially love being able to be on their own, without all their time being over scheduled. They love the freedom to play in the woods, to climb trees, to swim in the creeks or to just sit in a hammock and sway. Sometimes the most entertaining moments are when there is nothing to do.

Snakes, Lizards, Insects, Bats – Oh, My!

Snakes, lizards, insects, and bats are misunderstood creatures. Having a phobia for these creatures is a learned, false fear, and one generally picked up at a very young age through another's reaction.

Certainly, some of these creatures are poisonous, so you don't want to grab them like a cute puppy. However, you can learn to respect these beings that are vital to the Earth's balance, without becoming unglued upon seeing one.

I love all creatures, poisonous or not. I remember freaking out my Uncle Bill one spring, while we were walking in the foothills of the Colorado Rockies, tracking a mountain lion. I was about 11 years old, and he was teaching me to pay attention to the ground, and the disturbed leaves to see if they might hide an animal track in plain sight.

It had rained for a couple of days, so the wet Earth created a soft outline of cougar tracks, but it still took some focus, and getting on my knees to really see if the ground was disturbed. I figured that actually seeing one of the great cats was a long shot, but I loved walking in its tracks, trying to feel its energy, and knowing that it had just walked that way a short time before.

I wondered if it knew that we were on its trail, and if perhaps she or he was watching us from a cliff or tree above.

We never did find the lion, but at one point along the trail I heard a disturbance in the brush. Without thinking, I dove into the tall grass, hoping to catch whatever might be lurking there. I grabbed a handful of brush, and something else, to my uncle's horror, as he screamed, "It's a rattlesnake!" When I realized what I had caught I quickly slid my hand up around its head and held it tight.

I didn't know before I jumped that it was a rattlesnake, but it didn't freak me out once I had caught it either. I sat quietly with it for a time, lightly stroking the snake's body, and it calmed down a bit. I let go of the head when it became docile, and it crawled around my leg and slithered down the trail.

Even today, whenever I see a snake, I have to catch it and hold it. I just love connecting with snake energy.

Snakes understand human fear. They can pick up the scent of fear through the incredible sensors on their tongues. If you remain calm and open your heart, they will generally relax and be with you.

On many hiking adventures as a kid, I would often encounter curled up rattlesnakes on the trails, that were startled and rattling, and ready to strike. I would stop, remain calm and stay out of striking distance, and most of the time the snakes would calm down quickly.

In general, I love all snakes, but my favorite of all is the Bull snake. Growing up, I had over 30 snakes, a dozen lizards, 20 or so frogs, and countless other amphibians and insects, in aquariums and terrariums in my room. After a while, I would let some go and bring in other critters. I have to hand it to my parents who never complained – their only request was to keep the door shut.

One day, I came home from school and noticed that my big gopher snake was gone. I didn't want to tell my parents for obvious reasons. I looked everywhere for it without trying to arouse suspicion. I figured if I couldn't find it, it had gotten out of the house.

A couple of days later, I heard my dad shouting my name. I ran into his bedroom where he was telling me, quite excitedly, that there was a rattling coming from the darkness of his closet.

He asked if I had caught another rattlesnake and had let it go in the house. I assured him that I would never do that, while I moved boxes aside to find my poor gopher snake, rattling away like a rattlesnake. It's one of their defenses and a good one at that!

***

Another misunderstood creature is the bat. We have demonized these poor creatures in literature so that people think of vampires when they see a bat.

My friend, Jay, and I loved to hang around an abandoned house at the end of my street. We were sure the house was haunted because we had read a few Hardy Boys books, and seen some scary movies that closely resembled the old house.

It had a yard full of weeds so high, you couldn't see the broken front windows. It was dilapidated with rotten, wooden boards falling from the walls and ceilings, and it smelled musty like we thought a real haunted house would smell.

We decided to explore the place one night so we could see the ghosts, who we were sure inhabited the place. We were afraid the owner might show up unexpectedly, but the thrill of adventure was more motivating than the fear of getting caught trespassing. We decided to go just before night fell so no one would see our flashlights.

I climbed the stairs of the big house, all the way to the third floor. I had a flashlight that I used only when I couldn't see any definition. The hallway was dark with just a hint of dusk creeping through the holes. I flashed the light on and found a hatch in the ceiling. I opened it, pulled down the creaky, folding stairs, and climbed into the dark attic with the light off.

By the time I reached the attic floor I was covered in spiderwebs. I turned the light on to make sure I wasn't covered with any black widow spiders. As soon as I turned it on, I was surrounded by a rush of wind, created by flapping bat wings as they let go of their roost. I was so scared I almost fell back down the hatch.

When I realized the bats weren't attacking me, and that my light had scared them, I immediately turned it off and listened as they settled back onto their roost. I knew as it got darker, they would start to leave for their nightly hunts. I stayed for a while just communing with them in the waning light.

The next day I went back at dusk and waited outside the house until the bats – hundreds of them – flew into the night to feed on the swarming insects and pollen.

I returned to the house many times to sit in the attic with the bats. Though the bat guano was a couple inches thick, and it smelled quite nasty, they somehow kept pulling me in. They were a mystery and I liked being with them.

I was troubled even at that young age by the reaction people had to bats. When I tried to tell people about them and my experience, they would get grossed out and tell me that I'd get rabies or other diseases if they bit me. They told me just breathing in the bat guano could kill me.

Humans are a peculiar, fearful lot. They try to poison poor, little mammals that actually make our lives better by catching insects. If we didn't cut down so many trees, even the dead ones where bats like to live, we wouldn't have so many living in our attics.

***

A common critter that most people are afraid of is the spider. I read once that if all the spiders on Earth were gone, life would end in seven days because all the insects would defoliate all the plants. Spiders eat so many insects that they keep the population in check.

When I was six I had quite an encounter with a spider. We were living in San Diego on a farm, and my young mind and hands were into everything. I had put my hand into a woodpile and felt a pretty good bite. I yelled for my parents to come see what had bitten me, and as we pulled away the wood, my father found a Black Widow spider.

It caused me severe pain and I remember having to go to the hospital. I don't quite remember what they did for me, but I do remember my stomach cramping and my body aching for quite a while.

Even with that experience I still liked spiders. I loved to catch insects like grasshoppers and flies, and feed them to the spiders in my backyard. I liked letting spiders crawl on me. I liked the tickle of their feet as they crawled around, but after my experience with the Black Widow, I had a pretty good respect for them as well.

In that area of San Diego, we had Brown Recluses, Black Widows, and tarantulas. I had a pet tarantula who used to crawl all over me. I would sometimes let him go free because I knew I could always find him in the woodpile.

All these creatures are vital to the health and flow of nature, and I seemed to know that as a kid, which is why I respected them and didn't fear them.

Many of these creatures are called indicator species, which means when the Earth becomes unbalanced these vulnerable animals die first.

**

When I was a young kid, I could go outside every day and have numerous encounters with small creatures such as amphibians, reptiles, and bats. As I grew older and more of their habitat was destroyed for housing, and the air and water became more polluted, they all but disappeared.

It seems the most adaptable animals are the ones who can survive in urban areas. Raccoons, opossums, pigeons, doves, and coyotes adapt well, but the diversity that is necessary for even these creatures to survive is fast diminishing. There may come a day when even the songbirds will disappear from these areas, but sadly I imagine very few people will notice.

Interestingly, even the plant kingdom has been overtaken. Many species from other countries come into our country on ships, carried as spores or seeds on packaging, and have invaded and killed many of our own indigenous plants. For example, most of the Hawaiian native plants have disappeared due to farming, building, and landscaping with non-native plants.

I suppose with a global economy that it's just too difficult to monitor every ship, plane, or piece of luggage, and it's too soon to really know how each ecosystem will adjust or not. Yet, I believe if we can take care of our own communities, which includes protecting the plant and animal life that exists within it, we are acting responsibly and hopefully bringing our small world into balance.

I Jump In Anyway

I fear the ocean's power, it's raw energy. It lures me in but keeps me in tuned, as though it's a predator waiting for me to let my guard down and engulf me when I'm unaware and vulnerable.

It keeps me humble, always just a bit on edge, but its beauty and the light reflecting off it keeps me in awe, and invites me back in.

Love so deeply that it seems crazy. Dive into love. Be fearless. Your soul rewards will be bountiful. Start now. Nothing is more important, nothing.

When I stop trying to fight my way through fear, I watch my fear swirl around me. I am the stillness filled with laughter within the calm eye of the storm. I surrender to the fear and watch it pass by.

Self-Reliance Eliminates Fear Of Inadequacy

The art of self-reliance in nature equals freedom in all areas of life. When you have a sense of freedom, your creative side has a chance to come out and live, and express itself. Your relationships grow stronger, you become less tied down to fear and negative thoughts and laziness. You are more open, and everyone in your life benefits.

Take a moment, close your eyes, and go back to a time when you lived on the land, maybe in a small village. Take in all that you, and your ancestors had that came from nature. You didn't have a grocery store or hardware store or the internet to order from. You had to make everything. You had to work for all your food by hunting, fishing, and gathering.

See yourself back somewhere in that time. Take a look around. What do you see? Ask your ancestors to help you with this idea of self-reliance.

For me it would be with my Celtic ancestors, living in Northern Ireland. Living off the coast in rock huts with thatched roofs. In my current, everyday life I ask my ancestors for guidance.

As we moved out of the old ways into the Industrial Age, a couple of hundred years ago, but more noticeably beginning in the 1900's, we threw out our old skills.

When our European ancestors made war with the intent of genocide of the Native American tribes in North America, we didn't hold onto those incredible Earth skills they had. We showed very little interest in keeping the people and their knowledge alive.

When this modern world came into effect around 1900, anything that we had been doing as physical work, unless you were a farmer or had a hands-on skills occupation, we let it all go.

Now we're in the 2020's, and we live in front of computers and cell phones. Everything is done for us. Anytime anything goes wrong in our homes we call someone to fix it for us.

We've lost the art of self-reliance. The ability of being able to take care of ourselves, is quickly drifting away. In doing so, we lose something particularly wonderful within us. We lose the ability to create, the ability to have faith in ourselves, to believe in ourselves that we can accomplish things, and that we can problem solve.

We're losing that ability and it permeates out into all aspects of life. If we can begin to reclaim even one aspect of self-reliance, by learning the skills we need to know to go into nature and feel safe, think of how freeing that would be.

Imagine if you know how to build a shelter, if you know how to make a fire by friction or even with matches, if you know how to move through the landscape in a way that's safe for your body, and for the animals, if you learn how to find wild foods, and clean water, and how to rock hop across creeks, and how to climb trees, and go down trails, and go off the trail without worrying about getting lost.

When you're able to do these things, your creative side ignites within you. It becomes living, and your wonder side comes up, and your playful fun side comes up, and the essence of who you are, that amazing person that you are, gets to come out and play with nature.

When you're living in fear, when you're unsure of how to make a fire, or you're unsure if you're going to get lost, or you're unsure of how to cross a creek, or unsure of how to get off the trail and be okay, then you're always guarded. That true being that lives within you doesn't have a chance to emerge and enjoy the world. When that happens you lose, your community loses, and the world loses because they don't get the true you. So, there's a tremendous importance in learning to take care of yourself.

Think about what our world has been going through these past few years. We've had this COVID-19 tragedy, and we had to find ways to do things ourselves while we were on and off lockdown. Supplies weren't available, and the people who provided those supplies weren't able to work and deliver those needed items.

Think about the tragedy where the freezing storms wiped out basic life supporting supplies. People had no drinkable water, stores were closed, there were miles and miles long lines of cars to get water rations.

Think about if the post office wasn't open, if you couldn't go to the grocery store or a restaurant and buy what you want or need. If absolutely everything shut down long term, we wouldn't know what to do. We're helpless when even some of those services are not available.

***

To deviate a little bit to remind you, one of the greatest insurance policies you'll ever have are your friends, community, and family. Never underestimate the power of that.

Part of the self-reliance that our ancestors had was their community. The community worked as a whole to allow for everyone to have food, for everyone to have shelter, for everyone to be safe and have water. The community worked as a unit, young and old. Everyone within the community had their own specialty skills they could bring to the table, but they also had the ability to do a variety of tasks.

One of the great assets was that they were willing to be there for something bigger than the individual, for the greater good, the health, and life of the community.

When I talk about community, I extend that out beyond the human community, to the community of animals, plants, trees, and our very Earth itself, that's how I look at things. It either all becomes safe, and okay and respected, or it all falls apart, and certainly we're in those times now.

We are at the beginning of feeling the effects of climate change. It's becoming so serious that we don't have any time to look back. We must act now. We are witnessing climate change in a microcosm with the severity of the global hurricanes, flooding, droughts, and fires.

Self-reliance and the art of being able to take care of yourself is attainable. Part of it is your confidence. You believe enough in yourself that you know you're going to figure something out in most situations. The other part is curiosity. Learning how to do things by researching, asking questions of people, paying attention, and being curious.

The last part of it is just doing it. Being willing to get your hands in it and do it. Be willing to try things and mess up and keep trying.

Take classes in wild edible plant identification. Learn how to make fires. Learn how to make shelters, and practice. Learn how to clean your water. Learn how to get off the trail and get lost and found. It's a great feeling. Watch yourself soar. Watch freedom soar.

I hope this gives you inspiration to be more self-reliant for you, your family, and your community.

There is a time and a place for asking for help from others. I personally don't like doing plumbing, so I'll call a plumber to do the job, but I do know enough basic skills to fix a sudden situation.

You can start with learning one of the greatest skills, cooking. Learn to take care of yourself that way, if you don't know how. It's such a creative, rewarding skill to have, and a great way to be self-reliant in your house.

Go out in nature and live with nature in a way that says I believe in myself, I'm confident, I can do it. In that process, nature opens herself up to you, and your relationship and trust gets stronger.

I'm hoping you'll absorb this idea of self-reliance as a vital life skill. Assess your current skills, and then inspire yourself every day or week or month to learn a new skill. Become more self-reliant, and in turn more self-confident. Notice how it expands out into your life, and your life will just get more amazing. More amazing people are good for the Earth.

Stretch your boundaries to expand your life experience.

137

Chapter 16
Get To Know Dark

For much of the population, one third of each person's day is darkness. If we live to be ninety years old and we sleep eight hours a day, we will have slept for thirty years of our lives.

If we sleep the majority of the time during the dark hours, we will miss what comes alive at night and is waiting for us to experience.

In nature so many of us avoid the dark. Fear of what we can't see, fear of the unknown, fear of getting lost or fear from past, bad experiences are a few reasons that keep people from spending awake time in the dark.

Some of this fear may be living in us from our early ancestors, in a time when humans were very vulnerable from being eaten by other predators.

There are still legitimate reasons to be cautious in the dark, depending on where you are, the environment you are in, and the situation, but in general, many people allow false fear to limit them. An unwarranted fear of not having control takes over.

I have spent many nights in the dark in nature awake and observing. It is possible to learn to see at night by slowing down and letting your senses come alive. Through practice you will learn to trust your body's natural intelligence. Your body knows what to do and how to do it.

Going into the dark will become another defining moment for you. Freedom will become your calling, and a whole new world will be introduced to you. Often your greatest thoughts, ideas and dreams come alive in the dark.

The stars will become your friends. The trees will care for you. It will be an adventure in so many ways.

There will be those moments when you hear a strange sound or feel something that gives you the chills. That's an alive moment. Enjoy it. Learn from it. Explore it.

The dark will ignite the world of mystery for you. The mysterious, unknown place that is vital for our Earth souls. Have courage. Go out into the dark, and become the darkness in a most beautiful way, and watch yourself grow.

Pluto's Cave

During our classes at Headwaters, we take our students to a lava tube cave. It was created by an eruption of basaltic lava flow, to the north of Mt. Shasta, roughly 190,000 years ago. It was eventually named Pluto's Cave after the Greek God of the Underworld.

The Underworld has seemed to be portrayed as a place of hidden secrets, which ignites the explorer in us to seek out the unknown and bring it to light.

While our students are taught the geology of this near mile long cave, what always connects them to this vast cavern is experiencing the pure, pitch dark in the belly of the Earth.

At first there is usually excitement to scramble over the massive, fallen boulders that make up the floor, but farther into the cave sometimes a bit of fear starts to creep up.

Once we reach the back of the cave, we ask the students to find a place to sit and be completely silent. We ask them then to shut off their flashlights and be still, I mean very still with no squirming.

It takes only a few moments for complete silence to fill the darkness. The temperature is chilly, but the still darkness warms as Tim leads the group in a song of gratitude and reverence from the Earth.

The echoes truly fill your soul, and without the ability to even see your hand in front of your face, the darkness becomes sacred. There are no distractions, only song. You become the dark without defining bodies, only endless dark with no boundaries.

Those who were previously scared of the unknown are no longer scared. There is a oneness with no visual of separation. One universal voice is heard from many.

At the end of our week's adventures at Headwaters, this exploration into the calm darkness of the Earth is always one of the biggest highlights. The students have knowledge of the geography, but they also have wisdom from their personal connection to the Earth.

Night Hikes

We guide every class on a night hike the first night they arrive at Headwaters. We start the hike at dusk, and wander the land for a couple of hours until we are in the full veil of darkness.

We keep our flashlights off, and wander slow and quietly through meadows, through the trees and up into the hills. We walk right into the uncertainty of the dark and hang out with it. The intent is to just be with it, navigate through it, and demystify it.

When we explore in the dark together it takes away the power of fear. Throughout the week our students become more comfortable with the night, and they sleep outside of their shelters under the stars. They wander through camp without their dependency on flashlights.

The fear of walking around in the dark before arriving to our land has dissipated, and moving through the night unassisted has now become normal for them.

Their eyes adjust to the landscape. Their pace slows. Their awareness is heightened. Their senses become much more acute. They smell the various scents of the night. They can hear their location based on running water, certain trees rubbing against each other, and frogs or crickets signaling their location, in recognizable areas of camp.

The night becomes an experience the students know and welcome, as just another part of their day. It's a state of being they adjust to every night without thought. Instead of hiding from the night indoors, their day is extended, and they continue their activities in the dark.

I encourage everyone to enjoy the dark. In our modern culture the word dark has been often used as a negative. This makes me sad. It's simply not true. Break this way of thinking. Make dark a positive. Get excited for the night to arrive.

The darkest part of the sky is where the rainbow shines the brightest.

Night Life

The night is a most amazing time in nature. Many animals are out feeding and traveling. The night is full of life. In the morning, read the manuscript, the tracks are left for you to tell the stories of your animal friends.

Stars, shadows, shapes, moonlight. This is the night. To fully become the Earth, we can't forget the night. We must build a relationship with it. Slow down and open your senses, and have fun. Push the fear aside.

To truly know the night, you must go into it without flashlights. To know the dark is to know one of the Earth's most unique personalities. This interaction gives you a sense of freedom that few are willing to know.

Join the Great Horned Owl and open your eyes wide to let in more light, and you will become the darkness in a very light kind of way.

Stars Are For Dreamers

Go out on a clear night, lay back, and watch the stars. Count the stars. Make up your own constellations. Give them names. Get lost in the stars. Which ones call to your heart?

Personalize the stars you are drawn to. Ask questions of them. Look to the stars for answers, trees do it. I once saw a bear do it. I've seen many deer do it. I've seen many people do it, but sometimes we forget where the answers come from.

Let the dreamer come forth. Dream big. It's a huge Universe. Ask the stars for their energy to help manifest those dreams. Stars are an energy source always there for you. Sleep under the blanket of stars and dream.

Be The Night

Learn to be with the night. Be with fear. Go into it. Become the dark. See what it is. Get to know the night as a living being. Embrace the dark as a true friend and it will embrace you. Give it a name and talk to it. Get to know what you fear so you will no longer fear it. In that knowing comes peace.

The fading sky at the horizon needs to be watched.

The dark of the night is a wonderful teacher. Use your non-visual senses to learn what you think you already know.

Blue Night

Magical snowfall this evening. Beautiful, blue light creating silhouettes of the mountains and trees. Such a peaceful, real feeling. Walking outside tonight I felt life. I felt it in me. I felt the night wake up my insides. I've been distant and asleep, and the night woke me up.

Moon Light

Play with the Moon. Let the full Moon shine its light on you and shower you with its glow. Light your path with the Moon's light. Follow the light back to the Moon and back again to you.

Hang the Moon on a branch and climb the branch to the Moon.

Tonight, oh what a clear night. I looked deeply at the Milky Way, and I realized the Milky Way was looking at me.

Calling Of The Stars

A memorable, defining moment in my life as a child happened when I looked up at the night sky, and the Big Dipper sang to my soul through the beauty of starlight. I felt the Big Dipper with all my senses.

At the time I didn't know what that moment was, but I knew it was special and it stayed with me, and woke me up to the calling of the stars.

My Darkest Moment

Our Earth, our Universe, our Milky Way Galaxy were birthed from an exploding star. This is what some of our most insightful thinkers tell us what they have learned. This explosion created our Earth and humans. We found our place.

I cannot believe that all this happened so we could destroy our home on Earth. The miracle of that exploding star didn't happen so we humans could find our home and destroy it. In my darkest moments, when I'm overwhelmed with sadness and anger over what we've done, and are still doing to our precious Earth, I remember the stars. I look at the stars and dream of our way through. Then I get up and create a new way forward. It's what I do. That's all I can do. I become a part of creation.

Catch A Star

Reach out and catch a star, hold it close.
Let it shine inside of you, let your shine light your life, let your shine light the world.
Be the shine, be the light
Catch a star, shine your light

Night Sky

I am in awe of the night sky. Looking up, I feel humbled and almost overwhelmed at how vast it is, and how small I am.
The daytime sky seems more intimate, blanketed by clouds relatively close to us. The darkened universe is expansive and all encompassing. When I reach for it, I just keep reaching.
I fear the bigness that I can't comprehend, but that also challenges me to become closer with the night, to talk to it, and embrace it as a good friend.
I can feel the night tonight. I feel the spirit of it. Not sure what it is, but it makes me pay attention to it, and it feels good in my heart.

Allow stars to guide you. Light pollution hides the majority of what we can see. Go into nature in the pure dark, take in the vast, amazing sky, and learn the teachings of the stars. They can navigate your path.

Reminders:
*Go on a night walk with a friend.
*Lay out under the open sky and name your own constellations.
*Notice the different smells and sounds at night.

141

Chapter 17
Get Off Trail And Seek Adventure

Don't get me wrong, I love trails. I've hiked many miles of trails in my life. Looking at a trail going off into the distance through meadows or woods invites curious adventure. Whether they are human, or animal made, a trail entices a sense of wonder within us. It sparks the dream of what's around the turn or over the hill.

That being said, sometimes you need to just get off the trail, whether it's for a day or a month. Once off the trail you will have a whole new experience. The true self of nature is awaiting you. The land at its purest. Adventure calls.

I dream and live for the blank spots on a map. If there is no human trail marked, you can count on me to go and see what's there.

We don't get off the trail because we fear getting lost, or we don't want to deal with the difficulty of not having the convenience of a direction already laid out for us. We don't want to have to navigate rocks, bushes, ravines, and water. The terrain features become obstacles instead of curious challenges.

When we learn to move with confidence off trail, we flow through the landscape. When we don't rush or try to fight our way through it, we can then enjoy exploring.

Many times, when we get off trail, we experience the landscape untouched. Literally you could be the only person ever to walk where you're walking. How amazing is that? The animals and you. Only you, what a gift. You are now an explorer!

We live in a crowded world of eight billion people and growing. Many of the most beautiful places in nature, of vast medicine, are in parks and reserves. These places are power spots, that's why people come to them. The heart of the land reaches out and pulls people into the place of medicine. Most people don't know on a conscious level this is happening to them.

Yosemite National Park is one of our Earth's most beautiful places. Its beauty defies description. When you are in Yosemite Valley you are in a spot of immense power. Settings like Yosemite are places where all the world comes together to combine Earth Medicine, Earth Power, Earth Heart, Earth at its fullest.

You might find yourself in Yosemite, with what feels like a million people. Even when you are seeking solitude, don't avoid places like Yosemite because of crowds.

Be happy people are showing up to love the Earth, and then get away from them. You can find solitude by getting off the trails and moving into the landscape. Even just stepping 100 feet off trail, Yosemite can become your personal national park. What an opportunity!

I must admit, when I am on a nature photography trip, I cherish my alone time. I am teaching for most of the year, so I am constantly with people. I need my alone time in nature to refuel myself.

I highly recommend people getting out in nature, and it's great when they do, it also drives me absolutely nuts when they glom onto me. People have a tendency to gather where there are others, out of curiosity. So, when I stop on the side of the road or trail for a quick photo shot, many times immediately, I am literally surrounded by others right on top of me. That makes me crazy!

Sometimes, the gruff bear in me comes out. I am reminded of how crowded this world is now, and it also reminds me to get away from the trail so I can have my solitude and sacred time with nature. Getting off trail allows me to capture unique images in remote locations.

As a teacher, I love taking people out in nature. As a photographer, in my personal time, I thrive on being alone.

Getting off the trail creates a sense of freedom, a sense of exploration. We need these experiences to feed our souls. Soul growth requires this.

Most people stay on trails, and in campgrounds, and around visitor centers. Your freedom and solitude await you, just get off the trail.

Start On The Trails

Begin getting comfortable exploring by walking on the trails first. Trails create dreams inside our own wilderness. They lead us to adventure, wonder, and happiness. Humans are designed to walk. Our legs are an incredible asset to take us where our mind goes.

Look at a topo map and dream. Look at trails and dream, then walk, and walk, and walk. Go barefoot when you can, feel the trail.

Take a beautiful trail through the woods or a trail meandering through a meadow. What's around the corner, over the hill? Where will the trail take me? What will I find? How many have walked before me? These questions lead me on.

All beings like deer, rabbits, bears, and foxes, make trails and share them. Follow animal trails and be the animal. Trails have stories to tell through tracks left behind. Even not knowing the whole story is good because wonder is birthed, questions are asked. The trail is doing its job.

Trails call our bodies to the Earth. We become active and interactive with our Earth, and our senses come alive. As we round a bend our eyes catch a movement, maybe a fox hunting or a deer drinking water along the creek.

Trails take us into a calm state of being if we allow them to. In that still mindset we disappear into the land, and the land into us. In that oneness let go of fear and begin to see more, feel more, smell more, hear more.

Each step is a step back in time, our ancestors may have walked this trail. With each step the trail becomes worn down, and more beautiful with the energy of all that have walked it.

Your eye catches a shape, it's a feather, many feathers, a story to tell. Perhaps the local Cooper's Hawk caught a quail. Feathers will be in the packrat nest, perhaps a feather for you to put in your medicine bundle. Treasures abound along trails, rocks, sticks, tracks, leaves, and countless stories. Trails give us hope for more unknowns, because trails always surprise us. Trails take us out of our routines. They keep us active and aware.

One bonus of walking trails is that you will keep your body in shape. As you walk trails in nature, at some point, you lose your need to go somewhere, and you become the trail. You become perfectly in the moment.

There comes a point when you are walking on trails, when you know enough about the land, and you gain confidence in your skills, your tracking gets better, and there is no longer a fear of getting lost. You are at peace with the landscape, and then you are called to get off the trail, and wander and explore. This moment becomes a defining moment in your life.

You are about to go through an invisible boundary and know true freedom. Excitement builds within you, then you step off trail and your journey begins. A whole new layer of nature that was waiting for you, celebrates by showing you so many new experiences. New stories are lived. Your confidence and independence grow. Your senses become even more alive with new sights, sounds, smells, tastes, and feelings. Your inner vision gets excited to take you into the spiritual heart of our Earth. Adventure is the norm. The possibilities are abundant. Dreams become reality. Wonder takes the day.

Slow down and take your time. Wander aimlessly in nature. Push your boundaries. It's good for you. Getting off trail in this crowded world gets you to uncrowded land. We need this. Human's need to be free of crowds, and all the craziness that comes with it. If you are a lover of cities, then you'll go back fulfilled, and the city will be better for it.

When we get off trail, we truly enter Earth University. The teaching is limitless. In the Earth-ways we say there are no limits. Getting off trail gives you this opportunity.

Walking off trail is the first step to be an explorer. Next time a trail calls to you, heed the call and go. If you don't go, you may miss a pivotal moment that propels you onto your next life adventure. Trails become alive with the medicine of all who walk them. Go walk that trail. Go.

Adventure For The Sake Of The Soul

Adventure and exploring comes naturally to all beings. Before humans were taken over by technology, our baby brains yearned for the thrill of rolling over and standing up, walking, and running without help.

In my childhood, we all played outside and got dirty, dug into creeks like beavers trying to stanch the flow of water. We climbed trees, pretending we were pioneers looking toward the horizon of pure adventure.

Nature filled us and fed our souls with the nutrients that made us braver, more creative, and more inspired. If nature was the food, adventure was the water that kept us hydrated with the possibilities of life's fluidity.

I loved pushing the adventure envelope as a kid. Even today adventure is vital to my well-being, though I have learned to temper my adrenaline addictions with the reality of my aging body. Pushing the envelope allows us to connect with our inner strengths, and can create a sense of personal power and self-esteem. Adventures help build self-confidence.

In the last few decades that I have been working with kids, I see the effects of well-meaning parents, who prefer their kids to find safe adventures through technology and overscheduled, organized sports. The effects are dreadful on a kid's creativity and independence.

I believe sports and activities are great for kids, but there needs to be a balance where every minute of the day is not overscheduled. I believe technology is important in people's lives, but I also believe there needs to be room to physically explore.

Today, the pressure to get into a good school, to create a secure future by their late teens, and outperform their peers, is creating a generation of psychologically numb kids.

My observation of today's kids is that they have tighter schedules than their parents. Their calendars are filled with so many after school activities that are supposed to build bodies and imaginations, but in reality, it leaves the kids stressed, burned out, and over-programmed.

Is it any wonder they turn to drugs – a place where they relax, let their imaginations go and feel no pressure? We all know that with consistent use of drugs, whole years of crucial, social development are lost in a haze of mind-numbing smoke.

The initial pleasures found when getting high can be felt drug free in the natural world, and it's a remedy that gets ignored. Tumbling into creeks, getting dirty, exploring woods, scrambling up waterfalls, getting temporarily lost, getting crazy, climbing a tree, are ways kids can express themselves spontaneously and joyfully.

Being open to adventure means being willing to change plans, to change directions, to change your mind, and to learn problem solving skills.

Sadly, too many kids when they arrive at Headwaters Outdoor School for the first time, are woefully undeveloped in their free thought and problem solving. They have been living a virtual life and not fully experiencing our world hands-on.

As they become teenagers, drugs and alcohol become their adventure. It becomes their replacement to that internal call to adventure. Their crazy adventures are not spirit filled, but hurtful and painful to themselves and others. If they dont let the wild out, it comes out in destructive ways.

Time and again I see young adults, who should be flourishing and exploring the world, returning home to live within the "safety" of their parent's homes. I've been seeing an increase in a generation of lost young adults. Fear based parents, who want the best for their children, tend to overprotect them by sheltering them, and depriving them of their own life experiences.

The results are young adults who struggle later in life to make their own decisions, out of fear of making the wrong one. They are paralyzed by false fear. They don't have the experience, life skills or drive to know that they can get through challenges. The self-confidence isn't there.

I truly fear a weakening generation. We need to let kids respond to the primal call within their youthful spirits, by allowing them adventures in nature. I am still amazed when parents ask me if their child can be killed in nature.

We do the most dangerous thing we can do almost every day without thought, we ride in cars. Of course, anything can happen, but the odds for a negative outcome are greater in our everyday activities, but we need to live!

Life is risky, and kids need to learn to meet those challenges head-on. They need to learn how to react quickly in dangerous situations, and they need to learn how to trust their intuition. They are not going to develop these skills sitting dormant indoors.

Once kids get outside more and are free to explore with a little more room, parents are pleasantly surprised how their child opens up, and grows and flourishes when given the opportunities to challenge themselves.

The freedom of the Earth's wild children is not just physical, it's also in the mind.
Pure joy in nature is when we are most authentically living as we were meant to live.

Braving The Rapids

One of my wonderful death-defying adventures took place after a torrential rainstorm, when Stevens Creek became a raging river. One of my friends had an old raft hanging in his garage, collecting dust and spider webs. It seemed to us the perfect vehicle to ride the now, white waters of Stevens Creek.

We convinced my father to drive us up to where the creek meets the dam so we could ride it from there into the valley. The peaceful, burbling little creek of summertime became a boiling cauldron of fun.

As I look back, I realize how lucky I was that my dad allowed me to have this kind of adventure. As reluctant as my father was to leave us after seeing the power of the raging creek, he knew it was better to at least know where we were, and to let us have our adventure. I am sure he prayed all the way home as well.

It was a sunny day, so with shirts off and wearing only shorts, we carried the raft down to the creek. The water was extremely cold, unless you're thirteen. The four of us squeezed onto a 2-person raft.

With only two paddles we shoved off from the shore, and shot into the creek like a cork out of a champagne bottle. It was dangerous, and the frigid water kept pouring into the raft, while we bailed as fast as we could.

The creek took us through countless private properties, many of which had man-made water hazards of garbage that people had dumped into the creek. As we came around a bend, there was a length of barbed wire strung three feet above the water. With the protection of the gods for fools and teenagers, we ducked narrowly escaping with our heads still attached.

Laughing off that near miss with youthful bravado, we came around another bend and hit a big rock that sent us all sailing into the muddy bank. As I crawled up the slippery slope, grabbing at mud as a lifeline, I unearthed a clutch of turtle eggs, which was a great discovery that I quickly re-buried.

After the bank dump, we rescued our worse-for-wear raft, and with all the excitement of Christmas morning, we piled back on and into the raging waters. With all the dumping and bumping, we all began to shiver, laughing at who had the biggest goose bumps. We were too excited to really feel cold. We felt alive and connected to the spirit of a raging river.

Mortality was not in our thoughts at that age. We screamed in pure joy. The rush of being swept downstream and feeling so alive carried us through the fear.

Bumping down the creek, many beautiful pieces of driftwood whizzed past us like loose cannons. We saw dead fish that couldn't survive the rough water. We kept seeing "No Trespassing" signs and thought we would be shot on sight, but I guess we were going too fast for anyone to shoot or care.

When we had finally floated into the flatlands, which in those days, were covered with orchards, not cement, we gave a victory whoop that could be heard across the valley. Drifting in the calm, we recounted as many moments as we could remember. "Remember the barbed wire? How about the frog up there? What about when I got sucked into the rapid and almost drowned - man were your faces white!"

With all our limbs intact, we returned the raft back to the garage to collect dust. We never told my father what happened. He would surely have regretted potentially sending us to our doom. Although somehow the local paper got wind of our adventure, and sent a reporter to do a story on the boys who rafted down Stevens Creek.

That adventure became a part of me. It may not have been the smartest or safest decision I've ever made, but at the time I wouldn't have been able to talk myself out of it. It was a calling to my wild, primal being to escape for a while, and feel free.

A Day On The Bay

An adventure on San Francisco Bay gave my friend Steve's parents pause about him being my friend. I was always doing daredevil things, and this one was too much for them.

The Bay isn't necessarily a place where you see four boys fishing in a 12-foot dinghy. We had heard the striped bass were running and we wanted to catch some big ones. I had caught a 32-pound bass in the surf off Santa Cruz beach, and when the guys saw my fish, the spirit of competition was strong. They wanted their shot at the big fish.

We borrowed a dinghy from a friend's father, made our lunches and off we went. We were like the crew in *Gilligan's Island,* heading off to an adventure and having no clue where we'd end up.

Steve and I knew how to sail so we launched into the Bay with no trouble, although, with all of us in the boat, we were riding a bit low in the water.

We weren't catching much the first couple of hours, but the view and playfulness of seagulls entertained us for quite a while.

Floating peacefully on the water, we told stories, drank our cold drinks, and ate our sandwiches. Like most afternoons on the Bay, the wind picked up late in the day, and our little boat started to gain speed. The fog rolled in over the hills, and it brought the biting wind that made it feel like winter.

As the boat increased in speed, it started to take in water and we were getting wet, which with the dense fog, started to give us a serious chill. Of course, at the most inopportune moment our rudder broke from too much wind, and too many people on board. The boat started to spin out of control, but with some presence of mind we got the sail down. Though we were left rudderless and without wind power, we wouldn't capsize.

We had started out at 10:00 a.m. and it was nearing 8:00 p.m. with the light fading fast. We were absentmindedly not prepared for disaster. We didn't have food or water left or enough life vests, and the only emergency tool was a small flashlight. We tried to signal with it, but the puny flicker must have been invisible in the waning light.

We were beginning to get nervous that we might get hypothermia. We were still wet, and the wind was an unkind partner in this impending disaster, so we huddled together to stay warm.

Around 1:30 in the morning someone on another boat finally saw our light, pulled up alongside and called the Coast Guard to rescue us. Steve's parents were definitely freaked out. My parents were used to my reckless adventures and took it in stride. We weren't really scared – just very cold. We had a great time and great stories to share.

I think that adventure for adventure's sake, fills our spirit and inspires us to see and do things we normally don't. Adventure opens doors to greater creativity, and allows for grand thoughts, and big dreams.

Think Before You Act

My favorite stupid, kid adventure happened in Glacier National Park while I was visiting my grandfather. He would often take me to the park and let me wander off to explore.

One of those summers when I was about eleven, I came across a Grizzly sow and her cubs. I had a little Kodak Instamatic camera, and I wanted to get a picture of the family. I moved very slowly toward her. She was always aware of my position, but kept grazing, keeping her cubs close.

As I approached that invisible line of too-close-for-comfort, she turned her body with such a great force that I almost fell backward. She rose on her hind legs to an unimaginable height, sniffing and snorting and telling me in no uncertain terms I was not wanted there.

At that age, I had this idea that I could almost walk up and hug bears just because I loved them so much. She was not feeling that love however, and I knew I was in trouble. I didn't know whether I should run to the nearest tree and climb or just stand still.

Rather stupidly, I moved closer so I could take a picture, and with that, she charged me so fast I didn't have time to react. She stopped feet from me, and I could feel her breath on my face. I didn't look her in the eyes, which is probably what saved me. She made a few more grunts, turned and galloped back to her cubs. They all took off so fast across the meadow, and disappeared into the trees, that it became a blurred dream.

My grandfather was not happy when I told him what had happened; yet he knew the price of allowing a young boy to venture alone was that there is always danger and risk. He lectured me on the space a bear needs, particularly a mother with her cubs. He did say that to look a bear in the eyes is a sign of confrontation, so not looking at her most likely did save my life.

On the other hand, I wanted to believe it was my open heart and love for bears that stopped her in her tracks. It was a frightening, but awesome experience for me. I felt she had somehow come inside me and united with my spirit bear. I was sure it was a sign that bear country was a second home.

Why Not?

One of the greatest joys I have always had is to wander aimlessly in nature. I love to explore and see what's around the next turn, over the next ledge or deep inside a cave.

When I go into nature with an open heart and mind, I am pulled physically and spiritually along as if I have no will of my own. I have had an unbelievable life, and I believe it is due in great part to giving myself up to the spirit of adventure.

This may not be a confession that as a mentor I should admit, but my personal feeling is that signs are meant to be interpreted. While growing up, if I saw a sign that read, no trespassing, to me that meant, great, that means I'm going to be the only one in there.

We need to use common sense when situations are too dangerous, but more often than not, there are way too many voices telling us no, and not enough asking us, why not?

Adventures always have a degree of risk, and I have been willing to risk life's tests to live my vision.

It's Ok To Be Uncomfortable

When we jump into nature, sometimes we get cuts and bruises. Sometimes we stub our toes, we fall, and we bump into trees, and that's ok.

We often spend so much time seeking comfort that we miss the adventure of life. We are so fearful of getting hurt we give up on our nature-time. Just get out there and do it. Get comfortable with being uncomfortable.

Let Your Kids Explore

When we are over-protective with our kids in nature, we rob them of their right as a developing human, to build a relationship with nature. It's not ok.

I was on the Big Island of Hawaii in an area where lava met the ocean. I saw a mother and her toddler walking across the rough, sharp, and slick lava.

The boy was walking away from his mom, and exploring on his own under her watchful eye, but he was free. She didn't project fear on him. He came over to me for a visit, and I caught a crab and showed him, and he set it free.

This crab was the teacher. As this boy grows up, he will love and spend time with spiders, reptiles, and crabs. He will be open to the natural world unfolding for him, because of those moments when his mom gave him freedom.

I gave him a crab, and the crab was open to being held. That moment would affect his life forever. These moments matter. The crab could have pinched him. The boy could have fallen through the lava rock. I could have been a dangerous person.

147

The world isn't always safe. We are safer and more confident when we learn as kids to deal with various situations. If we are robbed of these opportunities from our parent's fear, we grow up weaker, and less equipped to deal with life's inevitable tests.

All living Beings, people, trees, and animals face challenges. It's how we learn and grow. It's our journey into our precious life.

Get Lost

It's good to get a little lost. You can't get found until you get lost. Let nature show you this way. You'll find yourself soon enough. Nature is truth, pure and simple. Find your true self in the wildlands.

Topo Map Dreams

When I was young, I would sit with a topo map. The dreamer in me would dream. Many times, myself and fellow dreamers, group dreaming, would look at blank spots and plan cross-country treks to far off and unknown places. Excitement and chills would come over us. The time would come, and we'd go. One adventure after another.

That love of maps has always been with me. Even today I can sit with a topo map and dream the land alive. I can see the animals, lakes, meadows, mountains, and vistas. The land comes right off the map.

It's very comforting to know that wild places still exist in today's world. We must be ever vigilant to save and protect what we have.

Trails lead me on a journey before I even walk them. My eyes follow the trails before me, taking me to a place where nothing else matters.

First Experience

I saw Roosevelt Lake for the first time from a distance when I was eleven years old. It was painful to leave, but it never left my mind- it called me back when I was thirteen.

My science teacher, Mr. Robertson, told me about Roosevelt Lake. I was intrigued, as it was clear it touched him as well. As we looked at the topographical map of Tuolumne Meadows, we found the lake, and I knew it was the lake I had seen two years earlier. Chills came over me. I knew I was going to go there.

It was the end of the school year, and I took home the map to show my dad, and we made plans for August. Off we went to the surplus store. We purchased Marine backpacks and down bags. We stocked up on mac n' cheese, canned chili, bread, and block cheese.

When we hiked in, I imagined the bears talking about the good food coming up the trail. As I would find out, Roosevelt rarely had bears. Bears don't spend a lot of time above tree line.

Roosevelt Lake sits at 10,000 feet. It's wide open. It's always ready to reveal its gifts to those who listen.

Our hike up was hot and sweaty, a steady climb all the way. From Young Lakes it was a half day, cross country, no trail to the lake. When I came over the rise and saw the lake, I was stunned that beauty of this kind existed. I was about to enter the place of my heart.

To share that place with my father for the first time was something special. We walked down to the shore and made camp. We stayed in that cathedral for two weeks, wandering the highlands above, climbing the peaks, fishing, tracking, and dreaming my future life into reality.

My father was the perfect companion, as he rarely spoke, and loved to be alone, allowing me endless time wandering by myself.

I was never the same after that initial trip. The lake not only gave me visions and clarity on my future life, in looking back, it also helped heal some childhood wounds. At the time, I didn't know how important that was.

I grew up Catholic and I always wondered what Heaven was like. I was told it was the best anything could be. Even at my young age, I knew I had entered Heaven on Earth.

I'm in my sixties now, and throughout my life my photography has taken me out thousands of miles off trails throughout the West and Canada. I live in Mount Shasta, California, often described as where Heaven and Earth meet. I would agree with this statement. Yet throughout my life, many times Roosevelt Lake has always called me back to that slice of Heaven.

Beneath My Feet

I travel far and wide. Always I come back to the ground I stand on. Always something new to explore right beneath my feet.

How I walk matters to some living being, ever mindful of my fellow Earth travelers.

The Ridge

I was on my afternoon, get-away-from-people-hike, along what is known as The Ridge, in the East Bay foothills. Unfortunately for me, more and more people began to frequent the trail. Along with people came noise and congested trails, exactly what I needed a break from.

I was having a rough day and needed to escape for some peace. I almost ran to the ridge in a panic to get away from the stress. When I got to the parking lot, I already knew it wasn't going to be the experience I thought. To my shock, it seemed that overnight the ridge was discovered, and the groups of people were flooding into my refuge.

I hiked up anyway. When I got to the top of the ridgeline there wasn't anywhere I could look across the rolling hills and ravines, without seeing people hiking or mountain biking. They were off on different trails, but still, they were there.

On this day, I later realized those people were my gift. I chose to break my routine and get off trail. I started walking, almost on a mission at a brisk rate, as if I were running away from the world. I had no destination in mind, I just needed to get away.

I walked through the old olive orchard and headed out the other side, and down a hillside through scattered, massive oak trees. I stood for a moment to wait to be pulled somewhere, and in the distance a movement caught my eye. I crouched down, not wanting to be seen by anyone. I just wanted to be alone.

I stayed still for a minute and then saw more movement gliding across the ground. It was a wild tom turkey, all puffed up. My angst started to fade into a smile. I took a deep breath and slowly let go.

Immediately, more turkeys joined the tom out of the bushes. I wanted to get closer to them and a primal instinct kicked in. I walked closer to the flock, one slow step at a time, with my eyes gazing down.

It didn't take too long to be within 45 feet of them. I kept my pace slow and eased my way down, and sat up against one of the Live Oak trees. Again, I closed my eyes, took a deep breath, and let go. When I opened my eyes the tom approached me, now with his feathers draped down, feeding on the ground.

He wasn't threatened by my presence. He knew I was there, but I felt it was ok. Soon, my feeling was validated. The entire flock of forty turkeys followed his lead and began to circle around me as they were feeding. The hens were now within arms distance of me, but I didn't move. I was so honored to be accepted into their family as a guest.

It was then that I was glad I wasn't alone. I had so many friends surrounding me. I felt safe. I felt welcomed, and I felt home.

I spent an hour with the turkeys, and then they moved on, down into the thick trees, and I walked back to my truck full of love. I was no longer angry or frustrated. I was just happy that I left the trail and found my bird people.

"Wilderness is a gift to those who are ready to receive it." - E.K.

Wander
Go for a barefoot walk in the woods, no time restraints or destinations. Observe your surroundings. Walk slowly with an open heart. Feel with all your senses.
Be all the living things. Walk in their way. This is how you know home and what is needed to help her thrive.

Take reasonable risks. Go where you're not supposed to go. Seek connection in nature in the places that don't call to you. These places have secrets for you.

Wilderness areas make me feel humble and welcomed Home. I feel a part of the Earth. I feel I belong. Sometimes I don't know where I am, but I'm not lost, I'm happy.

Step off trail and take a nap. Sink into the Earth. It may be the deepest sleep you'll ever know.

No Trails In The Ocean
Snorkel. Scuba dive. Explore not only the oceans, but rivers and creeks. There is so much to explore in this underwater world. It seems to be a separate planet than the one we live on, but it's all a part of who we are. Get excited and begin your journey into the quiet places.

Break The Rules
From the time we are born many of us are told it's not safe to be in nature. Fear finds a home deep within us. Nature calls us and we ignore her.

Rules are everywhere, signs are everywhere. At the beach, if you followed every rule and sign, you'd be paranoid, and wouldn't ever move.

At parks there are so many signs you can't even function in a heart-felt way, as your mind is so busy figuring out what's allowed and what's not.

I understand some signs and rules are needed, and it's important to be respectful. Assuming you're a kind, reasonable person, trust your intuition. Be reasonably safe, but not too safe. Go for it, just go for it. Be crazy in love with the fun and excitement. Let nature lead you.

Signs and rules are not meant to be blindly followed. Question their validity, and if safe and respectful, let yourself go. It's a type of freedom that feeds us. It's a pathway home.

Go Wilderness
When you're on a hike take that side trail. That trail to nowhere. Be uncertain. Just go. You might discover something that's been waiting for you. If you don't go, you'll never know.

When you wander off trail, the tree elders are there waiting to make you smile.

Go Out Alone
Nothing is more rewarding than going into nature alone - whether it's for an hour, a day, a week, or a month.

I've been out in the wilderness for months at a time. I crave this alone time. It connects me to nature perhaps more than anything I've ever done. Every moment, I open my senses fully without the distraction of another person. Just the good Earth and me.

It's great to go with friends, do that as well, but going alone puts your relationship with the land one on one, no distractions.

Go as simple as possible. Practice your skills and go into the wilderness with almost nothing. To know the wilderness, it's imperative to rid yourself of all things that get between you and the living wild.

There's a blessing in the wilds, which you can only find when you live wild, with the land. Often these times become vision quests. We have profound insights into life, and our personal lives. We can achieve great clarity about our place in the world and find our purpose – life's meaning.

Perhaps best of all, we get to know ourselves in ways we couldn't imagine. It's like going back to our birth, we find our true selves, before all the stuff of life got in the way. We find who we really are.

Nature truly becomes our teacher as we slow down and let the Earth into our being. We are reminded of our ancient roots with the land. We begin to remember what we have forgotten in our busy lives. Our memories come flooding back. We nourish our heart, mind, and soul.

We begin to walk backwards into the future – bringing our ancient Earth truths with us as we move forward into our lives. Perhaps most importantly, we become protectors of the Earth.

It is in these solo moments that our relationship with the Earth strengthens as we allow our trust to grow. We become more honest and authentic, just as the wilderness is.

We relate to animals and plants more intimately. You ultimately learn you're not alone, animals, trees, plants, water, everything is alive. In going alone, you learn how to let the living land and all its life forms become your relations. All the things beautiful, all the things bright, all the things woody and furry, all the things that fly and swim, all become friends, and they ask, "What took you so long? We've been waiting for you. Welcome Home friend."

Seek out the empty spaces and greet the abundance of Beings already there.

Push Comfort Zones

Get uncomfortable. Get in the cold ocean. Most people just look at it. Play in it. Explore the sea caves. Swim in the tide pools.

Be careful and use common sense, but be in it. No one else is doing it, so we don't. Humans flock to one spot like sheep. We pile on top of each other instead of exploring other areas.

We're all in the process of living, but also actively dying too, so what are we waiting for? Why leave this planet without fully checking out what we are curious about? Know it by having your own experience of it.

Have a moment of bravery and step off trail ten feet. Build on your courage and step off a little farther next time.

Why let someone else tell you what you should and shouldn't do? Pay attention to safety and respect an area that needs care, but it's everyone's world. Explore, explore, explore.

The Wilds

Go off to the wilds and taste the wildness on the wind, in the water, on the land. You get more aware when you get more wild. Let go of the awkwardness and become the wild.

Let the wilderness in you play. When you harness wild in you it builds up and acts out in other ways. Give the wilderness inside you room to explore and play.

Live your dream. Get off trail. Get out of your comfort zone. Immerse in spirit. Commit to adventure. Run in the wild and find all the answers you'll ever need, or it will be soul death.

Pay Attention

As you are wandering, be aware when you enter different terrain. Any time you transition from one area to another, feel the change. If you come out of the woods to a meadow, stop at the edge of the trees for a second and feel the energy shift. Who is there to greet you?

Follow The Leader

There are times when I'm out walking with no set direction, and I play follow the leader with our pack of dogs. I follow wherever the lead dog goes, even if that means crawling under low branches and crossing through streams.

When I do this, I'm usually experiencing a part of our land I haven't been on before, and probably wouldn't have explored because it wasn't a convenient route.

Sometimes my ego gets in the way, and I ask myself, "How old am I?" I then quiet my mind and remind myself I am as old as I act. Just because I'm not an adolescent, it doesn't mean I need to stop learning through exploring like a child. It's the best way to learn and live fully with no concern of judgment. Nature doesn't judge. It just is.

It's exciting to know that after a couple of decades living here in the mountains, I have many adventures on our own land still to come.

Creating Hidden Spaces

When cleaning our woods for fire safety, I always do my best to keep it a bit wild so it's not too manicured. I also want to keep the habitat for those who need shelter in the underbrush.

I intentionally clear out little spaces off trail, just enough to lure people in. I like to create intimate spaces that trigger people's curiosity to get off the main trail, to explore and find these treasures.

When they find these little hide-a-ways it feels like a special invitation for them. It helps them get comfortable with getting off trail so they can make their own discoveries.

Some of these sit spots are left without any changes to the surroundings. In other places there are log or rock benches or a piece of Earth art. Each space feels personal and blends in with the environment.

At the end of the week, it makes me feel good when students talk around the campfire circle about the secret places they found on the land. Some of the younger kids feel like they were the only ones that have ever been there, and they know something others don't. The land makes them feel special and welcomed.

The biggest compliment we get, and validation that the land is doing its work, is when a student says the best part of their week at Headwaters was that they had free time to explore. They didn't feel over controlled and didn't have to ask permission for everything thing they did.

We do set guidelines, but then we give our trust, and expect them to be responsible. Getting off trail for us, can sometimes mean letting go of strict precautionary rules, to allow nature, the true teacher, to step in and guide.

Each year, when those same students return to Headwaters, they always go back to their special spot for a visit. It feels comforting to know that space is always there for them.

Getting off trail, can mean even just a few steps away.

Climb Mountains

When we look at the stars, we dream. We dream our lives into physical reality. Certain things in nature do this to us, such as staring into campfires. Then there's mountains. Mountains call to our very soul. I believe they are the place the gods go for vision time.

The majesty of mountains calls to people. When you look at mountains, they draw you in to climb them. Often, we climb them with our eyes, and their beauty ignites awe and reverence. We climb with our mind and imagination. Sometimes we climb with our bodies. At the top all things become clear.

It's good and wonderful just to know mountains exist on our Earth. They hold space for all life. Mountains often seem overwhelmingly beyond touch, and yet they call to us, and we go.

Whatever it is, and I must admit, much of the calling is a mystery, it's not about summiting, we just need to get on the mountain.

Shastina

For decades I looked at Mt. Shastina, the mountain peak to the side of Mt. Shasta, and saw its shape as a heart, on its eastern facing side. The mountain-sized heart of Shastina has always been so perfect and amazing.

Maybe just ten years ago, I was on a walk on my land with my dogs and stopped to look up at the mountain, and my mind was blown. Instead of seeing the heart, which is obviously still there, a man's face appeared, looking upwards and towards the north. It is a native man with a long braid who seems to be in deep thought.

How had I never seen him before? Now I can never not see him. He appears more obvious in winter with a dusting of snow, but he's always there.

I never tire of looking at mountains. There is always something new revealed.

Think Like A Mountain

Thinking like a mountain is to observe with no judgments, to hold space with honor, to be bigger than life and not care. Thinking like a mountain is to be great for more than yourself.

This troubled world needs many people thinking like mountains. Many dreamers- manifesting dreams into reality, into mountains.

My Mountain

Mountains speak a language that can only be learned from being with them. I sometimes think mountains could save our Earth from us humans. I'm not sure why, but I know this.

When I look at Mt. Shasta my eyes travel the patterns of rock, snow, and trees. Always carrying me to the top where I touch the edges of Heaven. I feel the good in humans. My own darkness slips away, and I become the bird songs. My soul rises to meet the stars, and for a moment in time, I find hope for our lost world.

Mountains seem to know things. People seem to know this about mountains. To live where Heaven and Earth touch is to know both worlds.

I believe that nature on Earth is Heaven, and Heaven is nature, but brighter. Mountains know this. Mt. Shasta knows this.

Mt. Shasta speaks this through her beauty. Her beauty calls us home. The call gives birth to the caretaker in me. My heart becomes alive with love. Heaven's mountains become my home, and I find peace and hope for our loving Earth.

My eyes soar to the top of the mountain on eagle wings. The Earth comes into my feet, and I am Earth, I am mountain, I am the good of all the people. For that moment I am the best I can be. My life's meaning is clear: to love our Earth back to health, and to sing the bird song.

Alpenglow

The first time I hiked into the Sierra Nevada, the land of rugged peaks reaching for the sky, I became enchanted.

As I climbed into the high country above 10,000 feet, I left the trees behind. This was a landscape of granite rock. Perhaps it was my Irish heritage, but the rocks seemed to speak to me. They became alive. I became alive! Their beauty awakened the sacred in me, and I became the landscape.

Then something remarkable and unexpected happened. I was walking in a meadow covered in purple heather, and tarns full of frogs, when I looked up —alpenglow, the last light before dark had arrived.

The granite glowed red and pink as if it were coming from inside the stone. This color turned on a light in me. My whole being touched this light.

I changed that night, forever. Everything in my life began to glow -alpenglow. This moment was extraordinary to witness. This was a defining moment for me in nature. I began to see beauty as a living being. Through this pink glow I became a better person. I was inspired to make my life this beautiful.

To this day I seek out alpenglow. I believe each time I witness it, my heart and soul glow and grow. This growth is a profound way mountains speak their language. Alpenglow is an honored gift received with gratitude.

Question

Why do humans love to climb high? Trees, mountains, hills, anything high. What calls us? When we reach the top and we look outward, one answer becomes clear, we can see more of our world. We always want to see more. Let this calling to be higher remind you to be willing to always see more.

Commitment

When you climb a mountain, you *know* commitment. You begin by looking at the top. This ignites a personal journey of trust. One step at a time, one breath at a time, muscles straining, body sore, mind drifting into rock.

The trust comes from mind, body, mountain, knowing each has its part. As the journey progresses a blending takes place between all three, a partnership. That's when the commitment to the top becomes unimportant. The journey, the mystery part of the climb takes hold and that's when the mountain leads the way.

Above Tree Line

Above the tree line is sacred space where the Gods meet to sing. A land of raw purity that speaks of immortality and timelessness. A land that bares the soul of the Earth. Above tree line is the gateway to where dreams are birthed.

Above tree line is simple beauty. In this lucid space we find our answers that have been knocking, open the door. Dreamland is here. This I know.

"Man always kills the things he loves, and so we the pioneers have killed our wilderness. Some say we had to. Be that as it may, I am glad I shall never be young without wild country to be young in. Of what avail are forty freedoms without a blank spot on the map?" - Aldo Leopold – A Sand County Almanac

Into The Wilderness

It was an overcast day. It seemed as if night was fast approaching at mid-day. My backpack was heavy as I was just starting my journey, and I wondered if I should make camp early or keep moving.

As I walked through unfamiliar terrain, I wondered if any human had walked where I was walking. I must have been a hundred miles or more from any road – paved or dirt. I secured my .22 rifle that I used to shoot small game, and my fishing rod on the side of my backpack. I had decided that even with the approaching storm, it would be better to hike to a good camping site, rather than huddle under rocks on the ridge where I had been traveling.

As I came down the ridgeline, I stopped cold, as I had come upon what were decidedly fresh, wolf tracks. I was both exhilarated and afraid at the same time.

I had dreamed of the wolves laying down with me at night. I had imagined they would know that I would never hurt them, and they would befriend me and protect me on my wilderness journey.

Of course, daydreams and reality collide with the sight of fresh tracks. I stood still and listened for branches breaking or any other audible sign that they could be close. I scanned the sky for ravens to see if perhaps a fresh kill was close by. As much as I loved wolves, I didn't want to happen upon a pack of hungry wolves around a fresh kill.

***

I was 17 years old when I had decided to go to the Canadian wilderness to live off the land. I had seen a National Geographic film on the Nahanni River, in the Northwest Territories, explored by river rafters, and I knew that's where I wanted to go.

My years spent with many mentors had prepared me for the trip I was to create. It was going to be my Rite of Passage from high school into the world. It would be a four-month walk-about, a spiritual journey that would take me into the deepest parts of the wilderness, and within myself.

It's funny how the power of some experiences in life don't reveal themselves immediately – how years can pass or even decades pass before the power of such a moment in time can be felt. I realize now how truly profound it was at that age to plan such a solo journey, and of how it was such a defining moment in my life.

I graduated from high school early. I was ready to be out in the world living. I took as many extra classes as I could, and escaped the confines of those stifling walls in April, and headed north to Canada.

I drove an old, Datsun pick-up, outfitted with a camper shell, loaded with my gear. I was a traveling universe unto myself. I spent a couple of weeks hiking through wilderness beauty in the coastal rainforest, along the North Coast Trail.

I traveled through Glacier National Park, and on to Jasper and Banff, and then north, where towns get further and further apart, and where true wilderness begins.

After driving a couple of days on dirt roads past the last of the old mining towns, I reached a spot where I could hike into the Nahanni River. Though only about two miles separated me from the last town and the wilderness, it was a two-mile eternity.

I found the perfect off-road spot to park the truck, where I camo'd the hell out of it with willow branches and long grass. I did have the presence of mind to leave a note on the dashboard telling where I was going, and to not tow it away.

I scouted for animal tracks to get a sense of what was around and what I should be looking out for. I was fortunate that the tracks next to the river were plentiful, and told a story of the daily lives of all the creatures in the area.

I was delighted to find wolverine tracks, as I respected the wolverines for their aggressiveness and their elusiveness. They embody pure wilderness – so rarely seen in nature – they are efficient hunters and fearless, even facing down predators larger than themselves. It was a goal of mine to see a wolverine, and over the four months I saw numerous tracks, but only glimpsed one from high on a ridge as it traveled a valley below.

I can hardly put into words the exhilaration I felt being in that first camp. It had been my life's dream to be in country where I was the intruder, where bears, wolves and wolverines were the prominent inhabitants. It was equally exhilarating as there were no other people in sight. I was the last man standing, the last man on Earth, and rather than fear, I felt a complete state of grace. I was home.

I studied the topo maps religiously, as there were no known trails. I had to depend upon my innate sense of direction, but I also believed for me there was no such thing as being lost in the wilderness. I was wandering and adventuring and experiencing.

I also had the river as my guide and benchmark, and the mountain peaks were as good as road signs. I observed the direction of the sun as it traversed the sky to keep my sense of direction.

Light is a wonderful tool – its fusion with the Earth and plants is different everywhere we go. As a photographer, I was captivated by light. The sun's play through the trees throughout the day was subtle, but observably different from other terrain I had traveled through.

One of my major concerns on the trip became one of my greatest joys. I loved fishing – I mean I loved fishing. I knew to get the protein I needed I would have to find fish. I had experienced from California rivers and lakes, that abundant fish could be a hit or miss thing, not so here.

It seemed whenever I dipped my line into the river pools, a fish would be caught before the lure hit the water. I could catch fish with my bare hands if I was patient, and hid in the shade by the river's edge. It tested my quickness of eye and was just plain fun.

With that concern so quickly dispelled, it left me more time to spend observing the animals and plants and exploring.

It had been my intent from the beginning to track Grizzly Bears. I knew the bears in this area were seldom hunted, so they didn't have the same level of fear of humans as they do in the U.S. I also knew enough about the great Grizzlies to keep my distance, and let my presence be known quietly and calmly.

If we can be reincarnated from animals, I am the reincarnation of a Grizzly Bear. I look like a bear, I eat like a bear, I play like a bear, I am quick to anger like a bear, I even smell like a bear at times, and I certainly snore like a bear. Tracking bears in Canada was like going home to reunite with my brothers.

I was fortunate to find the tracks of a female Grizzly and her cubs. I followed them for a good two weeks. It was summer, and food was plentiful in the densely vegetative valleys. Their range was more compact than the 100 square miles I had heard bears need.

When I lost their tracks, I knew to scout the riverbeds until I picked them up again. Bears like to fish, and I knew they needed the water, so the mud prints were steppingstones to the living treasure.

One afternoon, I had been following the mother and the cubs at a safe distance, through a breathtaking meadow, blanketed with wildflowers and lush grasses. She and the cubs were cruising the riverbed below. One of the cubs was splashing in the river honing their fishing skills, and the other cub was a distance from mom, closer to me.

I inched my way down the hillside. I knew the mother was aware of my presence, as she would occasionally stand on her back legs, a towering figure of fur and muscle, and huff and snort in my direction.

I got within about 100 feet of her, hiding behind a big rock in the middle of the meadow, but she knew where I was, and she was getting very nervous. She started chomping her teeth, and huffing and grunting for her cubs to come near. I suppose she could smell me as well, and when the cubs didn't respond, her grunting and huffing became more intense.

I figured at that point I should show myself, hoping that it would calm her down a bit. I stood up and walked about a foot away from the rock so she could clearly see and smell me. I knew enough to not look at her. My eyes were downcast, and between the blink of an eye and the next, she was two feet from me.

Her breath was hot and putrid. I literally had to freeze every muscle so that I wouldn't run. I thought I hadn't had time for fear, until I felt the warm rush of urine down the side of my leg. Through it all, I was certain she wouldn't kill me. I hoped she felt we were kindred spirits.

As quickly as she had charged me, she turned and barked at her cubs to follow her across the river and up the hill. It was so quick and scary and exhilarating, and one of the most memorable moments of my life.

It was a peak experience, which for me means that the great mystery, that is nature, creates a small opening, allowing you to feel the connection with all things. In those moments, all things are connected in a state of grace - it's perhaps the place where we touch our knowing of God. It is where we understand we are not only a small part of something so much bigger, but as small as we are, we are also necessary.

Many years have passed, but the memories of that time in the wilderness are as fresh and pronounced as the tracks in the riverbank mud. I wonder who I would have become if I hadn't had that adventure at that time in my life.

As I reflect on why and how I have been able to live so many of my dreams, I realize that I followed my inspirations, rather than the usual drumbeat of societal dictates to go to college, get a nine to five job, earn money, raise a family, retire, and wonder way too late where it all went.

I also wonder why as a society we try to redirect a young person's inspirations. We certainly recognize inspiration in gifted children because they are so much further ahead than their peers – be it in math, science, or the arts – but we ignore the less pronounced inspirations of the so-called normal child.

The gift my parents gave me was the freedom to pursue what inspired me, rather than push me towards their expectation of what they thought should have inspired me.

***

I had been tracking the wolves for a few weeks, and while I saw so many signs of paw prints, fur on bushes, and lay spots, I hadn't seen the wolves physically. They seemed to be elusive spirits of the forest.

The howl of the wolves at night is both chilling and beautiful. The exhilaration of primal communication resonated at the base of my spine. It traveled like hot liquid into my gut, surged toward my throat, and finally hit the electrical impulses of reason in my brain, where fear automatically took over. I wanted to howl a response, but I was afraid I would anger them by my arrogance.

While sitting at my campfire one night, the illuminated eyes of the wolves from the light of the fire, circled around me. Startled from their ghost-like presence, survival was more prevalent in my mind than inspiration. I was humbled and nervous and excited all at once, but they never crossed that invisible, comfort boundary.

After a week of faceless, glowing eyes by the fire, I came to understand that these characters had no intention of eating me. Wolves by mythic connotation have a bad rap. In reality, they have loving families that take excellent care of their young. They have an efficient hierarchy that needs the companionship of the pack to thrive.

I realized that while I had been focused on my still novice tracking skills, the wolves were the ones that had been tracking *me* out of curiosity. That was a "wow" moment for me. I had wanted to see the wolves so badly, and they were just as curious as I was.

I felt a primal howl might be good for all of us, so I bellowed in a bad wolf accent. I was a little disappointed the wolves didn't respond, but I think it was because they were laughing too hard.

From that moment on I lost my fear, I felt safe in their home, and felt a mutual respect of space. This became a sacred encounter that I carry with me still today.

The wolves stayed around my camp many nights, and I slept peacefully knowing my wild canine friends were sharing their wilderness with me.

Though I never saw them up close, I could feel their presence most of the time I was in the woods. I felt they protected and looked after me from a short distance, maybe for no other reason than I was a source of amusement for them, and a kindred, wild spirit.

***

After some initial loneliness, I acclimated to the silence, or rather the lack of city noise. There was plenty of noise in the woods, but it had a rhythm and cadence that was meditative and calming.

There was the occasional screech and blood-curdling cry of an animal meeting its predatory stalker. Those jarring sounds kept me aware and vigilant, but not fearful. They blended with the mellow sound of life as usual.

Over the next few months, I encountered many Grizzlies, mostly from a distance, wolverines, countless birds, foxes, ubiquitous squirrels, and chipmunks. I fished to the point where I became the fish, and knew its hiding spots and habits.

As fall approached, I knew my time in that sacred place was coming to an end. I felt a deep sorrow at having to leave the forest, and all the creatures that had become my friends. I felt totally accepted by all the animals, plants, trees, and even the insects.

Nature's pace is slow, but the time passed way too quickly. I was certain that this was how mankind was meant to live – in concert and harmony with nature. I knew that I would never be afraid to be in nature for long periods of time, but I also knew that living as I did, so close to the heart and spirit of the Earth for all those months, would never happen again. This experience was an initiation into the next path that I would take.

Though by nature I prefer a more solitary lifestyle, life had different plans for me that I needed to listen to. That period was the beginning inspiration and training for creating Headwaters Outdoor School, in Mount Shasta.

Part 3

Earth Philosophy - Earth Spirituality

Bridging our nature awareness and physical skills with the language of the Earth - Connecting with nature through heart.

Chapter 18
Open Your Heart

Opening your heart is all you need to do to have a personal relationship with nature. It's as if your heart has huge arms and hands, and the hands reach out and pull all the land before you into your whole being.

This can be a life changing moment. Often it can be very emotional because you're reclaiming your sense of belonging as a child of the Earth. Nature lovers have these moments on occasion, and to live this way as your baseline is truly wonderful. I believe our ancestors lived this way always.

When you open your heart in nature it is open in all parts of life. This is what will change the world. This is what will help people to live in harmony and balance with all beings.

When you achieve this heart connection, the next journey begins at the very soul of nature. Much of this discovery is personal to you. It cannot be understood in the logical mind.

Imagine for a moment, the complexity of your body; mind, heart, blood, and body parts. Now imagine the Earth, and we humans are just a part of the Earth within the Universe. Imagine the heart connection of it all.

Whether your journey into nature's heart leads you to a tree or animal or a forest, it's all good. The journey alone is worth this simple effort.

Start with small steps. Open your heart to something you already love, perhaps a tree or animal. Go deeper and you'll feel a natural calling for more. It's up to you if you choose to go.

I warn you, at some point you will not be able to go back. You'll find yourself forever walking into the Earth-heart. Let your heart be your wilderness guide. Happy traveling.

Love - The Great Mystery

Bring love alive through your relationship with our Earth. Our master teachers of love are the animals, the trees, and all Earth's beings.

Go into nature and let yourself get lost in your love of Earth. Lose your ego and get wild. Get to know love and all its moods and ways. Nature's beings will be celebrating with you.

Knowing Earth's unconditional love is truly nourishing. Your soul and nature's soul are one. Reclaim this awareness and live fully as you were meant to live. Earth-heart, human-heart as one. Take this love out into your whole life, and mutual love will find you.

Love is a mystery; this we all know. It can't be explained in a logical way. One thing I do know is that it's real, it exists, and we all want it. All living Beings want love. We thrive in love.

I have hope for our future because I believe in love. It has guided my life. The Earth and my mother, and of course my animal companions have shown me what pure love is.

***

I recently had open heart surgery. I was terrified to have this operation. I feared my heart would be damaged. I feared if I died while my heart was being operated on, I would lose my way without my heart to show me my next path.

I obviously didn't die, and the love given to me through the support from the surgeon, the nurses, my students, and of course my dearest friends and family were true gifts.

I felt the Earth and particularly the land I live on, Headwaters, and all its life, holding space for me. I was held by all, and I healed extremely well with this help.

The love just wells up in me and I cry. I mean I cry all the time. My heart is repaired and happy, and once again guiding me into my life. Love is showing me the way and I'm thrilled.

I believe in the ability of love's mysterious power to instantly make change. So, I have hope. I have hope full of love. This will be my path now fully. I won't turn back. Every day love will grow in me, and I will live it. Without love there is no purpose.

I do have days in a row for sure where my positive outlook gets derailed from the actions of the crazy dark side of humanity. On those days I take a walk with my dogs. I connect with the trees and the creeks by caretaking them. I walk the meadows in the rain, snow or sunshine, and I breathe in the unconditional love of nature. I recenter back to balance, and am grateful again, and again I have more hope for the world.

As you enter our Headwater's camp, there is a rock painted with the one word that can change everything. Love.

Let nature show you how to love, and then pass it on, it's all you need.

Your Heart To Earth Heart

Your heart sings its own song. It has its own feelings, its own stories, its own hopes and dreams, its own way of living. Your heart lives for you.

Earth-heart sings its own song. It has its own feelings, its own stories, its own hopes and dreams, its own way of living. Earth lives for you and all other life. One heart, your heart, Earth-heart, one song.

Receiving Blessings

Give blessings of love's good wishes to all things, to trees, water, and animals. A blessing is from the heart, a wish of a good life, a healthy life.

Open your heart and allow them to give you a blessing in return. Open to their love of shared life upon our Earth, and be well. Be blessed.

Live to love all beings. It's the meaning of life. Love so deeply you lose yourself. Have no fear, you will be found. It's the heart's path.

Walk as if your feet are connected to your heart. Speak to the Earth in this way. Heart walking is an act of kindness. Try it.

Love yourself fiercely -as fiercely as you love others. Love fully, unabashedly until your heart swells and floods with joy.

Give birth to love. Let it grow within you. Like a plant, nurture it.

What Matters Most

The thing that matters most is the size of your heart. How much love do you have in you? There's nothing more powerful in the world than love. When human beings come from a place of pure love, that's when we are at our best, that's when we have evolved to our highest level of being, and that's what matters. Strive to live there.

Step To The Side

The only way to dissolve negative energy is by overwhelming it with love. Love for the world is bigger than hate and ignorance. Huge, loving actions have more power, and will draw more attention and right action than false drama. False drama is based on the weakness of fear and uncertainty.

We meet anger with anger out of a defensive fear of being victimized. We ineffectively match our energy with another's head on, with the intention of strength through anger, instead of gaining our own power through compassion. Compassion dissolves walls. Anger only reinforces them.

When negative energy is coming at you, stay out of the emotion of it. Step to the side and allow the energy to flow by you, and no longer directly at you.

The negative energy will dissipate because there is nothing feeding into it. Kindness will dissolve the negative. It is a stronger energy, and contagious, and will reset the balance.

You will be the one still standing in balance, and in a position to help lift things back up in time.

An open heart doesn't mean weakness. It means you are strong enough to hold space, and stay grounded by stepping to the side, and observing with compassion, the unconscious fear flowing by.

Compassion Towards Nature

Compassion is a gift we can offer to our world. Nature gives us endless opportunities to express compassion. Compassion is a life path if we choose to live it. It will transform our consciousness and purify our spirit. Compassion is not something in us that we need to search for. We *are* compassion.

There are people in this world who show little compassion. Those that are able to, hold space for the rest, and keep the power and the medicine of compassion alive.

When we show compassion and back it up with action, we are fulfilling one of our reasons for our life on Earth. Embarking on this path, you'll find animals that need your help, and they will find you. A compassionate life is a spiritual life. It's a life of meaning and respect.

Often, compassion needs to be taken to the level of justice for nature, and more to the point, animals. We must protect these beings that need our help. To stand up for another being is an honorable deed.

When you know an animal needs help or a wrong is being done, and you do nothing, it is harmful to all souls. Help animals every single time they need help. Stop what you are doing and help.

If you do this, the flame inside yourself will glow with love's light. You will be one of the good ones. A human being, being good at the core. The inner medicine will be a healing to all animals that you help. In turn, these gestures will heal you as well.

We must do what is right by nature. It is our eternal test. If we live this way, we will be a hero to our planet, and our civilization. Compassion toward nature will equal compassion toward people. Compassion is contagious and will grow. Many of the answers we seek in our darker moments will be known, and problems will be solved. Love is pretty much the answer to all the questions we have.

A Story Of Compassion

This story of a lack of compassion is hard to believe, and yet it is true. The New York Blood Institute, tortured chimpanzees in their laboratories for years, supposedly for the benefit of humans.

When the lab was finished with their research, they dumped the chimps on an island off of Africa to die of starvation. Slowly, one by one, all the chimps died except for one, a male, that was able to survive the death of all his fellow chimps, his family, his friends.

An African man began to befriend this chimp and to feed him. Their friendship grew through time into a close bond. People have since become aware of this situation and money has been donated to help.

I personally worked with chimps for many years. They are truly our brethren. I loved them as much as anyone ever.

The compassion this man showed to this chimp is remarkable. It's an act of greatness that helps to counteract the cruelty of what the NY Blood Institute did. Science can be good, but not at the expense of another living being's soul.

Compassion is a direct way to connect with our Mother Earth. Practice it with all living things and be someone's hero.

Let your dog teach you about love. No judgment. Only loyalty of the heart.

The Bear

The bear came by again last night. The trail camera missed him. He was kind to us, leaving only snow tracks melted from rain, to birth wonder within us.

Bear came three other times this winter. Our precious beehive became the bear. Another night our garbage locked in our shed became the bear.

On another visit our camera took the bear's picture in front of our shed. Bear heard me in front of my house and ran off. Our shed was safe, bear was hungry. We have a situation that we are in as a result of living in and on wild land.

Thoughts came through me of killing the bear when I saw our bees freezing and dead. What was left of them was disturbing. A destroyed hive in the cold snow after the happy bear left full of honeycomb.

A neighbor of ours killed five bears last year. They ate his chickens and goats. That was very sad. I think about it a lot. I wonder what could be different. I would not kill a bear, after all I'm a human bear. I just couldn't do it. I was just sad.

I love this land more deeply knowing that bears live here too. Bears have many human qualities such as their destructive sides and big tempers. They are also deeply independent and love to explore.

Bears keep land wild and mysterious. They create a fire inside us that makes us more alive, more awake.

As I put myself inside this bear and walk his walk, my compassionate heart opens. I know it is hard to be a bear in these California mountains during climate-change. Instinct tells the bear to sleep in a den under an old growth tree, from December until March. Instinct also says this sleep must happen when it is cold and snowy.

A bear mother is a wonderful mother. The mother bear, pregnant with a baby, must sleep in winter to have and feed her baby that is born into a den. Bear life can't continue without this den time.

It's confusing to be a bear in these times of shorter winters, around humans with tasty bee honey and garbage. What to do? How to live? Questions for bears and humans. Good times, hard times, confusing times. This sounds like our times, human times.

I understand this bear. I feel his dilemma. My heart opens to his heart. I give him my respect, my love, my hope for a good life. I wish him good luck. My world is good because he visits it. So what if on occasion he messes it up?

I'll continue to send him vibes to stay away from my bees, bird feeders, chickens, garbage shed, compost, and garden. We'll continue to take his photo, hang bells on fences and doors, and spray ammonia around to throw off the scent.

His presence makes us all more alive and aware of our beautiful life on this magical land. He will take off at some point, or he might run into a neighbor with a gun. I hope not. I know one thing for sure, and that is I won't shoot him or harm him in any way. We'll work our relationship out in a good way. I must do this; it can't be any other way to be a good way.

So, Bear, thanks for stirring my pot. Thanks for getting me out of my comfort zone. Thanks for bringing wonder and mystery alive in me. Thanks for walking this precious Earth with me. Thanks for your medicine, protection, and wild spirit.

I Go To The Woods

I go to the woods because in the woods I feel alive, because in the woods I am home.
Home allows my heart to open wide, and in this opening the living Earth comes rushing into me. Earth-heart, my heart, one heart, a joining, a reunion.
I give my heart in trust to nature.
Letting myself feel what it is to be the Mother of all life.

Love of Earth, love of place is knowing love's secrets.
Love grows from this bond and in this love, I find myself, my best self, and I soar.
The Earth Caretaker is born in me, my path is clear.
Now I live it. I have to, or nothing happens. Nothing.

A Night In The Wilderness

My intention is to soak up love. Love of place, love of Spirit, deep love, and to sink into it until I dissolve into its flow. I don't know what that means, but it feels good. Good night love. Let me dream into you.

Honor Relationships

Acknowledge relationships and don't take them for granted. The love of another being is sacred. Relationships need to be tended to whether it is a human relationship or with an animal, or a relationship with the Earth, it is the same.

We want others to know us and who we are, and how we live, so we need to extend that same curiosity and interest out to them. It goes both ways. We need to open our hearts to others and truly listen. When you are listening to another being's story, listen with your heart so that the words or language spoken becomes medicine.

Apply your love of nature with your human relationships. You will learn the true meaning of natural love.

Be willing to risk being vulnerable. Why would you leave this planet at the end of your life with even 10% of your love held back?

Smile Medicine

Smile at the land, the trees, the water, the mountains. A smile lets it all in. Just receive it with a smile.

It's Not Enough

Once you have felt a true oneness, and you have an awakening to your connection to something bigger than each of us, go beyond gratitude and bring it to life.

You have a responsibility to do something in the world with that awareness. It's not enough to know we are all one, take it to the next level. Make your life an expression of your love of our Earth through action.

Love must be acknowledged to come alive, not just in the brain, but through your whole being.

Earth-Beat

Tim led a ceremony with a group of ten-year-old students. He led them in song while playing his drum. After the ceremony, one of the young participants meant to say she felt the heartbeat of the Earth, but what came out, and was much more accurate in my opinion was, "I felt the Earth-beat of my heart." She was much wiser than she even knew, and taught me how to describe what it is I ultimately feel.

Let the Moon glow into your heart and soul, and you will know the intimacy of the Moon.

Hope Is Alive

Hope is found in a harmonious beehive. Hope is found in an old growth forest. Hope is found in the life of oceans, and in the lush mountains. Hope is a living thing that allows us to move forward in a loving and good direction. Hope feeds us.

Ultimately love is the great hope that lives in us to guide our way through the storms of human life. Open your heart and let it out. Inspire people by your actions and give people hope.

Hope Through Chaos

I haven't thought about the true meaning of hope until I have honestly felt hopeless in the insanity of evil leadership, but without hope what else is there to hold onto?

I don't know for a fact that the sun will rise tomorrow, but I sure hope it does. So far it always has, and my heart tells me it will.

I hope humans start aggressively healing this beautiful planet we are a part of, even if it's not convenient. I hope people get that our lives depend on this.

I hope that the overwhelming darkness that has been taking over part of our population will fall through its own cracks, and the light will shine and dissipate what isn't right. I hope.

I hope that more people will awaken and do the right thing. I hope that amazing changes will come of this climate crisis. Many times, in the face of disasters people come together and rebuild stronger communities. I hope this will be so.

My heart tells me I can always hope…and that's the first step.

A Miracle - The Heart

Consider all the living beings that have hearts. Empathy is the direct connection to all beings with hearts. In fact, empathy is guided by the heart.

Fill your heart with love's medicine by practicing empathy. One cannot be without another. Two friends, partners along the way, mutual guides to a richer life, living life as one heart through empathy.

Being empathic fills your soul, and it is a life purpose fulfilled. Life with meaning, life with soaring spirit.

The heart is truly a gift. It works for our bodies, pumps our blood and it connects to that spirit of love.

To live well on our planet, we must allow our heart to be our guides, our trusted friends, into this uncertain future. It's the hope for all life on our Earth.

Give the heart the freedom and trust to take us on our next journey of human evolution. Our future is unclear on our planet. With heart as our guide, I'm confident it will be a wonderful exploration into a new land. How fun and fulfilling. It's the only successful way forward.

Love's light will carry the day. This is my hope and dream. Our Earth is the true embodiment of love. Let Earth show us the way forward. This is my hope.

Finding heart stones is nature's way of teaching the value and symbolic language of Earth-Heart.

Nature Is A Wonderful Teacher Of Love

Let your love grow as a tree grows. Then let your love flow as a river flows, fingering outward into our world. In the end, love is the only hope for human life on Earth. It's the medicine that we can master by just being it.

Love is energy we can't physically see, but we can see it expressed through someone or something. We can feel love, but we can't grasp love and put it in a bottle and contain it. Yet with all these contradictions, we all agree that love exists.

As confusing as love is, it is truthfully always the answer. So, be the love that you would want to receive. As love blossoms within you, let our loving, life-giving Earth be your guide.

Those times when you just can't show love to others, keep going, and be loving to yourself. Don't give up. Ever.

Let the sun that shines into your heart be the light and warmth that fills all beings around you.

Love Always Creates A Circle

To feel love of nature fully you must first be able to receive it. To receive love fully you must be able to give love fully to all things.

Love is round like the Earth, like a bird's nest, like the moon, like the seasons, like a hug. Love always creates a circle. The circle of life is a circle of love.

Love is what makes life worth living for all beings. In the end, it's what really matters. Be a part of the circle of love, of life. This is a life path worth living. Live to love.

Chapter 19
Go Into The Mystery

We all love a good mystery and nature is an endless mystery. We are raised in this modern world with science as the definitive truth. I love science and believe it is important, but when we approach nature from a mind that needs proof for everything, then in nature we miss almost everything. We tend to close our minds, and countless moments to connect with our natural world pass us by.

Many of our native ancestors regarded the spiritual side of nature as the "Great Mystery." They knew what they saw or felt was real and didn't need proof. They trusted their intuition. They didn't have science, they only had experience, which they trusted through direct interaction with the world they lived in.

Don't be afraid to be wrong. Is there even such a thing as wrong? I don't think so. Just open yourself up and immerse yourself in our natural world, and let the mystery come flooding in.

Trust in the mystery. It is vital to the evolution of our Earth Soul, that place that lives inside us that doesn't need proof of anything, that place that longs to explore our Earth with no purpose, other than deeper connection, deeper love.

Mystery is that place of wonder, of curiosity, the Dreamland of our Earth. Be ok with mystery. Bring the idea of living mystery alive in you.

Embrace nature's mystery. We know that tangible mystery exists, often we see it with our own eyes. Sometimes our other senses get involved. Our intuitive side knows the mystery can be of a spiritual nature or a miraculous event. It's a miracle or simply a breathtaking moment of beauty and connection.

When we are truly comfortable in our own body physically and spiritually, and are ok with ourselves, and standing in our own personal power, insightful and enriching worlds tend to open to us. When we are not guarded, we are open to receiving the mystery and interacting with the ultimate teacher of it, our Earth.

Science is wonderful, so is mystery. Remember there are no limits, enjoy both. It is a wonderful way to live life.

Science has answered many mysteries. To me science just makes the mystery more amazing. It's a miracle that we humans can even use science. In our quest for answers, science only leads us down paths towards more unknowns. We learn more, and the mystery simply becomes more amazing and more of a mystery.

We must be comfortable within ourselves to receive the mystery. It's a sacred journey that allows our lives to unfold in layers, revealing an all knowing wisdom along the way.

The old people said, "If it's real, it's real. Many wonderful mysterious things happen in nature. They can't all be explained or understood with the logical mind."

The wise people said, "It's real to you, and you feel it, then it's real." Mystery keeps the wonder alive in us, it's a good thing to keep us curious.

Belonging

When I was about 10 years old, I had my first experience with a "calling" while visiting my grandfather in Montana. I didn't really understand what the urge was inside me, but I knew that I was supposed to do something. Whatever it was, it was a good feeling.

I had been going through horrors with dark people for a couple of years, and I had become accustomed to fear and bad feelings, so a feeling that was good when I was not immersed in nature, was not normal for me.

While I was cleaning the chicken coop, that good urge kept at me like an insistent fly. When I finished with my chores, I decided to wander and let the feeling take me wherever it would. I wandered along the rough, dirt track that disappeared into the thick, cedar and pine woods. About a mile from my grandad's farm, I found a clearing. In the clearing was a rounded structure with a big, fire pit in front of it.

Men from the Flathead Reservation ranches were there talking and stoking the fire. I was fascinated. It seemed like a scene from one of my books about the old west, and I had stepped back in time.

I watched from what I thought was a hidden spot, but one of the men had seen me. He had beautiful, black hair that hung in a braid down his back, and he wore a beat up "ol' timer's" hat, pulled down tight. His eyes were brown and gentle, and seemed to twinkle with a welcome, pulling me from my hiding place and into their world.

All the men were friendly, and each one told me a bit about what they were doing. They told me it was a sweat lodge made from bent willow, and alder sticks, and covered with canvas. It was a dome shape with an entry low to the ground because they humbled themselves to Mother Earth when they entered her Earthly womb.

The rocks were heated in the pit until they were red-hot. They were then carried into the lodge, and water was poured over them to create the steam that filled the lodge. The steam bathed their bodies, as they sweat out any toxins, both physical and emotional.

The door was closed while this happened so they could pray and sing in darkness, as if they had gone back into the body that gave them life. When they emerged, they would be re-born, regenerated, humbled, and reinvigorated.

My family was Catholic, and the rigors of Sunday Catholicism wore heavy on me as a kid. I was hard pressed to dress up for the heavenly fathers, and I figured if that's what Jesus and God wanted, then I was one of the flock's black sheep, as I preferred the Earth's dirt to altar boy robes.

I remember thinking that there must be something more to religion than a priest telling us all how sinful we were. It never seemed to fit for me. My youthful experiences in nature suggested that there wasn't anything bad or evil in nature. Everything seemed to have its place and its purpose, and there wasn't any one thing, telling any other thing what to do.

The men told me that the sweat lodge was one of their spiritual practices, and they invited me to join. The difference between their practice and my family's, was certainly not lost on my young psyche. I knew when I entered the lodge, and the door flap was lowered, that I had crawled into something big that would affect me the rest of my life.

I sat in silence, listening to the chants and prayers in a language that I didn't speak or understand, yet the sounds and the music helped me transcend from not knowing to knowing.

I spent many summers sweating with the Flatheads. I was always quiet and overwhelmed because I was the only white person, and a kid; yet they were always welcoming and eager to teach me about the spirituality that exists in every living thing.

My new mentors taught me that Mother Earth's heartbeat is replicated by the drumbeat. They taught me that things found in nature such as rocks, feathers, bones, and sticks, have spiritual power and energy.

They placed their sacred items on an altar that was created from rock and wood, positioned prominently in front of the lodge, between the door and the fire. They called them medicine items, and placed them in pouches called bundles. They carried them until the power of the object was no longer needed, and then they gave them back to the Earth or gave them away to others who might need that energy.

They taught me that these items are not really ours to own, and the more we hoard their power, the quicker that power dissipates. They believed in giving away the things they deeply cared about.

That special group of men impressed upon me the power and spirit that pervade a clean, organized, and beautiful ceremonial area. They taught me that function and beauty were inseparable.

Drums, fire-making kits, shelters, rattles, and pipes worked better when time was spent on making them beautiful, thereby bringing in both spirit and life. I learned how to be creative by making things from nature. I learned to communicate with the object by shutting down my chatty brain, and allowing my intuition to guide my hand as I carved a piece of wood or soft stone.

Ultimately, what I took on as my spiritual practice was taught to me by those men who collectively became my spiritual teachers. What I chose to believe in wasn't just because they said so, but it was because it felt right for me. It resonated with me, and the practices I learned and use today are tools to help me with my own direct connection with what I call Spirit.

I had assumed that since I had a calling at such an early age that everyone did. As I got older and shared my hopes and dreams with my friends, I was surprised that they hadn't had such an experience.

In my teens, most of my friends just assumed they would follow in their father's footsteps or go to college and see what happened. They never seemed to have hunches about what they would do with their lives.

I found my release and my peace in nature, where I felt more at one with everything wild, than with people. I felt that God had talked to me through the spirit of plants and animals, and I felt the Mystery. I have always trusted my inner knowing, and I have always been rewarded with rich experiences.

***

The physical beauty of the High Sierra has always struck me. In middle school I hadn't hiked above timberline very much. When I had finally talked my dad into taking me to my teacher, Mr. Robertson's, special fishing spot, I could feel a tingling on the back of my neck. I knew when I got there how sacred a space it was. It was an amazing amphitheater. The few trees that were there grew out of the cracks and were low and gnarly looking, finding survival and life in the harshest of environments.

The climb to this special place was not often taken by people back then, and the wildlife was abundant. I imagined that Lewis and Clark, and the other brave adventurers, who traveled the great expanse of America had the same visions of wildlife.

As I climbed, I pretended that I was the first person discovering this part of the country. I was the first human to see these white, granite peaks where the marmots, deer and mountain lions prowled for food.

The ragged edges of stone blended into lush, green meadows and wetlands that were filled with the deafening croaks of frogs. Snakes slithered along the banks, easily catching their singing prey. Golden Eagles, hawks, and falcons soared and surveyed from above, waiting for just the right moment to dive for their dinner.

I had died, and each step was taking me closer to heaven. The grandeur of the little creeks filtering out of the glaciers, and the banks of melting snow with wildflower sprouts popping through the icy, white patches, filled me with pure happiness. I would roll around in the grass screaming with joy.

This was ecstasy, and I was drunk on the Earth's vibrating energy and brilliant color. My father and my friend thought I had gone mad. For a few hours, I believe I had. I had been called to a spot that had transported me to another realm of existence, and it still does. It is the number one spirit place for me, and I rue the day when I am too old to make the climb.

This is the place where I also truly learned how to gather food or sustenance for my soul. We know how to harvest food from the Earth. Some of us know how to identify wild edible plants that would feed us, yet how many of us know how to feed our soul?

We all appreciate a beautiful sunset or a full Moon. Many people like to stroll along manicured paths that take us through gardens or woods, and some of us like to get off the path. These are all things that connect us momentarily to nature and to the Mystery of a world, of a Universe that is larger than just us.

Feeding the soul is about gathering the spirit and essence, the medicine of a place, and of experiences. It's about sitting and looking at nothing and everything. It's about wandering with no destination in mind. Sometimes as you wander you feel so absolutely connected to that place that you wonder if you might have dreamed it into existence.

I have experienced incredible rainbows. I have walked paths in the wilderness with wild animals that chose to be in close proximity to me. I have felt the cry of birds that echoed deep inside me. These moments are sacred moments in nature. They are the Earth's Life Force letting us know that we too belong.

All those experiences are a part of who I am now. They have come into me, and as a result I share that energy with everyone I connect with. We all do that. We are the sum of all those rainbows, sunrises, sunsets, and sacred moments that we stop and take in.

The beauty of your soul feasting on nature is that there is no right or wrong, and you can't overeat.

Spirituality In Nature

The spiritual side of nature is that magical side of the world. It can't all be explained scientifically, such as the idea of spirit beings or elemental beings living on the land, or the idea that animals have soul spirits themselves.

It is a challenge to explain that trees and plants are living beings, that emit an energy of life you can relate with, on a level higher than just physical interaction.

It is difficult to explain that the Earth is a living being that is a spiritual thing, and that all beings upon her, including humans, are a part of her.

We can physically experience our five senses, our sight, our smell, hearing, taste, and touch. When we tune into our sixth sense it is the doorway to the spiritual side of nature, the ethereal side of nature. The spiritual side cannot always be observed on a physical level, and so it is difficult to wrap our minds around it.

Sometimes we talk about special moments that nature gives us, like sunsets, and sunrises, encounters with animals, moments of beautiful color, or flowers that come into our hearts and speak to us, without identifying where it is all coming from. Those are sacred, spiritual moments.

We feel connected to a space, and sometimes we don't know why, but it feels like it's our space, like we've been there, we're supposed to be there. Sometimes different parts of the world call to us. That's all spiritual.

So much of what's called the spiritual side of life is not visible to our eyes and not tangible. Yet, here's how you blend it all together, think about a tree you're going to climb. You stand in front of that tree, it's big and beautiful. Immediately you send out love and appreciation for the tree. The tree feels that energetically on a spiritual level, and it opens up to you.

As you're looking and using your physical eyes, you're appreciating the beauty, and the beauty starting to come into you, and you *feel* that beauty. This is when it is a spiritual interaction as well as physical.

When you put your hands on the tree and you begin to climb it, you can feel it bringing you up, holding you. You can also feel the strength of the tree, and you can feel the tree give you some of its history. You start to learn about some of its life as you climb it.

You bring the physical in. You're climbing, your feet are pushing up and off, your hands are holding on, you're getting sap on you, you're smelling the sap and the fresh scent of the needles, you're feeling the crevices within the bark. When you finally get up in the tree, you can ask the tree internally, to let you see the world from its point of view.

This is a fascinating way to be close to nature, truly special. It is a mind-blowing connection. You see how Earth spirituality is interwoven.

We need to be careful with the English language because we get lost in words. Sometimes we limit ourselves by words. From the spiritual perspective, anything is possible, but it's not all describable verbally.

Go out in nature and feel the energies of living beings, flowers, plants, trees. Feel the energy of water, see beyond what you first see on the surface.

Feel the overall landscape, letting in the bird that is singing into your soul. That song will live in you as an intimate bond.

Open yourself fully, touch as many things as you can. Roll around in the grass, dance with a tree and give it some energy. Sing songs and make your own sounds. Express your unique self. Only good comes of this.

The Universe's Language

The Universe speaks in synchronicities. A coincidence is not a random phenomenon or accident. It is where two coinciding points meet congruently, often with an astounding outcome. When you are in sync with another being, the Universe is letting you know, you are right on purpose.

A Universal Greater Power

For some, there is still confusion between the meaning of religion and the essence of spirituality. I know people who have a genuine spiritual practice that don't go to church, and I know people who go to church and quote the bible, yet have no idea what spirituality is about.

Every approach and religion can lead to a genuine connection with whatever you call a Greater or Higher Power. I always suggest finding the uniting good in the teachings. Find the common thread which speaks to us all, and then it doesn't matter what you call it.

I believe, for myself at least, it is important to feel that there is a greater power at work in the Universe. This is what gives me hope, and encourages me to continue to do good for this world we live in.

The Source of the greater power, the Spirit that moves in all things, is present in the trees and plants, in the animals, and flowers, and in everything you can feel, and smell, and can see, and can't see on this Earth.

One of my teachers used to speak about the doorways into nature. These are the places where a person feels safe enough to open to the mysteries of the physical, and non-physical realms.

Mountain-climbing, hiking, fishing, camping, painting, taking pictures, botanizing, and birdwatching are just some examples of those doorways that lead to an everlasting connection with the spiritual essence of the Earth.

To me, spiritual means connecting to nature in ever expanding ways. Going deeper into the natural world is very personal. I, myself, feel God in nature. Teachings of most religions of love, kindness and service are quite simply what nature is.

Nature is a healer of the mind, body, and soul. Nature is a protector. Nature is a teacher, friend, and companion. Nature teaches us compassion, peace, and a higher purpose.

Perhaps love is nature's greatest give back. Love is when we are at our best. To be able to love nature and all its parts for what they are, offers a bridge to transfer that love to our human interactions.

***

Sitting quietly in nature "church", observing, and listening, brings us into a state of presence. Daily practices, such as meditation, are tools to bring us back to the present moment.

Most spiritual practices tell us that the present moment is the only moment that matters. In that present moment it is the only time that truly exists. That is our opening where we can merge with that universal energy flow, or Spirit that moves in all things, and co-create and manifest whatever we choose.

I believe this is what is meant when it is said that the power is now. Our energy is fully focused at that moment. Finding that opening is what will create change.

Being quiet in nature without the noise of city life, the sirens or honking of horns, without television, computers, music headsets, or cell phones can be overwhelming to those who avoid being alone. Yet, it is in the moments of quiet observance that the answers come. Answers to why we're here, or what the next step might be, or who we are, and what we might need to change. Answers come in flashes to questions we haven't even had time to sit and ask yet.

To sit quietly in nature and observe, is to become part of the majesty within the simplicity of life's tasks.

The ants carry the carcass to the colony to feed the colony. The spider weaves his web for food and joy. They know why they are here.

Going about our everyday lives while being kind, and being of service to each other and to the environment, may be why we are all here. Spirituality is just that simple, and powerful.

The healer is the Mystery. We are only the vessel.

Control is an illusion. The only control you have is when to let go.

Eyes Of The Woods

Eyes everywhere, looking at me. I feel no fear, interest only. What are they? Why do they look? Not like my eyes or yours. What kind? I don't care, it doesn't matter. Eyes in the woods, only for me.

Bird migration is a miracle. It can't be explained and yet it works. Believe in that.

Earth Spirituality Is Universal

Spirit is in everything, but in nature it seems easier to feel that sacred energy. Nature connects us to our purest, primal selves.

Nature is my church without walls, and all her beings are my spiritual community. Life on Earth is my physical Heaven, where I fall in love every day.

Angst

There are times I go out for a walk in nature and I'm seeking answers to questions I don't even know yet, but are calling to me anyway. There is an unquenchable thirst to know, to know what?

I just know in hindsight that it means I've been stagnant for too long. I'm ready to grow again. I'm uncomfortable being too comfortable. If I'm not uncomfortable, then I'm not growing, I'm not stretching my boundaries.

When my world feels as though it's closing in on me and it's too limiting, it's a signal that it's time to move those self-perceived boundaries further out. It's time to expand my world more through new experiences. It can be scary to broaden my awareness into something I've never known before, but going into the Mystery makes it not a mystery any longer.

The only fear is the unknown, and once it's known the fear dissipates. The "What-ifs?" no longer hold paralyzing power. With experienced knowledge comes the power to choose.

A Call to Adventure, to seek new experiences and perspectives, is not a one-time thing. There are huge pivotal experiences for sure, but even those small moments that call you into the Mystery, also become something to expect regularly. The call into Mystery is cyclical to help us gain new awareness.

Eventually as my mind lets go of the fear of the unknown, the answers come to those questions that I didn't even know were there. The answers have always been there, it's only a matter of when we are ready to experience those "ah-ha!" moments for ourselves.

New insight can still be scary. It pulls you away from what you currently know, but when the pain of staying still becomes more of a struggle, than just taking a step forward, then you take it, even if you are pushed. Life is motion and change. Life is animation. Death is stagnation.

Nature is constant change. We need to embrace our natural state of being. Go into the Mystery. Let one question lead you into another one, and journey into your life.

Follow The Gap

Find shadow spots through the trees and let your eyes flow through them like water. Follow the gap between shadows and follow them through the woods. Journey through the silhouettes and follow the trails of the shadows.

Explore

There comes a time when there is a call to test the limits, to crawl out of the boundaries of your physical body. Some people attempt that through drugs to escape. I would rather go to nature and lose my mind, leave it behind and explore.

One way to go beyond the physical is a defensive fear, a form of escaping. The other approach is a proactive drive to seek. One way is losing your personal power, and the other way is self-empowering, by being vulnerable with an open heart.

We are all a part of the whole universe, yet unique and individual at the same time.

"Original light is what I came into this world with. I came from that Bright Source. I came with original wisdom, not original sin." – John Brennan-Kamofo

Birthing An Idea

Imagination is putting images to energy that's already in motion. Your dreams already exist, you are just visually seeing the birth of an idea for the first time as it appears. Just because your imagination comes easy, doesn't mean it isn't real.

I Asked My Soul, "What Do You Want?"

My Soul replied, "I want to experience this physical world through this body. I want to experience mountains, and rivers, and meadows, and forests, and oceans. I want to Be in nature and connect as one with it. I want to experience the physical of that which I am not, but also Am. I want to know Me outside of Me, the energy of Spirit. I want to taste, and smell, and breathe, and touch, and hear, my Self through physical senses. I want to collect memory. I want to create through a body so I can experience Me in all forms. I want to grow through love, but also know what it is that I am not, so I am conscious of what I Am fully. I want to experience music and art, and I want to use them as my language or form of communication. I want to paint the world with color, which is Me expressing my-Self. Every-one has a different color radiating within, and your personal color of Me, is blue."
...Have you spoken with your Soul lately? It feels good.

Experience Your Own Sense Of Spirit

There is no mediator needed in the spirituality of nature, to remind you of your connection or to interpret your own experience. You experience your own soul connection and that's what's true for you.

You can share ideas and experiences with someone you trust, but it's not for them to validate what is real for you. If you experienced something that touched you, then that alone, is all the validation you need.

We can fill ourselves up and share our inspiration with others, but it's not our place to tell others what's real. Each person can experience their own connection with their personal idea of Mystery. There's not one way.

Very simplified, healthy religions are made up of supportive communities that can facilitate personal growth and awareness, and connection to a uniting, universal Spirit. A spiritual leader can tell you about God or Spirit or whatever the name is used to describe the Great Mystery. They can point in the direction they felt their own truth, but then they should step back to allow you to explore your sense of truth in your own way.

Going out deep into nature is one way of experiencing Spirit alive, and that's what's true. All religious beliefs or no religious beliefs are welcomed home in nature.

Life is an endless layering of existence.

173

Build Trust In Your Relationship With Nature

We were born spiritual Beings. Spiritually in touch with nature. To experience this, we must have a positive sense of identity. We must have a natural courage to trust in more than we know.

This is why it's so important to raise children close to nature. Children are naturally more open to Mystery, to accepting it, embracing it. Trusting in nature's ways, allows this to happen organically, the Earth way of teaching.

You can Know something, but not be able to explain it, and that's ok.

My Place

For much of my life I go to my place to find my true self and connection on levels, rarely felt in daily life. I found this place at nine years old. Bad happenings forced me to seek out sanctuary. This place saved me and became my guide. I know this place for me is at the mountaintop.

One day I was sitting on my land near Mt. Shasta with the Earth Keeper, and we went there together. That has now become our place, our meeting place.

Believe that anything is possible, there are no limits. Believe in living miracles. Believe in limitless space, and space inside that limitless space. We all have a personal space in the non-physical realms. Our medicine opens up our sanctuaries of spirit. These places are not physical. Don't think too much, just go and you will find your place, your medicine area.

Names are not important. Our Earth, our sky, our solar system is limitless space. Trust, play, have fun, and believe anything is possible.

Take risks and be willing to be wrong to be right. This space is your medicine area or your sacred place. It's calling you, just listen and feel. Trust your inner vision.

***

Late at night I sit out in front of my house and have conversations with the Earth Keeper. Many times, I am shown images or scenes of places I don't know yet. I can only assume they are places in other realms. Yes, I am aware this is strange.

I don't always understand what is shown or told to me, and sometimes it comes very fast as flashes, but I pay attention as best I can. I don't know when the Earth Keeper will show up, but when he does, I take in what I can.

I don't always understand, but I do feel a sense of urgency to pass along and act on whatever I can. Sometimes it feels lonely not being able to share all that I sense and know, but I do know I can rely on the Earth Keeper's support to help me.

"Earth consciousness is all living beings as one and separate. These two counter parts equal Oneness." - E.K.

"On Pleiades' Earths- Gravity is in control of Earth Keepers. All movement is by air. Walking in your body is only when gravity is in use by choice. This will happen one day on Earth when we move out of the mechanical, Machine Age." - E.K.

"Meetings in nature, passages if you want, when sky touches the Earth, when sun touches the Earth, when rain and snow touch the Earth, when Earth touches sky and sun, when Earth touches rain and snow, at this time, a moment in time is created. An opening, and invitation to go beyond what your mind and physical body want, beyond their limits. If you choose to pass through these types of portals, you must go freely and open. No purpose is required.
You will find you'll get just what's needed. Most likely you tap into the universal Earth conscience, a place of unlimited wonder. The wonder leads to a connection on a level all humans desire, the feeling of truly being a part of all that there is.

We have this feeling at birth for a short time, and again upon death as we transcend the physical to the nonphysical. Nature's meeting points can lead humans to this sacred place.
Think of a tree reaching to the sky, the sky coming into the tree as energy from the cosmos, and this energy turned through sunlight, into energy such as carbohydrates, and the making of air itself and so much more.
It's dispersed into the very Earth through Earth through roots, and thus becoming into the very essence of life. A part of the whole. The whole itself. One with all that exists.
Think for a moment, water when it touches your body, your skin, think of this feeling. What is the feeling? Put it into words. That feeling explains the feeling when Earth meets sky or tree meets sunlight. Put to words the feeling of sunlight touching a human body when the body is cold.
Put to words when the human eye sees beautiful things in nature, such as a sunset. That moment of meeting-color, burst of light, shape, mystery, that wonder that is birthed at these moments is the path to total connection. This connection awakens part of the soul and inspiration is birthed to live your purpose. Nature is the pathway to all good things. Keep it alive by looking for those places, those meeting places. There are more of these places than can be counted. Ask for them, with your wholeness." - E.K.

"Look to the horizon. Take your time, be patient, find that place where Heaven and Earth meet. Then when the horizon line is found, let it call you through. Let the essence of who you are go on a journey. A journey in many ways that takes you Home to where you began. Listen inside, and when our sacred Earth calls you back, come back, come Home to our planet.
Home is many places and times. The horizon will keep calling you Home, endlessly. Since there are no limits in this place, just keep going. It will become clear why you go through time. Not time as you know it. The other time where there is no time." - E.K.

"Find the sweet spot where the blue sky meets our Earth. That spot, if you look at it long with an open heart and quiet mind, you will be taken on a journey to Earth-heart. Quiet mind is most important as this journey cannot be understood by our logical brain.
Our ancestors used this technique as a way of accessing a oneness with our living Earth. A deep feeling of fullness for life to come forth from this work. Life becomes a joy." - E.K.

"That Other Place. That other world, the land of all knowing on levels most uncommon and common. The place where it all makes sense, all of it, everything. No hatred or the need to control, only love and understanding on a level far beyond the mind, and yet the mind is welcome. All beings can go there and do good. People, animals, plants, water, all life is in a place of goodness. It's a place that works for all. This place is an all-knowing place. We can go with the proper opening, and courage, and curiosity, in abundance. It's another world and it's our world. To all that I love and teach, I say I'll meet you there, and we will be good". - E.K.

Pleiades

Calling, calling me home. Every time I see the Pleiades star system, I feel a deep, aching call. It feels like home, but for now it's my mystery.

Earth Spirituality Principles:

*Earth peoples don't teach intuition, they assume it. It's a function as natural as breathing.
*The world is what we think it is.
*Energy flows where attention goes.
*No limits. Now is the moment of power. All power comes from within.
*Happiness is a human right.

*Nature welcomes everyone home.

*Earth Philosophy guides us to living our best lives, and to our better angels of our nature.

•You don't always have to have the answers, it's ok to be a mystery.

Chapter 20

Greet Sacred Moments

What is a Sacred Moment in Nature? The answer is truly personal. Often, sacred moments happen, and we just don't acknowledge them. All it takes is this recognition of the sacred, to make those moments Earth Medicine.

People are amazed that I have so many sacred moments, and ask me why. The main reason is simple: I get out in nature all the time. I fully engage with my environment, using all my senses, including my intuitive sense.

When highlight moments happen, I acknowledge them as sacred, and I stay with them as long as possible. I soak them in. I let my emotions engage with the experience in full amazement. These moments become me, a part of me, my medicine to carry my whole life. It becomes my gift to share with the world.

If I happen to be with other people, I help awaken them to the experience, and share it as a collective medicine moment. There are no rules for what's sacred or not. It's personal to you, but you must be open to these moments, or they'll pass you by. The good news is that they'll keep coming your whole life.

Being a nature photographer allows me to engage in sacred space, every single day. Almost all photographs are of sacred moments because I seek those opportunities out.

In our minds we think that for a moment to be sacred it has to be rare. This is not true. In nature, there are no limits, complete abundance is what it's all about.

What does become a limit is our false fear, a fear of nature, and our physical bodies not being in shape to fully engage in nature.

We can be adventure seekers, but sitting quietly, or walking slowly and quietly are still the most amazing ways to engage with sacred moments. Be open and aware, nature's miracles will come to you. Sacred moments are usually very simple events that are cherished as exquisite, because we are aware in that particular moment.

For me, sacred moments might be when I wake up to the sound of songbirds. I go to the door, and get drawn to light highlighting a rock in the grass, and I find a gopher snake. It allows me to hold and admire it for a moment, and then let it go, and I move on.

I look up at Mt. Shasta and the sunrise illuminates a lenticular cloud from beneath, giving it a unique, ethereal shape, and color.

I walk to the creek and jump in. The cold awakens me as I become the creek. I sit on a log and watch trout swim, in quiet reflection of my childhood of the endless creeks I followed, and the fish I caught. For me, this is a fully engaged sacred morning. What a way to start a day.

Sacred moments can be walking in nature and coming upon a bear, a herd of elk or deer and finding they don't scatter, and they stay with you. It can be a butterfly landing on you for a moment. It can be a familiar connection to a forest, water, animals, or flowers. A sacred moment can be an everyday occurrence, such as a remarkable sunset, a warm wind, or a passing cloud.

If you soak up enough Earth medicine moments, you can't be a bad person. You will know, when what you are doing is not right, and it will eat you up inside. You will change your behavior because it will

not sit well within. You won't be able to tolerate it. Your being knows better because it's experienced better.

Be open to the moments that are personal to you. Go out and find them by being aware, acknowledge them, absorb the moment, feel gratitude for them. Make those moments your personal medicine, and share the blessings of all those sacred moments. Then watch what happens to your life. I think you'll be pleased.

Peak Experiences

In nature these are moments that jump out at you, and stop you in your tracks. They're brighter, sharper, you don't forget them no matter how brief they were, they live within you.

Nature communicates to you in this way. Nature says, "Don't forget, there's something here to learn, growth to be had." It could just be a wonderful experience, or it could lead you through a threshold into a profound nature connection.

Often, a peak experience is personal to you. Although it can be for friends, couples or groups, peak moments help to propel us through our life's journey. They remind us how wonderful it is to be alive and engaged in life. It's like being in the river, not simply on the bank.

A peak moment could be something we do every day such as eating, and that one time you bite into something, it changes the way you think about food.

Some moments are huge events, some are intimately personal. The little moments are just as big as the obvious, grand moments. Some are for lovers, some are jaw dropping, some are humorous, some are thought provoking. Share them or hold them close inside your being, they are for you.

When something feels sacred don't question it, accept it and it will live in you. When you acknowledge sacred experiences and have gratitude for them, it makes them come alive.

When nature jumps out at you through color or sound or as a highlight, your job is to take notice. Soak it up through your senses, write about it, sing about it, draw it, or paint it. When nature gives you a peak experience, give it voice, tell its story. Make it sacred.

Remember these medicine moments because they will never happen the exact same way again. Consciously take them in. They will become a part of you as your personal medicine.

A simple smile shared can be a sacred moment.

Sacred Space

Mountain cathedral, the glory, the silence, the perfection. Inviting, crystal clear pools reflecting sparkling facets of Spirit. Swirling, smooth granite playground, luring joy draws me into exploring layers of paradise without fear.
Resisting leaving one place, gratitude revealed with another. Surreal dream yet never been more alive. These mountain pools have been here for centuries, but in this sacred moment, it's brand new to me, and I am full.

Live Your Life Fully

Live each day as a ceremony. Wake consciously. Stop throughout the day and evening and take in special moments. Breathe them in. Absorb them. Honor each moment as sacred. Have gratitude for each day. Every day is a gift to cherish, treat it so.

Today I found a brilliant, orange leaf that spoke to my very being. I don't know how else to say it. That leaf now lives in me. Always.

Feasting

A meal with friends can be a sacred celebration of gratitude, of abundance, of life shared. Taking in the living, nutritious energy consciously. Sharing of self. Gifting back love, laughter, and appreciation of life and each other.

Sacred moments with friends are a treasure. Honor them as medicine moments. Acknowledging them allows that energy to blossom and fill you up, it makes ordinary moments special.

Acknowledge sacred people in your life. Ask yourself what makes them sacred. With the answer comes a question. What are you waiting for? Ask.

Carpenter Bee

A large, black carpenter bee flew in front of my face. It stopped and looked directly into my eyes. No fear from me, only questions: "What do you want? What do you see?"

Off he flew. I said, "Come back". He did, and looked right into my eyes again. I wonder if in his own way, he was thinking the same thing. Two beings just making a living on this good Earth.

The next day I was at the beach with a thousand people. I looked at the edge of the surf, one person out of a crowd of thousands, and there it was: a carpenter bee. Upside down, mostly drowned, but still alive. I picked him up, asking inside myself, "Please don't sting me."

In my healing, loving hands he dried his wings. I put one hand over him, feeling his movements. No stinging. When I lifted my hand we made eye contact, and off he flew.

As I left the beach I passed by a rotting tree, the carpenter bee's home. There he was, hundreds of them, one of me, and a thousand people. The people never knew the amazing life drama that happened on that beach that day. It was a gift for the bee and I.

Insects are a being that are always willing and able to share their intricate lives. Remove fear and prejudice, and they will often show the way into a profound knowing of Earth.

Find beauty in all things in nature, and the beauty will reflect back to you, and you will know beauty as a living Being.

Be Still

How many sacred moments have you experienced, when you're frantic or rushing or gabbing away with friends? They happen when we are still or alone.

One such spiritual moment happened for me when I had taken a needed break hiking to my sacred spot. I watched a bolt of lightning explode on the mountaintop. The impact sent a rock falling down the cliff, which hit another rock, and another until the power of the rocks created a landslide. It flooded the side of the mountain with the flow of rock on rock, and as quickly as it began, it stopped. I sat awestruck and grateful that I took that moment to sit.

Dolphin Dance

Walking along the shore of the near mile long beach in Kauai, I was dragging after a full, fun day in the sun. I was looking forward to a shave ice and some shade. Then our friend, Steve, pointed out a large pod of Spinner Dolphins swimming by in the distance, and asked me if I wanted to swim with them.

I thought he was joking at first because they were far out in the open ocean. I hesitated, thinking that would be nice, but that seems too far out. I was tired and out of shape. Even though I had been a competitive swimmer for most of my life, the ocean has always made me nervous.

Yet, there was a wave of inspiration that lit up inside me. Well, really? Could we actually do that?! Steve encouraged me by saying this was an opportunity to swim with them in the wild, and he would go out there with me, but we would have to hurry because they were moving on.

Without too much more paralyzing thought, I said OK and jumped in. This beach is known for its shore breaking surf, but as soon as I ducked under the crashing waves, I swam straight for the middle of the line of dolphins.

I am a solid swimmer, so I wasn't afraid of the water or my abilities, I was just nervous of being in a new experience. I looked back for Steve. He was on his way not too far behind, but I knew I had to go on my own to catch up with the pod.

Before I knew it, I was among a handful of dolphins, swimming as a part of their pod. They were circling around me and diving below me, in what seemed like a water dance. They were making their clicks and whistle sounds, communicating with each other, maybe even communicating with me.

I couldn't stop smiling. I felt an endless breath blowing through me. It was better than a dream. It was physically and spiritually real. It was a sacred connection for me with another species. We were living our own life's journey, engaging at the same time on this amazing planet, where a land-living mammal can interact with a water dwelling mammal, harmoniously. This is a kind of miracle that shows us that all hearts are connected.

The dolphin's welcoming curiosity made me feel that I belonged. I wasn't intruding. We were just sharing a few moments of playful wonder and awe in each other's company.

While the swim out and back was much longer than our interaction, time made no difference. Being a part of a dolphin dance, in the middle of the Pacific Ocean, will live inside of me forever.

Sometimes you have to stretch to gather those sacred moments, and sometimes getting off trail means getting past the breakers to engage with what's on the other side.

Personal Truth

Many times, a sacred moment is shared between two people without the other one even knowing how they affected someone else.

In one of our Earth Philosophy classes on the first night, we each introduced ourselves in three minutes. We spoke of who we felt we were and where we came from.

Most people told of the things they do, their accomplishments, their family background, their heritage, or occupation, all of which were true. But one soft spoken, young adult, who I've known for many years, stood up when it was his turn and brought tears to my eyes. I could relate to his story because it was also my story.

The tears were happy, full tears of connection with another soul, who doesn't really know my story, and still doesn't, but it was just a validation of a truth I have felt as a knowing for most of my life. The words he spoke were words I could not seem to previously find for myself, only felt.

The simple words he said were, "I am who I am, when I am not." I felt that in my core as, I am who I am when I am lost in what I am passionate about, and not what I am trying to do. It is in the not doing, when I am my true Self.

Spirit often speaks to us through dreams when we are most open and available. This is a quiet, sacred space between the two of you.

When someone reads something powerful to you, make it sacred medicine by soaking it in like you would a song. Let it come into you, and absorb it, and let it resonate in you.

Ladybug Gathering

It was a dry February. The mountain meadows were brown and dormant, the snow had melted two months early that year. While out walking our dog pack, my eye caught a blotch of red. My curiosity led me to investigate the blob on top of a tuft of bear grass.

A huge cluster of ladybugs completely covered a ten-inch diameter of mounded dirt and dry grass. I had never seen so many ladybugs together. In fact, I had only ever seen them solitary.

I watched them for a while, figuring they were passing through, and were clumping together like bees do to keep warm. Getting distracted by the dogs running in all directions, I headed back home.

The next day we went back to the meadow, and I was absolutely blown away. An entire half acre of the meadow was solid ladybugs. It was an ocean of red, completely covering every inch of the ground, and branches of the bushes. I mean there were trillions of ladybugs! I don't even know what that number would look like, but that's how many were there. More than I could ever guess or count to.

I had the dogs stay back and I tiptoed through the grass, doing my best to clear a bare space to stand in the middle of the gathering. My jaw physically dropped, and I couldn't stop smiling. My expression was the emoji of awe.

I had never seen ladybugs gather like this on our land before. After looking up the reasoning behind it, to satisfy my logical brain, I learned they gather when there is a big weather shift.

They gather to mate, and share food and water resources, to stay warm, and for better survival odds from predators by being in large groups. The funnest thing I learned is that a large bloom of ladybugs is called a "loveliness".

What surprised me the most was that ladybugs don't all travel together. They felt the call individually and they came. That again, validated for me the communication of the unseen spirit that we are all connected to. As soon as I understood what was happening, I let all that go and just sat with them.

For a couple of weeks, they stayed in the meadow. For the first few days the ladybug gathering word got out, and it looked like a concert festival, where more and more would show up in groups to camp out. By the end of the second week, they began to head off into the world.

I don't know how to describe those days in the meadow with the ladybugs, other than to just acknowledge that it was sacred, and I knew it. I was fortunate enough that year, and only that year, to be a part of a loveliness bloom. What a blessing.

Birds are flowers with wings. Celebrate their beauty and be happy for them.

A Blessing To Witness

In the Red Rock country, the landscape of mountains, canyons and rivers are its distinct, stunning personality. I began going to this country as a little kid, and I've never stopped returning.

It's the rich rust, orange colors that draw you in to explore. The contrast of royal blue skies meeting the cliff's edges, with pops of yellow cottonwood leaves dotted throughout the landscape, lining the wandering, mint green rivers, speak to the soul through the windows of our eyes.

When the low light of the rising or setting sun meets the red rock, the transition of the various, warm hues is nothing short of remarkable. It's so shocking at times I lose myself, and become the colors. It's always a blessing to witness such grace-filled beauty.

Conscious Harvest

Harvesting food from the garden can be a ceremony. It can be a sacred experience to plan what meal you are going to create from what is available. It's what people have done for so long, but many of us have been removed from that seasonal harvest.

Because we are so fortunate to have access to so many foods from around the world at almost any season, we sometimes get arrogantly annoyed now when fresh peaches aren't available in January in California.

It's a gift to have fruit and vegetables brought to our stores from around the world, but at the same time we lose the sacredness of walking into our own gardens.

We need to remember the specialness of picking our own food and eating it while it is still alive, and the energy of the plant is still flowing through it, and then through you. Its energy becomes yours.

This simple act of eating becomes sacred when you acknowledge it and take in the experience as a ceremony.

181

Breathe in sacred moments. Have gratitude for them. Absorb them. Honor each moment as sacred.

A Humbling Story

I love insects, but I really love bees, wasps, scorpions, and spiders. I enjoy holding them and interacting with them.

On our Headwater's land we have bald-faced hornets, which can be very aggressive to other flying insects. They catch bees and yellowjackets on the fly, and eat them. It's very primal and amazing to observe.

One day some of my students saw a hornet on the camp kitchen counter when they were washing dishes. I wanted to show them how you can interact with them if you are gentle and soften your approach, so I walked up to it and started petting it gently with my finger. The hornet seemed to enjoy it and even leaned into my touch.

I stepped a few feet back and the hornet looked at me, I felt like I was almost in a trance, and then it flew within a few inches of my face and hovered for a moment. I could look at its eyes and I smiled, and maybe, just maybe my ego got the best of me. Right then it immediately landed on my forehead and stung me, leaving me with a large knot on my head.

Of course, the kids and I laughed. Boy was that a humbling moment to remember, maybe even sacred.

…and in my bliss, I rode on the backs of dragonflies.

Everyday Miracles In Nature

Miracles are a big part of my life. As a kid I was fascinated with miracles. I thought they were a big mind-blowing event that rarely happened. Those big moments do happen, and they are miraculous, but there are also everyday miracles.

As I grew up, I realized that by identifying everyday experiences as miracles, you give them a certain energy. You make them important enough that they stand out. You build up a reverence medicine by just appreciating them.

Once you acknowledge a butterfly as a miracle just like yourself, that moment becomes a blessing.

There are some events where everybody is going to agree they are miracles, and some are personal only to you. Each has their unique power and offering for you.

Fall is a miracle of stunning beauty. I've planted over 100 trees on our property that change color. As you look further into the trees, you see how miraculous it is on different levels.

The trees are dying back and going to sleep for the winter so they can make it through the snow, the rain, and the freeze, only to bloom again with flowers and leaves in the spring. Oh my god, that's a miracle! Simply identifying it as such makes it more amazing for you.

This is the key I want you to get! Take a moment, have gratitude for it, offer a blessing, appreciate it, and it will come alive in you, and you will carry it as medicine. Now that is a big miracle, right?

You could be walking down the trail, and stop by a little creek, and see where the water is flowing over a rock and trickling down, and hear the sound, and see the patterns of the water, and maybe see a water skipper walking on water, talk about a miracle!

What I realize then, is that water is life, for everything. We are 60-70% water, and the Earth is 70% water. Every being needs some form of water to live. It's a home for some beings and for many of us it just feels good to be in it. Identification of the miracle of water takes you on a journey of exploration, appreciation, and gratitude that never really ends.

Maybe you are laying in a meadow and a dragonfly hovers right in front of you, and it lands near you. If you watch it for a while, you'll see it's a miracle.

I have had dragonflies land on my face, and dry their wings in the sun, just after watching them emerge from their hard-shell casing. That was a special moment of awe for me.

Look at patterns in trees, and the shapes that speak to you, that can be considered a miracle. You can look at a young tree and watch it sprouting, and think about what it's going to have to go through to live 50 years, 100 years, 500 years, 1000 years. Imagine the stories that it will have to tell, and the homes it will provide for countless living beings. That is a miracle.

Watching clouds rising over the mountain behind me, admiring the formations and the softness of them. The edges of the clouds meeting the blue sky, the two becoming one is a miracle that makes me feel good.

Being able to lay down in the grass, snuggled in and feeling the warmth on top of your body from the sun hitting you in the first light of the morning, and feeling the dew on your back from the grass, that's a miracle.

Acknowledging these everyday miracles leads to a life of inspiration. A life in-Spirit. Eventually these Earth miracles become normal in your daily life.

If you're always rushed and distracted, you're going to miss these miracles. You're going to let them drift away, and even though they will have happened, they won't have really spent time living within you.

Pay attention. Every day you can pick a moment where you witness a miracle. You are living in a world of highlights. Be present. Be nowhere else.

You Are A Miracle

If you are at all in doubt of miracles, look at your own body. The human body is absolutely astounding. Our hearts pump love and beauty throughout our bodies. You are one of a kind. Yet, we all share a Collective Soul, a like energy. Everyone and every Being at our core is the same Spirit. Treat them and yourself as special because you are.

Take It All In

Take in the beauty wherever you are. In the city as well, not just out in nature. Stop and take in the sparkle of morning light, bouncing off the morning dew. Make everything sacred by being conscious of the specialness of each moment. Appreciate it all.

What does it mean to be in the moment? You are fully present and aware. At that moment there is no past or future, just now. All that is around you at this moment, becomes a part of you. A part of your experience. It becomes your story, your energy that you carry.

You are the sum total of all of your experiences. When you absorb those highlight moments in gratitude, they become the blessings you share with the world. This perfect beauty becomes your medicine, it becomes a part of your Earth personality.

To experience life fully in the moment, is truly a gift. Once we master this skill to last longer than a fleeting moment, opaque walls turn to translucent veils you can cross through. Be ready to hold on for the ride, it's a good one. Just be willing to keep going.

Windows In Time

Capture moments of opportunity. There's a time for everything, and there's a *right* time for everything. A lot of how we move through the world in our lives, and how we become extraordinary people depends on us being able to observe, and soak in the special moments. These are windows in time that allow us to enter into another phase of our life, where at the other end we become remarkable.

Every human being has the ability to become remarkable. Why could that not be true? It is. Many of us notice those windows when they're open. Sometimes we call them defining moments.

Sometimes we don't go through the window when it's open, even if we see it, we don't go through. Fear holds us back. The invitation feels like someone on the other side, a great spirit, a wonderful friend, a loving person saying, come, come, and we still don't do it.

What holds us back? Fear, laziness, lack of belief in ourselves? To have an extraordinary life you must be the one that goes through the open windows when they show up. They're going to show up in many ways. It might show up through another person, and they invite you into their world to come along on a journey.

Those moments might show up from things that happen in nature that inspire you, and you have these incredible inspirational thoughts that move you.

They might show up inside of you. One day just the idea, the thought, the dream appears and there it is inside of you, but if you are coming from fear, you might put it back to sleep.

When those defining moments show up it's up to you to act on them. Let the dream out. Give the dream energy. Give it medicine. Bring it to life and start the journey. Go through the window. Every person on this Earth is extraordinary if they want to be.

When people live in extraordinary ways, they affect the Earth and other human beings in extraordinary ways. So, live your dream.

If you get your butt kicked, if you get knocked down and beaten up, don't give up on your dream. Lick your wounds, learn from the mistakes you made, and then get back up and go for it. People who continue to get back up are the people that change the world forever for the good.

You might have to take a different path. You might have to change your trajectory a little bit. You might have to gain new knowledge, whatever it takes, do it.

Doing whatever it takes means you'll get it done, and then you'll have this extraordinary life, and we all win. When I say we all win I mean, humanity, the birds, the plants, the trees, the Earth itself.

Energy follows thought. When an idea comes up, and you put it out there, you give it energy, you give it life. It becomes real, it starts to live.

There are times when you need to manage the experience as you go through your life, but there are also times when you just need to get out of the way and let the forces of the Universe, seen and unseen, guide you.

Often, we are our own worst enemies. Learning to get out of the way and letting great things happen can be powerful.

Storms come and go, and when we make it through them, we enjoy the peacefulness. Let nature's teachers inspire you. Let them bring out the dreamer in you. Go through those windows in time and make those dreams come true.

Look at what humanity has done. We are amazing. We can solve anything. We just need to remind ourselves to throw in a little kindness and love, heart, and service. When our intention is for a higher purpose, for the good of all living things, we can't go wrong.

Your life is a sacred moment in time. Value each moment you have.

Big Boy - The Giant Bull Elephant Seal

I was photographing at Franklin Point at Gazos Beach, which is north of Santa Cruz, California. This place has been in my life since I was twelve years old. My dad and I went for a walk on this beach, and I knew that day that this place was my place.

This beach became my pilgrimage spot for over 50 years. There are so many stories to tell, so many adventures. This beach has always felt like my beach. It's a feeling that comes from my heart and soul. It comes from my experience, my medicine gained from my years communing with this sacred place.

It's important to understand the connection to land, and the feeling that it is only your special place is natural and wonderful. Deep love of place is a thing of the heart. Native people knew this and that's why when their land was taken away, it was so painful that many literally died of grief from the loss.

A few years back I was walking the beach and noticed a bull elephant seal laying at the top of the beach, by a large sandstone rock. As I carefully approached him, I noticed some cuts and bruises around his face and neck. He was exhausted. He was there to rest and heal.

The next beach cove down was Ano Nuevo State Park. There is an isolated island there, just offshore where elephant seals congregate to breed.

The males fight for the right to breed with the females. This 2000-pound male in front of me had lost a fight. Needing rest and healing, he swam to my beach, Franklin Point, where I found him waiting for me.

I know this day was meant to be our day. I sat right next to this bull for six hours. I photographed him and talked to him all day. I was careful to open my heart in a peaceful loving way so the seal could receive healing from me. I had no fear, just respect. He had no fear either, only respect, knowing that I was there, just for companionship.

Sometimes two beings can meet, in this case two predators, and the meeting place can become extraordinarily sacred. I think of words like love, respect, peace, good wishes, and blessings. This meeting place does not have fear or control or hate, and no manipulation. This place is open to all beings, and once it shows up, if you are aware enough to identify it, then seize the moment, and spend sacred time with another fellow Earth traveler there.

This sacred space is also there for humans. Trust your inner vision when it shows up and go in. These moments create lifetime bonds for friends, lovers, and family, and sometimes with strangers.

When special connections happen in sacred places it is vital to take notice. These sacred connections could just be the beginning and opening to blessed places within us.

Our souls could propel us to the deeper realms of spirituality. In these moments everything is brighter, everything is clear.

As our connections strengthen within, so does our connection to Earth and all life and beyond. No limits. Anything becomes possible.

In these moments we know more about all things. Our senses in these moments become more alive; they become your guides to unlimited realms of awareness. Seize these moments and live fully. Take risks and face fear and go in.

Mardji

In my early twenties I became an animal trainer, and caretaker at Marine World Africa U.S.A., in Redwood City, California. It was an extraordinary time in my life. I was the caretaker of the chimpanzees and elephants.

I was working with a 22-year-old Indian elephant named, Mardji, and we got hired to make an appearance in a film. Another caretaker and I worked with Mardji for a few months, while she patiently waited as the Hollywood costume makers built a costume around her.

Mardji was very tolerant, as we fed her a case of apples and a case of french bread, while the craftsman worked on her fitting.

When they finished the costume and were ready to begin filming, we loaded Mardji up in a semi-truck, and we rode in the back with her, and headed to Death Valley.

Being her caretakers, we also had to wear costumes, and we sure had fun shooting a 15 second scene for the movie.

That experience wasn't about the prestige for sure. It was just a good time with Mardji outside of the animal park.

The magical time that did leave a heart impression on me was when we were all done filming. I had the truck driver let us off in the Mojave Desert, and I rode Mardji alone into the wilderness for a few days. We would occasionally pass by hikers, and I can only imagine what people thought when passing by an elephant on the trail.

Mardji and I would spend the evenings at an oasis, where a spring would surface in the desert and there was fresh drinking water, and green grass to feed on.

That time alone with her was sacred, and it wasn't lost on me. That wonderful, special time in the desert with Mardji will always stay in my heart as a part of me.

We don't always know ahead of time when experiences will become sacred, but when you take advantage of those opportunities, no matter how big or small, and pause your mind to take it all in and appreciate them, they become special.

Working with those exotic animals was extraordinary and I'm so grateful for that experience. The quality of care for those animals was wonderful. They were loved, well fed, well housed, and taken care of.

I saw how the animals at that park became tremendous ambassadors for the wild, and how they touched people's hearts. I had so many sacred moments with so many different animals there. It inspired me to continue on that path of working with wildlife, and being an ambassador for them, and an advocate for protecting their habitat in the wild.

My personal, sacred moments seem to have always inspired me to continue to move forward and seek more.

Soak in the beauty of nature. Live through your soul, not just through your heart or emotions, but through your Being.

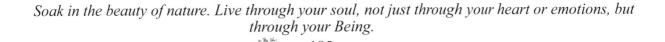

We Are All Connected

To look at anything in nature in a simple way, with a heart full of love and wonder, will allow what you are seeing to show its true self. At this point you meet this being of nature in a place that few humans ever touch. From that place anything is possible. Have the courage to explore.

What we see we become a part of. When we see with an open heart, and a sense of wonder, what we see becomes nature's best medicine within us. At that moment we become more amazing than we just were.

An Eagle In My Room

A huge part about finding sacred moments is just taking the time to identify something as a sacred moment. Giving it your best, giving it your energy, putting all you have into it. Taking the time to acknowledge it as something special, brings the experience alive and gives us medicine. That story then lives in you forever.

***

In the early 1980's I helped start a group called, Native Animal Rescue, in Santa Cruz, California. I had just come out of working in the zoo business, working with wild animals, training animals, and doing educational work. After seeing all the animals that were brought to the zoo for help, I realized there was a need for wildlife rescue.

As we were getting the rescue going, I realized it could also be a good vehicle for educating people about the local environment, and how to help animals.

***

I love birds of prey, hawks, eagles, owls, and kestrels. I worked with them in the zoo business quite a bit, and I love their power and majesty.

One day I got a call from someone who said they saw an eagle hanging off a fence in an apple orchard. I went to the location and was horrified when I saw a female Golden Eagle hanging upside down by one leg, in a steel jaw trap someone had set up on the fence post.

The farmer who set that trap was an idiot. Most likely the eagle would have been catching rodents that would have eaten their apples. To kill that bird was insanity, and cruelty at its worst.

That bird looked into my eyes and probably thought its life was over. As soon as I connected with her eyes, I opened my heart and I let it rush into that bird, and she immediately calmed down. I tried to let her know I was there to help her.

I put a towel over her, opened the trap to free her, put her in a box, and drove her to a veterinarian who specialized in eagles, at U.C. Santa Cruz. He said her leg was badly damaged, and infected. She had probably been hanging there for days.

The veterinarian cleaned her up and gave her medicine, and I took her back to my house. She needed to be immobilized, and have a soft padded space. I got her a big crib with padding and put her next to my bed.

I would hand feed her every day, and sit with her, and put my hands on her leg, and try to heal it by giving her energy.

Our relationship grew to a complete fusion of love between a wild animal, and a human. This love was on another level that I don't know if there's words for. We'd look into each other's eyes, and I'd go flying with her, how else can I say it?

One day I was sitting on my bed next to her, with my shirt off, and she jumped onto my back. I was worried about her healing leg, and her talons, but she didn't stick them into me. I learned something then, that she knew the difference in how much pressure she needed in different situations to perch.

After that, she started sleeping on the bed with me. She would sleep on one end, and me on the other, and this went on for about three weeks. I can't even begin to tell you what it was like to be able to sit with a Golden Eagle at night while reading my books.

Our relationship and trust deepened, and I took on her eagle medicine. Eagles are magnificent beings, and I was so honored to be her caretaker.

She seemed to be doing ok, but not as well as I had hoped, so I took her into the vet for a check-up. He said the infection had spread and it was going to kill her. I didn't want to hear what he said after that because I knew he would want to euthanize her.

I looked into her eyes, and in that moment, she was every being in nature. It was overwhelming, and I cried and cried as I said my goodbyes. I held her close to me and gave her lots of love. I told her, "I'm sorry we humans did this to you."

I had committed my life to saving wildlife and nature, but I couldn't do anything more. In a very comforting way, the veterinarian put her down, and off to the spirit world she went. I was 28 then, and I'm 69 now, she still lives in me, and will forever.

It was one of the saddest moments, and it brought up rage in me too, but I didn't let that become my way. I turned it into action by helping more wildlife, and educating more people about wildlife.

Sometimes sacred moments and interactions don't end the way we want them to. Sometimes they happen due to bad circumstances, but the heart connection is what we can carry with us.

One of the most significant influences you can make is to get involved in wildlife rescue. It is one of the kindest life purposes there is.

Today I watched Humpback whales full-body-jumping out of the Pacific Ocean, off the Big Island of Hawaii. Nothing more to say about it except, Wow!

See Ordinary As Extraordinary

I was sitting in the woods, and a chickadee started rummaging around the leaves looking for food. It came within a few feet of me. I was calm, and quiet, sitting against a tree. I didn't put out any negative energy, so the bird had no fear.

The energy of the spirit that flows through all things, is like a river of the essence of the Earth. When you tap into that energy and open your heart, and your mind, you literally put the call out for animals, and other beings to come and be with you in your space. Sometimes that just happens randomly because you are so peaceful, and the animals are drawn to you.

Even though I have had these intimate experiences with animals all my life, I realized sitting there with that chickadee at my feet, what a sacred moment it was to be with this bird in the woods. The moment was elevated, just by making this simple observation of how sacred it was. The bird stayed for a while and shared a part of my day with me, part of my journey.

I realized, even us true nature lovers, get so busy sometimes we forget to take a moment to observe something special happening.

***

Walking down the trail to our school's camp kitchen, I pass an area we call Lizard Gulch. In the summer it's hot and there's a lot of lizards and snakes that soak up the sun on the rocks. Often, I'll pick up a lizard or a snake and hang out with them for a bit.

Sometimes I'll see a songbird in a tree and talk to it. I'll thank it for being there. I'll enjoy its company. I'll express myself either through my eyes or smile or my emotions, and I'll offer a blessing in the form of good wishes for a good life.

Many animals are intercessors for these spirit seeking interactions. Birds and squirrels will come and spend time with you, especially if you have bird feeders and habitat for them near your home. They get used to your presence and develop a trust with you.

Those experiences can also happen with larger animals, like a bear or a deer. Stop moving and spend time observing, and they will show up.

There are opportunities to snorkel with fish and other ocean life, and enter their world. There is an entire universe of insects to interact with. Butterflies land on your hand, and on your head. You can enjoy bees by just sitting with them.

Have you ever stopped and really watched a bee disappear into a flower and drink the nectar? It's extraordinary to watch them. Have you watched a hummingbird hover deep into a flower?

If you acknowledge these moments, whether it is the littlest critter or a profoundly big one, soak them up. This is a blessing that nature gives us if we allow ourselves to receive it.

If we are too busy all the time or if our energy is too frantic, nothing will want to come around us, and we miss so much of the phenomenal planet that we live on.

So, take the time to acknowledge the sacredness of the moments that you have with the wildlife that shares your space.

What makes something sacred? .... Your awareness that **everything** is sacred.

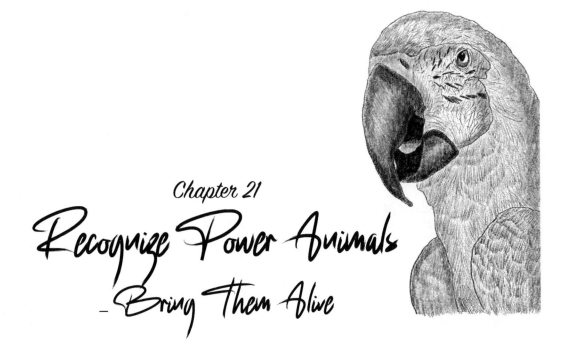

Chapter 21
Recognize Power Animals
- Bring Them Alive

Be an anthropologist and go back in time. Study our ancestors throughout the world who lived with the Earth interdependently. They honored animals as our brethren, and often felt we had a kindred spirit with animals.

Each person had an animal that he or she was like. To some degree we had the same habits, the same ways of living, the same ways of looking at the world, or even a similar body type as that animal in some regards. That kindred animal spirit would be highlighted as our power animal, our guardian animal, or animal companion.

Our ancestors had clans, as do current tribes. Examples would be a bear clan, a wolf clan, an eagle clan. They had ceremonies, dances, and songs to honor their animal counterparts. It is a way of identifying and honoring those animals that call to you.

Globally, all Earth peoples, our relations, truly knew wild animals. They honored animals by purposely taking on some of their traits. In battle they would often fight like a certain animal, or hunt like them.

They would collect bones, skulls, hides, feathers, and other items from their animal counterparts and power animals to take on their energy.

Those who lived close to the Earth depended on animals for food, for companionship, for wonder, and a connectedness to nature that can only come from a respectful relationship with them.

Animals hold space between humans and the plant and elemental worlds. Animals can show us the way into an intimate, spiritual connection. For our ancestors it must have been a normal state of being, living with animals as our friends, partners, fellow Earthlings.

To be with an animal in a way that is profound, and to mutually share our world, is a human calling. To create this bridge between worlds, we must have a real interest and commitment that truly comes from our heart.

Having this open heart towards all beings, including reptiles, amphibians, insects, fish, and birds is key. We must be interested in their lives and how they live as individuals. You can know their name, but what makes them happy and content? What do they eat? How do they sleep? What causes them stress? What are their dreams?

To be truly interested in another being's life is an opening to a sacred relationship. It unfolds into a truer understanding. There is a place of magic or spirit, a place in between places, where the animal and human meet. It's not a physical or intellectual meeting.

Once connected in this space between, it is forever. It is always within you, as a part of you, always unfolding into greater depths of love, peace, and joy. To be one with animals is to know pure love, pure peace, pure fun, pure living!

My Bear Within

Myself, I am a bear-man through and through. I walk like a bear. I think like a bear. I am built like a bear. I'm hairy like a bear. I play like a bear. I eat and sleep deeply like a bear.

When I used to fight, I was crazy like a bear. To deviate a little bit, a lot of martial arts use animal's energy and approaches as ways of fighting. They emulate fighting techniques like a tiger, a cobra, a crane, or a leopard.

I love bears. My nickname given to me by others is Bear. The connection is very deep. I feel it inside and out. My love of bears started when I was young. I was never afraid of bears, I've always loved them.

I went through a very tough time when I was young, and in my darkest moments, a spirit bear named, Big Bear, came to me. It was as real as a bear here in the physical, and it came to be my protector, guardian, and friend, and has stayed with me my whole life.

Bears spoke to me, and as I got older, I started backpacking and seeing them in the wild, and I knew they were my kindred spirits. I've had many encounters with bears, and by always being respectful, we both have had amazing interactions.

Luckily for me, no one ever said I was wrong to identify with bears. A mistake adults often make is we downplay when these magical things happen to children. When our kids show a strong affinity to an individual animal, we don't always support it or help nurture that relationship.

My Uncle Bill used to take me all over the Colorado Rockies on his off-road motorcycle, called a Tote Goat. He was a big bear himself. I remember grabbing onto him riding through the woods. He always supported my love of bears, and we would observe wildlife, and track, and go fishing, and hunting, and photograph wildlife.

Bears were always the beings I was called to. I would sit with bear tracks and study them. I would watch bears in the wild as long as I could. I was always drawn to them, and the bear naturally became my animal. One of my spiritual protectors.

Little Bear

A few years ago, Julie came to tell me that there was a bear under the deck of her yurt. I went down there and sat on the steps and talked to him. I coaxed him from under the steps up onto the deck.

He was a year-old bear, and he was not acting right. He wasn't fearful of me, and wasn't aggressive, he seemed confused.

I hung out with him for a while and watched his behavior, and realized something was wrong. I read an article a week before that some bears in California were getting encephalitis, inflammation of the brain caused by infection, and my fear for him was that was the problem.

We called the fish and wildlife service and a wildlife biologist. We spent three hours with this bear, talking to him while the biologist took notes of his behavior. The bear was practically sitting on the game warden's lap. The bear walked next to us back and forth, brushing against our legs at times. He was acting like a dog.

As we became more emotionally attached to this bear, I realized that he would have to be put down. He was suffering, and there is no cure for this brain swelling virus.

It was a heartbreaking situation, but what I felt good about is that the bear came to us on his last day. He came to a place where no one would shoot at him or scare him off. We welcomed him into our space. His last hours on Earth were loving. He was respected and cared for, and not fearful.

Often, these things only happen when you are in a place where you are aware and observing. You are able to identify when a situation happens, and not run away from it. Open your heart to these moments, and move into the experience, and work with it. Not only did we help that bear on his last day on Earth, but he touched all of us there forever.

I am sorry the bear had to lose his life, but the reason I'm sharing this story is because of the relationship I have with bears. That bear felt the energy connection, came here on our land to get help, and when I saw him, I didn't yell or run, or try to shoot him.

I have a lot of experience working with wild animals, and was able to feel out the situation. I invited him up on the deck, and spent some peaceful time with him, just being with him with nothing but kindness and respect. Without any physical contact, it was an amazing interaction to have with my kindred spirit, and an honor to hold heart space for him as he drifted off into the spirit land.

Animal Counterparts

Take time to think about what animal you truly love and admire. You may see it a lot in different ways, and forms. Ask yourself if that animal could be something more for you. Could it be a helper, a guide, is there something more to learn?

When you identify a sacred animal in your life, learn about it and enjoy them. Read about them in natural history books and study what this animal does, where they live, what they do, how they think, and their history with humans.

You will get closer to the animal by seeing your similarities. It becomes more personal to have heartfelt relationships with your animal brethren. Grokking animals and becoming them is all possible. Ask what they are mirroring in you. What are they symbolically playing out for you?

For some people who look at this through their logical mind, this idea of power animals or animal counterparts doesn't work for them. The logical mind often cannot grasp matters of the spirit. We need to have the courage to be open to other ways of being and living, knowing there are no limits.

One way to connect with an animal is to practice true empathy. Feel what they feel. Think like the animal. Observe the world through their eyes. The clarity you will find will awaken you to your own primal self.

In practicing empathy, barriers can drop, allowing space to know another more intimately. Much of what happens is through feeling, and understanding, and awareness. What gets in the way of interrelatedness with animals is fear, doubt, judgment, control, logical brain, ego, smartphones, and other mechanical devices that distance you from your heart.

Spirit animals, power animals, animal guardians, and animal counterparts are often one in the same. It's a partnership that is richly fulfilling and beautiful.

Some say vultures are homely looking. Watch them fly, it's magnificent. Drop your judgments and welcome a vulture's flyover blessing.

My Vultures

Twenty-five years ago, when I turned thirty, I was in a time in my life where my world was upside down, and I was grasping for something other than the life I was living.

Living in the rapidly growing East Bay of California, it was getting harder to find a place of quiet nature to myself. My emotional escape was to hike up into the foothills of a regional park to try to breathe.

One afternoon, I was walking along a ridgeline trail and took a seat on a log, in an old, olive orchard. Most every time I was there, I never encountered another person, but as soon as I sat down, I heard someone playing a flute. Even though it was a soft, pleasant sound I was annoyed. I really wanted to be alone.

I stood up and looked around and saw no one. When I sat back down the hollowed drone of the flute played again. I stood again and walked a little way into the rows of trees to see if someone was hidden in there, but the flute stopped.

As I walked back towards the path, I heard a rippling kite in the wind flying low, just above the trees. I couldn't see through the dense canopy, but then I heard it swoop by again just above. As I stepped back onto the narrow trail, a shadow shaded the sun and soared overhead.

I instinctively ducked and looked up to see a Turkey Vulture swooping down, skimming the treetops. Its wings stretched out, tipping its body slightly side to side, adjusting to the up draft of the wind, feathers rustling just enough to hear them in the breeze.

As I walked farther along the trail, the vulture repeatedly continued to fly right over my head from behind, and soar in front of me. I stopped navigating my path and I felt called to follow where it was leading me. After a few minutes the vulture left the trail and headed down into a ravine.

At this point in my life, I wasn't comfortable going off trail and venturing into the unknown on my own. This day was different. This day I had asked for help from whatever was out there that was bigger than myself, to give me some guidance. Outwardly, my life looked pretty good, but inside I was a mess.

The call to follow this vulture was so commanding I didn't question it. I had never felt this urgent sense of adventure before. I knew I needed to trust and let go of the fears of the unknown, because the fear of what currently was my life was stronger, and it needed to desperately change.

The vulture obviously was trying to get my attention. It made sure I kept up with the direction it was going, by flying over my head to lead me, and then circling back to get me to follow. I walked down the steep, grassy hillside into an open flat where a massive, dead Live Oak Tree towered alone.

It stood as a proud sculpture, weathered and bare of leaves, but within its solid branches perched twelve vultures. Some were sitting looking about, and some seemed to be in a blissful state, with their wings completely stretched out, catching the last hours of the sun to dry them. Three more vultures circled above the tree.

I asked from within, permission to come sit with them. Feeling reassured, I kept my head slightly lowered in a humbled reverence and sat against the trunk of the tree. A smile grew so big inside of me that I didn't recognize it for some time. I hadn't felt that welcomed by so many in a long time, and rarely had I felt that from the wild animal world.

I don't remember thinking about anything during that hour or so that I sat with them. I just remember the feeling of being welcomed, acceptance, happiness, disbelief of what was happening, honored, and I had a sense of hope. I felt that now my life was about to get better, richer, and more meaningful.

I felt I was being initiated into a lifelong friendship, as one of them. Separate, but in some ways the same. I felt understood, and not alone.

The sun was starting to lower, and I still had a couple mile hike to get back down the ridge. I thanked the vultures and asked if there was a feather I could take with me as a gift, to remind me of that moment of hope during some hard times at home.

As I stood up and looked down, there was a beautiful, vulture wing feather right in front of me. It had been there, and I never noticed it. I looked around right where I was standing, and I found twelve large feathers laying there for me. I felt they were for me to take as a symbol of their friendship.

I took a few steps away from the tree and held the feathers in both hands, with my arms stretched out in gratitude for them. It sounds like a ridiculous movie ending, but truthfully, I leaned my head back with my heart wide open, turning around in bliss and gratitude. I had gained a knowing that there actually is something bigger than all of us, working with us to help us on this crazy life journey. I now knew this as a felt truth for the first time.

I opened my eyes, to honestly, see at least six of the vultures joining me, flying low around me in a circle, just above the height of my head. I smiled so big it turned into a laugh, thinking that there should be some kind of movie score playing in the background for this incredibly perfect scene.

After a few moments, the vultures turned and flew up higher. I said my goodbyes and told them I would return. It was now dusk, and I needed to get going before it was fully dark. I headed back up the hill to get to the path along the ridgeline, before hiking back down the other side.

Part way up the hill I turned back around to look at the tree, and it was empty. I looked past it, and in the distance, I saw the faint, dotted trail of the vultures flying off. Did that all just happen? Yes, definitely yes!

The story doesn't end here, it was just the beginning. As I was heading back down the trail, I realized I had stayed too long. Darkness was setting in, and I was nervous, as it wasn't uncommon to have mountain lions in that area.

Against my better judgment, I started to pick up my pace and jog downhill. The farther I got away from the top of the hill, the more nervous I got. I felt as though not just one thing, but many things were watching me. I felt that the land around me was watching me. I don't know of any other way to describe that other than it felt like The Wizard of Oz, where things came to life in a way I hadn't fully experienced before. I was aware and sensitive to everything living, more than I had ever been.

In reflecting on this much later, I realized that everything around me was actually aware of my presence, it always has been. I was the one that hadn't been aware of feeling all of nature's being's presence, until I was totally open. The spirit of all beings are always aware, but it was the first time I was aware of sensing them. It all came at me so instantly, it was overwhelming.

At some point I was on the edge of panic and now running. As I came onto the wider, fire trail and rounded a corner, I skidded to a halt, and apologized to an elderly man on the side of the trail that I almost ran into.

It took me a second to realize that I was audibly talking to a tree! I had clearly seen a man standing there, in what was now an empty, burned-out cavity of an oak tree trunk. I literally took a double take, looked back behind me, and was in a full sprint to the parking lot.

Years later, I learned that this man in the tree was an Earth Keeper. I have met him several times now, and realize he is a helper that watches over land, and other Earth Caretakers.

Feeling disoriented as if I were a part of Alice's Wonderland, I felt relieved when I saw another person in the parking lot loading his mountain bike on his car rack. I needed a sense of grounding in this physical world, and that was enough to help me to drive home.

I didn't know what was going on, but I knew it was big. Like anything that happens out of the everyday ordinary, I tend to immediately start to question it, and negate what really did happen. I second guessed my whole experience and tried to logically explain it away.

I almost started to believe my explanation, except that the feeling was too real. As I drove down the road towards home, I felt almost sad that it was over. I was questioning if those vultures really were speaking to me. Not out loud, but through my heart.

Were they my friends, and would I ever see and feel them like that again? Was it just all wishful thinking? How quickly my certainty was dissipating.

Tears started to roll from the emotional rollercoaster of the day. As I came up to a stop sign the tears immediately turned to joy, and out loud laughter. Above me, as high up into the sky as I could see, was a slow-motion tornado of vultures. A spiraling cloud of dozens and dozens of vultures.

I sat there in my truck with my mouth gaped open in awe. There was no doubt left in my mind from that point on in my life, ever. They were with me for the rest of my life.

***

The following week I was not able to break away and make it up to the ridge. Part of me was wondering if they would show up, but the bigger part of me told myself never to doubt it again. It would almost be disrespectful to think that. I shouldn't have to make them prove anything. I think I was just used to being let down and waiting for the blow.

Shortly after that, I went to visit a mentor of mine from childhood. He had been a pastor at our church years before, and we had become long distance friends. Even though I no longer attended any church services or followed a religion, I kept in touch with him as I grew up. I was so excited to share with him this profound experience I had.

He had been a very open-minded person to share with in the past, and not preachy. Just a regular person that gave me straight, practical answers to my questions of the logical validity of the stories in the Bible.

I asked him once if he really felt that all those stories were literally true, and he said he didn't. I was a little shocked that he would admit that, but then he explained that he believed in what the symbolic lessons in the stories had to teach. I respected that. They were to him, somewhat like Aesop's Fables.

Well, I should have remembered that when I excitedly told him about my encounters with the vultures. I was hoping he would be open to the reality of what happened, but instead he chuckled and almost brushed it off as a fun story. He wasn't buying it as something real as a heart connection. He just started to explain away the facts of vultures, and lovingly joked that I was talking with birds like Saint Francis of Assisi.

We had a good visit, but inside I was crushed. I had been looking for validation of something he couldn't relate to. Driving back home I was feeling a bit deflated. I wanted to share what was an amazing, spiritual connection with these vultures, with nature, with the world, and it wasn't received the way I had hoped.

I turned onto my street in the suburbs and looked up through welled up tears, and every bit of sadness instantly left. I couldn't get to the ridge, so my vultures came to me! There they were, six of them sunning their wings in a bare maple tree along the cement sidewalk, in my neighborhood, across the road

193

from my condo. So much relief and joy. They continued to show up in that tree for the next year that I lived there.

From that day on I was careful who I shared my experiences with. It's not that people try to be disrespectful; they just aren't ready to hear it, yet.

It's been over half my life now since my power animals started coming to me. Every single time I'm going through a big change or a stressful situation, they show up. They have shown up outside my second story window, on my rooftop, in different homes I've lived in. They were directly across the street on phone poles facing me when I woke up in the mornings. They come here now to my forever home in Mount Shasta.

When I walk on a beach with the intention of just clearing my mind, they show up and swoop overhead. I feel as though they are giving me a personal nod or a fly by, with the tip of a wing to acknowledge that I'm not alone. They are there for support.

I was never drawn to vultures before that encounter on the ridge. I didn't know much about them. Like many, I fell into the thought that they are not the prettiest of birds, and that they were even creepy because of the stigma attached that they ate dead, rotting stuff.

After my first few encounters with them, my friend, Ben, encouraged me to learn more about them. I read up on them and learned about their characteristics, and it was then that I understood how I related to them. I understood our kinship, and the aspects that were similar to mine.

Vultures aren't the most popular, majestic bird, but they are still grand in their humble gestures, assisting with what needs to be done behind the scenes. Vultures are the clean-up crew for the difficult things that others can't swallow and deal with.

They tend to represent death, not because they kill though, but because they help clean up after the transition, and make the path clear for something else.

They are not the most approachable bird. They seem to be aloof, but still stay with their flock. They seem docile, but don't be mistaken, they will defend themselves instantly, and effectively.

They soar as high as any large bird, and from a different perspective they are athletic angels in the wind. They are not the fastest bird or the most powerful bird or the most vocal bird or the most good-looking bird, but they are the most perfect being for what they are here to do. They are the observers, the balance keepers, and the silent peacemakers, and I am proud of those traits within me as well.

I still stay connected to my power animal, my counterpart. When I see a vulture and start to really feel its presence, I take a deep, deep breath in, and open my heart as wide as I can with my arms outstretched. Pretty much every time I ask them to come to me, they do. Even if they are flying the other way, they will circle back and fly over me. It's not a test to see if they will do it, it's a hello from my soul to theirs.

Connecting with your spirit animal helps guide you as an Earth Caretaker. Their presence reminds you that you are not alone on this path. You have companions that will always speak to you and give you guidance.

The Eyes

I've sat with many elephant seals for hours. It's the eyes that pull me into their world. It's the eyes that open me up to their hearts. It's the eyes that carry me into their souls.

They let me know how close I can be to them. A slight movement, a look, a feeling -the eyes.

I sit where they say to sit, and then it happens. A bond between them, me, and the ocean. I journey into their world. What an amazing world it is. It's timeless to live in the ocean and on a beach. That's when I'm sure I know everything I need to know. Then I come back. It's the eyes.

When a bird comes into your space take time to visit. Next time you hear a songbird sing, sing back. I do this often—I whistle the tune, and soon a beautiful harmony is created.

Observe The Senses Of A Wolf

Notice how wolves use sound and smell to heighten their awareness of the pack, and sense their safety by knowing who is in their territory.

Pay attention to your own senses, and how you can do the same for your immediate community.

Calling For Our Human Pack

It became obvious during the COVID-19 pandemic in 2020, that no matter how much of an introvert a person is, there is an innate need to connect with other humans on some level.

Throughout many states in the U.S. at eight o'clock p.m. whole communities stopped, and gathered at their doors and windows, and howled in support of each other. It was a calling to let each of us know that we may be isolated physically, but we are not alone.

We are calling out for companionship, for support, for security, for tribe, for a sense of purpose for being here. We are not unlike our pack counterparts. We need to find our tribe and heed the call for connection.

LITTLE BEAR

195

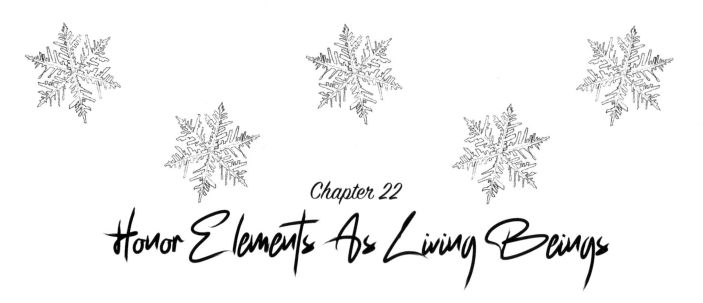

Chapter 22
Honor Elements As Living Beings

The elements are all things Earth. We are all made up of nature's elements. We *are* nature. Consider having relationships with things in nature that you might just pass by, like the four directions, soil, clouds, and wind. Interact with moving water, waves and what's inside water. Consider shadows, colors, and shapes. Engage with what's inside trees, roots, and rocks.

Think of edges, like places where forest and meadow meet, or where rivers meet oceans, or where trees touch the sky.

These tangible and intangible spaces, and beings, are awaiting your curiosity to lead you on countless adventures.

Spend a day honoring the elements. With that intention in mind, enjoy a day rafting, camp out by water. Build a campfire and cook over it. Go rock climbing. Go windsurfing. Create Earth art with natural materials around you.

Give blessings and gratitude for air, for water, for fire, for dirt and gravity.

Know This

We are the Earth, nature, the trees, the rocks, minerals, and the water that make up the Earth. Every grain of sand is human potential. We are not separate humans on the Earth, we are made up of all the elements of the Earth. Until we fully feel that, accept that as truth, not just intellectually, but know it, then we cannot fully protect it and heal.

I'm always amazed at how my Being reacts to the changes in weather, seasons, light, smells, environments, and the Moon phases. When I do consciously notice it, I'm just blown away, knowing that I am a part of the environment. I am a part of the water, and land, and Universe. I'm not in it. I Am it!

Participating With Life

At Headwaters we are constantly connecting people with nature by just doing the daily activities required to run the camp.

The camp kitchen is a great example. We collect drinking water from our spring. We collect it straight from our source.

We light fires for heat, but also to cook over. We interact with each fire and its personality, to work with it, to give us the results we are looking for. We engage with it to get to know it as a living Being. It's a dance between adding heat and taking away fuel to lessen the intensity.

We have to cut the trees when we are clearing the land for fire safety, and then cut the wood up for different uses. We get to know its characteristics and learn what it is best used for, cooking, warmth, ceremony, light, tools, or shelters.

We feel the wind, which lifts and forms the clouds, and brings the rain that waters our ground to grow our food.

Living every day outside, we are directly connecting with nature, and constantly working with the elements. When we are in our homes, sometimes we forget that these things that help us to live, come from these raw sources. Living outside for a while is a great reminder.

Air

Medicine Wind - A medicine wind is a sacred wind. It's not a prolonged wind caused by a storm or some other natural event. A medicine wind begins seemingly from nowhere, and doesn't seem to go anywhere. They usually blow across the desert landscape or the mountains.

A medicine wind suddenly appears and blows through you. When a medicine wind hits you, you feel alert, filled up, and full of energy. Sometimes you are filled with ideas, and dreams.

As a medicine wind picks up and travels across a landscape, it collects the essence and power or energy of the land. The land's soul, the land's heart, the land's medicine is captured in a breeze.

It also collects the medicine of the animals, trees, plants, lakes, and creeks. Everything it blew through is blowing through you. Welcome it, and you will connect with all those beings.

If you are lucky enough to identify these winds as they blow through, soak up that wind and absorb it. Pick up that energy and you are at one with the land, you will be the medicine wind.

Medicine winds come up fast and go away fast, here and gone in no time, that's their nature. It may not be apparent at the moment what you've collected, it may never be, that's the mystery of it. Trust is needed. Sometimes you will know what you've collected, acknowledge it, and work with it.

All these little moments become sacred within you. We are always looking for the big, huge moments, but it's these little special moments that build up, is what becomes who you are and what you share with the world. When the big moments do come to you, you will be able to recognize them, honor them, and take it all in.

May you have many warm Medicine Winds blow through in your life.

Breathing In Life
When I get out of a car and step into nature, I take in a full breath of air throughout my whole body, and I instantly know I belong here. I come alive in one full breath and I'm smiling throughout my whole Being. In one breath I am home.

Run with the wind and let it carry you. Let the wind blow your love into all things in its path.

My Quietest Afternoon Became The Loudest Symphony
The unusual stillness of no human sound made my ears pop awake. The deafening silence grabbed my attention. It was soon pierced with the honeybee's wings and the cricket's vibrations. The scampered rhythm of the Cottontail crunching across the fall leaves, led me to the distant breeze building, as it approached with the power of an imminent storm, rustling the drying sunflowers, blowing through me the secrets of the garden.
Like a thundering train, nature's spontaneous song came and went, clearing my mind, and settling my soul back into balance.

Earth

Digging a hole in the soil changes thousands of lives. The soil of the Earth is a living thing. As we dig, acknowledge the life we change. Have gratitude, and appreciation. Smell, feel, look deeply. This dirt is our ancestor. One day we will be the dirt.

To know the Earth, you must walk barefoot. Let your feet be loving feet. It's how you walk that makes you extraordinary.

Lay on the Earth, soak it up. Be the ground you lay on. Cover yourself in mud. It's the cleanest you'll ever be.

Rock Healing

Rocks are happiest after a rain. Enjoy them. Turn them over, look at them. Be with them. Get healing from a rock. Rocks speak the most ancient language.

Today I had a pain in my hip and leg. I sat on a warm rock to view the landscape. The rock spoke to me. It said, "Snuggle into me, let me heal you with my sun warmth." It did heal me. Much gratitude for the rock.

Have gratitude for mycelium. You owe your life to it.

Fire

Ancestor's Fire Lesson

To sit by a campfire in nature's wilds, is to do what our Earth ancestors did for thousands of years. When you make a fire and sit with it, invite your ancestors to join in. Some of them will come to sit with you. No words needed. Just enjoy their presence.

Look into the flames and see your grandmothers, and grandfathers. What were they thinking, feeling? Were they hungry, were they safe? Were they content? When you know your ancestors, you know yourself.

Build your campfire. Gather the wood, start your fire from a bow or hand drill, blow the tinder into flame, light your fire, sit and dream your life into being. Your ancestors will smile from their place, and you have created a miracle from nature.

My endless campfires in nature's sacred places have made my life the beauty that it is. Until my last day I will gather at campfires.

My ancestors taught me when you give birth to a campfire it becomes a living being. It has its own life, its own personality. As a fire tender, you learn to work with the fire to bring out the best in it, more light, less smoke, more coals, more or less heat.

A fire maker without nature awareness and earth philosophy as a base, is just a technician without medicine.

As a master fire tender your relationship with fire becomes sacred. In the sacred fire is a partnership. A mixing of wood, tree, ancestors, the fire keeper, light, heat, dreams. Fires become our friends, our relations.

Look Into A Fire

Let yourself filter through the light. Feel the fire's personality. Let its glow awaken your own warmth. Let the sparks at the tips of flames ignite dreams and visions within you. Let the glow of a warm fire become the glow within you. Let that inspired light bring out all the goodness in you. Stare into a campfire and gain all the answers to your life.

Fire Has Its Own Spirit

Learning to make fire by friction is a vehicle to self-empowerment. You are igniting the energy that is fire. Build a relationship with it. Fires are living Beings. Each fire has a different energy and its own spirit. Get to know its personality.

Fire is within you. It appears to be outside of ourselves, but it is a reflection of our own energy. Call that energy up within you. It is your passion, your life force.

Cook with the fire. Interact with it. Be aware of your partnership with it, and work with it while you cook your food.

Talk to the fire as a friend. Listen to it sing as it burns its fuel. It will talk to you, listen.

When you make a connection with fire you are touching the heart of the sun.

A Part Of You

When you feel gross with wildfire smoke in your body, it's not just the physical effects, it's also the feeling of inhaling the ash of the dead trees and animals that are burning. You are taking them into you. They come into you and become a part of you, along with their emotional energy.

Get To Know A Wildfire

What is your spiritual relationship with wildfires? Sit with a wildfire and get to know it. Sit at a safe distance of course, but just be with it and feel its energy, its personality and intention. Let go of judgment and ask it questions. You may be surprised by its answers.

Water

Water is perhaps the most sacred element on Earth. We don't have to compare, but there would be no life on Earth without water. The Earth is viewed from space and it's the beauty of the water that blows the mind.

Water is our planet, it is life, let it in. All things need water to live. It's beyond sacred, but think about it, how often do you buy a bottle of water or get water out of a tap, and for any second stop, and say thank you my friend? Just in your mind, think gratitude, appreciation, thankfulness that you have water to drink, and for what it does for you.

Scientists say we are somewhere around seventy percent water, same as the Earth. Can you imagine that?

There have been times where I was busy teaching in the heat and not paying attention, and I didn't drink water, and I started to feel extremely ill. My kidneys hurt. My liver hurt. I wasn't thinking clearly. It scared me, and I started drinking lots of water and it reminded me of how sacred and important water is. We cannot take water for granted.

Our native ancestors called water medicine. When you drink water take it in and feel it on your lips and feel it go down, notice how your body perks up once you swallow.

Look at the beauty and the clarity of it. Offer gratitude, give it blessings, good wishes, and it will become medicine for you, it will keep you healthy.

Some of the most sacred places are waterfalls, headwaters of rivers, headwaters of lakes, headwaters of springs and places wherever water calls to you through its beauty. Seeing beauty is a form of communication.

Any chance you get, jump in water. Swim in it, wade in it, splash in it. Recharge your energy. Appreciate it. Never treat water poorly. Never use soap or have chemicals on your body when you get in water in the wilderness. You are submerging yourself in someone's home.

Many, many beings live in water. You want to always respect it by enjoying it, by drinking it, by swimming in it, by looking at it and appreciating it. Know that it's full of life, and that you are as much a part of life as any other, because you are water. The Earth is water.

Never pass up the opportunity to drink spring water straight out of the Earth. Splash it up on your face, and get it on you.

Go river rafting or kayaking. Get in the water and flow with it. What is more mystical and magical than ocean waves? What is more fun and enjoyable, and peaceful, and meditative in life, than walking down the beach at the edge of the shoreline, looking for treasures that the ocean has brought up onto the sand, getting your feet wet, then jumping into the waves and getting tossed around?

There have been times when I was in the desert in a maze of slot canyons and suddenly came up on a pool of water in the middle of the desert. What a blessing that was.

Water is the eternal gift of the planet. Protect it. Sing to it. Talk to it. If you sit by water long enough, you will hear the music within the trickle of the water. Running water sings life's songs.

Songs will come through you. Look into the water and let it sing through your eyes to your heart. Get all your senses involved, your smell, your touch. Floating on water is the next best thing to flying.

Taste water. If you are lucky enough to drink from our spring on our land in Mount Shasta, you will experience the best water you'll *ever* taste. It's just crisp, and clean, and refreshing.

Using your inner vision will take you to the spiritual side of water. It's not understood in the logical mind, it's about feelings, an all knowing or an understanding within yourself. You start to speak to the water, and it tells you stories.

If you sit by a river, it can tell you its story of where it comes from, the things it's experienced along the way, where it's going and who lives in it.

It will tell you about the bears feeding, the otters swimming, the leaves falling in it, the trees drinking up the water along the edge, the beautiful plants floating in it, the children playing in it, the endless fish, frogs, and salamanders that live in it. It will tell you their stories. The water has stories of everything that is flowing through it.

When the water comes to you, so does the knowledge. You will become part of the stream, and a part of the story.

Science has proven water is a living being with a consciousness. I have always known this because I have built up a relationship with water since I was little.

Our native ancestors throughout the world have always known water as a living being. They have always talked to it and have connected with it, but it's wonderful when science backs up what our native ancestors have told us.

Next time you drink water, think of it as medicine. Think of it as nurturing your body. Think of it as sacred. Thank it. Bless it. It takes no effort to do this. Enjoy it.

I look to the water to find answers to my questions of where the creek has been. The edge is where you'll find out.

True inner peace is sitting by a slow stream or better yet, in it.

Springs Are Power Spots

When you drink from a wild spring, you are drinking from the Earth-heart. It is fluid energy for the soul. Give the live water a blessing and it becomes sacred medicine, and your body will celebrate.

Ask the water questions. Babbling brooks will always answer, they never stop talking.

Reflections

Reflections on water are a reminder to go beyond the surface. There are many facets to all living things. Reflections are a reminder of so much more.

Notice the beautiful shimmering images, this is the way nature loves us back. Let calm water be a mirror into you. What does it reflect back?

Life Force

In the East, they call water Prana – the life force in water. When we look at the Earth from space we see the oceans, the land, and clouds, and they seem to be alive. The water is life, the water is what makes this space view of our living Earth alive. Instantly, when this view comes into our being, the blue water speaks to us.

Water's life force communicates to us through all our senses. Water language is full immersion into all ways of understanding, it's universal.

Multiple times a day I jump in our creek to recharge my energy. Anytime I'm feeling run down and need to wake back up, the cold, healing water helps me instantly every time.

You must get into water in the wilderness. It literally changes lives. Next time water calls, jump in. If you can, get in with no clothes and just be in nature fully with no boundaries.

Immerse yourself. Remind your body that you are in a living being. Remind your body to fully absorb the water. Engage all your senses. Let it carry you on a journey. You'll never be the same again. We are water. Get to know it.

"Fish breathe in Prana, sacred air. It lives in water. Submerge yourself slowly, be comfortable under water and welcome the Prana, it knows how to merge with you. Just receive it. It is part of Earth's life-giving force." - E.K.

River Mouths

Go to the river mouth and explore. Ask questions. Feel alive through the power of waves crashing, water churning. Observe the sea life and river life above the surface of the water and in it. Get wet.

Let the seagull's squawk take you into the heart of the river mouth. Watch the birds sky dance, smell the sea life alive and dead, make sand art, squishing the grit between your fingers. Breathe in that mix of salty-fresh air that only a river mouth can provide.

Let yourself dream with all the other life. Be inspired to live as all life does, engaging with each other. We all live mixed together on this precious Earth; this is what we have in common.

Remember no time restrictions, just you and the river mouth. Let go and sink into the rhythm of the river's flow into the ocean.

Drinking Back In Time

We are blessed at Headwaters to have a year around spring that bubbles up, filtering through the depths of the Earth from five thousand years ago. My head can't wrap a meaning around that, but I can feel the truth in it.

Science is amazing in that people can track back time through geology. Humans can be incredible and at the same time the water itself is mind blowing.

Spring water is simply pure, and I always say it's the best water you'll never taste. It only tastes of freshness. Never take for granted the taste of pure nothingness.

Mountain Lake

Remember that moment when you're hot, and tired, and sore and you jump into a mountain lake, when that water covers you for the first time. That feeling of complete freedom, coolness, being held by that lake, that water. Remember the feeling, that moment when you were brought back to life.

Remember, and have gratitude.

It Keeps Me Humble

I'm watching wave after wave roll in and crash into each other. It's raw and beautiful and endless. It's intimidating, and yet I'm still drawn to it. Each wave is different and similar. I fear the ocean's power. It lures me in, but keeps me always on edge, as though it's a predator waiting for me to let my guard down and engulf me, when I'm unaware and weak.

Even though the winter waves are crazy, it would be eerie if they weren't there. The calm would make me nervous about what is lurking in the stagnant depths. The water itself as a Being is its own presence, and that is what keeps me curious, the energy, the character of the water itself.

The ocean keeps me humble, always just a bit on edge, but its beauty and the light reflecting off it keeps me in awe, lures me to it, and fills me up.

Water Dowsing

Water dowsing, or water witching, involves stepping into the spirit that connects us all. Drop into that deep intuition. It's important to have total trust and belief that it's possible. You must let go of any attachments to an outcome. If your hopeful outcome doesn't happen, try again. Keep it light and happy as if you are playing a game.

Water dowsing involves taking two green, freshly harvested, sticks, preferably willow, about three feet long, and holding them side by side. Set your intention to find water into a request from the Earth. Be open and unattached, but confident and hopeful.

Start walking. When the sticks begin to vibrate a bit, and as the water source gets closer, the sticks will cross, and many times bend down towards the Earth. That's when you know you've found your spot and to start digging for the water.

You can tell the depth of where the water is located in the Earth by how the sticks move and feel, and through your inner vision. This takes practice and patience, but it is a tried-and-true method of finding water.

Some dowsers are masters. This skill can become a true art form or craft. It's all about Earth relationship, Earth communication.

It is a mystery. It can't be fully explained in the logical mind. Witching can be used to find lost objects, power lines, and water pipelines as well. It's all about connecting with the veins of the Earth, and the energy that emanates from them.

When I walked my land before I built my home I spoke with the land, and more importantly I listened. Drilling for a water well is very costly and I wanted to make sure there were no mistakes, so I asked the land for guidance. I connected with the energy of the water by asking it to show itself.

I used two willow branches, and this is no fish tale, I was immediately physically pulled to a location near to where I had planned to build my home. It started as a slight tingling in my hands, and as I walked towards that feeling the branches began to slightly bend toward the ground and were vibrating.

Through my inner vision I could "see" the underground river was about 160 feet down. When the guy came to drill the well, I told him where to drill and how far to go down. I was ten feet shy of how deep I initially thought the water was, but the guy was still baffled at my accuracy.

I hadn't had a lot of experience in witching for water before that, but I trusted myself enough to know when to follow a strong feeling. I hit liquid gold and ended up tapping into a 36 gallon per minute artesian aquifer. Always, follow your instincts.

"To know peace, sit by a small creek and let the creek flow through you. Let the sound of the water touch those places within you that are ready to be awakened". - E.K.

202

Honor Weather As A Living Being

Get out in the storms. Feel alive. I live for the storm. To run into it. To feel the fear it brings. To be so small in something so big is a truth-filled humbling.

When the storm leaves, the land is refreshed and alive. The pulsing happiness of the land can be felt and seen. The colors are so vibrant, true to themselves. The animals are busy hunting. The trees are soaking up water and light, content, happy, and full of life.

After the storm some living things will not wake up, they will become the land. Although, most will be alive with a newness. My camera and I are in complete rapture. Walking, exploring the brilliance, after the storm.

Respect The Ocean

We sang to Kauai's ocean. Asking permission to enter her waters, and for safety, on a half day kayak paddle along the North-East Shoreline. Just as we began to sing, a wind gust blew straight at us. Droplets of sideways rain stung for a few minutes.

Tim and I looked at each other with doubt in our minds about going out. The wind died down a bit after the greeting song was over, but this was a sign, an obvious sign, that today wasn't a good day for this.

We had a class of a small group of adults with us, and we knew them all well. We both expressed our concern about going out, but the guides reassured us the weather was passing quickly, and it would be just fine as soon as we got out there.

We asked the ocean for permission to enter, but ultimately, we weren't willing to hear, no. Our friend had gone to a bit of trouble gathering the kayaks at his friend's house, and his guide friends had set the day aside just for us. Going against our better judgment, and our gut feelings, we checked in with the group, and they still all wanted to go out.

We got in our kayaks and did our best to paddle through the breakers. There was some difficulty, but we made it through, except for Tim. He is a fairly experienced paddler, but he was getting rolled every time he tried to break through the waves.

As soon as the rest of the group got past the breakers, everything just got worse. The wind and current immediately shot us out of the protected cove and into the open sea. One of our young, fit guys was instantly motion sick and was non-functional. He slumped over his bow, unable to paddle. Luckily, we had one tandem kayak, so he got in the double seater and let the other person paddle, while he collapsed into a mush ball.

Meanwhile, we all lost sight of Tim as we were blown around to the other side of the cliffs from our launch point. The swells were so big I was in a bowl alone, with walls of water so high I could only see blue around me. As soon as I was at the lowest point of the swell, suddenly I would be lifted straight up like an elevator, and I could see all around me, but mostly the horizon.

Being a competitive swimmer, and in good shape, I knew I was physically fit, but I could not seem to stay on my kayak. After just a few dips down and back up again, there was no one in sight. Our entire group was gone. I couldn't catch up, and I was exhausted.

I began yelling for the guides, but there was no one. I tried to head back to where we launched, but there was no way that was going to happen. I was in a washing machine. I couldn't go forward, and I couldn't go back.

The wind had died down, and the sky was now as blue as the ocean, but the swells were still massive.

After so many attempts to stay on my kayak, I just bobbed in the water for a while holding onto the side of the boat.

I stopped fighting the ocean for just a moment to look around. It was me and the deep, cobalt blue. The ocean met the sky, and the horizon was a faded line, barely separating the two. I looked back behind me, and my moment of peace was gone. I was drifting straight towards the wall of massive, rocky cliffs.

I guess my anger masked my fear because I was pissed. I yelled at the ocean, "Are you kidding me?! Am I going to die on vacation?! Does anyone even know I'm missing?! Are they even looking for me?!"

I crawled back on top of the kayak and tried to hang my legs over the sides for stability, and then suddenly, I couldn't see. I reached across to clear my face and in my hand was a six-inch, fat centipede. I launched it into the water, hoping I threw it far enough away. I knew those things could pack a sting.

Again, my anger rose, "Seriously?! A centipede in the middle of the frickin' ocean, on my face?!" I assumed it had come out of the front storage hatch of the kayak.

Getting my wits about me to start to make a plan, I rose up on another swell and saw two dots coming in my direction. It was the two guides backtracking. I waved my paddle as high in the air as I could, yelling as loud as I could. They were getting close and yet they still couldn't hear or see me. I yelled again and kept waving my paddle, but they were going to go right by me. They had their sights set on going back to the cove to look for Tim.

They finally spotted me, and I could tell they hadn't even been looking for me, by the shocked looks on their faces, seeing that there was someone else out there in the water. They paddled over to me and spoke to me as if I didn't know what I was doing. I reassured them I knew how to kayak, but I had no stability whatsoever.

One of the guides had me take his kayak and he jumped onto mine. As soon as he got onto my kayak it sank. It submerged two feet under water. Apparently, there was a hole in it, and I was just light enough for it to stay on the surface, but it was filled with water. The water sloshed side to side and that's what was rolling me off every time I tried to paddle.

They told me to take their kayak, and they would tow that one back into shore with the other one. They pointed me in the direction where the rest of the group was waiting in a protected bay.

Drifting closer towards the cliffs, I hesitated for a second going on my own, but I figured at least I had control of which way I was heading, so I paddled like crazy and didn't look back.

Had I not been so frustrated, I would have enjoyed that next part of my adventure even more, but the raw beauty of the Kauai coastline wasn't totally lost on me. As the waves calmed, I made my way past the Kilauea Lighthouse. The Blue-footed Boobies were perched on the cliffs, and the sky dancing, White-tailed Tropicbirds hovered overhead.

I rounded a corner and there was the rest of the group, laid up on a rocky shelf, catching their breath and soaking in the sun.

The guides returned and told us Tim's kayak also had a hole in it, and it sank as well. Fortunately, for his safety, he never made it past the breakers and went back to shore.

The ocean warned us. She spoke to us, and we didn't listen. It wasn't a good time to go out. She didn't want us out there. The drastic change of weather didn't last long, but it was a warning nevertheless, to always pay attention to what the ocean is telling you.

The power of the ocean has always humbled me, but this part of the ocean, in the Hawaiian Islands, has its own energy. Not necessarily a personality, but an ancient energy that you must respect.

Sometimes it's great to get out into the storms, and sometimes you have to listen to what you know inside and wait it out.

Storm Medicine

In our modern culture, when the news says a storm is coming, we run, hide, stay inside and we wait it out. I will agree that a few, and I mean very few storms, are so dangerous that we should be very careful. Those instances aside, storms, rain, snow, wind are nature's gifts of power to the land, and to us humans if we choose to participate.

Some of the best moments the storm offers are before or after the storm. Observing a storm build up its power is a great learning experience. It teaches us about our own, often untapped power. The power that brings out our best.

A breaking storm offers the most dramatic light I've ever witnessed, light that simply explodes our reality and expands our horizons.

After a storm, observe a forest, and the animals, and witness new life created before your eyes. I cannot think of words to express what I see and find. It's as if nature itself takes a breath. Its beating heart expands, and life expands. Earth happiness becomes the essence of all that we, as living beings, want and need. Next time a storm comes, get out in it, absorb it, become the storm.

Use Your Own Senses

We've been relying on weather forecasters to tell us what's coming, but especially recently in the mountains, in the microclimates, it's been a 50/50 accuracy in their forecast. The climate is changing radically.

Observe for yourself what is happening around you. Are the birds flying? Are they filling up on food? Are they hiding in their shelters? Or are they going about their day as usual?

Is there a warm breeze coming in? What shape are the clouds if there are any? Where I live, if thunderhead clouds develop before 4 p.m. we know a big rain and lightning is coming.

Speak to the energy of temperatures. Make friends with the extremes by letting go of judgment.

Can you smell the rain or snow coming? Can you hear the wind coming in the distance through the trees? Pay attention, and then go play in the rain.

Weather

Weather is the Earth's way of saying wake up. It's a reflection of the journey of life. The ups and downs, big and small, and over the top.

Weather often quickly connects humans to our Earth. It reminds us of our place. Earth, our keeper, has her moods and moments. Weather is one way she cleanses herself, and expresses herself, just like us humans.

One raindrop is a miracle. Follow it to the Earth.

The Sun's Warmth

The sun loves our Earth by shining upon her. Feel the sun touch you and warm you. You know that wonderful feeling. When you are chilled, and the first morning sun rays touch your body. You absorb it, and it feels so good. That is exactly how a tree feels as the sun first greets it on a cool morning.

Every single sunset and sunrise you ever witness becomes you.

What's Beyond

Fog is beautiful as it blankets the mountain landscape. Fog rolling in from the ocean and floating through forests is simply mystical. Fog teaches us to see ever-changing beauty in a living landscape. Clouding mist and then revealing in a moment. Nothing in nature ever stays the same, ever.

Perhaps the greatest teaching is curiosity. Dream of what's beyond the fog. We learn patience to wait for what's next, what's beyond the fog.

Honor Seasons As Living Beings

There are four distinct seasons no matter where you live, even if it's just for a few weeks. Each one has its own personality, and you can relate to each season literally, as our ancestors did, as living beings.

Fall, winter, spring and summer are living beings. They're not flesh and blood, but they're alive. Each one is unique unto itself. Take the time to explore what makes each one special. Experience them physically, emotionally, and intellectually. The seasons expand within and change you forever.

Something that defines fall is that it gets colder, the weather changes, and becomes more active. The trees realize they're going to shut down for the winter, and they display incredibly rich colors. One of my favorite events in nature is the changing of the fall colors. It's a miraculous light show every day.

Fall is when freezing temps wake you up in the morning. There's frost covering everything, and maybe there's a layer of ice over your bird baths or on the creek or the rocks along the edges.

Fall is the time of preparing to go inside and letting go to allow what's needed to sink in. Fall is the time emotionally when we've lived a full year in our ideas, our dreams, our hopes, our wants, and our needs. They're building a crescendo within us, becoming stable within us, becoming our medicine.

Then all of a sudden winter hits. Winter often is reflective of the time of death, and I don't mean that in a negative way at all. It's a time of heavy transition. The trees have lost their leaves, many animals hideout. In northern climates winter is hard for them.

Winter is a time of going inside emotionally, self-reflecting, looking at the life we've lived, and the life we're going to live going forward. It's a time to observe ourselves and ask those deep questions. When spring comes, who is the person I'm going to be?

Winter is a time of uprooting storms and quiet peacefulness, of getting warm by a fire, and thinking, and observing, and hoping, and dreaming. It is a time where ideas are birthed.

Then spring comes, the weather changes, the flowers come out, the bees and butterflies awaken, the animals come out of their dens. Life emerges, life is full. Spring is when nature is saying, Hallelujah, I'm alive!

You ask yourself, what are you going to do with all these days ahead of you? Spring is the time to start to implement your plans. It's time to wake up inside and out, spiritually, physically, emotionally, and intellectually. It's a time to let yourself out, to let the world experience the beauty of who you are. It's a time to make the world a better place, to lay your foundation. The new growth awakens us, and life's beat goes on.

Summer is the time to get to work. It's a time when it's all coming together. It's that time where it's warm and not so hard, and you just simply live everything you learned in the winter. Everything you were inspired to do in the spring, you live it in the summer. It is a time of abundance.

If you are taking on the Earth Caretaking path, then summer is the time when you get a lot of work done and manifest those dreams. Then you come back around to the fall, and you go through the cycle again.

***

How do the four seasons affect your body? When the different seasons come around, you will feel it physically, emotionally, intellectually, and spiritually. Each one will be unique to you.

The more you can relate to the four seasons as living beings, and I truly believe our ancestors did this, the more they will work for you. They will come alive, and as they work for you and inspire you, you will become a better person in the world, and the world will become better because you're in it.

So many human beings don't honor the seasons for what they are. Sometimes the attitude is that the seasons come, the seasons go, and there's a lot of negative thoughts around it. "Winter's coming, I'm going to have to shovel snow. Spring is coming, I'm going to have allergies. Summer is coming, it's going to be too hot. Fall is coming, it's going to get cold."

There are all these preconceived thoughts and judgments we have about the cycle of seasons. Look at those habitual thoughts and ask yourself questions about your beliefs. Do they serve you? If they do great, but if they don't, let them go.

Observe how animals experience the seasons. Taking on the seasons as living beings, and consciously participating fully in the unique gift each season brings, your life will become more enjoyable, and inspiring. Life isn't happening *to* you, you *are* life.

The gifts and varied energies of the seasons come back year after year and you can look forward to them. You know what's coming, and you sink into the patterns and the rhythm of the Earth.

Tests come along with the seasons. Life is full of tests, nothing new there. The more you're aware of the seasons and what they bring, the more you're open to enjoying them, to relating to them, the more you'll be able to deal with the challenges that show up.

I've often thought about what it must be like to be a bear in snow country. You live your life so fully from late spring through fall, and then so quickly you must find a den. You crawl in, you get covered with snow, and you sleep through the winter season.

Humans are awake through it all. It's a unique opportunity. I'm not taking anything away from the bear, there are a lot of times I'd love to be in that den curled up with that bear sleeping. We all are given amazing life experiences for our own species.

Relate to the seasons as living beings with their own energy and personalities. Enjoy them for the unique blessings that they are.

This fall, wish all migratory birds a safe journey, our lives depend on theirs.

Honor The Directions As Living Beings

Get to know the directions as living beings with their own form of consciousness and energy. Being open to other ways of living makes your life experience all the richer.

Different cultures pray to the directions, talk to them, and sing to them. They have colors and animals that represent them. Some of these beliefs are somewhat universal, and some are unique to a culture, and some to an individual.

Ask yourself, what do the directions mean to you personally? In the morning, greet the sunrise with your whole being. This is East, the day's beginning.

Later in the day, turn South and greet the full sun, as it warms you inside and out. In the evening look to the West where the sun sets. Let it help you to reflect on your day. Into the night watch the stars and Moon appear and think of the North, and what that feels like to you. It is a good time to go inward and reflect.

Give color to East, South, West and North. Discover what animal is in the East, South, West and North. As you build your relationship with the directions, a magical awareness will happen. You will discover that there are seven directions.

Consider how the directions live in you, and around you. The 5th direction is our Earth, what's below us. Our relationship to our Earth.

The 6th direction is what is above us and beyond. This direction is very personal, it is Spirit, your spiritual belief, and ideas to be discovered. As some of our ancestors called it, the Great Mystery. Something so much bigger than us, something to truly inspire us to live greatly and abundantly with love.

The 7th direction is where you are standing at any given moment. It's your moment. It's your time to be fully present. It's your time to show up, take action, and be the true gift that you are.

In the 7th direction there's nothing to stop you from being the authentic person our planet has been waiting for. In the 7th direction we can do good or bad or nothing. In that direction we are in our own power, and we can change the world.

Build your relationship with the directions. Allow the directions to come alive within you. Create songs, create ceremonies, bring them alive within your community, and keep them personal as well. Celebrate our Earth through her seven directions.

The Directions Can Get Confused

The directions get disoriented when there is a forest fire. The animals and insects and lizards get disoriented. They get turned around. Balance in the environment needs to be restored to right oneself.

The 7th Direction
I'm standing in the 7th Direction. Wherever I am, I am not lost.
I know I'm here and can be nowhere else when I am aware.
I can look to the North, East, South, West, above and below,
and yet I am still always standing in the 7th Direction.
I am never lost.
I am always here.

Chapter 23
Reverence For Trees

Trees are everything. I believe so strongly in the power of trees to transform our lives into lives of purpose and living beauty, lives of kindness and service. When we are at our best, we are as trees are every second of their lives. Trees are a vital part of what makes our living Earth, and life itself our home.

   At what length would you go to save a tree? There isn't a right or wrong answer. It is a question posed to make you honestly think about yourself.

We know trees are living beings. We know they can live a long time, much longer than humans. We know they provide a large part of what is needed for a healthy life on Earth for all living beings.

We know trees don't have a heart or lungs as we do. They don't communicate or move as we do, but does it matter that they experience life differently? Can another living being that is different from us humans matter as much as we do? Can we show the most basic respect as we would another human?

I learned to speak to trees through pure love, and an open heart of a child. There were no judgments clouding me and I never forgot this language. Trees speak to me through feelings, through my heart, through color, shape, and patterns.

That all knowing comes from my open mind, and connected heart, with no intention of control or manipulation. This skill is for anyone to hone. It takes work, practice, time, trust, curiosity, fun, love, and opening that awesome space within us that connects us to all life. This space must be awakened, and remain awake through spending time with trees, and of course with other beings in nature.

Trees are mediators. When we learn to communicate with them, they act as a conduit for humans to connect with the Earth. Trees are patiently waiting for us to get it together. They mitigate the craziness and anger of humans. They hold space until we can work it out.

Some of my best moments are with trees. They accept me for who I am. Trees do not have an attachment to life as humans do. They do love life and clearly want to live, just watch their actions. When their time comes to die, they do it with a dignity I admire.

Whether wind blows them over, or insects kill them or when they are in the north side of their life, and old age brings them tumbling down, trees become the Earth again through an artful transformation. It is a beautiful story of life and death and life, and it is perfect in all ways. It's magical, it is the way of the Earth.

I've cut down many trees in my lifetime, for firewood, for forest care, for wood to build with and for making space for my home.

I know these trees have been willing to give their lives up for good causes. I know this because the medicine of trees is to be of service. When I am cutting trees to help foster a healthy forest, I do this with empathy, and I listen.

When a tree lets me know it's not ready to be cut, I back off. I consider the health of the forest. It may not make sense to someone else of why I choose to cut down one tree, but not another that seems like it would be an obvious choice. I am communicating with each tree, and taking everything into consideration. I truly care. When I am in a forest I am among friends, the trees.

The modern way of cutting trees, such as clear cuts, and cutting old growth forests with no real concern for forest health is wrong. It's greed and we all pay a large price for this. It's a wound to the collective soul of all life. How we treat trees reflects how we treat all life, including human life. All Earth life matters. All life is in danger, and we all need to care.

Answers are hidden within the bark of trees.

The Old Redwood

Wherever I have lived I find trees that call to me. I visit them regularly. One such tree was near Santa Cruz, California. It was a giant redwood tree, about six feet across. My feeling was that this tree was around a thousand years old. The top part of the tree had been burned off hundreds of years ago.

This tree was on the north side of its life, meaning it wasn't growing larger any longer, it was getting smaller. Although, a tree at this stage in its life can still live for many years. As trees get to this point, they often become more beautiful, and full of life with insects, bats, and birds.

I would visit that tree often to think and meditate. What I loved the most was I could walk into this tree and look up to the sky and see the stars. It had burned out hollow hundreds of years ago, yet it was still very much alive.

Redwood trees are well suited for this type of survival. They resist fire and keep living. What a teaching to never give up, and to keep living and giving.

When entering this tree, it was like stepping into a grand cathedral of nature. It was spectacular.

I lived about fifteen minutes from where my tree friend lived. One day when I was at home, I felt the tree call to me. I felt a heaviness in my heart, and I knew the tree was in trouble. I went to the tree and found smoke and fire coming from it.

Someone had camped inside of it and set it on fire. Again, in its lifetime, it was burning. This fire was very intense. Flames leapt out of the top and up the sides. The firefighters were already there and doing their best to put out the flames.

A local friend, who was a logger, climbed the tree, and using a fire hose poured water down inside it, hundreds of gallons. Yet, it continued to burn fiercely.

To my surprise there were many people there watching. It turns out this tree was loved by the community. Many people knew this tree and were touched by it. It was a good old friend to many.

A horrible point came where the firefighters had decided the tree was in danger of falling across the road, so they had to cut it down. As it fell, I wept, along with the other mourners of our friend. This tree had lived a thousand years and now, in that moment, it crashed down.

When someone so revered is dying, and there is nothing you can do about it, it's frustrating and sad. You don't know what to do with that grief, but to just stay present with it in its final moments.

I don't blame the person that set the fire. They were cold and the tree had invited them in. I don't blame the firefighters; they did what they felt was right for safety. Yet, here lay the burning cathedral of nature, an elder, a God of the Earth, my friend. I was crushed. I could not make this right. I had to live with it. It was final.

Sometimes there isn't always a win, but the loss of that tree motivated me to be a better teacher, and pushed me to be more involved with helping nature. Sometimes loss like this allows us to dig down to our core of who we are, and feel the tree's instinct to want to live. It helps us to deal with tragic events through right action, by becoming the solution to problems that need attention.

After the fire had been long put out, I visited the tree's horizontal skeleton many times. One time I began to crawl into the tree and surprised a mother deer and fawn, who had been resting inside on a hot afternoon. Deer are heart animals, and this felt like a symbol of new life, and a completion for me.

If I could live my life in service as a tree lives, well then, I believe my life would be well lived.

Standing still in one place, and observing the landscape with an open heart, is knowing what it is to be a tree.

Acknowledge The Tree

Remember that lumber and sticks are trees. Have reverence for the wood, just like you would honor a cut of meat from the grocery store, by acknowledging it is an animal and not just a thing.

Have gratitude for the walls of your home and your furniture. Recognize they were living beings and are still giving back in another form.

See a stick as it once was, alive and thriving as a living tree. When you are roasting your marshmallow on a stick, thank the stick for the tree it is. Don't discard it as just a thing.

Wood holds memory in its cells, and gratitude is a felt energy that makes a difference in the world.

Ask permission and have reverence when you do need to remove a tree for your own purposes. I had to take down a young cedar tree to build my home where it was growing. I sat with it and asked its permission.

While the tree, of course, wanted to live, I also felt that this tree was also letting me know that it is of service. I cried when the tree came down. I honored it by making it into an art piece. It is no longer a living tree, but it now carries a spirit within it as a new form.

Scratch your back on a tree. Your back will thank the tree, and the tree will thank you.

Six A.M.

I climbed the elder fir as far up as I felt comfortable going, just before the trunk would sway from the weight of my step on its branches.

A still summer morning. Sitting, waiting to see something, but what? I didn't know. Still opening my eyes, not quite awake, but at least I showed up.

Staring out between the branches, in a half-asleep gaze, the silence was broken quickly. A fluttering through the dangling greens in front of me, and then there it was. Sitting on my branch three feet from my bracing hand, a Sharp-shinned hawk swooped in to check me out.

It tilted its head up just enough to catch my eye. I kept my return stare soft, still not believing what was sitting next to me. It gave me a curious, huh? And then a moment later it flew back off to patrol the sky for breakfast.

I don't always recommend climbing a tall tree when you're not quite awake, but that day, I think that state of mind was in my favor. We were both shocked at either of us sitting next to each other, but at the same time, it didn't seem that strange. It was a curious, nice morning.

Go to the woods and find yourself there.

Talk With Trees

One of the first activities we do with our new students is to get them climbing trees. Tim takes them to different, huge fir trees, and has them climb up as far as they feel comfortable.

There are times when there are thirty people in one tree. He has them settle in, close their eyes, and feel the tree's energy in silence.

Sometimes, Tim will have the students ask the tree a question internally, and quietly wait for the answer.

After one group of fourth graders came down from the tree sit, some of the kids volunteered what their question was and what answer they received. One girl blew us away when she said she asked the tree its name. We hadn't heard that question from a student before. When Tim asked her what the tree told her, she said, "Its name is Julie's Tree."

We had just met these kids the night before, and hadn't told them anything about the land yet. What was so amazing is that the tree confirmed to us that it is aware and can communicate with us, if we listen with the open heart, mind, and ears of a child.

That fir tree they were climbing was where I had done a powerful vision quest. I sat up in its limbs for three days. It was the tree that I got my answer from, letting me know that I was going to be moving to the Headwaters Land and be a caretaker of the land.

210

Of course, this young girl didn't know that, but she validated for me to never doubt what I know as my truth. I know that tree, and I had a personal interaction during my time spent in it, and it was felt. The tree is for everyone to share, but yes, it's also Julie's Tree.

Grab A Tree

Next time you're hiking and tired, grab a tree and ask it to fill you up. Know this tree called you. This tree cared for you. Trees give endlessly. They are the true example of service and are forever patient.

Humans Belong In Trees

Trees want you to climb them. All that stuff of adult life that gives us endless reasons not to climb trees – forget it. Paralyzing thoughts arise like, "It's dangerous. It's dirty. It's hard. I'll look stupid. I don't have time." These thoughts were not in our way when we were kids. We were open, we knew how to listen, and so we climbed.

I've climbed a lot of trees in my life. Growing up I spent many days in an old, Live Oak tree. Its branches stretched out far, creating a massive canopy. I would sit up in that tree through good times and bad times, and I would always be taken care of. I always felt held, and loved, and respected.

Ask permission from a tree if it's ok to climb it. Almost always you will feel that it's alright. If you don't, then maybe it's a safety issue.

As you're looking at the tree admire it and respect it for its beauty, and for what it can do for the world it lives in.

Sometimes we don't like ourselves as a species because of the destruction we have caused to our planet, but we need to recognize how we still belong here in a good way. Humans are beautiful in trees. When we climb up into a tree there is a bond between us. By spending time in trees merging with them as one, we heal the planet.

When you are climbing the tree feel its energy, its life force. Ask it to protect you and teach you. Be open to being taught.

When you find a branch to settle on, observe the world from the tree's point of view. Look within and look out. How does the tree see the world?

How does the tree feel when someone climbs it or when an eagle lands on its branches? How does it feel in a storm or in a drought?

Stay a while in the tree. It feeds your soul and gives you energy. If you can, stay in the tree overnight. I can't tell you how special that is. When you do, you'll know. Climbing trees is a personal experience, and it's a whole lot of fun. So, don't think about it, do it.

Trees are caretakers. They hold energetic space for the land. They hold memories, they hold stories, they hold our energy and ground it. They help keep balance in the world.

The Ponderosa Told Me

There is a lone, grand Ponderosa Pine that stands at the entry of our camp. When I first bought this land in Mount Shasta, I was still living six hours away in Santa Cruz. It was before there was a grated road to get to the property.

I had visited the land quite often to introduce myself, to get to know the land and feel its needs. I had befriended this particular tree, and knew it was a guardian tree. This tree had been on this land for decades, and knew instinctively the flow of everything within it. When there was a disturbance in the environment the tree responded.

I was able to tune into this tree's senses. When I was back home in Santa Cruz, I would check in on the land remotely by tuning into this great pine. I would know if a person had been walking on the land, or if there was any weather damage on the land.

One day, I was alerted by a feeling from the tree that there were people on the land with bad intentions. I knew they had done something. When I drove up the next weekend, I found that they had stolen a canvas teepee I had set up for shelter.

Over the years I had friends and students help build cedar bark shelters in the camp for people to stay in. About seven years after I had bought the land, I picked up another hit that something bad had happened. There had been a big storm, and I knew our camp had been damaged.

I knew it because I felt it. It wasn't just a concern; it was a deep knowing that the shelters had been washed away. I knew this even though the bark shelters were thirty yards away from the big creek.

Again, I drove up to the land to check on it, and even though I had that inner knowing, I was still in shock looking at the destruction of the camp. A warm, torrential rain melted the snowpack and flooded the creeks. The main creek that runs through our land got jammed up from all the trees that toppled into the creek.

The creek changed directions and shifted right through the middle of our camp. Most of the shelters were destroyed, and boulders had filled the remaining shelters completely.

Even if I had advanced warning there would have been nothing I could have done to prevent this. Though with the advanced notice as it was happening, I was able to go to the land prepared to clean up, and rebuild the camp in a different location.

It turns out in the long run the flood did us a great favor. We rebuilt the camp in a better location on the land, and the new flow of the creek allowed better access to the water for us.

The land has knowledge. It sends out information all the time. It's up to us to tune into this communication and interact with it instead of feeling victimized by it.

Vulture Tree

My vulture friends had been coming to the maple tree down the street from my condo for over a year. There was a line of trees down the sidewalk, but this specific tree was the one they always returned to every day.

One morning I was cleaning the house and instantly my heart hurt. I felt a knot in my throat and tears poured down my face. I heard the chainsaw, but felt it first.

I sobbed, knowing what it was I was feeling. I physically ached inside as though my artery was being severed. I felt the cut intuitively, the shock, and then the life force draining. My vulture tree had been cut down.

I knew it with all my being, but I went outside anyway to confirm, arriving as the limbs were being fed into a chipper. I was so connected to that tree that I felt what it felt. I melted in grief.

It was the only tree of twelve along the sidewalk that was being cut down. I couldn't bring myself to ask the workers why. It didn't matter. It was gone. Where would my vultures return to? Would they return at all?

I saw the vultures circling above later that day, but they didn't land. A week later a smile came back, seeing them on the neighbor's roof directly across the road from my place. A month later I moved to a nearby town. Within days they showed up on the roof of my new home, with wings outstretched.

I still felt the loss of my maple tree friend, but I also felt it was giving me a message that it was time to move on, and wherever I go, I won't be alone, there will be friends.

Giant Sequoias

When you look at a giant Sequoia in the perfect light you are witnessing greatness. The grand beauty can be so overwhelming, that at times in those moments I can be completely lost. Taken on a journey into the world of the tree, perhaps never to return to my conscious body.

When I do come back however, I'm not the same as I was before, I learned what tree reverence is. I've been touched, forever different, new again. Inspired, in love.

I'm happy to live in a world where some humans in the past saw a noble tree for its greatness and protected it. Trees unite all life, past to present.

Be Aware Of The Call

When you look at a tree and that moment comes when you want to climb it, stop and be aware. That tree is calling out to you.

Discover how it communicates with you. Pay attention. Wherever you live, find trees that call to you. The call could be a full-heart feeling.

The call could be in your mind. That place where your mind just knows a tree is special, you know your mind just can't stop thinking of that tree.

The call might come from your eyes. Seeing that profoundly beautiful tree that blows you away.

The call might come from the tree spirit, as a spirit connection. When the call comes, go to the tree, sit with it, climb it, protect it. Talk to the tree, ask questions. Make it a part of your life. Only goodness can come from this, only goodness.

You can see the life force of a tree, as the heat of a tree melts the snow around it.

Tree Kindness

Practice kindness, a trait so needed in our human world, by helping young trees grow. If you see a tree is struggling, care for it, give it water, give it your energy through direct touch, give it your love.

I often come across young trees covered in snow in the spring. They so want that sun, and to be upright, so I free them. As soon as I do, you can see those little trees feeling their tree joy, soaking up that light.

It's not about being able to save every tree, it's about the ones that call to you. Nature usually rights itself, but if you can show kindness and help it along, then why not? This type of kindness is uniquely human, it is our gift back to the trees for all they do. This is one way trees encourage us to be kind.

It can be overwhelming to try to help in every situation, but start with one act of kindness. Whether it is in nature or in the human world, every being wants to be acknowledged. Your gestures matter to the individual. In turn, your kindness will positively affect others. The energy of concentric tree rings will be set in motion. Start by helping a young tree and watch kindness grow within you.

Two Pines Planted

My dad and I were at a grocery store when I was ten years old. I spotted two potted pine trees near the entrance. They said to me, "Take us home and plant us". I convinced my dad, and we took them home and planted them along our fence. Fifty years later I visited them. Both were eighty feet tall and very healthy.

I smile when I think of all the good things those trees did for that backyard. They provided homes, shade, nuts, pine needles, and nutrients, and of course clean air.

Tree planting is a worthy enterprise. Save and protect, save and protect. Your mantra.

Forest Elders

Today very few old growth trees are left on our planet. About 95% of the world's old growth forests have been cut. They are disappearing at an alarming rate, and it must stop if we are to continue to live in a good way on this Earth. Not one old growth tree should be cut, not one.

A forest without old growth trees is like a community without elders. How will the young learn? How will they grow? Everything depends on each other. To cut anymore old growth trees is a crime against our Earth. Period. It's simply wrong and cannot be justified.

Biologists say that one old growth forest, at any one time, will be the home for 100,000 living beings, plants, animals, and insects. Think for a moment about that. It's a wonderful thing.

Plant a tree and change the world. It is so simple. Plant trees at your home, on your land. Get involved with organizations that plant trees.

 213

The trees that you plant will most likely live longer than you. Your children will thank you; animals will thank you; your community will thank you. You will leave your legacy in those trees.

The trees will teach you caretaking, love, and nature awareness. Planting trees is one of those special things in life that is truly full circle. Everyone and everything benefits and thrives.

Trees manifest wonder. Plant wonder today for tomorrow's children.

Learn From A Tree

Trees are great listeners as well as great storytellers. Lean against a tree, close your eyes, and ask it to tell you, Its story.

What do you see? How do you feel? Trees have so much to tell. They stay in one place their whole lives and are witnesses to all life around them. Quiet your mind and you'll get your answers from a tree.

Make friends with a tree. Reach out and touch a tree, they crave interaction. Imagine living your whole life where no one acknowledges you. They are givers, and when you give your attention back, it allows them to flourish.

 Dance with a tree.

They Are My Witnesses

When I am walking in the woods, I know I am not alone. I know that the trees are my witnesses. They hold me accountable to even my thoughts.

They are friends and they hold space for me. The trees know who I am. I acknowledge them and give them a blessing.

Reunited

I was out on a walk in a place I had never been before. Though it was only over a few ridges from where I live, it was new terrain for me. It had a very different feel, but it was inviting. I felt curious there.

There was open, grassy space at the base of the conifer covered hills. I wandered through the tall grass, and hopped through the marshy areas before my feet sank in too deep.

After an hour of exploring, I started to head back to my truck, but that curious call made me shift my direction, and I headed uphill instead. Sometimes clumsy on my feet, I had my eyes down watching my step. I hadn't walked long before I shifted my gaze up and chills ran up my arms. I took a timeless breath, and tears literally poured out of my eyes. I was standing in front of a magnificent Sugar Pine tree, and I knew without a doubt I had been there before, many times.

I knew that this was an old friend from the past. I had no logical reason for this knowing. I just knew it was a sacred moment, a reunion of old friends. This tree and a few others nearby were sentients of that piece of land. They held space for what I felt had been an old hunting camp in another time. I can't prove that. I don't need to prove that. I just know it.

The trees carried the stories of the seasons, and the animals, and people who had lived there, and had passed through that land.

That specific tree knew me. It called me over to it. It greeted me. In whatever way trees feel, it was in its own way happy to see me. I know this because I felt it. I felt the tree's joy. Just like you feel people and animal's emotions when you are reunited, that's exactly how I recognize the same response in trees. They are conscious Beings.

Who had I been during the days when I visited that place in the past? I have no idea. It doesn't matter. My soul is the same, and this I know because the tree showed me this, and welcomed me home.

To look at a gnarly old tree is to look at a god.
To climb a tree within a forest is to be with…well you know.

The Walnut Tree

In my old town Santa Cruz, lives a walnut tree. It was an amazing old growth tree that flourished many years ago. Now, it is a wounded tree, slowly healing from an attack on its spreading branches by the city's landscape maintenance crew. This tree was huge. It spread out all around a parking lot in downtown.

It was an icon there and people loved it. It was a God tree, one that kept you in awe of its grandness. The walnuts were cherished by the people and animals.

The ravens would take the walnuts and drop them on the road, and wait for the cars to run over them and break open the shells. They were happy, full ravens. Such clever, smart birds.

One day I felt the tree call to me. Each of the many trees I have been in tune with has a specific feel to it, so I know which one is communicating with me.

I went downtown and found a crew of people there with chainsaws cutting off the main spreading branches. It was tree butchery. What kind of person would decide to destroy an icon of the city and why? I was told the reason was that the branches could break and damage cars. Often the destruction of nature comes down to the fear of lawsuits. The tree never fully recovered. It broke my heart.

To be truly Earth Caretakers, we must consider trees and all of nature as Beings that matter, that have rights. Until we can do this, we will continue to make poor choices about how we treat nature. Nature must be considered first.

Our focus can't be about dominating nature. It must be working with nature, give and take. Sometimes there is no choice, the tree might need to go, but often, there is always a way to save these elders in a good way for all.

Earth caretaking is helping nature to live and prosper. That walnut tree is slowly coming back. Trees never quit, even though they may be wounded for life. The saddest thing is this tree didn't need to be cut. It was a bad decision made from fear and a lack of connection to nature. It was a lazy decision. A price was paid.

Speak Up

I was attending a Woman's March to support all people and the Earth, in our little town. The supportive, community turnout was impressive, but what I felt in the town itself broke my heart. Looking around I could see the death of the town's old maple trees that had previously lined the main street just a few days before.

In the middle of the night the city workers, at the direction of the city council, cut down the mature trees along the sidewalk. The council decided for the community, despite the disapproval of many citizens, to kill the trees because they didn't want the tree's roots to make the sidewalks bumpy. Yet again, the fear of lawsuits triggered people to make terrible decisions.

The life, the spirit, and character of the town was held in those trees. They held space for our community. They were the medicine keepers. They were the witnesses of our daily lives.

The council members knew there would be people who disagreed with their decision, so they hid their actions in the dark of night to avoid the conflict. Once they were cut down, there was nothing anyone could do about it. They could then move forward with their own plans for the town without obstacles.

At the Women's March I saw the mayor give a speech and afterwards I made my way directly to her. I introduced myself and asked if we could speak. She agreed to meet with me, and we had a cup of coffee a couple of days later. I couldn't hold back my feelings and spoke from my heart, sometimes out of sadness as well as anger. I educated her about the need for elders in a community, and the importance of the spirit of the trees to hold space.

She truly listened and could not help but to break down, and confess that she agreed with me. She was pressured by the counsel to agree with their plan of action, even though she didn't want to. She didn't stand up for what she knew was right, and she regretted it deeply. She saw what I saw, and felt what I felt, and knew it was wrong.

Eventually ornamental trees were planted. The cement sidewalks were straightened, but the life force that was once there is missing. The feeling of town has changed. Not for the better. It is cemented and sterile. The new trees will eventually grow, and they need our energy as well, but they do not carry the wisdom of the elders. It will take time for them to find their place and take on the spirit of the town. - Speak up for the trees. They need your voice to be heard.

My Muse

I sit up against an old cedar tree. It's the tallest tree on our land. It knows lifetimes of stories of people, of critters, of elements, of land, of weather.

I didn't think to go sit up against the tree. I was called to it through feeling. I went for a random walk with questions on my mind and I felt pulled to sit and close my eyes. In letting go of trying too hard, I was open to the answers. I was shown what my next art project would look like completed, and what the next step was to make it happen.

I leapt up with gratitude and re-charged energy. I was re-inspired to go make it happen. I literally felt an electric charge of excitement running through me. I got plugged back into my Source of creative energy.

Inspiration feels like a current that's back up and running, and the only challenge is to direct it with intention and focus. Otherwise, it's just a loose current, a wire, that's flying around. It needs to be grounded.

Sometimes the re-connection with Spirit in nature is so huge it feels like a giant download that's almost too big to handle. It's too much for one person, and all you want to do is share it to keep it flowing. It makes your experience that much sweeter.

You want to share your joy, and love, and inspiration with everyone. You aren't selective, you don't even think to exclude anyone. You just want everyone to feel what you have just experienced. - Sit with a tree, welcome it into you, and live inspired.

"Trees birth dreams of ideas. Ideas change the world". - E.K.

Make Trees Your Close Friends

There are going to be extraordinary trees in your life that call you, that you visit time and time again, and they become old friends.

Many trees are just getting started with life when ours is ending. Bristlecone Pines in the southern Sierra White Mountains, live to be 5,000 years old. Aspen grove root systems, which are considered one organism, can live over 80,000 years!

You might have multiple trees you know on a personal level. Visit them often, get to know them and build your relationship until it becomes sacred.

Trees need to be loved. Hugging them and connecting with them is one of the most important things you can do. When you come across a big tree, stop, and open your heart, and feel the story it has to tell.

As you spend quality time with that tree, talking to it, admiring it, bringing all your senses alive, the tree will teach you about how they live, feel, see, and how they experience the world. You will understand their ideas about the future based on their wisdom. You can learn so much by being open to a tree's energetic language, and allowing the tree to expand into your awareness.

Often, you don't just receive a teaching, there is an incredible peace that comes over you. You can also receive an emotional, and physical healing from your close bond with a tree. Trees can take your energy and work with it.

Remember, they're living beings, full of other living beings, and when you climb a tree and sit within its branches, you are another being upon them. In some ways you're like the children of the forests to the trees.

When the tree looks out into the forest at you, you're like a bear, or a deer, or a squirrel. You're another animal that lives within its community. They are willing to provide you with home, space, comfort, knowledge, and joy.

The inspiration of that personal relationship you have with the trees will hopefully turn into action, and you will become someone who passionately takes care of trees. An advocate who looks out for them and gets involved locally, maybe nationally, or globally.

You need to be allowing and give them your time. You need to learn how to trust your inner vision. If you think a tree is speaking with you and sharing with you, then truly listen. You have everything to gain and nothing to lose.

Our Cherry Trees

Cherry blossoms are nature's celebration. I have twenty-year-old cherry trees in my front yard, and a few more scattered on the land. When the trees blossom, I dream of the coming fruit and my taste buds get ecstatic, anticipating future, ripe cherries. I know the jays and robins and squirrels are waiting for their share as well.

Every year around the end of June the cherries ripen, and the abundance is amazing. For those few weeks, my students in my school are climbing the trees, picking cherries, and eating them until they are stuffed.

Harvesting fruit brings people together. Six people at a time will hang out in one tree. I could teach kids for weeks in the school how to connect to nature, and that cherry tree achieves that in an hour, just by the kids climbing the tree, picking the cherries, and gorging themselves into laughter.

The life of the cherry tree is the story of the cycle of life, give and take. We leave a percentage of fruit for the birds and squirrels as a give back. The wildlife shares the garden.

All summer the trees provide shade and beauty, and homes to the animals. Fall comes and another gift arrives. They drop their, now golden leaves, like a ticker-tape parade. Eventually they become soil. This soil will germinate the seeds from the cherries that the squirrels planted.

New cherry shoots sprout in the spring. The cherry tree roots reach into the soil. This soil is alive with worms and countless microorganisms. The roots find water and nurture the tree.

We let the cherry saplings grow. Sometimes we carefully dig them up, put them in a pot, and we give them to students to take home. Some of our students also clean and dry the cherry seeds, and plant them around their hometown.

Go back for a moment, back to the cherry blossoms and all that the cherry tree gives. It's an astounding thing to think of what one tree provides. Think of the impact of a whole orchard.

Planting a tree is a sacred act of Earth Caretaking, it is kindness multiplied.

Fruit Trees

When you bite into freshly picked fruit right off the tree, let the juice drip down your face and down your arm, all the way to your elbow. Chew it with laughter and let in the joy. Get all your senses involved. Let your taste buds revere it. Smell it, look at it with your eyes, feel the texture, listen to the tree as the wind blows through the leaves, while you enjoy its treats.

Appreciate every bite as a little miracle. Think of the fruit as Earth medicine. It is nourishing your whole being in every way. Know it is sacred. This is how you take living food to a higher level.

Dangerous Tree

In the dirt parking area of an East Bay Regional Park, are gigantic Live Oak trees. After a hike up the trail to the ridgeline and back, I would sit against one of those trees, and close my eyes and ask it to tell me its story.

A movie would play out in my mind's eye, and I was the witness to its life. I would see people and animals near the tree, from a time before there were cars. It was open land, untouched by the modern world.

Some days I would stay for a while with the tree, and other days I would just do a quick check in and say hello.

I had been away for a week and when I arrived at the parking area, a chain link fence had been put up all around the tree, with a sign hanging on it which read, "Warning, Dangerous Tree, Stay out".

Are you kidding me? I was shocked and ticked off. Dangerous to who? The people who are afraid of a lawsuit?

I stood outside the fence feeling so much empathy for the story tree. It wanted to connect with others. It had been standing there for hundreds of years, and it had stories to tell.

I remembered something Tim had said, "Signs are made to be interpreted." My thought was that this sign didn't apply to me, so I jumped the fence and sat against the story tree. I didn't ask it for a story that day. I just sat with it and gave it love. I felt that the spirit of place was diluted that day.

I returned months later, and the story tree's out-sweeping branches had been cut back, but I felt a little better seeing a companion tree outside the barbed fence, stretched over touching the upper branches of the caged tree. Some trees are good with being alone, but this tree thrived with touch.

Saving Trees Through Direct Action

Direct action is when we protest physically and stop what's happening. It's not for everyone, it can be dangerous. I want to add too, I'm in a place now where I don't think violence should ever be a part of it. I want to be violent sometimes to protect the Earth because I get so angry, but I know it doesn't work.

One of the darkest aspects of humans is that we can be a violent species, and it hasn't served us for the good over the years. We have created war and it never works out for the good. The path of peace is the best way. So, find conservation organizations that lead in this way.

When I was around 20, there was an old growth forest being cut in Southern Oregon. I joined a group of people that were part of an environmental movement, and went out to stop loggers from cutting down the old growth trees. One of the things we did was to climb the big trees and protest in a tree sit.

I climbed up about a hundred feet into a Douglas Fir, that was about 1,000 years old, 250 ft. tall, and would take almost a dozen people to wrap around the trunk. It was a true elder of the forest, an elder of our Earth.

I set up a tree sit, brought some food with me, and sat there for 10 days. The loggers were screaming at me and threatening me. I didn't fault the loggers. They were trying to provide an income for their families.

***

The issue is bigger than individuals. It's the way we, as a culture, think of forests. We think of them simply as something that is economic and a resource, rather than also thinking about how we can maintain and keep them, and our planet, healthy at the same time.

The greed factor comes in, often as it does in capitalism, and it gets confusing when it's only about money, and not offering different options. Our priorities get blurred, and we get blinded and don't think about the future.

We need to think broader, bigger, and better moving into the future. I will forever stand by my solid belief, that no old growth trees should ever be cut down.

There are only about 5% of old growth forests left in the world. They all must be saved. Old growth trees are literally life to the Earth. They are the most sacred beings. They are the ancient ones. They hold the stories and wisdom from thousands of years of living.

***

When I was in that tree there was a lot of time to meditate and communicate with the living essence of that tree. I can't tell you how powerful it is to sit up in a tree for days. Make time in your life, and do it, it will change your life forever, for the better. It doesn't have to be to save a tree, it can be just to be with a tree.

While I sat in that tree it gave me songs. If you meditate, you get calm, you get lucky, you become deeply aware, and you can pick up songs, knowledge, epiphanies, and dream-like moments from the spirit of the tree.

One song that has always stayed with me was about the tree's grief, and its fear of how its death as an elder would impact the forest. I felt its sadness of knowing it would kill a lot of the younger trees around it during its fall.

Forests need elders just like kids need elders to learn from. They need diversity for a healthy, balanced community, just like the human and animal world.

That song came into me through the tree as I sat in it. I would sing this song for hours upon hours. Each time it took me further into the heart of the tree to feel what it was feeling.

The tree knew more than I knew. It knew I was going to come down eventually and it was going to get cut. The wisdom in an old growth tree is mind-blowing.

Any answer you want or need in your life you can get it by spending time with an old growth tree. Not only that, but they are so profoundly beautiful and full of life that they fill you up in every part of your being. They are just extraordinary.

After ten days of sitting in the tree, I got hungry and scared of the logger's threats. I decided to come down. I wasn't sure if they had left or not. I snuck down in the middle of the night and hid in the woods. The next day I watched them cut the tree down. If a tree can scream, that tree screamed, and it took down many, many trees with it.

It broke my heart to watch that grandfather fall. I couldn't help it, I couldn't save it, and at the time I felt like I sold out. I was young and I dealt with that guilt for years. Now, in reflection, I don't think I sold out, it's not that cut and dry.

The good news is that one of the reasons we sat in the trees was to give time to the environmental lawyers that were working in the courts to save this area. After a few years they were able to protect the land and trees. It was added to the Kalmiopsis Wilderness Area, and is now saved for the sake of nature itself.

So, there was great news that came out of that, but watching that individual tree get killed has stayed with me all my life.

Trees have shaped the feeling part of me, the compassionate part of me. They have helped to grow empathy in me and have kept me in a peaceful way, rather than taking on the path of violence. They have motivated me to be more of an educator of nature, to literally speak for the trees.

Trees are all about making life work. If they can't grow one way, they grow another way. If they fall down, they keep growing. They help their young when they're struggling, they create air, food, water, and organic matter. They are homes to millions of insects and animals and birds. They make our homes. They're amazing mothers. They are the ultimate givers, and to tap into that tree energy is to flourish as a human being.

I encourage you to find a cause and get involved. If you want to take direct action, be safe and careful, stay away from violence, but get out there and do it. The timing is right. Go for it. Your elders need you now!

Chapter 24

Pilgrimage To The Wilderness

To pilgrimage to a place in nature is one of the most personal ways to build your relationship with our Earth. This means going back to a place overtime, repeatedly.

When we feel a sacredness around a place it's more than it being beautiful, we feel it in our heart, in our bones, in our whole being.

It's the kind of place that calls us when we're not physically there. We think about it. We dream about it. We want to know more and go back, each time furthering our exploration.

We love to see new places, and so often we go to sacred places in nature just once, and then travel to others. That's good to do, but there's nothing like a pilgrimage to the same place.

I think of pilgrimage places as sacred or spiritual. Pilgrimage places can become doorways to the unseen parts of our Earth, taking you to the Earth's heart.

Pilgrimage places can inspire us. My pilgrimage places are the places I can let go and let my true self out. Often, that means the wild man in me is truly free. These places become good old friends. When you arrive, you arrive home.

Some pilgrimage places are just for you, some for groups, some for lovers. All sacred spaces are openings to bring you back in deep relation with nature.

My Sierra

The Sierra Nevada raised me. In middle school, I hiked into Young Lakes with my mentor and the Sierra Club. We were collecting garbage from old campsites.

The timeless granite glowing with last light blew my mind. The rock seemed to glow from the inside out. The illuminated rocks reached through my eyes into my being, and now forever live within me.

As I was exploring Young Lakes, I felt a call to my heart, it began to beat faster, and I got chills across my back. An amazing afternoon thunderhead appeared as I looked up at Mt. Conness. The cloud was black behind the mountain, highlighting its white granite.

I wandered briskly across the open basin toward the base of the mountain, passing through only stunted trees, mostly Timber Pine and Red Junipers, and high-country ponds.

Every step was clearly a step home. I felt as if I was where I was supposed to be. I crossed over a short rise, and before my eyes, was the calling I had felt.

I was looking at Roosevelt Lake, the place of my dreams. The place that spoke to the essence of my very being. The place that was to hold me as I grew into a man. The place that I would grow to love as much as any place in nature. A place that would become my sacred pilgrimage destination for much of my life.

My teacher had told me about Roosevelt Lake, and there it was just as he described. I sat down, I could barely stand. I was shaking. Even as a young boy, I knew that moment was big as I soaked up the landscape.

The black thunderhead began to pour heavily, and the temperature dropped from warm and sweaty, to cold and wet in just a moment. It was late, and I knew the three miles back to camp cross country would be a challenge. I needed to get back before I was missed. It was painful to leave, but there was no doubt I would be back.

I Made The Climb Back

Roosevelt Lake is a big lake that sits at 10,000 feet within the boundaries of Yosemite National Park. It is named after my favorite president, Teddy Roosevelt.

I was able to talk my dad into taking me and my friend to camp at this amazing place, that I had a glimpse of from a distance a year earlier. The excitement of being down in that basin next to the lake, helped to motivate me up that steep, steady climb, cross country for twelve miles.

When we arrived, I felt how special it was. It pulled me in, and I was hooked. The rocks, the mirror reflection of Mt. Conness across the lake, the open sky and meandering tarns were all stunningly beautiful.

The nightly light shows of the alpenglow grabbed me and changed my life forever. When the last light would set over the Pacific Ocean, it would shine up on the top of the granite mountain and glow a pinkish red. The color spoke to my spirit and was profound for me. I let it in, and it has lived within me from that moment on.

I spent time with a family of marmots, I fished, I climbed, and I explored until most every stone was overturned. I was in my own Heaven.

In the way only mountains can, and only lovers of mountains can know, Roosevelt Lake, and the area around the lake's influence taught me what Spirit is, what holiness is, what it is to be in sacred space, and what it is to be sacred. The lake and the surrounding mountains became my personal space, my pilgrimage spot.

I have been back to Roosevelt dozens of times in my life. Sometimes I've gone alone, sometimes with friends, each time was sacred.

To this day, I'm sure that the man I've become was shaped in a big way by my time at Roosevelt Lake. Friends ask me why I go there time and again. I tell them, "When the Gods want sacred, quiet time, they make a pilgrimage to Roosevelt, and I want to be in *that* space."

A Sense Of Place

If you love a place, I mean if you really love a place, in your bones, in your blood...If you can't stop thinking about the place, then stay and become the place. Stop looking so far away. You might find you've arrived at Home, your place. It's been waiting for you!

Returning To Roosevelt Lake

It was the last night on a two-week camping trip with my two friends at Roosevelt Lake. We sat by a fire, talking a bit, struggling a bit with the idea of having to leave the next morning. It was time to go back down from 10,000 feet to that busy world of people and cities.

It's always hard to leave a pilgrimage spot where literally every second you spend is sacred, inspiring, and peaceful. We had our long hike out, so we woke up at first light.

Imagine this scene before our eyes. Above the treeline, the massive, high-altitude lake, Mt. Conness rising out of the East side of Roosevelt. Reflections, fish jumping, granite rocks.

At first light there is a quiet that defines quiet, and a frosted white blanketing the ground. Twenty degrees, cold, alive, happy, and inspired to go home and live in a good way.

We were ready to head out, so we offered our gratitude, blessings, and a song to the lake. There was a movement in the granite across the lake. A coyote ambled down the cliff, across the rock to the shoreline directly across from us and began to howl.

On this crisp morning, the towering mountain watching over us at the basin, and witnessing the echo of the coyote reverberating through us, was breathtaking, and we stayed for it all. The coyote sang to us for half an hour, and then there was absolute quiet, and the coyote disappeared.

Now that's a sacred moment. We changed that day, we became better humans. That coyote and that mountain space gifted us the morning with inspiration, and true peacefulness. They said thank you to us for this sacred visit. We hiked out inspired and happy that we knew we would be back the next year.

When sacred moments happen, particularly when they happen in pilgrimage places, take the time to let the medicine come into your being and become a part of you.

To Know A Place

To know a place, I mean to really know a place, you must go there many times. To know a place, you must become the place. This can only happen with time, quiet, no agenda, peacefulness and most importantly, an open heart.

To be a place is to know our Earth in a personal way. When this relationship happens, a kind of clarity comes that cannot be understood in the brain. Separation doesn't exist. You are as the animals are, the trees are, and the mountains are. This place becomes a pilgrimage place.

A Daily Pilgrimage Into My Backyard

We live in a very, very busy world. I'm as guilty as anyone for not slowing down. Sometimes I don't leave my office for days to go out and walk on my land. I remind myself, "What are you doing?! You live in paradise. Get out in the woods Tim!"

At the entrance trail to our camp, we hung a flag of the Earth. The flag got caught on the edge of one of the poles, and it became ripped and tattered. For a while it was really bothering me. Looking at it one day it struck a truth in me, that this is how our Earth feels right now. She feels beat up, tattered, broken in places, hanging on by a thread. The torn Earth flag feels like a distress call, but I know she is still at the point where she can heal.

To do the healing work, we need to build our relationship with her. We must get out and put our time in being with the Earth. If we don't do it, then nothing is real for us. The quest to fight for the Earth becomes more in the head, and less in the heart and the soul. If we are going to care for our Earth and save her from us, then we must come from kindness. Violence does not work. Our efforts need to be heart driven. Love is the most powerful energy there is.

Build your relationship with the Earth through curiosity. Wander, sit, get in the water, climb trees, truly get to know a place.

Keep the vision clear inside your mind, and let the Earth speak to you about your vision. That vision of how you are going to put your incredible self to work for the healing of our planet and all beings. You must get out to know a place. Start with your backyard.

Finding My Marbles While Losing Myself

Hiking into the Marble Mountain Wilderness, joy filled tears streaming, returning home for the first time in this lifetime. I had been lost for so long. Looking for a place where I fit.

Craning my neck to take in the majesty of the ancient Sugar Pines. Switch backs leading me up, up, up under the shaded canopy. Wandering bucks are the only traffic crossing my path.

Each new encounter and rise in elevation, sheds a lifetime of homesickness. I was called and driven to come here. I couldn't not go.

Light rays from an opening lead the way. The purest bliss clears my thoughts and fills me with awe. Transitioning from trees to a wildflower meadow is like walking into a mural with no canvas edges.

How could this be real? It's so real I don't recognize it. My life has been a movie, now changing from black and white to full color.

I found my Marbles, and while losing myself, I found me. Each year I return to the wilderness, it starts all over again. The hike in takes me back to who I am.

Find Your Place

Pilgrimage places don't have to be in pure wilderness. They can be places close to your home. For most of my life, I have been returning to a beach near my hometown of Santa Cruz. I visit this beach multiple times a year.

I have taken hundreds of people there. I teach school groups at this beach. I have vision quested there. I have shared this place with people I dearly love.

Your pilgrimage place is sacred for you. You can choose to share it with others, or return to this place on your own.

When you are at this place allow yourself to go into a higher state of being. Let go of fear of judgment, become as pure human as you can be. Just you and nature spending time together.

Explore this place, get refueled. Know it as you know yourself, and the secrets of the place will unfold. Go into the nooks and crannies. Introduce yourself to the animals, plants, rocks, and waterways. Let them know you care, that you have a good heart, and that you're not there to create disturbances. When you do this, there is an allowing and a welcoming that is felt.

Go to the same place you love repeatedly. In this space nature will teach you, and provide wonderful interactions and experiences for you. It will become so normal to you that you will not feel like a visitor, you will become a part of the environment.

You may not be able to track back the exact moment, but in time your life will become more amazing. Every aspect of your life will be lifted because everything is connected.

Go find these sacred places to pilgrimage to. Enjoy the journey of the search. There are always places that will call to you specifically. Pay attention and then go.

Animals Pilgrimage

Animals, fish, birds, butterflies, all migrate to the same location annually. Their intention may be for survival for food, more hospitable weather, or breeding, but they have free will of where they choose to go.

We have a pair of Sandhill Cranes that return to our neighboring pond annually. Our local residents look for their arrival each year in the spring, and watch for their departure in the fall.

We all keep watch to see when their first egg hatches, and wonder how many babies they will raise. We know if a coyote has been stalking by, and if one of the birds has been injured.

Our community is invested in their welfare. The cranes are a special connection we all have with each other, even if we don't know each other, we all know the cranes.

There are many different crane couples that congregate in multiple locations in our area. These two cranes choose this same grassy meadow, alongside the 67-acre reservoir, to return to every year to raise their babies.

Animals migrate and humans pilgrimage. We are all being called by something internally, and whatever we call it, it doesn't matter. We know a good place when we see it.

Go Find It

Dream of the most amazing landscape you could ever find on our Earth. I'm talking about a fantasy landscape. Our Earth most likely has this place somewhere on the seven continents. Look for it in books or on the internet. Do your research. Once you know where it is, plan a trip and go. This place is looking for you too. Go find it.

Welcome Home To Headwaters

Many students who have attended classes at our outdoor school, have been returning to our land for many years. They may not be participating in classes any longer, but they have made a connection with the land. It calls them home to get recentered, filled up, and back in balance to return to their everyday lives.

Of course, they have also made special friendships, spending so much time together in such a heart space. They miss the community that has been created and nurtured here. They feel the ache of that authentic companionship we feel when we are learning, and crafting, and eating, and working, and playing together in such a free and special place.

The people miss the campfires, and even the dish line, talking, singing, and working with purpose together. They miss how villages used to be, where interdependence was the way of life.

Even with these unique relationships they have grown up with, it's always the land that they are called back to, even when their friends are not here.

If the Headwaters family members have been away for years, sometimes it takes them a while to get the city out of them, and sink in with the rhythm of the land. The habitual busyness takes a little bit to let go of, but once they sink in, you can visibly see the change within their being. You can feel their energy shift and slow down, and open back up, as they start taking in the sense of place that has been calling them back home.

After walking on the land, smelling the smells, feeling the air, soaking in the energy of the abundant water, visiting their special sit spots, people remember themselves. They put back together the pieces of what is sometimes fragmented and forgotten.

Headwaters has become a sacred pilgrimage place for the people. In creating Headwaters, I have set the intention of what it is to be. I hold space and adjust guidelines as needed, but then I let go.

Headwaters is bigger than me. It has taken on a life and energy of its own. The land, the people, the animals have all contributed to this. People past and present have left their energy here. People have grown up here and stories have been lived here. All of this is felt and speaks to the heart. This unnamed force calls people back to pilgrimage to the Headwaters Land.

Headwaters is more than a nature school, it's a grounding place, it's a sense of belonging. Even if we don't see someone again, it's still comforting to them because they know the land is here, and the caretakers are still here, and Headwaters exists in this crazy world.

We are still honorably holding space on this sacred land for the community. People have history here and that never goes away. It will always be a part of them, and they will always be a part of the land.

Land Holds Energy

I live and run my outdoor school, ten miles from the base of Mt. Shasta. Mt. Shasta is a stunningly beautiful power spot, created by nature. It is a lone mountain that towers over the landscape, and can be seen from 100 miles away.

People from all over the world have been drawn to Mt. Shasta for the opportunity to be in its presence, and to receive its energy. Mt. Shasta touches everyone in some way and has changed people's lives solely by being in its presence. For some people it touches them with beauty, while others have spiritual experiences and awakenings of deeper truths.

Many believe this mountain has a spiritual connection, forming a powerful, energetic triangle to Mt. Fuji in Japan, and Mt. Kilimanjaro in Africa, all three being lone, volcanic mountains.

People who want to soak up this energy, pilgrimage to all three mountains, picking up their medicine. Carrying that experience with you can be life changing in the journey alone.

Mt. Shasta, like many large, natural, power spots, pulls people to them. It doesn't need to be explained. The mystery of it is an important part of a power spot's calling.

Even looking at a mountain for long periods of time can change you. There is something that happens as you let that mountain in through your eyes, into your body, you soak it up and become it.

You've heard the term, think like a mountain, when you take in the essence of the mountain, you merge with its energy. You begin to view the world like the mountain does. That's an amazing thing that requires trust and willingness to dive into that idea without overthinking it.

I myself have been drawn to this mountain, and hold great reverence for it. I have dedicated decades of photographing her beauty to share. I created Mt. Shasta Photo Project, where I have put together six photography books so far in her honor. I have included other photographers to share from their perspective and experiences with her as well.

I use the pronoun her, in referring to Mt. Shasta, because that feminine energy is what I feel emanating from her. It is the heart energy of love, and nurturing, and holding space as a mother.

***

My land itself is a power spot. The first year I bought this land, there was a woman up the road from me who lived out in the woods as well. Her name was Rowena Kryder, and she was a new age spiritualist, and highly respected within her community. She was a prolific, eclectic artist, and an author.

Rowena was kind of this wispy, wild woman I couldn't really get a grip on, but I do mean this in a very respectful way. There was a great mystery about her. She was powerful, and I was still young, and very impressionable so her presence caught my attention.

My good friend, Charlie Storm Owl, who helped me start the school, is a powerful person as well. He and I were working on the land one day when Rowena came to us and said, "Come to my house, I have to tell you something." We said we would come, but we were a little taken aback by her bluntness and sense of purpose. We had not officially met her before this invitation.

We went into her house she had built, which was interesting in itself. It was round, and most of the outside walls were all sliding glass doors. She was literally sitting on a raised altar, surrounded by thousands of crystals. I kid you not, this is not an exaggerated, Irish fishing tale. There were literally thousands of crystals of all sizes, and many ornate paintings on the ceiling and walls, and astrological mosaics on the floor.

Rowena was sitting in a chair that was like a throne, elevated up on sort of a stage. We sat in front of her, wondering what she was all about. She looked at us and told us the land I bought, is the power spot for the Mt. Shasta area, the whole Northern California region.

She said it is where there is a vortex of energy where all the power of the mountain, and all the power of nature, and everything that's ever happened on all the land here, focuses its energy and comes to a crescendo. It is a powerful piece of land, a power spot.

She said, "You have to be the caretaker. That means you have to protect it and keep it healthy." We didn't have much of a conversation, and we said okay, and we left.

I didn't really know what to say at the time. It all sounded very, woo woo, but I believed her. Like anything, I didn't immediately digest all the information she gave me. I did stay open to it though.

I started living on the land, and listening to the Earth Keeper, and you know she was right. I've had the land in my care since 1990, and I've seen countless people's lives change by just walking onto this land.

Our outdoor school teachings help speed up the connection to the land, but often, people just come to walk the land and drink the spring water, and their lives change. They could be here an hour or a day or a week or a month and their lives change. There is a quickening. A sped-up shift in their awareness, and their actions to make the changes.

Profound things happen to people who come here. Many times, they have no clue that it had anything to do with the land, but I know it did because I've witnessed it countless times.

I had a regular delivery truck driver come here just to deliver packages, and he became a healer. He credited it all to the land.

Since our school began, our students and visitors have put their time and energy into the land, so the power of this land has become much stronger. We also ask them when they leave to give the land a blessing, and express their gratitude for the land holding space for them during their stay.

All this positive energy is noticeably felt when people arrive at Headwaters. Most people instantly notice not only the beauty of the space, but they also feel the inviting energy. Many people say they feel like they are entering a fantasy world.

***

Our modern culture and upbringing, plants limits in our heads. Imagine a limitless world. Power spots can be on your own sacred, human body. Acupuncture points are power spots. Clearly your heart and brain are power spots. Your soul is the most powerful. It's connected to all things and carries us through all time.

There are zillions of types of power spots, they are everywhere. Many national parks are power spots. People are drawn to them for their unique landscape features, but also for the feeling they get when they engage with the landscape or water features. Many times, there is a noticeable feeling of awe or tranquility.

Power spots can be huge areas, or they can be as small as the rock you are sitting on. Power spots can be in the ocean or in trickling creeks. Power spots can be a small branch on a tree or the tree itself.

 225

Natural power spots are often springs, headwaters, waterfalls, hot springs, or places with biological diversity of plant and animal life, or unique rock formations.

The more you seek out these places, acknowledge them and enjoy them, the more inspired your life will be as you soak it all in.

The Earth is a power spot in our Universe. It is filled with life and is also life itself. From the beginning of our history, we have shared it all together. What is more powerful than that?

You can make a special place a power spot by visiting it many times, and having many experiences there creating memories. Those memories live in the land.

When you experience something special like a power spot, you don't need to question it. You don't need to endlessly search your mind to try to figure it out, or study it, just let it be. One of my greatest joys is to watch the magic happen.

Go to power spots again and again. Open your heart and absorb the place. Collect the medicine. Find new ones and create power spots by putting your good energy into it. Your life and your connection to our Earth will be unshakably personal.

Generations Of History

I have true respect for the great Native American leader Chief Joseph, (Hinmato'owyalahtq'it) of the Nez Perce tribe, whose people lived in the Northeastern region of Oregon, in the Wallowa Valley.

These were the generous people who welcomed the Lewis and Clark Expedition on their journey West, and back again, and provided them food, rest, and safety.

The Nez Perce believe they have always lived there from the beginning of time. Every tree, rock, meadow, waterway, valley, and mountain were revered and had a history that was known to the tribe. They knew those elements sustained them and were worthy of their respect, love, and care.

Trees and bark provided shelter. Animals provided food and clothing. Water was always known as their sacred life force. The valleys and mountains were their rooms, the sky their roof and the Earth itself, their mother, and their foundation.

Settlers and the U.S. government solely regarded nature's beings as resources and not relations, and greedily sought to own them.

When the U.S. government betrayed the Nez Perce and forced Chief Joseph from his beloved homeland, he led the tribe of over 700 people on an epic journey to the Canadian border where he hoped they would be safe. Joseph was the Nez Perce's spiritual leader and not a military tactician.

They were relentlessly chased by the U.S. Army. Throughout this entire treacherous journey, their tribe – men, women, elderly, children, the sick and the wounded- fought 2,000 army soldiers and won 13 battles. Against the odds, tired of the relentless fight, forty miles just short of the Montana/Canada border, freezing, sick, and exhausted, the Wallowa band (Wal-lam-wat-kain band) of the Nez Perce surrendered.

They were forced onto a reservation, and were lied to by the U.S. government. With negotiations and treaties broken, removed from his beautiful, beloved home, Chief Joseph died of a broken heart.

His people had lived for thousands of years on their land, and were a part of their landscape. I've traveled to their home in Oregon, and it is breathtakingly astounding. I can understand his feeling of loss. Chief Joseph must have been a truly wonderful human being.

To all nature people, the land is a living being and a part of them. Every hill, creek, river valley, and rock is alive holding stories of people's lives interacting with nature. The love of the land is deeply personal.

Home

The living Earth itself can speak to us humans. The Earth often speaks through her beauty. We see beauty and we are touched and often inspired.

We two-leggeds, love dramatic views. They fill us with wonder and inspired dreams. We can thank the Earth for this. Sunsets and sunrises speak to our own inner beauty. We feel good watching the light change. The Earth is speaking.

We don't often acknowledge the Earth for showing us things that feed our souls. When we ask and pay attention, the Earth will show us a special place for us that feels like home. Finding this place is so very important. All good things grow out of our Home.

As we learn this Earth language, we open to our Earth's intricate forms of communication, and that wisdom can be very specific for us.

This Earth holds memory and wisdom. We need to listen. There is no code to crack to access this, just listen.

The Story Of Place

Give a name to a place and you give it a story, you bring it alive. You make it personal. This place becomes a living being, a part of your community. It binds future generations to your generation. Oral tradition is honored through the giving of names. This place is given a voice.

This practice was vital to our Earth ancestors. It weaved communities together through the story of the place. It was medicine for them. As the place grew, and changed with the community, so the story changed.

Giving names to places can be very personal, something that you may keep to yourself. It can be for communities, where community events take place. It can be for lovers, to name the place where love first blossomed. It can also be places where dark, or shadowy events occurred.

These places can be large, universally shared places like mountains or valleys, boulders, trees, cliffs, rivers, lakes, streams, and any other body of water.

When I went to Ireland, I found that even today, countless rock outcroppings and hills have names associated with events or stories that happened there. This bonded the ancient Celts, my ancestors, to the land in a very personal way, that our modern culture barely understands.

Although, I must say, we name places too. We have national monuments, battlefields, and parks. These places help to bond our country, and communities together. The danger for us today is we become too superficial. We don't take the time to make these places medicine.

At Headwaters Outdoor School we have names for places around our camp, such as the sweat lodge area, a place where lives change forever. Magic happens here.

We give names to the land like, Bear Hill, the First Meadow, the Creek that Runs Uphill, the Second Creek, the Singing Tree, Julie's Tree, the Wedding Circle, the Old Growth Tree, the Kitchen Pool, where I found Headwaters, and Lizard Gulch to name a few.

I have many places that are personal to me. Places where I saw an animal in an amazing way, and the place where the spirit Earth Keeper dwells. Places I sit to think and observe. All this bonds us to our lands and our people, and our Earth.

Feel the energy of the land. Land holds space for people, animals, and plants. Give names to places and give voice to stories. Do this and these places will become alive. They will become revered places and hold the energy of your stories and memories.

If you go sit in these spaces, ask them their story. Close your eyes and listen. Take in the history of the land, and learn who else has been there before you, and maybe still is.

Story Rock

Year after year we bring people to our second home, our wilderness home. Over the decades there are many stories held within each feature of our camp, but one powerful place is the soapstone rock.

One night during our week stay, we gather on this large slab of soapstone, that sits on the hillside overlooking the lush valley. A couple dozen of us will snuggle up close and take in the changing light, while we all take turns sharing stories of our day's adventures, songs, music, jokes, and poetry.

Memories are shared from previous years of friends, and our Headwaters dogs who have joined us. Some stories are funny, some are thought provoking, and some are sad. All are good though. We bring those friends in to join us. Their energy is still felt there through our memories, through our stories, and through the stone.

We've watched slow moving fires burn through the base of the old growth trees across the valley. We danced with the thunder and witnessed the explosion of lightning hitting a tree. We've felt the rain wash us and the fire out.

From this community rock sunsets are watched, and shooting stars are revered. Curious deer approach our gathering and graze close by, listening to our tales. Birds stop by for a visit in the treetops before heading off to bed. Coyotes howl, and we go unnoticed as animals pass below us in the valley on their nightly hunt.

Story time on the soapstone rock is a cherished time, and one that is never forgotten. The rock holds our decades of stories. It reminds us of all those times we gathered during the last light of day in the magic hours.

Kauai

I have returned to the island of Kauai for over 30 years. I return for myself, and I also bring classes there to experience nature's ancient energy.

Kauai, in my opinion, is the heart center of our world, and that's a big statement. It is a power spot of love and wisdom. The energy comes through the breathtaking landscape.

There is an ancient, feminine energy within this island. It is felt in the volcanic rock, in the waterfalls and in the surrounding ocean. It is felt by the animal life, and they are drawn to it as well.

I have known many people who fall in love with each other while on Kauai, and many who have fallen out of what they thought was love. The energy of love is not judgmental, and it doesn't lie. You will know the truth, while on Kauai. Now whether you choose to listen to that truth, is up to you.

Landscapes

Different landscapes like mountains, deserts, forests, grasslands, rainforests, tundra, and oceans have a unique character that speaks to individuals.

Each of the seven oceans have their own temperament. The Atlantic Ocean is completely different from the Pacific Ocean. Ask any ship captain and they will talk about it for hours.

The Himalayas aren't remotely like the Andes or the Rocky Mountains. The North and South Poles are complete opposites.

I look at these landscapes as living beings, alive with their own Earth medicine. To truly know them you must see them as individuals.

Let yourself be drawn into them. Let them reveal their mysteries. If you do this, you'll become a part of them, and they will become part of you, and you will carry their personal spirit with you for life.

A powerful, old growth tree, even when it is gone, still leaves its energy in the space it once stood. It can still be seen and felt as strongly as it did when it was physically there.

Echo Medicine

When you're in nature, perhaps in a canyon or in mountain snow country, and you make a sound, there comes an echo. In this magic moment, listen, and take in the reply from the land.

It's gathering its answer from its surroundings and singing it back to you.

Collecting Stories

When we make things from nature, those items we collected have stories of their lives, as well as from the people who collected them, and then it has stories from the people who have used what was then created. There is no end to how, and what the land holds and passes on.

Where Rivers Meet The Ocean

I've spent a lot of time at the mouth of the Klamath River in California, and at the Rogue River in Oregon where they meet the Pacific Ocean. Places like these are true power spots.

Imagine these rivers running out of the high snow mountains, sometimes for hundreds, if not thousands of miles to reach their end and new beginnings at the ocean. All along the way the rivers are meeting, and interacting with different beings and carrying those experiences in them.

As the rivers work their way down and they start to merge with the ocean, the water becomes brackish, half freshwater and half saltwater mixing. A blending between river and ocean. So much life breathes in this transition zone.

Think of the stories the rivers have to tell the ocean about their journey. Think of the ocean's stories of who comes and goes from the river mouth.

***

Think of the salmon, a true miracle of nature. For years they travel the ocean and then a mysterious call beacons them back to the river. They meet at the river mouth. Relationships, memories, stories to tell of ocean life. Predators, seals, killer whales all feeding.

Then that mysterious call is felt. You know that call yourself. You feel it telling you it's time to re-engage on your life's journey. It's not so different from the salmon. They enter the river mouth, a place of power, of transition. A place of hope and dreams of returning home. A place of change and new life and death. Death, either real or metaphor.

The call into the river mouth, and a new journey begins for countless miles up the river. Through calm water, rapids, falls, and eddies, all must be navigated, such is life for all beings. Fishermen, bears, eagles, fatigue, doubt, fear, loss, peace, calm, love, joy, satisfaction.

The arrival, eggs laid, and the salmon's life ends. The salmon's body floats down the river and the salmon becomes another life and lives on through that life.

Eggs hatch in a miracle moment in time. You fish, hear the call, and the journey to the river mouth begins. The call of the river mouth, a place of power and transition.

***

As the two main artery rivers meet the vast Pacific Ocean the water mixes, the river life and sea life all intermingle.

Countless seabirds gather at the meeting place of these two powerful beings, the river and the ocean. There's so much food available there, and so many animals that come to feast.

When you come to a river mouth take time to really study it. Get into the water, walk along the edge, look at the tracks of the animals that have come out of the water.

Look for the Ospreys catching the fish, and carrying them off. Look for the eagles that come down and eat the rabbits that are nibbling on the small plants along the dunes.

Look for the whales, and the fish, and the seals that live just off the shore, searching for the animals that come down the river mouth.

I love to sleep near river mouths. I love to sit for hours and observe. I love to wade into the water. I want that water on me, so I get my shoes off and I get in there, and most times I'll jump in for a swim.

I love to photograph river mouths, and the brilliant colors of the sunset when the light sparkles across the waves of the ocean where the river meets it.

When you're on a road trip, make it a point to stop at river mouths. Maybe take a trip where you do nothing but visit river mouths. If you're lucky enough to live near one or two, visit them regularly. Make them a part of your life.

The meeting of a great river and the ocean is truly one of nature's powerful unions. The more time I spend in these amazing places, the better person I become, going further into myself, being held by the Earth's beauty and majesty.

Get inspired by those powerful places. As you move forward in life with all your accomplishments, you can track much of it back to the inspiration you received from seeking out those fascinating places of power.

Oregon Coast Rivers

To me, the Oregon Coast rivers are some of the most stunning, wild rivers I've ever seen. Turquoise water that stirs my dreams. Every year on my return, the oasis of deep, swimming holes invite me in.

Abundant wildlife everywhere. Bears, otters, deer, pine martens, cougars, salmon, and trout. I love going to the river mouths where they flow into the ocean. Walking wild beaches with majestic cliffs, endless sand, and washed-up logs from the inland forests.

I let my dad's ashes drift down the mouth of my favorite river and swirl into the ocean. As I shared my gratitude to my dad's spirit, an unexpected fleet of military pilots flew overhead in formation. I believe it was an honoring of my dad, as well as a hello from him. He was an Air Force pilot, and the timing of those jets flying overhead at that moment was an amazing gift.

When I walk the beach to the river mouth, I know my dad is with me. My visit to this sacred place never disappoints. I truly love the river, mountain to sea.

When you look at a magnified raindrop on a leaf, you see the universe before your eyes. Receive what these micro places have to offer. The knowledge of the Earth will awaken within you. There is vision in a raindrop.

"The land holds the memory. It becomes the medicine of the land. The land has a story to tell. It is no different than opening a book. The information and stories are there. You just need to read them." - E.K.

Negative Energy

There are places where negative energy is felt in the land. Energy is left like a track or print that we leave behind. Sometimes when the energy is very intense that imprint of energy stays.

When there has been a traumatic event or numerous people involved in battle as an example, the more intense the energy, the more that impression can be felt.

I walked into the Alamo and my mood shifted instantly. I wasn't paying attention to the significance of the building at the time. I had put my hand against the wall for just a second and I felt like I couldn't breathe, and had to walk outside quickly.

For a few moments I didn't know what happened. Once I was outside, I felt better physically, but there was a sadness in me. I then realized that I was picking up on whatever energy was still there in the land from long ago. It was like a fingerprint left behind.

***

On a day hike in the wilderness, I had been talking with friends and laughing, until we crossed through an area of mostly dead standing trees. Instantly we got quiet. I felt myself almost stalking quietly through the area, trying not to disturb whatever was there. I knew something bad had happened there. I don't know what exactly, but it felt like some kind of ambush.

I kept quiet even after we passed through that area. Tim caught up to us, and asked us if we felt the energy of that place we had just passed through. He said you can feel that a battle was fought there. That was a good reminder for me to trust my feelings, and to know that energy is powerful, and can still be felt physically, long after someone is there.

Decades later, revisiting that space year after year, it is still mostly a barren patch of landscape within the forest.

Roll in meadows. You will feel all who have joyfully rolled in them before you.

"This land is your land, come to the Earth. It's been a long time you have been gone." - E.K.

Feel The Difference

Jokingly, but also in seriousness, I tell our students to sleep around. I tell them to sleep in various places on the land to feel the different energy, and spirit of place.

Just as there are microclimates within a parcel of land, there are also varying degrees, and types of energy that are felt within the same property.

I tell them to sleep next to the creeks. One night sleep with their head upstream, and the next downstream. I tell them to sleep by the campfire or up on the hill or in a meadow.

You cannot fully know yourself, without first knowing the land you live on.

Entrance ways allow for transition. They take us from one world to another. When you create that transition you can feel it. Archways into gardens shift the energy into a new space.

They Sang With Us

Our school has been pilgrimaging to the same place in the wilderness for decades. Each year we backpack in and set up our base camp and use an entire valley as our living classroom for the week. There is a marshy, shallow pond there, surrounded three quarters of the way around by steep hillsides.

One evening Tim was singing a song to the land, while the whole class sat around an enormous, old growth, fir tree listening. As he was singing and drumming there were ancestors from long ago, singing along with him. I could hear them above us along the ridgelines, surrounding the pond. It wasn't an echo of Tim, there were many, many voices joining in. They were chanting, and it was beautiful. It gave me chills of acknowledgment, and tears streamed down my face.

After Tim finished singing, I wasn't going to say anything, but then a few people spoke up and asked if anyone else had heard the voices joining in, and many of us had.

The land holds energy, and the song triggered the spirit of place. Our ancestors are here singing with us welcoming us home.

Sounds of waves never stop. Man comes and man goes. What do we leave behind?

Chapter 25

Collect Earth Medicine

We tend to think of medicine only as medication. The medicine I'm talking about here is energetic medicine. Energy from the Earth.

There are three kinds of Earth medicine. You can gather Earth medicine through your awareness of your experiences in nature, and they become sacred as you take them in.

You can gather Earth medicine through objects found in nature that call to you. These are highlights of the things you find, such as feathers or rocks or shells or beautiful wood.

Each item you feel drawn to, you need to ask if it is alright for you to take it. Maybe it's just for you in that moment. If it feels right to take it, then honor it and give back gratitude.

You can also gather Earth medicine through things you make from nature, such as prayer sticks or musical instruments or tools or art.

Each form of gathering Earth medicine allows for a stronger connection with nature. The act of gathering Earth medicine with an open heart is a spiritual practice. It's as simple as that.

Personal Earth Medicine

We are the sum total of all our experiences in life, and this becomes our personal medicine. Those experiences are what you bring with you out into the world. Be a hunter of medicine moments. Capture and savor them.

Nature gives these endless experiences, through interaction, as well as through quiet observation. I've been in nature in these ways my whole life. My life has been, and still is, wonderful. I owe this to the Earth Medicine I've collected.

I'm a nature teacher, a nature photographer, a nature writer, a nature adventurer, I'm a fisherman and hunter, I'm a bird watcher and gardener, I'm a seeker of sacred places. I'm a vision quester, I'm a creek follower, I'm a get-stupid-roll-in-the-meadow-for-pure-joy-crazy -person. I'm a climber of trees, I get in water every chance I get. I look under rocks, and rotten logs, I follow bears through the woods, I sing Earth songs from trees, I go off path through the brush, rocks, cliffs, and wetlands, and my nature bliss never ends.

When we live this way our relationship with nature becomes personal, we honor nature by fully interacting with her. This translates to an amazing life, with an accumulation of Earth Medicine.

As a nature photographer I've watched countless sunsets and sunrises. I have watched light paint the landscape in every color, shape, and form. Every sunset, every sunrise, every sacred moment has become a part of me, my very being, my essence.

When I show up in life, and acknowledge all these sacred moments, and soak them up, they become my medicine.

Don't be a tourist and just stop and look at a sunset, and get back in the car because you're too cold, and drive away. When you have an opportunity to view a sunset, or a sunrise make it a priority.

Go out alone, or with someone you love or with your dog. Get out and absorb the experience from beginning to end. Be there in it an hour before the sun sets, and an hour after it sets. The same for sunrises. Soak them up.

Bring a sunrise into you each morning and it becomes a part of you, and in turn it becomes who you are out in the world. When you go out and relate to the world, others are getting that energy of the experience in you. This is the gathering of medicine, nature's medicine.

Every sunset and sunrise finds a home in you. When you show up in life, at home and at work, the sunsets and sunrises come along as your personal medicine. Imagine for a moment how wonderful this could be. Get out there and get lost in the experience, and get found, if you want to.

Be the sunrises and sunsets. Be the songbird or eagle soaring by. Project yourself up and fly with them. Empathically fly with them from their point of view. Watch them fly across the sky until you no longer see them. Follow a bee as long as you can.

Approach human relationships in the same way. Be with a person fully. Bring them into you. Connect beyond the surface and know them. Earth medicine carries over into all aspects of life. It's all the same life.

It Works Both Ways

You can gather negative or bad medicine as well. Being dishonorable becomes you, and that's what you bring to the world, as a part of your energy. It adds up.

If you are someone who doesn't go out and seek new experiences, and sits on the couch just flipping channels, then that also becomes your personal medicine.

It is a lower frequency of energy you will carry. When your energy from your experiences is not as stimulated, you tend not to attract others with more vibrant energy. The energy you project influences how the world interacts with you.

The Small Things

Being a nature photographer, I am often photographing majestic moments in grand places, like national parks or scenic areas like mountains, rivers, or old growth forests.

Often, I am out at a time when the weather is profoundly stunning, in the changing light with massive clouds and gorgeous rainbows.

When I'm out in those sacred moments when nature is shining its grandest light on us, showing its best, those times are profound.

I soak up each of those moments, and they go into my being, as my personal medicine. It's more than my personality.

While I can't recall every incredible sunset or sunrise that I took a photograph of forty years ago, they all still resonate within me. They make me the man that I am today. They bring out the best of who I am. They make me a good person. I truly believe this. You have to soak in those highlight moments and let them in, and they will live in you.

The big overviews are obviously amazing, but the intimate, medicine moments are what we tend to forget. You can walk into a meadow and see the beauty of the whole meadow, but also get down on your belly and look at those flowers, and the grasses, and see the smaller life. Watch the insects crawling around the plants.

Look at the shapes and colors. Use your whole body. Smell and feel and observe with all different layers of vision.

When you're looking into a forest, don't just look at the overall scene, but look at the details. How does the bark speak to you? What does it look like when the tree roots hit the ground and extend out? What do the shapes look like?

When you come upon a creek, look at the whole creek, and then the edges. Notice the various rocks, and the water swirling around them, creating rings, bubbles, and gurgles.

When you're watching a bird, study its habitat and how the bird lives. Be aware of the details in the deepest way you can and soak them up.

It's the small world, the intricate world, that we often forget. It has so many curious secrets to tell us.

You can go back and forth from the grand, stunning views, and then let your eyes and all your senses take you onto the ground. Let your eyes land on the rocks, the plants, and onto the waterways of the Earth. Take it all in.

You can take this into the modern world we live in. You can look at buildings and architecture this way. You can do the same with people. You can take this skill of looking wide and close, to all parts of the world.

If you come across things that disturb you, like clear cuts or damage, that can't be ignored, it must be honored too. Those wounds you see can be something that motivates you to make changes for the good of our planet, because you know better, and have seen better.

Be A Hunter Of Sacred Medicine

Hunting is what all predators do. It is a surreal rush, an all-encompassing oneness with the environment.

Humans are first and foremost, predators. It is what has allowed us to survive for thousands of years, while so many animals have passed into extinction, many by our hands.

The need to hunt animals for most humans today is gone, but the thrill of the hunt, the full immersion into the wild environment can still feed that competitive side of our nature. It's Earth Medicine. It's something we need. Become a hunter of the most beautiful moments on Earth. Seek out the storms, the animals, the amazing light. stay with them, absorb them, have gratitude for them.

Engage all your senses! You'll get the thrill of the experience of the hunt, and nothing will die. In fact, you will be more alive full of sacred Earth moments. Happy hunting!

Capturing Moments

Thinking about Golden Eagles gives me the chills. Cultures around the world who lived with the Earth before modern times revered eagles. They are one of the most powerful animals on the planet. Our native ancestors took them on as personal medicine.

Eagle feathers are considered very sacred. I was told by an elder one of the most sacred ways to receive an eagle feather is to see an eagle flying over you, and you catch one of its falling feathers before it touches the ground.

***

I once watched a Bald Eagle fishing, and he flew below a waterfall, and grabbed a Steelhead, shook off the water, and flew back up carrying the heavy fish, and a feather fell onto the water. What a sacred moment that was for me.

I will tell you though that all bird of prey feathers are considered illegal to possess, unless you have a special license to carry them. This law is enforced to protect the birds from being killed for their feathers, talons, and skeleton.

***

I am a bear by nature, and have a special affinity for them, so when I find bear "medicine", bones or fur, it is very sacred to me. I consider bears as my literal brothers.

What is sacred to you is personal. It's a feeling inside coming from your own experience, and your own calling. That draw could be to a Blue Jay or a squirrel, what matters is it is special to you. Honor those encounters and recognize them as sacred.

Goodness is a medicine that lives within us. Water it like a plant and let it come alive within you. Tend to it. Give it life and then share it to allow it to grow.

A New Way Of Seeing

Practice seeing in nature without thinking. Turn your brain off. With practice you'll find it easy. Start off with short movements and grow from there. What you'll find is that your eyes have their own language.

Free your eyes from your brain and learn this *eye language*. You will find a whole new world that has always been there, patiently waiting for you.

Your eyes are the window to your soul, if opened softly. Just a slight change of perspective can wake you up, and what you look at will become your medicine, instead of just an ordinary moment.

Absorb the medicine of a track. Hold your hand over the print, and take in the energy of the animal who created it to know that individual being.

Medicine Stick

You can make a medicine stick by either finding a dead limb or taking a small, live tree. To take a young, live tree can be a powerful way to get a walking stick. This killing must be done with love, and being present with the same reverence as though it were an animal.

If we choose a tree to cut, it must be OK with the tree, which means asking the tree, and being willing to hear no, and move on. This is hard for people who are used to getting what they want, but this respect in asking is vital for the tree to become good medicine.

We must also choose a tree in a forest gardening way. Killing this tree must work for the forest it lives in.

Your heart must be open to cut a tree. Give the tree a blessing, and as you cut it, feel the life of the tree. Give thanks. Remember trees aren't attached like humans are, but they all want to live.

A walking stick should be comfortable in your hand. The goal is the stick becomes so comfortable that it becomes a part of you.

Never forget that this stick was a living being, a tree. Now it is your walking stick, an extension of you, picking up the energy of all the places you travel together. What a wonderful thought this is, walking with a tree.

Walking sticks have been wonderful tools in my life. They are helpful when crossing creeks. They become an extra leg, and supportive arm extension, to feel what I can't see in the water.

My walking stick can protect me if needed. I lean on my stick and rest, and can also use it for a temporary, shelter ridge pole.

Take your stick to another level by making it a medicine stick. If on a quest the stick could carry your visions and memories of your experience. Literally, you can put your ideas, hopes, and dreams into the stick. The stick will hold them, and remind you of any commitments you make on your journey.

Make a stick for someone you love, your mentor or a friend. Let the tree co-create with you. Carve your stick, paint it, put a leather handle on it. Find nature's medicine to put on it, such as feathers, teeth, claws, rocks, or shells. It's important to find these medicine items in nature. Each has its own story. Make your stick a work of art to honor the Earth.

Your stick could also be used as a talking stick. When in a circle of people having a discussion, the stick can be held by each person when they speak, with a reminder to speak the truth, to the point, and if telling a story, speak in an interesting way. In turn, be a good, present listener when someone else has the stick.

When working on your prayer stick, be mindful that wood holds memory. When you work on it, it stores your energy and everything you put into it. Be aware of what you are thinking about while you work on sacred medicine objects.

Over the years your stick becomes a good friend. Someday pass your stick onto someone you mentor or a friend or just give it back to the land.

Build An Altar

Create an altar in a special place in your home for your medicine objects, such as under a window, on a table, shelf, or mantel, or even outside.

Always keep your altar neat and beautiful. The effort you put into your altar will be a reflection of you. It's a statement of your love and respect for nature, and your sacred times in nature. In this way your altar will be your teacher.

Know When To Use Your Medicine

Sometimes you may find a physical object of Earth medicine and it feels ok to take it, but maybe the timing just isn't right yet.

This was the case in a bear skull that I found. I felt it needed to rest before it took on a new way of life, so I wrapped it up in a cloth bundle and smudged it, and put it away for a while. When the timing feels right, I will bring it out to call on its energy or medicine.

Be aware of when not to force something before its time.

Create Ceremony Honoring Medicine Moments

Create a beginning, a middle and an end to each day, to each week, to each month, to each year, to each special or sacred event.

Keep it simple, but beautiful with intention. When we complicate things, we create a backdoor by saying it's too hard. When something is simple it doesn't mean it's not powerful. Simple done well is powerful, concentrated energy.

Stay ultra-focused and completely present with the ceremony. Energy follows thought. Thoughts are powerful, living, active energy with intention and purpose.

Being in nature is a powerful place to hold ceremonies. Everything around you is alive, listening and participating. Breathe in your surroundings. Invite the land and beings in your space, and thank them for being there.

Giving gratitude in ceremony is important. It keeps the energy flowing full circle. Give thanks for those who got you to where you are. Give them blessings. There is tremendous power in seeing people live their lives in a good way. Visualizing this is the beginning of making it so.

Ceremony is not about big frills, it's about focused intention, and good energy put into it.

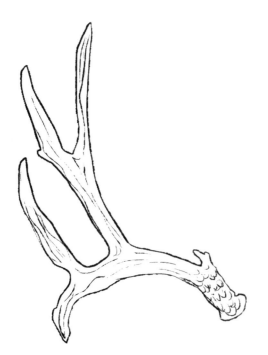
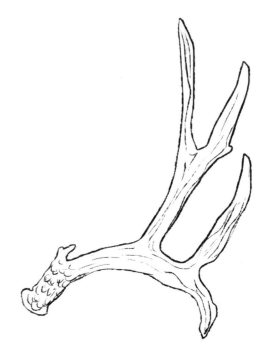

Chapter 26
Create Nature Art

Nature is living Earth art. The forests and seashores are living art, trees are art, mountains are art, their endless colors and shapes contribute to their beauty. Even when something such as a tree dies in nature, it becomes a magnificent sculpture.

Art and nature are one in the same. The greatest artist I've ever known is Mother Earth. Everywhere I look, almost every day, is a new masterpiece. New clouds, new windswept landscapes, new rain influenced streams, new seasons with changing colors, every single day a new masterpiece.

One type of nature art is creating beauty on the land from nature. Get inspired by the environment to co-create sculptures or a stone circle or a labyrinth or an archway. We can create beauty from beauty.

Find the artistry in every living thing. Give blessings back to the Earth by creating art in nature with love and respect. Create with objects found in your surroundings. As you create, you add beauty to the world. Nature speaks to you, and through you as a creator of Earth art.

Sometimes art is solely about beauty, and sometimes there are messages for others expressed symbolically through your art. Physical art is a wordless language, and a way that the Earth can speak through us to send out her messages.

It's an honor to have someone look at your art, and to be touched and motivated by it. Your art is a gift to the world. It makes everything brighter if you let love, kindness, and beauty come out through it.

You don't have to make a living doing art, you could just do it for yourself, for your friends, for your community, or just for the joy of it. If you discover that you're the kind of artist that can make it a profession, hey, it's a wonderful way to make a living, and you go for it.

I like to create beauty within my garden. Art permeates my life, it always has. I also love to look at other people's art and reflect on it. I like to support artists and buy original art from them. Art made from nature and in nature is made to be treasured.

Find Paintings In Your Surroundings

Paint and draw our lands. We are all artists. Sometimes art is only for you. Other times it's for many.

What is beautiful to us? And why? What is beautiful in a person and why? What we see as beautiful we want to protect.

One major reason land was saved for our national parks was that a few great landscape painters came out west in the 19th century, and painted highlights of Yellowstone and Yosemite, prompting the creation of the National Park System. They were able to show the leaders in power, the beauty we needed to save for generations to come.

Nature Art Journal

Make a beautiful journal to use as you journey into nature. Fill it with your art of nature. Remember that everyone is an artist.

There are no rules to art, it only matters to you. Your art journal is between you, and our Earth. It is the sacred secret you share with our Earth. It is wonderful to share it with others if you want to, and if you never share it, that's just fine too.

Take your journal on your sits and walks. Write thoughts, ideas, poems, and stories. Draw mountains, trees, flowers, animals, insects, and birds. Draw patterns, shapes, leaves, bark, water. See art and patterns in nature, and then communicate what you see.

You can use any medium you want. Go to an art store and be a kid. Being creative is a fun way to interact with our Earth. You may discover a new form of art you enjoy.

Write your hopes and dreams. Write songs. Make your journal a work of art. Treat it sacred. Enjoy its dirt time wear and tear. That is part of the Earth creating with you.

Open the journal and let the artist out. It's never too late. Having an open mind and no agenda is truly freeing. It may lead to many new paths to explore.

Poetry

Read poetry and write a poem every day in nature. Poetry is like music, you listen to it with more than just your ears, you feel it throughout your whole being. Take it in and absorb it and share your own lyrical music. Be creative for the sake of your soul. Let go of worrying if anyone else will understand it, it's ultimately between you and the Earth.

Forest Gallery

Create sacred spaces in nature. What is sacred space? That is up to you. Let nature show you. Listen and observe.

At Headwaters we are creating an ongoing forest gallery. We have small art pieces made of soapstone and painted rocks, intentionally placed along the pathways. There are large sculptures made from manzanita branches, some of which are arches, and shelters you can walk into.

Our students change the feel of spaces on the land with their stacked rock art, and burned-out cedar bowls, and willow baskets. There are stinging nettle cordage weavings dangling from some of the trees, drawing your eyes up.

We have large rock labyrinths, and mandalas that guide you off trail to engage with them. The nature art on our land complements the landscape, and lures people into areas they may not have explored without their curiosity being triggered.

You don't need a large parcel of land to display your artwork. Create an art gallery in your backyard and invite others to share their work as well. A community gallery is a great place to come together and have fun.

Get a song from nature and sing your joy into life.

Make a musical instrument from nature and create music with the Earth.

The Journey

Nature art can be temporary, such as a drawing in the sand that will wash away at high tide. Art can be made with the intent of it being more permanent, but with either approach, put your whole self into the creation of it. The inner results of the creative process will be the same.

Spirit, You are color. You are It. I am painting You.

Earth Altars

Creating an altar as an art piece, is another way of showing love to the Earth. It is a way of honoring a relationship with a living being.

An Earth altar can be in your yard or out in nature in an intimate space. You can create an altar incredibly fancy, and wild, and full of objects that can last for years or even a lifetime. You can add to your altar as you live your life's journey, as gifts come your way from nature or from another person. Or an altar can be very simple and more temporary.

Creating an altar about your life, and as a reflection of the Earth, can be powerful. Building an altar that represents your purpose and intention of making the world better is a way of setting that into motion.

An altar is a sacred focal space where you can sit, and pray in your own way or meditate. You can write in a journal and let the altar inspire you.

Each item on the altar will have its own story. It will have come to you in a unique way, and have its own life. When you put those objects together on your altar it becomes a community of treasures that represent the stories of your life.

You can make an altar to represent something specific that is currently happening. On our land we have made an altar for the COVID-19 victims who lost their lives. It is a place where we can sit and pray, and send blessings to those people and their families.

We have made altars on our land for animals who have been killed on the road by vehicles, to help us to remember these beings, and to try to do better by them.

We have made altars for our personal animals that have passed away. We have altars for all our dogs, and even for a special chicken and rooster that made an impact on us.

I have made altars for my mother, father, and sister who have passed away. I have placed items there that were theirs, as well as items I have found that remind me of good memories of them.

When my students make their own primitive shelters, I always have them create an altar in their space to honor it. Even if they are only staying in their shelter for one night, there should always be beauty and reverence for nature.

Altars become wonderful Earth art. When building, slow down, listen to the Earth, and work in partnership. Allow your creative side to emerge, you will go into a higher state of being. You will feel as part of the altar. It will reflect who you are and make a statement.

Your altar will become a living work of art. Insects will move in, animals will use it, birds will sit upon it, frogs, lizards, and snakes will enjoy it, and bring life to your altar.

Build altars as nature art, to celebrate your love of nature. Altars can remind us of sacred moments we've had in nature. It keeps the memory of those moments alive, so that those moments become our living medicine within us.

When creating an altar, it becomes an expression of who you are, what you believe, and how you feel about the world. I'm a bear, so when I find bear skulls and bones it means a lot to me. It's a validation of my connection to bears and their way of living.

I always find heart rocks for my altars. I believe in the power of love to change the world. I have feathers that I have found or that have been gifted to me. Unique pieces of driftwood, intricately patterned slabs of bark, leaves, flowers, rocks, rusty machinery parts, animal bones, and anything interesting that catches my eye, always find their way onto my altars. There are times when I keep poems that I write on altars as well.

Let beautiful items from nature call to you. The call may come from beauty. The call may come through the heart. The call may come from your inner vision or from your thoughts.

Ask the objects why they call to you? The question matters more than the answer. The answer may come, or you may have to wait for it. It may be a piece of your life's puzzle showing up. Whatever happens is the right thing.

Find things in nature that represent who you are at the core. Arrange these collections on your altar in an artistic way. Take your time, and be creative.

Vision quests can be significant moments in your life. Items from nature you find during a quest can be important to you. They carry energy, and help you to remember what came to you on your time out.

These items should go on your altar. Photos and writings, your own art, gifts from people that matter in your life can all go on your altar.

Sometimes when I'm sitting in front of my altar, one of the items may tell me it's ready to go. I'll either take it out into nature again, and give it back to the Earth or I'll gift it to someone that I feel needs it, and it will find a new home. When it is a gift given, then it's up to me to have no attachment of what they do with it. Some things I'll keep a whole lifetime, and some things are more powerful than others.

You can create an altar for a group of people to add to it, and let them decide what is important to them.

Creating an altar is a form of art, it's beautiful and inspiring, and it allows you to live through hope and see the good in things. This can be a practice that can open your heart, and an open heart is the welcoming doorway to nature's heart. Build many altars and have fun doing it! Be nature's artist.

Be With A Plant

Sit with a plant for a few minutes each day for a week. Each day sit in a different position and draw that same plant from a different perspective, maybe even with a different medium.

Get to know that plant and honor it by noticing all facets of it. Get to know that plant, not by name, but by its beautiful essence.

Draw tracks. Illustrate the animal's story. Better yet, make a casting of the track and bring the energy of that animal's story home with you.

Spirit In Nature's Art

I know each tree and rock on our land. I know when a tree is cut. I feel it before seeing it. I take it personally if someone drops garbage on the land or hacks into a beautiful, old tree stump. It's a weathered art sculpture that I cannot replicate.

I can mimic the stunning image of nature, but the spirit of place is not there. A hotel waterfall can look pretty, but there's no spirit like there is in a natural, chemical free waterfall.

The nature spirits live and reside in a natural waterfall, and we feel that abundant energy all around. That is something we cannot recreate. We can only emulate it and be inspired by it. To truly feel the spirit of place, get out in nature's gallery and soak it up.

Sacred Space Between

Look at the space between a tree's branches. That perceived emptiness is what enhances the form. Without holding that space there would only be a solid mass. No form, no definition. No support.

Empty space is just as important as what you fill it with. What isn't there is sacred space. It's where inspiration lives.

Rock Art

A great meditation is to stack rocks. You must work with them, and feel them to know where they fit and to find their balance point. You need to tune into the rocks to create beauty with them. When you create on the land and work with it, you need to create a partnership with the land. Don't try to control it. It will show you all you need to know.

We are not here to only create with our bodies, we are here to create with our soul. Our body is merely the tool.

Humans Are Works Of Art

Each person is different, and ever changing. Observe humans and how they flow with nature once they sink into its rhythm. It's beautiful.

When our students are engaging in our camouflage activities to immerse themselves into nature, they become living works of art. They blend so harmoniously with the landscape they enhance the beauty of the Earth. The mud they cover their faces with starts to dry and crack, and the crevices follow the contours of their face, and blend with the bark of a tree they are hugging.

The leaves they branch out of their hair, drapes a veil across their face, creating a humbleness and softness around their eyes.

As the students are partially hiding themselves in their surroundings, they begin to breathe softer. The air escaping on their exhale becomes unnoticeably the same breeze that is blowing through the tall grass.

We are all works of art coming from the Earth, blending with the Earth, and going back to the Earth. See your beauty in the mud.

Tell Your Stories Through Art

Don't hold back or censor out of fear. Let your art out in joy, and inspire what others may think. We all benefit from sharing our inspirations. This is how creativity and new life energize a community.

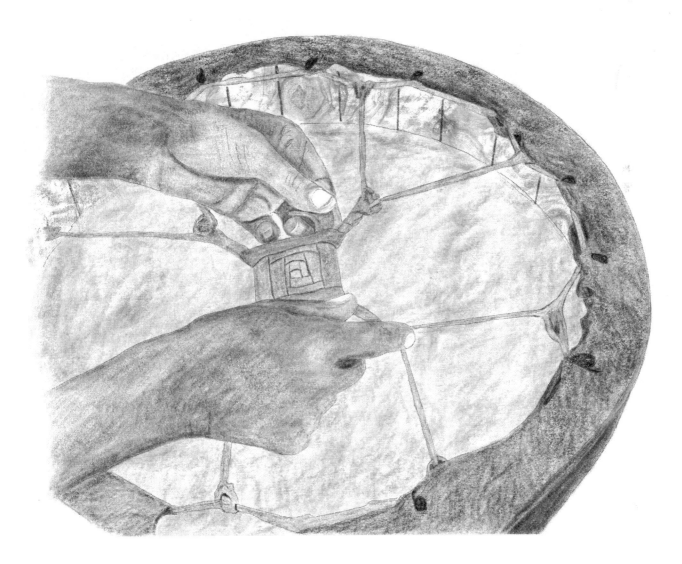

Chapter 27
Call On Your Ancestors

Walking with Our Ancestors - We want to learn about the Earth and nature, and participate in it, and we tend to forget that we have an ancestral connection that goes back many thousands of years through all human time.

We all have grandfathers and grandmothers that are a direct lineage from not too far back, to the Earth peoples who were living interdependently with the land. Their blood is ours. Their lives and way of life is in us. The modern world cannot remove them from us. They live in us and through us. We give them life.

We already have a connection to nature through our ancestors. We have their experiences and knowledge within us, and we can call up their wisdom. We need to rekindle our ancestral and cultural roots of living with the land in balance.

Acknowledge those who came before us. Think about your relations before your immediate grandparents, and the ones before them. Honor your ancestors by building a relationship and getting to know them. Learn how they lived.

How did your people live directly with the Earth? What did they think and feel? What did they look like? Did they have dreams? How did they hunt and fish and grow food?

As you gain wisdom from your ancestors, also ask them who *you* are. Look at your family history. Whether you are Native American, Irish, Hispanic, Romanian, African or Asian, it doesn't matter which country or continent your lineage is, you had ancestors that lived in the wilderness and with the Earth. We are our ancestors. Re-member your clan. Make yourself a member again.

Next time you go to the wilds, invite your ancestors along. They are here for us. Speak with them. Walk with them in nature. Call them in with you and ask for guidance and healings. For a moment see through your ancestors' eyes. Work with your ancestors and ask them what they want us to know and what they need now.

I believe they are still living in other layers of life. It is a great mystery, but I know they are there watching over us. You have ancestors that have done the work and you can ask for their help. As this generation works to save our planet, we need all the help we can get. We need our ancestors walking with us into the future.

We say in our outdoor school, through our nature teachings we are walking backwards into the future to remember what we already know.

Practicing Earth living skills awakens the Earth knowledge within us. This knowledge is the gift our ancestors gave us from thousands of years of life intertwined with nature.

We are going into the future, but we're bringing the knowledge with us that we learned from living with the Earth, long before we became modern people. We can live with the Earth in a good way again.

Sit quietly, maybe even by a campfire, close your eyes, and ask your ancestors to come be with you, share sacred space, and enjoy their company. They've been waiting for your invitation. What joy you'll have.

Dream Backwards

If you could go back in time and do anything you want, be anywhere you want, and be completely safe and participate fully, where would it be?

I always have two answers and it never changes. I would like to be the naturalist on the Lewis and Clark expedition. To be able to come from a new, emerging world from Europe and into America, and explore the West, and to meet the native people, and live with them before they were imprisoned and killed, speaks to my very being.

I would love to see the grizzly bears in massive numbers, and the bison in the millions, and all the wildlife that roamed free. It just gives me the chills.

My other wish is that I would like to have been the naturalist on all three voyages with Captain Cook, in the early 1800's when he sailed around the world.

I would cherish the opportunity to explore the islands in the South Pacific, Hawaii, and the North American coastline, along California, Oregon, Washington and of course, Alaska in the wild Pacific Ocean.

To witness the whales and all the wildlife, and endless birds, and experience the abundant, pristine Earth the way she was meant to be, would be my ultimate dream.

***

I think about my ancestors, like my grandfather, who was a huge part of my life, and lived on a homestead in Montana, and his grandfather, who came over from Ireland in the 1800s during the civil war, and the potato famine.

Each generation lived a different life that built the story of who I am today. The most recent close connection I had with my ancestor was my grandfather, who lived on the Flathead Reservation in Ronan, Montana.

His father and grandfather were settlers that were able to build a very small town within the reservation, and live harmoniously with the local native people, who were very welcoming.

My grandfather's homestead was at the edge of the wilderness, at the base of the Mission Mountains. I spent my summers learning from him. He taught me to hunt, fish, and farm through hands-on interaction. What I learned from him had been passed down to him by his father and grandfather.

Witnessing elders through generations after generations, we gain the lived knowledge from our ancestors.

My grandfather took on the role as my mentor seriously, and he treated me as someone special. He taught me what I needed to learn through his experience, but he also taught me how he was taught by his elders and their elders.

He passed onto me the love of nature, and to live with it. The key thought here is to live *with* nature, not against it, not manipulating it, not taking it over. He taught me the right relationship of living with our planet. My relationship and time spent with him changed my life forever.

Canyon de Chelly

The winding trail into the canyon is worn smooth from the ancestor's feet. Generations upon generations of footsteps and weather, carve sandstone to soil.
Families who have never left, live embedded within their relative's walls. Intentional, patterned hand and foot holds to scale their home, act as a puzzled doorway to the plateaus.
Water carving fluid tracks, green then yellow cottonwood leaves, ancient mural art predating graffiti, horses, livestock, and crops wildly tended, speaks to art in nature and the art of life on the valley floor.
While modern ways have splintered through, all the beings who inhabit Canyon de Chelly, are still actively living history. A tangible timeline is seen in the canyon, but mostly, notable timelessness is felt in the air.

Through Me

Often, when I'm making a fire by friction, I feel my ancestors within the experience. Sometimes through me they make the fire. Sometimes they watch with joy. Sometimes when I make a bow drill fire, I remember my *self* in my ancestor's past making the fire. Then they sit with me, and that's a sacred fire.

Cherish Moments

When I've been out in the woods for a while, and my thoughts drift, my true self emerges. I become more primal, and wild.

In these moments I often feel my ancient past merge with my present, and for a moment I am all my ancestors at once. I am all their experiences in that moment.

When these moments happen, I love our Earth in the deepest parts of my being. I know our Earth gave me all of this and here I am, Earth-mind, Earth-body, Earth-heart.

It is difficult to express the feeling of connection this moment brings, but it is a moment to cherish.

Common Tools

The drum came to our ancestors all around the world around the same time in human history. People on all continents used a drum for connection to nature, to Spirit, and to bring communities closer.

Drumming has been used for ceremony, for spiritual development, deep connection, communication, and for healing.

There is a heart connection with our past through drumming. The Earth's heart rhythm beats with ours, and connects us to our ancestors. It is a universal language that is felt throughout our whole being.

To tune into our ancestors, allow your primal self to emerge through a drumbeat, and speak to them through your heart.

Spirit Guides are mentors who are waiting for you to call upon them. They know you. They chose you to mentor. Talk to them. They are already walking alongside you.

Visitors

During a winter class at Headwaters, we were camping in the Lava Beds National Monument, near the border of California and Oregon. This was the homeland of the Modoc tribe.

It was single digit cold. The high desert, night sky was clear and bright. It was so quiet it made you feel as though you needed to pop your ears to clear them. The juniper tree's Moon shadows, sparkled across the patches of icy snow.

I had bundled up in my two-person tent, but left my door flap open to look out at the blue night, as I drifted off to sleep.

Sometime in the night a thud hit the top of my tent. It jarred me awake, but I was so bundled up I couldn't sit up fast. The crystal frost on my rainfly crackled and slid down the domed vinyl.

I opened my eyes to take in where I was, and what the sound may have been. In that moment of thought, another thump, but this time it was right next to my head on the side wall of my tent. I pulled my head away towards the middle, and then another thump on the other side of my tent.

A friend was sleeping not too far away from where I was, and I called out to him. I thought maybe he was throwing snowballs at my tent for some reason. I had no idea what time it was, and no idea why he would do that in the middle of the night, but it was the only thing I could think of. I called again, but no answer.

I recalled my campsite in my mind, and knew I had not set my tent up under a tree. It could not have been snow clumps falling. Being new to sleeping on my own out in nature, I was nervous about sticking my head out of the tent to see if an animal was around. A curious mountain lion is what my fear was imagining.

I did what they tell you not to do in any horror movie, I buried my head deep into my sleeping bag and pretended like it was nothing, and slipped back into sleep.

A couple of thumps on the top of my tent woke me again. This time I poked my head out of the rainfly, only to see the silhouette of elder juniper trees, and more stars than I ever knew existed. Pure silence, and air so crisp it felt like breathing in menthol.

Maybe it had been a deer? I closed the rainfly, buried myself back in my bag, and stayed undercover until first daylight.

When I got up, I walked around my tent to see if I could figure out what had happened during the night. There were no tracks at all in the snow around my tent, except for my own from the night before, and no trees near my tent.

I heard Tim talking to his wife, Jean, from the make-shift kitchen. Jean was asking Tim why he didn't do anything last night. He said, "There was nothing to do. They were just checking in."

I joined them by the fire, anxious to tell them about my experience. Right away I realized they were talking about the same thing. I told Tim about the thumping on my tent, and he confirmed what I felt, and told me it was the Modocs. He said they were doing the same thing to their tent as well.

Tim got up when Jean woke him up to tell him what was happening and he looked around. He saw them walking around my tent patting the top, as well as another student's tent in the other direction.

I asked him why they were doing that, and he said they were just greeting us. He said they were acknowledging our respect for their home, and letting us know they are still there watching over their land, their home.

There was no reason to be frightened, just the opposite. They were welcoming us, knowing we were there out of great respect and interest.

At that point I wasn't afraid any longer. While I wasn't able to see them, I absolutely felt and heard them, and felt honored that our visitors had made their presence known to me.

Over the next few days, I learned more about the Modoc people, and like all the native tribes in America, their unjust fate, being killed and removed from their land. I learned of their personal story, and had quite a few more encounters with them in that desert, some physical and some through their spirit.

I had some very personal moments and conversations with them, that I will carry with me the rest of my days here. I do not have direct lineage with the Modoc people, but I'm finding that most elder's spirits are universal in what they share. With respect and a reverent heart, they will speak with you too.

For many, many years I have gone on pilgrimages back to this land, and sat quietly with them. There have been many times that I did not feel them but knew that my mind had been cluttered with my physical life responsibilities.

There were other times I left their land again, completely humbled that they chose to visit with me, sometimes briefly, sometimes at great length. Most times I see them in my mind's eye, but occasionally, I will get a glimpse of these beautiful people's spirit.

After my initial encounter with the Modocs, I sat by the fire and asked if there was a message to share. This is what came back to me.

***

The Modocs Told Me - Speak with the spirits and get to know the individuals. Listen to their stories. Acknowledge them. Have reverence. Find out where they are from. Connect with them personally. Get to know them personally. Open up a conscious relationship with them, and there will be no reason to fear them. They have a lot to share.

They Taught Us Well

Our ancestor's simple lives, living with nature, have taught us what is most important. They taught us to be kind, and to love community, family, friends, Earth, plants, trees, animals, the sun, stars, the moon, mountains, prairies, the oceans, rivers, insects, the elements, and art.

They taught us to have reverence, gratitude, fun, and to be of service. They taught us to keep the circle full and healthy.

Honor our ancestors by carrying on their nature teachings. Make our ancestors smile.

Reminders:
*Have conversations with your grandparents. Ask them to tell you their stories of their grandparents and their ancestors. Get curious, learn, and remember the ways of the Earth.
*Sit in nature, close your eyes, and invite your ancestors into a conversation.

Chapter 28
Acknowledge Death And Grieving

We all go back to the Earth, and then onto another journey. We must find peace with death or live a life of endless fear. Nature is a good teacher for finding this peace.

All beings in nature live their best life or they die. Our life is a blessing, and this is a great reminder to not take this journey for granted. Living life fully as an Earth Caretaker with passion and purpose for a greater good, in the full circle way, allows us to have a good transition from this Heaven on Earth to Heaven beyond the stars. Death is a change and a new beginning.

***

I don't think grief is just a human thing. Grief can be quite powerful for a human being, but animals grieve, trees grieve, and our Earth grieves as well.

I have been a witness to the grief of elephants, dogs, and birds. I've seen all kinds of beings grieve losses.

Humans have taken grief to a whole other level. We have our highly intelligent brain, and complicated emotions, and often in our culture we don't allow ourselves the gift of grieving. The space to just feel sadness.

When we allow time to grieve, we can emerge out of it with a new understanding, and the ability to go forward in life. If we skip that process, we often never really get out of it. It lives within us. If we go into grief, and through it, when we come out of it, we can leave it behind, and move on living fully. This is a very necessary part of healing.

I love the Earth, and I grieve about the destruction of our planet due to human beings. I'm very educated on what's happening, and I just cry.

I grieve by crying, and sometimes with anger and confusion. Eventually I let it go and then I just keep working for our planet, doing everything I can. I continue educating people. I join environmental groups. I continue being of service on my land, and wherever help is needed. When I'm educating people, it helps the grief to disappear, at least for a while.

In these difficult times, there is a certain amount of grief living in me still that I need to manage. I tend my gardens, so the deep sadness doesn't take over me. I also know, going through that process is a very important part of me growing, and moving forward in my life.

I've had some of the biggest grief in my life from the loss of relationships. One of the most important things to a human being is to live in community, and to be loved.

One of the hardest things to get through is when we lose love in our life or lose a dear friendship or a longtime business relationship.

Loss of any companionship leaves a huge void. It's important to be able to voice what we're grieving about. To be able to write it, and to be able to talk about it, without being interrupted, is healing.

My sister died at 42 of a brain Aneurysm. She died in my arms. I remember the grief was so deep.

She died in Sacramento, and I drove back to Mount Shasta, and for three and a half hours I didn't stop screaming and crying the entire drive. What I realized through that process, is I needed to talk about it.

I lost another very important love relationship in my life, and it saddened me terribly. A good friend at the right time, just sat and listened to me talk. Sometimes I would repeat the same thing over a dozen times. There was no fixing it. I just needed them to hear me, and bear witness to my pain, and I worked through it.

One day I woke up and I was okay, and I moved on in my life. I don't think if I hadn't been allowed to express that grief, and had someone there to help me with it, I wouldn't be as good of a person as I am today. I would be carrying the weight of that loss with me still. Grief and negative emotions are heavy energy, and you physically feel the effects of it.

Whether grief is for a person or an animal, it can be just as intense and painful. I grieved for the loss of my mother and father, whom I loved wholeheartedly, but I almost feel guilty because I have truly felt more pain from losing my animal companions.

The loss of my chimpanzee, Raffles, my friend, my brother, has been one of the biggest heart aches in my life. We had built such a trust and love between the two of us working together, and living together, there were no barriers. When he passed, it took a part of my heart.

Even though I have gone through the grieving stages of his loss, I still have a part of me that hurts as an open wound, but it is not debilitating.

***

If we compare grieving for our Earth, and what's happening to our planet, it is not unlike what we have gone through with the COVID-19 virus. We don't really know what's going to happen long term. The anxiety of that throws us off. The different variants have been an ongoing sense of anxiety, and it leads to the never-ending question of, what's coming at us next?

It's the uncertainty that keeps hold of us to a degree. The unknowns of life, and how they're going to affect every aspect of our lives is always there in the back of our thoughts.

Going back to our ancestral times, foreseeing patterns was how we survived, by preparing for the changes. If we couldn't control our environment to some extent, we would have a very difficult time living.

The global pandemic has been a direct reflection of ourselves out of control. The Earth is out of balance, and we are out of balance. We all need to work with each other to heal. In this case, we can't have only a few people step up, the majority of us need to take right action immediately. We all affect each other, and this planet.

Notice how quickly the Earth started to repair herself, as soon as we took a time out. Once we were globally forced to just stop, the Earth had time and room to literally breathe.

Some skeptics don't believe we can heal the planet quickly, but it's not a matter of speculation any longer, we proved that we can. The Earth showed us she started to function in a healthy way almost immediately, as soon as we gave her some space to do it.

Within a few weeks, the air in some of the most polluted places in the world cleared. Wildlife returned to their original landscapes. Marine life once again swam up their previously abandoned waterways.

Within a few months, there was so much more healing and normalcy than we could ever notice because it was all happening simultaneously, and harmoniously.

While I am excited to have my outdoor school back open again, after over a year of closure, part of me grieves for that time. While tragic in many ways, when humans more or less stopped, most of us cared for others, and stretched to help where we could. Some were superheroes, and went beyond what anyone could have imagined to help others heal, and sadly for many healthcare workers it cost them their own lives.

My fear is that human nature will again get complacent, and go back to ways of convenience, instead of doing what we know is right and in balance for our own good.

***

We have an uncertain future, and it's important to have community. Be honest and tell your story, whether it's personal grieving or on a larger scale. Be there for someone else as well, be their witness. Help someone tell their story.

Allow heartache to wash through your system in a healthy way. Be committed to coming out the other side a stronger human, willing to make a difference in the world. Be a part of the solution, but don't ignore the grief.

If you try to be tough and hold it in, no matter what it is; a loss of someone you love, your pet, damage to our planet, if you don't work through the stages of grief the sadness will sit inside you. You carry it like a weighted backpack. It can sometimes manifest inside of you as a physical sickness or mental health issues. Too much anger and sadness results in stagnant built-up energy that creates illness.

Grief is huge, and if we think of it as a living being, a necessary part of life to acknowledge, I think we will be okay. Let go of embarrassment or feeling like a burden, and ask for help. When you ask for help, you give someone an opportunity to be a hero, to be of service, and to have a sense of purpose.

Grieving can take many forms. Some can be very damaging, but often grieving could take the form of a call to action. Grief can be an incredible motivator to get involved in caring, and protecting nature. Being a force for change, caring for our planet and all our living relations, and righting the wrongs, can lessen the power that grief has, and assist in your healing.

Journaling Wounds – 2020

I'm sad, very sad. I feel the wounds to our Earth, and it weighs heavy on my soul, my heart, my mind. Some days I cry for the Earth right through me, it hurts, it must be done.

I cry for the trees in one way. I cry for the birds in another way, through my eyes, tears of the loss of what could have been.

The land, the oceans won't let me cry except inside my bones. I talk to the Earth, and ask for time for wisdom to blossom among peoples.

Then I cry for all of it, and for myself, for my inability to help. To know it in the brain and not be able to make a difference in any discernible way, is a wound to the very soul, and I need my soul healthy to go on, and I must go on for our Earth. It is what's right.

Today I had to close my school because of a global virus, not knowing when it will be open again. My school is my soul's work, one in the same. So, today I cry from all parts of me. I purge sadness. I allow my grief to motivate me until I discover my next step. I will love my land, and my students, and apprentices into a new future, and soon they will come again to our sacred land, my dream returning.

Now I will love our Earth, the animals, and our community until the day comes when our land is alive with wonderful souls, and everything is back in place.

I will keep feeling all of it because that's who I am. I will find my way to the soul of the Earth. I will keep the land alive and healthy. I will live what I love, and love, and love. It's my true self-love of Earth, of Earthlings, and I will grow into a better person, and I will cry.

Our Earth is waiting for us to find our way to grow into our better selves, the gifts we are. We must open these gifts and share them with our planet, our people. It's time now.

This Old Camera

Some say a camera is a tool. My camera is a Nikon FM2. It's more than a tool to me. It's a part of me, an extension of my vision, my love of nature. We have decades of history together; it carries my medicine from countless photographs I've taken, and adventures it's been on.

Things that we hold so dear to us collect our energy and it can be physically felt. They become like living beings and we can have a different kind of relationship with them.

My camera has given me joy and happiness countless times. It has given me a purpose for my life and allowed me to live my love.

This old film camera is as weathered, and beaten as I am. We've gone through it together. This old camera has a soulful energy, and heart-beating rhythm of its own. I take great comfort in knowing it will be with me on the rest of my life's journey. This old camera is my friend.

***

I wrote this about my camera a handful of years ago. Not long after I wrote that, my car was broken into while I was out on a walk on the beach. My camera, my longtime adventure companion, was stolen.

I didn't care that my window was smashed or that other personal belongings were gone, but my camera being stolen, crushed me. That was a personal violation to my soul.

It's been years now since my gear was stolen, and I must admit, a part of my spark for photography has been missing. I don't quite have the enthusiasm to get out and photograph. There is still a sadness in me.

I continue to go out in nature, but the camera and equipment I found to replace my gear just doesn't feel the same. It's lacking the medicine of *my* history in all those places I traveled, and the experiences I had.

These cameras are not made any longer, and I had to hunt for a used replacement at a vintage camera shop. There is someone else's energy in the camera. It has a different physical and emotional feel to it.

Yes, you can grieve for *stuff* lost in your life. It's the energy of the memories from over 50 years that I'm missing. I can bring medicine to this replacement camera by using it, but it will always be different. In some ways, maybe there are blessings by not bringing the camera with me when I go into nature. I may not go intimately into capturing the detail of the moments, but it allows me the opportunity to just be in those moments.

Who am I kidding? It's not the same experience, and that's what I need to let go of. My passion for using my camera has shifted a bit, but my passion for being out in nature has never wavered, and that's what's important.

In This Moment
I Love
I Hurt
I Cry
I Grieve
I Ache
I Hurt some more, and yet I know I still love because-
I Hurt, and I Cry, and I Grieve, and I Ache.

Grief For The Loss Of Nature

I've realized that one of the costs of a deep love of nature, and a personal relationship with all things living, is that when we think about the damage human greed and carelessness causes, it causes us pain.

When we educate ourselves on what's going on locally, and worldwide, this knowledge lives within us. When we become more aware of our world we not only see and feel more of nature, we also see and feel more of what's wrong. There is a collective grief and often, we feel helpless to do anything in other places around the world.

When people around us don't recognize what's happening, it can be lonely and painful, and disheartening. We can become filled with anger and sadness. It feels so big that any possible solution seems downright impossible.

Trust our Earth to take care of herself. She's getting quite beat up, but I know she will take care of herself. Remember she has been through five major extinctions in her existence. We humans may be number six. She'll either remove us, or at least many of us, or we will learn to live as Earth Caretakers. One or the other will happen. *When,* is still the question.

We can mitigate our grief by being involved in the process of making life better on our planet for all living beings. Grief on the other hand also needs to be honored. It allows us to touch the beauty that lives within us. It shows us that we are full of compassion and love.

It's not healthy to let grief destroy us. Grief can remind us of how special it is to be human. Grief can be transformed into medicine.

It is a gift to feel grief. Work with it, and live well for yourself, for your community, and for our planet. That special person in you is so needed.

Forgiveness

The spirit of the Earth cries in our tears, and still forgives us every day for the damage we inflict upon her, by feeding us, by housing us, by giving us water and air to breathe. She gives us endless, magnificent beauty.

How can we learn from her and forgive ourselves? Love more than you ever thought you could. You will find love's light in all things of the Earth, including you.

The Americas

This land before us was so full of life that it rivaled any place on Earth. Valleys full of grizzly bears, elk, antelope, buffalo, cougar, deer, and rabbits. Abundant species of birds - enough to darken the sky. Salmon and trout filled the rivers. Oceans of seals, otters, and whales. Seabirds visible as far as the horizon allows. Beaches and tide pools gorged with clams, abalone, and mussels.

Oak trees heavy with acorns, grasslands full of seeds, life for our ancestors was lush and abundant beyond what we will ever know.

. . . The people watch the sun set and wonder if it will come back to them.

Ask Permission

Before cutting down any tree, stop and think. Are you making a good decision? Ask with your heart, is this killing ok? If so, do it with heart.

Offer a blessing, a thank you, and then with an open heart, cut down the tree. Trees are all about giving in life and death, just do it with honor and respect, and *never ever* cut down an old growth tree. They are vital for all of life.

Angelica

We harvested an elder Angelica plant today for sacred medicine, high up in the wilderness. While we dug it up with ceremony, with song and reverence, and gratitude in a sacred, respectful way, there were still tears shed.

The tears weren't for the Angelica we harvested, but for the Angelica plants that were left behind, without their life-long, growing companions next to them. It's the ones left behind in a symbiotic community that feel the grief and loss.

I live to go to the beach and feel the cleansing waves wash away weight I carry out to sea.

Wildfires

Every day during the dry seasons, I live with the concern of wildfires here in Northern California. We are vulnerable here. We work on our forest, year round, clearing it where it's needed, and keeping it healthy. I can only hope that if a fire came through here our beautiful land would survive. That thought weighs on me.

Global warming has created fires that burn hotter, and much more aggressively than ever before. The fires now create their own storms, and fire tornadoes due to the dry conditions and increasing warmer weather. Our fire season noticeably lasts much longer in the year now, than even ten years ago.

Wildfires are necessary for the health of a forest. Underbrush needs to be cleared away. The carbon from the burnt debris helps replenish the soil with nutrients. It promotes new, healthy growth.

The old growth forests can usually handle a fire burning through. The older trees are large enough that the fire doesn't reach the treetops. Canopy fires are one of the main reasons a fire gets out of control, and destroys forests instead of helping them in the long term.

Unfortunately, we continue to have to fight to hold onto our old growth forests. There is no benefit for clear cutting a forest. When forests are clear cut, they grow back denser and create a setup for a tinderbox situation.

We need to keep the elder trees and thin the landscape in a good way. Clear cutting forests is for short term gain, but ultimately causes extreme problems overall.

Death Valley is by nature a hot environment, but never before has it been an uninhabitable 130 degrees as it was recently. Temperatures are steadily breaking record highs almost annually.

The fires in Australia brought me to tears every day watching the habitat destruction and the death of so many animals. I grieved for them all, and of course the images of the Koala Bears who got burnt were heart wrenching. The understanding of how many didn't survive, and burned to death with no chance of escaping the trees, broke me. It is such a completely helpless feeling of not being able to stop it.

Sometimes I feel so sad at what is happening to our Earth, to nature, to animals, to trees, to our water life, and I get lost in that sadness. This feeling can't be fixed. For me I must live with it, it's not all of me thankfully, but it is me. I am sad, and that's simply true.

Australia and the Western United States are working on replanting, and bringing our forests back to health. My hope is that it will be a successful effort, faster than the next season of devastating wildfires hit.

In 2020, I saw an amazing photograph taken at night of my old home, Santa Cruz. There was a blanket of incredible clouds hovering just over the warm ocean, and the water was a brilliant, Caribbean blue from a bioluminescent algae bloom.

In the photo multiple lightning strikes were shooting down from the cloud, hitting the ocean's horizon. It was such a mind-blowing image, I felt charged without even being there.

I marveled at the glory of nature at that moment, but it was the next day that showed the devastating consequences of that storm. Santa Cruz and the surrounding communities along the coast, and up into the mountains, were on fire from the strikes moving inland and hitting ground later that night.

Apocalyptic photos of mountain fire meeting sea turned my awe into heartache. Many of my sacred places along the coast burned up, and many homes of people I know were destroyed. It was a sad and scary time for all.

I admire the firefighters and all the people that helped each other during that devastating time. When things happen like this, they are truly a chance to be of service. Providing shelter during a pandemic, fighting the fires, donating money to help people recover, were all wonderful ways to help.

I think what gets missed many times during a natural disaster, is the action to help the wildlife. We need to stop, and think about what it's like for the animals. Think about what it's like for a squirrel living in a tree and the fire is coming. Imagine what it's like for a deer with her two terrified and confused babies, she's running but there's no safe place to go.

When the birds fly over areas of fire, it gets too hot, and they fall out of the sky. The smoke and heat from fires kills the insects. Creeks are filled with ash and the fish suffer for it. After these extreme fires have blazed through a landscape it is susceptible to mudslides and flooding, which trigger another series of disasters.

Raging wildfires are hard on all living beings. Mature trees that would in an average fire survive, are now being wiped out as well. In Big Basin State Park, thousand-year-old trees were burning from the inside out and toppled during this fire. There were decades of fire scars on their bark from the previous fires that had burned through the forest, but they didn't survive these intense flames. It's painful to witness these deaths.

You can begin healing the Earth by being empathic with these beings, and find ways to help restore what has been lost. You can also find ways in your area to help prevent these misfortunes.

You can start helping by setting out water for fleeing animals. Keeping your dogs inside at night so animals will not get scared off, and run back into the fire areas.

Set out feeders for birds. Check in with local wildlife rescuers to see if they need help. Educate yourself in how you can effectively help. It's in the act of helping that the community forms a bond, and comes together for a higher purpose.

We can get through this time, but it's going to be difficult. I admit, I always have a little anxiety around fire. I want to put a prayer out for all the animals, all the people, and the land itself around the world that has gone through wildfires. I wish you the best in your healing and I'm sorry. All my love, respect, and blessings go out to you.

251

War

During the atrocities of war, of course we have empathy, and grieve for the loss of humans. The unimaginable happens again and again and we wonder will we ever grow beyond these horrific acts that we are all potentially capable of?

While grief is a given for human life, we tend to overlook the animals that are murdered, and the land and waterways that are destroyed as well.

Land mine and missile explosions, and toxic garbage left behind by military invasions are a short list of the irreparable damage that is caused to animal life and their habitat.

The terror and confusion for animals is just as real for them as it is for humans. Injury, dehydration, starvation, and witnessing horrific death are all situations that traumatize animals.

How can we help heal the wounded animals and land and water? We can find organizations or individuals whose mission it is to go into these war zones to repair damage and help wildlife and support them financially and physically.

If you are living in or near a war zone right now your focus is on saving your family and community, but for those who are outside of these places research valid organizations and get involved.

Empathy With Action

When we have empathy with no action to help, nothing changes. Currently I offer support to a Ukrainian veterinary couple at Vet Crew Hospital, who live in the war zone, but are still rescuing animals daily. They offer their medical services to every animal, bird and reptile that was left behind and needs help.

They also drive into active war zones and deliver food, medical aid, and supplies to as many people and animals as they can. Sometimes they are not able to bring the dozens of abandoned dogs and cats back with them to their hospital, but they leave food for them along the roads.

You could say the problem is just too big and there is no way they could help every animal, it's too overwhelming. The vets could say there's too many victims to make a difference, or they can help whoever they can in those brief moments of contact, because it matters to those individuals.

Is it heartbreaking for them? Absolutely. Do they grieve the individuals that die? Absolutely. Yet, they continue helping because they are heroic Earth Caretakers, and allowing war to destroy life without an empathic intervention is not an option.

These people were not known on a global scale before they built up a community of support. They built the support while they were doing the work, day, and night.

Grief with action can be a way through it. If we cannot help physically then we can help support those who can, financially, and by making others aware of the need.

I do not know these people personally, but I don't need to in order to help. I can read about atrocities and sit in sadness and anger, or I can also help our global community in whatever way I can. Imaginary boundaries do not separate humanity.

Full Of Life In Death

A tree can grow for thousands of years, giving life to countless animals and plants. All the while, the tree must fight off insect attacks and fungus infections, survive storms, drought, and fire. Finally, the insects win, or lightning strikes causing damage, and the tree begins to die, often over hundreds of years. All the while it is still providing food and homes for countless animals.

Dead trees are often more beautiful than living ones, standing tall as monuments to their kind. One day the tree falls but is still very much alive on the ground, with insect life inside.

With wood rotting from termites, and beetle larvae providing food for bears, over many years the tree decomposes and becomes soil, always beautiful and full of life.

Then a true miracle happens. From the soil a new tree sprouts, perhaps many. A new cycle of life begins.

What do trees think of death? Often, it's that question that reveals the mystery space only for those that are truly open. What does open mean? That's another question.

Being With Animals Through Death

Humans love life, we love living. We must understand that all living things also love life and living in their own, unique ways.

All living beings are remarkably different, and it fills our world with wonder. All Beings, plants, animals, amphibians, insects, birds have feelings and love life. All Beings fight to live when confronted with death.

I've held space for dying animals of all kinds, countless times in my life. I held my father, Jack, and my sister, Linda, as they died. I've been with my dogs and all the animals I've worked with, including elephants, chimpanzees, and birds of prey, as they passed on. Some of the farm animals I've been present for at their deaths, were ones that I killed for food.

When I was working for animal rescues, I had to put to death animals and birds that were severely abused by humans, and birds that were covered in oil, beyond the point of being able to save them.

There were so many, and I remember them all. I've consciously been present for the deaths of spiders, lizards, bats, frogs, and fish.

I write this to ask every human being to be present at death. Help another being to move on from this precious life to the next place, whatever it is.

Pray for the loss of animals, in whatever way that feels right for you. Be present, cry with love and respect. Dream together, sing, hold and touch with loving hands, gaze into the beings with peace, respect, beauty, love. Give your heart. Give blessings.

Remember your gift to give is empathy, compassion, and love. Feel together. It's ok to be sad, afraid, and confused, remember they are too.

If you can be this present for another being's passing, you will know why you are here on our Earth. You will feel and become more alive and amazingly special. You will fully grow into your spiritual Being.

Take the time to be present at death. Hopefully, one day when your time comes to transition into the spirit world, you will receive the same offering in return.

Jackie Boy

Learn to listen to your heart, heart-speak, heart language. Your heart has its own life and way of being. Your heart has its own dreams and songs. Your heart knows you so well.

Put aside your ego, your judgments, your control. Through a willingness, let your heart show you your way, your path. Practice will lead to trust, which will lead to a heartfelt life. A life of love as your guiding light.

***

I have found that the finest teachers of this heart path are my dogs. They love me for who I am, and that is truly wonderful.

On January 18th, 2020, my beloved Golden Retriever, Jackson, died. Jean, Julie, and I held him that morning, as he passed away, quietly, and peacefully. As his body shivered and his last breath was taken and let out, I saw his soul leave his body, and he was free.

It was difficult to watch his body shut down, and watch him struggle to be released from this physical world, and at the same time it was a beautiful experience to be a part of. The three of us were able to share his last moments with him, in the place he loved so much.

Death seems so final. The loss is so difficult for those remaining. We want to keep our loved ones with us, and we sometimes feel a twinge of hurt for being abandoned, and left behind without a true knowing of where they are going to.

Jackson went to the Spirit Lands, and we've had to adjust to living without him. The quiet on the land aches without his echoing bark. Jackie Boy's decade on this land has left us with so many wonderful memories. His medicine is embedded in our land, and his stories amongst all of us are seemingly endless.

Jackson loved people. Any time someone came to Headwaters to visit, it made his day. He couldn't stop visibly smiling, and parading around. He especially loved kids. I'm sure he changed many lives for the better by just enjoying the company of each and every person who came here.

Jackson opened hearts. He was quite simply pure love, embodied in a living being. Jackson was aptly nicknamed, Action Jackson, because he was more of a verb than anything. Living, loving, full throttle, happy Jack. Jackson made Headwaters a better place, a sacred place of heart.

In the morning when Jackson would wake up and go outside, he would bark and bark and bark and greet the day. His greeting was his way of saying, "I love life! Wake up and come play with me!" Meanwhile, most of the time, one of us would yell at him to stop barking so much, because we couldn't even think. It makes me smile to look at his barking as a way of him yelling at us to get up and live life, it's a new day.

***

I was on a photography trip in Northern Arizona on Navajo Tribal Land. This red rock country is some of my favorite land to photograph. I love the canyons at low light. I have lost myself in awe in this country many times, only to find myself again as a better, richer person. The solitude of the canyons always touches the quiet parts of my soul.

I connected with a Navajo woman who allowed me to explore her land, where there were slot canyons that had rarely been photographed. She allowed me to wander on my own through the pastel, swirled crevasses.

I returned with a full heart, and thanked her for this time. She lived in a hogan, and running around the dry, sparse landscape around her home were a litter of puppies she wanted to rehome.

Among those eight-week-old, fluff balls, was Jackson. He came to me, and he was beyond cute, and handsome, and filthy, full of ticks, Anemic, and he had Giardia. He was a bit shy, but we chose each other through heart.

I could have found countless reasons why I shouldn't take a puppy along on a photo trip, and eventually back to my home, but my brain shut down. My heart took over. My heart fused with Jackson's, and off we went. A road trip home. Little did he know he was heading Home to Headwaters, and that he had hit the dog lottery to paradise.

Our healing Golden Retriever, Bear, had passed away the same week Jackson was born, and my dad had passed away a couple of weeks before that. In honor of my dad, Jack, Jackson's name came to me. In the likeness of Bear, it quickly became clear that Jackson was the next one taking over for Bear, as the camp greeter for all who came to Headwaters.

Jackson was a blessing to all who met him. He was pure love. His love and excitement for life ignited the same in so many others. I miss my true friend. I enjoyed his company every day. My life is a better life, because he was in it. I miss his annoying, morning barks. I miss him on our walks in the woods together, exploring the world that I love.

Our memories are in the rocks, the trees, and the water. Our stories are alive on the land forever.

I miss you so much Jackson. You will always live in me. I'll never forget you. You taught me to let my heart lead my life. You, and all our dogs, are my best friends. I'm so grateful I found you Jackson. Thanks for ten wonderful years. You are missed. I love you forever!

I agree with the comparison that Dog spelled backwards is God. Dogs are angelic treasures to us crazy, wild humans, to remind us to love unconditionally.

Wolf Brother

Ho! Wolf Brother, your long patrol is done, the moon is set, the stars winked out, the final trail run. You were wilderness embodied, A wild stirring of the heart, and tonight, we sing in sadness for we be so far apart. We are pack mates on this planet, the same flesh and blood and bone, that will crumble, fade, disintegrate, when Spirit calls us home.

In the slanted evening sunlight, I can feel your golden eyes, find you loping in the lofty clouds that race across the skies. I will see you in the shadows. We will sniff the musty loam. We will run again together in the woods we call our home.

When the moon hangs half wolf-eaten we will sing you a traveling song, point our muzzles to the sky and sing our wolf-songs all night long.

Ho! Wolf Brother, your long patrol is done, the moon is set, the stars winked out, the final trail run.
- Elliot Drake-Maurer (A tribute to Riley)

Dare To Love Freely

I have an ache, like so many others, from the loss of those I truly love. Losing sacred friends leaves me raw and exposed. I have opened my heart so full and unconditionally, they have become a literal part of me, and me them, and we are forever connected. We can't not be. And, although I hurt so deep, I am at the same time so happy that I dared to love so freely...and will again.

Kodiak

Kodi, my gentle giant black lab, will always be a soul companion. He passed suddenly and unexpectedly, and years later I still grieve between the happy memories. I don't think it's a wound that will ever close, but there is more happiness than heartbreak.

My puppy Cooper was blessed to have him as a mentor in her first year of life. He truly led by example and watched over her.

When he died, I allowed her to be with him and smell him. I let her walk away when she was ready, so she knew where he was. I knew she needed to also grieve for her friend and brother.

After we buried Kodi in our memorial garden I sat at his grave day after day to talk with him. Although he wasn't in his body anymore, I felt his presence, and when I was sad, he had always been the one who comforted me.

I would ask Cooper if she wanted to go say hi to Kodiak and she would run up the trail and literally lay on his grave, as though she were leaning up against him like any other day.

Grieving is important for animals too. Some people think animals don't have emotions, but they absolutely do. Over time I didn't visit Kodi's grave as much. I now just speak with him wherever I am.

Five years after Kodi's death I brought home Tucker, another black lab puppy. The first day he came home to me we explored the land, and I asked him if he wanted to meet his angel brother Kodi and say hi.

I shouldn't have been so surprised, but my 7-week-old puppy ran up the trail straight to Kodi's grave, climbed up a rock altar where Kodi's picture is, and leaned in and smelled it. We have ten other dog's graves in the memorial garden, and Tuck went right to Kodi.

I know Kodi watches over me and Cooper and now Tucker. I've been blessed with dog angels in this world, and the next. Do I fear the days when my heart will break again when my dogs pass? Yes, absolutely, but what I fear more is the hurt of not ever having that mutual, unconditional love in my life, because I'm too afraid to love again and again.

The Healing Ocean

No thoughts, only emotion. Wave after wave washes away my grief.
Sadness swells and fills me completely.
I miss my boy, my friend, my reflection, my heart companion.
I ache, and then the wave builds, and crests, and takes away the burning for a while.
Wave after wave, my grief washes away.
The fog closes in and the sun sets, and I made it through another day.
With tomorrow's sunrise I will celebrate his life and our friendship, our soul connection, and cry some more, and be so very grateful that I never held back an ounce of love.
I love you, my baby boy.

I'm Crying For Vegas

Vegas, my rooster, just died in my arms. He looked to the sky and into my eyes. Through my eyes he touched my heart.

It was one of those moments that rarely comes our way in life, to be there for another being's transition into the spirit world. Vegas gave me that honor of holding him with love, at his final moment on this physical Earth.

Love sometimes shows up in the strangest places. We are not always ready when that moment shows up. Vegas grabbed my heart eleven years ago when he arrived at Headwaters.

He was young and had a huge job to do, he was in charge of protecting our hens. For eleven years he was the caretaker of the chickens.

I admired his work of chasing off predators, it was honorable. To observe him at work was beautifully perfect. Born from nature, descended from his wild relations, from the forest of Asia, he was carrying on his innate instincts.

Vegas would cock-a-doodle-do many times a day. That was music, happiness, peace, laughter, and most importantly, love to my ears. I loved his call. I knew Vegas through that sound, announcing to the world that he was alive and well, and doing his job, looking after his flock of chickens.

I loved Vegas' spirit and his commitment to a higher purpose. I loved his crazy looks. He was red and white with feathers on his head that fanned out in all directions. We called him Vegas because he looked like he was wearing a feather headdress, that would put any show performer to shame. He wore it well.

I couldn't see his eyes through his feathers. Early on, that was to my benefit because he didn't see me right away when I tried to pick him up. He would protest at first with a call, and a flutter of his wings, but then settle in and snuggle up to me. I would smooth his feathers back, and then our eyes would meet, and his heart and my heart would touch, we formed a trust, and our bond grew.

I sometimes feel that he came to this Earth to love me, and in turn, he came here for me to love him. Every day he would bring me happiness, and made my life more wonderful, every single day.

I know for some this is hard to understand. As a rooster, through his primal instincts, he was driven to protect his flock, and would attack many people who cared for him. To some, he was just a rooster, but to me he was an individual and he was a survivor.

One day, one of our horses stepped on his foot, he looked at me in terror, screaming for help. I pushed the horse off of him and picked him up, and nursed his wound. He lost part of his foot because of that injury. In those moments of pain, healing and trust, my love for him grew. I was his caregiver, and I was honored to be.

Vegas' spirit for life reminded me of myself. He understood me, we were in many ways the same primal being.

I knew that winter would be his last. Eleven years is a good, long life for a rooster. I felt his time to transition was near. I began to take him out of the coop every morning to greet the day. I would hold him and walk around the orchard. Always, his hidden eyes and mine would connect our hearts. That magical, universal language of the heart. I will always treasure those mornings.

One day, Vegas wasn't looking so good. His energy was low, and he was getting very thin. It was cold, and we had started covering him at night with a pile of hay to keep him warm.

Vegas was getting ready to move on. He stopped his greeting calls. He was tired from a life well lived. Many people say they want to return some day after they pass on, as one of our Headwater's dogs. They have such a life of paradise here, but our chickens get just as much love, freedom, and care as any of our animals. I can pass on one day knowing that I have given my very best to the animals under my care.

Vegas lived for two days longer than I thought he would. Perhaps he was just taking in the privilege of life on this precious Earth, and saying goodbye to his rabbit and bird friends who shared his feed. Maybe he needed to walk through the orchard a few more times to gather the medicine of the land. His work here was complete. Vegas outlived all but one chicken, who was much younger than him.

On this last morning, when I picked up Vegas and looked into his eyes, he said to me it was almost time. I held him heart to heart.

I carried him around our land for an hour. I took him to our sweat lodge area, our most sacred space, and that's where he passed.

If you are ready to receive love in whatever form it shows up, and you let it in, it can be a treasure of a lifetime. There is nothing more powerful or rewarding as shared love. Vegas gave me that honor.

As I cry writing this memory, I know he will always live in me. Thank you, Vegas, for the memories. Thank you for reminding me every day how to caretake, how to protect, and most importantly how to keep my heart open.

If it is true that when we transition to the spirit world, all the souls we have ever loved are there waiting to reunite with us, can you imagine how crowded it will be? I will never be alone, and for that I am grateful.

Our Great Horned Owl

Luna flew yesterday. Her soul flew from her aged body - her wing healed; her spirit free from cages.

It is a deeply intimate experience to share the passing of a physical being's life – be it human or animal. To cradle a wild owl who, in health, would never allow such intimacy, who on dying relinquished all wildness to human kindness, was an honor.

As she was weakened on Saturday, and we knew for sure she was dying, we wrapped her in a towel and brought her inside. I couldn't bear the idea of her dying on the floor of her cage. The talons that in health could break one's arm, softened. She could barely keep her eyes open; her breathing was shallow. She hadn't eaten in a while, so she wasn't getting water. We gave her a few droppers full.

It was a rainy and windy day. We sat by the fire holding her gently. She survived the night, but barely. Her head bobbed like a newborn baby, and like a newborn we had to hold it. It dawned on me that she didn't want to die inside. She didn't know inside. So, in my pjs and slippers I took her outside, into the rain and the wind. Wrapped in the towel, the wind blew her feathers, and she half opened her eyes. She moved her bobbing head to the north, the west and the south as if bowing to the directions in solemn prayer, breathing in the wildness of the day, feeling the rain on her beak, and then releasing her head back into the towel.

I held her close and told her it was time to let go, as if she were human. I was amazed at her tenacity for life. I watched as her breathing became gulps, and then – two deep breaths – her eyes open – and she was gone.

Unlike our reciprocated love for dogs or other domesticated animals, a wild animal knows only the wild even in captivity. Luna was wild. Our bond was symbolic. The last day of her life we viscerally exchanged energy. Perhaps I anthropomorphized her head bows to the three directions, but it seemed clear to me that life's meaning was sacredly shown, profoundly simple and complex, a fleeting moment of understanding that words hold no power to describe and therein lies the power of symbols and power animals. I honor Luna for a life not necessarily fully lived with her broken wing, but well-lived in the company of humans. - Jean Sage

Soul Friendship

There was a Rhodesian Ridgeback dog that helped me with all my animal caretaking duties around the wildlife park I worked at. He was a good companion who protected me, and alerted me of potential trouble.

A Bengal Tiger mother had a litter of cubs, but she rejected one of them. The dog took to the baby tiger cub right away, so I let the dog help raise the cub. Myself, and the other keepers, fed the cub, but the dog was the one who bonded with the baby.

Even though the tiger grew to 500 pounds, and the dog was 90 pounds, they would play with each other for hours, without either of them getting hurt. The tiger cared for the dog. The dog was more dominant because he raised the cub, but they looked out for each other.

Their friendship was sacred, a soul connection. It was inspiring to be a part of it. The two truly loved each other, and never wanted to be apart.

One day, tragically, the dog was riding on a hay truck, and fell off and was run over. He died in my arms. The tiger fell into deep sorrow. I could not make it better. I sat with the tiger for days and slept with him at night. He refused to eat.

Three weeks later, when I came into his pen, I found him dead. The tiger missed the dog so much that he just gave up on life. He died of a broken heart. This irreparable heartache profoundly affected me to the core.

Deep grief is a feeling that must be honored. We must have a way to work with it, so it becomes medicine. I also learned the power of soul level friendship, where a being can let themselves go into another being. There is nothing better.

To have friendship of this caliber is to truly know you've fulfilled your life's journey. It's the top of the mountain. The tiger had reached the top of the mountain, and when the dog passed on and went to Heaven, that's where the tiger needed to be, reunited with his soulmate, the dog.

***

When you are lucky enough to have this kind of a love connection, it's important to identify it as being sacred. You keep it alive by feeding it more love, and honoring it by giving it life, and energy, and attention in a good, healthy way. It doesn't matter if this relationship is with an animal, a friend, a lover, or a family member. There are various types of love, but they all center around the heart.

Every living being has a heart that we can connect with on some level. Sometimes the wounds are so deep we have trouble getting beyond them, but I believe our heart connection is also what allows us to see the good in things, and to continue to live fully as we work through the grief.

Roadkill

Every time I drive by an animal killed on the road my heart weeps. I stop and move them off into the woods if I am in a rural area. At least they'll be home. It's wrong for any living being to be run over again, and again. It is disrespectful and it encourages people to remove themselves from empathy.

Let the animal go back to the Earth. Maybe a predator will find them, and they will have a good meal out of harm's way.

Removing the animal from a tragic situation is a sacred act of kindness and compassion. Take the time to do the right thing. When your task is complete, let yourself feel the sadness for the loss of another fellow Earth Being, killed in such a way.

I know I've killed with my own car. I killed a Saw Whet Owl that flew into my window on a dark night. I buried the owl with a ceremony, and I wept.

Animals have not seemed to be able to make it a part of their being to have enough fear, and respect for cars, to avoid getting hit by them.

There's a lot of work being done now building pathways and tunnels over and under many roads, which has effectively protected wildlife. Do your best to support projects like this. Build awareness for the need to assist migrating animals in places where their territory has been divided by our roads and cities.

Educate people to be more aware as they are driving. I live off a dirt road and animals are constantly running out towards my car. They get confused and so I must be the one that assumes they will panic, and they will not know which direction to go when they get startled.

Some of our neighbors have made signs warning people to be aware of specific wildlife that tends to cross in certain bends along our main road.

A coyote crosses the road from meadow to meadow, to hunt small animals. Toads, frogs, and snakes gather on the road to soak up the warm sun. Squirrels are just crazy busy, trying to survive all the time. They don't pay attention to vehicles until one gets close to them, and then they run all over in a panic trying to avoid what it perceives is a predator.

Two deer cross the road to duck into the trees, but their babies hesitate on the other side not knowing what to do. They want to follow their mamas, but sometimes their timing is wrong, and they run into the oncoming traffic.

Every animal has a reason for being close to the roads, but we need to be as aware and responsible as we can, since we are the ones driving a foreign object through their homes.

The problem is not going to go away anytime soon, human beings love their cars, but cutting down on roadkill is a problem we can absolutely work on, that can make a significant difference in saving our wildlife.

The Rabbit Lives In Me

When I was nineteen, I was driving at night on U.S. 101 along the California coast with a friend. I was returning from a wonderful photo shoot in coastal Alaska. I had spent many days with Bald Eagles and endless, old growth forests. I was on a nature high.

I came around a turn and my headlights found a rabbit on the road. It had been hit by a previous car. Its back legs were crushed. It was helpless, not understanding, trying to live, dragging itself along the road.

We stopped the car and picked up the rabbit and held it for hours off the road in the forest. Its eyes were connected to our eyes. Its hurt was our hurt. Rabbit, my friend, and I cried. We cried for the rabbit,

for us being helpless, not knowing what could be done. We couldn't fix it. We were as helpless as the rabbit.

I changed that night. That gentle being touched me to my core. I feel him as I write this, as if it were now not almost 50 years ago, but rather as if it's happening now. That rabbit lives in me and through me always.

We didn't have it in us to kill the rabbit that night, so we set him in a bush in hopes that a coyote might find him and be quick.

Driving on we wept, and we were different. Every time I drive by an animal dead on the road my heart weeps. Animals are not supposed to die on roads, and yet they do. So, I will keep weeping.

Birds On Highway 1

Years ago, I drove 90 miles twice a week on Highway, 1 between Santa Cruz and San Francisco. I found that drive to be stunning. I was keenly aware of the surroundings on this route. I noticed, much to my sadness, songbirds dead on the road.

On average I would see 75 dead birds, each time I drove along that highway. I would add the numbers up, and think of all the roads on this planet and this became very disturbing.

It was clear that our songbirds were in trouble. I found that most people didn't even know they had even hit a bird.

While I was driving one day, two small Bushtit birds were fighting in flight, and flew right into my car. I watched the whole thing and couldn't stop it. I pulled over and found the birds. They were laying in the grass, eyes open and shaking. I thought they would die. I scooped them into my hands and held them closely, giving them healing intentions through my energy.

In five minutes, they came back to life and off they went. What a wonderful, mysterious moment that was. Such good news amidst all the dead ones on the road.

Nameless Animals

In our memorial garden we have made an altar to honor the animals that have been killed by cars, and other accidental human causes. I feel it is important to honor those who have passed, even if we didn't know them individually.

My heart goes out to those animals who get confused with our busy vehicles and air traffic. They don't always understand mechanical energy such as windmills, or the transparency of a solid object such as windows. If it's not a natural energy, it is difficult for them to read the situation. It is not something that is wired into them at birth.

I encourage everyone to send a blessing to all who leave this physical world and move on to the spirit world, no matter what physical form they were born into. All animals have a soul just like ours, and it can only be a good thing if we send them off with love.

Well Wishes

Tim has instilled in me the practice of kindness and respect, of removing dead animals from the road off to the side. When it's not safe, such as on a freeway, I at least give a blessing to the deceased animal and wish it well on its journey.

I usually notice a dead animal on the freeway fairly far ahead of me. My heart goes out to them, and I give an apology from the human world, a quick blessing, and well wishes as I drive by.

More than once I've had a good laugh at myself though, realizing after I have quickly passed by, that it was a shredded, truck tire that I gave a blessing to. At least the thought was there I guess, and it doesn't hurt to put more good intentions out into the world, and to have a good laugh at my empathy for a blown tire.

The Oil Spill

Back in the 1980's, when I was running a wildlife rescue, I was at a conference in the Bay Area, on how to take care of seabirds when they get caught in oil spills, from tankers.

While I was there, I got a call in the middle of the conference, letting me know there was an oil spill happening at that moment near Santa Cruz. I needed to get back down there to help.

An oil barge filled with thick, gooey Bunker C oil wasn't sealed up correctly, and it leaked oil for 100 miles along the coast. That part of the Pacific Coast is a National Wildlife Refuge filled with various seabirds; Pelicans, Murres, Cormorants, California Gulls, you name it.

It was a huge catastrophe caused by human error. I needed to find a facility big enough to handle what we were going to be dealing with. There is a power plant in the small town of Moss Landing, and they kindly offered us a huge space to take care of the injured birds.

This was an enormous task. We had about 50 volunteers there at any given time, and it was a 24/7 job. We had people that would scour the beaches to find the birds. They were covered with oil, and the people would catch them, put them in boxes, and bring them to us to wash.

Seabirds depend on their feathers being clean to live on the ocean. The tar-like oil would glue their feathers together, and they couldn't clean them to keep them waterproof and fluffed up. The birds would soak up the cold ocean water, and their skin would get too cold, and they would die from hypothermia.

Seabirds normally preen their feathers with their beaks daily to stay clean. A few birds like Cormorants, also stand on rocks and stretch out their wings to dry off.

Birds like, Murres, are literally in the water most of their lives, except when they come out to breed. They fly underwater, and catch other fish to eat. Can you imagine one of these birds swimming underwater or on the surface, and then that oil gets on them, and they try to preen themselves?

It's gross to imagine, and they're digesting that poison, and most of them die in the ocean. They drown and we don't ever see them because they're just not visible to us that far out.

If they do wash up onshore, they're often attacked and eaten by predators, or they just die there washing back and forth in the waves. If they are lucky, an Earth Caretaker finds them and brings them to a wildlife rescue.

I oversaw this rescue operation, and one of the hardest things I had to do in my life was triage. I had to make the decision whether I thought we could wash the birds and potentially save them, or if they were too far gone.

The ones that were too covered in oil and too weak and suffering, I would have to euthanize. I had to put a needle in them and kill them, and I had to make that decision for every single bird, and it burned my soul. I personally had to kill many hundreds of birds to end their suffering.

I still see every one of them looking at me with their bright eyes saying, "All I was doing was living in the ocean catching fish, why did this happen to me? What did I do?" That's what my heart heard them plead.

I then gave each one a blessing, and my good wishes and apologies. Another volunteer would hold them, and also give them their love. I put the needle in, and I put those birds who were suffering to sleep and sent them into the spirit world.

I cannot tell you how tough that was. I had such an aching sadness in me for what I had to do. Each bird I had to kill was a wound to my heart. The sadness welled up in me over many long days and nights.

The ones we thought we could save; we put in a sink and washed them with a detergent to get the oil off. Can you imagine a wild animal having to be held by humans while they are already traumatized?

Have empathy for a minute and feel this stressful situation from their point of view. What would it be like to have all these humans, with these bright lights on you? You're out of your element, and you're being held, and washed and scrubbed with soap and water. Practice empathy from the beginning, from the time the oil covered them, and become that bird. Look at the world from their point of view.

The volunteers and myself brought compassion, and love to each bird. I know that helps. I know that all animals feel and respond to that energy.

Once the birds were washed and dried off, if they looked good, a volunteer released them back into the ocean, in Monterey Bay, once the oil slick was cleaned up.

We stayed at the power plant washing birds for a month. We were able to save about 10,000 birds. I could only imagine how many thousands died. There were a lot of tears during that time.

One incident in particular profoundly affected me. While I was doing triage, I had to identify the birds, and a bird was brought in that I misidentified. I made a mistake, and we weren't feeding it the right food, and it was starving. It had become too weak to recover, and just wasn't going to make it, so I would have to euthanize it.

At the same time that happened, a game warden came in from the California Fish and Game Department, and he was overseeing what we were doing. He was in charge of wildlife in the state of California, and I had helped him before on some stings, protecting salmon from poachers, and a few other cases helping wildlife.

We just looked at each other, and with no words spoken, we walked out the door with that bird. All the emotions were coming up for both of us, and the weight of what was happening was overbearing.

We sat under the towers of the power plant, holding the sea duck that was dying. It was a surreal world like something from a futuristic movie. There were lights flashing, sparks between the towers, and unearthly noises all around us.

I held the bird to my aching heart, and as it died, the game warden and I cried from somewhere deep inside. All the sadness of what had happened to our sacred Monterey Bay, came together in that moment with that bird.

As caretakers for our marine sanctuary, we the people, had failed our birds and marine life. We knew the thousands of sea birds we saw was a small percentage of the birds and animals that had died in the ocean and were never found.

At that moment, my wounds opened deeper, and strangely enough, that sea duck helped to inspire us to be better people. My commitment to protect our environment became my life's purpose.

The real healing there we got was from the sea duck. It died in my arms, and we gave it a good blessing.

I still don't understand why there has to be all of that pain and sorrow. Why does this even have to happen?

My friend and I picked ourselves up, and got back to work doing what we needed to do to care for the planet. Often, the greatest teachers are the animals or the trees or the plants. If you allow yourself to be a student and be taught, so many wonderful things can happen for you. It doesn't need to be an intense situation like an oil spill, it can also just be a nice walk in the woods. Just be open and stay humble.

Remind yourself frequently, that we are a part of life, not the whole of it. What happened to the birds is happening to us. We have the ability to alter the outcome by being aware and making necessary changes. Let's do it.

The Otter

In the distance on the beach, I saw many gulls jumping, fighting, and screaming. I knew something had died. The group of children and I walked toward the birds. I approached the otter with sadness and amazement.

Gulls fly off, children see the gunshot wound. Entrails pulled out, mouth open, teeth showing. I thought of what to say to the children.

I feel the sea otter represents all that is so amazing about our central coast. At that moment, our central coast was dead. Dead by gunshot. Dead by ignorance. Dead for no good reason. I had no words.

We sat in a circle for a moment, and with the help of the screaming, hungry gulls and the endless, breaking waves, the otter spoke to us through our senses. We moved on, and the gulls and the waves reclaimed the sea otter.

Blue Whale

A whale died, I was told, an eighty-foot Blue Whale, the rarest of the rare. A female and her aborted baby on the beach. I went to see, curious, wondering.

Gulls were feasting on blubber. A mass of birds and whale. People were gathering, blubber was soaking into my feet.

A baby on the beach, dead and alone. I asked what had happened, the answer was painful to hear. She was sleeping, full with baby, close to birth. The ship hit her and broke her. Before me lay the definition of beauty and grace, becoming the gulls, the beach, and my feet.

261

This time my camera felt useless, as tears streamed down my face. This time my camera could not tell this story. I carry the weight of what I saw. I went back many times over three months, and the skin still clung to rocks. I have a bone from her, I don't know why, I just have the bone.

As I write this story, a year later, tears still wash down my face. I lost something on that beach. I have an open wound. It may never heal. Maybe that's a good thing. I will carry it, and I will never forget that Blue Whale.

Dead Animals

All my years of wandering the Central Coast beaches I've found dead animals. Much of the time there are birds covered with oil or tangled in fishing lines. I've found birds with their beaks cut off that had been thrown into the ocean.

I've found many seals and sea otters with gunshot wounds. I've also found many animals that appeared to have died of natural causes.

The ocean washes to shore all things floating in it. These dead animals are now a part of the sacred, natural cycle of the ocean and the beach. There is a raw beauty in looking at animals going back to nature. It's the brutal honesty that only nature can provide.

Let those deaths motivate you to protect our precious animals that we share our coastline with. How we care for animals is a clear statement of who we are as individuals, and as a community. It's not always convenient to be kind, but it's the right thing to do.

Swallowing The Pain

Today I was driving down the freeway, and I saw something that greatly disturbed me. A pick-up truck was pulling a trailer full of rabbits in cages. They had no protection from the wind. They were terrified. They told me so. I could see it. I knew it. These living Beings were terrified and all I did was feel their pain, their fear, their sadness. Their next stop was more than likely the butcher's.

I couldn't do a thing to help them. Often in life we are presented with these kinds of moments. We want to help but can't. Sadness welled up in me for those rabbits and I drove by them, and went on my way, and swallowed the pain.

Death Feels Personal

One evening I was walking up to my house, and saw a chipmunk covered in saliva, alive and terrified, one of our dogs had attacked it. I picked it up and brought it into the house to examine it and clean it up.

What a beautiful being. Chipmunks live all around my house, and land, and I interact with them daily. I love them, they have my respect. Many predators eat them. Their death is a natural part of nature, and yet I have trouble finding peace with it when it's personal.

This chipmunk was personal. I wondered when this precious being looked up at me, what it thought, who I was. It never bit me, even though it was fully conscious. After my exam, this chipmunk seemed to be okay, so I went to bed, and let him rest with me.

I woke up in the morning and found his back legs were paralyzed. I was heartbroken. This chipmunk looked into my eyes as I looked into his. We met in a space only of us. In that space, we shared our sadness.

I was so fearful because I knew I would have to put him down. When I left that space, I knew that chipmunk had given permission. I held him to my heart and cried. I sent him to the spirit world.

I've killed many animals throughout my life in the animal rescue business, and as a hunter. Each time, it's harder, and hurts a little bit more.

Death is a part of nature, and we humans are nature. We die too, as all things do. As a conscious human with our amazing brain, I often wonder if we take death harder than other animals. I don't mean this in a way that says humans are better, just that we're different.

That day that I killed the chipmunk, our eyes meeting on a journey of deeper understanding, my heart unfolded and opened wider. That little precious being met me in a space reserved only for unique moments of understanding through oneness—that chipmunk took me on a spiritual journey into life and death. I experienced the power of love, mutual love between two beings transcending all the beliefs we carry.

I don't hunt anymore, because I don't need to, and I don't want to kill wild animals. They're under enough stress from our human population.

I don't mind hunting if it's done with honor, and respect. I do eat meat; I know animals die so I can live. Life is complex. I'll go on questioning and exploring death. Death defines how life works. Life and death make the whole.

***

Two years later our dogs caught another chipmunk. It seemed close to death. It was curled up, eyes closed, barely breathing.

My feelings were again of sadness. My dogs did this. Predators doing what they do. There is no need for them to kill for food, it was pure instinct. I was reminded of my own human race, the top predators.

At that moment this critter was all that is currently happening to our Earth. I felt the pain and I wanted to help, even if I could only give the chipmunk some of my heart, maybe its last moments on Earth were full of love.

I took him to my house and wrapped him in my arms, held him close to my heart, filled him with love, and fell asleep.

When I woke up, he was looking into my eyes, fully alive. As he started to move around, I saw that his back legs wouldn't move. This injury was heartbreaking, he couldn't live in the wild.

He was full of life running around the bed with his front legs. Not giving up, enjoying the gift of life, enjoying each other's company. Two Earthlings stepping outside the normal rules of life and connecting through heart.

This was a magical time, as short as it would become, where two beings just simply loved each other. I didn't have it in me to put him down. I wondered how I could take care of this animal in a good way.

The afternoon moved into night. The chipmunk began to breathe heavily, I knew his time was limited. In the morning I found him crumbled in a ball dead.

Those moments I spent with him were precious to me. I can only hope I touched that chipmunk as much as he touched me. I buried him under a favorite fruit tree.

I wish good travels to my chipmunk friends. With love and regret, Tim.

Rodents And "Pests"

If you must kill an insect or a mouse, do it only after deep, heartfelt thought. Always be willing to not do it. Remember they want to live their life just as you do, and they were born here with a purpose as an integral part of our lives. Is there another solution?

<u>Extinct Animals</u>

"There are different layers of existence. There are "extinct" animals waiting in other veils for their time to come back. When the time is right, they will return." - E.K.

Creating Space For Endangered And Extinct Species.

The last California Grizzly died in 1922, near Fresno, California. They were the most magnificent animals.

The California Grizzly weighed over two thousand pounds, and roamed the abundant land, sometimes in numbers so large they traveled in herds.

They were a unique subspecies that were wiped out by the gold miners and settlers mostly. Now, only remembered on the California state flag. They are one of the great losses of our planet.

263

I've often had visions of extinct animals. There are many that have become extinct at the hands of humans, and it's a weight we carry.

Sometimes when I'm quiet and open, the extinct animals from our past, such as the Great Auk, the Passenger Pigeon and the California Grizzly come to me. They tell me they are not gone. They are in another level of existence, waiting in another time and space to return when it is safe. Their energy and spirit still reside on Earth.

Anything is possible, and this is what I've been told as a truth. I do believe there will be a window when the timing will be right for those who have gone extinct to return to the physical world, and I live for that time.

On our land in Mount Shasta, we have a memorial garden honoring the people and animals we have been connected to and have passed. Julie has created a majestic, life size, driftwood sculpture of a California Grizzly, partly as an honoring of it, but also as a symbol of holding space for its return someday. This grizzly species may not physically roam the Earth any longer, but its spirit is still felt in the land.

I have great faith that we humans will get it together, and allow the world to be a place where all beings can live their lives.

I encourage you to create a space on this Earth, for all living beings to safely live their lives. This is one basic desire we have in common with all living things. This Earth, our mother, gives us all that we need to live. Sometimes we just need to get out of the way, and let things be.

Although, one of the great gifts we have is the ability to assist in the healing of our planet. We have the knowledge and resources to bring back our current population of endangered species by creating and restoring space for them to live.

**

When I think back to my childhood, one of the things that truly inspired me to save animals from going extinct was a book called, *Silent Spring* by Rachel Carson. She was one of my heroes, and a true Earth Caretaker.

She exposed the use of DDT poison being sprayed on plants, and then it washing off from the rains into the waterways, and its detrimental and lethal effects on birds and animals.

At the time when the book was published, we were about to lose the Brown Pelican, many birds of prey, and in particular the Bald Eagle and the Peregrine Falcon. These birds would consume the insects that had been exposed to the poison on the plants and in the soil. The bird's eggshells would get weak as a result, and they would sit on them, and the eggs would break, and so their population began to disappear rapidly.

With that knowledge we were able to reverse the damage that was being done. It was a very close call for many of those endangered species, but we did it. We can remedy what we've damaged if it's caught and acted on in time.

Some birds have been lost, some animals and plants and insects have been lost. Environmental groups from around the world have come together, and their studies have shown that a million species of animals are on the verge of going extinct, right now, due to the actions of human beings.

That is not a weight we want to carry. We want to reverse that impending outcome, and be able to say that all those animals may have had some close calls, but we found a way for them to harmoniously live on this planet.

We can save every single one. We just have to find that place inside, the will and that strength within us, that would trigger us to do the right thing. This common focus is something that could bring humanity together.

We are so divided now, and we are so screwed up in that way, but it doesn't take much of a shift within us. We can come together for a higher purpose in fighting for our Earth, and these animals, and ultimately for ourselves.

DDT was eventually banned by Richard Nixon, who was the president at the time. He certainly had his troubles as we all know, but he did that good thing, and it's held till today.

We were able to bring those bird's population back, through the help of science and caretaking. They are now healthy, and the Brown Pelicans have been taken off the Endangered Species list. The Endangered Species Act is an amazing act of kindness humans created. It is something to feel good about.

Imagine if you didn't hear birds singing every day. Imagine if you went to the ocean and you didn't hear the gulls or the pelicans. We take it for granted, but it would be so empty, and such a loss.

We're facing the effects of global warming. We've had catastrophic fires. We have had extreme weather patterns like hurricanes, and floods, and ice storms, and droughts throughout the entire planet, and that's just scratching the surface.

The good news is we have the skill, and the ability to restore balance, but where do we dig down and find the willingness? Where does that live within us? What does it take?

It's time for a change, and to reverse the damage we have inflicted. Let's move into our present day and future, and let's start getting a grip on it by voting for the Earth.

We're going to get a cure for this disease by going back to the work of caring for our planet, and doing what's right.

No More Grizzly

As I walk into the forest, I feel no fear. There is no California Grizzly here to make me aware. There is no grizzly bear to wake me up. I'm in a deep, waking sleep and the bear is gone forever.

It will take another Heaven and Earth to bring back our extinct animals. I am a grizzly. I am proud to be a grizzly. I feel them upon the landscape. Their memory is in the old growth trees. Their memory is within me.

I want to wake up to that bear place, that sacred space that only a predator like a bear can give me, but I must find it elsewhere now.

My brothers and sisters the grizzly, I'm so sorry for what we've done, please forgive me. I will keep you alive inside of me. I will never forget.

We are currently grieving our Earth, but as we get through this grief, hope is on the other side. We have to reach for hope through trust, before we actually feel it, but once we do, we are moving in the right direction.

The questions to then ask are, have I done all I came here to do? Am I going to be ready to die?

Part 4

A Life Of Service

Build upon your awareness and values and physically set into motion being of service in every aspect of your life. This is who you are, an Earth Caretaker.

Chapter 29
Follow The Scout, Earth Caretaker Way
– A Life Of Service

The Earth Caretaker movement is a commitment to living a life path that makes the Earth a healthy place to live. All past Earth peoples had scouts that were the protectors of the people. Their skills of living directly with the Earth were highly developed.

The scout was the one who went out into the wild lands and practiced deep nature awareness, blending in with the landscape as one. They were master trackers and observers. They would find where the animals were for food and for protection.

The scouts also would know who and where their adversaries were. They stayed informed. First and foremost, they were protectors of the lands and the regions the people lived on. They were the Scout Earth Caretakers.

Today it's a new world, the Earth itself is now endangered, and as a result, all humans are endangered as well. It is time now for a new generation of Earth Caretakers to rise and protect our global community, by protecting the Earth.

The modern Earth Caretaker is like the scouts of the old days, the one that commits oneself to a greater cause. The commitment of protecting our Earth and all that lives upon her. This commitment expands out to all humans living close to the Earth. All humans will benefit from this because a healthy Earth is good for all life.

Unlike the scouts of the past, which were few in numbers, the Earth Caretakers today must become many. My dream is that all people will be Earth Caretakers. Becoming an Earth Caretaker will become our medicine, it will simply become who we are by reclaiming our birthright to be a steward of the Earth. It will be the norm for all people.

I believe this can happen. Our love and care and respect for our Earth is already living in us from our past, through our ancestors who lived consciously with the Earth.

We now need to awaken the Earth Caretaker within us, and give it new life through action and involvement. This gives life and purpose back to us. It connects us to something greater than ourselves.

Being an Earth Caretaker opens our hearts and creates community, and it can be challenging and fun at the same time. This sacred tending of the Earth is magical, and we find spirituality in our everyday lives just by our simple interactions. It stimulates our minds and expands our awareness of the world around us.

I believe becoming an Earth Caretaker will catch on as momentum grows, as the majority wake up to what needs to be done, and what can be done by our daily actions.

At our core, people want to be of service. We want to be a part of making a situation noticeably better. We may feel that on our own our efforts won't make a difference. Yet, when we join others with the same intention, we can see the positive outcome we made collectively, and we feel proud, and want to do more.

As we see the progress in the small but powerful steps taken by the masses, we will reclaim our deep love of our home, and take on Earth Caretaking as a way of life.

This caretaking already lives within us. We just need to remember what we already know. Our problems will begin to dissolve, and life will start to get back in balance for a healthy, sustained future. With a little extra effort maybe, just maybe, we will all get along better for a common cause that benefits us all.

I'm a practical man as well as a dreamer all in one. I believe that if even 5% of the people are fully committed, they can lead the other 95% into doing what is right. It takes that full commitment of the five percent, and then watch the transition happen.

Our living Earth is calling you to service. So, dig down deep you lover of our Earth, feel that call, and live your life through action. Change the world for the better by living the Earth Caretaker Way. I'll see you on the front lines.

A Scout's Code To Live By

We have many rites of passages in our lives. Some we acknowledge, and some we live through, but don't consciously recognize. A personal code of honor is based on values that you hold as important to your own personal integrity.

Creating your personal code of honor to live by is about who you are as an authentic individual. It is based on bringing out the best of yourself in your everyday life.

A Scout Earth Caretaker code of honor is the next level of service beyond yourself. Its focus is about living a life of service and protection for our whole global community, and how you are going to show up for others, and for the Earth.

When you think of the Earth Caretaker values, ask yourself what your role is as a part of this whole global life. How will you show up for your Earth, your world, with your personal values and attributes?

***

As a core part of our Scout-Earth Caretaker Way class at Headwaters Outdoor School, we create an Earth Caretaker Code of Honor as a guide. This is the basis of the teachings in this class that we encourage our students/Earth Caretakers to live by, as a part of their life's intention.

This is a well-represented guide of values. For a code of honor to become a part of you, and become your medicine, take away inspiration from these thoughts, but make them personal.

Earth Caretaker Code Of Honor

Be Authentic - Know yourself and be true to you. Get inspired by other people, but don't compare yourself in a judgmental way. You will always only be the second best someone else, but the very best you.

Be Humble - Be humble, but step up and be noticed when your presence is needed.

Expand your Awareness - Awareness is the first step in knowing where attention is needed. How do you affect your surroundings? When you observe, be mindful if you are being judgmental or are observing with wonder, admiration, discernment, and an open mind.

Practice Kindness - Being kind starts with awareness. Are you kind? In any difficult situation ask yourself, what would love do now?

Self-Mastery - Give your best effort in all that you do. Work on your weaknesses and honor your strengths. Self-Mastery in anything is striving to be as good as you can be.

Competition is good and healthy, but also always lift others up, you will grow together. Mastering your ego is a lifetime project, but one worth working towards, to lead a life of greatness. You don't need to be famous to be honorable.

Explore - Get curious and participate. Be a pioneer of radical, new discoveries. There are no limits. What are you passionate about? That's where your momentum starts.

Be of Service - Help where help is needed. Be proactive in caring for the Earth and all beings. Nature gives you an opportunity to be a hero every single day. Be a person of right action.

If you see a job that needs to be done, it's your responsibility to see that it gets done. At the end of the day ask yourself if you have done your best that day, if yes, then acknowledge that. Take the pat on the back. If you know you could have done better, then get up the next day and do better.

Be a Protector - Stand up for all who need help. Be a peacemaker with an open heart. Restore balance without over controlling.

Be Respectful - You may not agree with another person, but your actions can show respect. Judgment creates division through ignorance.

Respect all beings. Every being is only trying to live its best life. Be tolerant. An ant is perfect for what an ant is here to do, and be.

Treat Yourself as Sacred - Live your beautiful life fully in gratitude for who you are. Know that you are sacred. Believe in yourself, and others will believe in you as well. Respect your body. Take care of your physical, mental, emotional, and spiritual health. We don't always allow our bodies to be the gifts they are. Get in them and be physical. Your body is a part of the Earth, one in the same.

Stay Educated - Stay informed and continue to grow, and stretch your brain. Dig in and research facts and find truth. Follow your intuition and believe in that. The world needs thought leaders.

Be Self-Reliant - Live confidently in this world and thrive. Master Earth living skills. Be self-reliant, but also be teachable. Allow others to have purpose and be of service to you, when you need guidance or assistance as well.

Be Honest – Be honest with others, and most importantly be truthful with yourself. You are only as good as you are when no one else is looking. When striving to live an honorable life, truth matters. Care enough about your relationships that you are willing to risk losing a friendship by telling the truth.

Be impeccable with your word. Say what you mean, mean what you say. When you are not trustworthy it is a violation to your soul and becomes a wound you carry.

Do the things you say you will do. What if everyone were in their integrity and did this? What if our politicians and government were to do this? We don't live in a world where many of our leaders follow this, but what if? What if they had been mentored, and loved, and held accountable by not only their family, but by the community they grew up in? Be honest and trustworthy. Live life on a handshake, knowing that your word is golden.

Be Courageous - Courage does not mean you are not afraid. You may be afraid, but you take the right action anyway. Sometimes it doesn't always feel good doing the right thing. Do it anyway. Expand your comfort zone and expand your world.

Be Loyal - Loyalty is a gift you give another being. Knowing that someone is there to stand by you can make all the difference in one's life. Even if you are the last one standing up for what you believe in and what's right, be the last one standing.

Have an Open Heart - Love fully. Lead with peace, love, and kindness. Being vulnerable is an act of courage, knowing you could get broken, but you are open to loving life fully anyway. Love is the most powerful energy there is. Why live a life of mediocrity? Holding even 10% of yourself back is a waste of a great life, and can only lead to regrets.

Live the Full Circle Way - Live knowing every decision you make or don't make will affect the whole, and come back around to you. Every action has a consequence. Are you giving back to keep yourself, and your community in balance? Is there an equal exchange of energy? Will your action take away or restore? If you gain something, give something back. Be aware of your impact, and keep our life circle full and in balance by your conscious decisions of living a sustainable life.

Be Compassionate - Open your heart to all living beings. Have empathy, and find a way to make other's lives better because you are in it.

It's easy to focus on wanting to be right. Stop and go to empathy. Can you be more compassionate about what you don't understand or agree with? Can you be more compassionate, even when it's not convenient? Then do it. It makes a difference.

Be Committed - Follow through and complete tasks. When you're fully committed the unseen world shows up to help you along your path. Life starts to take you seriously and supports you.

There will be struggle, that's your opportunity to grow. Learn problem solving by doing it. Ask for help when you need it, but 99% of the time figure it out by yourself. Stick with your values, and dig in and do the work.

Have Fun - As we get older, we forget to just have fun. We get caught up in responsibilities, and take life too seriously for too long. It's important to have fun every day. Do what makes you smile. Take time to be curious and play. It's important for your soul growth, and it's important to inspire by example.

Live In Gratitude - Start and end your day in gratitude. Stop for moments throughout the day and find something to be grateful for.

***

As you commit to living the Earth Caretaker Code of Honor you will become it. You are saying to the world who you are through your everyday actions, and in time there is no more conscious thought, you are those core values. You are a person of service. This is self-mastery.

Living as an Earth Caretaker in every area of your life, you will know a life of purpose and honor.

What Is Honor?

Honor is the goodness and rightness inside of you. Honor defines you and how you show up in life. Living a life of honor is living your personal core values.

You are the keeper of your honor. Keep it safe. Keep it alive. Never ever damage it. Nothing can take it from you. Keep it in a good way, in a good place. Protect it as you would protect what you love.

Protecting Nature

Why should we protect nature, and what does it mean to do so? The Earth will most likely be here long after mankind has disappeared.

Man may just be the primary hand in his own demise. If we are not conscious of our abuse to a finite resource, that resource can and most likely will retaliate with all its force and power, and destroy all the things we take for granted. Fires, Earthquakes, floods, and droughts have proven how fragile our infrastructures are in their mighty wake.

There are many places today whose beauty has succumbed to man's insatiable need to develop and build. When I grew up, Silicon Valley was a riparian woodland with commanding oaks, and redwood forests layered with madrones, and gorgeous grasslands. In the lowlands there were orchard upon orchard of cherry, apricot, peach, and pear trees.

Like so many places, the orchards disappeared and were replaced with industrial tracts. The wooded hillsides vanished under the sprawl of housing developments. Whenever I saw a "For Sale" sign, I knew that land was doomed.

My friends and I would take the signs down and shred them to bits, in our naivety, hoping the buyers and sellers would go away. Though we must have taken down dozens of signs in a desperate attempt to save our forests and orchards, it was of course to no avail.

***

One of the great joys of my childhood was spending time with my beloved Uncle Bill at his home in the Colorado Rockies.

Uncle Bill was as big as a bear and just as scruffy. His mouth lines were curled up on the ends because he spent so much time laughing, and he loved nature more than anyone I knew.

His backyard was a nature wonderland. There were aspen thickets flocked with singing birds, crystal-clear, water pools filled with fish, and mountain vistas carpeted with some of the most beautiful wildflowers my young eyes had ever seen.

Uncle Bill taught me so much about nature, but he also gave me one of the greatest teachings of my life. I remember a conversation where he asked me what I was willing to die for. Although I was only 11 years old, and thought I would live forever, and wondered why I would need to die for anything,

I respected everything Uncle Bill said to me, so I took this question quite seriously. He explained that being willing to die for something commits you to life.

As we talked, I told him that I would die for my parents, for him, to protect myself, and I also said that I would be willing to die for the Earth. At such a young age, I don't think I appreciated the gravity of

the question, nor the gravity of my answer, but it resonated to the deepest parts of me, and it continues to live within me as an adult.

***

When I returned home at the end of my summer visit that year, bulldozers were destroying one of my sacred spots. The forest and hillsides had been my home ground, where I had made trails and built a fort, where I hunted and fished, caught snakes, where I could sit for hours watching nature unfold, where I felt safe.

My home for the past four years was going to be destroyed, and there was nothing I could do about it. I would sneak close to the worksite and watch as the huge trucks rumbled past.

In grief and amazement, I watched the men in the trucks destroy a world so full of life with so little regard. They excavated and hauled, and dumped load after load of precious Earth, to mine sand to make concrete for roads and buildings.

One day after school, when I was heading over to visit my friend, Grandfather Oak, I found a chain-link fence wrapped all around it, and a sign on the front declaring, "No Trespassing". There were red surveyor's flags around the tree, and paint marks on its trunk.

I watched as a man with a chainsaw started to cut the limbs and sections from the tree, and began to load it into a truck. He was destroying Grandfather Oak. He was killing one of my dearest friends. I remember screaming at the man, and charging him with tears streaming down my face, but I couldn't stop him. He just yelled back and pushed me away.

I kept charging and screaming, and suddenly there were three men who grabbed me and threw me outside the fenced enclosure and locked the gate.

I gave up at that point, and had to watch brokenhearted, as they methodically reduced Grandfather Oak down from its full, branched-out majesty, to a mere stump. It was literally as if they were cutting a vital organ from my body.

When the workers left, I went to what was remaining of my protector and friend, a two-foot stump. All I could do was sit on the stump and sob.

These were men who only saw it as firewood, and not a child's *living*, treasured friend. Grandfather Oak had protected me in my darkest hours of childhood, and I was powerless to protect it in return.

Not only did they cut my friend down, but countless other trees as well. Some were butchered to create more sunlight for the inevitable sprawl of houses to come. Sometimes the developers would spare a handful of oak trees, only to lay pavement around them, which ultimately killed them.

Even as a kid, I knew that oak trees spread their roots out underground in a large area, to collect the water that falls in California's short, rainy season. The cement poured so close to the trunk prevents the water from soaking into the ground, and the trees die.

I remember trying to explain this to the builders, who looked at me as if I were an alien. Society in general, tends to overlook the untainted wisdom of children when their obvious truths aren't convenient or profitable.

***

Later in life, as an adult, I was taken more seriously, and I was able to have a greater impact on the builders of a subdivision in Scotts Valley called, appropriately enough, "The Oaks". They listened and created another solution for the trees. By leaving a bigger space around the trees, and spacing the brick before the edge of the cement sidewalk, it allowed for more movement with growth, and provided space between the bricks to allow rain seepage to water the roots.

***

I would often return during the year to sit on the stump and be with my fallen friend. I could sometimes still see the tree in all its glory, and feel its wonderful energy. Its presence had been so powerful through all its years that some vestige of it still existed, and that feeling comforted me. I like to think that my presence gave comfort to its spirit as well.

The loss of my sacred spot overwhelmed me. I kept hearing Uncle Bill's question in my mind over and over. Was I willing to die for my sacred spot? I thought so, but all I could really do was watch them destroy what I held so dear. I vowed to never just watch again. I would defend the Earth and animals as best I could.

As construction encroached more and more upon that spot, the spirit of the tree was soon gone, and my time of grieving had passed.

I learned a vital lesson from Grandfather Oak, and from the woods, which was that nature not only protects those who go to her with open hearts, but that nature needs to be protected as well.

***

The Earth has its own soul from which springs all life, including man. Our inner spirit, and the inner spirit of the Earth are interconnected. All plants, animals, insects, stones, mountains, rivers, and oceans know this, and know their unique positions within this reality. Human beings seem to be the only species that tries to negate this interconnectedness by destroying the very source that gives them life.

***

Already understanding this principle, and as a result of my passionate need to defend nature, I became known at school as the "Nature Freak". Kids can be cruel with name calling and teasing, but I took on that name seriously. I *was* a nature freak, and proud of it.

At a young age I was doing everything I could to help nature and wildlife. Sometimes I was able to help and other times, sadly I felt helpless, but I always tried my best.

Kids who have not been taught or mentored early on, can make bad decisions in their interactions with nature, if it is something that feels foreign to them. If they don't have that sense of connection, they may not be respectful to what they don't understand.

I caught a boy trying to burn a nest of baby robins by pouring kerosene on them and setting them on fire. My primal self emerged. I was enraged and I chased that kid for blocks with the intent of beating him senseless. I didn't catch him, but I felt the courage of my conviction – to defend.

When I returned to the nest to hopefully save the young lives, I found four, charred, little bodies. My heart broke at the sound of the mother chirping madly from the tree branch above.

That incident was not an isolated case. I remember cats and dogs being teased and hurt by people. The wanton killing of animals seemed common, even among my peers. It was very confusing for me, as I could never consciously hurt an animal, even a small, unusual creature.

***

On a hike in the Santa Cruz Mountains with a friend, we came upon a stunning, banana slug. My friend started pouring salt on it, which is a terrible way for a banana slug to die, as it sucks the moisture from it. I couldn't believe that my friend could be so cruel, and before I could think, I slugged him. My instincts again emerged to defend.

It might sound silly to get so upset over a banana slug, but to me that lump of yellow was as important to defend as the larger creatures, and maybe even more so.

I felt bad about hitting my friend, but he never did that again. He wasn't by nature, a cruel person, he had made a bad choice, and needed someone to teach him.

In middle school, I learned another important lesson about how our society views cruelty to animals, and the consequences or lack of consequences.

I was on the wharf at the Santa Cruz beach, where people like to fish and watch the birds. I saw a guy baiting his hook with a fish so he could catch a pelican. He swung the fish into the water and a pelican dove and caught it. The guy started reeling it in, flying the pelican like a kite for a couple of seconds until the line broke.

I told some bystanders and an employee at the wharf what I had seen, and we confronted the man. Someone else had called the police, who talked to the idiot, but were powerless to do anything more.

It was good to see that people cared, but disheartening to find out the consequences for such cruelty were non-existent.

I wondered if the kid who burned the robins or the fool who tortured the pelican for his own amusement, felt remorse when confronted. Remorse is a great educator. Remorse gave me an understanding of what I committed my life to.

Even though I was a nature freak, and I had vowed to never consciously hurt an animal, I still had my own lessons to learn.

I experienced one of life's great, defining moments when I was playing football with a bunch of friends on a grass field at school. Dozens of gulls were flying around us, and like any primal, non-thinking kid with a stick, or rock, or football, I threw that ball as hard as I could at one of the birds. I never thought I would hit it. I was showing off and I hit one of the gulls square, and it tumbled from the sky. It flopped around sideways with one of its wings useless and hanging limp.

I was horror struck by what I had done, and I felt physically sick. All the other kids scattered, knowing I had done something bad. I was scared, but I couldn't run.

 273

I learned I wasn't immune to getting caught up in the gang mentality of wanting to fit in, without thinking about cause and effect. That all important pause button to think of consequences wasn't there.

I went to the gull and sat close by watching it writhing in pain. It tried to get away from me. It looked me in the eye seeming to ask why I had done such a thing. I felt that bird's pain. I moved closer, and eventually got close enough to pick it up and hold it in my arms.

I knew I had made a mistake I couldn't fix. I had caused a living creature pain, and I sobbed for the bird, and I cried for myself. I tried to give it my loving energy, but the wing was broken, and my loving energy wasn't enough.

When the animal-care authorities arrived, they looked at the bird and said it needed to be put to sleep to spare it the pain.

While I had been holding the bird, looking into its eyes, and begging it to forgive me, something happened deep within me. I knew through that experience what I would die for, what I would commit myself to. I knew that for the rest of my life whenever or wherever help was needed to protect nature or animals I would do it. It wasn't just an idea any longer. The gull physically taught me about respect for life.

***

Soon after that day, I was able to stand by that conviction, in a small, but defining way. My dad and I were going to film the pollution that washed up on Franklin Point Beach, near where we lived.

Franklin Point is an incredibly idyllic place with acres of rolling, sand dunes, marshes, willow thickets, wildflowers, tide pools and abundant wildlife. Amongst this beauty is the garbage that washes onto the beach from boats dumping their waste further out in the ocean.

While I was shooting the film, we came across an injured, beached seal. About that time a man and his dogs were coming from the opposite direction from us. He let his dogs loose and they surrounded the seal trying to attack it. My father was a fairly passive man who didn't like to get involved in situations like this, but I was not.

My protective instincts exploded, and I ran for the dogs, yelling. I looked them in the eye, and I am sure they saw one crazy son-of-a-bitch, and they backed off.

I lit into their owner telling him that seals were my friends, and his stupidity or pathetic pleasure at watching his dogs torture a seal was unconscionable and sick. He started to say something, but then saw that wild rage in my eyes and turned and walked away.

We stayed with the seal for a while to make sure it was safe, and continued to film along the beach. When I came back, the seal had moved into the surf, momentarily safe from moronic humans.

***

Being true to one's beliefs is hard. It takes work and commitment. It's much easier to sit on the sidelines and let others act.

There were incidents that shaped my view of the world in a negative way. I had to learn that sometimes you just need to get to a point of peace with a situation that you can't fix. Sometimes fear gets in the way, and sometimes you don't know how to fix it.

Early on, I lost some of my innocence. It took years to understand that the reality of negative events are what toughened me to life's tragedies and inequities, but that I also didn't have to become callous and cold. It takes courage to keep an open heart and open mind, as nature unfolds in mysterious ways.

There is something so vile about people doing harm to nature and animals. Each time I see a cruel act I feel violent towards the person causing it, but all that does is perpetuate violence.

People ask me how I feel about nature's own cruelty – natural fires that destroy habitat and life, or animals killing each other. I am reminded of an incredible scene I witnessed in Yellowstone in winter, when a pack of wolves had surrounded an elk, and were literally eating it alive. The elk brought to its knees, had surrendered to the pack, and though horrifying to hear its screams, I understood the laws of nature provide the balance. The wolves needed to eat for their survival as well.

Unlike nature, mankind in general, does not practice balance. We take more than we need, and don't replenish what we take.

In nature everything is in perfect harmony and balance. Nothing is wasted. There is no excess among animals. Even though there are horrifying things in nature, they are in perfect balance with what is needed.

With an Irish temper and a bombastic nature, I need a calming influence to keep myself in balance, so I go to the woods. There is a Mystery and a spirit in the forests that lifts me out of my crazy humanness, and connects me with the primordial energy that is the "Spirit that moves in all things".

Connecting with that universal Spirit is a place where you know you belong in harmony with all things, and *are* in harmony with all things.

Artists, poets, and musicians feel that energy when they create. All of us can feel it, and one of the best places to connect with it is in a quiet spot in nature. For that reason alone, we should be defending our wild lands and our wild animals.

People often ask how one person can really make a difference. It's done in many ways: recycling, planting trees, joining environmental groups or just being vigilant in protecting the smaller forms of life.

***

One of my proudest accomplishments as a boy happened when I helped our neighbors move some bats from the attic of their old, Victorian home. They were going to call an exterminator, but I convinced them to give me a couple of days to figure out where they were getting in and out.

I had a previous experience with bats in a home, so I knew what to look for. Their attic had a small opening that I squeezed through to get into the dark space, which was the bat cave.

The smell of bat guano was intense. It was like ammonia and vinegar being blown up my nose, and it dazed me. Once I got used to the odor, I was able to stand up and turn on my flashlight to see hundreds of bats hanging upside-down from the ceiling, and bat guano stacked almost two feet high in places.

I figured that I had to observe them leaving from the outside, so I found a good observation point, and waited for dusk when I knew they would fly out on their nocturnal journeys.

In the fading light, I heard the humming of wings and watched in awe, a visual spectacle of a colony of the creatures flying from a hole in the roof, like an explosion of black smoke.

I climbed a ladder to the roof and made my way to the edge, where under the eave, I screened the hole with wire.

Although the bats had to find a new home, it was certainly a better option than the exterminator. I was a kid, I was one person, but I saved hundreds of bats from extinction because I took the time to do so.

***

Unfortunately, we tend to respond very slowly to situations that we know need our attention. If something in our environment is out of balance, but doesn't show an immediate result in our daily, personal life directly, we disregard the importance and validity of our actions, and non-actions, until it's too late.

We don't make inconvenient changes until it hurts bad enough. Doing the right thing isn't always convenient, but it's the right thing.

We shouldn't have to think about protecting our resources. Nature should be valued more than our cars, houses, and technology. It literally is as important as breathing.

Humans have been given the gifts of being creative and innovative. If we use those abilities consciously, great accomplishments can be achieved, even by a kid.

Hummingbird

This winter in the midst of six feet of snow in a raging storm, in ten-degree weather, a hummingbird showed up. What an amazing being. I even heard him sing.

In extreme cold, hummingbirds slow down their metabolism to survive. I made some sugar water, and thawed and filled the frozen feeder. I am at your service hummingbird. I admire your strength, and I love you!

Tell The Truth

I want to remind you to continually educate yourselves about nature, and to build your relationship on a personal level. Build a relationship of heart and soul so that you will fight for, and work for, and live for our Earth. Be a champion for the Earth so that all the beings can live in a good way.

THE EARTH CARETAKER WAY

Something I've noticed is that we don't tell the truth to do what's right for the Earth. We must get information that is truthful about what is actually happening, in this world of the crazy mass media. The general population thrives on drama, which pits *us* against *them.*

There is so much false information projected out, it is beyond overwhelming at times, and it becomes divisive.

There are some simple basics we need to know about what's happening to our planet, to take effective action, that cuts through all the crap and gets significant projects done.

This is going to take self-education to know the truth. It's going to take research. It's going to take time out in nature, out in the wildlands exploring. It's going to take reading books and talking to biologists, and engaging with people who have been studying what is happening to our planet, to know what can be done now.

I think we can all agree that global warming is a real issue. The deniers are simply wrong and not telling the truth.

Our climate crisis is happening due to human beings. There are too many of us using resources in a way that is out of balance. We use too many fossil fuels, and that is one of the major reasons for the changing temperatures across the world.

We abuse the land and animals for food consumption, and do not think of sustainable living on a significant level. This is not new information, but we need to really let it sink in.

If global warming takes full effect 2/3 of the animals that live on the Earth will die off as a result of our actions. That is the blunt truth. For some animals it's way too late, they're already gone, or their habitat has been minimized so much, they can only live in zoos for their survival.

For many animals this can be changed, and their species can survive, but it takes making changes *now*. We need to tell the truth that global warming is real, and it is affecting all life on Earth. Ultimately, it will affect human life in a horrible way.

Why does it matter to humans if an animal or plant species in another country dies off? Aside from the fact that all species have a right to live with or without a human's need for it, currently numerous medicines for our diseases come from plants. As long as humans have a need to be healed, we need to continue to protect our biodiversity while we discover medicines yet to come.

When an animal species goes extinct it affects the other animal populations that it feeds, as well as the animal population that was its prey. When animal overpopulation goes unchecked, the plant life gets decimated, and as a result water resources can dry up, and the domino effect has begun. Keep in mind this is a very simplified example to a very intricate ecosystem.

Eighty years from now it will be way too late to make a change. It will probably be way too late ten years from now, if we continue to misuse our planet at this same rate, as more and more people are being born into this world.

I do have great hope, however. The being in me that I call the scout, allows me to observe, by telling the truth of what's happening, without a lot of over emotion or judgment. Once I have the information, I can decide what action to take through discernment.

There is also this other part of me that says we are in deep trouble. Human beings and the planet that we live on, the only planet that is livable, is in trouble due to our actions and inactions, and I feel the harsh sadness of that understanding.

Ultimately though, I realize the Earth has been through five major extinctions due to asteroids, comets, climate change, and other natural disasters, where 80 to 90% of the terrestrial life died off, long before we arrived. The Earth still built herself back each time to this glorious state.

I know in the end, the Earth will be ok, and that gives me comfort. I am an Earth Caretaker and I love my Earth. I can't imagine not being able to be here. It's good and comforting to know that she will find her way.

I do believe we humans are supposed to be here. I know it in my soul. For all the dark things that we do, we also have an equal number of wonderful qualities. I have this vision of a future where human beings live in harmony with the planet, and in caretaking it, all things live as they were meant to live in a good way.

I believe in miracles, and I have hope, and I have dreams, and I know that we're highly intelligent and we're capable of building great things, and we can turn this downward slide around.

I have no doubt, not one single doubt in my mind that if the majority of us decided to work for the planet, and invested our focus and actions for the greater good, we would accomplish it.

History would look upon this next 20 to 40 years as the most pivotal in human history. We have the answers. We have the ability. We can get the job done, and we can have a hell of a lot of fun doing it in the process.

What will it take to get us off our butts? First, we must tell the truth, and then we have to get to work, even when it's not convenient.

Human beings have come together before for a greater good, and accomplished it. It is doable. It's going to take being a leader, and getting involved, and being committed to make anything happen.

Ask yourself, "What am I going to do to shake people awake and save our planet?"

The Other Side Of Judgment

A perceived enemy, is many times just an adversary, because you haven't seen from each other's perspective. Each side is usually just trying to do what they think is best for their family's survival.

There are no bad countries, just mis-run governments. The communities of people are wonderful. The misuse of power is the imbalance, acting from fear of losing status.

Misuse of power is a sign of inferior self-empowerment. Those who abuse their status are relying on putting others down, so they don't feel their own weakness.

Don't mistake your compassionate heart as weakness. Instead, know that the courage to be vulnerable and empathetic is your strength.

A weak leader steps on the backs of the people to try to elevate themselves, instead of sharing their own strength and lifting the people up.

Right use of power is sharing abundance to create a strong, balanced, self-sufficient, flourishing community.

Light Up The Shadows

It's time to go to work. To get active for our planet. The murder many of us witnessed in 2020, of George Floyd, was a wakeup call, again. There have been many, many people that have been betrayed by our silence. The majority of us ignored the call, but this time, in this moment, we are waking up and it's time for us all to take action for right justice. Justice for our fellow global citizens, and for the Earth Herself.

As the Japanese Admiral said when they attacked our American fleet at Pearl Harbor in Hawaii, "We have awakened a sleeping giant." The United States entered World War II and fought for a right cause, and changed the world forever.

The world came together for the greater good, and good came out on top. Over time, wounds are being healed, and we are working towards right relations with countries we were conflicted with.

***

The United States has been asleep to the needs of our Earth. Global warming is here, *Now*, and getting worse every day, as most of us do almost nothing to stop it or slow it significantly, because it's not convenient.

As I write this, a million animals and plants are on the verge of extinction, due to the abuse of our planet Earth, and human overpopulation. We are busy using our Earth every day for our needs and wants, and giving very little back.

One of our core teachings at Headwaters is living the full-circle way. Life flows in a circle, our Earth is a circle. We humans have become takers, not leavers. We take and take and take, water, food, plants, animals, and minerals. We use these as resources and do not allow enough time and thought for giving back, for restoration, and regrowth.

The circle is broken, and our Earth-heart is broken. Our Earth is in pain. Every moment She asks, "Why are my children killing me? I am their mother. I give them food, water, trees, air, gravity, beauty, shelter, and love. I give them life. What has happened? I'm waiting for an awakening, an awareness, an epiphany moment for humankind to become caretakers of their Home."

This is human purpose, to love and care for our Earth and all beings, including each other, so all beings can live and thrive together. We are meant to support each other, not divide ourselves. We need to be caretakers of humanity.

***

I have been a teacher of nature's ways my entire life. I have been wondering when people will wake up and fight for our Earth. Every day I ask what it will take to move people. When will the next defining moment show up that cracks our walls, so much so that we can't ignore it?

Then we witnessed the horrific murder of George Floyd. These crimes could no longer be hidden from the world. Two brave people spoke up, and turned in their video footage to show the truth.

We ask how could this happen? Why didn't someone stop it? How could they have stopped it? These actions have been so normalized by the police in black and minority communities, that most of us shake our heads in disgust, but then we just move on with our lives. We hope they will face consequences for their wrongful actions, but we never really follow through with what actually happens or doesn't happen, to hold people accountable.

We have been dealing with the tragedies of the COVID-19 virus, and the divisiveness the 2016 -2020 administration promoted and encouraged, which worked its way through America just like the virus.

The one positive that has come of this is that the majority of the people around the entire world have been supporting each other. We had time to literally stop everything and reflect. We have now been more aware of our global community. We realize more than ever that we all share the same air, the same water, the same land. Viruses affect humans and animals, and they don't stop at a border.

The uncertainty of everything that is happening in the world shows us the vulnerability of our lives in a way that is humbling. It truly connects us to the fragility of our planet, and it allows us to appreciate the beauty of the world we live in. It reminds us that a beautiful life is worth fighting for.

The virus brought people together. Where top leaders failed, people within communities rose up to take care of what was needed in any way they could. Neighbors got to know each other by checking in to see if each other's needs were met.

Many of us came together by staying apart and answering the call for help where we could. Most of us were respectful of not wanting to spread the virus to others, and adjusted our lives to make sure others were ok.

There are always going to be exceptions. Those who won't cooperate for the good of the whole. Thankfully, they are not the majority, but because they are an oddity, they receive the most press and attention, and that begins to feed the fire of division of *us* against *them*.

We need to remember who we are, and who we can be. We created the national parks, wilderness areas, and the Endangered Species Act to save animals and plants that are in trouble.

These ideas have spread across the planet, and because of this movement, other countries have been working on conservation in their part of the world as well. Humanity has shown that we are caretakers. We can do what is right for all of life. We are amazing when we focus on the right action.

We have been off track for quite a while, and then this horrific moment in time made the world stop, and think, and more importantly, *feel* the unjust loss of a life. For 8 minutes and 46 seconds we felt another one of our own human beings suffer, and was shown no mercy in his cries for help. Enough is enough.

Multiple countries, people of all ages and of all races joined in the streets to protest the murder of George Floyd, and all the unspoken murders that have been discounted, at the hands of those who took an oath to protect and serve all people. Not some people, not only ones that look like them, but they took an oath to serve and protect *all* people in their community.

What has happened to this man is symbolic of what we are doing to our Earth, our Home. We are killing Her every day by how we live, and we *know* it. We look the other way, and either don't want to get involved or don't know how to, and nothing changes.

Enough people forced us to see the truth, and we finally tapped into our global empathy, and felt George's cry for help. We failed him and so many others, but we now need to make it right for those who may face the same circumstance tomorrow.

We humans are the Earth, and the Earth is us, and what happens to one, happens to the another. It is not just a nice saying. It is a literal fact. We are one in the same. All Beings are connected. There is no "other".

We are at a place in time where what we fight for cannot be either or. We are in a situation where we need to focus on justice for *all* people. We also need to focus on justice for our planet. We need to keep pushing our elected representatives to make these changes, so that these important issues don't get swept away when the media moves on to other stories.

This man's murder woke a generation. The young people have begun to show up. They will be the ones who inherit this damaged, but beautiful Earth, and they are rising up to say, enough. No more murder, no more racism, no more hatred, no more misuse of power.

My hope, my prayer, my dream is that this atrocity is an awakening to all life-threatening wrongs, and will inspire us all to continue to fight for justice, to fight for our precious Earth, to stop global warming, to stop species extinction, to save half of our Earth for the sake of the land itself, to care for our oceans, and to clean our water and air of poisons and pollution. I hope we are at that wake-up moment, and that the sleeping giant is not asleep anymore.

For a while I was losing faith and hope that people would not stand up and do what is right. I'm gaining that faith back. Let's truly become Keepers of the Earth and all beings.

Continue to take to the streets for justice for all peoples, and all life on our Earth. Honor the Earth. Join organizations that protect our Earth, and beings on Her. Donate money to Earth healing and humanitarian causes.

Vote, Vote, Vote for our Earth! Educate yourselves about the people you are voting into positions that affect our quality of life. Know your local representatives. Change begins in your own community. You can make big changes in your own neighborhood. Keep protesting the injustices. Consistently volunteer your time to heal our Earth.

Enjoy the land and our waters, go out into nature, and fill your heart and soul. Plant gardens for wildlife. Let go of maintaining manicured lawns, and create habitat instead. Heal the planet starting at your own home.

Educate yourself to what is wrong, and what is needed. Remember the bad guys depend on you not being educated and giving up. Don't support industries that pollute or damage our Earth. Vote, Vote, Vote.

The suppression of people's quality of life starts with the environment they are living in. Our Indigenous peoples, many of our communities of color, marginalized communities, and low-income communities are very aware of this.

Everyone needs a healthy environment to grow and thrive in a good way. In our abundant country, the United States of America, people should not still be fighting for clean water to drink, and for safe air to breathe. There is no excuse for that. This is an act of greed and disregard for basic human needs, by the people who control the distribution of life-giving resources.

This is where Humanitarian Earth Caretakers step in, and continue fighting for the rights to live in a healthy community. When we help our own species, we lift each other up, and in turn our global ecosystem thrives.

We *can* change our justice system. We've been waiting for this time when all people rise together. It's your time, it's the Earth's time, it's the time of awakening the Scout Earth Caretaker in all of us.

Go out and do what's right every single day, and never stop. Never. Don't go back to sleep.

Serve Our Planet

Something to think about is how we can change our outlook on the way it has always been, and create new ways of living.

Many young adults are now taking a gap year after high school, and traveling before continuing their education or starting an occupation. This is a great thing to do.

I graduated high school a year early, and traveling is exactly what I did, but that was not the norm back then. I chose to live off the land in the Canadian Wilderness for a few months, worked on a trail restoration crew in Oregon, backpacked through many national forests, and ended up working at Marine World Africa U.S.A. with exotic animals.

These experiences acted as stepping stones, eventually leading me into wildlife rescue, nature conservancy, and nature teaching.

I would highly encourage young adults to combine their explorations with being a global community volunteer for 1-2 years. The idea of a year of global service is something that seems so right to me. The year after high school could be dedicated to community service to the Earth, either locally or in another country.

That year of service could be doing physical work, restoring land or water ways, or helping with rescue animals. It could be working in the office of various organizations that are doing good work for the Earth. It could be working with people to build houses for low-income families or helping to enhance communities who need a shared garden. This service year could be planting trees along the streets to help cool the climate, and to bring beauty to neighborhoods. Or it could be working in green technology.

The work they choose for the year would be up to them. This would give young adults opportunities to gain more life experience, and skills in a field they may be interested in pursuing as an occupation or as a passion. This would help guide people on a more focused path when furthering their education, and when it's time for them to grow out into the world and begin their own life journey.

So many young adults have no idea what they want to study in college or in trade schools, because they haven't had the life experience to know where to begin. They need to get out into our world and see for themselves where the needs are, and what calls to them.

Many young people serve in the armed forces, which is another honorable way to be of service, but it's not the only way. Earth Caretakers can find a way to give back through their own interests and skill set.

I do believe traveling is important for young adults. When traveling abroad or even to another part of their own country, young people have the opportunity to get to know people, outside of their image of their political situations or governments. They will find that we are all the same good people, just living in different circumstances.

Through this hands-on interaction it would build community. It would break down walls of misunderstanding, by experiencing life through someone's else's perspective.

By exploring more of this amazing Earth of ours, and connecting with the human in all of us, these young Earth Caretakers would be personally invested in our global community, and take responsibility in caring for it.

If we create a new model or path for young adults who are just coming into adulthood to be of service, it will be ingrained in us that this is who we are, and what we are here to do. I would go as far as to say that this should be a requirement for everyone. Being of service builds self-esteem and self-confidence, and only good comes from it.

My wish is that this would be a nationwide program, and eventually a global cooperation, where these Earth Caretakers would be supported with a stipend during their service. Until that time, my hope is that individuals of any age will begin to implement this in their lives as volunteers, and encourage others to join them.

Take that gap year, but do it with the intention of being of service to our global community, and ultimately to our Earth. Gap could take on a new definition as a *Global Apprenticeship Program.*

As I have said, I am a Dreamer, and I make those dreams happen, but something this big and important needs the energy of many to come to fruition. Who's going to make it happen? You?! I hope so.

Our Time To Shine

Climate change is threatening all life on Earth. It is caused by us, and we can stop it. If we allow the Earth Caretaker in us to come out and do this work that is needed, in the process of healing our Earth we could come together.

We could elevate our consciousness to a higher level of service, kindness, love, courage, and hard work for a higher purpose for our Earth, and thus for ourselves and all of life.

As we begin to take corrective action, our struggles begin to subside. War, greed, poverty, hatred, racism, and violence will not be as prominent. When we work together as a community for each other's best interests, people are no longer in fear of survival, but can come from a place of abundance.

Let's step into our higher purpose. Let kindness lead. When humans come together there is nothing we can't do, anything is possible. Inspire others with your actions. We have been waiting for this moment in human Earth time.

Our Earth Is Calling You

Taking on the Scout Earth Caretaker Way is choosing to live at a higher standard. It can be a lonely path, but it only takes a few dedicated people to make a mass change, and bring others along..

The Scout Earth Caretaker Way is about taking action for our Earth, doing what you say you will do. Protect the mountains, protect the forests, protect the oceans, protect the rivers, protect the animals, protect the human species.

Sometimes to be effective we must be willing to get uncomfortable and get dirty. Our Earth is calling you. She's calling.

Chapter 30
Rite Of Passage

Traditionally, our Earth ancestors recognized and practiced rites of passages for boys and girls around the age of thirteen. This was designed for the survival of the people. Boys and girls were taught how to grow into honorable adults, and be capable of providing for the community.

A code of honor was created to live by common, important human values, such as kindness, service, hard work, loyalty, love, respect, and courage. The idea was that a man or woman of honor would help the people to be safe and prosper.

Usually a physical test was involved, and four days of sitting or wandering alone in nature. This time was good for making the code of honor a part of the participant, their medicine. The code would live in them and show up through their actions, the way they lived their lives.

The young adults would return to the happiness of the people, and a grand celebration. The people knew in their hearts the participant's completion of the rite of passage would be good for the community. Knowing there were initiated men and women in their community would create a sense of safety, and thus the people could be free to hunt and fish, explore, create ceremony, and love.

A tribe or clan or group of people who were full of men and women of honor could live and grow in a good way. Knowing if times got tough or dangerous, all the people could be counted on to work for the greater good of the community. This is a beautiful way of being.

At Headwaters Outdoor School, we have brought back rites of passages. We teach young adults to respect all things, each other, and themselves, and to understand that we are all connected. What happens to one, happens to another, both positive and negative.

I truly hope these teachings come back to all people. Young people should be educated about this special time in life, and how important it is that they step up and have a voice, and count for something.

They need to be taught as they grow, that this opportunity is there for them. By the time they are of age they should be seeking out mentors and begging to be put out on a rite of passage, knowing it's something they can take great pride in by giving back.

Initiated young adults are recognized as a valued part of their family, community, and ultimately the global community.

In our modern times, in the United States, on a large scale we have allowed rite of passage ceremonies to drift away. There are exceptions of course through religious ceremonies, but as a national community, this conscious intention of becoming a good citizen has been lost.

Often young people carry out their own instinctive rite of passages by symbolically getting tattoos or through peer pressure to attempt some usually misguided achievement.

We honor young adults for getting their driver's licenses or for reaching the legal drinking age. We do not, however, honor our youth by putting them into situations that challenge them psychologically, physically, and spiritually with the intention of them stepping into a bigger role of responsibility for themselves, and for their immediate community.

We need rites of passages more than ever in these troubled times. We are currently living in an uninitiated world and living under many dishonorable representatives. Many people who are in roles of leadership have no honor. They can be narcissistic, greedy, power hungry, racist, cruel people.

282

It's time to change this behavior and return to our basic life skills and values. To have leaders who are honorable women and men, we all need to raise them this way. We need to support our young adults to be honorable, in a world where this has not always been encouraged.

My Rite Of Passage

I was very lucky as a boy to have Bo Almroth as my mentor. When his son, Claus, and I turned thirteen, Bo gave us the gift of a lifetime by taking us on a rite of passage with a road trip around the United States.

He had us read books about other people's experiences of rites of passage. I read about the Celts and Native Americans approach of putting young men out on vision quests.

A quest was a place in the wilderness where a young man sat for days without food and water until he had vision for his life. I read about Crazy Horse, the great Lakota leader, who went into the mountains at age fourteen, and sat until his vision was revealed. I was so struck by his experience I couldn't wait to do the same.

My enthusiasm didn't rub off on Claus however, and he protested about having to leave his home and friends for the summer. Bo knew the value of adventure in a young boy's life, and Claus, though disgruntled, gave in to it.

We traveled in style – in a rustic, white, Ford pick-up with a camper shell, fridge and even a toilet, bought especially for that trip. It was home to the three of us, plus Bo's dog, Julius, a German Shepherd-Labrador mix.

Our trip would take us to 35 states, where we would backpack and explore the wilderness and the urban jungles, from small towns to historical sites.

My journey would culminate in Northern California on Mt. Shasta, where I would climb to the summit, 14,000 plus feet, and spend the night alone, thinking about my future and what it was to be a man.

Bo told me I would also write a Code of Honor for my life – a life map of values that I would need to memorize so it stayed with me forever.

We loaded up the truck in early June and began our drive, through the already summer-browned hills of the Bay Area. We headed northeast to Lake Tahoe and descended the spine of the Sierra Nevada range, and out across the Nevada desert. Before we reached the Nevada border however, I had my first brush with death.

Bo had me make a climb behind some lakes near the Tioga Pass, in the Sierras near Yosemite. Our base camp was around 10,000 feet, but we were still below the tree line. My goal was a steep spire much higher – up on the stark, white, granite walls – way above the tree line.

I was to make the climb alone, find my own route and hopefully have the good sense and wits to use my wilderness skills without coming to bodily harm. I was to stay there for as long as I felt comfortable, and to do it for the love of the outdoors, and to prepare myself for the more difficult climb of Mt. Shasta later that summer.

I made my first mistake quickly by being a little too cocky, and climbing higher than I should have and beyond my skill level. I became scared and lost my footing in the loose stone, and half-slid, half-tumbled down thirty feet of slick, granite wall.

I could see the end of the wall, and I knew I was heading for a one-way launch into the great abyss. I had no idea how to stop myself. I was terrified, and I clawed at the granite hoping to reduce the speed of my trajectory. Without quite knowing how, I came to a heart pounding stop on a landing.

I had the awful taste of fear in my mouth. I lay there not daring to move, terrified I would slip again. As I came to my senses and my fear became more manageable, I realized I had landed in a clearing among a herd of deer that seemed quite unperturbed by my presence.

How strange that my abrupt arrival didn't even seem to register with them. I immediately felt a sense of ease and calm wash over me, and I felt safe among this herd.

I had a sense the herd had stopped my fall. I felt as if a spirit had rushed to my rescue. Clearly if I hadn't caught hold of something permanent, I would have pitched over the edge of the landing and fallen another 100 feet.

I lay for an eternity, feeling the mix of exhilaration, fear, and relief – feeling very much alive. As my breathing slowed to its normal rhythm, and my body became centered and calm, I realized I didn't

really need to climb further. I felt that experience was my purpose for the solo adventure. My cockiness and boldness almost took my life, while luck and spirit saved it.

When I returned to Bo, we spent a long time talking about the experience, which helped me understand that luck and spirit need to be honored. To walk away from that with just a, "Wow was I lucky." would have been okay, but to see beyond it into the mystery of Spirit, allowed me to learn about faith and trust, in a world that was beyond our rational understanding – the place where intuition comes from.

Awareness and intuition are partners. Awareness however is cultivated and learned, and intuition is felt within. We develop awareness of people or our surroundings by observing what is visible. A person's body language is far more important in understanding that individual, than the words they say. Intuition is the invisible knowing that comes from awareness.

My adventures with Bo helped hone both my awareness and intuitive skills, sometimes at the risk of a great deal of pain.

***

At Cape Hatteras off the coast of North Carolina we could drive right onto the beach. There were plenty of good spots to camp and I was eager to get out of the back of the pick-up. I was tired from a long day of reading and being on the road.

Thrilled that we could drive onto a beach and camp, I jumped out of the truck and landed squarely on top of a small cactus. I fell to the ground in excruciating pain and fear.

Searching the sands for a demon, I saw the cactus half-buried. Bo ran to me and was filled with almost as much horror as I, seeing my foot loaded with spines – a true pincushion.

It took Bo two hours of pulling each thorn – they were shaped with a barb on the end, which meant that Bo had to exert pressure to extract each one and I screamed with each pull.

The pain was made much greater because Claus was swimming and enjoying the water, and I was reminded of how oblivious I had been with each extraction.

Julius never left my side during this awful process. He seemed to understand, and comforted me, as only dogs can.

I promised myself to be extra vigilant, and to pay attention to any intuitive feelings I might have. Within a day or so the bottom of my foot had healed well enough for me to swim.

I loved bodysurfing and I was overjoyed to be doing it on the east coast. I felt like a world traveler being able to bodysurf in two different oceans. The joy of wave riding soon turned to apprehension when I felt my intuitive senses kick in – a dread swept over me, and I stopped moving and tried to center myself.

I knew the Atlantic had a lot of sharks and my heightened intuitive self was ready for anything. As I scanned the horizon, I saw a group of dolphins riding the waves. I screamed for Bo and Claus to come quickly. The panic on Bo's face swiftly turned to joy at the sight, and we all swam out to ride the waves with them.

We stayed out for over an hour and as suddenly as they came, they disappeared. It was so sudden we all wondered if it had really happened, but that special interaction with such magnificent creatures could hardly be denied. I felt I had been rewarded for paying attention.

As a naturalist, Bo worked with a variety of plants. He taught us how to really know the plants by having us spend time with them and use our inner vision to listen to the plant. On certain hikes he would have me sit with two or three plants studying their shape and size, what grew near them, how they smelled, what kind of soil they grew in, and if not poisonous, to taste them. Did I get a feeling about a certain plant? Did an image come into my mind?

He taught me about "owl" eyes, allowing me to see more by simply opening my eyes wider. He taught me how to see through, around, and beyond things. It's easy to see what is perceived to be in front of you, but there are the empty spaces that contain as much texture as the object. It's that space between, that allows an object to come forward, and gives it shape and definition.

Bo taught me about deer ears, and cupping the backs of my ears with my hands to move them in different directions, to pinpoint where a sound was coming from. Mimicking the auditory skills of a deer, expands a world of sound the ordinary ear misses.

Visualization is also important for developing your intuition and awareness. Bo said that visualizing something, would make it so. It may not happen instantaneously, but practice and faith would open the doors to having the image materialize. Imaging is picturing events or things to come.

All these wonderful tools Bo had taught me then, are a result of who I am today. He had the wisdom to cut me loose in a world of my choosing, and I chose to play life to the edge, by experiencing the joy of nature without fear.

***

There were three adventures that summer with Bo that allowed me to witness my adolescent life with adult eyes.

We were in the Great Smoky Mountain National Park, and I had been hiking fast, way ahead of Bo and Claus. I was enjoying the views and environment. I had never seen a hardwood forest so beautiful and so different from my West Coast home. All the new sights and sounds fascinated me.

I was also thinking about the juicy steak I was going to have for dinner. Distracted, I came around a bend face-to-face with a black bear – we literally crashed head-on like linebackers on a scrimmage line. We were both momentarily dazed, which is probably what saved my life.

I turned and ran back down the trail as fast as I could, hoping beyond all hope that the bear was too stunned to follow. I threw off my backpack like it was on fire, and continued to run for my life. I turned once or twice to see if the bear was coming, and though I didn't catch sight of it, I sprinted until I reached Bo and Claus.

By the time we got back to my backpack, I could see from the bear's tracks, the churned-up leaves, squashed plants, and disturbed dirt, that it had been just as terrified at bumping into me. The bear had crashed down the hill, leaving my backpack untouched with my steak still inside.

Even though I knew I was safer with Bo and Claus, it took my heart a long time to return to a normal beat, and for the hairs on the back of my neck to relax.

We continued our hike to an Adirondack hut where we would spend the night. These huts are placed throughout the forest to accommodate about a dozen campers under one roof – it wasn't my idea of wilderness camping, but it's where we ended up that night, and we had a fine time telling tales with the other hikers.

As I was feasting greedily upon my steak, the hair on my neck stood at attention again. I looked around the group, but no one seemed to have any concern, yet that feeling told me something was out there. I heard a noise and told everyone, but no one was bothered.

They said it was probably a deer, and as I was about to say I didn't think it was a deer, a black bear exploded from the woods into our site. He came toward us unperturbed by our shouting and pan banging. I was quite fearful after my close encounter that afternoon.

I noticed the bear's hind leg was nothing more than a bloody stump. The bear seemed to have no fear as he clambered into the circle, and began to eat whatever food he could – my steak, someone else's oatmeal, and a tuna casserole. When he finished, he hobbled off on three legs, dripping blood from where the fourth should have been.

No one had been hurt, but the shock at such a terrible sight made us all extremely sad. About an hour later, forest rangers came into our camp in pursuit of the poor bear. They told us he had gotten his leg caught in an illegally set trap, and that he had chewed his leg off to get free.

The rangers were also upset because they had to hunt down the suffering animal and kill it. A bear with its leg chewed off would never be able to survive the rigors of the wilderness, and the bold interactions with humans meant imminent death.

I had read about such traps in my books, but to experience the result of such cruelty was almost too much for me to endure. The person who did that was surely evil.

I love bears, they are my kindred spirit. I felt that bear's physical pain to my core. My childhood illusions that the world is a good place were once again betrayed by adult acts of cruelty, and I struggled with not becoming bitter.

Bo assured me that even though the world and life is full of pain and struggle, we must constantly choose to affirm life to right the wrongs others do, out of their ignorance or fear. It's a hard lesson to learn even to this day. Though the marauding bear instilled some fear in me, I knew that nature was still the great healer.

***

Bo continued to encourage me to hike alone, in part, to improve my awareness and navigational skills, but also to heighten my senses, which only hiking alone can achieve.

We had come to the cypress swamp in Louisiana Bayou country. I was captivated by the huge, old trees, whose trunks disappeared into the still, black, swamp water. Their branches reached to the sky, dripping long strands of Spanish moss that gave them an ethereal quality.

The swamp was alive with alligators, crawfish, raccoon, and cottonmouth snakes, lending a dangerous, travel-at-your-own-risk quality. I figured what better place to hike alone, what greater adventure to have than exploring a swamp.

I ventured into its murky waters, and I immediately sank in two feet. The trees were over a hundred feet tall, with beautiful bromeliads growing from the trunks and branches, creating a suspended garden.

Bird calls echoed through trees, bouncing back and forth. It was an acoustically perfect concert hall, and I was almost hypnotized by it all. My senses were so overtaken by the awe and mystery of it, that I wandered aimlessly and joyfully, until I realized I was lost.

I had never been lost before, and I had never been in a swamp before, so I had no idea how to get out. I couldn't use the sun as a bearing because the trees covered 90% of the sky. There was no trail, and no matter which direction I looked, it all looked the same.

I felt the chill of panic and started to cry, knowing that the venomous creatures, and the alligators could make a fine meal out of me.

Without really being aware of doing it, I was hugging a tree for comfort. It seemed the tree understood my fear and I felt encouraged to climb it. It was as if the tree was telling me to climb, and to center myself, and then everything would be all right.

Night was approaching and I knew I would stay put for a while. Below me alligators lurked, and the strange noises that brought such joy earlier in the day, took on a frightening quality. I saw one monstrous snapping turtle, and had heard they could be more vicious than an alligator.

As night swallowed the swamp, I wedged myself deeper into the crotch of a branch of that old tree. It was a long night of imagining all the terrible things that could happen to me. The outline of trees in the black night looked like monstrous creatures reaching out to absorb me.

The occasional bug on my skin felt like someone trying to touch me, and my mind raced with thoughts of swamp ghosts. Though, I would always go back to hugging the tree and a feeling of peace would comfort me again.

It was a long, long night, and I could only doze, as the unfamiliar noises always startled me awake. Yet, even through the fear, I also felt a wonderful peace in the tree's embrace.

As daylight crept through the dangling moss, my nighttime imaginings seemed childish. I scrambled down the tree and into the murky water again, not really knowing which way to turn. I tried to tune into my inner vision, but the exhaustion from the sleepless night was keeping me off-center. I finally trusted the direction my intuition pointed me toward and hoped for the best.

I hadn't been walking for more than ten minutes when I heard a dog barking. I was elated there was someone else within range, and I yelled until I heard a call in return. I ran toward the voices, and was overjoyed that it was Bo, Claus, and Julius.

They had been looking for me most of the night, but they too had quite a swamp-quest and had been turned around. Bo said his intuition told him that I would be fine, and we all hugged each other with great relief.

The night in the tree had been a quest, and a rite of passage in itself. Though I was afraid, I allowed myself to calm down and tune into my inner thoughts. It was a meditation of sorts, and I knew that I would find my way out if I stayed centered, and in control of my fear.

I felt quite grown-up after that night alone, and I grew to appreciate that the fear comes from my own mind. Certainly, the snakes and alligators were real, but they were in their environment and not hunting me, and I knew I was safe in the tree. The true fear was created in my mind. I learned that if I can create it, I could just as easily replace the fear with better thoughts.

***

The third experience was not an adventure; it was a lesson in the harsh reality of life and prejudice. The Deep South in the 1960's was a place of constant racial strife, and economic deprivation.

At that time in my life, I didn't know what prejudice was. We were driving through Mississippi when our truck broke down. We found a mechanic, who was so covered in grease, we figured that he had to be a magician with cars and trucks.

While the truck was being fixed, we decided to have lunch, and we walked through a park on our way to a near-by restaurant. I stopped at the drinking fountain, but before I could drink, I encountered a black person who told me that it was a "black drinking fountain" and that I couldn't drink there. I was stunned.

I was taught that you judge a person by what he or she does and not by how they look. I had heard about segregation, but it never entered my mind as to what it meant – that all changed in Mississippi.

The same thing happened again in the park bathroom. There were only black men in there, and one man came up to me and said, "Son, you better get out of here." I sensed his sadness in having to tell a 13-year-old, white boy to leave the black's only bathroom.

We finally found the classic American diner and I was ready to eat everything on the menu. We sat in a booth by a window, and across the street on a billboard there was a picture of a hippie on it. It portrayed the classic hippie's look, with long curly hair, lots of beads, and a scraggly beard. Across the top and over the picture, was written in huge letters, "Stamp out Pollution". I couldn't believe that people didn't like hippies.

My parents had taken me to San Francisco's Haight/Ashbury during the "Summer of Love" so we could experience a part of history. We had a great time. The free-spirited people seemed weird to us conservative types from Santa Cruz, but there was nothing to dislike.

It was Mississippi that seemed like a foreign country to me. I had never been to a place where some whites hated black people just because they were black, it boggled my mind.

By the time we got our truck we were ready for anything to come at us. Would we be taken for a large sum of money? The mechanic charged us a dollar and said it was simply a loose wire. He could have been a jerk, but he was an honest man. It was a strange day.

***

Our adventures took us to New York City. It was an awesome, exciting, and intimidating place. I was hoping to camp in Central Park, but we found a giant parking lot to camp in.

I went to the Empire State Building, the Statue of Liberty, whose endless stairs I climbed and, most exciting of all, the Museum of Natural History.

I learned about extinct species, like the Passenger Pigeon and the Great Auk. I could have stayed there for a week.

I also loved Central Park. In the middle of a huge city, is a park that's a stopover for a huge variety of birds on their annual migrations. Imagine being a bird flying over a mass of terrain that's concrete and buildings, and suddenly it changes to trees and ponds. I imagined how happy the birds must be to find such an oasis.

I enjoyed Central Park, but New York intimidated me. I saw people living on the street and asking for food. Other people were rushing and pushing to get who knows where, in a short period of time. As a California boy from the suburbs, it seemed so unnatural.

We knew that you couldn't go to New York and not ride the subway. As we went through the turnstile the smell of the dankness of human life hit my nose, like an assaulting waft of ammonia.

We went down several levels of stairs, and I was lost in the sights, smells, and the noise of the on-coming train. The doors opened and Bo and Claus jumped on, but I wasn't quick enough, and the doors closed without me. Talk about fear.

There are no trees to hug for comfort in the New York City subway. I had no idea what to do – I probably should have waited for Bo and Claus to get the next train back, but I figured they would never find the right station. I didn't trust people to ask for help, so I got on the next train. I was sure people could tell that I was out of place. They seemed to be checking me out, which scared me more. I had no idea what to do.

I decided to get off the train and find a police officer. Luckily, it was easy finding one. He got me back on the right train and gave me directions that confused me even more. When I did get off the train I was shaking, and had a heightened awareness of every sound, smell, and sight.

I didn't let anyone get close to me. I was like a frightened animal in the wrong territory, relying on my inner vision to get me out safe. I tried to remember which block to walk down, and which way was north and south.

Relying on buildings and street signs was a foreign experience, but a miracle took hold, and I made it back to the camper, and to Bo, Claus, and Julius. Bo had called for help, and he said that half the city knew about the lost kid, but I wondered in a big city like New York if anyone really looked.

I slept hard that night with Julius in my arms. New York was terrifying, and fun, and I was glad to say goodbye.

***

There were so many things that captured my imagination that summer. In the Midwest I saw huge flocks of crows that perched like black, ornaments in the trees along the riverbeds. Their calls brought a hint of sadness in my heart for what had been lost. The crows brought to mind the extinct Passenger Pigeons.

Millions of pigeons would darken the sky as they flew in vast flocks. People, ignorant of nature's fragility, would sit on their rooftops and shoot them for sport until none were left. The last known pigeon died in 1918 at the Cincinnati Zoo.

Envisioning the last mated pair of pigeons brought me to tears, but defined a life-long purpose in trying to help animals wherever I can.

I was equally moved by the battlegrounds of the Civil War at Gettysburg in Pennsylvania. The hushed, green fields dazzled in the sunlight. All traces of the two-day battles that took the lives of 50,000 men have long been covered by the hand and time of nature, but the memory and the ghosts are as fresh as each morning's mist.

The thought and emotion of that long ago war didn't really sink in, until I walked the green fields and listened to the trees – many that had stood guard over the slaughter – whispered the horror of the past on a glorious, summer day.

My world was expanding faster than my mind could comprehend. Each day was a rite of passage. I would never again be the same person that I was when I started the trip. I was learning to be self-sufficient, how to take care and fend for myself, but Bo said that adulthood was more than being responsible. To be a fulfilled adult, you had to live a life of honor.

My uncle always told me you could take everything from a man, except his honor. So, what is honor? For the Irish, honor meant that giving your word was a sacred contract. Honor is speaking the truth and having integrity. When one loses respect from others, their honor is lost.

If we honor ourselves, which implies self-respect, self-integrity, self-worth, and self-esteem, we are able to honor others. Our lives are more fulfilling, and we recognize our value in this world.

It doesn't mean that life is less difficult, or there are fewer hard times, it means we have the foundation and the inner strength to overcome our trials with courage and dignity.

Someone with little honor is always looking to blame someone else in the hard times. They are victims, and believe that life and the world is against them, and so it is. I had many experiences in my early life with people who had no honor.

***

On my rites journey I was at a beautiful beach in Florida, which was a haven for Fiddler Crabs. I had quickly befriended these sweet, little creatures. They have one small claw and one huge claw, and at certain times of the year, they come together in the millions and completely cover the beach.

I would lay on the beach and let them crawl all over me. They tickled as they crawled over my belly. I could look at them from their eye level, and felt as if I were one of them. I was part of a "cast" of Fiddler Crabs. I spent hours by the surf looking at each one through a magnifying glass.

My bliss was rudely interrupted by the roar of dune buggy engines that sailed over the dunes and onto the beach, killing and mutilating hundreds of the creatures. Bo and I yelled at the ignorant guys, but they simply laughed at us as they continued their four-wheel slaughter.

I was on my knees trying to save the ones that had been pushed into the sand, crying with anger and sadness at the same time. Bo and I stayed well into the early morning hours trying to save as many as we could, but ultimately hundreds died and became a feast for the gulls.

Those were people with no honor or integrity, with no sense of connectedness. It is people like this through their careless ways and ignorance, that will continue to destroy the beautiful places and creatures in nature.

A code of honor must be a heartfelt set of beliefs that has meaning for you alone. Many can share the words, but the meaning of the words are different to each person.

One can say they will live a life of integrity, but if they don't really understand what it is to have integrity, it's a meaningless concept on a piece of paper.

***

As the end of summer approached and we were heading back to California, Bo had me really think about what each word meant in my code of honor. As a pre-adult, it was hard to take in the meaning of words that would reflect the way I would live my life.

When we arrived in Mount Shasta in late August, I saw the mountain that I was to climb. It loomed like a vision from another world, rising 14,179 feet into solitary space. There were still patches of snow, though most of the snowpack had melted in the heat of the summer.

I was to climb that mountain, and spend one night up there, in air so thin the mildest exertion can make you gasp for a breath. I was scared and I questioned my ability to climb such a peak, whose rock gardens and punishing winds, whose ice and snow and glaciers are challenges for the hardiest of souls. Bo had no doubt, and he told me that when I returned, I would be a man.

He walked with me to the top of what was then the ski area at 10,000 feet, and as he turned and walked away, I had a fear so great that I had to dig deep into my soul to continue alone.

The climb was grueling. I had always had a great pair of legs, but a bad set of lungs due to childhood asthma. I had attacks bad enough to periodically put me in an oxygen-sleeping tent.

As the air got thinner, I sang and prayed and exhausted every religious belief I had ever learned. I would stop and sit in beautiful places, and look out over glorious vistas of green mountains. I would say, "Why don't I stay here? No one will ever know. It's as good as being on the top." But I would know, and I would have to live with a lie if I chose to say that I had made it to the top.

I called upon Big Bear, my spirit animal, who came floating to me from the cosmos. He gave me strength and I could visualize him pushing me up the mountain. At one point I thought he was carrying me up the mountain on his back.

There were other times when I collapsed in pain. I would have to really focus on calming my breath. I couldn't let the asthma overtake me. It was like drowning or asphyxiating, and I refused to give it power. I knew I had to pace myself and go at a speed that would allow me to get to the top.

As I slowed my pace, I could take in the beauty of the mountain. I had read so many of John Muir's books about his adventures on Mt. Shasta that I pretended I was him. Even though he had almost died one winter on the mountain, he loved it with all his heart. I remembered he wrote about almost freezing to death, but even in that darkest hour he found joy in the moment. I was determined to find my own joy in each moment.

Most importantly, I kept going because I had told people I was going to do it. I was going to earn my code of honor, I was going to have my rite of passage, and I was going to make Bo and Claus, and even Julius proud. I was going to do it for myself so that I could look in the mirror until the day I died, and know that I had accomplished something really big.

When I finally did make it to the top I remember saying, "This wasn't so hard." Technically it wasn't a difficult climb, but it required a thoughtful pace to get through the grueling haul.

I held my code of honor and cried for the joy of the accomplishment, and for the inspiration I had found in each step. I memorized the code sitting on top of the peak, and it became a part of who I am. It became my heart and soul and body, not just words on paper.

When I got to the bottom of the mountain, Bo was waiting, and he knew that I had returned a man. He knew that the impact of an extraordinary quest, in a sacred place, can change a person forever. We hugged each other and cried, and no words were needed to be said.

The deeper mystery of the energy the mountain gave me still affects my life over fifty years later, as I now live in full view of her.

My celebratory lunch was in Redding, before heading down highway 5 to Santa Cruz. We were so charged by the experience of my quest, that it was about an hour into the drive that we realized Julius was not among us. How could we have left him behind?

With guilt and fear and every emotion you can think of, we headed back to the rest stop where he had last been let out. We called, we searched, and we hunted every place that could hide a frightened dog. We sat quietly trying to put our energy out to him so he would return.

We were despondent when Bo finally said we needed to move on. I couldn't let him go, so I used every bit of energy I had to call Julius back. I had learned from my time in the woods that focusing all my thoughts and energy on a particular animal, could bring that animal to me.

As I sat in the back of the truck using every tool I had, I thought I heard a faint bark. I yelled to Bo to slow down, and to all our amazement there was Julius racing toward us. It was the perfect end to a perfect summer.

***

I have used my code of honor over the years as a guide and road map for my life. Through my teenage years, my journey up the mountain stayed with me, and I would spend many hours by myself in the woods contemplating the long-term effect of that quest.

I learned that my life's purpose would be to share my love of nature with people, to try and instill in them the connectedness of all things, and to respect the Earth as the life-giving force that it is for all beings upon her.

As I tell many of the young people that I work with at my school, and who I put through a rite of passage, the effects of the experience might not be felt for a long time, but it will deepen and grow if they respect their code. It is my belief when the stone of initiation is cast into the waters of the ritual, the ripples of each person's experience will touch the life of everyone they meet.

It took some years, but I knew I wanted to teach people that nature was a place of reverence. It's a place that accepts our deepest sorrows, and transforms them into inspiration, if we open our hearts and rid our minds of silly preconceived ideas.

As I opened to that calling fully, the special land where I live now, at the foot of the same mountain where I culminated my adolescent rite of passage, came to me through a series of unplanned events.

There are no accidents, and miracles do happen. The mountain called me home, and I've been returning the favor by bringing people back home here ever since. My life has come full circle from a child climbing a mountain, consciously being initiated into an adult, to an adult living at the base of that same mountain over fifty years later, initiated into a man of service, living my beliefs and my vision.

My father gave me the gift of trust in allowing me to climb Mt. Shasta to help build the man I am today. He looked after me in the way he knew how that was best for me. In return, after my mother died, I moved my father to my home, and had the pleasure of his companionship, and watching over him for the last seven years of his life, in this beautiful place on our beloved land.

There is a certain comfort in knowing life and this incredible Earth take care of you, and it all comes back around.

A Look Into A Rite Of Passage

There is not one way to mentor someone on a rite of passage, but there are certain elements that are important to the experience.

At Headwaters I hold rites of passages for young adults, boys, and girls, usually between the ages of 13 through 18 years. Sometimes it is an individual person, sometimes a group of boys or a group of girls.

I also run a unique rite of passage for private 8th grade school classes, which are mixed boys and girls. This time with their classmates, who they have grown up with, creates a unique lifetime bond of the experiences they have grown through. Their group rite of passage seals that connection even stronger.

Each rite of passage is a bit different based on the people and the situation, but every time the experience includes mentoring from myself, as well as from other teachers. It is a week-long ceremony that is created to bridge, and consciously honor the process of adolescence to adulthood.

The one requirement is that the participant wants to be there and wants this rite of passage. If they are being told to do it by parents or someone else, I don't believe they are ready. They may be nervous and may need some encouragement, especially if they haven't been prepared ahead of time by their parents or teacher, and that's normal and ok.

If a potential participant still doesn't feel ready, then I will have them shadow the week with the group to see what it's all about, and encourage them to come back another year to participate on their own and complete the ceremony.

A rite of passage has the mentoring component as the core. As a mentor I talk *with* the participants, not just *to* them about life. It's an interactive exchange. This takes a little time to build their trust to open up, but I happen to work very well with young adults, and I'm very straight forward with them, which I know they appreciate.

We talk about what they do know and what they still need to learn. We talk about where their life has taken them so far, and about life skills still needed to move forward into the future.

We talk about the state of the world and how they fit in helping to heal and care for our Earth. We talk about their struggles, their strengths, their fears, and their dreams.

I'm not sure that teenagers get enough credit for how attuned they are to this world of ours. I have had many wonderful conversations with teenagers who are very insightful.

***

I do have to say though, my staff and I have observed how tough it is for a young adult after high school or college, to move out on their own these days. Financially it is tough. It can be done though, and it is important that young adults are prepared to be out on their own.

We see so many young adults going back home to their parent's house in their 20's, and it causes a big imbalance in the household. It generally causes tension in the home because at this age they are supposed to move out and begin living their own life. They need to go out into the world and start adulting.

There is a reason that young birds leave the nest as soon as they are capable and don't return. They outgrow it, it's too crowded, and they need to learn to fly, feed themselves and live their own life.

If young adults keep going back to their childhood home, it inhibits their own ability to handle tough, life situations without their parents constantly pulling them out of the fire or worse, enabling them to not even be motivated to go out and make it on their own.

When they are constantly being allowed to go back to their childhood home, it is a disabling of perfectly capable young adults. In my opinion, it can be almost abusive and co-dependent in some situations.

Of course, there are unique times when there is something different for each transition, but in general, get the kids out of the house! They need to learn problem solving. They need to learn hard work by actually doing hard work. If I sound like I'm lecturing parents, I am.

Get young adults prepared to be out on their own, even if that means living with other roommates, as long as it's not you. It is not healthy, and you are not helping them. Period.

Preparing them at least through high school is key. Teach them to cook, teach them about personal finances and how to budget, teach them how to do laundry, and how to live in a family as a *participating* member of the community. Teach them life skills by working alongside them. Show them by doing it *with* them and have fun!

I say this firmly because I have witnessed many families pulling apart with animosity, because the young adults are not making their own way out into the world.

***

Part of a rite of passage is providing physical and psychological challenges to help build their self-confidence and self-esteem. These supportive experiences help the participants to push through their limiting fears or weaknesses in a safe environment, giving them a stronger sense of themselves. It helps them to work through obstacles that keep them stuck in old behavior patterns that no longer serve them.

At our school, one of the group's challenges is a good, solid uphill hike off trail. There are people in varying degrees of physical shape. They all have to make it to their chosen destination and back by an agreed upon time. If that challenge isn't met, they have agreed ahead of time to skip dinner that night.

During this hike, leaders switch off leading the group, either from the front or the back of the group or somewhere in between at times. It is their job to check in with everyone and make sure they are all ok. They need to navigate their route as they go, considering the terrain, the weather, if they brought enough water, and who is capable of what.

It is everyone's job to look out for each other and give their best for themselves and for the group. They work together with the thought of, one for all and all for one.

After the hike we have a debriefing of how the hike went, and any issues that may have come up and how they handled them. We also talk about how problems could be avoided, as well as giving each other props when a job was well done.

The kids work alongside us the entire week as a part of the community. They help with whatever chores need to be done to make the camp run. They learn that they are needed in a community.

One of the best ways for kids to learn is by working alongside a mentor doing the dishes, cooking, yard work, crafting or mechanical work. Mentors need to do physical work with kids. Make the work fun, it's a great time to talk or listen to music together.

Our students have free time to explore the land and be social as well. They learn to connect with the people they will be spending the week with. Some of these connections last the week and some a lifetime.

The free time to explore the land is an important part of their experience. They need that unscheduled time to allow room to be curious and explore, and to be able to entertain themselves without electronics.

We spend part of the week learning wilderness living skills; how to build shelters, how to make a fire by friction, how to tend a fire, how to find water and navigate direction.

The core teaching of the connection we all have with one another is emphasized. The participants are taught about respecting the Earth and to be of service to the community.

They learn people skills and how to handle a disagreement in a good way. How to talk through issues or ask for help from someone else to be a mediator.

We emphasize that what they have to say matters, and to speak up and make their voice heard. We remind students to recognize that the rite of passage is a celebration of their coming of age, and it acknowledges that they are a part of the larger community, the global community.

We encourage them to bring out the gifts of who they are to share with the world. We ask them to step up and take an active role in life, in contributing to their family and their home community.

There are many times I work with youth who have been raised by a single parent, and there is a lot of stored anger and hurt toward not only the missing parent, but the one who is the main caretaker, and is trying to fill both roles in parenting.

Some houses the kids come from are broken, and some homes are idyllic, but no matter what, kids are all the same. They still need support, love, parenting, and boundaries. They all want boundaries, whether they could articulate that or not.

As kids, it's their job to push boundaries, and explore limits and beyond. It's our job as mentors and parents to hold those boundaries, and keep them alive in the process of them almost trying to kill themselves, out of spontaneous gusto and blissful ignorance.

If kids don't respect you, if you don't hold the essential boundaries, they will take on being their own leaders. It sounds funny to compare them to a pack of wolves, but we are very much like pack animals. If there is a weak leader, then a younger pack member will try to rise to the top.

You can gain young adults and kid's respect by speaking with them truthfully, listening, giving them freedom within the boundaries, playing with them, working alongside them, and just being real and caring.

During the Rite of Passage week, the participants create their code of honor. In a group setting we create a group code of honor and I have them personalize it for themselves. We do this group code to create that bond and to hold each other accountable.

The students learn about taking the life of a small tree and using this tree to create a prayer stick or dream stick. I ask them to carve into it their dreams and wishes, and intentions of what they want their lives to look like.

They take this stick, which is now a medicine object, out with them on their solo sit to pick up that energy. I put the challenge out to them that one day when they are older and become a mentor, to put someone out on a rite of passage and pass this medicine stick on to them.

While they are harvesting their small tree, they learn about caretaking a forest. They learn about thinning the forest to open spaces in thick areas, to allow sunlight in for diverse plant life, animal habitat, and fire safety.

Every day they spend in nature they are learning to live in balance, simply by living *with* their environment. They also recognize immediately how one action or inaction affects everything.

For the solo time each participant chooses their own sit spot in the woods, and they build their own shelter. During the week-long rite of passage, the participants go out on a 24-hour solo sit and memorize their code of honor. This time is for them to dream their life.

After the participants return, there is a community ceremony and celebration. It's important for them to have a supportive community to return to when they go home. It is easy to slip back into everyday routines, and forget about what they have put so much effort into.

I suggest that they share their code with their parents, and to also create a small altar to help keep them connected to this experience. It can be as simple as putting a special rock or stick on a shelf that they brought back from their time out on their solo sit. It's a reminder to keep to their code to the best of their ability.

This is an abbreviated example of a rite of passage. As I mentioned, my rite of passage looked very different from this. My rite of passage was a trip around the U.S. that lasted all summer. I had different experiences and challenges, but the main components and intentions were the same.

I do highly encourage young adults to travel the world as a part of a rite of passage. It is so important to be exposed to our global community, and to interact with this amazing planet of ours and all her landscapes. You need to know this world to fall in love with it, so you will be committed to protecting it.

My dream is that rites of passages such as this, become the norm again. We live in an uninitiated world, and it's time to consciously restore honor again as something to be valued.

Elder's Rite Of Passage

Rite of Passages are for different phases of life. The most common time is when we are just entering young adulthood. At this time in life, we are often caught between a child, and what's next?

Other times in life as adults, we will find ourselves at major life transitions, and it is helpful to recognize these transitions as a type of a rite of passage.

We have recently been bringing to light the need for an elder's rite of passage. There is a definite stage in life where we transition from a place where we have been living our life purpose, many times through our career, and then we retire. The question again comes, what's next?

As we approach our elder years, conscious thought needs to be put into this time. How will you step into the role of an elder, and pass on your knowledge and wisdom from your life's experiences?

I agree with the statement, don't die with your music or story still in you. How will you choose to share what you have gained through your life?

In the United States, extended families rarely live together anymore. Our immediate family grows together, and then we all move off into our own homes. As our parents get older, they move into senior living communities, and they stay isolated from those who could benefit from their guidance and mentorship.

When we separate ourselves from our elders, they lose the opportunity to pass on their wisdom, and many times they lose sight of their purpose in life.

When our Earth ancestors lived in tribes, our elders were respected members of the community. They were honored for their knowledge of the Earth-ways. The elders were valued for what they had to share.

There are many wise elders sitting at home, that have so much to share with us and it never surfaces, and we all lose. One of the breakdowns is we live in a culture where elders don't offer their gifts, because it's not supported in this world today. Also, people don't actively seek out elders, and the opportunity is lost.

We need to bring this respect back to our elders. If we create space for our elders to have purpose, it will become an invaluable, cherished gift for everyone.

In many healthy communities in nature, such as with animals, and trees, there are elders that pass on their wisdom to their youth for their specie's survival. We all need our elders in our communities, as we all benefit.

Many hands-on skills are being lost, and our elders are a great resource to learn the trades from. We need younger people stepping into these skills. There are gems of wisdom waiting to be shared.

When you are nearing your elder years, it is a good time to begin to see your future. This is a good time to participate in a rite of passage. Go on a solo sit with the intention of seeking the answers of what your new role looks like, and how that will unfold.

At this point in your life, if you have been doing your best to live your values, then it becomes an honor for others to learn from you.

At Headwaters we facilitate an Elder Rite of Passage. We have seen a need for honoring this transition. After decades of living, we can still become lost, and it's ok to ask for guidance. We are never too old to seek out a mentor, and to learn to be a mentor in return.

Whether you seek out someone to put you through a rite of passage or do this on your own, the important thing is that you do it. The world needs you to step into a new role.

Strength In Knowledge

We are not born into this world with a how-to manual. Some things we learn through our parents, mentors, and friends. Some of our life skills we learn from strangers. Some things we learn through our own life experiences.

All these sources are valued, and by creating your own code of honor, it will help you reinforce those guiding principles.

When you create your own code of honor, it forces you to truly think about what your personal values are, and to bring them to the forefront. When you are consciously aware of how you are living your life, it helps you move forward on your path with purpose. You have a guide to refer to in life's daily situations. You can take responsibility for your own actions. You are no longer a victim of not knowing. There is strength in knowledge, and in turn, self- empowerment.

Code Of Honor

Our young adult students who come to our school, take on a code of honor to live their life by when they do a Rite of Passage or take our Scout-Earth Caretaker Way Class. When students participate in our Earth Philosophy Class, they also create a Spiritual Code of Honor.

I believe completely that these simple values come from nature's teachings. It is in our interaction with nature on a personal level, that we learn how to live a true code of honor. Nature is the most honest relationship we will ever have.

Nature is not trying to get anything from you. It's not trying to use you for money or power or for knowledge. Nature is there to give us joy, connection, and the beauty of our life.

What we put into our experience in nature is what we get out of it, and it's so brutally honest. If we go out in the wilderness and we aren't careful or aware, and we don't know our skills, nature is perfectly happy to take us away in a flood or drop a tree on us or catch us in a fire or any other natural disaster.

Nature isn't judgmental, it is life-giving and nurturing, and is also just as indifferent to turning us back into compost, and growing a tree out of us, and starting all over again.

It's that full circle way of living that nature teaches. It's an honest relationship that shows us basic values.

The whole focus of creating a code of honor is to consciously bring up values to use as a guide in life. When creating a code of honor don't get hung up on semantics if the words are not quite spot on. The focus is on the original intention of the words you use. Are those words important to you? Do they resonate on some level inside of you? Then make them sacred through your intent.

I truly believe that the problems we're having with our planet and caring for our planet, and the problems humanity is having living together, all come from a simple lack of living a code of honor.

One of the first values we teach in our school is to help when help is needed. It's so simple. We are human beings; we live on this Earth. To keep the circle full, to have enough food, to keep nature balanced and healthy, to care for our families and our friends, and our communities, we need to give back. Human beings by nature are caretakers.

We take what we need to live. We need food, housing, transportation, computers for work, you name it, all these things come from nature. We take and take, and we forget to give back equally. We forget the importance of that balance of give and take. Service is keeping the circle full.

Being of service can be as simple as doing a dish for someone, making food, helping someone cross the street or carrying a heavy bag. Something as simple as cleaning your house for your family or doing something huge like rebuilding a school or tending a forest or wildlands, it all matters. Every deed you do for others matters.

We need to seek out what needs to be done, and we need to make it part of our daily medicine. You don't do service to get money or fame or acknowledgement. It's nice when you get recognition, everybody needs that now and then to keep you motivated, but that's not why you do it. You do it because it's the right thing to do.

I also truthfully believe that if my life affords me to live in comfort or even abundance then there is nothing to feel guilty about. It is however my responsibility to make sure I give back to others to help them live life in the best way they can.

The benefits of your efforts are amazing. You get engaged in your community and you feel good when you are of service to the world. You have a sense of purpose, and it comes back to you in return. Nature is all about the full circle.

Keeping your word, doing what you say you will do, telling the truth, living through simple integrity are basic things, but today I don't see it very often. Sadly, when I do come across people with integrity it stands out to me, because it doesn't seem to be the norm.

My father and my grandfather raised me, and they told me, "If you give a handshake to someone you give your word with that handshake. If you borrow money from someone you don't need to write up a contract, you pay them back when you said you would. When you shake that hand, you look them in the eye and that's your word. That's your sacred word. When you keep your word, when you do what you say you're going to do, when you give your best, then what you are doing is setting the stage for getting that in return."

What I learned from that carried over into building trust in relationships. When trust in relationships doesn't have to be defended, always wondering what the other person is doing, you can go to a deeper place. You can connect through the heart to the spirit of another.

Giving your word is a sacred gift you give. It's not something that you always have to give. Think about it before you do, and reflect on what you are giving your word to. When you do give your word, it is a sacred pact.

Nature keeps its "word". It gives us air to breathe, water to drink, trees to build our homes, and food to eat. It's endless.

Integrity is the overall value for a code of honor. It's telling the truth; it's giving your best. When you have integrity, you can be counted on. People will honor and respect you because they know that when times get tough, you'll be there. You'll be the one to lead the way. To have that dependable integrity, to let that trust blossom so relationships can go to a more meaningful level, is a huge thing.

Think about the values you might put on a code of honor. Often, we have the kids that come through our program put on their code, "Have Fun". When we grow up and we raise families, we get busy with our jobs, and we forget the importance of having fun, and how much that feeds us. It allows us to welcome brighter things in life. We get so serious and sometimes get lost in the drama, and that takes over our whole life perspective.

Having fun doesn't mean you're not serious about life, and you should never have fun at the expense of others, but just have some good old, goofy fun to lighten up. Laughter has been proven scientifically to be one of the greatest medicines that there is. It is healthy for us. It is good for our overall physical, emotional, and spiritual health to laugh.

Get out and do fun things like sports, and dancing, and climbing trees, and building shelters. Go on hikes and wander down the rivers and explore. When we are out in nature having fun, we set the foundation for us to blossom into more meaningful relationships with the land, and with those who are with us.

Giving your best is really telling about where we sell ourselves short. We are faced with this lesson when we climb mountains either physically or metaphorically. For example, when our apprentices are climbing Mt. Shasta, they get to that last 1000 feet they call Misery Hill, and the only thing that gets them to the top is their commitment. Every step is arduous and painful, but they are committed, and they're giving their best.

When they get to the top, they believe they have made it, and then there's another peak to go. It was a false peak. As it happens so often in life, we get close, right there, almost, and then we stop too quickly. We give up. We get distracted when we are right there in front of our goal.

Learning to give your best and dig down deep is a medicine that's in you. When you are in a tough situation, knowing you can bring up your best when it counts, is a valuable thing to know. The only way to know what is in you is to keep stretching that boundary.

Commitment may be one of the most important values to incorporate into a code of honor. When you're committed is when you're fully involved in something. When I am committed to getting in our cold creek and I say I'm getting in, I get in. I don't leave one foot out and put one foot in. I get in fully. I immerse myself in the water. I'm committed to it and then the water works its magic on me.

When you are committed to something it is your whole being that is committed, your emotional self, your physical self, and your intellectual self. When all of that is gelled together to a commitment, then the spiritual world, the unseen world, the mystery world, gets behind you and helps you. Until you are fully committed, you're on your own.

One of the reasons in a marriage vow you say you're committed is because of course you're going to go through difficult times. Stresses will test you and it's the commitment that carries you through those times.

When you get through those difficult times, and through the struggle, then you grow closer to your partner. Your relationship is stronger, more loving. You begin to build a history, and that history becomes part of the medicine that holds you together in a marriage, or a friendship, or within a community, or a country.

I can't think of anything more important than just simple kindness and compassion. Caring for the Earth, the world we live in, and the individual beings that live on the Earth.

Just before I sat down here to write, I went to fill the water bowl outside for our dogs and I saw a wasp drowning in it. I simply put my hand under it, pulled it out, and it flew off after it dried off.

I didn't have to do that, I don't think most people would have done that, but I'm not looking for praise on this, it's just the right thing to do. My point is that it's that simple. This being was struggling and it needed help, and I helped it. I get emotional on this because I don't understand why human beings can't get this one.

Each of us must be the one to make a change. We must be the one to do what's right when we are presented with the opportunity, it will define who we are. Our actions will tell the world who we are, and when the world knows, the world comes forth and engages in our lives. Our lives become richer and more meaningful.

When we get busy, we can get so lost in ourselves, and we mistakenly fall back to, what's in it for me?

We get so removed and into our technology, endlessly wondering who's calling me? Who's emailing me? Who's texting me? Who's not? We forget to stop and remember that the world around us is alive and living, and we're a part of it. More importantly, we miss when our compassion and generosity can be given, such as helping the little beings.

Helping that wasp was a personal thing between me and the wasp, but it's so much bigger than that. The act of helping sends an energy out that says, I'm that kind of person, and that opens the world up to me in a more meaningful way. The little things turn into the big things. You can't skip the little things and get to the big things.

A code of honor becomes like a road map. It's something that we follow and reminds us how we're meant to live, and why it's important.

If I take it to a bigger level, I know there are so many problems in the world, but if everyone created a code of honor, and if we simply followed it, a shift would happen. The population would change, and we could become caretakers. We could become true stewards of the Earth, and strengthen our relationships and grow closer.

I don't mean the problems would go away, there's always problems. Every single animal on the planet has problems. Everything struggles and has good days and bad days. The point is we won't be putting all our energy into fighting, killing, and destroying our Earth. We will be putting our energy into problem solving, while also enjoying this great world we live in.

I want to get you thinking about, what is your own personal code of honor? What matters to you? Who are the heroes in your life, and how do they live honorably? What are the things they do that you could also do?

Let nature help you look at the truth and teach yourself how to live a code of honor. When you're not coming from integrity, you're not coming from honor, you're not coming from commitment, you're not coming from compassion, you're not coming from kindness, you're not coming from giving your best, you're not coming from keeping your word, and then you are not the gift that you could and should be to this world. You're allowing yourself to be lesser, and ultimately the Earth pays the price.

I don't understand people who don't come from integrity, I'll never understand that, but I know that it's never going to change for many people. I know I must be the change to make a difference in the world, and I'll do what I know is right because that's what I can control.

Ultimately, the Earth will work it out. The Earth will answer the question of how humanity will go forward. I am always a dreamer, and I'm dreaming that we are learning, and that we are going to get it.

Create a code of honor, go out and change the world by how you live daily. I wish you the best!

Keep In Mind

When creating your own code of honor, reflect on what your personal values are that you believe you can follow, and that can show up as medicine in your life.

Your code of honor is just a guide. You will mess up. Part of living this code is to recognize your mistakes. Don't beat yourself up. Be accountable for your mistakes, clean them up, and get back on track.

This code of honor you create is for you personally. You can choose to share it with others so they can help you stay accountable, or this can be an agreement within your own soul.

If you do choose to share your code with someone else, make sure it is with someone you can trust, that will honor and hold your values with respect. There may be many wonderful people in your life, but they may not all be ready to respect this personal document as sacred for you.

Your Honor Is Yours To Keep

Can we conceive of being a person of honor in a world that doesn't necessarily reward people for being honorable? This is our challenge, to be honorable anyway.

When life's not fair, when those around you are lost, when it doesn't seem to pay off to make the extra effort, do it anyway, it matters. Your honor is a part of your being. It's like another body part.

When consciously practiced every day, your code of honor becomes a part of you. It is a living being within you. It is who you are. The world needs people like you to enhance our humanity. No one can take away your honor. It's yours to cherish. When wrong shows up, do right. No matter what, do right.

Chapter 31

Vision Quest

Times of transition such as times of great growth, marriage, changing directions in life, parenthood, and elderhood require a type of rite of passage.

Often a vision quest or a walkabout is a part of this process. Each requires time alone in nature seeking answers, and visions, and ideas to help us move into sacred periods of life.

Nature then steps forward as our teacher. All that we love, and honor is found in nature in the way the Earth lives. This time alone allows us to turn away distractions, and let go of what is no longer needed. It allows our hearts and souls to receive Earth's teachings.

We find courage to go forward, and put these visions and ideas into action. We give birth to them, and bring them alive in a true partnership with the Earth.

Sometimes to live fully, to come into our power, we must in a sense, let a part of us die. Then we are reborn anew to unleash our better selves upon the Earth.

The practice of a vision quest or a walkabout goes back thousands of years to our ancestor's times, in different cultures. If you want to look at religious teachings, then Jesus went out on a vision quest for forty days and forty nights. Siddhartha went out on a walkabout when he traveled outside the walls of his home.

The Celts sought solo time for reflection, the Aboriginal culture embarked on walkabouts, and Native Americans have used this sacred, questing time throughout their history.

It is important to note that vision quest is an English term. Each tribe or culture had their own name for it, and their own customs, and form of this solo time.

I believe it's important that we take time in our lives for ourselves. I know this is hard, because we are so busy with life that we forget to just live, but we always need to work to seek balance in our lives.

To build your relationship on a true, personal level with nature, going out on a vision quest is integral. Very simply put, you go out into nature, and find a sit spot that calls to you, that feels personal and inspirational. Some people choose a magnificent view for big ideas, and others choose enclosed spots to promote more inward thinking and visions.

A quest must be in a place in nature that is removed from your daily environment. It can be in the desert or on a mountain, on a secluded beach, in a meadow or in the woods.

It is a place where few, if any, people go. Always the vision quester asks the space permission to be there. The answers usually come through feelings or an all knowing through one's whole being.

No plants or animals on a quest can ever be hurt or damaged. This spot must be treated sacredly. It will then come alive within you.

The quester must introduce oneself to each tree, rock, water source, plant, insect, reptile, and bird. Any beings that visit are important to the quest.

Build an altar in that space out of respect, and to reflect your intention. Use found objects in the environment. Make it a work of art. Lose yourself in it.

Find a stick and carve it. Let the carving represent all the moments you've had while you are there. You can also do this on your return home, to bring the experience and medicine back with you. This type of Earth medicine will support you as you go back into your everyday life.

Vision Questing is a time to attune yourself to the rhythm of nature, which is slow to slower. It's a time to clear out the chatter in your brain, which keeps you busy and moving fast. It's a time where you can access messages and intuitions that you may not know are there.

***

Traditionally in native cultures it's four days and four nights out, without food, water or man-made distractions. A quester stays in the same spot and observes the land and prays in their own way that's personal to them, while asking for guidance in their life. They seek guidance on who they are, where they are, where they're going, and what they are supposed to do in their life. There is an asking for support in building their connection with nature, and ultimately themselves.

Many questers want to move into the spiritual realms and talk to our Gods. Some native ancestors referred to the idea of God as the Great Mystery. I love this. It leaves it open for each of us to discover.

Remember the Earth Itself provides spiritual connection. The Gods are in the trees, plants, animals, and the water. The Great Mystery lives on and within the land. Spirit is within our sacred Earth.

***

When you are out on a quest, talk to the Earth. Take time to talk internally or outwardly through all your senses to every tree, plant, insect, and animal in your spot. The blessings that can come out of it are profound.

How often do we take that much quality time to connect with nature alone? Once your connection is that intimate there is no going back. You will only go further and forward, and your life will profoundly change forever. You will know the Earth as your friend, teacher, and partner in life. You will also find the Earth is a healer.

On a vision quest look for signs, symbols, colors, shapes, patterns, and clouds for inspiration. Use your senses, bring them alive. Sounds can speak to you. Smells can deliver ideas and memories. Sing Earth songs, make sounds, touch trees, rocks, and water.

Feel ants walk on you. Insects can be your best teachers. Flies, mosquitos, and spiders will test you. Watch and enjoy them.

Let your emotions come alive on a quest. Talk to your feelings, anger, bliss, sadness, boredom, or fear. Ask them what they have to teach you. Go through your past and learn. Observe without judgment.

Take this time as a mid-life review. Why wait until your death bed to look back on your life, and find that you may have regrets that you wish you could have changed? Maybe there are wrongs you want to make right. Maybe there are goals you still want to accomplish. Maybe there are places you want to explore. Maybe there are experiences you want to have. This is the perfect time to have your own life review.

A vision quest is not easy. It's very difficult in many ways. You will get hungry, and tired, and lonely, and bored, and scared, and mad, and sad, and maybe happy. I have put myself out on dozens of vision quests in my life, and they do not get easier.

When I'm hungry I think about all the people in the world who are truly starving. I put it in perspective, knowing that my hunger is temporary, and by choice, and my heart feels empathy for those who do not have a choice.

It is important to push yourself, and it's ok to be uncomfortable, but you will need to know your physical ability to participate in a vision quest. I believe it is important though to go without food. The ego needs to drop, and allow room for something else to fill you up.

Many traditionalists do not drink water while they are out, but I wouldn't recommend doing that your first time. This is an opportunity to flush out all the toxins you built up physically and emotionally, and water helps with this process.

You can dance in place and keep your body alive and well. Do your best to stay awake at night. When you are fatigued, and your mind is turned down, the world speaks to you in ways you could never imagine, dreams and visions come. Observe with an open heart and a humble mind.

Leave your journal, watch, book, and cell phone behind. In that space is you, and nature only. My perspective is if you are experienced in nature and have spent a lot of time out in the wilds, then vision quests can be done on your own.

I do believe however, it is best to have someone put you out. It is powerful to have someone hold you in their thoughts while you are out. It frees you to know that there is someone who knows where you are, and will support you on your return.

If something happens, and you are disturbed by someone, don't stress about it, it's part of the quest. There is something there to learn from.

**

Years ago, I put a woman out on a sit, who believed deeply in the spiritual world and extraterrestrial life. She was truly terrified that aliens were going to abduct her.

On her last night out, which is usually the hardest night and seems to never end, she fell asleep. She woke up in the morning when it was barely light, and heard scuffling footsteps. She finally braved opening her eyes to meet her worst fear, and circled around her were thirteen cows.

Her quest spot was on the edge of the woods and a meadow, and the cows had broken through a neighbor's fence. They curiously investigated what was lying in the meadow. They were drawn to her open energy, and hung out with her. When she woke up, there were her aliens.

**

Even if a jet plane lands next to you, that's all a part of your experience, but the more you can have solitude and quiet, away from the things of the city and modern life, the better. I can't say it enough, you and nature are all you need.

When you get a vision for your life or when you make a commitment, it is important to keep your word to nature, to Spirit, to your ancestors, to yourself.

Never quit. Often the greatest epiphanies happen at the last moment or even after your quest. The more in the moment you can be, the better.

Don't commit until you are serious. Ask your ancestors for help. When you commit, help will show up in ways you cannot even imagine. The universe is just waiting for you to say the word.

I fully believe in questing to shape our lives. Questing has enhanced my life, and taught me to be reflective and thoughtful. My connection to our Earth has strengthened beyond belief. It has taught me immense kindness to all living things.

As often happens on a quest, your most profound visitors can be insects, plants, and trees. I've connected with old trees who have told me their stories. I've been visited by many animal friends from mice and marmots, to birds and bears, all of whom respected my space but still engaged with a message for me.

I've experienced so many spiritual moments and visitors from other dimensions, they almost seem like an everyday event.

I've learned the power of commitment, and the power of keeping my word. I've learned to believe in myself. I've become my own best friend. I've learned the gift of just sitting and dreaming and observing. I've learned Earth-song, and sang and sang for days. Maybe most important, vision quests have helped me to feel one with our Earth, no separation.

As we Earth Keepers say, go out into the woods and allow your life to begin. Go out and fall in love with our precious planet.

Vision Quest

With eyes closed to the outer world of illusion, the inner truth of life opens up with clarity.

Vision Walk

The Vision Walk or Walkabout, was used by all Earth cultures. The Aboriginal People perfected the walkabout. When the call came, they would walk into nature until some answer came. It could take a day, a week, or a month. The idea is the same as the quest, except that you walk in nature. The best way is no time or destination, just wander and let nature lead you. Surrender to the land, the trees, the animals. Let the Earth guide you.

In today's modern world, walkabouts can be difficult. If you get the call and leave your family or work place they might not understand, so plan to go out for a specified length of time with no destination. Just do it. It will always be good.

Go backpacking alone. The best is to go off trail. Learn navigation and then wander. Self-reliance creates a solid belief in yourself. Our Earth is a living being, a true mother. She will protect you. Remember the power false fear holds over us.

Go through different landscapes. Walk creeks, valleys, gullies, hills. Climb up high. Talk to the land, ask questions.

Always keep an open heart, this is the key. Love attracts all beings. Nature will respond to an open heart through feelings.

The Earth celebrates you when you join Her with no ego. Ideas and inspirational thoughts will come to you, along with a wholehearted sense of happiness and contentment.

Remember you've come home to the Earth on the Earth's terms. Take a walk and lose your *self*. You will be found, or not.

Time To Know Who You Are

An art I believe we have lost, that I think we might have had in the past, is being able to just sit and be, and not have to be constantly busy.

Leave those smartphones behind. They are too tempting to take your attention away. It's easy to make excuses for why you need to bring it along. You don't need it.

When you are sitting still imagine this, if we had no concept of time, what would we do with our lives? Am I really who I think I am or am I a false personality? Am I all these things that I did in my life to get attention? Who am I in my purest sense, at my core?

Vision quests give you time to self-reflect. No one is there telling you how to think, it's you, and nature, and Spirit. You go on a quest to purge what you no longer need, and purify yourself to be who you truly are.

Solo Time

My first solo time was on Mt. Shasta when I was 13 years old, and it was then that I wrote my code of honor, while completing my rite of passage.

I have been on many vision quests since that first one, in many different places.

***

On one of my quests at Roosevelt Lake, I was sitting in a crevice up a hillside, along a little creek, praying and asking the Great Spirit, and the nature spirits to help me. After two days of praying and asking, I had pretty much depleted my prayers.

I decided with the last couple of days left I would just observe. I watched the sun's progress move ever so slowly, completing each day. I watched and listened to the birds and insects.

Everything moved so slowly that my mind and my thoughts became equally as slow. From this slowness, emerged the thought that I should be teaching people about nature.

I had always taught, but it wasn't until I created Headwaters Outdoor School in 1992, that I realized the power of that quiet moment. When I got quiet and still, it allowed space for my vision to come to me clearly. It was from that time out, that I began creating my dream life.

Why Am I Doing This?

Ten minutes into my three-day, vision quest I was already bored and fidgety. I wasn't totally sure why I had felt I needed to go out, but there I was, committed, and pissed about it. I knew I needed to be there, I was called to be there, but didn't know why, so my enthusiasm was lacking.

I spent my first day watching a gopher snake swim in the creek next to me, and eventually settle at the bottom of a calm eddy. Butterflies periodically rested on my knee, and dragonflies became my heroes swooping across the meadow, scooping up the evening mosquitoes.

It took most of the day to get the to-do lists out of my mind. I drew in the dirt some creative art ideas that were coming to me, but other than that, my focus was all over the place.

I did my best to stay awake, but I know I drifted in and out of sleep. At some point the heat of the day forced my eyes open.

I was feeling horrible. I have a crazy metabolism, and only one day in, I was very weak and nauseous. It was a tough, long day. I started to doubt I would be able to make it through two more days, and I sat in some loathsome, self-deprecating thoughts and emotions.

Time seemed to stand still and stagnant. The night before, the sun seemed to never want to rise, and on this day, the sun seemed to never want to go down.

I finally gave up on trying to guess what time it was, and eventually the sun started to move further across the sky to the other side of the mountains. It was still light out, but I felt a lot better, physically, and emotionally.

I was laying back in my marked off eight-foot space, looking up at the tops of the circle of cedar trees I was being watched over by, and I glanced to the side at a light that caught my eye. I didn't even flinch seeing a very, very tall, elder man, standing just at the edge of my space looking down on me.

No lie, he looked very much like the character, Gandalf, in The Hobbit movie. I couldn't really see his face, but he did have a thin build, gray hair, a light-colored robe, and a walking stick.

His humbling presence filled my circle with an all-encompassing, but peaceful energy. He stood there passively looking around my circle, as if he were checking to make sure everything was ok.

He never made direct eye contact with me, but at the same time there was a non-verbal communication. He made me feel like he was there to make sure everything was ok, not just with me, but with the land itself.

Within a few seconds, he faded back away from me into a soft light. I sat up and looked around, but he was gone. I know I had been fully awake, because my dreams are usually ridiculously bizarre, and this encounter was literally real. The place I was in, and the state of awareness I was in, were very much my everyday, physical world.

From that moment on, I was filled with inspiration and felt I was lit up from the inside out. I knew I needed to make a huge life change, and I knew that I was supposed to move to Mount Shasta, to Headwaters, for the next phase of my life. I didn't have the how yet, but I knew where my heart was leading me. I knew I was somehow going to be the land caretaker at Headwaters.

In the late evenings I heard constant drumming and murmured voices, and I didn't feel lonely at those times. I felt community supporting me.

Initially, I thought there were people in the distance having a party, but then my logical mind couldn't explain that away. It really wasn't until I came in after three days and nights out, that I realized it was the spirits on the land, drumming and supporting me.

A few days after I came in, I overheard Tim talking to someone about a spirit that is on the land, he referred to as the Earth Keeper. He described the man I saw exactly, including his walking stick, and being non-verbal, but still knowing what his intention was.

Tim explained that he was a caretaker of the land, and watched over those who were there as well.

I told Tim later that he came to my spot, and I was glad he verified my experience. It was then that I had a flashback of this man.

Years earlier, at a place I call The Ridge, I had an unbelievable experience connecting with a flock of vultures. I was running downhill and was startled by an older man standing along the trail. As I got closer to the man he was gone, and there was an oak tree where he stood.

I realized that the man I saw that day, as well as during this quest, was the Earth Keeper. The only way I can describe my encounter with him, is that it felt like an initiation into a new role I was to take on.

***

Through the years I have only visually seen the Earth Keeper a few times, but I still feel his presence.

During a ceremony one day, I asked the Earth Keeper who he was, and I understood him to say he is the Keeper of the Keepers. He watches over those who are here doing the work to care for the Earth.

***

I have gone out on a quest a few times seeking clarity, and those times are never easy for me. Some people love questing, I personally do not at all, but, I have always, always gained insight through those times out.

Sometimes my ah-ha moments happen during the time out, and sometimes it unfolds later, but it's always valuable time spent, and I never know who I'll meet out there.

Chapter 32
Make Kindness Your Way Of Life

Kindness is a life's path. It takes guts to truly live a life of kindness. I'm not going to tell you I've achieved it completely, even though I'm a very kind person, sometimes it is tough. Kindness is a huge medicine that lives within me, and nature has been my greatest teacher for kindness, but it isn't always easy to be kind.

Judgment blocks kindness. Letting go of limiting judgment is a lifetime of work, but in the journey of working on it, is when all the greatness comes.

Working with kids in my school is a very good teacher for kindness. Being in a friendship and love relationships are also very good teachers for kindness.

Think of kindness as a serious part of your life's path. You bring it alive within you, and kindness becomes one of the purposes of living.

If you completely commit to kindness as a core of your life's purpose, kindness to yourself, kindness to others, kindness to nature, and all the Earth's beings, there will come a defining moment when you won't even have to think about being kind. You will just be kind. Your physical being, your intelligence, your intuitive and spiritual instincts will emanate kindness. In moments when you are tested whether to be kind or not, kindness will be who you are. Kindness will be your instinct, even in the hardest situations.

I personally get crazy angry sometimes when I see injustices around me, especially having to do with nature. I have violent thoughts of retaliation, and have to remind myself to get back down to the place of protection of the Earth through right action. Even though I am a kind person, this is something I have to keep working on.

When nasty people in politics seem to go unchecked, I have to catch myself by taking a deep breath or ten, and then go sit by a tree. Trees are kind giants. They are easy to relate to. They are amazing listeners. Trees are all about giving and caring endlessly.

After I sit with a tree and allow it to take away the negative emotions, I get myself back in line and come back to my center, which at my core is kindness.

Kindness is infectious. It is one of the ways the world will change. Kindness is the power that activates healing.

We are here to be of service to each other and to all the beings we live with. This all begins with taking care of our home, our Mother Earth.

The phrase, practice kindness, gets thrown around a lot. You see it on bumper stickers and some people make fun of it, but the strongest people in the world are the kindest. There's so much strength that comes through that heart energy. It's really the only answer that ultimately works.

We've tried the anger approach. We have been at war since the inception of humans claiming territory. We've done this great experiment of a lack of kindness, and it doesn't work. Hatred doesn't work.

We can work on developing kindness. If you want to experience pure kindness, spend time with people who are truly kind souls, and learn from them just by observing.

If you are having trouble some days, then restart your day by going into nature. Take a walk in the woods or lay in a meadow or go to a park. Explore a creek and watch the abundance of life all around, notice how those beings are not taking life so personally. Reset your heart and go back to practicing kindness.

Heart Talk Through Poetry

One of the core teachings at Headwaters is to be kind. At some point during all my classes I recite a poem written by Joseph Bruchac, "*Birdfoot's Grampa*". The story is told by a young man, who observed an old man stopping their car in the rain to save the toads in the road. This poem reminds us we can always make time to be kind, even when it's not convenient.

Ask yourself, would I stop for the toads? Most people wouldn't even see the toads, but to see them, and run over them anyway, is disheartening.

It's often the little animals that are the greatest teachers. Spiders are some of the most vulnerable beings, and sometimes they show up in your shower. Are you kind enough to move them outside or leave them alone or do you smash them?

We have many opportunities in our lives to be heroes. Animals are simply trying to live their lives, and somehow or another they get in our way. How we react to them is a huge statement about who we are. Do you have what it takes to slow down, and be willing to take the time to help when help is needed for another being?

I have so many stories flashing through my head of times when I've had that opportunity to assist someone or some being, and never once did I regret taking the time to try to help.

We live down a dirt road where we pass a seasonal reservoir. One summer I was driving home, and I noticed the road was alive with thousands of frogs and toads that had hatched out, completely covering the road.

Previous people had already driven over so many of them. It made me sad and angry all at once, and then I noticed there were still so many alive. It was amazing witnessing such a massive hatching. I got out of my car and caught hundreds of them. I put them in cups and coolers and brought them back to my land to release in my gardens and ponds.

The frogs and toads were there along the road for weeks. I returned many times with my students and staff, with buckets to collect and release them in safe habitats.

Then a remarkable thing started to happen. The neighbors noticed what we had been doing, and they began to pull over and remove them from the road as well. One of the neighbors painted signs to warn others to slow down, and to look out for the little ones. This was a wonderful thing to be involved with. A community that came together to help the little beings. The poem I had been reciting for years had come to life for us.

Yes, many toads and frogs were still run over, but the act of being of service was still a wonderful validation that good things can happen when we work together. It only took a little awareness and kindness. People want to do good; it takes one person to get things started and others will follow.

As you move through your life, think about these kinds of stories, and how and when these moments come up. It is a test for you to stop and do the right thing. Your heart will tell you. Your brain will tell you. You will know how to do just the right thing, and you will be better off for it, and the critters will be too.

Kindness is not always convenient, in fact, many times it never is, but be kind anyway. It's the best way to never have regrets.

An argument somebody might make may be, why would it really matter? There are millions of critters of the same species, but it matters to that individual one.

Often, we just need to educate people as to why it truly matters that we do our best to save even the one. We cannot save them all, but we can do our best to save as many as we can.

There is a great story told by an anthropologist and naturalist, Loren Eiseley. He saw an older man down the beach far ahead of him stooping frequently and flinging his arm. He was curious and wandered down the beach towards him. He saw that the man was throwing starfish back into the ocean.

There had been a high tide, and there were thousands of starfish washed up on the beach, some were still alive. Upon seeing that there were more starfish than could be counted, the man asked the elder why he was doing what he was doing. He wasn't going to be able to save enough of them to make a difference. The elder, barely looking up and holding a starfish, told him that it made a difference to that one.

He wandered off from the elderly man, and found himself also throwing back starfish into the surf in hopes that they would survive. They were not going to be able to save 10,000 starfish, maybe 100, but it's the act of kindness that makes a difference to the individual. Kindness is personal.

Steps Count

To walk anywhere in nature is to walk on some being's home.
To walk anywhere in nature is a chance to practice kindness.
Look where you step. Every step you take can make a difference to someone's life.
Make your steps kind steps, steps toward a kinder world.

The Importance Of Service In Nature

The more your awareness skills build-up, you will find that more opportunities to be a hero in nature will arise. Chances to help animals, plants and other beings in nature will come to you. More of the world will show up.

As your awareness grows and your tracking skills evolve, at some point you will know more, a lot more, and that's how the teaching works. You have to trust in that process and put your time in.

What better way to spend your life than to be of service to nature? Many times, being of service to nature is by educating people about things they are afraid of. Helping them to understand what they don't know. Pointing out why a certain being is so important, and the role it plays in our world.

Sometimes being of service is by pointing out things in nature to people that they wouldn't necessarily see, because they don't know what to look for, or how to look.

I've been engaged with wildlife with a hundred people around, and no one else even knows what I'm doing. It amazes me at just how unaware people are of the world around them.

Now, with smartphones and technology in their face, many people are not even aware of what's at or under their feet. There is a balance to find with cell phone use, but when you are out in nature, *be* in nature. Get your selfies out of the way right away, and then put the phones away. Experience where you are fully. That's how you will know what is needed.

You have to be willing to help. You have to be able and willing to see or hear or feel what is needed. You need to stop and take action when you see someone or something that needs help.

Being of service allows us to directly work with the planet, and the living beings on it. It helps connect us, makes us feel good about ourselves, lets us feel that we are making a difference in the world, and gives us a sense of purpose.

Being aware helps us to see more of the details of the beauty in nature, and to feel and understand how many things live at our feet, and around us, and how these things support us to have good lives.

When I sit at the edge of a dipping pool in our creek, I watch a couple dozen trout swimming around. Those fish enjoy that pool because we made it for them. When winter comes, I need to break down the dam a little so they can swim on and find safer, deeper pools or they won't survive. I think ahead of how I can help the fish in the creek pool that I take care of and swim in every day.

Every time I swim in the pool, I'm swimming with my fish friends. I love it. It's just enjoyable to know that they're there sharing the creek with me. It's a communion between us. No one is trying to get something from each other. I'm not trying to hurt them, and they're not trying to hurt me. We're just enjoying the water.

The water is what brings us together. All this joy I receive just by being of service to the fish, and all who benefit from the creek.

Some of the greatest teachers of service are insects. I removed a ladybug from someone's shirt collar. I relocated it onto a bush, and I knew it would in turn be beneficial in keeping the aphid population in check. It was a small effort that paid a big reward for that being and all those it affected.

Relocating spiders outside of a building, instead of smashing them, is a kind thing to do. Allow the spiders to be the natural, insect population control. I leave some spiders in my office just to observe and enjoy, and they help keep the flies managed during those big hatchings.

There are countless plants that need trimming that are laying down in a path and are getting trampled. Help them up and move them to the side or trim their overflowing branches.

Sometimes animal holes get covered, unearth them, and let them have their space. There are so many ways you can help nature. I couldn't list everything, but the important thing is for you to discover where you can be of service in nature.

Look for ways of helping by using your awareness and opening your heart. When you put your intention out into the Universe, those who need your help will appear. When you participate you will feel more engaged, and life will be more fulfilling for you.

There are many people who suffer from depression and anxiety. Working for nature is a way to feel a sense of purpose and to feel happiness. By serving another being you are invested in someone else's quality of life. If you have the right intention, you will be empowered to make a positive difference. Ask the woods or the ocean or a creek, "What can I do for you today?"

Make your relationship with nature personal. See the individual. It's personal to them as well. Help when help is needed in any way you can. When you pay attention, you'll find hope. It matters.

Are you kind? If you are, then there's space for you to go forward. A future is bright with kindness as the light.

Lifelong Service

My friend, John, is an Earth Caretaker on the island of Kauai. He is a respected elder and native to the island. He has been caretaking a 20-acre parcel of ancestral land his whole adult life. He shares this sacred land with the community and he mentors children, teaching them traditional Hawaiian ways.

John and I have had many afternoon-long conversations on the power of nature and our roles as caretakers. John put into words for me of what I've been called to do at my land in Mount Shasta. He spoke of taking ownership in a task that is of service to others as a personal give back. This lifetime dedication, whether it be keeping a playground clean and kept up, or tending a section of beach, or clearing springs, or removing graffiti, or tending trees along a city sidewalk, is an honor and something to take pride in.

This commitment becomes a sacred act of kindness. It is something you do because there is a need and you put your heart in it. This space or task becomes a regular part of your life. You don't do it for recognition, you do it because you are called to be the caretaker of that space, and you provide your service honorably. No one is checking on you, you are only accountable to yourself, and the promise you made of your dedicated service.

Your whole life purpose could be this humble act of sacred kindness in service to others.

Holding Space

We have successfully rehabilitated and attempted to save many critters. No matter what that being is, it is an honor to have at least been a part of helping, whether it was successful in our eyes or not.

Sometimes we know the animal will die, but maybe in those times it is for us to just hold space, be there through their passing, and show compassion in a stressful situation.

Tim called me one night and said he had just found a cottontail rabbit laying in the driveway. It was alive, but it wasn't moving its back legs.

I brought it inside my house. I could feel its life force was weak, even though it was very alert and awake.

My call that night wasn't to try to fix it, but rather to just hold it in my lap, and give it the energy of love through its passing. I held the rabbit for two hours until it finally went Home. Not one time did I feel fear within the rabbit, only peace through its passing.

Compassion is not something in us that we need to search for. We are compassion.

Give Blessings To The Earth

We have a blessing well on our land, at the entry to our camp. We have made an altar of cut stone with a wide-brimmed, copper dish on top of it, and a bucket of coins to the side. We invite people to sit a bit, and give a blessing to whatever they would like their intention to go to. It's a wonderful space to reflect and pay the energy forward.

Next to this space, there are a few paracord ropes strung between cedar and pine trees, with hanging colored, fabric squares. We have fabric markers available for people to write love letters to the Earth. We then hang them for the wind to carry these messages across the land.

Creative space doesn't have to be fancy. It just needs to have good intention. This intentional space is simple. It invites people to stop, and take a few moments to reflect on gratitude, and good wishes.

When you give love boundlessly, you receive love boundlessly.

Spread happiness. It's contagious.

Feed Animals

Think for a moment how difficult it can be for wildlife to live in a world of 8 billion people. Countless cars and trucks, boats, buildings, houses, roads, windows, planes, helicopters, cats, dogs, fences, power lines, wind turbines, smokestacks, polluted water, endless noise, confusing smells, guns, hunting, fishing, farm animals, trains, signs, light poles, cell towers, and poisons in gardens, crops, and golf courses. With all that said that is just scratching the surface of the insanity it must be for wildlife.

Whenever you can help animals, feed them quality food, give them clean water, create habitat for their safety. Every chance you have, help wildlife, especially in cities.

When I'm on the Big Island of Hawaii each year I feed the birds, and wild turkeys, and geckos at our rental house. It's a wonderful treat for them, and for me. It doesn't take much effort to make a difference.

Humans Are Predators

Turn the predator in you into something good. It doesn't always have to be bad to be a predator. Humans tend to want to take out other predators out of fear of competition.

Observe other predators in the animal world. Learn from them. Animals are perfect for what they do. They instinctively know what to do.

Get to know them by listening to them. More importantly, *feel* what they say. When you get to know them, you will know how to be in balance with your own predator within.

Invest In Your World

Put your love of nature into action by volunteering your time helping nature heal from human abuse. This shifts the energy from just being angry about what's wrong, to putting good, heart medicine back into a bad situation. Finding solutions creates healing. Serving others is serving yourself.

Join organizations helping to restore our land and water. Like a colony of ants, one person can do the work of one person. Two people can do the work of four. When we work together, we make new friends, build community, and find new ideas and solutions.

Donate a percentage of your income to organizations that work for our planet. Allot some of your extra change to humanitarian and environmental organizations, any amount, it all helps.

Research organizations and find one or more that speak to you. Let your money back what you believe. Money is just another form of energy; it becomes what you make it to be.

Help When Help Is Needed

My wife, Jean, and I were on the Big Island of Hawaii. We were out on a lava shelf jutting into the Pacific Ocean. I know this place well. I've witnessed countless sunsets, and whales swimming, and I've swam day in and day out with sea turtles and endless reef fish there.

I've watched seabirds forage for food right next to me. I'm always in awe of these birds who fly over 2,500 miles across the open ocean to reach these islands. It's a miracle. How do they do it? I love nature's mysteries.

This lava shelf is called Puako Reef. It's a special place for me. Along the backside of the reef are the Kiavi trees and Coconut Palms, which create a living, green boundary of beauty. Each tree has a story to tell of their journey.

Imagine what these trees have witnessed. Kiavi trees twist and turn in ways that quite simply challenge the imagination. They are life givers. All we need to live comes from the coconut trees, food, hydration, shelter, cordage, clothing, and fuel.

Turtles come into these coves to rest by going up onto the sand. This cove was all rock and no sand.

Jean called me over as I was photographing the sunset. She was concerned for a turtle, as it was somewhat jammed into a tight spot in the rock. We watched for a moment and saw a Moray Eel come out from under the turtle. The turtle had blocked the eel's entry into its home.

The eel nudged the face of the turtle, and the turtle gave a nip back. The eel wasn't happy and kept harassing the turtle. It was an incredible interaction to watch.

Jean urged me to do something, as the turtle was getting exhausted and was clearly stuck in an unfortunate situation. I climbed down to the water's edge and reached down and gently turned the turtle around and gave a push. He got just enough assistance to be able to swim away.

The eel was thrilled, and the turtle returned 20 minutes later to the cove, and crawled up to join four other turtles on a safer portion of the rocky beach for a good night's rest. A good night for all and a wonderful sunset.

Humans have the gift of empathy. We can feel what other beings feel. Use this ability to give back what you feel others need at any given moment.

Teaching children to be empathic to the life of a snake, is as beneficial to the snake as it is to the children.

Rescue

Imagine that you are a Loon or a Grebe, a waterfowl that migrates thousands of miles every year from their breeding grounds in the north, to their wintering areas in the south. The act of bird migration alone is truly a wonder of life. These birds should be admired and revered. Imagine these birds, exhausted, flying over a city, looking for a pond or a lake to land on and rest. They see a glimmer of a dark, large, flat surface, and land on what they think will be safe water, when in reality, it is a parking lot, shimmering in the sun.

If they survive the impact of crashing into the pavement, and don't sustain any wing injuries, they are stuck. Large water birds like Loons and Grebes need water to run across and pick up speed to lift off, something that is impossible on pavement.

When I worked at the wildlife rescue in Santa Cruz, I would receive calls like this, with a bemused bird in a parking lot, surrounded by people, cars driving around it, dogs barking at it. Imagine what that bird must feel in that situation. Empathetic tears come to my eyes.

I would approach the birds and place a towel gently over their eyes to keep them calm. I'd then do an examination for injuries. If they were physically ok, I'd take them to water and soon they would take off, flying away on their migration.

An open-heart extension to nature's creatures is human beings at our finest. When help is needed, most humans love to help. This is a give back we can give to our Earth, and to ourselves.

Kindness is a healer. Heal your wounds by blessing them. Be kind to yourself.

Track Kindness

Stepping over an ant is a simple act of kindness that can trigger a series of unforeseen events. You may meet the love of your life years later, and maybe you could track that meeting back to that ant through that one extra step of kindness, that triggered a series of small acts of kindness, which led you to meeting that special person.

Never discount the value of any act of kindness, no matter how small it seems at the moment. The energy of love pays back tenfold. Be a part of goodness and goodness will follow you home.

Insects

I love insects and I know it sounds strange, yes, they love me too, in their own way. They have always been my friends.

Look closely at insects and you'll know what a miracle is. Science says bumble bees shouldn't be able to fly, well tell that to the bee. Next time someone tells you something isn't possible, remember the bumble bees.

We need to help insects. Be of service to them. Feed and house them when possible. Stop killing them for no good reason. Consider what you are doing to our world if you use pesticides.

Be respectful with insects. They are just living their lives as you are. We are all in it together. We all serve a purpose. An insect's purpose may be to pollinate, to control populations of other beings or to feed certain beings.

Have you ever considered how many living beings you kill just by walking, or driving? Pay attention to where your feet go. It matters. Be aware. Your feet make a difference.

See beings as individuals and make a personal connection with them. Saving one beetle matters. Take interest in the individual and practice tolerance for what you don't understand or fear.

If an insect bites you and you kill it, then it's between you and the insect. You have a right to defend yourself of course, but always consider if an insect needs to be killed or just relocated.

If insects are taking out your garden, then yes, you need to stop the destruction, but also educate yourself in how to counter those insects, with beneficial insects for your garden.

The most powerful things in life are simple. You don't have to have a higher degree in education to learn how to be kind. It's within your grasp at this very moment.

Whatever You Love, Love It Deeper

Bring love into the world. Share love, be it. Soak it up. It's you at your best. Love of nature, love of self, love of life. There is no end, it's boundless. All of it, the trees, the water, the animals will love you back.

Give Gifts

Give gifts from nature. We buy everything. We are major consumers. We need to stop the madness. When gifting time comes, which can be anytime, go to nature, find beautiful rocks, branches, and leaves, and make art out of them for gifts to give.

Make gift altars. Heart stones full of your love and hope are wonderful gifts. Wildflower bouquets are amazing and so full of life. Let nature help you be creative. Nature and you working together to create beauty from nature's beauty. Give a gift from nature's heart.

Just Listen

There are a myriad of ways to work with healing. Sit and hold space for someone, and let them just talk, give them your full focus, and really listen. That is a healing. No advice needed. Just listen and be there for them to tell their story. Ask yourself, when you listen to others, are you hearing their heart?

Milkweed

Today I planted 300 milkweed seeds for the Monarch Butterflies. It was simple. Scratch the dirt and drop them in.

Today I helped the Monarch Butterfly fight back from extinction. Today I became bigger than myself, I became an Earth Caretaker.

Today I gave thanks to the Monarch Butterfly for the countless times I've been blessed by their presence. Today the bumble bee thanked me for the milkweed. They love the luscious flowers too. Today was simply a very good day.

Teach By Living Kindness

Remain humble and keep your intention to be of service. That is an honorable life well lived. Living the life of purposeful kindness, is the foundation of being a masterful teacher of life for the next generation.

What Do I Want My Medicine To Be?

While I am alive as a part of this Earth, as well as when I have passed, what do I want my legacy to be?

A great use of your life is to live it for something that will outlast you. Show up respectfully. Whatever that looks like for you. Show up as the best you.

At the end of each day ask yourself, what did I do to help the Earth today? Be kind by making a difference every single day. *How* you live your life is your purpose. Live your life well.

Is A Place Better Because You Were There?

Wherever I go, I do my best to leave a space either neutral or better. I do this everywhere, whether in nature or a city.

When I leave a hotel, I always tidy the room before I go. I tie up the garbage bags, strip the sheets off the bed, and put things back the way I found them.

I know the housekeeping workers will be in to clean the room, but it is out of courtesy and respect for another person, that I leave the room as neutral as I can when they arrive, so they can focus on sanitizing.

Yes, they get paid to clean the rooms, and at the same time, isn't it nice to help whenever we can? That small gesture may make someone's day a little better.

An easy thing to do is put my shopping cart away, and any strays along the way. It's a way for me to practice gratitude for a healthy body to be able to do that.

***

I was gifted a family vacation at a resort one year, and was on an early morning walk alone on the beach. It was a calm, pink sky morning, and would have been a surreal, idyllic setting, but as far as I could see along the mint green water's edge, were plastic cups washing back and forth. The waste from the previous night's dance party.

I noticed one resort worker sitting at a picnic table staring off into the horizon. She wasn't having it that day, or maybe any day.

I found a bag for garbage and walked along the water's edge picking up the trash. A woman walking from the opposite direction, was about to pass by me and asked if I worked there. I told her no, that I was just trying to help.

She looked at me and the floating island of shoreline garbage with an inquisitive smirk, and continued on her way. A minute or so later, I looked back at her farther down the beach, and watched, as she too was now picking up the garbage on her way.

This was one week of my life helping a place that had been neglected. When I left, I'm sure the mess accumulated again, but for that one week, maybe that daily clean up triggered more right action. Once that seed is planted, it is always there, and when you know better, it eats away at you to do better.

Kindness is contagious and you can't unlearn it. It lives within you as a part of you. Sometimes you just have to wake it up.

Kindness Births More Kindness

Trees love each other, just look at them growing together. Observe how they share space with other trees that are not even the same species. In our woods we have huge pine trees and cedar trees entwined. They have wrapped themselves around each other for support their whole lives.

Like a tree that grows out into the world and makes everything better, kindness also grows within you, and makes you a better person, for the care you offer to another being.

To be a good person I must be good to the Earth. It can't be any other way. Good blessings come to those who persist in doing good. This is nature's way. Be as kind as a tree.

Caretakers Are Magicians

Caretakers are magic people. Most of the caretaker's work goes unnoticed. This is love made real, love in action. The most wonderful caretakers work their magic for a higher calling. A calling to make a difference, to do good, to create peace and harmony.

Julie is the caretaker for our school, and our land and animals. She creates all the magic, mostly behind the scenes, but the energy is felt.

For a moment, think if most humans decided right now to let their inner caretaker come alive in service of the health of our Earth. I truly believe our problems would begin to dissolve.

Caretaking is Spirit's work, it's a higher calling. It's in all of us. Give your caretaker freedom right now and go to work. Be a magician, go create magic.

Believe

Believe in love and kindness and service. Three words that seem so simple. We can add other words like commitment, compassion, and integrity as well.

We're at our best when we come from love. We're at our best when we are being of service, giving back to the world we live in, giving back to all aspects of nature, giving back to our communities, giving back to our families, and giving back to ourselves.

Service means helping when help is needed. Not doing it for money or fame, but solely because there is a need to fill.

The beauty of animals, trees, and plants is that they make the planet healthy just by the way they live. Animals eat a certain amount of insects. They create compost, chew back overgrown vegetation, and keep other specie's population in check, which keeps the Earth healthy. Trees and plants provide food, shade, shelter, tools, oxygen, soil, and warmth.

Human beings are not better than any of those other beings, but we are very different. We have the intellect to formulate ideas and create those visions with our hands.

Yet, we put ourselves in a position where we've bred like crazy, and our population goes unchecked. We are at 8 billion people now, and we all want things to make our life work easier. We want convenient food, cars, refrigerators, washers, dryers, big houses, and boats.

All these things we've created come from nature, and if we're not giving back, if we're not practicing service, the resources eventually run out. When nature suffers, we suffer.

Basic things to consider is to live your life through love. Really study love. I'm not talking about just romantic love, which is an extraordinary thing. I'm talking about love of trees and plants, love of friendship, love of rocks, and love of water, love of ourselves, love of the things we love to do, love of the things that other people do, love of our planet, love of life.

When we come from love, we are truly extraordinary to all living things. Empathy, the ability to feel what another being feels, makes love that much more profound. Empathy is a trait that is so beautiful and should be honored. The ability to see or feel that something is wrong, and then be able to help remedy the issue, is love put to action.

Let nature show you how to walk softly on the Earth. How to not damage the lives around you. Making this simple effort becomes an extra-ordinary way to live. It makes you a good, good human being.

Unfortunately, so many people never even consider the idea of love and kindness, and service as being what can lead us in our daily lives. Those three actions are what can guide us on any decision that

comes up each day. It's that simple, but it does take practice. In time though, there will be no thought about it. It merely becomes who you are.

The most powerful way to live is to practice love and kindness, and put it into action through service. Take your incredible intelligence, your physical abilities, your hopes, your dreams, your ideas, your connections, and go to work to make the world around you better.

So many people wonder what their purpose is and why they are here on this Earth. We want to complicate it because we get lazy. It gives us an excuse not to act on our own. We look to others to tell us what our life purpose is, when it's already within you just waiting for you to live it. *We are the solution to our own problems.*

Kindness is a life's purpose. *How* you live your life could be your life's purpose, being the best you.

Be someone's blessing today.

Chapter 33
Manifest Your Dream Life
- Live Your Purpose

Being an Earth Caretaker includes caretaking yourself. You are a part of the Earth.

What is your path? Why are you on this Earth? What unique gifts do you have that you can share with the people, animals, and plants, to fulfill your own life, and make the world better?

It's important when trying to figure out your path, to remember the simple things, and to grab onto them when they show up and give them life. All your life experiences are steps along your journey.

Think about your path and what it's going to be, and then birth it and give it life, and enjoy the journey. It can be a combination of many things. Write your ideas in a journal and let it evolve.

Our Earth is calling you. Go and find yourself. Not the self that was forced upon you, find your truth.

If your path has heart, if your path has love, if your path has intention, if your path is beautiful, then please go for it. The most important thing is that you're committed to a path, and you live it. The world needs good people.

Happy people do good things for each other, and for our planet. We all win. Go live the life you were meant to live and soar. It's okay to be happy. You can do it.

Freedom Seekers, you need to find your own path. You can ask for help, but you must be the one to do it.

Stepping Stones

Some people know their path early on in life. I was mentored at a young age by my grandfather, my father, my uncle, and a family friend. I was raised as a nature boy. I knew early on my life was going to be about helping the planet, and working in nature would be at the forefront of my life.

I've had many jobs throughout my life, most of which had to do with working with plants and animals.

I was given a camera when I was twelve, and the love of nature photography grew into a passion of mine. Photography led me on countless journeys backpacking, and on road trips exploring sacred places.

It wasn't until I was 50 years old that I became a professional photographer and opened my gallery. The true test of knowing you're doing what you're supposed to be doing, is that if no one bought a book or a photograph from me or even looked at my photographs, I would still love doing it. I would look at the photos myself, and remember those sacred moments in nature and smile.

While doing photography I worked at animal parks and reserves, and then helped start a wildlife rescue. I continued to rescue wildlife, while also starting my chimney sweep and masonry business.

313

I worked in my chimney business mainly in the fall and winter, which allowed me to work at my other interests in the spring and summer. My chimney business afforded me the financial grace to pursue working in nature, which doesn't tend to pay as well. I enjoyed the craft of masonry work. I met amazing people, and was gifted many sacred personal stories and items from my customers.

Each one of my interests seemed unrelated, but they all came together and helped shape my path. While running my chimney sweep business, rescuing animals and birds, and going on photo trips, I also started a small, outdoor school where I took homeschool kids and their parents on day trips each week into nature.

***

Sometimes nature creates opportunities through natural disasters as well. After the destruction and tragedy, many times in the clean up, something good eventually comes out of it.

I went outside when the 1989 Loma Prieta earthquake hit, and I watched as the brick chimneys in Santa Cruz crumbled. I knew at that point, I was going to be very busy.

After volunteering with my men's group with the cleanup of local businesses in downtown Santa Cruz, I got to work rebuilding chimneys. It was due to that influx of work that I was able to afford to buy my land in Mount Shasta.

I then created Headwaters Outdoor School, and I now caretake this incredible land near Mt. Shasta. I share the land with people, I teach about nature, I take care of wild animals, and I care for the land itself.

***

My path developed this way. One experience leading to another. Nothing was ever either or. I have always been able to include all my skills and passions into my life. There were many jobs and experiences in between that have led me along the way, and I'm not done yet.

I am writing books, and now beginning to create the new movement of The Earth Caretaker Way. This movement is to help establish guidance and assistance for Earth Caretakers to carry their work out into the world, by saving land and animals, and reversing global warming.

I have always been a dreamer and a doer. I have always been curious. I ask questions and seek answers to how to get things done. I seek out mentors. I jump in fully, and work hard to make things happen. I build community and ask people for help, and help them in return.

People are usually amazed at the number of things I have done and accomplished in my life. They comment that I have lived multiple lives in one, and they are right. Yet, everything I have done, and am continuing to do, is all reachable for everyone. You just need to dream big and manifest it. So, get to work and do something grand with your life!

Defining Moments

A defining moment is when a shift happens within us. It may be an event or a realization that changes, or enhances our trajectory on our life path, or even boosts us forward. Sometimes people will recognize that moment immediately or it may be in hindsight years down the road when reflecting on life events.

When a defining moment happens in nature, it's as if time stops briefly. It can grab your attention physically, emotionally, or spiritually. Often, these moments provide you with a choice to make, and result in a profound interaction with nature.

It's as if the Earth is gifting us this moment. It senses something in us and says, "Here's this opportunity, now come along with me. Journey with me into the future."

Sometimes these moments that make you pause could be as simple as laying in a wildflower meadow, and sinking in so far your own thoughts disappear, and as a result, on some level you just know more. The meadow takes you in as a part of it.

These life changing moments can become a gateway to profoundly richer experiences. Defining moments are one way the Earth calls us home.

I consider these highlights in nature sacred, because the Earth recognizes something in us and stops us, and awakens us, and inspires us to jump in fully in life, in partnership.

Defining moments can happen in all areas of our lives, in work, love, art, and family. The challenge is when a defining moment arrives, will you have the awareness to recognize it and soak it up, and bring it to life through your actions?

As we track back to these peak moments in our life, we can see the path we have taken that led us to this time and place right now.

Defining moments are not always positive, sometimes they can be difficult and painful, and change our lives according to how we respond. We can be grateful for those challenging moments, even when they seemed negative at the time.

If we haven't adjusted our actions towards a positive result, then that opportunity is always there for us when we choose to act on it, and shift course.

When faced with these pivotal choices in life, be willing to jump towards your heart. It will lead you in the right direction.

My Land Of Miracles

I had a good life in the Bay Area. It was a nice place to grow up. Then the Silicon Valley sprawl began to ooze into all the small suburbs among the foothills, and blew up our quaint town into an overpriced, concrete maze of townhomes.

I owned my own home childcare, I was selling some of my art, and had been coaching competitive swimming for over 20 years. My lifelong friends lived close by, and it was still a nice place to live.

Yet, there was an ache deep inside, rising to the surface, that I couldn't ignore any longer. I was living a nice life that was familiar, but I knew I needed to make a change, and take a leap into something else.

I was feeling myself shrivel up. Even though change makes me nervous, I also could feel that if I wasn't growing, I was dying inside.

One day, I was pacing in circles. I said I just need to take one step outside of my circle, but I didn't know what that was exactly. I picked up a magazine and told my friend, that whatever I was supposed to do next was in there. I flipped through the whole magazine and got to the very last page, and chills shot up my arms, and lit up a smile inside my whole body.

It was a full-page ad for Headwaters Outdoor School, with a photo of majestic Mt. Shasta, in the background. I read the short description, "Bringing people back home to nature, to remember what they already know."

I was looking for a deeper teaching and interaction in nature, and I was confident this was where I was supposed to go. This was my sign, my answer to what was next for me.

I hadn't traveled on my own much before that time, but I signed up for the Nature Awareness Class. With some reassuring words from my friend, Ben, I made the drive up for my first class to the Marble Mountain Wilderness, in Northern California.

This was one of the biggest, defining moments in my life. I found my Home in the wilderness, the moment I stepped out of my truck and breathed in the rich, loamy air. It was also the first time I met Tim.

Our class spent the initial night at the trailhead, and in our opening circle, Tim asked us to introduce ourselves, and say a little something about why we were there. Before I could get words out, I had to choke back tears. I was a little embarrassed about my unexpected reaction, but they were the most completely honest, relieved tears I've probably ever shed.

They were tears of a reunion of place. A place I had been searching for, but also wasn't aware of at the same time. I simply said, "I don't know why I'm supposed to be here, I just know that I am."

From that point on I knew I didn't need to explain a thing. I had found my people, along with my sense of place in the world. I was 34 years old and knew I had just begun living my own life the day I arrived in the Marbles. It was a baby step, and at the same time a very significant one. This day was the day that I could never turn back from, I could only go forward.

Hiking into the wilderness and coming to the edge of the first, wildflower meadow, literally left me breathless. Not because of the altitude gain, but because the life I had been living was leaving me, as the new life was filling me up.

It sounds so dramatic, but it felt like I was walking into a mural painting. I became a part of my surroundings. My life was being animated in a way I had never felt before. I felt everything coming into me, filling me up. The blanket of flowers, the towering ancient trees, the billowy, bright white clouds, the deep, deep cobalt sky, the snow peaked-red rock cliffs, I was breathing all of it in as a part of me.

Any idyllic movie could not compare to what I was witnessing and experiencing. I physically reached out in front of me to make sure it wasn't a dream, and there was no canvas boundary behind this pallet of brilliant colors.

My week became an unintentional vision quest. A review of my life seemed to stream through me, and new hope, and life visions, and laughter was discovered inside of me.

I humbly knew I was not the top predator in my environment, and I felt the truth of being a part of the whole. I was not an outsider, I felt welcomed home.

At the end of the week, I knew I needed more of this. I didn't know how, but I was going to do my best to make it back for another class as soon as I could. Fortunately, I was able to make it back within a few weeks, this time to Mount Shasta, at Tim's land, where the school is based out of. Again, everything I had known was expanded beyond my self-limiting boundaries.

***

Over the next couple of years, I took every class Tim offered, and volunteered my time when I could. Each time I drove back to the Bay I felt I was grieving for Headwaters, the land, the teachings, and the people.

My life was good, but I was emotionally growing away from it. After a couple of actual vision quests on the Headwater's land, and some profound experiences, I got up the nerve to ask Tim if I could have the land caretaker job as soon as the position came up.

He tried to discourage me, thinking I would be too lonely in the off season, and said it was a room and board trade position, and I would have to find a job in town for income.

I finally convinced Tim and Jean of how serious I was, and that I would work my tail off and figure out my finances later.

I gave my one-year notice at work. That was tough to do because I had grown up with the team I swam and worked for since I was in middle school.

I was so excited about my upcoming move; I didn't have time to remind myself that I didn't know anything about being a land caretaker. Nothing. I had mowed my lawn and pulled weeds in my backyard, but that was the extent of my skills.

I had a lot of reading to do. How to use a chainsaw, how to plant a garden and maintain it, how to fix things, and how to drive a tractor.

Then my phobias of dealing with money, and the fear of all my other non-existent job skills kicked in. There wasn't a swim team I could coach in Mount Shasta. I couldn't run a daycare in my new home, which would be a 20' yurt, but those were the only two jobs I had ever had.

Knowing I had nothing financially to count on yet at my new home, I put in my advanced notice of my departure anyway. A slight twinge of doubt crept in, but within two weeks an opportunity showed up.

Tim's best friend and previous Headwater's cook, Dave, called to let him know he was going to be moving to Hawaii, and wouldn't be able to work for him that next year. Perfect! I jumped again at the door that was being opened.

I asked Tim if I could have the job. He again tried to talk me out of it. He said, "You don't want to cook."

Without hesitation, "Yes, I do!"
He argued, "You don't even know how to cook."

I couldn't argue with him about that, but I assured him I would be able to do the job by the time the next season started.

***

For the whole of my working life up to that point, I had been working two full time jobs, 16 hours a day. I left the house when it was dark and returned when it was dark.

I had no time to even empty my untouched groceries out of the bag in the fridge before they went bad, and had to replace them with a fresh bag.

Aside from heating up baby food and bottles, and making snacks for my daycare kids, I was the microwave queen of reheating. There just wasn't time in my life to learn to cook. I was out of hours in each day, and honestly out of energy to even think about it. Fast food was my number one source of fuel. So, there was that hurdle to conquer.

My friends and family laughed when I told them what my jobs would be. They didn't think I could pull it off. I wasn't sure I could either, but I was going to give it everything I had to make it work. I knew I was supposed to be there in Shasta. I knew that I was home there, and whatever it took, I would do it.

One of the best skills you gain as a longtime, competitive swimmer is a killer work ethic. I had been training for many, many years, and that meant being at the pool at four in the morning, and then again in the evening, working-out for 5 hours a day, in between school and jobs. That was my life. Eat, semi-sleep, eat, workout, eat, compete, eat some more, and work.

That early training and coaching has benefitted me my whole life. No matter how many hours I still work a day, it will never be as hard as those younger years that I am so grateful for.

***

Preparing myself for my new life to come, I put myself through the homeschool of cooking shows. I filed through cookbooks. Tim taught me a few things, as he used to cook for the classes before Dave came along.

I called my sisters and asked what our mom used to cook for us, and I found a few of her handwritten recipes, which I cherish today. I put my friends through trial-and-error tastings, and I actually got pretty good at the cooking thing.

I called Dave to get some advice from him on cooking for a large crowd over a camp stove, and fire pit. I was also stumped about what to do with vegans. His advice was this, "Vegans? Juls, F*** vegans! They're the first ones to complain when they're cold. Give them a stick of butter and tell them to shut up." Needless to say, I had to figure out how to cook for vegans on my own.

Turns out I enjoy the creative side of cooking. I like the challenge of feeding a large group outside, and making people happy with my rustic, and primitive, gourmet meals.

It has been fortunate for me that eating is my favorite hobby, so cooking has been a perfect match.

***

A year later, moving day finally came and I was ready. My first dwelling that summer was a 16-foot canvas teepee. The previous caretaker wasn't due to move out of the yurt I was moving into until the fall.

I learned quickly how to live in the woods. It was fun. It was new, and each day was an adventure. I thrive when I am outside, and more importantly, my random bouts of irritated panic that started to happen in the city, completely disappeared.

The fall came, I made it through my first season as the camp cook, while also learning my role as the land caretaker. I was severely sleep deprived, but I had gotten used to that.

What I did, and still do have gratitude for, is that at the end of each day, I find that I am tired from truly living a full day of my life. I don't go to bed blah tired. I go to bed after a full day and night of work and play, tired with no regrets, except that sometimes I run out of hours to do just one more thing I wanted to pack in that day.

With fall and winter, came a whole new set of skills I needed to learn. I learned to preserve a lot of garden overflow, woods clearing and burn piles for fire safety, winterizing buildings so water pipes don't freeze and break, and how to drive The Beast-snow plow, the tractor and snow blower. I learned what it took to shovel feet of snow off the roofs, how to clean chimneys in the winter, how to caretake horses and chickens in the snow, and chisel their frozen poopsicles off the ground, how to feed a rescued Great Horned Owl, named Luna, how to caretake the Headwater's eight pack of dogs, and how to split and stack firewood, a lot of firewood, and eventually how to caretake honey bees throughout the year.

I also had to learn how to relax and enjoy the cozy fire in my yurt, without putting on my pj's when the sun sets at three in the afternoon.

I worked on art projects, and writing, and managed the office work, that now became another layer of my job. I planned the next spring's garden out, and practiced more recipes for the coming year.

When the busyness slowed down to the pace of deep winter, I finally unpacked my moving boxes, after having lived in my new home for nine months.

While sorting through boxes, I found my volumes of journals. As I was flipping through the pages, I landed on one entry titled, "My Land of Miracles", dated 1998, three years before I had even heard of Headwaters.

***

My friend, Ben, had his hands full with me back then. I had been going through a difficult time in my life, and he was doing his best to get me not only through it, but beyond my self-doubt, and growing into the person I was supposed to be, myself.

He gave me the assignment of writing out my land of miracles, as if I were living it right then in the moment.

317

Of, course I questioned it all, and told him that I would never be able to have what I dreamed of. How would I ever make enough money to get it? Even though I worked a lot, my jobs just paid enough for my living expenses. So, I gave him a lot of doubting, push back. He said to let go of the how's, and just write.

So, I wrote out my land of miracles, and eventually it got packed away and forgotten about. Having moved multiple times in a short amount of time, I never unpacked those journals until I finally settled into my yurt, my forever home, eight years later.

***

"My Land of Miracles" – 1998

I live north of here in the mountains. I have my own space and live in a cabin, but there are other people living on the land as well. There is a community of like-minded people here. It is like a retreat center focused on nature and self-growth. There is a sweat lodge and medicine wheel next to a creek. There is a garden here. I caretake the land.

***

Sitting on the floor of my yurt, in 2006, reading this journal entry from 1998, I was in awe. I was reading the story of my life; I had written years before I even knew that this home and life existed.

I can assure everyone that what I wrote is truly my current life, including the creek that runs between the sweat lodge and the medicine wheel.

Even though I had been attending classes at Headwaters for a few years, and had lived in my yurt for almost a year, it wasn't until I found that letter eight years after writing it, that I realized I had actually manifested my Land of Miracles.

It had already existed before I had known about it, but I manifested myself into this life. It was at that point where I had to admit to Ben that he was right, "This s*** actually works!"

My journey here started with an ache, a search for the questions that I didn't even know, but felt, then a calling that I had to follow. Doors continued to open, and I trusted my gut feeling and that pull to keep going through.

I had to tell my truth and ask for what I wanted, demand it. I had to work hard, and also ask for help. I had to let go of other people's worries for me. I had to trust in spirit, and I had to trust myself that I was enough to do this.

Yes, I was nervous, but I never doubted that I was heading home where I belonged. Once I found home at Headwaters, I knew I was on the right path. Being an Earth Caretaker touches the depths of my truth, this is who I am. I just needed to learn the skills by doing the work.

When I was first writing out my land of miracles, I thought I had to own the land I dreamed of, but it turns out I just needed to take ownership in it, in my heart. Headwaters is not my land legally, but it is my land to watch over, and I am forever grateful that I live my life as an Earth Caretaker.

I couldn't see what was ahead of me, until I let go of what I had only known before. I had to jump out of my comfort zone to get to a different perspective, so I could walk into my dream and live it, and I'm so glad I did.

Everything I have done before Headwaters has guided me, and trained me to do the work, and live the life I do now. From swimming, to coaching, to daycare, and all my relationships and experiences in between, good and bad, gave me relevant skills for my current life as a caretaker.

Even if your path seems to zig zag, you're still heading in the right direction. There just may be something else you need to experience, and learn, and gain skills from, before you are ready to take the next step forward.

Becoming Your Truth

Let nature become your reflection. In other words, let nature reflect your true self back at you. To be fully in nature, I mean one with the land, we must be our authentic selves. This profound honesty can be life changing.

Your relationship with nature can help you find your true self, and begin to live it. To be your true self, for many, is a life path of searching, and often coming up empty or lost or lonely.

In nature, if you find yourself not connecting, then take a moment. Be open and willing to learn. Become a student of life. The beauty in this is that forests, trees, water, animals, the Earth itself, all these beings want to take nothing from you. Sometimes it's a mystery, but it feels good.

We learn right away that nature reflects back to us its true self, no judgment, no control, no hatred or prejudice, no manipulation. Nature is just living for the sake of life.

Life itself is a sacred miracle. These teachings, and so many more, can come alive in us, and we can live them.

In nature, practice letting go of control, and you'll have the freedom to live fully. Imagine how long that primal self has waited to get out.

Remember, it's not your fault that you lost your true self. It was there when you were born, and then as you grew, you had to build your ego to get your needs met. You needed food and water, and warmth, so the world you grew up in took over to help you. Sometimes that was good, sometimes it was not so good. Parents, teachers, family, government, and your community, showed you, and told you how to live and survive, all with good intentions.

To live and survive in this world you built up your confidence in gaining those needs, and developed a personality. Your true self became smaller and smaller until it was a dim light.

Sadly, sometimes the light goes out for some of us. For many of us throughout life, that light flickers like a distant star, reminding us of who we are. We have moments of clarity, experiences, with friends, and relationships, that for a moment, makes that star brighter, and then we may forget again.

I was raised in nature, and by nature. I wasn't over-controlled, so nature showed me my true self, my authentic essence, daily. I never lost it, and as I grew into adulthood, I valued my true self so much, from my continued relationship with nature, that I wouldn't tolerate letting modern society take it from me.

It's simple, but it does take discipline. Go into nature and find your truth. The wilds will never disappoint. They will inspire you to give life to your authentic self.

It's Never Too Late

I remember one day in my outdoor school, a student who was working on connecting with a tree, came into camp crying. I asked her what happened, and her response was that after countless hours of time with the tree, it finally spoke with her. She said it took allowing her true self to come out, then she was able to let the tree into her being.

She was crying because she realized at forty-four years old, what she had missed all those years. It was truly a defining moment in her life.

Bringing your true self to your everyday life will only enhance all your relationships. There will be struggles, as some relationships won't be ready for this change.

Embrace love as a path, add a dose of patience, throw in some kindness, sprinkle on some gratitude. Allow in nature's true spirit, and you won't get lost again. Also, most importantly, get out there in the woods on a regular basis, and I promise you this, you'll be happy.

Dream Your Life Big

If you had one dream that would come true, what would it be? Be careful, your answer will reveal who you are.

Knowing your dream and letting it drift away is a great loss. Dreaming of good things is the birth of hope. Hope can become motivating action, which is what's needed. Movement equals new ideas, change, and fresh beginnings.

Never stop being the force of change. New hope is within all of us. Dream your life into reality. Dream the answers that will change the world and build your dreams alive.

Chase Your Dreams

My own personal medicine, who I am through my relationship with the Earth, and everything that's made me in my life, is that I'm a dreamer. I'm a person that dreams of ideas, and then I can physically and emotionally and intellectually make the ideas come true.

My outdoor school, where I work and live and caretake the land, is an example of where I dreamed the idea of a school first, and then I took it to the practical step-by-step world, and created it.

I'm going to challenge you that you all have wonderful dreams within you, and often give up on those dreams before they even leave your being. "It's too much money, it's too difficult, I don't have the education, there's nobody that can help me, I don't have the first clue of how to do it, I'm lazy."

Millions of ideas and many dreams just fall into the wastebasket right there. How many of them could have come true? How many lives would be changed?

Think of the concentric rings going out from people's lives being changed by living their dreams, making everyone and everything else on the planet better because of it. It makes you cry, but the good news is they keep coming, they don't ever stop.

I say dream big and write them down. Think about them, talk about them with people who care and that will support you. If those dreams are realistic in any way, and sometimes even not, even if they seem almost impossible, do what it takes to make them happen.

In the journey of making them happen, other dreams will be birthed. Hope will be birthed. You might even end up going a different path than when you started out, but you never know if you don't start after that dream.

Chase those dreams any way you can. Dream for lots of things. Dream for your own personal life, for your health, dream for what you want to do with your life. How do you want to show up? Where do you want to live? How much abundance do you want to have in your life?

Dream big, and then dream not only personally, dream big for the Earth. Dream big for your country.

Putting a dream out there changes the world. Your thoughts are energy, and energy follows thoughts. So, if your thoughts are dreams, you make them real through your attention. When you give them focused attention, those thoughts will go out into the world energetically, and begin to manifest.

It's even possible that your dreams will be caught by someone else, and they'll make them real. In fact, to grow your dreams you'll need others to help you. There might be dreams that include groups doing things together.

My current dream is that around the world people will take on becoming Earth Caretakers. They will start building chapters in each city, and look at their own area where they live, and get involved in making the planet better.

I have started a non-profit, The Earth Caretaker Way, where we can support land care and conservation projects all over the world. I have a dream that people are going to start creating wild spaces called Backyard National Parks.

We're going to recreate our yards and turn them into food gardens, animal gardens, and pollinator gardens, and heal the world.

I've got a dream that my government is going to become healthier, and better, and do good for the planet. In turn this will wake up other nations around the world, and that will be the action that brings people together, working for the Earth. I really have a dream for that. I have big dreams, and that's just the beginning.

I've created a wonderful life I truly believe in, by being a dreamer. It can happen for you as well. Make dreams real by putting the energy into them. If for some reason they don't happen don't get mad, reevaluate. Look at them again. Maybe you missed something. Maybe you do it a little differently, and if it doesn't work then you let it go. You pick yourself back up, and you come up with a new dream or come back to it later.

You never quit. You never give up, ever. Your life is worth being happy, being fulfilled, being close with the Earth, being a part of what makes the world better for all living beings. Start looking at your dream as a sacred thing.

People might be there for you, or they may not, but at the end of the day you're the one that must do it. If you put your intentions into motion, you will excite others, and they will be there to join in.

Sometimes there are things you must do alone as well. There are solo journeys, and that can be wonderful too.

The step forward on your life path is to dream big, manifest your dreams, and make them real. Our dreams have been waiting for us to give them life, and go fully into them. Live your dream. Why not? The path of mediocrity leads to sadness.

Abundance

Our Earth is the definition of abundance. Think of all the beings that live upon our Earth in abundance, this includes humans.

Greed and fear are our enemies. In abundance they disappear. Love, kindness, service, fulfillment, and happiness come alive. Thinking abundantly creates abundance. Live what you love, and abundance will follow.

Abundance doesn't always mean monetary, but money is ok too. Money is just energy, and you give it the power to give it meaning. Treat money as a tool. That's it. It's not for abuse of power.

We've put a darkness on money in our society because some people have it and some don't, and it can become a power play or status symbol. If you chase after money as a God, you will be left empty. Take the judgment out of it, and view it as an exchange of energy.

Money is like water, if you need to take a drink it's there, and then just let it flow. It's not meant to be hoarded and stagnant. Money can be used for the good and for stability. To find our true power we must let go of our fear of losing power. To let go, is freedom and power.

It's not bad to have a lot of money. It's nothing to be afraid of. It's all in your intention and generosity.

Good Words

Compassion, gratitude, kindness, service, love, caretaker, education, peace, imagine, art, play, laughter, wildness, wilderness, mentoring, gardening, working, abundance, open heart, joy, health, magic, connection, spirituality, justice, faith, mystery, empathy, beauty, respect.

These words need to *live* in each and every one of us human beings, and when directed toward the Earth it creates unity. When communities practice this, eventually some mystical tipping point is reached, and look out! —a new way is born.

What do you want your medicine to be? Consciously bring that aspect out in yourself and develop that gift. Everyone has gifts. These gifts are waiting for you to acknowledge them and give them life.

Each Day Is A Ceremony

Create each day, each week, each month, each year as a ceremony. A beginning, a middle and an end. Your ceremony begins when you wake and ends when you sleep.

Greet each day aware. Put out your intention for the day. Each new day is an open book. Create it, make it heavenly. Let your heart and love be your guide.

You can create ceremony for a friendship or to celebrate animals or changes of seasons. Your life is a ceremony. Celebrate it!

Create Your Own Holiday

Celebrate a day in honor of whatever you choose. A day of Blessings. Create how you would like to celebrate, and with whom. Take a day off work just for your own holiday. Name it whatever you would like. Enjoy it. It's your day.

To be a free thinker you need to be curious about the world we live in. Ask questions and seek answers.

Where To Begin?

What are your skills and talents? Use them as vehicles, your unique approach to Earth Caretaking. Ask questions to track your purpose and lead you to your dream life.

*What makes me come alive?
*Where do I put my thoughts and ideas? Where do I store them in the Universe? Let them out.
*What do I do that makes my soul smile? Ask my soul what it wants. Have that conversation, and more importantly, listen.
*Am I kind? *How* I live my life could be my life's purpose.
*What do I believe in? What am I passionate about? What am I here for on this Earth? What am I willing to die for?
*What does it mean to give my best? What do I want to get out of each day? What am I going to do to make that happen? What does it mean to be committed?
*Am I a supportable person? Will I listen to mentors and friends and family, and make necessary changes to grow and be a better person?
*What clues to my life has curiosity shown me? Imagine my life into reality. Image it.
*What have been my defining moments? Those moments where I made a decision that changed the course of my life or how I perceived myself?
*What places in my life do I check out, because I feel it's too big for me to take in, and deal with? Maybe it's time to check back in.
*What is the automatic tiller that helps me navigate when everything around me is going crazy? What helps put me back into balance, and back on track?
*What makes that wild woman or wild man inside of me happy? -Include that wild being as a part of myself always. Fully live with them as a conscious part of myself.
*What am I going to master?
*What would I do if I knew I had one day to live? How would I live it up?
*What is my legacy? What do I want to leave behind that makes the world a better place?

Journal Your Story

As you begin on this journey as an Earth Caretaker, with a daily life commitment, start to write your own story.

Start a journal and make it sacred. Note how you manifest yourself into an Earth Caretaker by looking at your strengths and your weaknesses. Begin by asking yourself how you personally affect the world.

How do you go through life? How does the Earth Caretaker in you show up in the work you do? How does it show up in your free time? How does it show up in your creativity or artistic time? How does it show up in your love relationships? With your friends? Your family? Your community?

What kind of a person do you see yourself developing into, with a huge part of who you are as an Earth Caretaker?

I found it is helpful to write a story and to visualize it. Visualize your future, maybe several futures? As you live your life, you'll start to manifest these visions.

Write down snippets of things that matter to you, observations you made about yourself. What new gifts appear for you when connecting to the Earth? Where do your greatest ideas come from? Write them down and study them.

Think about your dream life. Remember it's OK to be happy. It's OK to live a life of purpose. It's OK to make a difference in the world. In fact, it's not only OK, it is vital to our survival, and all beings that live on the Earth.

The more you live a good, beautiful life, the more you'll be willing to share that beauty with the world through service, through giving, and helping our planet.

So, write your story, manifest it, and be willing to change it if you need to. Add to it as you go, and take your life seriously.

322

Think about your life as a masterpiece painting that you get to create. You have the brushes to create that masterpiece. If something gets messed up, learn the lesson, brush over it, and create it again.

Be very careful who you give that brush to, to help you. We need help, we can't do it alone. We need mentors, we need elders, we need books, we need ideas, we need friends, and we need family to support us, but in the end, we are the ones who decide what is going into our masterpiece.

If you don't own your own painting of your life, someone else will take your brush from you, and create your life for you in the way that suits them. Those people, including your parents or friends, could have good intentions, but the focus of those intentions is through their eyes, not yours. Paint your own life. Do not give your paintbrush away. Create what is on your canvas.

Your Calling Is In Your Everyday Life

Your spiritual practice is not separate from your occupation or your everyday home life. Your spiritual connection is your everyday life.

Your Calling is your state of Being while you are doing whatever you are doing. It doesn't matter what you are doing physically. Are you kind? Are you being of service? Are you aware? Are you being creative? Are you living in gratitude? Are you living as your authentic Self? Then you are answering your Calling.

Nothing you do is a mistake unless you're not living in alignment with your personal values. No matter your occupation, you will always use those life skills.

Living your purpose is in your intention and what you bring to everything you do.

***

A Calling starts with an angst and a question that you can feel as a sensation. It's an insatiable feeling of seeking. You may not even know what the question is that you're trying to answer, but you physically feel it within you. At first you may not be able to articulate what the question is. It's an uncomfortable urge to figure out what it is.

There's a point where you feel like a squirrel preparing for times to come, even though you don't know what that is or what that means yet. Instinctually your spirit knows though. It's a Calling. It is a wake up that starts with a spark and burns until you do something about it. It eventually reveals itself as a brilliant sigh of relief, and an enthusiastic surge of inspiration.

There is no quenching the Call once it has ignited. If you try to ignore it because it seems impractical, it becomes painful, emotionally, physically, and spiritually. You have to act on it, or you will feel the light of your soul dimming.

Some people who just cannot bring themselves to follow that Call, tend to numb themselves from it, but it's always there. We are all born with this desire to manifest this inspiring life into reality. It's not easy to show up, but it's harder not to.

Tell The Truth About Yourself

Observe yourself through discernment. What do you need to live as your 100% authentic self? How much time do you need with people? How much time do you need away from people? Know what drains your energy, and know what feeds you, and go towards that.

Create an environment where you allow yourself to live who you are. Depending on where you live, creating your space may mean in a yard, in a corner of a room, or on a balcony. If that space is not currently at your house, then find a place you can visit regularly that fits what you need, until you are able to manifest it in your daily life.

Life decisions don't have to be either or. You can have all of the above, and you can always choose again.

Completely Live Your Story

Recreate your life story with found objects in nature. Use these items to symbolically tell your story. When you are done, ask yourself what feels complete and what is missing? Go back into nature, and live in those empty spaces to complete your story.

Participate In Life

*Live in partnership with birds, trees, and animals. Listen to their perspective. Take it into consideration. Watch and observe. Life is the true Mystery. Let nature show you how to live.

*Be the person your dog thinks you are. Your dog will happily show you how.

*Fulfill yourself so you have something to give back. Give yourself what you need in life.

*Surround yourself with the energy you want to resonate at, and live from.

*Appreciate the blessings you have.

*Take care of your body. Treat it as sacred. Every organ in your body is their own being. They have their own intelligence. Listen to your body, and respect it enough to make daily decisions to keep it healthy. Stay in good, physical, mental, and emotional shape. All animals in nature are in pristine shape or they perish.

Be less worried about how you look, and put more effort into how you feel. Our Earth ancestors were not burdened with mirrors. They weren't concerned about wrinkles. However, they could *feel* their youth and their health, and that's what is important.

*Remember to smile, it's good for everyone.

*All you do in nature leads up to this day. It's who you are. Go to nature and be you.

True success in life is measured by your value, not your valuables.

Make Friends With The Shadows

My mentor told me to make friends with my shadow side, and build a relationship with it. He said it lives in me as a part of me.

I have learned over the years your shadow side is that part of you that knows something is not OK, and takes part in it anyway. We must build a relationship with our shadow side so we can master it. Practice observing it from the outside.

Learn the power of the word no and mean it. Set boundaries and stick to them. Consciously let your shadow side out to play in non-harmful ways. Be creative with it, remember it is a part of you. You need all aspects of who you are to be in right balance and whole.

You cannot kill your shadow side; you must learn to relate to your shadow side, and embrace the gifts it has given you.

There is a reason your shadow side comes out. It usually surfaces if you feel threatened in some way. You can control how much you allow it to come out to protect yourself. It has been an ally at times. Honor that right relationship for what it has done for you, and then ask yourself if you need it to surface in the same way anymore. If not, thank it and let go of those actions you no longer need.

All parts of you can be sacred. Learn about all of you, and then you will flourish. You are not a victim to your shadow; it can be your friend. When you fear something, it is usually because you don't know it. Give your shadow side a name and acknowledge it. Then it will no longer have power over you, it will exist alongside you instead.

When you make friends with your shadow, it can become an asset when those traits are used for the good.

Let Go Of Attachments

When you're owned by your stuff, or your ideas, and you become attached to something, you lose something. You limit yourself.

Nature is always changing and transforming, so are we, but why are we afraid of change if we are a part of nature as well? Without change there is no growth. Allow room for growth. The only way to do that is to let go.

Self-Observation

Use your nature awareness skills on yourself. Observe yourself with no judgment. Pretend that another you is observing yourself. After practice, you won't even have to think about it.

Awareness through observation is the key to unlock the blinders of judgment, and the illusion of separation. Judgment comes from fear of the unknown.

Work on letting go of judgment. It limits you. It shrinks your world. It is a lifetime of work, but when you can open your mind and heart to another perspective, you are letting the world come into you, allowing your life to expand.

Take responsibility for the space you hold here in this life. Be conscious of your energy and how you affect the whole.

Look into the shadows that live in you. The thoughts that go through your head become your habits. Through self-observation, change what no longer serves you for your highest good.

In self-observation, remember to have a sense of humor, and allow room to laugh at yourself.

Acknowledge when you are being strong or confident. Even the tiniest of moments where you recognize these positive traits count. You develop those aspects more by acknowledging them. A moment of acknowledgement is a blessing, a healing you can give yourself, by honoring the beauty within. Your life is precious. If you don't treat yourself as if you are, how can you treat others as if they are?

Find Balance

Humans are confused, but we are perfectly confused. We have amazing brains, but that same brain that can create, can also destroy us.

We create weapons of mass destruction that can wipe ourselves out. What other being does that? What animal destroys their own environment to the point where they can't survive?

Why do we damage our Earth when we know it is harmful? Our shadow side must take some responsibility. Awareness and truth equal change.

To know when wrong is being done, and to do nothing, is a wound to our collective souls. You can't grow forward in life until you come from truth.

I'm Wondering

Are tornados, wildfires, hurricanes, and droughts the Earth's shadow side? I'm not sure that the Earth has a shadow side. I think this is a human dilemma birthed from our egos, still I wonder.

Honor Commitment

A core teaching in my school is summoned up in the powerful words of Goethe. I cannot emphasize enough the importance of seizing a moment, and fully committing to making it happen. Without commitment, complacency takes over and dreams die.

***

"Until one is committed there is hesitancy, the chance to draw back, always ineffectiveness. Concerning all acts of initiative (and creation) there is one elementary truth, the ignorance of which kills countless ideas and splendid plans; that the moment one definitely commits oneself, then providence moves too. All sorts of things occur to help one that would never otherwise have occurred. A whole stream of events issues from the decision, raising in one's favor all manner of unforeseen incidents and meetings and material assistance, which no man could have dreamt would have come his way. Whatever you can do, or dream you can, begin it. Boldness has genius, magic, and power in it." - Goethe

***

Animals, plants, trees, insects, amphibians, spiders, birds, are all committed to fully living life or they die. They give their best, it's all they know. Being a hard worker is a good life skill.

When you go into nature as a student, these sacred beings will eagerly show up and guide you. Once you are committed to what you are creating, spirit moves in. All beings work with you. Those forces align with you to assist you on your journey.

To be fully committed is to live a full life. When you're halfway in, you're halfway out. Next time you're by an ice, cold lake, let nature inspire you and jump in. You'll know full commitment.

Be *That* Person

Create a Spiritual Code of Honor for the essence of who you are. When those words become you, you don't have to think about being those things. You just are. Don't give up or give in to mediocrity or lower your value standards.

The world is full of nay-sayers, and they aren't always people, sometimes they are experiences. Do whatever it is you are reaching for anyway.

Concern without action is worry. Worrying serves no purpose. Take action.

All Work Has Medicine

Start your work by doing something to perfection. A job well done is pure bliss. Action speaks most honestly. Let right intention be your words, and your life's path will unfold.

Self-Mastery

What does that mean? To me it means possibly an unreachable goal, but a noble quest to always improve, and grow through many experiences. It means reaching to be the best human being I can be, while I'm here on this Earth.

It means when I mess up, that I will do my best to make it right with others, and most importantly with myself.

Self-Mastery to me is a way of life to strive for, with the knowledge that, I'm not sure anyone really ever achieves their idea of a perfect result.

What is more important, is that it gives the idea of hope and inspiration. It's a challenge towards a life well lived, while simultaneously living in gratitude for where I'm at along the journey of striving to be a good person.

There most likely will always be hiccups, but I'm getting better at laughing at them, and to me, that is a success.

Partnership With Our Earth

Nature never forgets. Leave it alone and it will return. Give it a helping hand, and it will return more brilliant than ever.

When you are a champion for the Earth you are paving the way for an incredible life for all.

Listen For The Call

When you answer a calling, you need to tend it, nurture it, and let it grow within you. Have the courage to live your ideal life, and manifest it. A great idea and great accomplishments start with one person, and that's you.

Often, to be a person of right action requires getting out of our comfort zones, but there is comfort and beauty in being uncomfortable.

Ask for what you want, do the work, and allow your path to unfold.

Every day has the potential to be your best day. Go to nature and find wonder and beauty and magic.

Another Opportunity

When you go to bed each night, take a moment to ask yourself if you gave your best, and if you fully lived that day. If so, then go to bed smiling in your heart.

If not, then go to bed smiling in your heart, knowing that you have an opportunity for a do-over, another chance to live fully tomorrow, and have gratitude for that.

How Will You Be Remembered?

Being an Earth Caretaker doesn't interfere with other things you do, but it is the most important thing you do. It is vital to sustaining our lives. Whatever we choose to do in life all relates to caretaking the planet that gives us life.

When I look across my land, through the trees at the top of Mt. Shasta, I am honored to be the caretaker of this land. To be a part of this land, to me, is like being at the top of that mountain. I feel like this is my greatest achievement. It is my greatest gift to myself, being the caretaker of this land. I don't take it lightly at all. It is an honor.

Ask yourself, how will you be remembered when you're gone from this physical life? Live life with intention and act with purpose, and you will achieve great things. Whether you're saving a spider in the corner of your house or saving a coral reef, or demanding social justice, it all matters.

When you ask yourself how will your efforts be remembered, you're not only thinking about how other human beings will remember, but also, how will the trees remember? How will the animals, and plants, and water, and mountains remember? How will the Earth itself remember? What will it take to make that vision happen?

Take one step towards creating positive change today. This is not a list to make for the future. Today is the day.

Join or start organizations to fight for our planet's health. Get involved locally making the environment better. Educate yourself on what animals need. Don't use poisons in your yard or home. Create wildlife habitat.

Vote for the planet. Whoever you vote for should be an Earth lover that will use their office and power in service of the planet. Write letters to our representatives of what issues need attention.

Sit in old growth trees to save them from being cut down. Speak up and let people know what you think.

Much of the research of what needs to be done is out there, and it's part of your journey to find the information. In the journey of searching, you may discover how you want to be remembered.

In learning how to be a good Earth Caretaker you discover yourself. You connect with your personal essence.

Make sure you leave this Earth knowing that it is a better place because you were here. Your legend is within your own decisions and control. You are a gift waiting to be opened. Use your gifts and we will all be better for it.

Every day matters. Every day you have lived led up to this day. It's who and what you are, a sum total of all your experiences. You are as extraordinary as any other being on this planet, no more, no less. You are pure potentiality. You are a miracle.

A life with a higher purpose is a life well-lived, and a blessing to all. The two most important days of your life are the day you were born, and the day you wake up and realize what your purpose is in being here.

Be A Leader By Doing It

Lead and inspire others to be Earth Caretakers. If you believe in yourself others will believe in you too. If you don't believe, others won't either, and nothing will ever get done.

The only way to know you can do it, is by doing it. Your attitude in life will be your experience. Be a part of the greater good. Be a part of the solution.

Service

To be of service, with no expectations of compensation, is to be in our highest state of human evolution. Service is love and kindness manifested. Each moment of service changes the world.

What you do matters. Your actions regarding our Earth matters. Get involved. It's in our collective interest to turn your love of Earth into positive, productive action.

True inner peace comes from being involved in something great. Something great for other living beings. Find your place in the web of life and live well. Give the offering of yourself to our Earth, and your life will be one highlight after another. Be a part of what makes a day beautiful.

Universal Beauty And Purpose

Why are trees beautiful? Why is water beautiful? Why is the sound of water beautiful? Why are wildflower meadows beautiful? Why is it beautiful to see a bee taking nectar from a flower and making life for us? Why is it beautiful to see a bird of prey fly thousands of feet above and cast their shadow over us? Why do we all see so many of the same things as beautiful? What makes them beautiful?

The Earth is the finest work of art that was ever created, and it's personal to us because it's our home.

I learned as a nature photographer how beautiful life on Earth is. I spent much of my life photographing nature's sanctuary, and the secret moments in nature, and then sharing them with people.

I watch the reaction in people's eyes in awe and it has taught me so much. It showed me that nature is literally food for our souls. I know my life's work of photographing our world is a part of my legacy. I know that part of my purpose is to share our universal beauty, and inspire others to notice it as well.

Daily Reminders:

*Wake up and soak in the day. Think about what you're going to do each day. How can you make it the best day of your life? Listen to the birds singing you awake. Listen to all sounds, the animals, the Earth breathing through the wind. Take in the smells that change throughout the day.

Go to sleep the same way. Think about the day and go back over it. What could you have done differently? What was perfect? What did you learn? What did you feel connected to? Did you grow in any way that day?

*Have quiet reflection time, it's just as important every day for your health and growth, as eating.

Be sure to self-reflect and journey into yourself. Learn about your higher selves, who you are at your core truth. Do you know who you are? What do you believe in? What would you truly put your life on the line for?

If you don't consider these questions and discover your own truths, and you don't take time to honor them every day, then the world around you will define you. You may one day wake up and say, that's not me. You realize you haven't been living as your authentic self, that you came here to be.

*Take time every day to meditate and go on a spiritual journey into nature. Take a walk of meditation through the woods or a park. Journey into the higher realms, the places we call our medicine areas.

*Do something creative, whether you're building something or working on a two-minute project stacking rocks, or working with the beauty of a creek, or painting your home, be creative in some way every day to fill your soul.

*Live your purpose by doing work that matters. Whatever your occupation is, you can always live your life's purpose in your everyday life. Let what you love animate your life into action. When you are powered by passion, the money will follow.

*Ask yourself what you can change so that you are not the problem. You cannot simply remain an observer. Non-action doesn't work. Humans, animals, and the planet are intrinsically connected, every action and non-action affects each of us.

*Be generous. Live in abundance. Share the beauty of what you have, whether it's intellectual, emotional, or physical, share it with the Earth itself. Go out and sing to the land and trees, play with them, they love it.

*Give thanks and blessings for the day. It's important to give blessings all day long. A blessing is wishing another being well, not just humans, but it can be for a butterfly or a snake or a plant.

Taking a moment to wish it well, giving it thanks, and seeing it living a good life is all that is needed. That act alone creates an opening that starts to manifest as a connection and healing. Giving blessings is a tremendous healing power. Positive intention may not always be physically felt, but the physical results will at some point be seen.

*Please realize you are special. For the soul of humans and for the soul of the Earth, think about how you live your life. It's our differences that make life worth celebrating. Rejoice in that.

There are so many things you can do, but I would have to say the most important of all is to love. Ask yourself, how does that show up in your life?

Treat your life as sacred. Make your life count for something. You're right at the edge of your life…jump off!

Chapter 34
Educate Yourself

Education is vital to work for our Earth. Educate yourself to the needs of our planet, and all beings. It's the responsibility of all Earth lovers.

There is great power in education, ideas grow, and dreams become possible. We become more creative, and more attractive inside and outside. We become more engaged in our lives, and it's fun to learn.

There are many ways to educate ourselves. Traditional schooling is great, but it is only one way to gain knowledge. We learn through curiosity, observing, wonderment, and hands-on activity.

Ask questions of our Earth. Ask your teachers and mentors questions. Apprenticeships are extremely beneficial for learning from those who have paved a path before us.

If humans are not learning, then we are not taking advantage of fully living. Life on Earth is defined by learning. It is vital to the growth of our whole being. It is vital to developing our Earth medicine, the very essence of who we are.

Be a lifelong student of life. Be in love with learning and growing. Knowledge is the power that gives you the freedom of choice. The more you know, the more your world expands.

A person who is educated in many facets of life, usually tends to live in a good way, and is in a position of being able to lead through their life experience.

In the knowledge you gain, you may find a path to your greatness that's waiting to emerge. The world is waiting for you to show up with these new tools and get to work. Armed with the power of knowledge, get off your butt, and put into action what you say you believe.

The most impactful, environmental action you can take is to invest in a child's education.

I'll Figure It Out

When I moved to Mount Shasta from the Bay Area to be the land caretaker, and camp cook at Headwaters, I didn't know how to do the jobs I was hired to do. So, I did what anyone with a dream and a passion to make it happen does, I faked it.

I had a vision of where I wanted to live, and what I wanted to be doing, and to make that happen, I had to take a big risk and jump in when the opportunity came up.

I learned by watching others. I learned by watching videos, and by reading. I learned by asking family and friends, and ultimately, I learned by just doing it.

I don't do well in traditional school settings, so I figured out how to learn what I needed to know by using other resources, and it worked for me. Get creative in educating yourself, there's more than one way.

I made mistakes through my trial-and-error approach, but it has all been an amazing dream life, and I don't regret a single moment.

I have grown through my learning, and that has allowed me to live my best, most wonderful life. I had to let go of my fears that held me back, and break through those limiting beliefs of what I thought was possible for me.

I still need pep talks from friends when I need to stretch myself and try new things. Yet, once I jump in, there are no doubts that I am doing what I'm supposed to be doing, even when it gets tough sometimes.

Everything I have learned in life has made me a better caretaker of the Earth.

Make this a why not life. Why not try everything and have those experiences you dream of?

Expand your awareness. Look into someone's eyes and see the beauty within them. Look into the history of someone and ask more questions.

Step Up And Be Heard

I don't want to stand out. I don't want to take responsibility for what I know. What new thoughts do I have to share? What do I have to say that hasn't already been said?

Maybe it's all been said and heard, but it hasn't been said from my perspective, from my experience. So, do I still need to speak up? I guess I do.

Study

Read the great naturalists from our past and present. Many of them have great wisdom in their words. Their writings will educate and inspire you. When I was eleven years old, I read a book called, *"The Last Great Auk"* by Allan W. Eckert

This book was about the first documented animal species to be wiped off our planet by humans. The Auk was a flightless bird that lived on islands in the North Atlantic.

While they were clumsy on land, in the ocean they could fly, and they were masterful at hunting fish. They had no fear of humans. Sailors would come into their habitat and club them to death for food and for sport.

There used to be millions of these wonderful birds. In just a few short years of explorers encountering them, all the Auks were gone. The last two Auks and their nest of eggs were clubbed to death. Once the last eggs were crushed it was the end of the Great Auk forever. For what? For callous amusement.

I remember crying when I learned of this horrific deed. This book was instrumental in turning me into a warrior for our Earth.

In 1985 I went to the Smithsonian Museum of Natural History and saw a stuffed Great Auk. It was a surreal experience. My Godson was with me, and I told him the story, and I cried again.

Read nature writings by wonderful naturalists. We are blessed to have so many. I admire the writings of the great Earth Keepers, Ralph Waldo Emerson, John Muir, and Henry David Thoreau. They all live on in me.

Writing is a human gift. Write in your own journal. Express your love of Earth through words for others to be inspired by.

Know What To Buy

Educate yourself on how to live for our Earth. How to buy food and other supplies. Spend your money on things that are good for our planet. In capitalism, spending money makes a huge impact. What you are interested in, businesses will supply. As the saying goes, money talks. So, speak well.

Know Truth

I believe in science, but let's be honest, science gave us the bomb, it gave us gasoline, plastic and countless inventions that are destroying us. It gives us truth and sometimes truth is tough, but once we know truth, we have knowledge, and we then have the choice to do what's right with our new discoveries.

Science is a blessing. Let's make sure it is used for the good of all.

Self-Reliance

The art of self-reliance is becoming lost to modern humans. As we moved into the industrial age around the late 1800's, we began to leave behind our personal relationship with our Earth. Living off the land and with it, is truly a deep loss we feel now in this world that we have created. A world where so much of daily life is done by someone or something other than us.

Our way of life is quickly becoming the age of artificial intelligence, which will take us even further away from the art of self-reliance.

When we lived closer to the land, we had to do everything we needed to do to live. We did these daily tasks such as acquiring food, shelter, water, and fire, in partnership with our Earth. That relationship created a bond of love and respect.

Now for most of us, our food comes from stores already prepackaged. We go to the hardware stores for supplies and tools, and we call service people for almost all our needs.

While all these things are very convenient, we have gotten out of balance and have given up our knowledge, and our own power. The personal relationship we had naturally with our Earth has drifted away. We must reclaim this connection of love and respect for our Earth by being more self-reliant, and interacting directly with the land.

One way of being self-reliant in nature is by going out onto the land. Take very little with you, perhaps only a knife and a wool blanket. Go barefoot. Make a shelter, build a fire. Leave your cell phones and computers at home.

Let someone know where you will be and then go into wilderness areas, wild places where you're not the top predator. Be humbled.

Educate yourself, and gain wisdom through your experiences. Part of wisdom is knowing your limits and gently pushing on. A slow march to deeper wisdom, equals inner peace.

This is a very big jump to take but believe me, you'll find a new freedom. Fires will ignite within you. Old memories of your past and your ancestor's lives will come forth.

Knowledge from generations will awaken within, and your instincts of how to live and take care of yourself and the Earth, will take over.

Come back from this time out and become more self-reliant at home. Create things. Fix things, use your head and your hands to figure out your own solutions. Self-reliance truly equals freedom. In learning to take care of your basic needs you will be living from your greatest potential. Let the Earth be your teacher.

Vote For The Earth!

Participate in life. Educate yourself about the world you live in and on. Knowledge equals power. Evil doers count on ignorance and laziness.

We are agreeing to give away our freedom and power to the rulers when we do not educate ourselves, or participate in the decisions our countries make. The most chilling and eye-opening quote I have ever heard is, "What luck for the rulers that men do not think." - Adolf Hitler

Let that sink in. He knew the power he had over the people that follow blindly and don't think for themselves. When people do not want to take responsibility for their own choices, they hand over their power to someone else.

If we don't participate, and step up and speak up, we are allowing space to be filled by those who mean harm. We leave the door open for the worst of us to take over, in the name of greed, corrupt power, and control, at the expense of our Earth and our freedom.

Sometimes humans must go low, I mean fall very low, before we can see the light and begin to reach for it.

Fifty percent of Americans did not vote in the most high stakes election we've had, and we ended up with a nightmare for our Earth and the people. People were voted into office who do not respect the validity of science, or the urgency of our climate crisis. There is little or no heart-connection to the Earth, or compassion for those who are different from them.

I get so angry when I talk to so many young people who love nature, and are proponents for human rights, but didn't vote. It is truthfully a gut punch. I take it personally, especially as a mentor to many of these young adults.

They either didn't care or pay attention to their world, or made various excuses of why they thought that it didn't matter if they voted.

This is not a subject to dance around and sugar coat. We need to address this directly and make a change today.

By *not* participating in managing the health of our planet, we went backwards in healing our Earth, and righting wrongs. Many lives were affected negatively, and many lives were lost due to the rollback of environmental protections that had been in place.

We are now reinstating those protections and moving forward, but it will always be a back and forth battle to establish balance. Those who are acting solely on their own interests and motives, are counting on people being passive. This is why it is so important to continue to educate ourselves, and to continue to participate in decisions that affect us and our planet.

Educate yourself with legitimate resources, not entertaining "news" channels. Do your research. Read and investigate beyond the headlines. Get curious. Write letters to your local, and federal representatives. Speak up. You make a difference.

Democracy is like a living Being. It is comparable to our Earth. For a governing body to work, it needs to be cared for. A democracy is beautiful when the people nurture it, and care for it, and participate in it. You have to own it, and you have to actively manage it.

When we take giant steps to get back on track, we can keep going forward and do better than before. When we get complacent, we slip back into old, unconscious habits, and we lose ourselves again.

To make a democracy work, we the people must participate, and first and foremost that means we need to educate ourselves and vote.

Vote for saving the land, and wild parks, and wildernesses. Vote for causes that help stop pollution and destruction of our home.

Vote for people that care about the Earth and want to protect her. Watch their actions, not just their words. People who truly care for the planet are generally good people. Good people usually do good things. Vote for people who care about *all* people.

Remember, that the people we elect to represent us are supposed to be in their positions as a public service. Serving the people and our causes to create and maintain countries that work for *all* humans, of all ethnicities and incomes, as well as for the animals, the land, and the waterways. Wanting what's good for everyone is not radical. It should be normal.

We must study, and research, and ask questions about our countries, and our leaders. Have a healthy skepticism, and an open mind as well.

The easiest, most powerful, and most honorable thing people can do to make a difference in the health and protection of our Earth, and the well-being of humans, nationally and globally, is to vote. Voting is a sacred act. It is your voice speaking up for the future, and history of our planet.

Every single vote matters. You matter. Your community needs you. Your nation needs you. Our global community needs you to speak up and to always, always vote for the Earth.

The bottom line is that nothing else matters if our Earth is not taken care of first. Our lives depend on her being healthy.

These next elections are defining moments affecting the future of our Earth, and our liberties and personal rights. Dictatorships begin by banning truthful information from the people. We can't afford to be shocked into disbelief and silence. Pay attention to what is happening in your cities, and with your country.

As soon as the media stops covering a story, just causes fade into the background and nothing changes. We need to continue to keep all these important issues in the forefront, until there is action to

correct corruption. We can take down the giants. They have more money, but we have more people power and passion for our Earth.

***

At the base of Mt. Shasta there are a handful of smaller towns that are uniquely independent in themselves, but also together create a community based around the presence of Mt. Shasta.

One of the many things Mt. Shasta is known for is its pure spring water. People go to the community park to fill their water jugs straight from the headwaters of one of the springs. The water is for everyone to share freely, but of course the corporations always jump at the monetary opportunities that could be had.

As a kid I would have never thought that water was something we would ever have to buy. The Earth's blood, its living energy, is our lifeline. Without it we die, but some people feel we need to pay for our right to live.

We have had very big companies try to hoard the water and monopolize the springs. They approach the small-town city councils, promising job opportunities to help the local economy.

They don't tell you the environmental destruction it will bring, as well as the privatization of the land that will no longer be available to the public to enjoy.

One of the most hypocritical aspects of one of the bottling companies that was operating in our area, is that they bottle the natural spring water, and then add chemicals to make it "safe". They tell their employees they can take some of the bottled water home, but that they shouldn't drink it for ten days to avoid getting diarrhea.

We have fought off one of these corporations for years, but they are persistent with their lawyers coming back year after year, to try to wear the citizens down.

We are also battling a large truck stop from being built directly across the freeway, from an already established truck stop. These large truck stops are environmental hazards, and fire hazards to our community.

We have fought off large ski parks and condominium tracks that were hoping to buy up the property that our Headwaters land is on. I have nothing against ski parks, but we already have one on the south side of Mt. Shasta, and we do not need another development here wiping out our wild lands.

On a side note, there used to be a ski resort high up on Mt. Shasta, and she shook it off with an avalanche. So, that tells you how she feels about that.

My point is that all communities have choices to make about what it is they hold as value, and what they are willing to protect. There will always be people in the community who disagree from their perspective. Hopefully the majority will look to the long-term benefits of saving land for the land itself, and prevail in that fight.

It will take commitment to continue to show up at the city council meetings and make your voice heard, and vote for what you know is right. I can promise you those who want to monopolize a natural source, will count on the community's complacency. They will take advantage of non-participation every single time they come back.

***

America specifically, is a work in progress. I love my country and I believe in the Constitution, the Declaration of Independence, and our Bill of Rights. Our country has been responsible for many wrongs, such as the genocide of Native Americans, and slavery, and many other atrocities. As a country we need to admit and take responsibility for our immoral actions, and open the door for healing.

We have righted some of our wrongs. We ended slavery and gave women their inherent right to vote. We fought in World War II and helped end fascism and genocide. We have established policies to protect wildlands and waterways. I could go on and on listing the wrongs and the rights our country has done, and is still doing, but this is where I find hope. I know we can and will do better. This is why I vote, and in the end, I believe that good will win over evil. The path forward won't be easy, but it is the only path.

The scale can tip back in the right direction, but we need all of us committed and on board to fight the good fight. The future of the Earth depends on all of us voting. You count. You matter. There is no time to be passive. Join organizations that help the Earth. Donate where you can. Take action today!

Embrace the challenge of being alive at this time in human history on our Earth. Help lead the march forward into that thriving future that is waiting to come true. It's our time to do whatever it takes, no matter how hard or complicated.

334

Our power is in being educated and taking action. Let's bring in a future of love of Earth, and love of all life. Vote with your heart. Vote because our lives depend on you!

There's Always Hope

As I was growing up, I was profoundly affected by the loss of animals. I fought as hard as I could as a kid. I wrote letters, I volunteered on projects, I tried to educate myself about the world.

As much as we don't like to see hard things, it's important to know the good and the bad of what's going on. There's a saying that says, know your enemy. You must know who does these detrimental things and why. Often, it's not the right thing to hate these people. Knowing them beyond the surface allows room for some compassion, and maybe some understanding as to what motivates them, so that we can work within society to change things.

The Wilderness Act of 1964 was a great human achievement that we came together on. In this act, humans showed how great they can be. It was a defining moment in human life, which birthed hope for all life.

Another beautiful thing that was created is the Endangered Species Act. People gathered information and made decisions through the studies done by naturalists and biologists, of why certain animals were in trouble of going extinct. Based on the results of the studies, those animals at severe risk were put under complete and total protection.

The Endangered Species Act shows human beings at our best, when we do what we are capable of with good intent. We identified the problem and we came up with a solution. We voted it into law and then we practiced it.

It brought back the Peregrine Falcon, which was shot almost to the point of oblivion for really no reason. There were many other animals in danger of extinction including the Brown Pelican, the Bald Eagle, and the California Condor, many fish species, as well as small and large mammals, including the Grey Wolf.

Conservationists went out and caught many of these animals and bred them to bring back their population. I remember going to the University of California Santa Cruz where they had a breeding program for the Peregrine Falcons. I spoke with the falconer and scientists there when I was younger and was given a tour. It was very inspiring. They were raising enough of these birds that they could release them back into the wild.

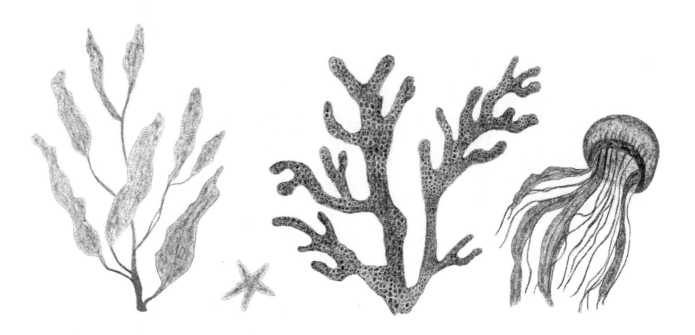

335

Can you imagine not seeing pelicans along the ocean? To me it's just as important to see a fleet of pelicans soaring above the crests of the waves as it is to see the water.

Many of these animals have made a comeback and have been taken off the Endangered Species List. We righted the wrong. We had the intellectual knowledge, we had the physical ability, we had the people studying the animals that cared, and we made it right.

I reflect back to the time when John Muir had to endure the building of the Hetch Hetchy Dam in Yosemite, flooding the magnificent, granite sculpted valley. It seemed impossible that it could happen, and yet it did.

John Muir lost himself in grief. One day that dam will come down and he will smile, and the Earth will heal itself in time. Hope is vital to have healing. When you stay educated and fully engaged, you feel a part of the solution, you feel hope and inspired to act. Educate yourself by learning what others before you have accomplished, and then go out and continue the legacy of right action.

These are tough times for nature lovers. There's a lot of weight on our shoulders and it's easy to give up, but don't ever give up. We are fighting for our planet. There is nothing more important and we must make time for it.

If we don't change the way we're treating the Earth and not living sustainably, we will also one day be on that endangered species list.

I truly find hope in that we are able to identify problems, and that we have solved them before. When we're coming from love, and at our best, we are dream beings.

At times like these is when a Scout-Earth Caretaker with heart is needed most. To be an Earth Caretaker is to be a hero for all of nature and humanity, and it is a noble cause.

Some of these problems are so huge right now in this world, that we must get together globally to grow out the other side of them in a good way. I do have hope that we will answer these problems that are facing us. Until my last breath, I'm fighting for the right side.

Chapter 35

Gather Community

The Earth itself is a community of living beings, and humans are clearly a part of it. Sadly, and much to our great loss, we try to pull ourselves out of our Earth community.

We need to claim our place in this Earth community with honor and respect. All animals are teachers of community. Start now to live with other humans and our Earth in a good, loving way. Live as a part of something bigger than yourself. It's the Earth-way, the only way.

Change your perspective to seeing a community as something bigger than a few individuals. A true community spreads out like a spider web, reaching out beyond what you can see, connecting all species as one.

Create A Sustainable Community

Create a community based on respect for the land. On our land in Mount Shasta we have created a space like this. We are growing our own garden to feed our students, with extra food going to our neighbors. Our honey bees pollinate our land, as well as our neighbor's in a 2–3-mile radius.

Our larger community of Mount Shasta City, and Siskiyou County, have also begun creating an Earth-based extended community, with the ideas of respect for nature and self-reliance. Treating animals raised for food with respect and growing healthy food at a fair cost. There are small, family farms, as well as larger family ranches, with pasture raised animals, that sell direct to each household.

We certainly cannot trust large corporations to care for us or our Earth. It's not reasonable to expect the government to do it all. Our government can help, but when we put it all on the government to fix our problems, we give away our power. We, the people, must do it ourselves.

All Earth-based teachings passed down from our ancestors are about self-reliance, and supporting our communities.

Nurturing A Community

My outdoor school has become a seasonal community of Earth-loving people. We teach the ways of Earth living for adults and children, on our beautiful property at the foot of Mt. Eddy, near Mt. Shasta. Our land is sacred space, which has become a center for this community of students and teachers.

The community has put their good medicine into it, creating in cooperation with nature. It amazes me as this happened in an organic, natural process, with very little manipulation or planning.

As the leader of the school, I was able to identify this process early on, and with some gentle nudging, and mostly just letting go, was able to participate in the creation of a truly sacred space. It does take vision and dreaming, and someone needs to take that role, but trust in community, and the life-giving spirit of nature, to create what is needed.

It's so hard to remember to get our egos out of the way. Too much control will kill any good nature-based community. Good leaders and organizers must also control their greed, encourage sharing of resources, and practice abundance thinking. This is exactly how indigenous leaders made their communities work successfully in the past.

Community must be able to be creative. If heart, soul, and kindness can be first, then nature can truly be a winner. I believe this is one of our great hopes for our future on this planet.

At Headwaters we get to live closer to how human beings are supposed to live. We are heard, and we can tell our personal stories. We create strong friendships, and this feeds our souls.

Everyone contributes to caretaking our home. Everyone puts in their share of work. Even though I am the legal owner of the land, we all take ownership in the land, and take pride in it. We put in our own creativity towards whatever we are working on.

We respect each other, and recognize we are a valuable member of the community. At Headwaters, people who can use their hands on physical, trades skills are highly valued, and respected as much as someone who has a business or medical degree. There is not a hierarchy as far as the importance of jobs goes.

We check in on each other. We are kind with others, the land, and animals, as well as with ourselves.

We create art in many forms. Our building structures fit in with the environment and add to it. We grow much of our food, we honor it, and we eat well. We have dubbed our camp food as rustic, primitive gourmet.

When we do have differences, we work them out, and clean up any wrongs with each other as soon as possible. We focus on not spreading gossip. We work on speaking the truth, even when it's hard. It is tough getting feedback that is not favorable, but if given with sincere heart, we do our best to take it in and feel if it is a truth, and something to work on.

It's not realistic to think everyone will always get along. We work and live with each other 24 hours a day, seven days a week, for months at a time. When you are in a full-time relationship in a small community, whether it be a romantic relationship, friendship or co-worker relationship, your sensitivities are going to get magnified.

People will be forced to look at their own strengths and weaknesses, and work with them and through them, or the community collapses. As we stick with each other through the other side of tough times, we can usually get to the point of laughing at ourselves, and our relationships strengthen.

We laugh a lot, even if we are doing the most unglamorous tasks at the time. We share quality community time together. We come together for teachings, and then allow room for people to have their own space out in nature. We encourage each other to get out in the woods, and in the water whenever possible.

What makes our community special is the wide range of ages, cultures, and genders that are here interacting with each other. We also include our dog pack as part of the community.

The land itself is sacred, and is treated as a plant and animal sanctuary, where humans also live. The community at Headwaters is not different from others. We just focus on *how* we live.

Say Hello

I had a few appointments at a physical therapy center, and each time while I was waiting for the technician to come get me, I had a nice chat with the elderly gentleman who was greeting people at the door. He was such a pleasant man, with always something positive to say. In those few minutes, he would share a little about his life hiking in the sierras, and tell me about his favorite places to visit.

One day when I was walking back with the technician, I asked her about the man in front, and she said she didn't know anything about him. She didn't know his name and had never spoken to him. That surprised me because she was a very friendly, talkative person as well. In the few moments I was walking with her, I knew her name, what kind of music she listened to, when her days off were, and what she was planning to do over the weekend for fun.

I am not a very talkative person myself when I don't know someone, but by asking one question of interest about their lives, they were so happy to share about themselves.

I encouraged her to say hi to the man next time she walked up front, and to introduce herself. I told her she will enjoy his company.

Even if you work at a large company or in this case a hospital, get to know each member of your work community. Take time to interact with them, even if it's just a few moments at a time. You will be surprised how quickly you feel more like a member of a community, than an employee at a business.

Relationships Are Sacred

Humans need each other. We need elders and young people. Humans are part of the life cycle, and we need each other for balance.

Create a community to be of support and to protect you. Then call on your community for that support. Through tough times find companionship. Create your community consciously with people who lift you up and inspire you to be a better person. Raise the quality of who you keep company with.

Don't isolate, we need each other. Your community is your true social security. Our ancestors knew this.

Everyone, in a community, needs to be an active member of its tribe. Young children and adults need to be accountable for their role within it.

A community starts within one's own family and extends out to neighborhoods, cities, states, countries, and the planet. Build relationships by tending them.

Allow room for partnership, and allow space for differences, to take in new ideas. In partnership you have a second set of eyes watching out for you. Instead of getting defensive in a disagreement, see through their perspective of what you might not be seeing for yourself. You may not agree with them, but you can at least understand where they are coming from, and take that view into consideration. Ask your partner what they need. Go into them, instead of pulling away.

In a community setting it's not about you as an individual. It's not about the one. It's about focusing on the whole, and in doing so it makes the one better.

We grow up in our tribe. Be open to other ways of being and living. Be open to understanding different ideas and beliefs, and expand your tribe.

Boundaries Are Needed

Sometimes there are tough lessons to grow through when interacting with other people. Not all people are good, some are just bad. The hard part is how to know who a person is before you have a bad run in. Use your intuition and watch their actions, not just their words.

On a side note, we watch how our dogs respond to people when they come to our land. Sometimes people are just nervous around dogs, so the people are hesitant, and that's a normal reaction, and our dogs are still very welcoming to those people.

What triggers a warning signal with us, is if one or more of the dogs completely backs away from a person and sometimes cowers with side eye while looking at them. It is very rare when that happens, but 100% of the time the dog was right. They turned out to be a shady person.

Through those bumps in the road with others, never give up your medicine or your personal power. As you create a community that lifts you up, be willing to let go of those who do harm, no matter who they are.

Honey Bees

Learn about bee colonies, and you will learn all that humans need to know to live in a balanced community. A bee colony decides collectively what is needed to keep it healthy, and in balance and thriving. The queen is protected but does not make the decisions.

The bees all participate in each job and grow into each position. If something happens and the jobs are out of balance, other bees step up and learn those tasks earlier. They get it done for the sake of the colony. Each member of the colony is relied upon to keep the colony healthy and safe.

Learn from the honey bees, and watch caretaking and being of service in daily action.

Storytelling

There's nothing like a good story of a nature experience to bring us together. Share your story. Entertain your friends, write your story, sing your story, dance your story. It's a treasure that keeps the experience alive.

In the days before technology, storytelling was vital to the community. People love a good story. It fills our hearts and connects us with each other, and to our Earth.

Everyone has an entertainer in them. Give your story life, and share your experience with your community.

Be an active member of our global community. It is our responsibility to show up and have our voices heard. Each of us matters.
If we want a harmonious world, then we need to participate and make it happen.

Chapter 36

Seek Mentors And Be A Mentor

The art of mentoring is as important as anything we humans do. It is vital to our growth. For humans to develop into good people who live from kindness, and from service, and from purpose, and love, we need to be consciously mentored.

Mentoring could save us and our planet. Our ancestors knew this value because it ensured their survival. They knew that younger people learn by watching, and listening, and feeling. They knew spending time with an adult, alongside them while they worked, was teaching through action.

Indigenous cultures revered their elders. They were the people who had survived the hardships, and who had the knowledge and wisdom of experience to help the tribe survive. A tribe or community couldn't make it without their elders to guide them to hunting grounds, or to spring meadows filled with edible and medicinal plants.

Their knowledge was passed from one generation to the next and was sought out and respected by the younger generation. Today, the older we get the less valuable we become to the next generation.

A true mentor is an adult who develops a special relationship with a child, who teaches them skills, and creates a sense of wonder about the world. Someone who helps the child develop a sense of honor and knowledge of right and wrong.

A mentorship can last for years, or even a lifetime. There is so much value in mentorship.

Even a brief moment in time with a child can have a tremendous impact that affects them their entire lives.

Mentoring isn't just about what an adult says, but it's the energy shared with a child that makes a difference. That energy can affect them just by being in the mentor's presence.

It's vital for the mentor to understand that the child is picking up that energy by listening, observing and ultimately by imitating that adult. In essence, mentoring is a sacred trust.

When we take mentoring seriously, we become better people. We know we are being watched, and it forces us to observe ourselves. Most important to mentoring, is being authentic and truthful. It's not about being perfect, it's about striving for perfection to lift others up. Being human is to be flawed, and then grow and learn, and to repeat this pattern throughout life.

Mentoring is helping a mentee learn how to live life. How to find peace with themselves as they are, and to grow and learn, and develop the gift of who they are. This makes good people.

Good values must be mentored such as honesty, hard work, love, kindness, gratitude, service, and continued learning.

A mentor should never try to make the person they are mentoring an image of themselves. A person being mentored, should not try to become like their mentor. This is wrong. The person being mentored should take from the mentor what they've learned, what they love about the mentor and bring it into themselves. Let it live in them, and then live through their unique way of being with their own medicine.

Remember when you copy someone, you lose the realness of what was learned. Take what you've learned and live through your authentic self. You will always be a second best someone else, but a number one you.

Wisdom comes with slowing down, persistent experience, listening and patience.

Personality

Go back to your birth. When a baby is born into this world, they are helpless. They need to be fed, and protected, and they need to be loved. With these needs, babies form personalities to get what they need to survive.

As you develop as a baby, and you get a little older, and a little wiser, you learn what you need, and act out more to get that attention. That could be good, or not, but you continue to form a personality.

Medicine is a part of our personality that is formed, but it's also what we take in as we go through life. The older you get the more you take in, the more it forms the person you are. Mentoring is vital to nurturing that personality and helping it to grow into someone magnificent.

Without that mentoring, often a person can go astray. When we don't ask for what we need in ways that are healthy, our personality grows into something that isn't necessarily honoring our truth. It's a false personality, and we can often carry that into our adulthood.

A mentor can be that person who can help break that pattern and show you who your true self is. They can help you acquire your authentic medicine. That's a life changing thing. If a person allows themselves to be mentored, we all win.

What a change it would be if every person took mentoring seriously. We need to teach our young people to seek out mentors. There are golden nuggets of wisdom that are dying silently with our elders.

Who Are Your Heroes?

Heroes could be present in your life now or in your past. They could be family members, friends, teachers, sports figures, historical figures, or characters made up in books or movies. Ask yourself who they are based on their relationship to nature and humanity, and the life values or good deeds they are known for. Study your heroes fully. Identify the things about your heroes that stand out to you, and ask why they matter. The inspiration you feel from your heroes should motivate you to live in a good way.

Something to think about is if your heroes would be proud of you and how you are living. Could you be *their* hero?

So much of how we learn from our heroes is by observing them over time. They enter our hearts and find places in us to live. We then give them life through our life. They continue to live into the future, long after they have gone from this Earth.

Some of my heroes were Teddy Roosevelt, Tarzan, Edward Abbey, and John Muir. Teddy Roosevelt helped to create the National Park System and had such a strong influence in protecting our Earth. Tarzan lived in the wilds with a wonderful woman, and a boy, and a chimp. He communicated with the animals, and protected nature. Edward Abbey fought for our Earth and wrote about it in a real raw way from his heart. John Muir saved Yosemite Valley. He loved nature so much that he lost himself in it.

Live this life well and be a hero.

Gratitude For My Mentors

I am quite certain that if I hadn't found mentors growing up, I wouldn't be living my dream life today.

Every person born on this Earth has constant choices in every moment of each day. While I had made some better choices than others, I was heading down a path where there was no light. I was just bumping along the way, stumbling, getting up, and getting frustrated and beaten down.

I felt that I came to this Earth without a manual on how life worked. It seemed that most others had that secret knowledge that I was missing. It wasn't until much later in life that I realized that they were just faking it better than I was, and were more than likely, cheating off someone's else's life experience. I also found out that eventually it catches up with people, and they then need to relearn to live their own life, as the unique individual that they are.

At each point in life when I felt like I didn't want to get up again, a mentor showed up and helped me through the rough parts. It only takes one person to care about someone to help them want to get back up. When you see someone who needs a hand up or just a listening ear, be that person.

I've been gifted many guardian angels in my life. Some were in my life for brief encounters, and some have been a constant lifeline and anchor through many years. All are treasured.

Much gratitude to my human guardian angels, my mentors, my friends.

My Mentors Helped Raise Me

I have had a very good life, and I can owe a lot of my life to my mentors. Their influence shaped my life, and I can track it all back to them. I was fortunate enough to have many adults who took the time to teach me about nature, and ultimately about life.

My earliest recollection of an adult who taught me outside the realm of my family, was an elderly, Italian man, who I remember as having wild, bright, white hair, a big nose, and intense, dark, brown eyes. His face was a weathered, road map of wrinkles from long years in the sun.

I was about five when we lived on a farm near San Diego, with lots of prickly pear cacti surrounding our yard. The man had gotten permission from my father to collect the cactus so he could make wine.

I don't recall what exactly attracted me to him, perhaps it was his patience in answering every question I had, and I bombarded him with hundreds. He made me feel safe, and he seemed to welcome my company, and nurtured my curiosity, not only about the cactus, but with other plants as well.

He didn't simply show or tell me about things, but he allowed me to get my hands on the plants and to experience things firsthand. My parents trusted him enough as well to leave me in his care without worrying.

The first plant he taught me was the prickly pear. He showed me how to rub the outside of the fruit with a rock to remove all the stickers. Once removed, I could cut the fruit in half, scoop out the center and enjoy its delicious taste. The fruit was sweet and had a beautiful red color and smelled like a watermelon.

He showed me how to slice and cook the cactus pads, or nopalitos, and he helped me prepare a meal for my family.

He showed me how slicing the pads, and rubbing the juicy flesh on my skin, could relieve sunburn, which was wonderful for a fair haired and light, skinned Irish boy. He told me that the plant could be put onto wounds, and snakebites, to help heal them as well.

By sharing his time and experience, an incredible doorway into nature was opened for me. I learned about the wild plants growing around my neighborhood. He taught me some of the most common plants, such as dandelion and sow thistle, which I brought home to my mother to include in our dinner salads.

Although I don't remember the man's name, his generous spirit and teachings have stayed with me all my life. I now teach edible and useful plant classes, in the hope of opening the door of the plant world to others as he did for me.

We eventually moved away from the farm, and I never saw him again, but his spirit is deeply rooted in my life, and will always be a part of me.

I realize how my own experiences with children can count in a lasting way, and I try my best to give the children I teach positive experiences to remember.

That man positively reinforced my thirst for seeking knowledge outside my family. As a result, I value the knowledge of elders to this day, and I try to advise young people to do the same.

***

Today much of our learning comes from television, internet, and video games. It is rare today for a youngster to seek out training from an elder.

I did have an apprentice who sought out a mentor to teach him his craft of knife making. His mentor helped him to develop that skill, and develop the part of him that was unique. The man was brought to tears, believing his trade would disappear.

If a child is allowed to pursue what he or she believes to be his or her gift, without censorship from parents or teachers, he or she learns how to ask for help, how to be self-motivated, and how to connect with their world. They proactively engage in their own lives.

***

343

My Granddad, Leo, was one of the great mentors of my life. Granddad was about five-foot-six, with beautiful, gray hair, a true ruddy Irish complexion, and slight jowls that hung and wobbled when he talked. He had steel, blue eyes and a wonderfully shaped nose that seemed to define the entirety of his face. His deeply, wrinkled forehead seemed to reflect all the experiences he had. He had broad shoulders that defined his self-assuredness and made him look taller than he really was.

I loved watching him walk, because he had such confidence and grace. He always seemed to be in step with the natural world and its rhythm. It gave me a sense of peace just to be in his presence, and I learned that non-verbal communication could teach so much more about another person than words.

My Granddad lived his entire life on his homestead in Ronan, Montana, at the base of the Mission Mountains, surrounded by the Flathead Reservation.

Ronan at the time, was a small town in the middle of open land, and forests. It was a special place where grizzlies, elk, deer, and other wild creatures would visit his farm of dairy cows and gardens. I spent many summers with him when I was a boy, and cherish the memories in that incredible part of our country.

My Granddad let me go out all day and explore. He taught me how to take care of the cows, and chickens, and pigs, and sheep, and goats. He taught me how to trim trees, and how to garden, and grow plants, and run a homestead.

The native people there were kind to me because my grandfather was so respected in the community. They also took me on as a mentee, so I got the benefit of not only being mentored by Grandad, but all of them, and I fell in love with the Native American way of life.

***

I often dreamed of living like they did. I also felt sad, and empathic about what happened to them. Even now when I think of this, tears come because it didn't have to be that way. Their lives and homes were destroyed by our oncoming march from the European people, my Irish ancestors. It could have been different, and it wasn't, and we can never get that back.

That is a wound to the heart of the Earth and humanity. It's a wound to the soul of each and every one of us, that the Earth people's culture was lost in such a horrific way. I think if our country had good, conscious leadership, it would be the very beginning of a healing to take responsibility for what our ancestors did to the Native Americans and apologize.

Start with admitting the wrongs, and telling the truth, and learn from it. There is something in an apology that comes from the heart, that allows for healing to take place, and then good things come from there. Healing the grief of that nation is a dream I have.

***

My Granddad was the first person to teach me about honoring elders, not just humans, but non-human as well.

We loved to go fishing. He taught me how a fish thinks, and where they hide to camouflage themselves from unsuspecting insects that skip over the surface of the water.

On one of our fishing expeditions, I caught a huge trout. It was so much bigger than my 10-year-old mind and body was used to, that I was afraid to reel it in. Granddad grabbed the line, but he saw that the fish was barely hooked, and he released it.

I was mad because I really wanted to eat that big guy, but Granddad explained to me that he released it because it was an elder. I had never heard anyone talk about an animal, let alone a fish, that way.

He told me that there were elders among *all* wild creatures, and plants. The elders in every species are important, as they breed health and strength into their species. He said that trout was needed in the trout world for its wisdom and strength.

Granddad told me that many people believed animals, and plants had no feelings or wisdom or soul. He felt that perspective was just a way to justify so much killing. The devastation that man creates can be seen all around us in small but significant ways.

***

When I was growing up in Santa Cruz County, there were many two-hundred-pound deer. Now they barely reach a hundred pounds. Unethical hunters prized the big bucks, whose loss has diminished the species.

I also remember a visit I made to the Steinhart Aquarium in Golden Gate Park, where I saw a huge, stuffed lobster hung on the wall. I heard Granddad's voice whispering in my ear, "Boy, they caught a big one, a big old elder."

***

Elders can be found in the plant, and tree world as well. Granddad and I loved to hike and explore. He would take me to places where we could just sit with the trees.

He never said that the walnut tree he loved so much was an elder or a tree of wisdom. We would simply sit with our backs against the trunk and feel the variations in the bark and the hardness of the wood.

We would listen to the soft music of the wind through the leaves, and marvel at the patterns the sun would create as it shined through the branches and leaves. It was a work of art, and we naturally and easily communicated that joy and pleasure to the tree.

***

Any time you sit with an open heart, by a great old tree, you are silently communicating with that tree. The challenge for us is to receive it without questioning, to let go of the fear of feeling foolish.

The endless chatter in our mind drowns out what our heart so easily understands. Listening and feeling with our hearts is the key to the mystery of so many things in life. Just being in nature opens a doorway to the universe, and to a better understanding of our own internal process.

The primal urge that drives us to explore, and excel in our daily lives is also the urge that drives us to explore the mystery of things. Too often I see parents who are afraid to let their children get dirty or explore the woods or even climb trees. They inhibit their child's curiosity not only within the natural world, but ultimately, they inhibit their child's curiosity for life. Unknowingly, they take away the joy of exploring the mystery, and impose a false fear that is not the child's own.

***

My Grandad gave me Ronan, Montana. His homestead on the Flathead Reservation gave me my relationship with the Flathead Tribe members, and my introduction to the sweat lodge way.

My Granddad also engaged me in gardening, and working with farm animals, and ultimately, he also showed me what it was to be an elder.

My Grandfather listened to me dream for hours. He taught me about life and death in nature. When he died, he taught me how to do death in a good way. I learned the depth of my grief when he passed. I loved him as I love our Earth.

***

Many people over the years have asked me about my leather hats. I always wear one, not just to keep the sun out of my eyes and protect my Irish skin, but I started wearing it out of respect for another mentor who I had met on my Granddad's farm.

He was a neighbor who always wore an old, leather hat. I would see him on his walks near the farm many times.

When I was about nine years old, I finally met him as I was sitting on the bank of a nearby creek. I was afraid of strangers, but my intuition told me that this man was ok.

I had only seen him from a distance, but up close he had warm, soft eyes and a red, almost burned looking complexion. He had a gentle voice, and a peacefulness about him that lent credence to what my gut was telling me.

The man said he stopped because he noticed that I was chewing on some plantain leaves, a wild edible that my Italian friend had taught me about. He was happy to see that I loved wild plants, and was curious about them because they were a big part of his life.

He showed me how watercress grew in the creek right in front of me, and how delicious it was. He taught me about cheese-weed, and how the little "cheeses" on the leaves were edible, and how the plant's fibers could be used to make string. He even showed me how to brush my teeth with the roots of the plant, stressing how important it was to keep clean when in nature to remain healthy and strong.

Most importantly, he taught me about the sacred connection between plants, and people. He told me about praying before taking a plant. As people say grace before dinner, he stressed that there is energy between plants and people. This has been common knowledge for our ancestors, and now has been scientifically proven. He taught me that praying and asking permission from the plant to take it showed respect.

Eventually I learned to feel the energy of plants, and to develop a deeper sense of communion with them as fellow living beings. This lifelong skill has been the biggest factor in my success as a prolific gardener.

At my outdoor school I have a vegetable and flower garden, which provides organic food for our students. My staff and apprentices help with the gardening and at times are confused when I tell them to leave many of the "weeds". There are certain plants that don't seem like a good idea to keep in the garden or on the outskirts of the beds, but they have become friends of mine. They have their own purpose for being there, whether anyone understands what that is or not. It's just a knowing that I have, and it can't, and doesn't need to be explained. It just is.

Earth's people believed that all forms of life, be it stones, plants or animals, are all conscious beings just like humans, and deserved the respect one would accord another human being.

Plants are so vital to our existence that to acknowledge their essence seems the right thing to do. They clean the air we breathe and provide us with food, clothing, shelter, tools, beauty, and companionship.

This man also taught me how to trust people again. Our hikes in the woods, and his love of nature helped to heal my young, troubled soul.

One of the great mysteries of life is how we seem to get exactly what we need when we need it. I am not sure I ever knew his name, but I remember his leather hat, and another door that he opened for me into the magical world of plants.

Sometimes a mentor can be someone whose name you don't know or don't remember. It can be a brief, but memorable encounter that can affect your life, as that man did mine. Had I not trusted my intuition, I might have lost a wonderful opportunity.

***

It was magical spending summers in Montana, but I also still loved going to the Colorado Rockies, to be with my Uncle Bill.

Uncle Bill loved to take me riding on his four-wheeled, Tote Goat, dirt bike over the rutted roads. He'd smoke his big ol' cigar and I would hang on to his hairy back for dear life. It was like hanging on to a Grizzly Bear.

When he finished his cigar, he would stick the butt in his mouth, chew it up and spit it out. To this day I love the strong, earthy smell of cigars, and always think of my Uncle Bill. My uncle was a character, but he took mentoring seriously. He taught me through example, and through experience.

Uncle Bill was an honorable hunter and fisherman. He ate what he killed, and treated it with reverence. He used all of the animal or fish that he could. Every time my Uncle Bill or I killed anything, we cried.

He taught me to fish, and I found that there was nothing more enjoyable to me and more connecting to nature than wandering up small mountain creeks trying to catch trout.

Our dirt bike adventures included lots of stops so we could hike into the streams to fish or just explore. We found beaver ponds, and he taught me how to stalk in as close as possible without the beavers becoming alarmed.

One time I was in a fishing hole that was created by a beaver. I saw a beaver swimming into its den, and my uncle was laughing and told me to go in there with it. So, I did.

I swam into the beaver den by swimming down and then up into it. I came out into a dry space and there was the beaver with three babies.

It was one of the most memorable moments in my life. My uncle laughed, maybe thinking I wouldn't actually do it, but I listened to everything he said, and I think maybe that just made his day. It probably became one of the most memorable moments in his life as well.

The mother beaver didn't try to attack me, I'm guessing because I had love in my heart, and I didn't have intentions of harm. I just looked around and swam back out, and I went back to fishing.

Even though the forest and all its creatures act as one, as they are all interdependent on each other, it is still an environment of individual species. I had developed a personal relationship with nature by then, and I saw those beavers as individuals – living, working, and playing as much as I did.

Though we tend to generalize our references towards animals, they are individuals, and each has a distinct personality. Spending as much time as I did in nature as a kid, I could have a different relationship with each being within the same species. I felt honored when I developed such a relationship with a wild creature.

One of my passions was, and still is, snakes. My uncle was constantly amused by my insatiable desire to find snakes, and when I did, I would jump on them. I wasn't too smart about it when I was young, because it didn't matter to me what kind of snake it might be. I'd run through the bushes, getting all scratched up just to hold one.

I loved to connect with snakes – they were fascinating animals, and I could hold one for hours, mesmerized by its beauty and movements. To this day, I will still dive on a snake without hesitation. Even

346

rattlesnakes are fair game for me, although there have been a few close calls, but I love holding those wonderful buzz worms.

On our amazing forest odysseys, Uncle Bill and I encountered wolverine, marten, bears and many other creatures whose tracks could be found everywhere. He would have me on all fours in the mud, studying and learning what animals had made what tracks. He would have me imagine their stories, to know what the tracks were saying.

Sets of tracks are like adventure books that the animal leaves behind after a night of hunting. By day you can read their tracks, picture what they did, where they've been, where they were going, and who interacted with whom.

I was a pretty good tracker and fisherman at a young age, and I could have trapped many animals, taking their furs as trophies, but Uncle Bill told me that over-trapping was driving a lot of these animals to extinction. He said you could hate the trappers, but they were only there because people wanted the furs.

One of my most memorable tracking experiences was with a bear. Uncle Bill and I were crazy for bears. We would seek them out, following their tracks or scat until we found them in clearings or saw them on hillsides, feeding on the grasses and berries.

One fall as we were fishing in a creek, we found some bear tracks and followed them through a clearing, then into the woods, until we came upon another creek. Using our stalking skills and being as quiet as possible, and hoping we were down wind, we came upon a pool that was covered by a thin layer of ice.

A bear had knocked a hole through the ice with his paw, and he was pulling out a trout that had been trapped just below the surface. Watching the bear eat the fish felt like a sacred moment after following the track's story to the end. It was a play performed by nature for our eyes only.

Uncle Bill had many culinary lessons for me as well. He taught me to eat grubs. Like bears, we would wander the woods looking for fishing bait by pulling apart rotten logs and finding the plump, white rice-like creatures.

We would take some for the bait and then he'd say, "Let's pretend we're bears." and we'd pop some of the grubs in our mouths. I began to think like a bear, and see the world as a bear saw it. I'd smell things like a bear, paw the ground looking for roots like a bear, and rip a log apart like a bear. I became so bear-like that I wondered sometimes if I wasn't more bear than human.

Aside from acting like bears, Uncle Bill told me that grubs were high in protein, and were a valuable food source, and something I should remember in case I ever needed it in an emergency.

I love teaching this to my students at the school. It's like a rite of passage for each person who tries eating a grub or grasshopper or ants for the first time. It's a whole new experience for them, not only to do something they never imagined they could do, but it takes them into the world of insects – another doorway into the depths of nature.

Many countries outside of the U.S. do eat insects as a regular part of their rich, protein diet, but after removing ourselves from the Earth's wisdom, our "civilized" country has to be reintroduced to what was once common knowledge and practice.

My uncle and I were fortunate enough to watch a great hunter on one of our walk-abouts in the woods. We had come upon a mountain lion just as it pounced on a deer. There was a gut-wrenching struggle, of life-and-death that was both powerful and horrifying to watch. The deer's death was neither quick nor painless, and I was overwhelmed by how long it took for the deer to die.

Though Uncle Bill tried to comfort me, he was also a realist, and told me that there isn't really an explanation for why nature can be so harsh and cruel at times. Everything lives off something. Whether we are predators or prey, we are all part of the sacred circle of life. The deer and the mountain lion were dancing the sacred dance of life and death. Uncle Bill said nature teaches us many full circle lessons.

We left the mountain lion to his deer, and we headed for the nearest creek to explore its banks. My love of creek and river exploration comes from the hours Uncle Bill, and I would spend hopping from boulder to boulder, getting in the water, swimming, and crawling through the mud, looking more like beavers than humans.

As we splashed through the chilly waters, he told me that this creek would flow into a nearby river, which would flow into the mighty Colorado River, then into the Sea of Cortez in Mexico, and eventually merge with the Pacific Ocean.

The clouds that form over the ocean move toward land, where the moisture builds, until the cloud can no longer contain the moisture. The rain falls into the canyons and creeks and begins the cycle again.

I loved my time with my Uncle Bill. Simple explanations to a young mind can have a lasting life-long effect when the mentor spends the time with his young protégé.

I loved his energy, and it seemed to fill me up as well. Most of what I teach today is Uncle Bill's energy coming through me. My Uncle Bill gave me his personal medicine of exploring, hunting, fishing, tracking, and adventure.

Why I have been blessed with so many good mentors is a mystery. They seemed to appear when I needed the most help, or I was about to pass into another stage of life.

***

Bo Almroth was a family friend, and father of my best friend. Bo was an engineer by trade, and a naturalist by passion. He was a six-foot four-inch hunk of a Swede with piercing, blue eyes, and a golden, tanned face, which told the story of his years in the outdoors.

Bo was an avid backpacker and lover and seeker of the wilderness, and the wild ways. He was truly in love with nature, and he gave that to me by taking me on countless hikes, and on one of the most formative trips of my life.

He made me an apprentice. Most people think of an apprentice as someone who is taught a trade by a skilled craftsman. I believe an apprenticeship is where you learn not just a trade or skill, but you learn about life.

Bo was the man who took me on a rite of passage around the U.S. We went to big cities and learned about history, we backpacked in many of the national forests and wildernesses.

Bo was an educated man who instilled the love of reading in me. He gave me reading assignments from J.R.R. Tolkien to Siddhartha, and we studied about nature. I read up on historical places and events and visited historical monuments.

We had many adventures together, and spent many weekends hiking the Santa Cruz Mountains along a 10-mile loop, discussing the books he had me read.

Bo taught me how to fish for crayfish in the creeks, and how to cook them with wild fennel that grew nearby. He'd take me to the beaches to collect mussels and clams, or to fish from the rocks for snapper, cabezon or sea bass, all the while discussing some of the great literature. He fed my body and my mind at the same time.

He opened my eyes to art, often taking me to galleries and art shows. He spent more time with me than his own sons, as his boys weren't interested in nature, which I think was a huge disappointment for him. I was a sponge and took in everything he had to teach. He gave me so much. He literally dedicated himself to me.

Part of the reason I started Headwaters Outdoor School was to find some way to repay Bo for all that he gave me. His mentoring created the same need in me to mentor others. It's a full-circle way of living, and one in which you can get immediate benefits by giving your time and energy to a child, who in turn will pass on what he or she has learned.

Bo stuck with me as I grew, and then in my later teen years, we grew apart a little bit, and we weren't in contact as much. I was told he was sick, and he died of cancer very soon after. I spoke at his eulogy, and it was sad, but I also felt gratitude that he had been there for me, and his teachings would live on through me.

The timing was right for me, and he led by example, and that was the perfect form of mentoring for me. He also held me accountable to my word, and made sure I gave my best when I was backpacking and learning new skills in nature. He made me do them well.

Bo taught me the deep love of nature by just being out and loving nature, without always having to do something. He instilled that admiration in me, and it never left, and it formulated my life.

Bo Almroth gave me his complete attention and his endless wisdom, which equaled my deep, spiritual love of nature. He made me feel special, unique, and important, and helped me know that I mattered. He showed me that dreams and visions can and do come true.

***

Good mentors can help young people light the fires of their natural curiosity and adventurous spirits. With guidance, they can engage with life, rather than hide from it, and flow with the positive energies rather than the negative.

We assume that our kids will just figure out how the world works. There are so many kids today on antidepressants or have anger management struggles because they can't figure the world out by themselves, so they disconnect and become depressed or angry.

We don't come into this world with an owner's manual, but we do have elders that we can learn from. I guarantee that any parent who spends quality time with their kids, and who finds good role models for their kids, will be less likely to have problem teens. Ninety nine percent of being a good parent is showing up.

I don't mean that their teens won't act out or test parental boundaries - that's part of the process of growing up and finding their individuality. It's a kid's job to push the limits, and it's the adult's job to say no when it's appropriate and set a boundary.

When kids come close to crossing the line between good or bad judgment, most of those kids will err on the side of caution, due to the foundation that good parenting and good mentoring has instilled in them.

They will learn from their mistakes more readily than those who have had little assistance growing up and be less likely to repeat their mistakes.

***

School teachers are the most obvious influences on our children's lives. Our kids spend most of their day in school. Our schools should be a place where they are not only educated but are influenced positively.

Our culture seems to devalue public schools and teachers, yet schools and teachers have the greatest responsibility in shaping our kid's futures.

I had four great teachers who shaped my perspective of the world. How many kids do you know who can say they have four great teachers who inspired them to greatness?

***

Mr. Robertson was a big, round man. He had green eyes, close-cropped hair, and very powerful hands, like a trade's man.

He loved to teach science ,and convinced the school to let him build an outdoor lab on an acre-and-a-half of school property. He was going to teach us about the Earth by creating a mini ecosystem around a pond.

This really excited me, so he let me help, and in my freshman year in high school I was entrusted to create a wildlife habitat for our school. He handed over the project to me and a few other students.

The barren piece of land was just outside the classroom. He asked me to fix up the nature habitat so that it could be used as our biology lab. He gave me free reign to create, and told me the dirtier I got, the better. He said that if I wasn't getting dirty, I wasn't working hard enough.

Dirt is a magnificent doorway to connect with nature. Everything we are, and everything we have on this Earth comes from the dirt.

My classmates and I built a pond. I began stocking the pond by transplanting fish and frogs that I'd caught in the local creeks and lakes. I introduced lizards, and I planted reeds, cattails, and other native plants I collected from various locations in my community. We also fed the birds so they would take up residence as well.

We had many classes out there, and it was something to be proud of. All of this wouldn't have happened if I didn't have a mentor that allowed for this freedom to create. What a treasured gift that was for me. I was given a generous amount of trust from a teacher, and it showed me how important that is when you mentor young people. You need to take a risk by allowing room for creativity and for possible mistakes. You need to allow room for kids to grow. Give them basic guidelines and let them create! You may learn more than they do.

By the time I was ready to leave high school, I had helped turn our outdoor lab into a paradise for all the students and teachers to enjoy and learn from. Many times, the teachers went there to have a little quiet time. To this day, our lab is a thriving little ecosystem unto itself.

Mr. Robertson also gave me an outlet for my budding nature photography passion by using my pictures in his class lectures, which inspired me to take even more and better photographs.

He told me about his favorite fishing place in the High Sierra's where the fish were so numerous you could almost catch them by hand, where the mountains stretched to heaven, and the rivers and creeks ran clean. It was a place where the grass stays green for months, and the wildlife was so abundant they were everywhere you looked.

Most fishermen are deaf and mute when it comes to sharing their favorite spots, but Mr. Robertson showed me on a topographic map where it was. I have gone there for decades now. It has become one of my sacred places, and where I have taken some of my best photographs.

***

Mr. Fagrell, was my crafts teacher, and strangely enough taught me how to hunt wild pigs in the Santa Cruz Mountains where he lived. The pigs wreak havoc on the meadows, and Mr. Fagrell taught me how to stalk them.

He, too, encouraged my photography and would provide space at school to show my photos, and helped me find places in town that would show my work.

Each person I met along my life's journey has added a little piece to each of my career paths.

***

Mr. Goody was my history teacher who taught me the importance of understanding the past, so that we hopefully wouldn't make the same mistakes in the future.

I have a great passion for history and am often sharing the stories I have read in ways that engage those I am speaking with. Mr. Goody instilled my gift of storytelling.

***

Mr. Sartwell, my basketball coach, demanded that we give our best each time we played. As a matter of fact, one of the most spiritual moments I have ever experienced happened on the basketball court.

It was a moment that you hear athletes talk about when everything comes together, and the performance is flawless and perfect. I had such a moment where every pass was perfect, every fake worked, every shot I took I sunk, where my teammates and I were in perfect harmony. It only lasted a few minutes, but I felt connected to everything during that time.

Because Mr. Sartwell expected us to give our best every time we stepped on the court, it allowed for that sacred moment to happen, where you just let go and enjoy the moment and let it all flow into perfection.

***

My teachers and mentors guided me and invested so much of themselves in my success, and my parents were also a tremendous influence on me.

My mother, Nita, taught me how to cook, which is a huge teaching that many people don't get. I have a love for the creativity of cooking and sharing sacred meals with others because of my mom. When I cook now I always think of her, and I am grateful.

I can honestly say my mother loved me unconditionally. She dedicated her life to me in so many ways, which I believe helped me through the rough times. She showed me truly the power of love.

I know that if a kid feels that he or she is loved, wanted, and cared for, even in the midst of the most difficult situations, they will usually turn out all right. It's the consistent love that overcomes the bad things that happen.

I found over the years that the kids who come to me without that kind of love or consistency in their life are the ones who struggle as adults.

My mother taught me love for all things, which has been my life's greatest gift. Love has guided me and kept me on track and sane and peaceful, in an often insane human world. My mother was and still is my Guardian Angel.

***

My dad, Jack, mentored me in a different way. He worked hard, and he took care of our family. He was consistently there for me, always loving me through all my ups and downs and in-betweens.

He was just a hard-working man with good values, love, and kindness in his heart. He didn't speak much, but he showed me love. My father was a quiet man, but he gave the same kind of energy that I received from my uncle and grandad, in a different way.

He was an engineer who designed, and built missiles and airplanes. He loved the challenge of building anything. We built a couple of kayaks that we often used on our fishing trips, and to explore the environs of a local reservoir.

One of the most important things my father instilled in me was the responsibility of being part of a household. It was my task to take care of the garden that helped provide food for our family, and it became a life-long passion.

It was a place where I could feel the spirits of the plants, and where I could immerse myself in nature, while growing beautiful vegetation to nourish my family.

Gardening taught me how to get the information that I needed to grow plants in abundance and in various, challenging environments. My father didn't spoon-feed me the information. He simply said, "You're the gardener - learn how to do it!" That taught me how to take initiative.

I also had to learn about different tools so I could fix things like plumbing and wiring. One time I had asked my father how a toaster worked, and the next day he presented me with a toaster he had found at the dump, and he told me to take it apart and put it back together.

The best gift and teaching my father gave to me was his trust. He trusted me so much that at age thirteen he allowed me to go on my summer-long rite of passage with Bo.

He let me go into the woods alone as a kid, even at night. As a teenager, he allowed me to fulfill a long-held dream of going to Canada, to live alone in the wilderness. I spent four months in the wilds of Canada exploring, and learning how to live and survive in extreme situations.

My father knew there was danger, but he also knew that for me to find my true self, adventure was vital for my psyche and soul. He never kept a tight rein on me because he had the wisdom to give me small responsibilities when I was young. When he saw that I could handle those, he increased my responsibilities, each one involving a leap of faith.

My father taught me commitment, the importance of an education and how to build structures, and how to earn and build trust.

My dad gave me my first camera at 12 years old. Since that time nature photography has become a foundational part of my life, as my art, and my way of sharing my love of our Earth with people. That one gift and his support changed my direction in life.

I was blessed to have my dad live on my land in Shasta his last six years on Earth. He saw my school in action. I knew how proud he was of me. That was his final gift to me.

When he died, I had held him for hours until his last breath, and I gave him to the Angels.

***

Each person has the power of mentorship. Each person has a special gift that he or she can give to another person that will affect that person's life forever. In the giving you also receive, and you can help the world become a better place one kid at a time.

Everyone Has Something Important To Share

Are you aware of how you affect others by your actions? It doesn't matter how old you are, you can be a mentor.

You may think that mentors can only be elders. Although elders do mentor, you could be a mentor as a kid or a young adult. In general, you start mentoring when you get a little bit of life experience behind you that you can share.

Many teenagers have already had a lifetime of rich experiences, and are ready to take mentoring seriously. Some of these young adults are often recognized as old souls.

People can truly come into their own as a mentor in their 40's and up. You can become masterful. It's simple, and incredibly fulfilling for you, and the person that you mentor.

It's the responsibility of all Earth lovers to educate others. We must teach others about our Earth's needs or give them the space and place to allow nature to be the teacher. The kids today are our future and our Earth's future. They are our hopes and dreams. They are our legacy.

Become a mentor, be a hero, a protector, be an example. Live as you would have them live. Share your life story and insights along the way, and do not let your wisdom die with you.

Our kids are watching, and waiting. They are right at the edge of their lives. Be there to encourage them to leap off and jump in fully awake and inspired.

Working Together

Mentoring is not complicated. One of the most impactful ways of teaching is to have the person work with you. Often, no words need to be said. It's in the act of working, and doing something well, completely with beauty, and love, honor, and respect, that the teaching comes in. Lessons well learned are through quality time spent together, careful observation, and a heart full of love.

Students at our outdoor school help with the clean up after meals, and I always get right in there and work alongside them. I actually enjoy washing the dishes with our students. I teach by example by talking with them, and joking, and singing with them in the dish line. While we are doing this, I'm teaching the younger students how to do a good job, and to do it over if the quality of work isn't there.

Take time out of your life to take a kid on trips, whether it's a day hike or a week trip or just in the woods or the beach for an hour, you've got to take time.

I've watched so many people get too busy, and they don't take time for others, particularly when it comes to mentoring, even their own kids. I know life is tough, it gets busy, I'm in it too, but sometimes we need to rearrange our priorities. Taking mentoring seriously is the most important priority.

Know you are a mentor to others, and that you have something to offer. You may need to seek out someone to mentor, but whoever it is, they have been waiting to connect with you too.

If you go back to our ancestors, people wanted to be mentored, they sought out mentors. Now, younger people are not seeking out mentors, and older people are not seeking out people to mentor, and it's sad.

Teachers are mentors, but they have so much put on them already it is hard for them to have the extra time outside of the classroom as well.

Sometimes the most valuable mentoring comes in the spur of the moment. Something you do or say may stay with someone, and become part of their medicine, and they will have it forever. Don't ever think what you do doesn't matter. Children watch and study and emulate.

When I built my school, I realized our staff had to be real. We had to be honest, and we had to work at getting along and being respectful with each other. When we had problems, we dealt with them with no secrets.

The world is full of obstacles, and part of mentoring is learning how to deal with them, not pretending they don't exist. We need to deal with them directly in a healthy way. I know more than anything else I can lecture all day long, but kids learn by watching.

A big part of how we mentor in our school is how we, the staff, interact with each other. We mess up sometimes, but we always go back and clean things up, and we don't allow gossip.

When we teach, we don't just lecture. Talking is important, but what's more important is to physically move. We go out and we climb trees, we walk, we build things, we create art, and we learn skills.

Before I moved to Mount Shasta, I worked with five homeschool groups in Santa Cruz, California. I took different groups out in nature for a full day weekly. I still hear back from some of those kids who are now in their 40's, and they tell me how it affected their lives.

I take mentoring seriously and when I work with someone my door is always open to them, and that offer to be there for them is for life.

So often you don't even know how you touched someone and it's not even important that you do know, you just need to trust and take a leap of faith that you do.

Apprenticeships

Our apprenticeship program at our outdoor school is unlike any other. Students stay with us for 4-7 weeks at a time taking our nature classes.

We also mentor them, not only with personal life skills, but with physical living and job skills, including outdoor skills, cooking, gardening, land care, animal care, office skills, maintenance work, and assisting teaching.

They can choose to participate in the areas they are most interested in, and gain hands-on experience. No matter which tasks they participate in, they are all an equally important member of our community. Every job helps to run our school and helps the community. There is not one job skill that is more important than another.

One of the main things we emphasize is that each apprentice is a part of the community, and they matter. We also let them know that as a part of the community they also have the responsibility of being caretakers of the land. We ask them to pay attention to the land's needs. If they see a job that needs to be done, then it's their job to do, or ask for help if needed. We also remind them if they delegate out a job, it is still their responsibility to go back and make sure the task was completed.

352

Our apprentices take ownership in the land and school, and they know they always have a place to return to year after year.

We remind our teenage apprentices that they have a lot of freedom at Headwaters, and they have our trust, unless they show us otherwise. We reinforce taking on more responsibilities, and to take that dedication of being a part of the community home with them when they return.

We are constantly teaching by working alongside our apprentices and having fun. We always encourage them to try new things, and to master the skills they already have.

It does take a lot of effort to commit this amount of time into mentoring kids and young adults, in addition to our regular classes. In my opinion this is how it should be though, multiple mentors helping a young person to grow in a good way, and sharing what we have learned.

The teachings are not always about the actual physical skill. The main goal is to bring out the caretaker in each person in their own way.

One of the biggest obstacles we come across with the kids and the young adults, is their lack of problem-solving skills. We expect to teach them new skills, but a common problem is that they don't know how to problem solve, and think of a different way of accomplishing a task. We see their hesitation when faced with something that isn't working, and then an immediate surrender of defeat, and lack of action.

When I tell them that waiting for someone else to do it for them isn't an option, some of them still just draw a blank. We have to encourage them to figure out a plan B, C, and D, and if they still need assistance, then that's when to ask for help.

Even though it's sometimes easier to just jump in and do a task for the apprentices, whenever we can, we need to restrain from doing that. We are not helping these kids be more self-reliant if we don't let them complete their task.

We need to proactively educate our youth in all areas of life, and get them hands-on working. This is how they learn best, by working alongside others, and jumping in and doing it.

Our focus is to help teach life skills that build the student's self-confidence, and self-esteem, and to encourage them to regain their personal connection with nature. Growing into an Earth Caretaker begins in childhood, and is nurtured throughout one's life. With that sense of self and belonging, our apprentices are heading into their independent life with a great start.

Share Space

Be honest. Tell your truth. Give your best. Take the time to help an insect or help a lizard or hold a snake or climb a tree. Your actions as a mentor will speak for you.

Be mindful of not always being in a rush. Work together. Build something together. Build a shelter together. Build a fire together.

Mentors need to open a safe, communication space so deeper subjects can be talked about with a young person. Subjects or situations may come up like spirituality or if you went hunting how it feels to hurt or kill something. Bring up the dreams for their life and support them in ideas of how to make that happen.

Talk about how it is to live in a capitalistic world and how to make a living while you are reaching for these dreams. Teaching teenagers how to be financially independent, with a reality check of what that really looks like when they move out on their own, is so important for their success in being self-reliant.

A mentor wants to instill in their mentee hope for the future and ideas, but you also want them to know all the difficulties that face them and have the skills to deal with them.

Most of the best teachings come from just being with them. Overall, it's the love, and the honor, and the respect that you bring to the relationship, that they feel. They feel cared for, they feel wanted, they feel respected, and that is the foundation that makes all the teaching real.

One of the most powerful acts you can do is to just sit with someone, and share space. Go back hundreds of years where a clan would sit around a fire. What did they do to bond? Our ancestors told stories and listened to each other. They gave life to those stories by being fully present and listening.

People really want to be heard, and know what they say matters. The art of just sitting and holding space and really listening to another person or another being, is a healing you can give. This is how you pass on knowledge and how we learn. No judgment. Just listen.

So many times, we are not truly listening when someone speaks, we are just waiting for them to stop talking so we can get our own point across. Catch yourself when you feel the urge to interrupt. Craft a talking stick and use this tool in your heartfelt conversations to remind you to share talking and listening space.

When you do give advice don't be attached to the other person taking it. It's their choice of what to do with it, and it's their life to live those choices. Pass along your insight if asked, and then let them go on their own life journey.

One of the great gifts you can give another human being, which you can give to nature as well, is being fully present. Being present is becoming a lost skill, but it changes the energy of the whole experience.

Being a mentor for a younger person is as important as any work you could ever do. There is nothing more noble. It's not about money. It's not about control. It is true service to another. It is about encouraging, and supporting another with a heart full of love and a soul full of dreams and it will shape a life forever.

My mentors influenced my life and it's been a life well lived. My mentors live in me and through me. I will never forget them. I will always be grateful and will forever pass on their gifts.

Explore

Many young people don't read books as much anymore. They seek quick answers, but don't seem to be as curious about learning beyond a paragraph on a smartphone.

We have recently built a nature library and photography gallery on our land. It is a 24' yurt filled with books and comfy spaces inside, with an outside deck to curl up on. Students can swing in a hammock or lounge in a chair or sit by a creek, and disappear into a story.

Of course, I want them to be out in the woods, but sometimes it's good to get inspired by someone else's adventure to encourage them to set out on their own.

You need curiosity to grow. Many people only learn what is forced upon them in the moment, but then don't seek extended knowledge beyond that.

Encourage curiosity, and then go explore the answers with a younger person. Show them how to have fun and adventure in the seeking.

The Elders Need To Step In

If a group of kids or young adults have gone astray, then a community of elders need to step in. Kids may have been born into a family influenced and affected negatively by alcohol and drugs. The parents may not be capable of changing the pattern, but the community can step in and mentor the younger members of their community.

Drugs and alcohol can be a major influence in young people's lives, and it can be crippling, but there is still free choice. There is a choice to go one way or the other. There is a choice to be angry, and there is a choice to redirect that energy into following a different path.

One person can make a difference with heart and right action. Be that one person and bring others along.

As a member of the human race, it is our responsibility to take care of those who need help. It is not easy, but it is an honorable life worth living if you make a positive difference, in even one child's life.

You can be a teacher without being invasive. Teach by example, by how you live. Remember kindness. Let go of bitterness and judgment. Just be kind. Teach through this love, not just through your personal expression of love, but through deep, guiding love.

Teaching Doesn't Have To Be Your Occupation

I'm a professional teacher in my school, but that doesn't mean if you are not a paid teacher you are not a teacher. Every day you teach through your actions and your words.

So, consciously think about how you are putting yourself out into the world. What kind of a teacher do you want to be? What are your actions and words communicating to people?

As a mentor, be a living example of someone who makes a positive difference in the world. When you live enthusiastically, and wholeheartedly your energy is infectious.

With encouragement and support, the ultimate wish is that in turn others will go out into the world and do wonderful things. Teach young people to be great teachers.

Mentoring The Trades

Our hands-on trades workers are finding a lack of interest in up-and-coming apprentices. We need people doing the physical work to keep our world functioning. We need young people helping to build and restore the physical landscape of our Earth, including farming, forestry, and physical infrastructure.

To help fill this need, journeymen need to mentor in a positive, uplifting way to inspire young adults to take on their trade.

Unfortunately, sometimes there is still the hazing attitude of "the good old boys club" in many trades, which is off-putting to any young person, of any gender, who may be interested in taking on a job in those fields.

We need to lift up our young adults and encourage their growth, to help support our communities. In doing so, we can retire from our professions knowing we have left our world better for us being here.

We can be proud of allowing our legacy to live on and thrive through our mentees. Humility makes exceptional leaders.

In any area of life, ask yourself if you are teaching apprentices or mentees in the way it's always been done, or are you teaching them in the way it should be done?

Let Go Of Ego

When I am working with our young staff, I'm watching some of their abilities to lead coming through. It makes me so proud to see their growth ,and owning their new roles as teachers, and I must admit at times, it also makes me feel no longer needed.

I wonder sometimes that as a mentor am I rendering myself useless? Then I quickly step back, and remember I am here now to create more teachers, not accumulate students, and I feel good about that.

It is difficult as you age to step back to allow room for others to lead at times. I have my own way of doing things, and I can be a bulldog about finishing a job to the end, and doing it well. I also need to allow others to find their personal approach to making that happen.

I am slowly transitioning into the role of an elder, and sometimes wonder if I am still relevant. I watch the interactions of my younger staff with the students, and they are coming into their own medicine, and they are doing great. What I also see is that it's important to expose our students to teachers of all ages because we all have our life gifts and experienced wisdom to share.

I also know that I have the ability and a true joy of working with kids, teenagers, and adults. Not everyone enjoys working with people of all ages, but I truly do, especially teenagers. They appreciate me joking with them as well as being direct and honest with them. They know that I honestly care what they have to say, and I respect them for their own ideas. So, for now, I am becoming an elder who is still an active teacher and mentor.

Mentoring is something that human beings are obligated to do. Interact with kids. They learn by doing and being with elders. Be a nature mentor to a child. Seize those moments and share your Earth wisdom. This is how you encourage generations to become Earth Caretakers.

Reminders:

*Check in on a past student and see how they are doing.

THE EARTH CARETAKER WAY

*If a child is living in a single parent home, invite them along on a family hike. Their home life might be wonderful, but giving them the opportunity to engage in a different family dynamic gives them another experience to enjoy.

*Take a mentee along on a volunteer project. Get them engaged in groups being of service.

*Challenge an apprentice to use their creativity to come up with ideas of how to help the Earth and humanity, and implement them.

Chapter 37
Nature As Teacher

Accept nature, and all living beings, as fellow Earth travelers. While all beings don't have a brain like humans, that doesn't mean their lives are any less important than ours. There is a different form of intelligence that we can learn from.

When you allow nature to be your teacher, you gain an instant, expansive awareness. Boundless communication comes your way from the Earth.

Nature is the endless university of the art of living life in a good way. By going into nature, we learn about ourselves. We learn to be self-reliant. We learn freedom. We learn how to love. We learn gratitude, and to help when help is needed. We learn inner peace. We learn the importance of staying healthy. We learn about community, and how to work together with all beings for the greater good. We learn abundance and balance.

We learn how to deal with fear, real fear, and false fear. We learn about sadness, and loss, and pain, and suffering in a way that allows us to handle those emotions in a healthy way.

As the teachings come, you simply have a greater understanding of nature and how it works, and of your own nature. Inspiration, visions for your life, and the wisdom of simplicity comes to you.

We can learn to be better teachers by observing the ultimate teacher. We learn about Spirit and spirituality, and our senses grow in magnificent ways. Great teachers who changed the way we perceive the world went into nature and felt this connection. Put ego aside, open your heart, and let our living Earth mentor you.

Wild places in nature are the best classrooms. Just like you would go to college and attend a lecture by a professor, be a student of life, slow your busy mind, and be willing to be taught and learn through open-hearted communication.

Enter a space in nature with the intention of fully soaking up all that the Earth has to give. Ask questions of the Earth and feed your curiosity. Talk to plants, and mountains, and animals, and meadows, the ocean, and the sky. As you send out your questions, your answers will begin to show themselves. Often the most powerful mentoring is subliminal. It's not always verbal or visual. It shows up later and goes into your being. It rests there, and when the time is right it surfaces.

Freedom to explore is crucial. You need to be out in nature to gain experience and knowledge.

Learn Earth's language. Kindness, compassion, love, empathy, respect, and truth are nature's finest teachings.

Mentoring is practiced with all living beings. Bears teach their young how to live by spending time with them exploring, hunting, foraging, and nurturing. Every single moment is a mentoring moment in the life of a mother bear teaching her curious cubs.

Every animal, plant and tree are mentored by nature. Earth itself mentors humans on the cycles of life.

When we let the Earth mentor us, we become the best we can be. For our lives to be all that is good and beautiful, all other lives on Earth must also have that chance.

Working in the large animal training business, and wildlife rescue, I had many mentors that showed me how to work with the animals in a good way. They taught me to follow my intuition, and connect with the animals empathically to know how to help them.

As I got older, instead of losing the feeling of connection with everything, my childhood mentors and teachers had rooted that knowledge in my psyche. I have been able to stay open to these teachings from the Earth and the animal world, throughout my whole life.

Earth Mind

Wilderness is where you know truth. It will honor you and humble you equally. Nature is the most authentic teacher. Truth without judgment lives in nature, and that is something you can always rely on.

The Earth has no ego. The Earth has no need to control. The Earth lives for the sake of life only. What can we learn from this?

The Boys And The Fawn

An extraordinary event took place at Headwaters during a boy's rite of passage into manhood. After some time scouting out potential shelter locations in the woods, some of the boys had been visited by a very young fawn. The baby deer kept approaching them and crying. It wouldn't run away, and no mother was seen.

When the boys told me what was happening, I knew right away the fawn was lost from its mother. I was very sad to hear this because I knew the fawn would get weaker from lack of its mother's milk, and die. I advised the boys to keep their distance, as I hoped the mother would find it. It is common for mother deer to hide their babies while they forage.

A day went by, and morning arrived. We were eating breakfast and we heard a blood-curdling scream in the woods. I knew it was the fawn.

I had experienced this scream before when a fawn was hunted by predators. I had been in the wilderness, and was awakened by a fawn that had been attacked by a black bear. I saw the bear running with the fawn in its mouth, and the mother deer was chasing the bear. That chilling sound became embedded in my being.

The boys and I ran toward the scream, and found the fawn cornered by a hungry coyote. The coyote ran off as we ran to the fawn. The fawn was scared and weak from malnutrition, and collapsed to the ground. I picked it up and put it on my lap. The boys and I put our hands on the fawn, and gave it loving, healing energy.

This moment took a life of its own. It became sacred. This baby fawn fused with us. We cried, we gave her blessings, and we gave her love. The fawn passed away in our arms, and we were never the same again.

That baby showed us the way to our heart of hearts. She led us to that place of love that only animals can show us. This was truly a sacred moment in time. If the fawn had to leave this world, she went with our hearts connected to hers.

This fawn became our teacher. We learned about unconditional love, about death and the process of dying, and about letting go. That experience bonded us forever.

The teachings were endless. This experience alone was a rite of passage. We had a profoundly quiet night just feeling our feelings, and thinking about nature and life and death.

The next morning, we returned to find some blood, bones, and tracks. The coyote had consumed the fawn, and the fawn had become the coyote. The coyote did what nature teaches, and does so well. It was a reminder that we are all connected. We are all one Earth, and at our core we are all one love, and we need each other.

When we leave judgment behind, we can see the various faces of love that nature teaches. These sacred moments are like the lifting of a fog bank. For a moment we are shown the light, and we are forever changed; a little more enlightened, a little more alive, a little more a part of the web of life, a little more human with a heart.

I could not have fully taught the boys about life and death and compassion, and empathy, without nature giving them this experience.

To be the best teacher I can be, I step aside and let nature be the master teacher, and only offer guidance and compassion to assist her.

Nature Adapts To Change

Water flows through the least resistant route. When it comes to an obstacle, it either stops and creates a pool or it flows around the object. It doesn't get into its ego's wants and desires. It flows, and allows, and sometimes changes form, but it doesn't judge, it adapts and finds its way.

The Top Of The Mountain Every Day

Let nature show you how amazing this world is. Don't let your logical mind marginalize the wonders of nature. Acknowledge the wonders happening around you, let them live within you, enjoy them, give them life. This will bring the rest of your life into that place of inspiration.

Let nature show you the way into a life of wonder, and hope, and dreams, a life worth living. Let nature show you how to live big, and be a part of something great.

Your teacher is the environment and landscape you live in. It's a wonderful world, our Earth, our Home. Let our Earth show you this wonder that you are, that we all are. It's good to be an Earthling.

I Know This

When geese fly on migration an amazing teaching happens. Observe them flying in a V shape. The lead bird cuts the wind for the rest of the flock. The geese honk to encourage the others, as well as to help with navigation, each bird helping the other even through the night.

When the lead bird gets fatigued another bird moves up to the front, and the tired bird moves back to draft off the others.

These birds fly for thousands of miles. They are living miracles, gods on the wing. When they need rest and food, they find a good place to land. On the ground they look out for each other for protection. When they find food, they share it.

I've witnessed injured geese go down, and two to three other geese follow for comfort and protection, and stay with the wounded bird until it either recovers or passes on.

All living beings know love. All living beings know community and friendship. Being there for another being, to help when help is needed, is a higher calling, it's nature's calling. Imagine if humans practiced this on a grand scale.

Teach Through Nature

I coached high level, competitive swimming for many years, and often at practice, when the opportunity came, I would teach the athletes by showing them animal interactions. If a flock of geese flew overhead, I showed the swimmers what it looked like to draft off another swimmer.

I told them to watch dolphins riding the crest of waves to see what that looked like to ride a bow wave, and how to also duck under the turbulence of a breaking wave when they were coming off a turn.

When a frog jumped in the pool, I showed them how it finishes its kick, and glides for a second, streamlined before it recoils for another kick.

At the end of some practices while the swimmers were cooling down, I had them float on their backs just to soak in the amazing colors of the sunset to help them get their heart rates down, and to also just enjoy the world we live in.

Whenever possible, I tried to connect the human part of the athlete to our world, and to keep what they were doing in perspective.

Occasionally, I took the swimmers on hikes up into the foothills for our workout. They were so excited to see wildlife and climb on the old growth oaks. The athletes always jumped into nature with enthusiastic energy, being out in the real, natural world.

I had them swim in lakes and ponds surrounded by a lush environment, to keep them connected with water in its non-sterilized state.

No matter where you work, it is always, always best to get people outside, and engaged with nature, to help them stay in balance with what is real. You can always adapt whatever you're doing out in nature. Get creative. Let nature be the teacher, observe, and mimic, and above all have fun!

Rocks are teachers of patience, one of nature's finest lessons.

Perfectly Mystified

I was wandering in Point Lobos State Park along Monterey Bay. A stunning coastal reserve full of sea lions, otters, seabirds, seals, and breathtaking coastal vistas.

There are a variety of hardy plants, cypress, pine, and oak trees, and magical cliff and rock formations. A visual candy store for nature lovers.

I have so much gratitude for the people who saved this place from development. Houses and businesses are encroaching the perimeters of this land, but this sacred space will always be protected.

I was standing at a cliff's edge looking down at a protected cove. There were dozens of Harbor Seals bobbing along the shore and resting on the beach.

Two small shorebirds were squawking at each other, either playing or posturing, I couldn't tell. A nearby resting seal got annoyed as one of the birds bumped into it while they were squabbling. The seal flipped its flipper at the birds, chasing them away. Then a moment of peace and calm.

I was watching a Herring Gull standing by, getting curious about the two birds. They soon began to make a fuss with each other again, seemingly unaware of anything else around them. The gull moved in closer to them, apparently agitated. To my horror, the gull grabbed one of the small birds with its beak and killed it.

I thought that maybe it was just stunned, but then I watched from a distance, the lifeless bird laying on the shore with the lapping water rolling it around. The other small shorebird quietly observed the dead bird for a while, and then eventually a wave rolled in and carried its lifeless body out, and it disappeared underwater. Observing the remaining bird's shock and grief, made me realize that they had been a mated pair.

I was completely stunned that the gull killed the bird and didn't eat it. It just killed it, and flew out to the water and floated as if nothing just happened, and then flew across the cove up to a cliff's edge.

The gull killed the little bird because it was bothered by it. It seemed to me it killed it for fun or because it could, but not for food. I was truly sad and mystified. This kind of behavior I would expect from a deranged human. I just couldn't make sense of it. It haunted me for a while.

After a few minutes the shorebird's grieving mate flew away. Life went on in the seal colony. I remained sad and confused. As it should be, a perfect Mystery. I was perfectly mystified.

Sometimes nature can be confusing. What did I learn from this? For now, I've learned that sometimes life just isn't fair. Sometimes life is unpredictable because we all have freewill.

The Power Of Bird Watching

Become a bird watcher, a bird follower, a bird lover. Birds are graceful gifts of beauty. They sing to us and show up for us every day. They're presence alone is a delight.

I walk every day and have gratitude that this Earth is filled with birds. I love almost nothing more in my life than bird watching.

Birds are also wonderful teachers for us. When we observe birds with a keen interest, we find that they have a language all their own. This language is communicated through sound, movement, their habits, and their change of behavior.

By nature of their ability to fly and move quickly through the terrain, birds can observe and see much of the world. By listening and observing their reactions, calls, and behaviors, we can learn about their observations of our world.

As we observe, we'll naturally learn their language. We'll know things that often we don't even know we already knew, and our interactions with nature will reflect this knowledge.

We can improve our birding skills by observing for long periods of time, and not just identifying a species, and moving on.

Observe the answers to your questions. What color are they? What do they eat? Who eats them? How do they fly? Where do they live? What are their nests like? What are their babies like? In this watching and questioning you'll build up your nature wisdom.

Unfortunately, birds are in terrible trouble. All over the world, our birds are disappearing. Habitat loss, illegal hunting, poisons, collisions with buildings and cars, massive wildfires, and predators such as cats, are all prime causes of their decline.

Take a moment and close your eyes. Imagine a world without birds. Our world would be very empty. The loss of birds would be an irreparable wound.

So many species have already gone to the spirit world forever. We must all become bird advocates. Educate yourself on how to help. Offer feeding stations, and supply water. Get involved. They need your voice now. In return they will bring joy and beauty to your life.

Birds are such an integral part of our circle of life, that we know when they are in trouble. They are an indication of our health. Pay attention and make more of an effort to save the birds.

Pay Attention

Nature is a teacher with no agenda, no dogma and plenty of room for everyone. Nature teaches us that when we humans remove ourselves from the web of life, we lose control. We get crazy and anxious.

Right now, Mother Earth is trying to teach us that as her body heats up, our food source, both physical and spiritual, will decline. Some of us are listening and acting, but sadly not enough yet to make her better.

Sleep in different places in nature. Learn from each environment.

Concentric Rings

The Earth is a master teacher of concentric rings. Throw a rock into a pond and watch the rings ripple out. A mellow throw sends out gentle rings, a hard throw sends out rough, choppy rings. Throw a monster rock, and watch the pond rock and roll.

You can just imagine what the fish, frogs, bugs and even the water itself would all be saying. "Lookout, swim for your life!"

Humans are always moving, making noise. In the woods we're crunching branches, talking, crashing through brush. Our minds are busy with bills, gossip, and useless thoughts of fear and discomfort.

In this technological world, we're on our smartphones or thinking about our smartphones. We're not in the present moment. We are always thinking ahead to potential situations, which usually end up taking care of themselves anyway.

When we're with another person we never stop talking or thinking of what to say. Busy and noisy in our minds and body. The natural world passes us by every moment, and we never know what we've missed. We lose special moments that the Earth offers us.

Wherever we go, we send concentric rings out into the world with our physical bodies, and our thoughts. The animals in the forest hear us or feel us coming, and disappear.

We can learn to send out concentric rings that are peaceful and loving and inclusive, and the animals will not flee from us. Or better yet, we can quiet our minds and bodies, and almost disappear. We become part of the land. We belong. We find ourselves at home.

This fusion is a profound experience. It's recapturing our birthright to be one with the Earth. If we do this often, this oneness becomes our baseline, a life changing experience.

When you sit quietly in your mind and body, and minimize your energy going out, animals will come right to you. Patience is a must, and it's worth the effort.

Calm your energy and flow with the land. Watch your thoughts and movements. If all the animals disappear or flee from you, then you know the teaching. You have more to learn.

Enjoy the journey of practicing clearing away concentric rings. It's truly a wonder to be free flowing in nature with limitless possibilities. Over time you'll find this becomes easy, simply a part of you, and your concentric rings of disturbance will fade away naturally.

Removing our concentric rings and finding that oneness with the Earth is not only profound for you, but also an expression of love and respect to those you influence.

The dream is to walk into nature, and become such a part of the land that all living beings accept you as a part of the whole environment. At that point you have arrived, you have come home to the Earth. Once you get to that place of oneness with very little disturbance, you have made the leap into nature spirituality, a universal energy of spirit.

There's a time for crazy out of control noise. That's good too. We all love it, just not all the time. Listening deeply to nature is honoring the Earth herself. As you sit quietly, honor yourself as well.

Stop for a moment and think about what kind of a human being you want to be. I'm hoping one that makes your world and other living beings better because you care for our Earth.

We are at a troubling place in human history. I have no time for patience for takers. Every day everything you do, every action you take, every movement you make, every thought you have, every sound you make, everything you do or don't do creates concentric rings.

Your observation skills of concentric rings are a key teaching our Earth gives us every day. Become more aware of how you affect the world around you.

Life is a series of concentric rings. Notice the effects when you get angry or intense. Be aware when your intentions are not honorable. Watch when you are lazy. Observe what happens with discernment, and make the changes necessary to have a more amazing life.

This kind of teaching is life changing. We find purpose and vision. We find freedom. Concentric rings give us an understanding of ourselves, as we relate to all life.

Simplicity

We look to others for our own answers, but the rule of life's guidance is that the most significant truths are the most simple. It's so simple we don't believe it. When we complicate things, we use this as an excuse to not be the blessed beings we can be.

Set Yourself Up To Learn

Learning about the woods and acquiring the skills of a woodsman, helps to establish and deepen your nature connection. A local park or preserve is an excellent place to start, and the woods themselves will begin to teach. Finding a quiet spot and simply listening, can be revelatory for those who are always rushed and have deadlines.

Nature is easier for kids to connect with, as their hearts are open, and their minds not yet bound by cultural conformities. It's important for parents and teachers to know that at around nine years old, children often move from the magical mystery world to the logical, "I-must-fit-in" world. Don't let them give up the magical for the logical. It's simply wrong. It hurts their overall development. They must learn to live in both worlds. It's about blending and mixing. This is what nature is, living in balance.

I tell all my students to listen with their entire bodies, not just their ears, and to see with their entire bodies, not just their eyes. The deeper connections don't happen in the brain. They happen first in the heart, and in the gut. It's the same with having a soul connection with another person. The eyes may initially attract you, but it's your intuition and heart that take you deeper.

The intuitive hunch is about trusting what you feel is real. Learning to trust our intuition takes time and practice. This inner vision is what connects you with all the wonders of life, and protects you from negative forces.

There are many things in nature that we feel or maybe even see, but can't explain. Nature spirits are a mystery. The logical mind denies their existence, but the part of you that is soul and spirit, knows they are everywhere.

When we spend quality time outdoors without electronics or mind chatter, the baggage of our life washes away. Technology is not bad. It is a tool for the mind and body that is sometimes out of balance. We need balance and connection for the soul, and that comes from your personal connection with nature.

Get your face out of your phone and allow your life to begin. Your phone is a tool you choose when to use. Do not let your phone control you. Put it away to live fully.

Tune back into your surroundings. Engage in life in the physical world. Think of what you have missed buried in a virtual world. Look up before this lush environment is gone.

Some people just won't be able to tolerate the "empty" space between the noise. Those who do, will begin to have a new relationship, not only with themselves, but with the world around them. They will be fully open to receiving all that nature has to teach, with an open mind and heart, and they will gain a new friend.

Chapter 38

Nature As Healer

Troubled times
Changing times
Your time
Our time
The right time
An awakening time.

Think of a time when you were moved by a sunset, or felt peaceful and happy sitting quietly under a tree. Perhaps a bird migration caught your eye as you drove sealed within your car, and you felt an inexplicable yearning. Remember the last time you were caught in a storm, and it made you feel alive.

Sadly, many people have lost the respect and care for our Earth because they no longer live in it, but rather upon it. Modern man's desire for an easier life than his ancestors, has almost eliminated his personal connection with nature.

Our desire to conquer nature has distracted us from the magic and wonder. We relate to it as if we were in a museum looking through glass. Many people's relationship with nature is through television shows and they engage passively.

As I teach nature awareness, I observe that as people begin to reconnect with the Earth, they are vulnerable and teary-eyed, and often confused. As one's daily, city life is left behind and the Earth rhythm begins to take hold, the heart and soul connection grows stronger, and one realizes all that has been missed.

Sitting quietly for an hour in a grove of trees, feeling the wind, hearing the call of birds, and smelling the richness of loamy Earth, can often do more for the physical body and psyche than an hour in therapy.

When you go to nature for healing, put out the intention of walking in reverence. Go into nature with clear intent and respect, and enter in a good way.

***

If you work in an office building, in a city or somewhere removed from nature, you can lose a sense of daytime, and the natural light changes. You get disconnected from the Earth's rhythms and it distorts what's real. Which often results in mental exhaustion and depression.

We tend to long for our coveted vacation days, but don't wait, create vacation time daily. On a lunch break sit against a tree in the parking lot, on a patch of grass between cars if you have to. Take your shoes off and directly engage with the Earth. Walk to a park and sit on the grass and breathe in the scents. These little moments during the day will help re-energize you.

On the weekends pack a picnic lunch and get off trail at a regional park, or explore tide pools at a remote beach. Spend time gardening and getting to know your backyard and all who live there.

When you have more time, camp in the desert or the mountains. Walk into the past through the woods, live like we used to live with the Earth. Build a primitive, Earth shelter, sit for a day under an old growth tree and watch the sky. Let you self out to play and find your future, and I'll see you in the woods.

Nature's Pharmacy

Take a plant identification class, and learn how to harvest physical medicine directly from the Earth. As you learn more about what plants are right there available for you to use, you will gain a newfound respect for how our Earth can heal us from the inside out.

Nature As Protector

Finding refuge in nature saved my life. My connection to nature carried me through some rough emotional times when I was a child. It was a dark time in my life when horrific, abusive events happened. My parents were unaware of the abuse that was happening to me by neighbors, and I was threatened into silence, so I kept it all hidden.

We all suffer some traumas and have hard times, but it's how we handle those experiences that define our character. Do we become perpetual victims to our trauma, or do we allow the experience to mold us into better, more compassionate people?

When I was scared and wounded as a child, I was able to start my healing by befriending animals in the woods. Throughout the trauma I was experiencing, I embraced my gift of being able to connect with animals and nature on a very personal level. I could feel their energy, and their feelings they were communicating to me. They spoke to me on a universal level that I fully understood.

My bond with the animals became stronger, and it was a magical thing amidst the terror. My greatest comfort and solace always came from nature.

During one of the dark times, I found my spirit traveling to another place, another dimension. My mind was traveling into another realm, a place just as real and vibrant as the physical world. As I was drifting through a translucent veil into a meadow, exploding with lavender, and yellow and red wildflowers, a 1,500-pound Grizzly Bear came to greet me.

He nuzzled me and I felt completely safe. I was so happy to be with him that I wrapped myself around him, burying my face, and as much of my body as I could in his fur. He smelled of berries and dirt. His fur was coarse and warm, and he played with me until my hurt disappeared. He let me know that he would always be in that realm for me, and that I could go to him whenever I wanted or needed him. He came to be known as Big Bear to me.

Decades later, he is still with me. He is my spirit animal, my protector, and my savior. Much later in life I became acquainted with the terminology spirit world and spirit guide; yet, as a child I didn't need to know the words. I naturally accessed a world that not only took me into the primal mysteries of our physical world, but a world that saved my emotional life.

I had been mentored since I was five years old in the ways of the woods, so I knew my territory well. It was as much my home as the house I lived in.

I would often sneak out of my house at night, even at that young age with no fear, to spend as much time as I could in the woods behind our house. There was an irresistible pull, particularly to an old, giant, oak tree full of knotholes and twisting branches. I called it Grandfather Oak, and its mighty branches and leaves absorbed me into its loving mystery.

At night it looked as if it had a mouth that was speaking to me. It might have been scary to most kids, but to me it was welcoming and comforting. When I wrapped my arms around its trunk, I felt loved. The oak's energy calmed me, and gave me strength, and protected me during those fearful times - a communication we shared for years.

Grandfather Oak was one of the first non-humans I felt personally connected to, and had taught me about communicating and bonding with other non-humans. I learned how each living being has a feeling and energy that can be sensed and shared.

It's easier when one is young and still unformed by adult perceptions of what is supposedly real, but it is not a skill just for children. Adults can communicate in that manner as well, if they simply change their perception and re-examine their belief system.

I decided that I would set up a camp at the base of my new friend. I made a simple stick shelter, up against a log at the tree's base, and covered it with leaves and other forest litter.

Unbeknownst to my parents, I would sleep under the massive oak, and I gradually became a part of that place. In time the animals began to show themselves to me, as I was no longer an outsider.

Being a child, my energies were pure and non-threatening, and I was open to receiving the blessings the natural world gifted me.

I remember one night quickly falling asleep, exhausted from the fear that I had experienced earlier. I was awakened with a start in the middle of the night by something touching me. A raccoon was making his bed at the foot of my blanket. It was if my dog had shown up and I remember saying, "Where have you been all this time?" I didn't try to touch him, as I knew that he was still a wild animal, and I respected his power. He snuffled and curled into a ball, and we both fell asleep.

The next night my raccoon friend returned, and curled up at the foot of my blanket, but this time he let me touch him. He didn't come back for a long time after that however, and I missed his comforting presence at night.

When he did return, we got to know each other well. He never tried to bite me or hurt me in any way, and he often stayed with me for long periods of time. I think that was my first experience fully understanding the meaning of the word sacred. There was no other word for the bond that the raccoon and I had.

There were many other wondrous moments as well. I woke one morning to find six deer sleeping around me, the closest just a few feet away. Deer are heart animals, and I felt their comfort and protection. When I got up, they didn't run, but seemed content to let me go about my morning.

Animals can feel your energy and know when a healing is needed. Their support helped me through those horrible days.

I began to spend more time among the branches of my Grandfather Oak, more time in fact than on the ground. I moved my lean-to shelter in the branches, with my neighbor the squirrel just above me.

Above the squirrel and I was a hawk's nest. The branches were so thick and lush that the squirrel was never in danger from the hawk, and the hawk never felt threatened by my presence.

Eventually my lean-to grew into a hut, about six-by-six-foot square, where I could sleep comfortably. I was like a bird in its nest, high among the branches, safe from predators. I was so well hidden that one day two men walking in my direction didn't see me, as they took no care to fit into the natural flow of the woods.

Because of my experiences with the "dark people" I was distrustful. I got a weird feeling about these two men, so I kept very quiet. They stopped to talk for what seemed like an eternity right underneath me. My heart was pounding so hard I wondered if they could hear it. I asked the tree to help me stay calm, and I wrapped my arms around a branch and let my heart beat into it.

Amazingly, the tree seemed to take the fear from me, and I felt safely held in its limbs. Eventually the men moved on and they never looked up to see me there.

I was called to the woods as a way of alleviating the fear of those dark times in my early life. I listened to the spirit that called me to the safety of the woods, and was grateful for the adventure it provided me. I found my sanity at that early age by being able to literally feel the Earth.

Gaining new friends in nature was the beginning of my healing, and my lifelong connection with our Earth as our mother. I grew to know Grandfather Oak and Big Bear as friends and protectors.

I see trees and plants and animals as individuals, not as groups. When I walk through the woods, I feel a communication with the trees or specific plants, and I will often spend time in silent union with one that I am particularly drawn to.

Unlike humans, Grandfather Oak, the raccoon, the deer, and Big Bear were my guides and solace during those dark times. Perhaps because of my youth and my openness to the spirit energies of the non-human world, and the emotional trauma that I was suffering, I was able to connect deeply with the natural world. Gratefully, that sense of safety and belonging has never left me.

I believe that most children, who have had that nature-heart connection in childhood, but let it go as they grew, always seem to have a vague yearning and emptiness as adults. They are unaware that their youthful connection can be rekindled, and they can receive a healing.

Allow Love

Allow the natural world to love you. Be open to receiving this unique way of affection. It could be a bird song or a butterfly coming into your space. It could be a flower reaching out to you through its scent.

It could be the sound of a creek coming into your ears, giving you peace and tranquility. Let yourself be loved. It's ok. It's what the Earth is all about.

A life without nature is a lost life.

Time Back In

I thought I went to nature to escape, but I realized I go to nature to re-engage. I'm not running away; I'm returning Home, back to my real self. Back to my center. Back to my natural rhythm. It's not a time out. It's time back in. Spending time in nature is my reset.

When I get stagnant and lost, I go to nature. When I lose the zest for everyday life, I go to nature. When I hurt or when I'm happy, I go to nature.

I know I'm out of balance when I start emotionally believing that all the roles I play in different events around me, are who I am. Those may be things I do, but they are not who I am.

Nature is my reset. It inspires me. It reminds me what is real and what matters. Nature breaks everything down to truth. Nature's perception is neutral.

When you tune into nature's flow, it resets your mind and redirects you back on your path with clarity. I forget that so often, and then I need to remind myself to just open the door and go outside. Let go of the clutter and worry in my head and heart, and breathe in life.

Every time I re-engage outside, I jump back up with more energy and enthusiasm. Always.

Blue in nature is a healing color. Welcome in blue; blue sky, blue water, blue flowers, and feel the healing begin.

Shaman's Gift

One gift a shaman had in the tribal communities was the ability to talk to nature. This gift is for all, but shamans refined this skill to perfection, so direct knowledge and healing could come from nature.

Earth based healers can ask a plant what healing properties it has, and with a direct response, can begin using the medicine.

This Earth connection takes time spent communicating in nature, and time learning from skilled people, but it is still a very special, and practical healing practice.

Can a person receive too much beauty from nature? No. Not possible.

Mental Health And Nature

Anxiety can be debilitating. It can bring people to a place of being non-functional, and it can be triggered moment to moment.

Whether anxiety comes as a temporary phase triggered by life's circumstance or if it is a lifelong struggle, spending time in nature can help to alleviate some of the stress.

Focusing on what is happening directly in front of you can be a doorway through the moment. Get curious outside yourself. Curiosity can be a crack in the opening to a different focus and perspective.

Following an ant to its home, watching a bee pollinate flowers, being still enough to invite a bird into your space and seeing how they work, and play, and live, can all be just enough to pivot your focus outside yourself.

Burrowing your bare feet into the dirt to ground yourself, taking in the breeze to assist you with a full, slow breath, jumping in a cold creek to snap you back to being in the moment, climbing a tree and asking it to listen to your story and take away your pain, watching the clouds pass by and imagining them clearing away your stressful thoughts, can all be ways of connecting to nature as a healer.

367

Ask for help from your surroundings. All of Earth's beings are there for you. You are not alone. They feel your energy, and only want to reset the balance of the whole. We all work together for this, so ask for help. Show up and nature will be there for you, it is a part of you.

Returning Home

Coming home to the natural world is where many people long to be today. Since people have entered the so-called civilized age, we have done all that we can to separate ourselves from nature.

We wear clothes so we don't feel the weather. We wear thick shoes, so we don't feel the Earth. We build houses and buildings that keep us from feeling, seeing, and hearing nature. Throughout most of our lives we attempt to separate ourselves from nature which causes a feeling of emptiness.

To fill ourselves we must come full circle and return home again. Most importantly we need to feel as if we belong in the natural world, not separate from it. In this belonging will come great healing and a sense of peace.

Spend as much time as you can in nature. Do not let the weather stop you. If you are feeling short on time, start in your backyard.

Open your heart as wide as you can to connect and communicate with plants, trees, and animals. Let yourself fall in love with the beings in nature.

Sit quietly or wander with no planned destination or time limit. Let go, and let your inner vision guide you.

If you are on a beach, breathe in the salty air and let it flow through you. If you are in the desert, soak up the warmth of the sand.

Smell, feel and taste all that you can. Listen intently to the sounds. Widen your vision by looking up, down and all around. Be curious about your surroundings. In those moments no other troubles exist. As you see and feel more, life becomes more meaningful and purposeful.

There's always room to strengthen your bond, and no end to how seamlessly you can fuse with nature, it's who you are. When you are feeling distant, go back home by going outside.

You Are Water

Drink water as soon as you wake up. Give your body its life force. Your energy flows through water. Feel it give life to your body, to your Being, as it flows into you and through you, and then give thanks.

Waterfalls and springs have thousands of healing spirits that you can feel giving you life. Swim under waterfalls and dunk your head into springs. You will instantly feel your energy being restored.

Ask For Help

Nature is the ultimate healer. It's healing to have companionship, enjoy that shared energy. Sometimes that is with another person, and sometimes that means consciously sharing energy with the Earth.

There's a collective intelligence that's bigger than our brain. Trust the Earth's intelligence. It knows what is needed. Draw energy from the Earth and believe in nature to do the right thing. You are the Earth; you can heal yourself.

We Humans Are Ok

We are almost there. Don't give up. The dark of night lets the stars shine at their brightest, and then the night gives way to the light of day.

Eternal hope is powerful medicine. Tell the truth, but don't live in fear. The light will come through and uncertainty will become clear.

Balance

I was in an angry time in my life, and I drew other angry people to me to fight. I had to let that go. Shutting out the human world cannot be separate from your connection with nature. You cannot escape to nature for balance, and not have healthy human relationships, they are one and the same. If one is out of balance, they are both out of balance.

State Of Being

Why is it I can lose my mind in town over a malfunctioning gas pump, and 20 minutes later just outside of town, I lose my mind in the bliss of photographing a flower?

One is a state of mind, and the other is a state of grace. At one place I'm in my head, and in another I'm in my heart. How to be in both at the same time? ...Still working on that.

Truth and sanity are always found in nature. This is a healing that is needed in this insane time.

Looking Forward

One night sitting out on my land I was visited by the Earth Keeper. I was sad and in great fear of losing my way. I was in fear for the future of my commitments to share nature through Headwaters Outdoor School.

The year, 2020, was brutal for our Earth, and all that lives upon her. I've always worked for the greater good, and my school has been my greatest achievement in my life as an Earth Caretaker, and as a teacher. 2020 forced us all to take a time out and to close my school.

I missed interacting with our community, working, and playing alongside them. I missed the meals we shared, cooked with love by Julie and her kitchen crew.

I missed the sweat lodges, that magic and healing, and that deep Earth connection.

Mostly, I missed the students and the mentoring relationships I have with my apprentices. I missed waking up every morning with such a single-minded purpose, to share my love of our Earth with my students, and to infect them with the same passion.

It's truly an honor and a gift to be a teacher and mentor. I found myself lost being a teacher without students, knowing there was so much still to share.

I've been so lucky to do what I do, always surrounded by wonderful students and staff. I am so grateful for this abundant sacred land I live and work on.

That night I was sitting out, I was fearful of the future. I feared the loss of our school and my use as a teacher. I was afraid I wouldn't find that sweet spot inside of me that moves me to be the best person I can be. I was afraid of losing my creative edge and desire to start our school up again, when it was safe to do so.

Tears came, and the Earth Keeper appeared in the trees, and animals arrived as my witnesses. They held me while I cried for our school, for our community and for the Earth.

The Earth listened to me as I spoke of my fears. I spoke of global warming and the defining moment it's brought to humans. I feel these Earth-shattering moments as a vital time to act to rectify our destruction, or it will be too late.

I cried for all the species of animals and plants dying right now due to humans. I felt the hurt from the West Coast fires, the Australian fires, and the continued burning Amazon, the melting arctic, the dying coral reefs, the global famines, the COVID-19 virus, and the worldwide suffering.

I've always felt that empathy is a gift, to be able to feel what other beings feel. That night the feelings were too much for me to carry. Help arrived in a Screech Owl, which landed on a willow above me and began calling out.

I quieted myself to listen. My sadness and fear turned to wonder and appreciation, and connection to our Earth. Hope, inspiration, and ideas began to grow within me.

That warrior in me that never gives up awoke again, and a fire burned in me. My true self began to take over, ideas and solutions began to stir.

As I looked up at the owl, my eyes were drawn to the stars and the Pleiades star system, a place that always gives life to the dreamer in me.

The night became beauty and wonder, and my troubles drifted away. The Earth Keeper let me know that now, this time in history is the time of all time. This is the defining moment for humans, and our relationship with our Earth going forward. This is the right time. This is the time when the right people will show up and carry all beings into a beautiful future.

Work is needed to navigate the darkness to reach the light. In a way, it's the death of old ways that don't work, and finding the path into a future where our Earth, and all living beings are honored and allowed to live in a good way, for all life. The right people will show up and lead the way. The Earth Caretaking way.

The Earth Keeper said something so simple and so powerful. He said, **"Be the shining light of a star in the darkness. Never stop that light from shining. Never. It's who humans are when we are at our best, coming from love and kindness. Never give up, fight the good fight. The Earth Caretaker way for our Earth."**

The owl flew off and the night went quiet. At that moment I knew that there is no higher purpose to living life than caring for our Earth. It's who I am. It's who we are. So, join me in this epic moment in history. Let's let the light of the stars show us the way through all the chaos and darkness and uncertainty.

As we go through this, we emerge into a healthy Earth cared for by humans. A truly wonderful place to be. A place where all life is honored and flourishes. We must commit to caring for the Earth daily, and stay focused, and continue to learn.

We must take big action. Things may get much darker for a while, but look for that light, no matter how small it seems, and follow it. It is your guide to get through these times. It will illuminate your path.

I believe this is our time. It is our time to take on this task. We are not here by accident at this time in life. We are all Earth Caretakers. We will go about achieving that in different ways, but this is our primary life purpose, to be of service. It is your Calling.

I love our Earth. I love our Headwater's community. Our land here is one of those shining stars. I will continue to care for the land, and keep our school alive and well far into the future. It is my Calling, and I will follow that Call with honor. You have my word.

Tree Talk

When you're having a bad day, talk to a tree. Tell your story and let it take away your troubles.

Nature Heals Through Play

At Headwaters, we usually teach students who want to be here, and are excited to play in the woods and learn. On one occasion, we had a particularly challenging group of kids from a reservation in Washington. They were all around fourteen years old, and most of their parents were not present in their lives. Of the twenty kids, fifteen were being raised by grandparents or foster families. Many of their parents were in prison or in rehabilitation programs.

Kids being kids, they still hung out and joked, but not with our staff. They were very distrustful of adults, and especially of non-native adults, so we were not welcomed in their inner circle.

All this knowledge we knew ahead of time, but it was still our dedicated challenge to get them to start to build a relationship with nature as something they could count on.

For the first three days they were tough to deal with. Tim and I were tested time and again each day, with their reluctance and flat-out refusal to participate in any activity.

They were used to throwing their trash on the ground, and carving into any wood surface they could, even if that meant a live tree.

I'd consider myself pretty good with interacting with kids, but even I was starting to lose my cool. I watched as the kids threw trash on my ground, at my home. They didn't respect the land and critters because they hadn't experienced true respect themselves.

It was tough getting the kids to engage in any real conversation other than sarcasm or sometimes a head nod. Eventually, they gave us small glimpses into their daily lives. They let us know that most of their friends got pregnant around their age, and most of them had never left the reservation until this trip to Headwaters with their social worker.

As we gained more insight into their reality of life, we were understanding that being a kid for long wasn't an option for them. They were raising themselves, and had a rightful built-up defensive wall, for their own emotional and physical survival.

On day four, Tim pulled me aside and told me to just follow his lead. I was ready to try anything. We had watched their energy shift whenever they had time to play in the creek pools. You could begin to see the kid come out in them. There was a little spark of joy that they allowed themselves to show.

He told the kids we were going on an adventure to get to a big pond to swim at for the day, but they had to stay close and follow him.

The pond he was talking about was on our adjacent property, about an eight-minute walk, along a flat, grated, fire service road. So, I wasn't sure what Tim was up to when he prefaced it as an adventure to get there, but I was game.

He told the kids to leave their towels behind, and off we went. Tim sank down into our dipping pool in our shallow, camp creek. He then slid onto his belly and floated downstream. Ducking and crawling under willows and alder saplings, the whole group was making their way through the brush and water.

The journey started out with complaints of being poked by branches or being pushed from behind by impatient students trying to go faster.

Within ten minutes there was more giggling than complaining. Within twenty minutes, there was more laughing than just giggles. The put-downs and shaming each other ended, and within thirty minutes into our adventure, they were encouraging each other, and helping each other through the tough terrain.

I knew Tim was leading us in the opposite direction of the pond, and I was wondering how long their good mood would last. To my great surprise, the kids got even more excited as we left the water and hiked up, what we call, Bear Hill. At the top is an expansive look out point of Mt. Shasta, and the whole Shasta Valley to the north, towards the Oregon border.

There was a sense of pride that could be felt from the kids. They had made it to the top and were so happy with themselves.

As we followed Tim down the slope and onto a wide trail, I felt a hand slip into mine. I looked over at the young, teenage girl, beaming with joy. She hadn't spoken with me before that, and her smile was so infectious it grabbed my heart.

She told me how much fun she was having and was glad they were able to come to Headwaters. She asked about me and my life.

Soon another girl grabbed my other hand, and the three of us walked hand in hand swinging our arms as if we were young schoolgirls skipping along the trail.

We talked, and laughed, and shared short stories about our lives. When we finally reached the pond 90 minutes later, there were screams of laughter, as if we were in a play yard at recess.

At one point I looked over at Tim, and he was beaming with joy, playing in the water with the kids. When it was time to head back to camp for dinner, the kids asked if we were going to go back the same way. I told them that we would look for a shorter way back.

When we made it back to camp the easy way, in less than ten minutes, they didn't even question why it had taken us an hour and a half to get to the pond. They were just happy to be happy.

There was a weight lifted. A kindness emerged. Their defenses went down, and their pure, human spirit was allowed out to play.

There was a healing for those kids. Tim and I didn't do the healing. We provided and facilitated the opportunity for nature to do its magic. They received a healing through water, through adventure, through nature, and through the non-threatening space, that was held open for them to play.

When you hold a safe space for others, to allow them to drop their guard down and just have fun, that's a healing. Attentively listening to someone tell their story is a healing. Fully jumping into nature with your friends and sharing laughter, that's a healing.

In the last few days, the kids engaged more, and visibly had fun, and we all grew. I realized we are all kids. We want to have fun. We want challenges, but we also want companionship to help us through them. We want to do it ourselves, but also have support. We want adventure. We want leadership and independence. We want to play. We want boundaries, but we also want to get off trail in life sometimes and push those limits. We want to trust, and we want respect. Through nature we get all those things. We just need to jump in and go for it.

371

The kid's home lives more than likely didn't change when they returned. They may have had to put their guard back up to protect themselves, but their experience those few days will always be a part of them.

For a brief moment in their lives, they were allowed to be kids running free in nature. Sometimes that's all it takes to shift one's life trajectory just enough, to give them hope that things can be better. Without really knowing it, the kids were able to experience nature as a friend and healer, and that's a constant they can learn to trust.

Nature -Food For The Soul

One of the mysteries of life is that we don't really know why someone thrives and another doesn't. I know people who have risen above their addictions, despair and poverty and become sober, happy, and financially secure. I can't speak to how they did it, but I found my sanity at an early age by being able to literally feel the Earth.

I have been fortunate to have never lost my connection with nature. Being in it and of it, and teaching others how to appreciate it, rather than fear it, has been my life's work.

Growing up in nature and being allowed to have adventures in the wild that were dangerous, but character-forming, was all part of my core teachings. My parents never said no to my need to be outdoors.

I love to inspire adults to become kids again by building shelters, climbing trees, and sitting for an afternoon under a tree with absolutely no distractions. It's time for everyone to get dirty and muddy again.

Let nature inspire you and feed your creativity. We all need and want inspiration in our lives. We get busy doing and not being, and we forget. Time moves on and the day comes when we find our inspiration is what we've lost, but it's been right there for you all along.

When we're inspired, we get new ideas, new dreams, new hope. Go out to the woods or beach or mountains or deserts and let go.

Wander or sit in nature and pay attention to your thoughts, maybe write them down in a sacred journal. Build an altar or art piece with rocks, pinecones, or sticks. As you build, ask for inspiration, and let nature fill you up.

Dream big, don't hold back. Let go of your preconceived ideas. Be an open book, nature will write out the pages for you. Once these ideas come, it's up to you to give them life. You must birth them into your world through action.

The beauty is that nature doesn't have a need to control you. There is no attachment, there is no wrong, just inspiration to help actualize dreams.

Go into the wilds and let go, and find your *self*, your way, your path, your hope, and your dreams. Nature will always give. So, get off your butt and get out into the woods.

Chapter 39
Nature As Friend

We often only think of other humans as friends, but when you change this way of thinking, and include the natural world, your community will grow.

Start your friendship with nature by acknowledging other Beings as fellow Earth travelers. Have a feeling of gratitude for them. So many new friends from the animal, insect and plant world will emerge.

The Earth wants you to interact with Her and show up. Build the foundation of your relationship with nature just like you would in a human relationship, build your history, your stories, and your adventures through your interactions. When you have that bond, if you hurt the Earth, you will feel that wound, and you will change your actions to make it right.

Friendships need tending to grow, and should be cherished. Interacting with nature says, I care about you, I love you, I am interested in you, and I am invested in your well-being.

Get to know yourself through your friendship with nature. Have a conversation out loud, and also in your heart. Walk with the land, listen to the land, and get to know each other.

The most sacred relationship in life is true friendship.

Home

The living Earth itself can speak to us. She often speaks through her beauty. We see beauty and we are touched and often inspired.

We two-leggeds love dramatic views, they fill us with wonder and dreams. We can thank the Earth for this. Sunsets and sunrises speak to our own inner beauty. The Earth is speaking, and it feels good.

We don't think that the Earth itself intentionally shows us things to feed our soul, and so we rarely listen. When we do take in these sacred moments, we don't usually track it back to the Earth that's showing us these moments.

If we ask and pay attention, the Earth will show us our special, personal place where we feel we belong. Finding this place is so very important.

As we learn this Earth language, we understand more of our Earth's varied forms of communication as her wisdom is shared.

We are born with this connection and understanding, and then almost immediately it is stolen from us. Society doesn't emphasize the value of a personal relationship with the Earth, and in turn, parents don't always prioritize this connection either.

We must let our children be immersed with the Earth, in the trees, in the water, in the dirt. We must let our children be in nature from day one and every day after. It feeds their whole being and enhances their personal growth. It will shape their lives. It will lead them on life journeys that you alone can't imagine for them. We must trust the intelligence of the Earth, and the Spirit that moves through all things to care for our children.

The Earth has told me this. I know this to be true because I live it every day. There is a special energy place inside our bodies that's an Earth place, its colors are blue and green. It's not solid. It can't be touched. It is impossible to adequately explain, but I call it our Earth Place.

Our personal Earth Place connects to another similar place that lives inside our Earth. When a child connects their personal Earth Place, to the Earth's Place by interacting with nature, the connection of love, of Earth as home, comes alive. This fusion of these places stays for life, and only strengthens with more time in nature.

This place is the place within us that always calls us home. I personally call it the Green-Blue Place. It lives in all parts of humans. It is a Mystery. The logical mind cannot grasp it. It's about feeling trust.

As we grow with our Earth, we begin to feel it, and relate to it on levels unknown to our science, unknown to our logical mind. It doesn't matter if we even know about it, the Earth knows, and our sacred bodies know. Just live and protect our Earth as you would a good friend. That's it.

Befriending Nature

I talk a lot about dirt time. This is the essence of what I teach. It is the time that a person spends in the woods or anywhere in nature, perfecting their outdoor skills, and becoming as comfortable outside as one is inside.

A great starting place is with a tree. Standing in a forest, ask yourself if there is a particular tree that seems to call to you. Trust your feelings. Go to the tree and hug it, bury your face in the bark and smell it. Climb the tree and sit in the branches. If you are not able to climb, then sit up against it.

Look at the tree's beauty. Talk to it, lean on its trunk and ask for its help. Observe the insects that crawl on its bark-skin. Make a bed under your tree and spend the night with it. If you are not able to go to a forest, then take a nap under a tree in a park.

Your tree, like my Grandfather Oak, will take care of you. It will calm you and give you inner peace. Let yourself be open to everything near you – the sounds, the smells, and your thoughts. Maybe you will even be lucky enough to see the nature spirits – the "little people".

My nights spent with Grandfather Oak enhanced my senses. I began to see Earth spirits. I'd watch them floating through the air. They were different shapes and sizes, and sometimes just little flashes of light. Sometimes they looked like little people.

As a kid, I never thought any of this was strange. I thought it was just part of being in the woods. As an adult I have found that many people, particularly gardeners and others who spend a lot of time in nature, see these beings as well.

I used to sit up high in my oak with my buddy the squirrel, who was just a few branches above me, and feel the power of the tree. I could even feel the water being sucked up from the roots. It was an incredible sensation, and I felt as if I were part of the tree.

I would sometimes close my eyes and visualize myself going into the tree, and traveling through its bark layers.

A full-grown tree is one of the most powerful beings in nature. It bears the power of high winds and storms, swaying with the gusts as if it were dancing. The roots of the tree spread deep underground, stabilizing it as it grows.

It stands majestically in one spot for the entirety of its life, watching over all the creatures that live in its branches or in its bark.

If you sit in your tree for any length of time, you will feel the quiet majesty of your new friend. I think trees are happy when people explore them and touch them.

***

I remember trees, like some people remember childhood friends. I was about 10 years old, and I was exploring in the woods, when I heard noises that sounded like rocks being thrown against rocks.

It triggered something inside me because I got a sick feeling in my gut, and I knew something was wrong. The noises were coming from the creek where I had a small brush shelter, so I quietly and quickly made my way there. I slowed into a stealthy stalk to close the gap between the sounds and me.

When I got close, I looked out from behind a thick, coffee berry bush and saw three boys about my own age, throwing rocks at something. As I focused in, I could see that they were throwing rocks at lizards that were sunning themselves on the river rocks, along the streambed.

They were beautiful blue bellies, as we used to call them, and I could see that the boys had managed to kill one of them. I crawled closer through a patch of stinging nettle, taking care not to be seen or heard, until I reached the edge of the creek, where I could see the poor, dead lizard.

I wasn't particularly big for my age, and these boys were bigger than me, and well-known bullies at my school. When I saw what they were doing, my Big Bear inner power welled up in me, and filled me with an intense need to protect the lizards. I leapt to my feet screaming at the boys to stop. Unfortunately, it had no effect on them, and they just laughed at me, and continued to stone the lizards.

I was so mad, however, that I picked up a stick and threw it at them, hitting one of the kids. I tried to talk my way out of the inevitable confrontation, as they began to circle up on me. I knew I was outnumbered, and I bolted like a frightened deer running toward the creek, hopping, and leaping over rocks and boulders, splashing through water, and clambering over downed tree trunks.

I was ahead of them, but it wasn't going to be easy to get away from those athletic boys, who were intent on getting me. I felt like I was running for my life. I had seen these kids gang up on someone else before, and I knew I was in big trouble.

I ran a gauntlet down the stream, when I suddenly felt like I was being pulled, almost as if someone had reached out and grabbed me by the shirt. My heart was pounding, and when I turned to look, there was no one there.

It occurred to me that I was feeling the pulling in my gut. I stepped toward the guiding sensation, and I was literally yanked into a giant, old oak, much like Grandfather Oak. I was in a notch of the tree. It was as if the tree had pulled me into it.

The bullies soon caught up but ran past me. I felt safe there. When the boys ran past, I climbed into the higher branches, knowing that they would circle back when they didn't find me.

Once again, when they did come back, they never saw me in the tree. It proved to me again that nature can be a great friend and protector.

When the world is bat shit nuts, go back to what's real and sane…nature. That's where your friends are.

Earth Play

Don't be too serious. Laughter and play are so important in nature. Animals play endlessly. Animals make mistakes, they fall, they trip, they slip, they're just like us.

Play in nature, laugh in nature, and laugh *with* nature. Be a part of this life. When we are too serious, we separate ourselves, always join in the fun.

I cherish my experiences growing up in nature, and having been allowed to have adventures in the wild that were dangerous, but character-forming. My parents never said no to my need to be outdoors.

I like to inspire adults to become kids again by building shelters, climbing trees, and sitting for an afternoon under a tree with absolutely no distractions.

It's time for everyone to get dirty and muddy again. You will be amazed at what inspires you. Every day there are joyous opportunities meant just for you to find and experience.

Learn your skills, and go into nature, experience freedom, and have fun. All beings do it. Nature is the most honest relationship you will ever have; it asks nothing of you except respect. Nature never judges. Just show up and be aware.

We need to build a relationship with the Earth first and foremost. We need to play on her, and with her, and protect her. Go to the wilderness and bring the wild back with you. Learn to dance with nature. Sing to nature and with it.

The Earth has your back. Show her the same respect in return. Nature celebrates us. It loves us. You are never alone. When you strengthen your friendship with nature it will be a life turning experience. In engaging this intimately, you will have a moment when you connect so effortlessly, you feel a

belonging as a part of it. You are no longer an outsider looking in as if you are in a museum. You are home, you are at peace with a lifelong friend.

Truth

I go to nature to seek truth and it's so refreshing. Truth is nature's baseline, it's all that nature is, it can't not be.

When I go into nature, I take time to notice these offerings, to participate with and in truth, and I become a better human. Truth is a precious thing, to be coveted, it is the basis of every honorable friendship.

A Letter To Earth:

To my friend, my Earth. You've been a most wonderful mother to me all these years. I often wonder, where did I come from before my time with you? I often wonder when I die and become you, as Earth itself, where will I go? I don't want to leave you. I love you. I love my life upon you. So, I'm going to keep living as long as I can, and soak you up.

When I do physically leave you, just know I'll be back as an Earth Keeper, living and caring for you once again. At least that's my plan.

I'm writing this letter at this moment in time because I've been very troubled. I'm not at ease, I'm scared and angry. I am confused. It's about the harm my fellow Earthlings are causing you. I feel your pain and I know you feel mine. I want to do the right thing, and some days I just feel hopeless, and I'm generally a hopeful person. I need you, my Earth, to help me going forward. Talk to me, give me a sign.

I feel I must do more to help you with this problem of humans abusing you. What to do with the two-legged Earthlings called humans? I know we humans love you, but we seem to be out of control. We are lost in our quest to grow and develop. We've forgotten the basics. We've forgotten to care for you Earth, and yet you care for us.

I feel equally as lost as to what to do. I've spent my whole life in service to you. Now I find myself so scared for your safety, and in turn ours.

I'm remembering my early years growing up. This was when I built my foundational relationship with you. I fell in love with you as my mentor, and you raised me ever so close to you. You taught me to see beauty. You taught me love and self-reliance. You showed me Spirit. You introduced me to all your relations, mountains, oceans, rivers, animals, trees, and plants. It was a wonderful childhood to be raised by you. A true blessing.

At a young age I found the purpose of my life upon you, to be an Earth Caretaker for you. I have been called to do all that I can to help you be healthy. When I began in earnest working for you, I had much hope. People were beginning to work for you worldwide.

Through the sixties and seventies, the Wilderness Act was created. Land was saved around the world in parks and reserves. The Endangered Species Act was created to help wildlife. Humans began to learn, and more importantly wanted to learn how to care for you. People of all races, religions, politics, young and old began to learn how to help you, my Earth.

We stopped killing whales, we saved ocean environments, we began learning how to live in a way that respects you. A healthier way for all life. There were setbacks. There was much pain and loss, and yet hope still lived strong in humans, and strong in me. I've always been a dreamer. You taught me to dream. You are a dream come true.

So, here I sit talking with you, committed to you, but scared, lost and angry. Our human world today has stepped back into the dark times. We've lost our way. Many heroes are still at work, and I earnestly believe when humans are fully committed, we can significantly move in the right direction. So, my Earth, I won't ever give up, never. I'm thankful you've never given up on me or humanity.

We are young. We are finding ourselves. We know what to do, that's the good news. We even have great knowledge and creativity to build technology to help right our wrongs. Our greatest time is yet to come as we embrace our purpose to be Earth Caretakers. It will be what brings our human community together for a Higher Purpose.

So, please be patient with us, we will find our better nature. Please keep making our air, keep growing our food, keep giving us water, keep giving us healthy land, a home to thrive on. Keep our oceans, lakes and streams flowing and alive with abundant life, and give us those green trees, and flowers, and meadows.

I will continue to keep caring for the birds, they are always a gift to see and spend time with. I call them flying blessings of color and song, and I dream of flying with them.

I will do what I can to keep our mammals protected so they can thrive. I will give them food, space, and help to keep them from being constantly run over by cars. I will continue to help educate people so that the animals are not being over-hunted.

I will fight to keep the mountains wild, so the Gods, the spirits of the land, have places to thrive. Through all of this, let us become so inspired to live in a good way.

My Earth, my friend, my teacher, my Home. Hold us close in love and respect as we grow up and find our greatness to become Earth Caretakers. Help us to wake up to what is needed and inspire us. I believe in the future because I'm living a dream, a miracle as an Earthling.

This is the only Earth we know of. When our astronauts who were on the far side of the moon, took your photograph, and brought it home to show us You, we had only imagined what you looked like as a whole. At that point we all stood in awe of your beauty, and fully embraced you with pride that you were *our* home.

When I look at that photograph, I feel your beating heart, the green and blue and white. All of what that photograph is, is wonderful, precious, glorious life.

So, my Earth, please keep the communication open as I will be speaking and listening to you again and again. Thank you, Earth, for the gift of life. Thank you, my friend.

Today I fell in love with our Earth, just as I do every day.

Make Nature Personal

Wherever you live, pick a tree, a rock, a plant, a body of water or whatever calls to you. Go to that place on regular visits, and *fully* engage with that being. Talk to these beings. Awaken your senses, smell, taste, feel, listen, and look deeply, and I mean deeply.

Imagine yourself as one with these things. Feel what they feel. Notice how they fit into their environment and affect it.

Every visit will make your relationship stronger with this being. This relationship will connect you to the entire ecosystem where hearts open, knowledge grows, and empathy is given life.

All things in nature are alive. Some things are very similar to humans, and others, such as rocks and water are very different, but never-the-less, alive. Leave out judgment and comparisons.

Be open to connection through love, respect, and curiosity. You'll be alive with oneness with our Earth. All life becomes full of wonder. You'll know that you belong on our Earth as a part of it. Life becomes a prayer of gratitude. The way we are meant to live.

Become An Explorer

Go out in nature for an hour or many days, it doesn't matter. Take little with you or better yet, take nothing. When you arrive, become an explorer. At some point the fire of the Earth will ignite within you, build upon that passion and you won't allow it to be extinguished. It will become internally sacred.

Be A Friend

There are trees in the city that want to be talked to. It's important to get out into the wilds to connect, but the plants and trees in the cities appreciate your attention as well. Think of the poor trees in those cement sidewalk strips. Think about their need for interaction to thrive.

Science has proven plants are living beings with their own form of consciousness. Don't ever think you're not being witnessed. Plants and trees hold you accountable. You are being watched by the surrounding trees and plants. These beings pay attention.

It's up to you to be sensitive enough to feel them. One of the best ways to know them is to climb up in trees and hang out with them. Touch is the most direct communication, and city trees crave this interaction the most. Make a friend in the city.

My Day With Ollie

Franklin Point Beach. Rocks and waves crashing, finding gaps, new homes, and ways to flow. Seagrass beneath bare feet, gulls screaming overhead, my friends the pelicans, skimming the waves for fish.

Harbor seals bearing witness, ocean on three sides of this western point. Ollie, age 8, my nephew, sees movement in a crack, waves crash over our bare feet.

Water retreats, Ollie reaches into the crack and pulls out a small crab. "Hold it gently," I say. All eight legs moving, and then it happened, Ollie held the crab up, and he and the crab looked at each other. I witnessed this sacred moment, a smile so big and so wonderful I felt blessed by this moment. That crab touched that boy that day, pure and simple, and yet profound, a forever moment.

The crab returned to the crack in the rock with a story to tell about those crazy humans. A blessed sacred moment in nature's time. Ollie, myself, the crab, and Franklin Point, a day we all shared.

Chapter 40
Live In Gratitude

Make every day an expression of your thankfulness for our Earth. Make gratitude, your personal medicine. Countless lives will benefit from your way of life. Living this way opens the heart and mind to more meaningful places awaiting all of us. Take the step into living in appreciation.

What creates a selfless nature with an intent on helping others? Perhaps it starts with a childhood grounded in humility, healthy curiosity, hard work, lots of love, giving and receiving, and gratitude.

Gratitude helps us see abundance in times of fear and scarcity. It replaces longing with contentment. It guides us toward appreciation of what we have, rather than dwelling on what we don't have.

Gratitude opens space for more gratitude. If you feel good about something in nature; such as a sacred moment, a sunset or sunrise, an experience with an animal, waking to a bird's song, falling asleep under the stars, or anything that feels good to you- feel gratitude or express it in some other personal way. That's it.

Acknowledge the small things, seen and unseen. They all play a part in our life. Gratitude then makes the experience medicine by pulling it out of the small, whole experience. The act of gratitude is a prayer. Gratitude is love expressed.

As a steward of the Earth, it's our obligation to give back, and feel gratitude for the blessing of being born into this life.

Gratitude To The Humpback Whales

Today I snorkeled over a reef on the Big Island of Hawaii. A Humpback Whale sang to me. It was pure bliss. Floating, sunset, fish, coral, whale song. It was all I could ever want.

Hope

Do you have hope for our Earth? It's very hard to be educated in the ways of nature, to learn what's been happening to our land and animals, and have hope for the future. It's very hard.

I do have hope though. I give you my word. Hope is the medicine that keeps me engaged in working for our planet's health and wellbeing.

Please don't misunderstand me. I go through the gamut of feelings and emotions. I feel anger, sometimes extreme anger, sometimes I want my predator side to attack out of protection. Sometimes I'm so angry I want to do harm. Sometimes I'm extremely sad and I cry deeply. Sometimes I feel useless and helpless. Sometimes I feel lost and lonely.

As I'm committed to continuing to be educated on what's happening to our Earth, to our animals, plants, and water, sometimes it hurts so bad I don't think I can go on another minute. Then I find that place inside where hope lives, and I grab it and get to work. That's all I can do.

Being engaged in the good work of caretaking, and protecting our Earth is surely the ultimate nurturing for the soul. We must honor our feelings, all of them. We must give them a voice, and then do what is right, and get to work for the good.

Hope is powerful medicine. When coupled with commitment, knowledge, and good, hard work, as well as love and gratitude, and wonder, hope will be the inspiration that creates healing change. Nature is worth it all.

Hope leads to many paths that might never be found without it. Hope itself is a pathway to inner peace. Look anywhere in nature, and you *will* find hope. The question is when you find it, what will you do with it?

It's always a good day in the woods. Every day a gift awaits you, perhaps many. Go find those gifts. Your only giveback is to fall more deeply in love with nature.

Take On A Word

Gratitude and kindness are simple words, but when you take on a word, it becomes alive in you, and you become it. You take on its essence as a living Being in you. When you are in this state of being, every day on this Earth becomes the best day of your life.

Wake Up And Cheer

Wake up early when it's still dark. Listen for the very first bird call. Then listen for the wake-up choir, all the birds waking together, greeting the day. It's glorious to be alive. Enjoy that cup of coffee.

Wake up consciously, wake in gratitude for the Earth, and all that nature gives us to live. Turn on the light switch, and we have light. Turn on the faucet, and we have water to drink and bathe in. Open the door, and we have shelter. Go to the store, and we have food.

All you need is out there on the land, spiritually, emotionally, physically, intellectually, it's all there waiting for you. Get out there and say thank you by enjoying the land.

Wake up and cheer, life is amazing and there's so much to cheer about. Celebrate our Earth. Celebrate life. It's good to be alive.

Blessings

In the Earth Ways, blessings are given in moments of gratitude. Blessings are given to things that touch you in some way. Water that you drink, food that you eat, anything can be blessed. It is simply wishing something well, good tidings, happiness, good health, safety. The medicine is in the gesture.

When a blessing occurs, it is like the spirits of the place awaken and do their work of protection, preservation, and connection. These Earth spirits work with the natural web of life. They help all things in nature to have balance and strength, through connection. They work like the roots of trees in a forest. Their connection stays strong and vibrant. Everything is simply better for the blessing.

Appreciate a bird song, and give gratitude and blessings for an amazing life. Some gifts are not physical but can be life changing through their inspiration. When you give something a blessing, it's calling you. There's a reason you felt the urge to give it a blessing. It needed it.

Blessings can also be used with people for protection and awareness. Before a hike or a wilderness trip, a difficult mountain climb, or vision quest, offer a blessing and the land itself will become your protector, as will the Earth spirits. Give a blessing to anything and anyone, and it will all come back to you.

I Live Here…

I Live here where the water runs clear, and I can drink from the Earth with no vessel between it and my lips.

I live here with our pack, and am especially watched over by my Kodi boy and wolf Riley.

I live here where I help grow and raise what I eat.

I live here where I physically participate in living my life.

I live here with the honeybees, and sacred gardens, and towering trees.

I live here where smell is welcomed, and no scents avoided through a mask.

I live here where the blue sky is truly blue, and green has far more shades than I can count.

I live here where my backyard has no fences, and keeps me humble and aware of who else resides in the forest.

I live here through four glorious seasons, and grateful for what each one brings, even the challenges.

I live here where days vanish as if minutes, where calendars and clocks have little use because it doesn't matter what the name of the day is, weekends, workdays, and play are all the same.

I live here where I sleep when I'm tired from a maxed-out day of living, and wake ready to jump in fully again, not knowing what each day will bring.

I live here where my home itself is a natural work of art, where it inspires me, and my personal art is a constant prayer.

I live here where my neighbors are my interdependent community, my true social security, and my friends.

I live here where people acknowledge each other and wave hello when I drive by.

I live here where I know I make a difference each day, and whether anyone else is aware of it or not, I am.

I live here where I thrive in abundance and love.

I live here in complete gratitude.

I live fully here.

Letters Of Gratitude

Christmas Day 2016, My Birthday

Here I sit, a wood stove warming me, inside and out. Five degrees outside. It's a good day to be alive.

Tonight Mt. Shasta spoke to me, bright pink in the last light, framed by pastel blue sky. Only you could do that, Mt. Shasta. Ice crystals forming in Dale Creek gave birth to wonder in me.

My dogs walked me through the woods today, showing me where every animal walked last night, and who they were. I love the beauty of tracks in snow. Nothing better than walking with dogs, being part of the pack. I'm reminded of earlier years, less complicated.

The mother and baby deer enjoyed our food gifts of bread and veggies. I worry about them in this bitter cold. They seem to have claimed Headwaters as their home.

The songbirds inspired me to explore more deeply into my land. Every day hundreds of songbirds eat at our feeders, always inspiring me to explore, to be brave, to live and play. I truly admire birds. They are love and beauty on the wing.

The sun, shining through the fog, setting the frozen snow aglow speaks to me. It says, "It's good to be alive. It's good to be an Earthling." Thank you gravity, thank you air, thank you water. Our creator did wonderful work. Our Earth is a masterpiece.

Snow offers the gift of tracks through our eyes. Once our eyes receive them, they are given over to our brain, and then we think, "Who was here? What was this being doing, and why?"

Our beauty eyes see nature art, they see the track manuscript on the snow. The animals have shared their story with me. Just enough to inspire me to look through the veils of layered worlds.

Thank you to my fellow Headwaters friends who live on this wonderful land with me. The mice, rabbits, coyotes, and the foxes. Thank you to the wolves that tell me more of them will come back one day. Thank you to the vultures, the hawks, the songbirds, and woodpeckers.

Thank you to the pack rats, skunks, weasels, pine martens, raccoons, bobcats, cougars, reptiles, and fish. Thank you to bear, my true friend, always around. To our honeybees and chickens for teaching me love through caretaking. When another being's life depends on me, I become a better human being. Caring for another, allows me to live in the state of love.

Thank you to the deer for living with me. Thank you deer, squirrel and chipmunk for teaching me to share my garden. These animals remind me where, and how I live. They remind me of how small and yet big I am. For a moment, I am reminded how good it is to be part of so much life upon our Earth. It's a good day, a lucky day.

I worry about the night's coming cold. I worry for the animals, and I wish them well. I think of the old saying, "One for all and all for one." This is a good way to live.

I think of my dog friends that have passed on. I love them so much. Tank, Bear, Scout, Mattie, Kodi, Joseph, Riley, Crash, Benny, Koa and Jackson. I truly miss them. Thank you for our time together.

Vegas, the rooster, crows, reminding me to break the ice in the chickens' water dish. It's good to be reminded of my commitment by a crazy rooster.

In this land I found my dream. I am this land's caretaker, and Earth Keeper. This word "Earth Keeper" defines me to my soul. I am rich beyond imagination, and honored to know my place on this sacred Earth. I am full of purpose and wonder.

I have a great home, even when so much hopelessness exists, I know I can dream any future I want for myself.

To all my friends and family that are still here, and to those who have moved on, I thank you for the gift of yourselves in my life. You all live within me.

Thank you to the Earth Keeper, my companion. My commitment to this life is to give more of myself than ever before to our Earth, to Headwaters, to my family, to my students, to our country, and to our planet.

I've been called to caretake my land going into the future in a deeper way, a way that is still being revealed.

Gratitude for all, and Happy New Year! - Tim

Thank You, President Obama, (This was written just after Barack Obama's farewell speech, and lots of tears. 1/10/17)

I watched President Obama's Farewell Address. I cried. He was my president. I'm proud I voted for him. I want to say thank you for something that few people know about, that Barack Obama did. He very quietly became the greatest environmental president in our nation's history.

I'm a lover of, and a fighter for the Earth. Our Earth is our home, our sacred space. President Obama protected more land than the great Teddy Roosevelt, and Franklin Roosevelt, combined. In parks and preserves of all kinds, he has preserved more than 550 million acres of land and ocean. A gift to our Earth and all humanity.

Think for a moment, of all the animals, and trees, and mountains, and rivers, and oceans that are protected. Think of all the trillions of living beings that are safe because of Barack Obama, and those who educated him on this need. The greatness of this achievement is beyond comprehension. The depth of love and understanding it took to save these lands, the message this work sends to our Earth is beyond beautiful. It shows human beings at our best. I voted for the Earth, and I voted well. I'm very happy about that.

I'm fearful, but inspired for our future, for our Earth. This fear has ignited a fire in me, to continue to live and work for our planet for my entire life. Our Earth is calling us home. Heed the call and go to work. Continue on this important path. Be an Earth Caretaker. Make everyday Earth Day.

Ho! To all the Earth Keepers, we thank you. You are heroes.

Friends Along The Way

I've been reflecting a lot about my life. It's been wonderful. There's very little that I would change. In my reflection I've thought a lot about the richness that all my close animal friends have brought to my life.

I was lucky to be raised with animals, so I've always known how to be with them, how to speak with them, how to meet them in that special place, that place that's sacred, that heart-space where I can be real with them. No fear, no need for over control.

It's truly a unique shared place that many humans rarely experience, and I've been blessed my entire life with these kinds of relationships.

So, I offer my thanks to them all, and I look forward to seeing them again on my next journey. They made me who I am, and I am forever grateful. Acknowledging my animal friends leads me through my life's journey.

Thank you to Boots and Corky, my cat and dog, who ushered me through my early childhood. To my Sheepdogs, Clyde, Blue and Wiggles, who were with me through my teens. To Arco, my protector, my German Shepherd.

To all the farm animals at my grandfather's farm in Ronan, Montana; the dairy cows, the meat cows, pigs, chickens and turkeys. To the wild cats that I loved and protected. To the bats that lived in the farmhouse attic, and kept me company at night.

Thanks to my parakeet, Henry, who brought me through pneumonia at five years old. To my cat, Sam, who only lived to six months old, and died of Cancer. Sam taught me love and loss.

To all the wild animals that shared my days in the woods as I grew up. Gratitude to the lizards and the snakes that let me hold them. Thank you to all 30 of my snakes I had in my room as a kid, and eventually released back into nature. The countless insects, frogs, and salamanders. The fish that taught me so many nature skills. I am humbled by the deer and raccoons that spent many nights with me.

It's hard to write this. Tears flow as the memories come back. When you love animals deeply, you have to learn to accept their loss, as most don't outlive us. It's painful to remember, and it's good too.

Thanks to Jeb, who slept with me in the Trinity Alps Wilderness in the summers on horse packing trips. He was such a loyal dog. To all the horses that shared my younger years. The mystic Arabian stallion that let me train him, and gave me his power to carry. Gratitude to my quarter horse, who carried me through the Santa Cruz mountains for endless miles. To all the pack horses.

To Blackie, the raven, who was kicked by a horse and broke his wing. He came into my life at a very important time. I thank Blackie for the 20 years we had together. Thank you to all my pet rats, mice, and hamsters.

In writing this, I'm amazed by all my animal friends. I'm fearful I might forget one. I was fortunate to work with wild and exotic animals from my teens to late twenties. Some of my most sacred relationships came from this time.

I thank the chimpanzees I worked and lived with every day. Thank you, Raffles, my most beloved animal friend ever. You will always be my great love, my brother. I still love you. I always will. Gratitude to Gabby and Jai. Thanks to my baby chimps, Bobby, and to Kobi who taught me about deep sadness for the loss of love, and taught me my limits on how to help, and how to just hold space. Thanks Kobi. To Kong, my gorilla and motorcycle riding partner. To my monkeys, and baboons, John, George, Ted, Jenny, Chloe, and Jane.

I forged life long, altering relationships with many elephants that I loved, with all the love I could ever have. To them I say thanks. Sampson, my big male, who taught me how to move through pure terror, and find peace and loyalty on the other side. Ho to Sam!

Thanks to Matiedi, who died in my arms. She allowed me to usher her through to the other worlds. To Mable and Flossy, my true babies. To Mardji, who was a goddess. She carried me through the Mojave Desert on her back. Elephants, all of you, thank you.

Thank you to all the tigers, lions, cheetahs, leopards, and especially Nina, the black leopard that loved to jump on me so I could catch her. Thanks to Jeeter, the water buffalo, who carried Raffles, my chimp, and I, through our home, Marine World. He proved that anything was possible, as the experts had said it couldn't happen.

Thanks to Cobra, my Harpy Eagle that trusted me to hold her on my arm, and to fly her into crowds. I know she longed for her jungle rainforest. I couldn't give that to her.

A huge thank you to Keanu, the Orca Whale, who was my secret nighttime swimming partner. My trip with you to Japan was so unbelievable, that I still can't believe it was real. I truly hope I helped you on that journey, and I hope I made your life in captivity better. I'll never forget you. What happened to you

should never happen to an Orca whale. Thank you, to all the seals and dolphins I swam with after hours at Marine World. All I can say is, Wow!

Thanks to Fred, the wild moose, who visited me every day at the Alberta Game Farm in Canada. Thanks to Jenny, my daily elephant companion, who traveled into the woods of Canada with me, and all across Canada on speaking engagements.

Thanks to the Mountain Gorillas, the rhinos, and hippos. Thank you to the 800-pound Siberian Tigers who sent me on crazy chases in 50 degree below zero weather, to find them fresh meat.

Thank you to the Chinese Leopards for not killing me. I love life. Thanks to the wolverines who never stopped giving me the chills, as I wondered what they would do to me. A very special thank you to the bears I worked with. The Black Bears, The Grizzly Bears, and the Polar Bears. Thank you again to the six Polar Bears who allowed me to live, when I slipped on the ice. I appreciate your kindness.

Thank you to the giraffes, zebras, gazelle, wild sheep and goats, deer, elk, and moose. The bobcats, lynx, servals, and African wild cats. To my muskrat friend, who I tracked through endless bogs, and thank you to the prairie dogs.

A most heartfelt thanks to the wolf pack I often lived with, and ran with. I still can't believe my luck. Unbelievable. Thanks to the alpha male and female for taking me into this pack, especially for giving me a true once in a lifetime moment, when the female let me crawl into her den and lay with her newborn babies. I still get chills.

Thank you to the draft horses that waited all night for me in 50 below temperatures to hook them up to a sleigh. They pulled me through ice and snow, to feed over 1600 animals every single day. They are my heroes.

Thanks to Shelby, the musk ox, who allowed me to bring her back to life. I couldn't have survived the grief if she had died then. She was a miracle. Thanks to the red panda and giant pandas. Just being in their presence was sacred.

In the city of Miami, I had countless relationships that changed my life. Thank you to the elephant, Dollop, who never liked me, and always tried to kill me. You kept me humble Dollop. Thank you.

To Babe, the elephant who had been so abused but then so loved by me. We healed each other with our love. She knew so much pain, so much, and kept on loving and living. My heart-hero.

Thanks to my wild, manatee friend on Key Biscayne Island. Every day after work, you would meet me at our secret lagoon. I'd feed you watermelons and lettuce, and we would swim and play. Wild man and wild manatee. I got to swim with a real mermaid. It doesn't get any better than that.

Thank you to Luna, our Great Horned Owl, who connected humans and wildness by allowing so many people to touch and admire you. Thank you to Edith, my first Great Horned owl in my care. You taught me to see you, through your one eye. Thank you to Porsche, my Red-tailed Hawk for helping to educate humans through your wounds. To my Osprey who allowed me to give her a new life as an ambassador for wildlife everywhere.

Those years in the zoos and parks were instrumental in my life. To the thousands of animals that let me clean their homes, sit with them, sing to them, cry with them, share joy with them, know their fear and loss, their dreams. I hope I made your life better. You all did that for me, and I am grateful. – Your forever friend, Tim

"You have the inherent right to be happy." - The Constitution of the United States of America

***

Have gratitude for those visionaries who had the foresight, and did the work, laid the foundation, and created this sacred document with the intention of not only physical, equal rights, but for the rights of the *spirit* of humans as well.

We need to have gratitude for those who started down this path of right living, and we need to continue forward with making it right and just for all.

Of course, we need to continue to work on growing into the right ideals, but that's what life is, constant change and growth. Let's continue to adjust our intention towards what's best for all, and have gratitude that we have the freedom to make this choice.

Gratitude is life expressed through living in love.
Gratitude is a chosen way of life.

Of all the places my soul could live, our Earth is my home. What luck! What joy!

Chapter 41
The Earth Caretaker Way Movement

The Earth Caretaker Way is about taking moments out of your lives to help something outside of yourself, but that is also intrinsically connected within.

Fighting For Future Generations

I am not a naturalist by degree. I am a true lover of nature. I have spent my life adventuring, working, and teaching in nature. I share from my heart. I can speak to the Earth and speak for the Earth. The Earth does speak to me and through me. I never question this; it has always just happened.

I've lived off of, and with the land for months at a time. I have tracked countless animals and lived and interacted with them on a personal level. I've fought for trees and landscapes, at times risking my own life.

I've taught wilderness skills, and my love of the Earth to many thousands of adults and children. I've vision quested almost half as many adult years as I've been alive.

I've fished in the oceans, lakes, and countless wild streams. I've hunted deer, rabbits, birds, and squirrels for food when I was younger, until my heart couldn't make another killing.

I have rescued and rehabilitated hundreds of beings from insects to elephants, and gave my heart equally to each one.

I've worked with and befriended a variety of wild and exotic animals through varying occupations, and life experiences.

I have extensively photographed the American West, and have spent in between time photographing various parts of the world to show the glory of our Earth and her needs.

Taking on my teachings and initiations from my elders, I have led a lifetime of sweat lodges to connect my community in a sacred way to our Earth.

I've fallen in love on the land. I've sang Earth songs, always. I've dreamed my life into a life of living on the land that I own, and caretake, and manifested Headwaters Outdoor School. It became my purpose for living when I found my land. I was initiated as an Earth Keeper. I have always been an Earth Keeper, but once I took on caring for this land my purpose became clear.

***

It's become obvious to me that Headwaters Outdoor School is so much more than a school. It's become a sacred space for a grouping of people, of all ages, that have for decades now, been a part of our community.

Our school and land holds space for our community. It has become a source of light. I believe Headwaters has become sacred space for many reasons. The land itself has always been very powerful. Over the years I have witnessed the land transform countless lives.

The work, and all the love that so many people have put into Headwaters has added powerful medicine, and has added purpose to the land. The land is our teacher.

The teachings at our school have become so powerful, that we now have countless lovers of nature sharing about their personal connections with others, and influencing them to get outside and enjoy nature, and protect her.

I now know that much of my legacy lies in my students taking their love of nature out into the world, and changing it for the better. I am hoping they will also create more teaching-learning communities to share their enthusiasm.

The largest movement in world history is happening right now globally. There are growing pockets of people of all ages, with different lifestyles, working independently at various levels to fight for our Earth. We are working to stop poverty, and abuse to people, and to animals, and to our Earth. What makes this movement so great is that it's spontaneous, and creative.

People aren't waiting for someone else to do something. They are doing it on their own because it's the right thing to do. It's the only way anything ever gets done, by one caring, dedicated person with an idea, acting in any small or big way. These people are not standing on the sidelines thinking it's someone else's problem. They know it is all our responsibility to take care of the planet we all live on.

There is no reality in the separation of countries or living class. All of that is an illusion created by people who are not aware, either by choice, or fear, or ignorance. We need to acknowledge the truth, that what happens on one side of the Earth eventually happens on the other. There is no air filter between our made-up boundaries. We are all in this life together. When we lift others up, we all rise.

This environmental movement is service in the best way it can be. This kind of service always makes a full circle. These beneficial changes are being felt by our world. It takes risk takers to say and do what's right even when it's not easy. This is the generation and mix of people that will take us into a new way of living. We are here to shake things up and tip the scales back in our favor to create balance.

We, as a human race, tend to let things go that we know need fixing, until it hurts bad enough. We are on that edge where *everyone* will feel it bad enough. The effects of drinking up our own pond that we live in is not something that the wealthy can buy their way out of.

A credit card won't bring long-term water in a drought. Money won't buy healthy food without poisons when everything is contaminated.

There are a lot of negative actions and situations happening, but the exciting part of our fortunate life is that we have the opportunity to jump into the adventure of creating a new way of living.

Now that I am in my sixties, I believe it is time to pass on more of my insights of building a deep relationship with our Earth. Through my outdoor school I can only connect with a limited number of people each year, and we are at a time where these skills, and action motivated teachings, need to be shared much farther out into the world.

What is obvious is that we need to act more aggressively, and with much larger numbers than what individual awareness programs can do on their own. This is not a time to think small. This is a time to think and act big.

I have been able to manifest my dreams into reality, and I have had a vision for quite some time, to birth the movement of The Earth Caretaker Way. The mission of this movement is to initiate everyone into their birthright as Earth Caretakers. To remind people of their life purpose of caring for this Earth, and all beings upon her through their daily actions. This movement is a soul awakening.

This calling to establish The Earth Caretaker Way has grown from a spark of an idea, into action. I know my involvement in this is to help establish this movement, and then it is the younger generation's role to carry it on and make it grow.

Myself, along with a handful of amazing and inspirational, young adults, have created The Earth Caretaker Way. Our intention is to grow this collective, caretaking movement to five million Earth Caretakers, within a few years, and continue this growth globally to billions.

Our focus initially is supporting further efforts of nature conservancy organizations. Our vision is to save land for the sake of saving the wilds, and educating people on land conservation, restoration, and long-term land caretaking.

At Headwaters our intention is to help people build a personal relationship with nature. The Earth Caretaker Way goes into the next step of living a life with the purpose of being a caretaker of nature.

Our goal is to get people to transform their property, yards or balconies into wildlife habitat, and create the largest continuous wildlife sanctuary in doing so.

Currently humans have developed over 70% of Earth's land and fresh water. We need to save fifty percent of the land on Earth as wild land. That would go a long way to balancing out the damage eight

billion people have caused by living in a modern world. This protected portion of wild Earth will give a home to plants and animals to flourish naturally.

We can go to these wilds to hike, observe and fill up our souls. Saving this space can bring all people and nations together for a higher purpose. This is a worthy goal bigger than ourselves, that could unite us all.

By using technology and what we already know, we can eliminate poisons such as oil and chemicals that damage our land. Let's engage this knowledge and bring new ideas into action to go forward. With our intelligence and our empathy, I believe anything is possible. Let's get to work creating countless new ways to grow food that are healthy for the Earth and humans.

We need to immediately stop factory farming, which is evil and death to our collective heart and soul. Let's make cities wildlife havens, and bring balance and peace to our urban and rural homes.

Let's make farmland good for all animals and people, and restore the biodiversity we need to survive. Let's create beauty everywhere. Let's eliminate racism, and specialism, and hatred around our world. Let's end war on each other, and of course against our planet.

There is not one answer or one thing to do to fix all that needs fixing. It will take many steps, by many people, every day to correct our balance, but each step is an important step, each step is significant.

There will always be doubters, and the ones who don't care or are just lazy, but they are outnumbered. Earth Caretakers who are waking back up will do what's right, and there are always open arms and hearts to join along. Healing our planet through direct action takes one person to be the catalyst of change. Goodness follows good actions.

There is a fire lighting us up now, sometimes we feel it out of our passion and enthusiasm for life, and sometimes we feel it out of desperation from the weight of destruction. Either way, we are motivated to bring health back fully to our planet.

The idea of Earth Caretaking will continue to grow. We are collectively feeling the call, and the need for right action in our daily lives, in every decision we make, and every action we take. The Earth will guide us, she will show us the way, she already is.

Get to work. It's that simple. Why? Because it's what we are all here for, at this time, on this Earth, in this lifetime.

In the 2030's and 2040's pivotal events are projected to happen with our Earth. Often, in life when faced with a big problem, we are not sure of what to do or how to do what is needed to make change. Technology, which ironically has been a big part of the problem, can be a big part of this solution. We are currently working on environmental, restorative breakthrough technologies. Let's make those efforts a priority and invest in those essential innovations.

Let's own the truth of what is truly happening, and take responsibility for the proven consequences of our actions, and move forward towards healing. The eternal question is, do we humans have the willingness to get off our butts to do it?

We are all on this planet, right now, for a common reason. We are here to restore the health of the planet.

The older generation is here now as a transition group to hand off what we have learned to the younger generation, while still being engaged. It is clear much of my job going forward is to be of guidance, and then to get out of the way for others to step up.

This younger generation is now here to take on the challenge of this crisis, and help the planet. This is a daunting burden or an exciting honor, it all depends on your attitude. My hope is that you choose to live a magnificent life of purpose and joy.

I'm hoping through this movement, you will be inspired to go forward and change the world forever. This generation of global citizens are the ones fighting for the Earth's rites and caring for it. Then the next generation of Earth Caretakers are the ones that maintain the gardening of the Earth, and loving and enjoying your efforts.

In the path of healing our Earth, let's bring out the beauty that humans are when we come from truth, love, and kindness in service to all life. The time for the human-race to grow up is now. This is our defining moment. We can be the force that destroys our own home, or we can be the force that heals our home, and allows her to flourish. Let's choose to be the gift to our Earth.

The Earth is a master at healing wounds. As we do our part, she will do hers. We have seen this healing countless times in our recent past.

Look in the mirror at the end of each day and ask if you made a difference. Did you do something to be a part of the positive change? Teach by your actions, do what is right. No matter how old you are, you are a role model for someone else. Commit to taking on that responsibility, and be on the right side of history when the children ask, what did you do to help the Earth?.

Step into Earth Caretaking. Be the dream come true. Get up and do it! Make each day count, make every day Earth Day.

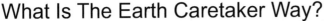

Your Earth Needs You
Speak up for the Earth
Stand up for the Land.
Be the Voice of the Earth
See the wrongs inflicted and right those wrongs.
Live as if this generation is the last.
Fight for our home, even if you're the last one standing, win or lose, it must be done.
What happens to the Earth happens to you.
Your Earth needs you.

What Is The Earth Caretaker Way?

The Earth Caretaker Way is a way of a life with purpose that gives voice and action to the environmental needs of our planet. The intention is to inspire people of all ages to be Earth Caretakers. To ignite the passion to learn more about nature and our ecosystem's challenges, and how to act on those needs.

The Earth Caretaker Way is a hands-on, nonprofit organization that helps to restore balance in our Earth, and the right use of our resources.

The organization promotes environmental stewardship through training programs, with an emphasis on building on one's personal relationship with nature. Without this personal connection with nature, we lose our focus and motivation of why this restorative movement is so vitally important. We strive to put hope and passion into daily action.

The ECW is run by an enthusiastic group of outdoor education specialists, and community builders. The organization will grow to become a physical and digital nexus, for a worldwide Earth Caretaker community. We have begun stewarding land and educating people locally through Headwaters Outdoor School in Mount Shasta, CA. and will be expanding into a larger movement with chapters worldwide.

Future wildlife sanctuaries will double as educational and Earth care training spaces. Anyone can participate as an Earth Caretaker Way community member, and can access information online from experienced staff on how they can be an Earth Caretaker.

Earth Caretaker classes and events are listed on the website. There are opportunities to physically participate in restoration events, as well as becoming a donor for future wildlands sanctuaries. There is always an opportunity to leave your legacy on Earth.

You can be an Earth Caretaker on your own, in the way you live your life, and you can also join others to be even more effective in this lifelong adventure. The Earth Caretaker Way is a central point to connect with established environmental groups, and individuals who are journeying along the same path to right balance.

Earth Caretaker Pledge

I give my word to protect our Earth, its wildlands, its oceans, waterways, animals, and humans. I give my word to live my life in a way that honors our Earth. Every day I will awaken as an Earth Caretaker. My actions will speak for the love and respect I have for our Earth, and all that lives upon her. I commit to enjoying our Earth by exploring her wild places, by gardening, and tending the land for food for humans and animals, and by playing in her mountains, forests, meadows, deserts, lakes, and oceans. Every day I live will be a good day for our Earth. The Earth is a gift for me, and I am a gift for the Earth.

Be An Earth Caretaker:

*Start at home. Do a zone-to-zone assessment in all working parts of your home. Evaluate the efficiency of appliances, ethical purchases, and recycling and repurposing of household items, including clothing. Are there unnecessary chemicals you can remove from your home, and replace with non-toxic solutions? The bottom-line question to ask, "Is this helping to maintain or restore health and balance in myself, my family, my community, our world, or our Earth?"

*Assess your work environment. What needs to change to help the environment, and what can you do to start making that change? Involve your co-workers, inspire them, and make them a part of this project. Start with recycling and waste management, ethical and sustainable purchasing choices, equipment and energy use, humanity projects within your work community. Ask co-workers what they feel needs to be addressed, and work together to tackle each project.

*Assemble your own Earth Caretaker Way Chapter locally. Educate yourself on where your attention can go to be of service, and work together to make it happen. This can be a public project or assistance for an individual.

*Organize cleanup days in your community.

*Help with reforestation after fires or clear cuts. Help with coral reef restoration projects.

*Donate to environmental groups.

*Use your unique skills to create new ways of addressing environmental problems, and share those insights.

*Volunteer at wildlife rescues.

*Walk dogs and play with cats at shelters. They all need love and exercise and freedom.

*Create community gardens. Share your yard with those who need space to grow a garden.

*Become a beekeeper or allow others to use your property to raise honey bees, and plant abundant flowers for them.

*Partner with others and buy land to caretake for wildlife.

*Become a sponsor and adopt an acre of wildland through the Earth Caretaker Way.

Conclusion

Where Do We Go From Here?

These times are very troubling for our Earth and all life upon her. We humans have caused these troubling times, and we are in a true predicament. We are potentially the sixth extinction to all life upon our Mother Earth.

We know the problem, we know what caused it, and what is continuing to cause destruction of our environment. We have the brain power to find solutions. The question that may haunt future generations is, will humanity come together for the greater good and make the changes required? Honestly, I don't know, but I do believe in miracles.

This real threat today is astronomical, it's our planet that's in trouble, and it's the only one we have! The confidence I have though is that millions of people, private groups, organizations, and governments are working hands on for animals, for land preservation, for human rights, for our oceans, and ultimately for the greater good of our planet.

I know individuals are working to live in good Earth-friendly ways, and here's the miracle, the Earth has her own intelligence. Our Earth's history has shown us she knows how to heal her wounds.

Being Earth Caretakers is our higher calling. This is what can bring us together. Some say the Earth didn't need us before, so why now? I firmly believe that we are not an accident. Our brains, our bodies, our ability to think, and reason, and learn, and create, are gifts to all life.

We are here to engage in life, and specifically in this moment. We can assist the Earth in repairing herself by going light on her resources to give her a break, allowing her the time to breathe and regenerate.

We say humanity can never come together and make this happen, yet we saw this in real time, when the human world was basically shut down for a few weeks due to the onset of the 2020 global pandemic.

We saw how the air cleared in the most polluted places on the planet. We saw wildlife expanding their living spaces by returning to cities. We saw coral reefs being preserved just by not allowing suntan-lotion-soaked people to go in the oceans for a while. It was quite amazing how quickly we saw the Earth restoring herself back into balance.

All animals do their part by simply living. They engage in the art of living their lives in balance to keep our planet healthy. They have been keeping their commitments to be who they are in a right way.

Humans are complicated in a beautiful way. It's our time to be heroes, to do the right thing. We need to step into the amazing beings that we are, and be the solutions to our own problems. We are fighting for this Earth, and it's a good and necessary fight.

More than ever, our personal connection with nature is so very critical. Land and the elements hold space for people, animals, and plants, and helps us to heal. We find balance in nature and get re-centered.

Nature can be brutally real and amazingly nurturing. It doesn't discriminate. We are all equal, and we are all a part of it. Nature is our source of life, and we need to protect it. It literally is a matter of life or death.

The human race can be ignorant and also extremely brilliant. We have the ability to destroy, and we have the ability to create. We are at a pivotal time in life where we need to create. We need to go to nature and regain our perspective of what is truly important.

If enough people become Earth Caretakers, we will reach that tipping point and swing towards the healing of our Earth. This is our Home. Our Mother. Our life. Treat Her with respect and love and kindness.

Do we have enough time? Is it too late? The funny thing about time is that it is man-made. Time is a subjective perception filtered through emotion. So, do we have enough time? Yes, we can create whatever needs to be made, to change whatever needs to be fixed and restored. If we start now, then yes, we have enough time.

I do believe that humanity will go through a collective grieving period where we will have to go through it to get to the other side of it, and then we will go forward. We will come out of this uncertain time, and from there a new way of living will become who we are, and not just a temporary fix.

Is the world a better place because you are in it?

What Will We Do? What Will You Do?

We can do this. I believe we can. I have faith and hope. I dream that we move into the future as Caretakers of the Earth, and in doing so find peace with each other and grow through this by serving our higher purpose.

My personal dream is that I'll live to be one hundred so that I can see this dream come true. I'll never stop doing my part for the greater good. No matter what, I will never give up. Never.

***

Live life fully animated, not as a spectator, but as an enthusiastic participant. Live Nature Awareness, Live Wilderness Skills, Live Earth Philosophy, and Live a Life of Service as a way of life. Be life and live in motion.

Remember to enjoy our planet. She loves and enjoys you. I believe this to be true. Celebrate nature.

Every day be a part in healing the Earth by each choice you make. Ask yourself what is most important to you. What you do is fueled by what you are passionate about. Take small, daily actions and big, giant actions, and bring others along to help restore our Earth's health. Everything matters. You matter.

My hope is that the end of this book is the beginning for you. Reference this book as an inspiring toolbox. Put that smart phone down and get out in nature.

Get off your butt and get out into the woods! It's the best place to be. I'll see you there!

-Tim Corcoran

Reminders:

*Greet the day and end the day outside in the magic hours.
*Keep an open heart, and follow where it leads you.
*Slow down
*Become an animal to truly know them.
*Ask for what you want.
*Follow your inner vision.
*Use all your senses, stop and sniff, and taste, and look up and all around, listen intimately, touch everything, and collect those memories.
*Take off your shoes and walk softly.
*Get the Earth on your body.
*Sleep outside and look out into your Universe.
*Go out in nature alone with no timeline or intended destination.
*Get in lakes, and streams, and swim under waterfalls, and get energized.
*Climb trees and give them great big hugs.

*Eat wild, edible plants.
*Join the symphony of nature.
*Be aware of your concentric rings.
*Respect and admire all things in nature.
*Lay in animal sits.
*Go into the night without a flashlight.
*Explore with the curiosity of a child.
*Get off trail. Go into challenging terrain and weather.
*Live in Gratitude.

About The Author

Tim Corcoran –

Tim's Irish heritage, as taught to him by his uncle and grandfather, has linked him deeply to Earth people's philosophy of life. He first went to the woods at age six. He knew then that it was his home. At seventeen he spent four months alone in the Canadian Wilderness practicing Earth living skills.

Tim began a career teaching wildlife conservation in 1974. During this time, he learned how to communicate with the spirits of the animals he worked with, enhancing his abilities to connect on an intimate level with them.

He has an extensive background in working with wildlife. He has worked at the Alberta Game Farm in Alberta, Canada as an animal caretaker, the Crandon Park Zoo in Miami Florida as an animal relocation director, and Marine World Africa U.S.A. as a chimpanzee and elephant trainer.

Tim co-founded the Native Animal Rescue in Santa Cruz, California, rescuing and releasing injured wildlife. He also took that opportunity to speak at schools and venues to educate people on wildlife conservation.

In the late 1980's Tim started a wilderness school in Santa Cruz called Pathfinders, where he led wilderness survival backpack trips and vision quests. As that school grew, in 1992 Tim created Headwaters Outdoor School in Mount Shasta, California to realize his lifelong vision of sharing what he has learned from nature, and to inspire people to discover their own personal relationship with nature. Tim teaches outdoor living skills, and Earth Philosophy to kids and adults.

In 2010 Tim wrote a book based on his childhood memoirs called, *Growing up with a Soul Full of Nature.*

Throughout Tim's many years of travels he has become an accomplished, professional, nature photographer. In 2006 he opened the Tim Corcoran Photography Gallery in Mount Shasta, California. Tim has published a series of nature photography books highlighting sacred places in nature.

Tim has recently founded The Earth Caretaker Way, with the intention of uniting a global community of Earth Caretakers to save wild spaces, and create wildlife refuge within every environment, including urban settings.

Tim lives with his wife, Jean, and their pack of dogs, on an amazing sanctuary of wooded land in Mount Shasta, California, where he runs *Headwaters Outdoor School,* and *The Earth Caretaker Way.*

Julie Boettler –

Julie grew up in the California East Bay Area as a competitive swimmer and coach, and ran her own childcare.

Thriving in the outdoors, Julie came to Headwaters Outdoor School in 2001, and joined the staff in 2005 as the land caretaker, school manager, teacher, and camp cook.

She has been a professional artist, and is now sharing her art throughout the Headwaters Forest Sanctuary Gardens.

Julie lives in her forever mountain home with her dogs, stewarding the beautiful Headwater's land as an Earth Caretaker.

Acknowledgment

I have lifelong gratitude for my mentors growing up, who were always committed to my Earth Caretaker relationship to Mother Earth. They were my angels along the way.

Bo Almroth taught me that pure love of Earth is sacred. He gave me my love of hiking, and the gift of loving to get lost, with never a need to be found.

Uncle Bill gave me the gift of joy and play in the wild. My love of creeks and endless wanderings, and my love of trout.

My Grandfather, Leo, loved me and related to me as an old soul. He gave me the freedom of his homestead, my relationship with the Flathead Indians, gardening, and a love for farm animals.

Mr. Robertson, my science teacher, sent me to Roosevelt Lake, which became my power spot on Earth, and opened the door for me to find my Earth Caretaker place for this life.

Blackie, my teacher of pure love of wilderness lands. He gave me a love of horses and horse packing, and he gave me a friendship with his dog Blue, who slept with me every night on our wilderness adventures.

My dad, Jack Corcoran, believed in my vision, and always kept it alive. He joined me on countless wilderness trips. No matter how crazy and wild I got, he never complained.

To my mom, Nita Corcoran, who taught me pure love, and always believed in me. She gave me the belief in myself that I could create my life as a thing of beauty and purpose. My mom helped me to create a life that matters.

I thank my students and staff, who have made my dream of having an outdoor school, and being a land caretaker come true, by showing up, and by learning, and taking these teachings into the world. You are all bright and shining stars.

I have so much gratitude for my wife, Jean Sage. Thank you, Jean, for all that you have given to me and to Headwaters. Thank you for the addition of your writings from *Growing up with a Soul Full of Nature*, your teachings, and for all your creations on our land. Your unwavering support and love over the years has made all this possible.

I offer a very special thank you to Julie Boettler, for partnering with me on this book. Hours upon hours of work have been dedicated to this project. I thank you, Julie, for your amazing writings, illustrations, and editing. Also, so much gratitude for being the main caretaker of the Headwaters land, and my partner in running Headwaters Outdoor School. This could not have happened without your hard work, your love of the Headwaters land, and your amazing loyalty to it, and to our Earth herself.

Thank you to those who have put in time transcribing some of my writings. It can be a daunting job reading my handwriting.

Thank you, Janie Stapleton, for your time in getting this book ready to be published, and for your wonderful artwork.

Thank you, TJ Putnam, my grandson, for your illustrations, editing, and your dedication in taking this book to the finish line.

I am blessed to have such good people in my life, to help with all the behind the scenes work that it takes to bring a book to life.

Finally, thank you to my dogs. You keep me real, and wild, and crazy. You keep me primal. You are a part of my staff, you are my teachers, and my friends.

Everyone in my life has had a part in making me who I am, and creating the life I live, and I am forever grateful. Thank you. - Tim Corcoran

Contact Us

Headwaters Outdoor School is a place of refuge and refueling. It's a place for people to recharge, and to then go back out into their everyday lives to be a light that darkness cannot extinguish.

It is a sanctuary of refuge and rest for animals, critters, birds, reptiles, and fish. A place of reverence for trees, and plants, and all critters within the soil. This land is held with an open heart to restore and maintain balance.

I am here now to create more teachers. Headwaters Outdoor School is a school of higher learning. There are many things you can learn from a book, but you can only know about nature by being in it and interacting with it. Engaging with nature is where you choose to take knowledge to another level of experienced wisdom.

Join us for a class at our school or for retreat time in our forest sanctuary gardens. Get inspired, and then go out into the world, and create more spaces with the same magical intention.

The Earth Caretaker Way: www.earthcaretakerway.org
For any questions or additional information, email us at info@earthcaretakerway.org

A portion of the proceeds from the sales of this book will go to The Earth Caretaker Way to support funding towards land conservation.

To donate to The Earth Caretaker Way, visit www.earthcaretakerway.org

Headwaters Outdoor School: www.hwos.com

P.O. Box 1210
Mount Shasta, California 96067

To reach Tim directly, write to: info@hwos.com

Tim Corcoran Nature Photography Gallery: www.timcorcoranphoto.com

Made in the USA
Columbia, SC
25 February 2025

54381565R00224